Handbook of EMDR for Children and Adolescents

Handbook of EMDR for Children and Adolescents

Edited by

Renée Beer and Carlijn de Roos

OXFORD
UNIVERSITY PRESS

OXFORD
UNIVERSITY PRESS

Great Clarendon Street, Oxford, OX2 6DP,
United Kingdom

Oxford University Press is a department of the University of Oxford.
It furthers the University's objective of excellence in research, scholarship,
and education by publishing worldwide. Oxford is a registered trade mark of
Oxford University Press in the UK and in certain other countries.

Published in the United States of America by Oxford University Press
198 Madison Avenue, New York, NY 10016, United States of America

British Library Cataloguing in Publication Data
Data available

Library of Congress Control Number: 2025941337

ISBN 9780198918400

DOI: 10.1093/oso/9780198918400.001.0001

Printed and bound by
CPI Group (UK) Ltd., Croydon, CR0 4YY

The manufacturer's authorized representative in the EU for product safety is
Oxford University Press España S.A. of Parque Empresarial San Fernando de Henares,
Avenida de Castilla, 2 – 28830 Madrid (www.oup.es/en or product.safety@oup.com).
OUP España S.A. also acts as importer into Spain of products made by the manufacturer.

MIX
Paper | Supporting
responsible forestry
FSC® C013604
FSC
www.fsc.org

Table of Contents

Foreword

I am honoured to contribute a foreword to the *Handbook of EMDR for Children and Adolescents*, a unique and timely resource in trauma treatment. This book arrives at a critical juncture, as the mental health of our children and youth faces unprecedented challenges, with a significant rise in mental health-related concerns. Authors Renée Beer and Carlijn de Roos—world-renowned trainers, researchers, and clinicians—convey their unparalleled dedication and extensive expertise in this handbook, guaranteeing its emergence as a vital and indispensable resource for the EMDR community. This handbook also brings together other leading experts in the field, offering a wealth of knowledge and insights to advance theory, clinical practice, and research.

The handbook offers a thorough review of the growing body of evidence supporting EMDR therapy's effectiveness in treating post-traumatic stress disorder (PTSD) and the broader constellation of trauma-related symptomatology in children and adolescents exposed to trauma.

The authors provide a comprehensive coverage of the model, methodology, and procedural steps of EMDR treatment, offering clear guidelines on necessary adjustments to ensure that the benefits of EMDR therapy are optimized for children and adolescents at every stage of their development. The authors underscore the importance of proficiency in developmental psychology, legal frameworks, and systemic contexts, supporting clinicians as they adapt EMDR procedures and protocols to align with their young clients' neurobiological, emotional, and cognitive stages of development.

The handbook explores in depth the symptoms, diagnosis, and assessment of the complex phenomena arising from early trauma exposure, along with the intricate interplay of protective and risk factors that shape the neurodevelopmental pathways of children and adolescents exposed to trauma and adversity. A cornerstone of this handbook is its detailed discussion of case conceptualization, which is crucial for effective clinical decision-making. The authors offer clinicians a robust and comprehensive framework for identifying relevant treatment targets, utilizing multiple pathways—intrusion, timeline, flashforward, emotion, and belief—to develop individualized treatment plans.

Moreover, the handbook goes beyond clinical techniques to address the critical question of when and for whom EMDR therapy is most effective by examining specific symptoms, contexts, and conditions where EMDR proves beneficial—whether as a stand-alone intervention or as a complement to other therapeutic modalities—the authors equip clinicians with the knowledge needed to make informed decisions.

The practical value of this book is further enriched by the inclusion of case studies that illustrate how theoretical principles translate into real-world scenarios. These case-based narratives bring the complexities of trauma treatment to life, offering clinicians step-by-step guidelines and insights. The authors pay thorough attention to contraindications and critical factors for treatment planning, ensuring clinicians can navigate trauma work's intricacies while remaining grounded in intentional therapeutic decision-making.

Multiple authors thoroughly address the interpersonal and systemic nature of trauma and healing. They provide a comprehensive theoretical and research review while offering invaluable guidance on mapping parental reactions and understanding their impact on the therapeutic process. This book explores when and how they can support their child/adolescent, when therapy for the parent is warranted, and when involving the entire family is essential.

In sum, this handbook is an essential resource for EMDR clinicians, providing a comprehensive guide to effectively delivering EMDR therapy across diverse populations, settings, and situations. This volume's practical approach ensures that the insights and knowledge presented can be readily applied in clinical practice.

Francine Shapiro, the creator and developer of EMDR therapy, was deeply committed to her vision of supporting the healing of humanity and future generations. This volume honours and aligns with her vision, upholding the collective efforts of thousands of EMDR practitioners worldwide who share a common mission: to accompany children and adolescents on their path to self-discovery, integration, and healing.

Renée Beer and Carlijn de Roos provide a comprehensive resource to support new and experienced EMDR clinicians, consultants, and trainers. This volume is poised to become an essential guide and a source of inspiration for current and future generations of EMDR trainers, practitioners, and researchers.

Ana M. Gómez, Psychotherapist, MC, LPC
EMDRIA Accredited EMDR Therapy Trainer
AGATE Institute Director and Founder
ISSTD Fellow
Author of:
EMDR Therapy and Adjunct Approaches with Children: Complex Trauma, Attachment, and Dissociation
The Handbook of Complex Trauma and Dissociation in Children: Theory, Research, and Clinical Applications
EMDR-Sandtray-Based Therapy: Healing Complex Trauma and Dissociation Across the Lifespan

Foreword 2

For any EMDR therapist working with children and adolescents, this handbook is much more than just a foundational text. It is your companion and your guide, the basis of your learning, and a source of support and clarity. Within these pages are global voices of expertise and wisdom brought together to guide you through clinical complexities and advise you how to move with a child along their unique healing journey. Working as an EMDR child therapist, holding a child as they courageously heal is one of the most rewarding, honourable, and humbling professions. At times we may be overwhelmed by the task at hand. This textbook will be a source of insight, affirmation, and hope in those times.

In this extraordinary handbook, editors Renée Beer and Carlijn de Roos have integrated state-of-the-art knowledge of all things related to EMDR therapy for children—theory, empirical evidence, case conceptualization, and clinical application—with a wide array of presentations, populations, treatment settings, and contexts. This cutting-edge volume coherently brings together expert knowledge, a wealth of experience, and stories of recovery from leaders in our EMDR therapy field. Each author has not only generously taken time to comprehensively share not just what they know; each chapter also presents insights and wisdom in specialty areas derived from careers passionately dedicated to the healing of children across our globe.

This book is beautifully structured and organized in a way that takes any clinician, through the foundational theory of trauma formation, impact, evidence for treatment, standard EMDR therapy application, and adaptations required for younger clients, including integration of EMDR therapy into the complexities of working transdiagnostically, all the while considering family, systems, attachment, dissociation, and this work's ethical, legal, and forensic contexts. Each chapter is a reminder that effective therapy incorporates an understanding of the theory, mechanisms, human development, attachment, and systems in which we learn, live, and grow, and an understanding of the impact of trauma on the developing mind and body of a child. The depth and breadth of the texts in terms of content, theory, clinical interventions, practical suggestions, and attention to specialty areas—such as EMDR for children with autism, hearing and language problems, mental disabilities, BPD, and ADHD—makes this book the most comprehensive text of EMDR for children in our field to date. It is globally relevant, including for clinicians working with children and adolescents here in the Australian context, where the development of a separate trajectory for this target group had a later onset.

As an editor of the *Oxford Handbook of EMDR*, I am convinced this text will be a valuable, complementary resource for EMDR child & adolescent clinicians, consultants, and trainers, and will facilitate the application of EMDR therapy as a psychotherapeutic approach to healing young clients in need: children who have suffered and are now being offered a space to heal, develop, and grow to experience the life they deserve.

Dr Sarah Schubert, Clinical Psychologist, B.Psych (Hons.), M.App.Clin.Psych, PhD.
EMDRAA Accredited EMDR Therapy Trainer (adult and child and adolescent)
Northumbria University, Newcastle, UK, and EMDR Therapy Training Australia
Editor of the *Oxford Handbook of EMDR Therapy*

Preface

This book is devoted to the treatment of children and adolescents (C&A) with EMDR therapy and provides information on trauma and trauma processing within this context. EMDR training courses for C&A therapists have been offered in Europe since 2000 and are increasingly yielding results: EMDR is being used more frequently, in many countries, for the successful treatment of various psychological problems in C&A. The development of EMDR for C&A has progressed at varying rates in different regions. The aim of this *Handbook of EMDR for Children and Adolescents* is to share knowledge and expertise, which will hopefully promote and facilitate further international development.

This book paints a picture of the 'state of the art'. It offers a compilation of instructional information for therapists in training (to become C&A EMDR practitioners), practitioners, and even experienced practitioners. We hope this information will inspire C&A therapists and trainers and guide clinical practice and training. The content of this handbook demonstrates that empirical and experimental research is required to answer outstanding questions about EMDR therapy. For researchers, the book might be a source for retrieving research topics. This book intends to provide a valuable complement for C&A specialists to the *Handbook on EMDR* (Farrell et al., 2023).

Inspiration

Two milestones in the evolution of EMDR gave a solid impetus to develop its use in C&A.

The first was the publication of three books in quick succession in 1999 by US EMDR C&A specialists:

- *Through the Eyes of a Child* (Tinker & Wilson, 1999)
- *Eye Movement Desensitization and Reprocessing (EMDR) in Child and Adolescent Psychotherapy* (Greenwald, 1999)
- *Small Wonders* (Lovett, 1999)

Before that time, limited attention had been paid to the adjustments required to make EMDR accessible to C&A. These books encouraged C&A therapists to consider EMDR as a therapy option for traumatized children.

The second impetus came from the 2000 conference on EMDR for C&A, organized by the British Association of Child and Adolescent Mental Health in London at a historically significant location: the building where preparatory discussions on the founding of the United Nations had once taken place. During this conference, the foundations were laid for an EMDR Europe—Child & Adolescent Section, formulating several objectives for the following years. The most important of these was to establish 'gold standards' for EMDR C&A training and develop a European training model. The intention was to enhance the availability of EMDR for traumatized children across Europe and to support colleagues internationally in implementing EMDR for C&A in their country.

This goal has been achieved in recent years. A European model for the curriculum of C&A training has been established. Quality criteria were also established for EMDR Europe C&A practitioners, consultants, and trainers. Furthermore, a curriculum has been established for a trajectory to become a C&A consultant and, likewise, an EMDR C&A trainer. An additional aim was to stimulate international research on the effectiveness of EMDR in C&A, so results from larger client populations could be obtained and compared.

Since the 2020 COVID-19 pandemic, global cooperation has emerged alongside European cooperation through the Global Child EMDR Alliance (www.globalchildemdralliance.com), a group of EMDR C&A specialists that distributes resources digitally for children, adolescents, parents, and clinicians. These resources relate to global themes and threats, such as war, disasters (natural disasters, climate change), ACEs (adverse childhood experiences), and pandemics.

Content

This book contains general information that C&A therapists are instructed on in their EMDR training and specific information regarding target groups that C&A therapists may frequently encounter in their clinical practice. A range of psychopathologies is covered, which is, however, non-comprehensive. In creating this handbook, we selected topics and target groups because of their relevance to clinicians and the available expertise and research data. More flowers bloom in the field, but not all have been elaborated sufficiently to report on at this stage. The book contains chapters written by us and by guest authors. These authors are experts in their fields and, as editors, we collaborated intensively with them on the content and format of their chapters to forge a coherent whole.

Structure

Part I provides information regarding the proper application of EMDR to C&A, which is covered in C&A training. It also incorporates essential background information, such as the impact of trauma on children and research on EMDR with children. Two perspectives that C&A therapists must always consider are integrated: the developmental psychological perspective and the systemic perspective. Consequently, the first part informs the reader on protocol adaptations for different developmental phases and how to involve parents in EMDR therapy.

Part II focuses on the application in C&A with specific psychopathologies: children who are reluctant toward EMDR; children with ADHD (the most frequent diagnosis in C&A psychiatry); children with communication problems (i.e., children who are deaf/hard-of-hearing or have a language development disorder); children with autism; and children with an intellectual disability. The authors of these chapters advocate concretizing and visualizing the information for their target groups wherever possible, and they provide creative solutions for typical problems therapists encounter in their work with these groups. The next two chapters discuss how to do EMDR with C&A with a dissociative disorder and with adolescents with a borderline personality disorder.

Part III focuses on EMDR treatment in different (family) settings: adolescents in the setting of forensic C&A psychiatry or youth care; (young) children together with their parents, using a dyadic, playful approach; families with a child that was maltreated within or outside the family;

children with attachment trauma who are placed out of the home and/or separated from their biological parents; children in refugee families; and, finally, children receiving therapy together with their parents in an inpatient setting because outpatient treatment is not possible.

For ease of reading, we have aimed for a consistent structure of the chapters in Parts II and III, with deviations as needed to convey the content best. Each chapter starts with an introduction, followed by a description of the target group or the clinical presentation of the group addressed in the chapter. Following this, the authors describe treatment according to the guidelines for the group involved—if existing—culminating in a rationale for why EMDR is essential for this target group as an alternative or supplement to mainstream treatment. After presenting the empirical evidence for mainstream treatments and EMDR (if available), the authors discuss relevant focal points, distinguishing between general points that apply to the entire treatment and specific points per phase of the EMDR Standard Protocol (SP) for children and adolescents aged 4 to 18 years.

Terminology

This book concerns EMDR therapy for children and adolescents until age 18 and their families. In two chapters (18 and 19), the age group extends to 23, as treatment of these groups usually occurs in settings with adolescents/young adults up to 23 years. We use either 'children and adolescents', or abbreviated 'C&A', or the collective term 'children' for readability to refer to children and adolescents between 0 and 18. In all chapters, we use the term 'client' for the person receiving therapy and 'therapist' for the person applying EMDR. For gender neutrality, we have avoided the terms 'he' and 'she' wherever possible and substituted they/them as a singular, third-person pronoun. Where avoidance was impossible, the term 'she' was chosen when referring to the therapist and 'he' when referring to the client.

The goal of this book is to be a resource for C&A therapists and trainers worldwide. Therefore, the terminology must be compatible with what therapists have learned or are learning in their training. As Laliotis and colleagues (2021) stated in the position paper of the Council of Scholars, 'Innovations in the field continue to develop, which makes consensus definitions essential'. Therefore, we will explicitly define some terms used in this book. We adhere to internationally agreed definitions but give room for 'cultural diversity' within this context, where relevant. Throughout the book, it will be indicated explicitly whenever a deviation or alternative option is mentioned, and the suggested deviation will be explained and motivated.

For ease of reading, the definition of EMDR therapy is presented in Figure 0.1 (Laliotis et al., 2021, p. 187).

A definition warranting special attention concerns the preparation phase.

Laliotis and colleagues (2021, p. 200) suggest the following interventions and goals for the preparation phase: 'Education on EMDR therapy and mechanics, including informed consent; establish a therapeutic alliance; and access readiness for processing. Provide stabilization strategies as needed.'

We introduce a non-standard differentiation between the regular 'preparation phase' (phase 2), which takes place after history taking and treatment planning, and a more extended phase, called the 'preparatory phase', which involves strategies that make trauma processing possible. This extended phase occurs when complete case conceptualization is not—or is only partly—feasible because there is no motivation, readiness, or preparedness for (trauma) treatment yet. Chapters 10, 12, 17, and 19 describe interventions for this phase.

In these cases, preparatory interventions are implemented to create or optimize readiness for treatment; there is no agreement yet with the child or the parents to do EMDR in these situations. By contrast, in the preparation phase (phase 2), all interventions prepare the child and the parents for EMDR after having achieved 'informed consent'. This differentiation was already inserted in the first edition of this book,[1] where we proposed the term 'preparatory phase' for what is usually called the 'stabilization phase'. We prefer the term 'preparatory phase' to explicitly indicate that this phase aims to enhance the 'preparedness for (trauma) treatment'. The therapists should be motivated to move on with the client to the trauma processing phase as soon as possible. We made this differentiation because the interventions provided in this phase cannot yet be called EMDR.

A second term regards the bilateral eye movements or their equivalents. In the literature, different terms are used to indicate what we do, such as 'bilateral stimulation' (BLS), 'dual attention stimulation', 'dual tasks', 'distracting tasks/stimuli', and 'working memory taxation' (WMT), which is confusing as these terms refer to different mechanisms of action (such as interhemispheric coherence or working memory taxation). Until now, there has been no conclusive research on what the working mechanism(s) of EMDR may be (Laliotis et al., 2021). Brain studies have found little evidence for interhemispheric coherence (Pagani et al., 2013), and most empirical support has been established for the WMT hypothesis (see Chapter 1 of this book). Therefore, it may be premature to redefine the term for this component of the procedure. Laliotis and colleagues (2021) propose 'dual attention BLS' as the definition for this component, which aligns with Shapiro (2018). For convenience and recognizability, in this book we use the following acronyms interchangeably for the eye movements or equivalents, 'the engine to set the information system in motion': BLS/WMT or EM$^+$.

EMDR therapy is an integrative, client-centered approach that treats problems of daily living based on disturbing life experiences that continue to have a negative impact on a person throughout the lifespan. Its Adaptive Information Processing theory hypothesizes that current difficulties are caused by disturbing memories that are inadequately processed, and that symptoms are reduced or eliminated altogether when these memories are processed to resolution using dual attention bilateral stimulation. The resolution of these targeted memories is hypothesized to result in memory reconsolidation. The standard application of EMDR therapy is comprised of eight phases and a three-pronged approach to identify and process: (a) Memories of past adverse life experiences that underlie present problems; (b) Present-day situations that elicit disturbance and maladaptive responses; and (c) Anticipatory future scenarios that require adaptive responses. There is strong empirical evidence for its use in the treatment of posttraumatic stress disorder, and it has also been found to be an effective, transdiagnostic treatment approach for a wide range of diagnoses in a variety of contexts and treatment settings with diverse populations.

Figure 0.1 Definition of EMDR therapy (Lialotis et al., 2021)

[1] This book is a revision of a book published in Dutch in 2017.

Finally

May this book inspire many EMDR colleagues in their important work of increasing opportunities for better futures for traumatized children.

Renée Beer and Carlijn de Roos

List of Contributors

Jacqueline van Baar MSc, health care psychologist, family therapist, Private practice, Netherlands

Estie Bar Sade MSc, educational psychologist EMDR Europe Senior C&A trainer, Private practice, Psychological Services Israeli Education Office

Renée Beer MSc, clinical psychologist, cognitive behavioural therapist, EMDR Europe Senior C&A trainer, Private practice, Netherlands

Lieke Doornkate MSc, psychotherapist, EMDR Europe consultant, Stichting Doof & Co, outpatient mental health treatment centre for deaf and hard-of-hearing adults, Netherlands

Anneke Eenhoorn MSc, clinical psychologist, cognitive behavioural therapist, Regional mental health care (GGZ-NHN), child and youth, Netherlands

Tirtsa Ehrlich MSc, child psychologist, EMDR Europe consultant, de BOSgroep, Youth, Netherlands

Ana Gomez MC, LPC, Psychotherapist, EMDRIA Accredited EMDR Therapy Trainer, AGATE Institute Director and Founder, ISSTD Fellow

Laurian Hafkemeijer PhD, clinical psychologist, cognitive behavioural therapist, EMDR Europe consultant GGZ Delfland, Netherlands

Kirsten Hauber PhD, psychotherapist, associate professor, Curium-LUMC, Private practice, Netherlands

Irma Hein MD, PhD, child psychiatrist Levvel, Academic Center for Child and Adolescent Psychiatry, and Amsterdam University Medical Center, Netherlands

Mirjam Heinemans MSc, psychotherapist, family therapist, Private practice, Netherlands

Jeantine Janse MSc, CBT therapist, EMDR Europe practitioner, Stichting Doof & Co, outpatient mental health treatment-centre for deaf and hard-of-hearing adults, Netherlands

Agaath Koudstaal MSc, clinical psychologist cognitive behavioural therapist, GGZ Delfland, Netherlands

Esther Leuning MSc, clinical psychologist/psychotherapist, EMDR Europe consultant, cognitive behavioural therapist, Karakter, Child and Youth psychiatry, Netherlands

Steven Meijer MSc, clinical psychologist/psychotherapist, EMDR Europe senior trainer, cognitive behavioural therapist, Private practice and National Organization for Mental Health Care (HSK), Netherlands

Liesbeth Mevissen PhD, clinical psychologist, EMDR Europe consultant, Private practice, Netherlands

Trudy Mooren Professor by special appointment, clinical psychologist, family therapist, ARQ Centrum '45, Utrecht University, Faculty of Social Sciences, Department of Clinical Psychology, Netherlands

Joanne Morris-Smith Consultant psychologist, AFBPsS EMDR Europe Senior C&A trainer, CYPS SW, SABP NHS Foundation Trust Surrey, United Kingdom

Caroline Ploeg MSc, health care psychologist, cognitive behavioural therapist, EMDR Europe practitioner, Accare, child and youth psychiatry, Netherlands

Thimo van der Pol Dr, forensic psychotherapist, senior researcher Levvel, Academic Center for Child and Adolescent Psychiatry, and Amsterdam University Medical Center, and Arkin, Netherlands

Carlijn de Roos PhD, clinical psychologist/psychotherapist, EMDR Europe senior trainer Levvel, Academic Center for Child and Adolescent Psychiatry, and Amsterdam University Medical Center, Netherlands

Nathalie Schlattmann MSc, clinical psychologist, family therapist, EMDR Europe consultant Levvel, Academic Center for Child and Adolescent Psychiatry, and Amsterdam University Medical Center, and Arkin, Netherlands

Henriët Scholts MSc, clinical psychologist, EMDR Europe consultant, cognitive behavioural therapist Accare, child and youth psychiatry, Netherlands

Sarah Schubert M.App.Clin.Psych, PhD, Clinical psychologist, BPsych (Hons.) Murdoch University, Western Australia; Northumbria University, Newcastle, United Kingdom; EMDR Therapy Training Australia Pty Ltd.

Michel Silvestre Dr, clinical psychologist, family therapist, EMDR Europe Senior C&A trainer, Private practice and University of Aix en Provence and Metz, France

Petra Spuijbroek MSc, health care psychologist Family Supporters, Netherlands

Arianne Struik Msc, clinical psychologist/family therapist, EMDR consultant, Institute for Chronically Traumatized Children, Australia

Ariane Tjeenk-Kalff Dr, clinical neuropsychologist, EMDR Europe practitioner, cognitive behavioural therapist Levvel, specialized Youth Mental Health Care, Netherlands

Femy Wanders MSc, clinical psychologist, cognitive behavioural therapist, Accare, child and youth psychiatry, Netherlands

Debra Wesselmann Psychotherapist, MS, LIMHP Private practice, The Attachment & Trauma Center of Nebraska, USA; EMDR Trainer, EMDR Institute

Gerarda Jeannette Wieten MSc, clinical psychologist, trauma therapist, EMDR Europe practitioner, Private practice, Netherlands

Barbara Wizansky MSc, clinical psychologist, EMDR Europe/Israel Senior C&A trainer Retired, Israel

Lysbert Zeinstra PhD candidate Erasmus University Rotterdam, Erasmus School of Social and Behavioural Sciences, Youth & Family, Netherlands

PART I

Trauma and EMDR with Children and Adolescents (C&A)

Starting Points

RENÉE BEER AND CARLIJN DE ROOS

1

1.1 Adaptive Information Processing Model

The foundation of EMDR therapy is the Adaptive Information Processing (AIP) model: 'the general model that provides the theoretical framework and principles for treatment and an explanation of the basis of pathology and personality development' (Shapiro, 2018, p. 26). This model hypothesizes that various forms of psychopathology result from how information is stored in memory. The assumption is that the natural information processing system can get blocked due to overwhelming events, so the information linked to these event(s) is not assimilated and subsequently not stored adaptively. Instead, according to the model, this information is stored as dysfunctional information, 'frozen' in fearful images with dysfunctional meaning, negative emotions, and physical sensations. Memories thus stored can be triggered by stimuli or situations in everyday life that recall the disturbing events, leading to psychopathology. Hase and colleagues (2017) call such memories that form the basis of various mental disorders 'pathogenic memories'.

The AIP model theorizes that the EMDR procedure restarts the blocked process of information processing so that the information can now be 'taken towards a state of adaptive resolution and functional integration' (Shapiro, 2018, p. 28). After treatment, the information is assimilated in an adaptive form and restored in long-term memory—a process known as reconsolidation. Shapiro (2018, p. 28) speaks metaphorically about 'digesting' or 'metabolizing' the information. We do not know yet how 'memory' works nor how it can be influenced directly. Several areas of the brain are involved in memory, and different memory systems are distinguished (sensory memory; short-term memory, a part of which is working memory; and long-term memory). 'We think in metaphors about our memory—we cannot think otherwise' (Draaisma, 2015, p. 1).

Shapiro (2018) proposed the existence of memory networks with associated information as a working hypothesis. She used the metaphor of a node—or a 'target'—to which various channels are connected, with related memories, thoughts, emotions, and bodily sensations stored in these channels. Shapiro posited that in EMDR therapy the client focuses on the 'target' (node) and then runs through the memory network via associations, which results in 'cleaning up' the memory channels. This process is supposed to be stimulated by the dual attention of the client, meaning that they focus internally on arising reactions while simultaneously focusing externally on a

Renée Beer and Carlijn de Roos, *Starting Points*. In: *Handbook of EMDR for Children and Adolescents*.
Edited by: Renée Beer and Carlijn de Roos, Oxford University Press.
DOI: 10.1093/oso/9780198918400.003.0001

secondary task or stimulus. This process aims to gradually establish new connections between neural networks, allowing functional information to replace dysfunctional information.

1.2 Mechanism of Action

Since its discovery, EMDR therapy has been the subject of much empirical and experimental research. Intrigued by its effectiveness in clinical practice, researchers put much effort into finding explanations for these effects by initiating research projects. When we know how and why EMDR works, we will eventually learn how to enhance treatment outcomes. However, to date, it is not known precisely how psychological therapies work, and this includes EMDR. Our explanations are only hypotheses. For a better understanding of these hypotheses, it is helpful to differentiate between mechanisms, mediators, and moderators (Kazdin, 2007; Leeds, 2016a, b).

Mechanisms encompass the steps—or factors—of a process, explaining how, why, or through which changes a treatment brings about results. These steps are responsible for the observed results (i.e., psychological and neurophysiological changes). *Mediators* are the intermediate steps (or variables) that affect a causal relationship between treatment and treatment outcomes. However, they do not explain the effect or the process that produces the effect (e.g., the dual attention in EMDR). *Moderators* are variables that influence—enhance or reduce—the extent to which treatment (therapy) generates treatment outcomes in a specific group (e.g., for children the availability of support figures). This chapter provides an overview of the most broadly discussed hypotheses regarding the proposed mechanisms of action, revealing that it is sometimes difficult to determine whether the variables involved should be seen as mediators or as (part of) separate mechanisms. Moderators are beyond the scope of this chapter and will be discussed in Chapter 2.

Most studies on mechanisms of action concern the effect of dual attention tasks. Lee and Cuijpers (2013) concluded in a meta-analysis comparing EMDR with and without eye movements that eye movements appeared to contribute significantly to treatment outcomes. It remains to be shown why this is so, and if this is true for children alike.

An array of hypotheses for EMDR's mechanism of action have been studied and, to varying degrees, enjoy empirical support (De Jongh et al., 2024a; Landin-Romero et al., 2018; Leeds, 2016b; Shapiro, 2018; Van Pelt et al., in prep.). Landin-Romero and colleagues (2018) differentiate three types of models: psychological, psychophysiological, and neurobiological. However, most models seem to have effects on several levels. The following subsections highlight the main features of the dominant hypotheses and their empirical support. We recommend that readers who seek further details on this topic read the publications mentioned.

1.2.1 Psychological Models

1. *Working memory taxation*

The hypothesis with the most empirical support concerns the taxation of working memory (WM), and is based on Baddeley's (2012) model of WM. According to this hypothesis, the WM is a cognitive system consisting of multiple components (phonological loop, visuospatial notepad, central executive, and episodic buffer) responsible for selecting, organizing, remembering, and integrating information. Together, these components ensure functional cognitive and affective executive control and the ability to control predominant responses and inhibit irrelevant information. The WM can perform several tasks simultaneously, such as planning tasks, solving problems, and facilitating memory reconsolidation. This is a process where retrieved long-term memories become unstable, are updated with new information, and then re-stabilized, allowing them to become reconsolidated as altered long-term memories (Baddeley, 2012). However, the WM capacity determines how much information the WM can select, organize, remember, and integrate simultaneously. This capacity is limited. When this capacity is overloaded—due to competing tasks—one of the tasks loses quality in favour of the other (Landin-Romero et al., 2018; Van Pelt et al., 2025).

In EMDR, dual attention typically involves two competing tasks—that is, simultaneously focusing attention internally on a specific memory and the accompanying flow of associations, and externally on a (distracting) task or stimulus, such as tracking moving fingers from side to side with the eyes. EMDR therapy requires the client to focus on a negative memory with associated vivid images and intense negative emotions. Attention to these memories and what they trigger consumes a lot of WM capacity. When combined with a secondary task, competition arises, and the memory loses its vividness and emotional intensity. After EMDR therapy, these transformed (i.e., less vivid, and affect-neutral) memories have been stored in the long-term memory. This transformation has been demonstrated in numerous experimental studies by different research teams (e.g., Barrowcliff et al., 2004; Gunter & Bodner, 2008; Lee et al., 2006; Van den Hout et al., 2010, 2011, 2012; Wadji et al., 2022). Moreover, both the nature and the speed of eye movements or other dual attention tasks have been shown to influence changes in memory (Lee & Cuijpers, 2013; Littel et al., 2017; Matthijssen et al., 2018; Maxfield et al., 2008; Van Veen et al., 2015.).

There is support from neurobiological research for the hypothesis of taxing WM as a potential mechanism of action (Van Pelt et al., 2025): 'Taxing working memory has been shown to suppress the activity of the amygdala, the brain structure that acts as the brain's alarm bell and plays a central role in the storage and reconsolidation of memories' (De Voogd et al., 2018, p. 11; Pierce & Black, 2023). This effect is not limited to eye movements. Research has shown that any intervention taxing a client's WM can cause a weakening and desensitizing effect on emotionally charged memories (de Voogd & Phelps, 2020).

The fact that eye movements are more effective than other WM-taxing tasks in alleviating trauma symptoms puzzled Wang and colleagues (2024), who explored possible explanations for this. One could hypothesize that eye movements tax the WM more than the other tested tasks; however, the authors assume other explanations must exist. Their experimental findings suggest that eye movements facilitate information processing by increasing information transmission of concurrent perception and memory and enhancing neural activities in the brain. They argue that information facilitation rather than disruption by WM taxation might explain eye movement's efficacy.

2. *Orienting response*

The orienting response (OR) is a reflex to assess whether a new situation or unfamiliar stimulus is dangerous. First, an arousal response occurs, accompanied by changes in the autonomic nervous system (a chain of physiological and neurobiological responses, such as accelerated breathing and heart rate, increased blood pressure, and skin conductance), meaning that the sympathetic nervous system is activated. When no danger is detected, de-arousal replaces the arousal response. Several physiological effects (such as decreased heart rate, blood pressure, and skin conductance) indicate a predominance of the parasympathetic nervous system, which returns the body to a calm state (Landin-Romero et al., 2018).

Based on this phenomenon, Armstrong and Vaughan (1996) proposed that eye movements elicit an OR, facilitating access to the traumatic memory without avoidance, followed by rapid extinction after discovering that there is no threat. Arousal increases, followed by rapid de-arousal once it is evident that there is no danger because the eye movements are predictable and follow a repetitive pattern. This phenomenon could be explained as a form of classical conditioning, or contra-conditioning, whereby an adverse memory is presented together with disconfirming information, thus forming a new association between certain stimulus aspects of an unpleasant memory and the automatically elicited relaxation response—the response aspects of this memory representation (Van Pelt et al., 2025). This state of de-arousal is assumed to make re-evaluation of the traumatic memory possible. According to this hypothesis, the ultimate consequence of this state change is that functional meaning can enter the cognitive system and adapted attribution of meaning can occur. This hypothesis is supported by, for example, Barrowcliff and colleagues (2003) and Lee and colleagues (2006).

1.2.2 **Psychophysiological Models**

3. *REM sleep*

One of the first theories was the analogy with REM sleep, pointing to similarities between the client's brain state during EMDR and REM sleep. Shapiro wrote in her early publications that saccadic eye movements presumably cause an anxiety reduction when confronted with memory material, parallel to the desensitization of dream material by rapid eye movements during REM sleep (Shapiro, 2001).

Stickgold (2007) proposed that the eye movements in EMDR, possibly through recurring ORs, move the brain into a memory-processing mode akin to REM sleep, promoting the integration of episodic traumatic memories into general semantic networks. Shapiro (2018, p. 373) writes that 'some of the physiological changes associated with eye movements are characteristic of the de-arousal correlates of the OR (decreased heart rate and skin conductance, increased heart rate variability)'. It is remarkable that 'physiological data collected during EMDR sessions offer support for the presence of both ORs and a REM-like state during desensitization of traumatic memories' (Shapiro, 2018, p. 373).

The function of REM sleep is information processing and memory consolidation. REM sleep deprivation leads to detrimental effects on concentration, memory consolidation, and learning. PTSD can be partly understood as resulting from disturbed REM sleep because traumatic memories have not been processed adequately (Stickgold, 2007). Therefore, activating a REM-like state while awake is assumed to aid in integrating episodic memories into general semantic networks (Landin-Romero et al., 2018).

Studies addressing the REM hypothesis directly are limited. Pagani and colleagues investigated the role of slow-wave sleep rather than REM sleep (Landin-Romero et al., 2018). Slow-wave sleep is crucial in memory consolidation and the reorganization of distant functional networks. It leads to weakening of traumatic memories and reconsolidation of new information (Landin-Romero et al., 2018). Empirical studies have found conflicting results or can be interpreted differently, so further research is needed to test this hypothesis (Landin-Romero et al., 2018).

1.2.3 Neurobiological Models

4. *Interhemispheric interaction and changed activation*

Neurobiological models suggest that the effects of EMDR therapy can be explained by either new or increased connections between areas in the brain, or increased or decreased activity of specific regions. The hypothesis of interhemispheric interaction posits that horizontal eye movements facilitate access to episodic memories and promote interaction between the brain's two hemispheres through the corpus callosum. However, EEG studies showed that vertical eye movements are not less effective in reducing the vividness and emotionality of memory images and that horizontal eye movements decrease interhemispheric interactions (Gunter & Bodner, 2008; Samara et al., 2011). An extension of the interhemispheric connectivity hypothesis has been suggested, including a two-stage cortical coherence model whereby intrahemispheric changes in the right hemisphere may occur along with interhemispheric changes. Leeds (2016a, b, 2023) proposed additional hypotheses regarding intra- and interhemispheric activation, including temporal binding via the thalamus, prefrontal flexibility/ mindfulness/ meta-cognitive awareness.

Over the past 20 years, much research has explored neurobiological changes as concomitants of EMDR; see Shapiro (2018) and Landin-Romero and colleagues (2018) to learn more about these studies. At this stage, it is unclear how much guidance we can expect from this type of research for clinical practice.

In summary, several interacting mechanisms are likely responsible for the observed clinical changes. It is unclear whether these may point to mechanisms or mediators (Leeds, 2023). At this stage, we know no more and no less about mechanisms of action for EMDR than we do for other psychotherapies. Hopefully, future experimental research results will shed cumulative light on this allowing us to better understand what we are doing and learn how to do it even better.

We conclude with a pertinent quote:

> To date, research on the working mechanisms and mediators of therapies has always been correlational, and to establish that a mediator is indeed a causal factor in the recovery process of a patient, studies must show a temporal relationship between the mediator and an outcome, a dose–response association, evidence that no third variable causes changes in the mediator and the outcome, support experimental research, and have a solid theoretical framework.
>
> (Cuijpers et al., 2019, p. 207)

1.3 Memories

This section discusses essential principles relevant to every EMDR C&A therapist.

1.3.1 Memory Components

To do EMDR, the child must be able to retrieve memory images of a specific event. Intrusive images (flashbacks, nightmares) are a hallmark symptom of PTSD (Brewin, 2015); thus, usually it is easy to retrieve. However, assessing a memory without images is challenging, though possible—for example, when children report having no images or suffer more from other memory components than intrusive images, such as smell (alcohol, semen, sweat) or a sound (a siren, screeching car brakes, certain music). Then these components are used to activate the complete memory. A prerequisite for applying EMDR is that components can be identified to fully activate the memory in the assessment phase. In cases where symptom-related memories have been identified with the help of the parents, while the child cannot (yet) verbalize (components of) these memories, the therapist can use the storytelling method.

1.3.2 Here and Now Perspective

Dealing with memories or fantasies from the here-and-now perspective is central in EMDR, including when working with children. However, children aged under six years still need to develop sufficient awareness of time to detect the difference between past and present. Therefore, the questions in the standard protocol have been adapted for this age group.

1.3.3 Reliability and Validity of Memory

Memory representations are subjective perceptions, as are conclusions derived from these representations. EMDR treatment aims to alter maladaptive perceptions, interpretations, and conclusions so that adaptive meaning connected to these memories is stored and consolidated in long-term memory (reconsolidation). As a result, the symptoms associated with these memories will disappear. Sometimes, this process must be clarified for the client. Consider situations in which, for instance, an adolescent asks for EMDR treatment not only to get rid of symptoms, but also to find out what exactly happened during an event. Such a request for help is possible when symptoms have arisen after an event (or series of events), and the person involved does not remember what happened, perhaps because they were drugged or drunk. In such situations, the following explanation could be considered:

> The fact that specific memories lead to symptoms says nothing about these memories' validity (or truthfulness). Symptoms do not result from events, but from the perception and interpretation of those events. Our memories are only mental representations of experiences as we have stored them in our minds, and they are subject to change over time. Therefore, the fact that we have symptoms does not prove that events occurred as

we remember them. Additionally, the reduction of symptoms following EMDR is no proof that the events occurred as we have stored them in our minds.

Shapiro (2018, pp. 298–301) wrote the following about the validity of memory:

> The very attempt at memory retrieval as a therapeutic goal may establish the belief in the client that a memory of abuse exists, that it should be revealed, and that there was indeed a perpetrator. Thus, this scenario could provide the perfect condition for eliciting 'false' or mistaken memories. When a memory is reported during EMDR, there is a possibility that (1) the image is a symbolic representation, (2) the event was only vicariously experienced, (3) the image is a result of trickery (e.g., a perpetrator in disguise), (4) the image is valid.

In short, memories may not be valid as objective and accurate representations of what occurred, for various reasons. Instead, they are valid as subjective representations of what happened and how the person stored this in their mind.

For these reasons, it is essential that the therapist only follows the client's association process and refrains from asking about details or interpretations of events that the client reports during the process. The therapist should inform clients about the unreliability of memory without disqualifying their experiences. Clients should draw their conclusions in response to their (surfaced) memories and not be directed by their therapist to do so (Shapiro, 2018). It is essential that the therapist realizes the above and explains this where necessary. Therapists can explain that EMDR is always aimed at symptom reduction and not at truth-finding. In most countries, therapists also have national guidelines, directives, or ethical codes to which they should adhere. We recommend that EMDR child and adolescent therapists are familiar with these directives. Everything that arises during the desensitization process is relevant for understanding the symptom(s), and for reducing them, but of no value for discovering the truth. EMDR always focuses on what is in the mind, and not on what actually happened.

1.4 Concluding Remarks

The AIP model serves as a working hypothesis, providing the foundation for EMDR therapy. The most prominent hypotheses regarding potential mechanisms of action—and the evidence supporting them—are discussed: working memory taxation (WMT), OR, REM, and neurobiological models that involve activating specific brain regions or strengthening connections between parts. Differentiating mechanisms of action and mediators is challenging, as is distinguishing the hypotheses across various levels (psychological, psychophysiological, and neurobiological). Further research is needed to gain a better understanding of this. Perhaps we will never fully understand how and why EMDR works. Nonetheless, we see in clinical practice that EMDR therapy is a powerful therapy that helps alleviate the suffering of children and their parents. For careful and proper application of EMDR, therapists should consider the principles discussed in this chapter.

2 The Impact of Trauma on Children

RENÉE BEER AND CARLIJN DE ROOS

2.1 Introduction

Many children (between 25% and 68%) experience one or more traumatic events before the age of 18 (Copeland et al., 2007; Lewis et al., 2019; Woolgar et al., 2022). The range of reported percentages can be due to differences in defining what constitutes a traumatic event, cultural norms, different instruments used for measuring, and various sources of information (Fairbank & Fairbank, 2009; Smith et al., 2019). Only a small percentage of children exposed to potentially traumatic events (16%) develop post-traumatic stress disorder (PTSD), with the rate varying by gender and type of event. PTSD appears to be significantly more common in girls than in boys, and it correlates more often with interpersonal trauma than with non-interpersonal trauma (Alisic et al., 2014; McLaughlin et al., 2012; Smith et al., 2019).

The experience of potentially traumatic events in childhood is a risk factor for the development of various problems related to mental health, such as impaired maturation of the brain and nervous system, difficulties in attachment, and the formation of negative cognitive schemas about oneself, others, and the world (Bastien et al., 2020).

Prevalence studies on the impact of trauma on adolescents within the clinical population in the United States demonstrated that adverse life experiences had preceded the onset of a psychiatric disorder in 44.6% (Green et al., 2010) and 58.3% (McLaughlin et al., 2012) of cases. This percentage was even higher (85%) in a retrospective assessment of files for adolescents admitted to a residential care facility in the Netherlands (Kroneman & Beer, 2013). These studies indicate that there is a moderate to high likelihood that children seen in child and adolescent psychiatry, mental health care, or youth care services have experienced traumatic events in their past.

In contrast, only a small percentage (16%) of children in the general population develop PTSD or other trauma-related psychopathology after traumatization (Alisic et al., 2014). Most children can cope with negative experiences on their own or with support from their environment. However, this is not true for the many children living in war zones (more than two million worldwide), as they are at high risk of developing psychopathology due to the limitation of protective factors, such as the support of parents, friends, neighbours, and the social infrastructure that is usually in place to ensure their safety and provide support (Danese et al., 2020, 2024).

Renée Beer and Carlijn de Roos, *The Impact of Trauma on Children*. In: *Handbook of EMDR for Children and Adolescents*. Edited by: Renée Beer and Carlijn de Roos, Oxford University Press.
DOI: 10.1093/oso/9780198918400.003.0002

The aim of trauma treatment in all circumstances is to reduce symptoms that have arisen due to stagnated information processing. One of the options for evidence-based trauma treatment is eye movement desensitization and reprocessing (EMDR).

This chapter explains why EMDR is essential for children who have developed trauma-related symptoms. It describes which types of traumatic events children can experience, what consequences these experiences can have, and what factors protect against or increase the risk that problems may arise because of stagnated trauma processing.

2.2 Traumatic Events

Events that can lead to trauma symptoms are referred to by various terms, such as 'shocking', 'overwhelming', 'intense', 'potentially traumatic,' or 'traumatic'. These events can be classified by the frequency of occurrence, the nature of the event, and the mode of exposure to it. These variables can affect the consequences of having experienced these events. Here, we discuss the most common classifications. See Box 2.1 for a brief definition of psychological trauma.

BOX 2.1 Psychological trauma

Trauma literally means 'wound'; in a medical context 'trauma' refers to a physical wound or serious physical injury, and outside the medical context to an internal state created by experiencing an event. The same event can lead to trauma symptoms in one person, but not in another. In this chapter, we refer to events that have led to trauma and trauma-related symptoms as 'traumatic events or experiences', following the DSM-5 (American Psychiatric Association, 2013). The symptoms are referred to as post-traumatic stress symptoms or trauma-related symptoms. Events that may lead to these symptoms are called 'potentially traumatic events'.

Firstly, the best-known classification of traumatic events is by their frequency of recurrence (Terr, 1991). Type I trauma refers to an event that has occurred once, such as an assault or a rape. Type II trauma, or chronic traumatization, relates to events that have occurred repeatedly over a long period, such as sexual abuse or neglect. A characteristic feature of persons being chronically traumatized is that they feel helpless and powerless, sometimes over many years—feelings from which there is no escape (Gersons, 2013; Wamser-Nanney, 2016). This classification covers a continuum from having experienced something negative once to multiple occurrences.

Secondly, De Bellis and Van Dillen (2005) proposed a classification based on the nature of the event:

- *Interpersonal traumatization:* trauma caused by human actions. This includes all forms of violence, such as war violence, terrorism, and robbery, and all forms of child abuse, such as emotional and educational neglect, domestic violence, physical abuse, sexual abuse, and exploitation.

- *Non-interpersonal traumatization:* trauma not caused by human actions. This includes events such as natural disasters, fire, confrontation with a life-threatening illness, and sudden and unexpected loss of a loved one. Medical interventions are initiated by other people; however, they are not intended to harm or hurt the child.

Interpersonal traumatization is common worldwide, and children exposed to it are at risk of developing PTSD and other psychiatric disorders (D'Andrea et al., 2012). The occurrence of several types of chronic interpersonal traumatic events from early childhood within the family context presents a risk that brain and personality development may be affected (Teicher & Samson, 2016). Because of the potential impact of this specific form of chronic trauma, the term 'complex trauma' has been proposed to describe this. This term is not included in the DSM-5. See also Section 2.4.2 of this chapter.

A third way to classify traumatic events is by the mode of exposure. The DSM-5 distinguishes between direct and indirect exposure of a person to a traumatic event (DSM-5, American Psychiatric Association, 2013). Indirect exposure means that the person was not present at the event but was informed about the event, which took place elsewhere. In contrast, witnessing the effect of a traumatic event on another person is considered a form of direct exposure, which is potentially even more traumatizing than being affected oneself. This may be due to the powerlessness experienced by watching the victim actively trying to survive (fight, flight, or freeze).

A specific form of indirect exposure is secondary traumatization, also known as vicarious traumatization, compassion fatigue, and empathy-based stress (Kim et al., 2022; Rauvola et al., 2019). This refers to symptoms that people may develop because they are repeatedly indirectly exposed to the traumatic experiences of others. This can include therapists or other professionals exposed to their clients' traumatic experiences and parents of children who have experienced traumatic events. The term secondary traumatization is also used to characterize the specific symptoms that children whose parents are victims of war may develop; such children may develop trauma-related symptoms through indirect exposure by being confronted with the functioning of their traumatized parents (Bachem et al., 2018; Dashorst et al., 2019; Greenblatt-Kimron et al., 2021).

Children frequent our practice because of PTSD or other trauma-related symptoms after direct or indirect confrontation with one or more types of traumatic events, single or chronic, or combinations of these types of events.

In cases of chronic trauma, it is sometimes the most recent event that causes the 'trauma bucket' to overflow and for PTSD symptoms to become visible. For example, a child who is being abused frequently and has experienced a fire recently may have nightmares about a fire. The content of the PTSD symptoms—in this case, the nightmares—relates directly to a specific recent event. Often, it is not possible to quickly ascertain which event has caused PTSD symptoms. For this reason, it is important to ask clients carefully during intake about the traumatic events they have experienced, as well as to explore their symptoms (both PTSD and beyond). This information is relevant for the therapists to formulate hypotheses about the development of symptoms and their possible relationship with (maladaptively processed) memories of traumatic events. It is essential to keep in mind that symptoms do not always appear immediately after a traumatic event (delayed onset).

2.3 Consequences

Traumatic experiences can lead to symptoms that disappear as the child processes their memories of the event adequately. Such processing typically consists of an alternation between reliving and avoiding aspects of or full memories of events. Re-experiencing and avoidance reactions can be intense and overwhelming at first. However, the reactions diminish in frequency and intensity until the memory is no longer emotionally charged. During the final phase of standard processing, children can pick up the threads of their lives and refocus on the present and their further development.

However, if the processing stagnates, physical and/or psychosocial problems arise, which can have repercussions on a child's social, cognitive, and emotional functioning, as well as on the family dynamics when family members are affected by daily exposure to the child's symptoms and the effects on their behaviour. This is when trauma treatments, such as EMDR, have a role.

Knowledge about many aspects of trauma-related disorders in children has increased enormously over the past 30 years. It is now well established how trauma-related symptoms can manifest themselves in various developmental stages (Beer & De Roos, 2017a; Cohen et al., 2010; Copeland et al., 2007). Factors and mechanisms that influence the likelihood of the emergence of trauma-related symptoms following traumatic events have been identified (Smith et al., 2019). McLaughlin and Lambert (2017) noted that disruptions in threat processing are a critical neurodevelopmental mechanism underlying the associations between child trauma and the onset of psychopathology. Research by Hiller and colleagues (2016) showed that natural recovery is unlikely if symptoms persist for six months after experiencing an event. Trauma treatment is then needed.

2.3.1 Symptoms at Different Developmental Stages

Traumatic experiences can cause a variety of reactions in children, and sometimes even mental disorders, according to the DSM-5. Children's reactions vary according to their developmental stage. Diagnosticians should be familiar with the diversity of children's potential responses to traumatic events so they can recognize these. During the diagnostic phase, age-specific reactions must be identified as the answer to the question of whether there is standard or stagnated trauma processing. Below is a list of typical age-specific trauma reactions. They may start as usual, transient reactions to an extreme event, but if they persist therapy is needed (Beer et al., 2021; Beer et al., 2024).

- ***Babies and infants (0–1.5 years)***

Dysregulation is the primary response to distress in babies and infants. It features inconsolable crying, overstretching, problems with drinking or eating, restlessness while sleeping, not seeking comfort when in pain, separation anxiety, and an apathetic or anxious expression in their eyes.

- ***Toddlers (> 1.5–3 years) and pre-schoolers (4–5 years)***

Very young children may experience feelings of helplessness and generalized anxiety. These may be expressed in (post-traumatic) play; regressive, aggressive, or destructive behaviour; difficulty with separation from parent(s) and clinging behaviour; fear of going to sleep; and nightmares about monsters.

- ***School-age children (primary school) (6–12 years)***

Children aged 6–12 years may experience physical symptoms (headaches, stomach aches) or sleep problems (fear of falling asleep, sleeping alone, fear of nightmares). They may become preoccupied with their actions during the event and their possible responsibility for what happened. Dysfunctional guilt can lead to concentration problems, inevitably resulting in the deterioration of school performance, and thus potentially damaging consequences for self-esteem. They may also develop aggressive and anxiety-inducing fantasies. They may endlessly repeat (in play, drawings, or conversation) what they have been through, become overwhelmed by sadness and fears, and continue worrying about them. 'Omen formation' can occur: the child becomes convinced that they missed omens that could have allowed them to predict what had happened. They believe they can avoid new traumas by being alert and recognizing warning signals. Omen formation is also found in older children and even adults.

- ***Adolescents (13–18 years)***

Characteristic for children in this stage of development is an internal struggle between a need for autonomy versus feelings of dependency and fear. If they are ashamed about what has happened to them, they can present a tendency not to want to communicate (they hide or conceal their distress), or they pretend nothing is wrong. They can be (significantly) focused on others, which may serve to help them escape from feelings of anxiety.

Another possible reaction in this group is to mirror the behaviour they experienced during a traumatic event (re-enactment behaviour). They may be dysfunctional at school: performance, behaviour, or truancy. They may seek refuge in 'thrill-seeking' behaviour, which gives them a kick and thrills and distracts them because of the risks involved (e.g., joyriding or dangerous sexual behaviours). Substance abuse can enable them to escape negative feelings and sensations. Fantasies about revenge and penance can dominate their thinking processes. Young people who have experienced prolonged violence or oppression and who closed themselves off from their inner processes are particularly vulnerable to this. This puts their community at risk. Their mistrust of others and their desire for revenge make them susceptible to the influence of terrorist organizations (Joshi & O'Donnell, 2003; Siegel et al., 2019).

2.3.2 ASD, PTSD, and CPTSD

This section includes some points of interest regarding the criteria for an acute stress disorder (ASD) in children, an overview of the criteria for PTSD, as set out in the DSM-5 (American Psychiatric Association, 2013), and a description of the requirements for complex PTSD (CPTSD) according to the ICD-11 (World Health Organization (WHO), 2019). It concludes with some reflections on the A-criterion for the traumatic event as described in the DSM-5.

ASD and PTSD are both classified as psycho-trauma or stressor-related disorders in the DSM-5. Box 2.2 shows an overview of all disorders falling under this heading.

BOX 2.2 Psychotrauma- or stressor-related disorders in DSM-5

- Reactive attachment disorder
- Disinhibited social disorder
- PTSD
- ASD
- Adjustment disorders
- Other specified trauma- or stressor-related disorder
- Unspecified trauma- or stressor-related disorder

Source: American Psychiatric Association, 2013

- ***ASD***

The DSM-5 describes the specific manifestation of several symptoms of ASD in young children. Table 2.1 shows symptoms in adults in the left column and symptoms in children ≤ six years of age in the right column.

The DSM explicitly mentions some examples of events that can lead to ASD in children, such as non-age-appropriate sexual experiences without violence or injury. Re-experiencing symptoms may manifest in children ≤ six years of age in the form of nightmares or repetitive play that directly or symbolically refers to the event. Young children do not necessarily

Table 2.1 ASD in adults and children according to DSM–5

Adults and children > 6 years	Children ≤ 6 years
Recurrent, involuntary, intrusive, and upsetting memories of the event	Repetitive play expressing themes or aspects of the event
Recurrent upsetting dreams, in which the content or affect is related to the event	Frightening dreams, where the content is not recognizably related to the event
Dissociative reactions (such as flashbacks) in which the person concerned feels or behaves as if the event is happening again	Dissociative moments during trauma-specific re-enactment in play

Source: American Psychiatric Association, 2013

demonstrate anxiety during exposure to the event or symptoms of re-experiencing. Finally, preoccupation is also possible, in addition to avoidance of situations that remind of the event—for example, a child who talks incessantly about dogs after being bitten by a dog yet no longer dares to go outside for fear of encountering a dog.

- ***PTSD***

Box 2.3 lists the PTSD criteria in the DSM-5 for children over six years and adults; criteria for young children (< six years) are indicated by '*'.

BOX 2.3 **PTSD criteria DSM-5, A-H**

PTSD DSM-5, Criterion A

A. Exposure to actual or threatened death, serious injury, or sexual violence, in one (or more) of the following ways:

1. Experienced the event(s) personally.
2. Witnessed the event(s) that happened to others.

*Especially primary care givers.

NB: Excludes events witnessed through electronic media, TV, film, or photo.

3. Hearing that the event(s) happened to a close relative, or close friend(s). For an actual or imminent death of relative or close friend(s), the event(s) must be violent in nature or involve an accident.

*parent or caregiver

4. Experience of repeated or extreme exposure to horrific details of the event(s) (such as emergency workers having to collect mortal remains; police officers repeatedly confronted with the details of child abuse).

NB: Criterion A4 does not apply to exposure through electronic media, TV, films, or photographs, unless such exposure is work related.

Criterion B

B. One or more of the following intrusive symptoms are associated with the event and started after the event occurred:

1. Recurrent, involuntary, intrusive, and disruptive* memories of the event(s).

NB: In children over six years old, there may be repetitive play reflecting themes or aspects of the event(s).

*NB: Spontaneous and intrusive memories need not necessarily appear as deregulation but can be expressed in the form of re-enactments during play.

2. Recurrent upsetting dreams in which the content and/or effect of the dream is related to the event(s).

NB: It is sometimes impossible to determine whether the frightening content is associated with the event.

3. Dissociative reactions, such as flashbacks: the affected person feels or acts as if the event(s) are reoccurring. Reactions vary greatly in intensity, the most extreme manifestations being a complete lack of awareness of the current environment.

NB: Children may re-enact the event(s).

4. Intense or prolonged psychological disturbance when exposed to internal or external stimuli that symbolize or resemble an aspect of the event.
5. Distinct physiological responses to memories of the events.

Criterion C

C. One or more of the following symptoms that start or worsen after the event(s) must be present. These symptoms include persistent avoidance of stimuli associated with the event(s) or negative changes in cognitions and moods associated with the event(s). (Only one of the symptoms needs to be present in young children.)

1. Avoidance or attempts to avoid painful memories, thoughts, or feelings about, or strongly associated with, the event(s).

*Avoidance or attempts to avoid activities, places, or physical aspects that trigger memories of the event(s).

2. Avoidance or attempted avoidance of external aspects reminiscent of the event(s) (people, places, conversations, activities, projects, situations) that evoke painful memories, thoughts, or feelings about, or strongly associated with, the event(s).

Criterion D

D. Negative changes in cognitions and mood, related to the event(s), that started or worsened after the event(s) occurred, as evidenced by two or more of the following characteristics. (Only one of the symptoms needs to be present in young children.)

1. An inability to remember an important aspect of the event, usually due to dissociative amnesia, excluding other factors such as head injury or alcohol or drug use.
2. Persistent exaggerated negative beliefs, or expectations about self, others, or the world.
3. Persistent, distorted cognitions about the causes or consequences of the event(s), leading the person to blame themselves or others.
4. Persistent state of mind, for example fear, disgust, anger, guilt, or shame.

*Strongly increased frequency of negative moods, such as fear, guilt, sadness, shame, or confusion.

5. Markedly reduced interest in participation in major activities.

*Including strong reduction of play.

6. Feelings of detachment, or alienation from others.

*Socially withdrawn behaviour.

7. Persistent inability to experience positive emotions, such as inability to experience, happiness, satisfaction, or loving feelings.

*Persistent decrease in expressing positive emotions.

BOX 2.3 **continued**

Criterion E-H

E. Changes in arousal and reactivity associated with the event(s) and started or worsened after the event(s) occurred, as evidenced by two or more of the following features:
    1. Irritable behaviour and outbursts of anger (with little or no cause), usually manifesting as verbal or physical aggression, including extreme tantrums, towards people or things.
    2. Reckless or self-destructive behaviour.
    3. Hypervigilance.
    4. Exaggerated startle reactions.
    5. Concentration problems.
    6. Disruption of sleep, such as difficulty falling asleep or restless sleep.

F. The duration of the disorder (criteria B, C, D, and E) is longer than one month.

G. The disorder causes clinically significant dysregulation or impaired relations with parents, siblings, peers, or other caregivers or at school.

H. The disorder cannot be attributed to the physiological effects of a substance (such as medication, alcohol) or to a somatic disorder.

Source: American Psychiatric Association, 2013.

CPTSD

For many years, several authors (e.g., Cook et al., 2003; Van der Kolk & Andrea, 2010) have advocated for a revision of the term PTSD, believing it to be far too narrow to capture the heterogeneity of outcomes that may result from specific types of chronic traumatic experiences in childhood, referred to by the term 'complex trauma'. They proposed the term 'developmental trauma disorder' to describe the types of traumas that can affect the child's development on several fronts. However, this proposed classification has not been included in the DSM-5 because empirical evidence to validate this theoretical classification is provisionally lacking (De Jongh et al., 2016; Resick et al., 2012). By contrast, the ICD-11 (World Health Organization, 2019) includes the classification 'complex PTSD' for children who meet the criteria listed in Table 2.2.

Table 2.2 CPTSD according to ICD-11

A CPTSD diagnosis requires that all PTSD diagnostic criteria are met (exposure to at least one traumatic event and one symptom from each of the three clusters), along with at least one symptom from each of the three DSO symptom clusters.	
PTSD clusters	+ Disturbances of self-organization (DSO)
Re-experiencing the traumatic events	Emotional dysregulation
Avoidance of the trauma reminders	Interpersonal difficulties
Heightened sense of threat (hypervigilance, startle response)	Negative self-concept

Source: Phelps et al., 2022; World Health Organization, 2022

2.3.3 The A-Criterion

The DSM-IV posited two criteria for a traumatic event:

- A1—Objective criterion: The person concerned has been directly or indirectly exposed to actual or imminent death, serious injury, or a threat to physical integrity.
- A2—Subjective criterion: The person concerned experienced or reacted to the event with intense fear, horror, disgust, or helplessness.

The A1 and A2 criteria had to both be fulfilled for an event to qualify as traumatic. This implied that if a child showed more than sufficient PTSD symptoms to meet the criteria but had not experienced an event that met both the A1 and A2 criteria, they could not be classified as having PTSD. Verlinden and colleagues (2013) showed that children can also develop PTSD after adverse life events that do not meet the A1 criterion: for example, being bullied, parental divorce, the death of a grandparent, or the loss of a pet. Children who had experienced events that met the A1 criterion were twice as likely to develop PTSD as those who had not. In contrast, the subjective A2 criterion proved to have a much greater predictive value for the development of PTSD: children who had experienced events that met the A2 criterion were nine times more likely to develop PTSD.

It is remarkable that in the DSM-5 the A2 criterion has been removed. The reason for this is that studies in adults showed that the A2 criterion had no added value over and above A1 as a predictor for PTSD (Verlinden et al., 2013). However, these studies had mainly involved police officers and military personnel who, by virtue of their profession, might not readily say—admit?—that they reacted to an event with fear, horror, or disgust because they typically feel that this is what they have been trained to deal with. For this reason, they might therefore indicate that they 'can handle it'. The study by Verlinden and colleagues (2013) convincingly showed the added value of the A2 criterion as a predictor, at least for children. The removal of the A2 criterion from the DSM-5 has increased the risk that children for whom trauma therapy is indicated will not receive this therapy and will maintain symptoms for an unnecessarily long time.

Thanks to the well-known study by Felitti and colleagues (1998), the potential consequences of adverse childhood experiences on physical and mental health have become more widely appreciated. Adults who experienced four or more adverse childhood experiences in their youth were found to live, on average, 20 years less and to face many more physical illnesses than those without these experiences. This knowledge makes it evident that recognizing and treating symptoms resulting from adverse life experiences as early as possible is necessary.

Therefore, during the intake and diagnostic phase we recommend always asking if there have been what Shapiro (2018) calls 'big T-trauma' or 'little T-trauma' events. If we limit ourselves to the DSM-5, A-criterion, children will continue to carry the burden of under-recognized trauma-related symptoms, the risk of undertreatment, and chronic symptoms. Diagnosticians should also be aware that the development of partial (sub-clinical) PTSD in children following a traumatic experience is the rule rather than the exception and can be as disabling as full-blown PTSD (Meentken et al., 2020; Smith et al., 2019). And, lastly, it is essential to realize that symptoms may occur both immediately after the event(s) as well as later (delayed onset). Effective trauma therapy is therefore needed also for these children.

2.3.4 Comorbidity

PTSD is a disabling disorder and often goes together with other psychiatric disorders, such as mood, behavioural, and anxiety disorders. Children may develop comorbid psychopathology next to PTSD or any of the various disorders within the category of trauma and stressor-related disorders, especially after chronic traumatization. Thus, PTSD is just the tip of the iceberg and can be accompanied by problems with emotion regulation, attachment, negative beliefs about themselves and others, impulse control, executive functions (attention and concentration), and stress regulation (Jonkman et al., 2013).

Furthermore, it is demonstrated that children with PTSD have a higher risk of developing comorbid disorders than children without PTSD, and that they are more likely to become victims of additional traumatic events: that is, re-victimization (Walker & Wamser-Nanney, 2023).

Untreated trauma symptoms can have a significant impact on social, emotional, physical, and educational outcomes, thus presenting as a substantial threat to a young person's overall developmental trajectory (e.g., McDermott, 2009).

So, early identification of PTSD and psychiatric comorbidity is of great importance to providing children with appropriate, timely therapy (Verlinden et al., 2015). Fortunately, we often see that effective trauma therapy leads not only to the reduction of PTSD or other trauma-related symptoms but also to the reduction of comorbid symptoms.

2.4 Risk and Protective Factors

Based on research, a picture is emerging of the factors that influence the development of psychopathology (Beer & De Roos, 2017b; De Roos, 2021; Kraemer, 2016). However, many associations remain hypothetical. The relationship between the type of event and the resultant consequences does not appear to be linear. Symptoms are not necessarily more severe the more drastic or the longer the event. Outcomes are determined not only by the nature of the event but also by child, family, and environmental factors. Knowledge of relevant (predicting or moderating) variables helps us predict which children are at increased risk of developing symptoms after experiencing a potentially traumatic event.

There are two types of predictors: risk factors, which increase the likelihood of developing trauma-related symptoms, and protective factors, which decrease the likelihood.

Research has been conducted on the role of 'fixed' factors (cannot be influenced), such as a child's age, gender, and ethnicity, as well as on the role of 'amendable' (modifiable) factors, such as cognitions, coping styles, and competencies. The role of environmental characteristics, such as social support from family or friends, has also been studied. Table 2.3 presents factors that influence the likelihood that trauma-related symptoms will emerge. These factors are explained in Sections 2.4.1 and 2.4.2.

2.4.1 Risk Factors

The following list presents explanations for the risk factors listed in Table 2.3 and their effect on the development of psychopathology.

Table 2.3 Risk and protective factors for the development of psychopathologies

Risk factors (Exacerbated by social isolation: environmental factors)		
Event	**Child**	**Parent–family**
Immediate separation from parent(s) Seriousness of consequences: - Permanent - Tangible or intangible - Physical injury - Loss of loved ones - Increased exposure to media reporting and legal proceedings	- High peri–traumatic stress - Previously traumatized - Previous psychiatric or psychosocial problems - Limited coping skills - Fragile temperament - Dysfunctional meaning-making (appraisals)	- High peri-traumatic stress in parents - Processing stagnated in parents - Previous psychiatric or psychosocial problems in parents - Changes in family functioning
Protective factors (Enhanced by social involvement and support: environmental factors)		
Event	**Child**	**Parent–family**
Proximity to parents during events or immediately afterwards	- Problem-solving skills - Social skills - Adequate impulse control - Positive self-image (self-efficacy) - Extravert - Functional meaning-making (appraisals)	- Support from parents - Adequate coping by parents with situation and reactions of family members

Sources: Carlson et al., 2016; Cohen et al., 2010; Grant et al., 2006; Pat-Horenczyk et al., 2008

- ***Event***
  - Being separated from the parents

If the child is with their parents during the event, they can ask for protection or the parent can offer it, which can lower the stress levels of both. If the child is separated from their parents, they may worry about how their parents are during the event, which can increase their stress level. Conversely, parents may worry about their child, which affects their reactions to the child afterward.

  - The severity of the consequences

In cases of permanent loss (for example, of a family member) or permanent damage (for example, of a limb), the child not only faces the task of processing the event but must also learn to cope with the loss resulting from the event. This increases the risk of developing trauma symptoms.

  - Increased exposure to media reporting and legal proceedings

In the case of indirect exposure to the event, confrontation with the event by exposure to media reports or legal proceedings may increase the likelihood of the development or persistence of psychopathology. Exposure to images and other information about the event through the press activates memories. It also sometimes creates new ones or adds new aspects to the memory due to the additional information provided. This frequent activation of the traumatic memory hinders the completion of the natural trauma processing.

- ***Child factors***
  - High peri-traumatic stress

The degree of emotional stress experienced during or directly after an event can be expressed through extreme panic or dissociative reactions, such as derealization, depersonalization, or amnesia. These reactions are a risk factor for the later development of PTSD (Cohen et al., 2010; Memarzia et al., 2021; Peltonen et al., 2017).

  - Previous traumatization

If the child has been traumatized previously, there is a chance that similarities between the events will result in increased psychopathology. However, in some cases, repeated traumatization results in the opposite: that is, an increase in resilience.

  - Previous psychiatric/psychosocial problems

Pre-existing psychiatric or psychosocial problems increase the likelihood that the child will develop symptoms in response to the new event. This happens because the child lacks specific skills or due to circumstances that inhibit the child's ability to solve problems.

  - Coping skills

Research has yet to yield consistent results regarding the role of coping skills as a predictor. Possibly, this is related to unclear and inconsistent definitions of 'adequate coping skills'.

- Vulnerable temperament

A child who tends to react strongly to emotional stimuli will also be more susceptible to traumatic stress by reacting more intensely. This increases the chances of developing psychopathology.

- Appraisals

Appraisals are cognitions related to assessing the event and one's own reactions. Parents and children give meaning to the event and their reactions (appraisals). Depending on its content, an appraisal can be a protective or a risk factor. Therapists regard meaning-making by parents and children as one of the most important predictors of whether PTSD will develop (Hiller et al., 2021; Meiser-Stedman et al., 2019).

- ***Parent and family factors***

- High peri-traumatic stress in parents

The extent to which parents were upset during or directly after an event correlates highly with the severity of the child's symptomatology and is considered a significant predictor. Consider the phenomenon of 'social referencing' (see Section 10.3.1).

- Stagnated trauma processing in the parent

When trauma processing has become stagnant in parents, it may interfere with their functioning as adequate educators. Several studies have found a positive correlation between the incidence of PTSD in mothers and in their children (Afzal et al., 2023; Bronner, 2009; Morris et al., 2013).

- Previous psychiatric or psychosocial problems in parents

Another risk factor at the family level is pre-existing psychiatric or psychosocial problems. As a result, parents may not be emotionally available to the child (Greene et al., 2023).

- Changed family functioning

When an event upsets family members to the degree that the family functions differently and previous structures no longer work (even if temporarily), support for the child is inadequate, the child feels insecure, and psychopathologies are maintained.

- ***Environmental factors***

- Social Isolation

A lack of support from the school, family, the circle of friends, or the neighbourhood, which may isolate the child or family, increases the likelihood of psychopathology.

2.4.2 Protective Factors

Fewer research studies are available on protective factors than on risk factors. Many of the protective factors are simply opposites of the risk factors. The following factors seem to promote resilience in children.

- ***Events***
  - Proximity to parents

When parents are present, they can offer protection and comfort.

- ***Child factors***
  - Problem-solving skills, social skills, adequate impulse control, a positive self-image, and extraversion

These skills and personality traits can protect the child against the development of trauma-related symptoms. See also the discussion of meaning-making in Section 2.5.1.

- ***Parent and family factors***
  - Supportive parents

Parents can stimulate standard trauma processing and offer support through proximity and provision of care.

  - Adequate coping by family members

The ability of family members to handle their stress reactions adequately and, if necessary, to ask for and receive support from their social environment is also an essential factor in promoting resilience.

- ***Environmental factors***
  - Support

Social support reduces the risk of isolation and resultant psychopathology.

> **Recommendation**
>
> Based on the knowledge summarized in this chapter, we recommend assessing not only symptoms but also protective factors and risk factors in the diagnostic phase. This additional information enables the therapist to deduce whether other interventions besides EMDR are indicated to strengthen protective factors.

2.5 Concluding Remarks

This chapter describes the impact that trauma can have on the lives of children and the chance that they might develop various symptoms in response to traumatic experiences. Whether these symptoms develop depends not only on the nature of the event but also on factors specific to the child, their family, and the environment. It is well established that children with PTSD are more likely to develop comorbid disorders in childhood and mental disorders in adult life. The development of partial PTSD after a traumatic experience is the rule rather than the exception in children, and it can be just as disabling as full-blown PTSD. Research data and clinical practice experience have generated a consensus in the field that early identification of and therapy for trauma-related symptoms are of great importance to provide the child with optimal developmental opportunities. Once trauma-related symptoms are identified, prompt delivery of effective trauma treatment can lead to the elimination of already-present developmental delays and prevent new ones.

3 Empirical Research

RENÉE BEER AND CARLIJN DE ROOS

3.1 Introduction

Numerous studies—including more than 30 randomized controlled trials (RCTs)—have demonstrated that EMDR is effective for the treatment of PTSD in adults. Thanks to these studies, EMDR has been designated as one of the first-choice treatments in many national and international guidelines for the treatment of PTSD (De Jongh et al., 2024a). For PTSD in children, the evidence base is steadily growing, although the number of good-quality studies still lags behind the extent of adult research (Beer, 2018). The efficacy of the treatment of PTSD in children has now been tested in 10 RCTs, and EMDR has been adopted in several sets of international guidelines for children (ISTSS, 2019; NICE, 2018b; World Health Organization, 2024). Nevertheless, additional research is urgently needed. This chapter provides an overview of the published effectiveness studies conducted in children and adolescents (0–18 years).

We include an overview of effectiveness studies in children and adults with an intellectual disability (ID) here because much research has occurred in this target group. These clients are treated using the EMDR protocol for children and adolescents, and the therapists involved (preferably) have attended EMDR C&A training. Chapter 16 provides information about treatment aspects for this target group.

This chapter encompasses an overview of controlled studies, such as RCTs and single case experimental design studies (SCEDS), on paediatric PTSD. RCTs must meet the criteria of good research projects and the international standard for journal editors to assess research publications. These criteria are defined by the Consolidation of the Standards Of Reporting Trials (CONSORT) statement, a guideline updated in 2025 and developed by a consortium of epidemiologists, researchers, editors, and statisticians. See CONSORT Statement. See CONSORT Statement (Hopewell et al., 2025). Standards for replicated SCEDS are defined within the Single-Case Reporting Guideline in Behavioral Interventions (SCRIBE; Tate et al., 2016) and the What Works Clearinghouse (WWC, 2022).

Non-controlled studies for PTSD and case reports are not mentioned in this chapter because they contribute little to the guidelines' evidence base for EMDR. Nonetheless, these studies have great value and show promising results; they are included in other reviews of

Renée Beer and Carlijn de Roos, *Empirical Research*. In: *Handbook of EMDR for Children and Adolescents*.
Edited by: Renée Beer and Carlijn de Roos, Oxford University Press. © 2026, Oxford University Press. For the English edition.
DOI: 10.1093/oso/9780198918400.003.0003

EMDR studies for children with PTSD symptoms (see, for example, Adler-Tapia & Settle, 2009; Barron et al., 2019; Beer, 2018). However, this chapter does include summarized non-controlled studies on the effectiveness of EMDR in areas beyond PTSD, where research is still in its infancy, to indicate the preliminary results of studies in these areas. Chapter 11 discusses effectiveness studies on group protocols, and Chapter 8 discusses studies using the storytelling method.

This chapter covers the following topics: evidence for the efficacy of EMDR treatment of PTSD (regular and complex) (Section 3.2); its efficacy for other conditions, such as depressive disorder and conduct disorder (Section 3.3); challenges for future research (Section 3.4); and practical recommendations for new researchers (Section 3.5).

3.2 **Efficacy for PTSD**

3.2.1 **RCTs**

For the treatment of PTSD in children (aged 4–18) with EMDR, 10 RCTs have been published. Table 3.1 presents an overview.[1]

The evidence base for EMDR therapy as a treatment for PTSD has grown gradually over the years. Most studies compared EMDR therapy and wait-list control conditions (Ahmad & Sundelin-Wahlsten, 2007; Chemtob et al., 2002; De Roos et al., 2017; Kemp et al., 2009). Other control conditions were care-as-usual (Meentken et al., 2020; Soberman et al., 2002) or psychoeducation (Jaberghaderi et al., 2019). However, five of the 10 RCTs involved a comparison between EMDR therapy and trauma-focused CBT (de Roos et al., 2011, 2017; Diehle et al., 2014; Jaberghaderi et al., 2004, 2019), with sample sizes ranging from 19–139 participants of various ages (range 4–18 years). Only two studies also included preschool-aged children (de Roos et al., 2011; Meentken et al., 2020). The types of traumatic events that children included in these studies had experienced were single trauma, multiple traumata, sexual abuse, interpersonal violence, and natural or man-made disasters.

All but one RCT found that EMDR therapy was associated with a significant reduction in PTSD and comorbid symptoms or a loss of PTSD diagnosis compared to wait-list, psychoeducation, or care-as-usual (CAU). Treatment results occurred in relatively few sessions (3–8). The only RCT not showing a significant decrease in the severity of PTSD symptoms was the study by Meentken and colleagues (2020). This might be because children with full-blown PTSD were excluded, so there was little room for a decline in PTSD symptom scores across the treatment and compared to the control group.

Furthermore, the five RCTs comparing EMDR therapy to trauma-focused CBT showed no difference in the reduction of PTSD symptoms between either trauma treatment, meaning that both were equally effective. The only apparent difference between the two treatments is preliminary evidence from four of these five RCTs (de Roos et al., 2011, 2017; Jaberghaderi et al., 2004, 2019) showing that treatment results were achieved with EMDR in fewer sessions than with a form of trauma-focused CBT (range = 25–50% more efficient).

[1] References pertaining to the measures mentioned in this Chapter (in Tables 3.1, 3.2.a, 3.2.b, and 3.3) are omitted from the bibliography, as they can be found online.

Table 3.1 Overview of RCTs on PTSD with children and adolescents

Author(s)	N	Setting	Intervention (number of sessions)	Outcomes/dependent variables	Measure(s)	Results
Ahmad et al., 2007	33	Children 6–16 years who experienced at least one traumatic event and grew up in a condition with physically or mentally unavailable parent for several reasons	EMDR (8) vs WL EMDR: n = 17 WL: n = 16	PTSD symptoms Treatment session measures	DICA PTSS-C	EMDR > WL Significant reduction in PTSD symptoms
Chemtob et al., 2002	32	Children 6–12 years who have experienced a hurricane	EMDR (3) vs WL EMDR: n = 17 WL: n = 15	PTSD symptoms Anxiety Depression Number of visits to school nurse	CRI RCMAS CDI	For both treatments, significant reduction pre- to post-treatment and pre- to 6 months FU in PTSD symptoms, anxiety/ depressive symptoms, and health care visits.
De Roos et al., 2011	52	Children 4–18 years who experienced an explosion of a fireworks factory	EMDR (max. 4) vs CBT (max. 4) EMDR: n = 26 CBT: n = 26	Post-traumatic stress Anxiety Depression Emotional/behavioural symptoms	UCLA PTSD-RI CROPS PROPS BDS MASC CBCL	EMDR = CBT: Significant reduction on all measures: PTSD, anxiety, depression, and emotional/ behavioural symptoms post-treatment and at 3 months follow-up. Mean number of sessions: EMDR < CBT (3.2 sessions vs 4 sessions).

De Roos et al., 2017	103	Children 8–18 years who experienced a single traumatic event	EMDR (max. 6) vs Cognitive Behavioural Writing Therapy (max. 6) vs WL EMDR: n = 43 CBWT: n = 42 WL: n = 18	PTSD diagnosis and symptoms Anxiety Depression Emotional/behavioural symptoms Somatic symptoms Negative trauma-related beliefs Quality of life	ADIS-C/P CRTI- C/P RCADS-C/P SDQ- Y/P CSI-C-P CPTCI Kidscreen27 C/P	EMDR> WL CBWT >WL EMDR = CBWT Significant reduction post-treatment in PTSD, anxiety, depression, emotional/ behavioural symptoms and negative trauma-related beliefs, maintained at 3- and 12-month follow-up. Mean number of sessions: EMDR < CBWT (4.1 vs 5.4 sessions).
Diehle et al., 2014	48	Children 8–18 years who experienced a single or multiple traumatic events	EMDR (8) vs TF-CBT (8) EMDR: n = 25 TF-CBT: n = 23	PTSD diagnosis and symptoms Anxiety Depression Behavioural problems	CAPS-CA ADIS-P CRIES-C RCADS-C/P SDQ-P	EMDR=TF-CBT Significant reduction in PTSD post-treatment Mean number of sessions EMDR = TF-CBT.
Jaberghade-ri et al., 2004	19	Girls 12–13 years who have experienced sexual abuse; 14 completed pre- and post-treatment	EMDR (max. 12) vs CBT (max.12) EMDR: n = 7 CBT: n = 7	PTSD symptoms Problematic behaviour in school	CROPS PROPS Rutter Teacher Scale	EMDR=CBT: Significant reduction in PTSD symptoms and behavioural problems post-treatment. Mean number of sessions: EMDR< CBT. (Mean 6.1 vs 11.6).
Jaberghade-ri et al., 2019	139	Children 8–12 years who were victims of domestic violence	CBT (6 to max 12) vs EMDR (3 to max. 12) vs Control CBT: n = 40 EMDR: n = 40 Control: n = 59	PTSD symptoms Problematic behaviour exhibited in school	LITES CROPS PROPS RTS	EMDR = CBT > Control Significant reduction in PTSD post-treatment. No change in behaviour in classroom Mean number of sessions: EMDR < CBT (mean 5 vs 9)

continued

Table 3.1 *Continued*

Author(s)	N	Setting	Intervention (number of sessions)	Outcomes/dependent variables	Measure(s)	Results
Kemp et al., 2009	27	Children 6–12 years who have experienced a motor vehicle accident	EMDR (4) vs WL EMDR: n = 13 WL: n = 14	PTSD symptoms Anxiety Depression Behavioural problems Memory-related distress	CPTS-RI PTS-RI/P STAIC CDS CBCL	EMDR > WL Significant reduction in PTSD symptoms (CPTS-RI), clinician-rated PTSD diagnostic criteria and SUDS. Gains maintained at 3- and 12-month follow-up
Meentken et al., 2020	74	Children 4–15 years who experienced medical trauma	EMDR vs CAU (mean 3.5) EMDR: n = 37 CAU: n = 37	Subthreshold PTSD symptoms (CAPS-CA/DIPA), anxiety, quality of sleep	CRTI, SCARED-NL, CDI-2, SSR/CSHQ	EMDR > CAU. Significant reduction in symptoms of blood-injection-injury phobia, depression, and sleep problems. EMDR = CAU: subthreshold PTSD symptoms:
Soberman et al., 2002	29	Boys 10–16 years with conduct problems in residential or day treatment, multiply traumatized	CAU vs CAU + EMDR (3) CAU: n = 15 CAU + EMDR: n = 14	PTSD symptoms Behavioural problems Memory-related distress	IES-8 CROPS PROPS PRS BRS	CAU + EMDR > CAU: Significant reductions in memory-related distress (SUD) post-treatment. Significant reduction of problem behaviours at 2-month follow-up.

EMDR: Eye Movement Desensitization and Reprocessing; ADIS = Anxiety Disorders Interview Schedule (ADIS-C and ADIS-P for DSM-IV; Silverman & Albano, 1996); BDS = Birleson Depression Scale (Birleson, 1981); BRS = Behavioral Reward Scale, C/P/A = Child version/Parent version/Adolescent version (Butler & Lord, 2021); CAPS-CA = Clinician-Administered PTSD Scale for Children and Adolescents (Nader et al., 1996); CBCL = Child Behavior Checklist (Achenbach, 1991); CBWT = Cognitive Behavioral Writing Therapy; CDI = Children's Depression Inventory (Kovacks, 1992); CDS = Children's Depression Scale (Lang & Tisher, 1978); C-PTCI = Child Post Traumatic Cognitions Inventory (Meiser-Stedman et al., 2009); CPTS-RI = Child Post Traumatic Stress Reaction Index (Frederick, 1992); CRI = Child Reaction Index (Pynoos et al., 1987); CRTI = Revised Child Response to Trauma Inventory (Alisic et al., 2012);CRIES = Children Revised Impact of Event Scale (Verlinden et al., 2014a, 2014b); CROPS = Child Report of Posttraumatic Stress Symptoms (Greenwald & Rubin, 1999); CSHQ = Child Sleep Habits Questionnaire (Goodlin et al., 2008); CSI = Child Somatization Inventory (Walker et al., 2009); DICA = Diagnostic Interview for Children and Adolescents (Reich, 2000); IES-8 = Impact of Event Scale (Horowitz et al., 1979); LITES = Life Incidence of Traumatic Events Scale (Nilsson et al., 2010); MASC = Multi-dimensional Anxiety Scale for Children (March et al., 1997); PROPS = Parent Report of Posttraumatic Stress Symptoms (Greenwald & Rubin, 1999); PTSD = post-traumatic stress disorder; PTSS-C = Post-Traumatic Stress Symptom Scale for Children (Ahmad et al., 2000); PRS = Problem Rating Scale (Mooney et al., 2005); PTS-RI = Post-Traumatic Stress Reaction Index (Steinberg et al., 2004); RCADS = Revised Children's Anxiety and Depression Scale (Chorpita et al., 2000); RCMAS = Revised Children's Manifest Anxiety Scale (Reynolds & Richmond, 1985); RTS = Rutter Teacher Scale (Resanov et al., 1998); SCARED-NL = Dutch Screen for Child Anxiety Related Emotional Disorders (Muris et al., 1998); SDQ = Strengths and Difficulties Questionnaire (Goodman, 2001); SSR = Sleep Self Report (Steur et al., 2019); STAIC = State-Trait Anxiety Inventory for Children (Spielberger, 1983); TF-CBT = trauma-focused cognitive behavioural therapy; UCLA PTSD-RI = University of California Los Angeles PTSD Reaction Index (Steinberg et al., 2004); WL = wait-list.

It is noteworthy that the methodological quality of the RCTs conducted varies. Some study limitations are small sample sizes, the absence of a diagnostic interview for PTSD, the lack of appropriate treatment fidelity checks, and no long-term follow-up assessments. Accordingly, additional methodologically rigorous RCTs of EMDR therapy for PTSD, meeting the CONSORT criteria, should be conducted and reported in the coming years.

So far, studies into the effectiveness of EMDR for children under the age of eight years are limited, but results of pertinent research projects are forthcoming and will be published in due course. More research is needed with children (specifically pre-schoolers aged 0–4 years) into the EMDR storytelling method for the treatment of preverbal trauma. For an overview of studies regarding the effectiveness of EMDR for PTSD in young children (< eight years), see Chapter 8. In summary, we can conclude that these studies show a decrease in PTSD symptoms and emotional and behavioural symptoms post-treatment and at short-term follow-up.

3.2.2 Meta-Analyses and Guidelines

- ***Meta-analyses***

Several meta-analyses have analysed the effectiveness of varied psychological and psychosocial treatments for PTSD in children (8–18) exposed to a range of traumatic events (single and multiple) (Bastien et al., 2020; Gutermann et al., 2016; Harvey & Talor, 2010; Kowalik et al., 2011; Morina et al., 2016). The findings show that trauma-focused interventions (i.e., EMDR therapy, prolonged exposure therapy, trauma-focused CBT, cognitive therapy for PTSD) yield effect sizes in the medium–large range relative to no-treatment control conditions for the symptoms of PTSD and comorbid conditions (Smith et al., 2019). The effects of these treatments were maintained at follow-up, and relapse rates were low. Findings of a meta-analysis regarding the feasibility of EMDR and other trauma treatments demonstrate that dropout was not higher in trauma-focused therapies than in non-trauma-focused treatments. Thus, trauma-focused treatments are well tolerated (Simmons et al., 2021).

To determine the relative effectiveness of a broad range of psychological interventions for PTSD, Hoppen and colleagues (2024) conducted a network meta-analysis (NMA). This type of analysis allows estimation of the relative effects of treatment that may not have been compared directly in RCTs. This NMA is the most comprehensive one to date and included 67 RCTs and 5,297 children and adolescents with full or subthreshold PTSD. Five groups of interventions were evaluated: TF-CBT, EMDR, other trauma-focused interventions, non-trauma-focused (non-TF) interventions, and multidisciplinary treatments (MDTs). Most RCTs (73%) examined TF-CBT, followed by EMDR. The findings of this NMA analysis showed that post-treatment TF-CBT, EMDR, MDTs, and non-TF interventions were all effective in treating PTSD when compared to passive controls with significant pooled effects (all Hedges' g[2]>0.84). A sensitivity analysis (i.e., a refined secondary analysis) including high-quality trials showed that only TF-CBT and EMDR outperformed active control conditions. Regarding mid-term results (up to five months post-treatment), EMDR yielded the

[2] Hedges' g is a measure for effect size: >0.84 means a large effect size.

highest treatment effects, and TF-CBT was second. Regarding long-term efficacy (beyond five months post-treatment), TF-CBT yielded the highest treatment effects. The authors conclude that more long-term data and multiple-event-related PTSD data are needed for EMDR, MDT, and non-TF interventions to draw firmer conclusions regarding their efficacy.

Another NMA, including 32 trials and 2,260 participants, found that trauma-focused CBT, in particular individual forms, appeared to be most effective in the management of PTSD in youth (Mavranezouli et al., 2020). EMDR was also effective, but to a lesser extent. For children and adolescents exposed to natural or man-made disasters, a third NMA (26 studies, 4,331 participants) reported that EMDR was the most effective treatment for reducing PTSD and depression (Xie et al., 2024).

- ***Guidelines***

Clinical practice guidelines (CPGs) are recommendations based on the available evidence and input from the relevant stakeholders (e.g., healthcare providers/organizations, clinicians, and client organizations). CPGs are designed to support healthcare providers in service provision planning, and to assist clinicians and their clients in decision-making about treatment. The most influential CPGs for PTSD are published by the National Institute for Health and Clinical Excellence (NICE, 2018b), the International Society for Traumatic Stress Studies (ISTSS, 2019), the World Health Organization (World Health Organization, 2024), and the Australian Center of Excellence in Posttraumatic Mental Health (Phelps et al., 2022). For persistent PTSD in C&A, both NICE and ISTSS recommend trauma-focused CBT interventions, including prolonged exposure (PE), TF-CBT, and cognitive therapy (CT) for PTSD as first-line treatments. However, the recommendations for EMDR therapy are not consistent: ISTSS (2019) strongly recommends EMDR therapy for children and adolescents, while NICE (2018b) gives a conditional recommendation to use EMDR therapy only if youngsters do not respond to or do not engage with trauma-focused CBT. Likewise, the Australian PTSD treatment guideline recommends EMDR for children and adolescents with symptoms of PTSD 'where trauma-focused CBT is unavailable or unacceptable' (Phelps et al., 2022, chapter 6, p. 2).

The discrepancy between the recommendations in these CPGs results from differences in the inclusion criteria[3] of the studies considered relevant when the guidelines were last revised (Dominguez & Lee, 2019). With regard to the research studies related to C&A being in-/excluded, Dominguez and Lee state (p. 257):

> While there is an argument that some studies should have been included in the NICE guidelines and that this would likely have resulted in a higher recommendation

[3] NICE had stricter inclusion criteria for treatment studies, such as a minimum number of participants per treatment condition, a minimum percentage of participants fulfilling the diagnostic criteria for PTSD, having clinically significant PTSD symptoms indicated by mean baseline scores above the threshold on a validated scale, and the ability to extract necessary data. Consequently, NICE included only four of the eight available RCTs (Ahmad & Sundelin-Wahlsten, 2008; Diehle et al., 2014; de Roos et al., 2017; Soberman et al., 2002).

equivalent to ISTSS, the fact that two or three missing studies impact the analysis underscores the importance of further trials in this area.

Therefore, hopefully, this appeal will be noticed and adhered to in the EMDR child and adolescent field before the next revision of the guidelines (Beer et al., 2024).

3.2.3 Complex PTSD

A subgroup deserving special attention is children and adolescents with complex PTSD (CPTSD). CPTSD is a distinct classification in the International Classification of Diseases (ICD-11; Maercker et al., 2013; World Health Organization, 2019), contrary to the DSM-5, where it is not (yet?) adopted as differentiation from PTSD (see also Chapters 2 and 10 of this book). CPTSD involves exposure to severe, repeated, or prolonged interpersonal traumatic events within the family, along with core PTSD symptoms (i.e., re-experiencing, avoidance, hyperarousal, negative alterations in mood and cognitions), as well as additional symptoms including disturbances of affect-regulation, self-image, and interpersonal relationships (Cloire, 2021). With the introduction of the classification of CPTSD in the ICD-11, the validity of the PTSD–CPTSD distinction has become a significant topic in the trauma field. The critical question is whether enduring symptoms in the domains of affect, the self, and interpersonal relationships are just an indication of a severe form of PTSD or indicative of a qualitatively distinct disorder (Bryant et al., 2012; Resick et al., 2012; Kotov et al., 2017). An additional question is whether these extra symptoms require new treatment elements or more extended treatment with the same elements. For this vulnerable group, a phased treatment approach has been proposed with a stabilization phase before the trauma processing phase. The authors suggest that phased treatments run the risk that effective interventions for PTSD might be (unnecessary) delayed, thus increasing the risk of dropout and poorer treatment outcomes. Chapter 10 argues why trauma treatment for these children should start as soon as is possible and feasible. A new trend is the implementation of (intensive) trauma-focused treatments for this group without a prior stabilization phase. Fortunately, some studies have already been conducted and published, and show positive results.

When trauma treatment is provided to clients with complex PTSD in the traditional weekly session format, the dropout rate is high (range = 30–62%; Ragsdale et al., 2020). Reasons for this high percentage of attrition are varied but include barriers to care, such as avoidance behaviour, which is part of PTSD symptomatology. During the last decade, intensive treatments for PTSD have emerged for adults and youngsters to increase retention and accommodate more rapid recovery from symptoms of PTSD. These intensive or 'massed' treatments provide a dose of evidence-based trauma treatment within a condensed time frame (e.g., one-, two-, or three-week treatment formats), including one or more first-line PTSD treatment and additional services—for example, physical exercise, psychoeducation, or sessions with family members (Van Woudenberg et al., 2018). Findings from a systematic review based on 11 studies that included intensive outpatient programmes for adults (Sciarrino et al., 2020) were supportive of the notion that intensive delivery of trauma treatment can be an effective alternative to standard delivery, and can contribute to improved treatment response (significant weighted mean effect of treatment, $d = 1.57$) and reduced treatment dropout (5.5% pooled dropout rate across studies).

For C&A with CPTSD, only a few studies have addressed the efficacy of trauma-focused treatments so far. This is partly due to the lack of validated measures on this condition. In intensive treatments for adolescents, several evidence-based trauma-focused therapies are combined—for example, EMDR plus physical activity and family-oriented (systemic) intervention. Clients are referred either because prior treatments were unsuccessful or because too many complications were expected.

In the first published study on this topic, the effectiveness of an intensive trauma-focused inpatient treatment programme for clients (n = 27) suffering from complex PTSD was assessed (van Pelt et al., 2021). Treatment consisted of daily sessions of PE therapy and EMDR therapy supplemented with physical activity (13 days on average). Of all clients, 81.5% (n = 22) showed a clinically meaningful response, of whom 63% (n = 17) no longer fulfilled the diagnostic criteria of PTSD at post-treatment, as established with the CAPS-CA IV (Lindauer, 2014). The results were maintained at a three-month follow-up. During treatment, neither adverse events nor dropout occurred.

A second study assessed the results of a six-day intensive outpatient programme for young people (12–25 years; n = 74) with PTSD. The treatment consisted of PE, EMDR therapy, and physical activity. Relatives and friends participated in the programme (Rentinck et al., 2025). The findings showed a significant reduction in PTSD and depressive symptoms from pre-treatment to one month after treatment. A clinically meaningful response was demonstrated in 70% of clients one month after treatment, and 65% no longer met the diagnostic criteria for PTSD. The dropout rate was 4%, and no adverse events occurred.

In a third study, Van Ee and colleagues (2024) also found significant symptom reduction in adolescents with PTSD (12–21 years; n = 22) who were treated in an intensive treatment programme consisting of a combination of interventions, including EMDR. The researchers recommend going beyond clinical symptom change to assess treatment efficacy when dealing with adolescents. As childhood trauma can affect identity development, a more holistic approach could be beneficial for this group, whereby interventions are incorporated in the programme aimed at reinforcing developmental milestones and assessing how changes are experienced and relate to their identity development.

Given the deteriorating and longstanding effects of severe or complex PTSD, there is an urgency to further develop and implement evidence-based PTSD treatment in an intensive format to improve treatment retention and enhance outcomes in a limited time frame.

3.2.4 Efficacy for Treatment of PTSD in Clients with ID

The evidence base for EMDR for PTSD in persons with ID is steadily growing (see Chapter 16). Research on the applicability, safety, and effectiveness of EMDR therapy in persons with ID has accelerated, and existing studies cover a range of functioning levels, varying from mild to severe ID. Overall, the results are promising, as illustrated by Tables 3.2a and 3.2b.

Table 3.2a Overview of RCTs on the effects of EMDR in outpatient settings

Author(s)	N	Age	Level of ID	Design	Treatment condition(s) (Number of sessions)	Measures	Significant results
Mevissen et al., 2017	2	10 years; 18 years	Mild	Multiple baseline cross-subjects design	EMDR (mean 3, max 4, 60 min each). On PTSS	Adapted ADIS-C-section PTSD for children with MID-BIF*	In both participants PTSD in remission PTSD symptoms and daily life impairment decreased
Karatzias et al., 2019	29	Mean = 42 years	Mild (n = 24) & Moderate (n = 5)	Randomized controlled feasibility trial	EMDR (mean 6,75, max 8, 60 min each) + TAU (n = 15) versus TAU (n = 14) On PTSS	Events Checklist Childhood Trauma Questionnaire Post-Traumatic Stress Disorder Checklist GAS-ID GDS-LD CORE-LD	EMDR + TAU > TAU a higher number PTSD in remission EMDR + TAU > TAU general anxiety decreased
Penninx Quevedo et al., 2021	6	Between 31 and 60 years	Mild	Multiple baseline across subjects design	EMDR (mean 7, range 2–9, max 12, 90 min each). On PTSS and psychosis	Adapted ADIS-C-section PTSD for adults with MID-BIF* PSYRATS (Dutch version) BSI (Dutch version) (HoNOS) (Dutch version)	In 5 of 6 participants PTSD in remission PTSD symptoms, psychotic symptoms, and general psychopathology decreased

continued

Table 3.2a *Continued*

Author(s)	N	Age	Level of ID	Design	Treatment condition(s) (Number of sessions)	Measures	Significant results
Verhagen et al., 2022	9**	Between 34 and 53 years	Mild	Multiple baseline across subjects design	EMDR (mean 7, 13, range 3–12, max 12, mean 68.2 min. each, range 26–111 min.). On PTSS and psychological and psychosocial problems	Adapted ADIS-C-section PTSD for adults with MID-BIF* BDI-II-NL (HoNOS) (Dutch version) BSI (Dutch version)	In 6 participants PTSD in remission PTSD symptoms, depressive symptoms, general psychopathology, and overall mental health problems decreased
Hoogstad et al., 2024	3	30, 31, and 35 years (+ resp. cerebral vision impairment, Down syndrome and ASD)	Severe	Multiple baseline across subjects design	EMDR- storytelling (resp. 4, 6, and 8). On PTSS	DITS-SID VAS for dysfunctional behaviour BPI	In 2 participants PTSD in remission after treatment In 1 participant PTSD in remission during baseline PTSD symptoms, behavioural problems, and dysfunctional behaviours decreased

Adapted ADIS-C-section PTSD for children with MID-BIF: Adapted Anxiety Disorder Interview Scale-Children for Children with Mild Intellectual Disability or Borderline Intellectual Functioning (see Mevissen et al., 2016); Adapted ADIS-C-section PTSD for adults with MID-BIF: Adapted Anxiety Disorder Interview Scale-Children for Adults with Mild Intellectual Disability or Borderline Intellectual Functioning (see Mevissen et al., 2020); BDI-II-NL: Beck Depression Inventory—2nd edition (Dutch version) (Van der Does, 2002); BSI: Brief Symptom Inventory (De Beurs, 2004); BPI: Behavior Problems Inventory (Rojahn et al., 2001); CORE—LD: Clinical Outcomes in Routine Evaluation—Learning Disability (Marshall et al., 2013); DITS-SID: Diagnostic Interview Trauma and Stressors—Severe Intellectual Disability (Mevissen et al., 2021); Events Checklist (Gray et al., 2004); Childhood Trauma Questionnaire (Bernstein & Fink, 1998); GAS-ID: Glasgow Anxiety Scale for People with a Learning Disability (Mindham & Espie, 2003); GDS-LD: Glasgow Depression Scale for People with a Learning Disability (Cuthill et al., 2003); HoNOS: Health of the Nation Outcome Scales (Dutch version) (Mulder et al., 2004); Post-Traumatic Stress Disorder Checklist (Weathers et al., 2013); PSYRATS: Psychotic Symptom Rating Scale Interview (Dutch version) (Haddock et al., 1999); VAS for dysfunctional behaviour: Visual Analog Scale for dysfunctional behaviour (see Klimek et al., 2017)

Table 3.2b Research on the effects of inpatient trauma treatment

Authors	N	Design	Treatment	Measures	Significant results
Mevissen et al., 2020a 2020b	6 families 9 parents (6 with mild ID of whom 2 mild ID + ASD) 10 children (all with mild ID of whom 5 mild ID+ASD) All with trauma-related symptoms 7 parents with PTSD 2 children with PTSD	Replicated single case experimental design	KINGS-ID* Step 1: 6 weeks inpatient: EMDR** parent(s) followed by EMDR** child(ren) followed by parenting support Step 2: 2 weeks outpatient (at home) **in each family member disturbing memories, as set with the DITS-ID event section, were targeted.	DITS-ID SCL-90 OBVL	PTSS in remission in all 7 parents and 2 children PTSD symptoms and daily life impairment in parents as well as in children decreased. General psychopathology and parental stress in parents decreased.
Ooms-Evers et al., 2021	33 children (6 up to 17 years) with mild ID All with trauma-related symptoms 22 with PTSD	3 measurements during intervention: at intake, start, and end of treatment	Intensive clinical trauma treatment: 2 weeks 4 days per week Each day 1 session PE, 1 session EMDR, and a physical activity in a trauma-sensitive environment.	DITS-ID SDQ	PTSD in remission in 14 participants. Trauma symptoms, emotional and behavioural problems decreased.
*also see Chapter 24 on KINGS					

DITS-ID: Diagnostic Interview Trauma and Stressors-Intellectual Disability (Mevissen et al., 2018); SCL-90: Symptom Checklist (Arrindell & Ettema, 2005); OBVL: Opvoedingsbelasting Vragenlijst [parental stress questionnaire] (Vermulst et al., 2015); SDQ: Strengths and Difficulties Questionnaire (Goodman et al., 1998)

3.3 Efficacy Beyond PTSD

The central role of trauma in the development and maintenance of mental health conditions beyond PTSD has received more attention lately (Sara & Lappin, 2017). This renewed insight has generated a series of research projects examining whether a trauma-focused intervention, such as EMDR therapy focused on reprocessing symptom-related memories, could reduce the primary and the comorbid symptomatology. In recent years, multiple RCTs involving EMDR have been carried out with adults, showing that it may be effective for a broad range of disorders, including chronic pain, depression, psychosis, obsessive-compulsive disorder, and eating disorders (Maxfield, 2019; Matthijssen et al., 2020; Valiente et al., 2017). However, research on this topic for youth is still largely lacking.

3.3.1 Major Depressive Disorder in Adolescents

In C&A mental health care settings, therapists are regularly confronted with adolescents suffering from major depressive disorder (MDD) who do not react with sufficient symptom reduction or who do not recover after one or more first-line psychological treatment(s), such as CBT or interpersonal psychotherapy. Although there are several treatments for adolescents with MDD, of which CBT is the most frequently studied, current treatments show limited effectiveness (mean effect size = 0.29), including high rates of dropout and relapse post-treatment (Weisz et al., 2017). Therefore, there is an urgent need to develop, test, and disseminate additional treatments that may be effective for adolescent MDD. Given the role that distressing memories play in depression, the high prevalence of MDD in adolescents, and the limitations of existing treatment, a pilot, non-controlled study of EMDR as a stand-alone treatment with depressed adolescents was conducted (n = 32; Paauw et al., 2019). Treatment consisted of six weekly 60-minute individual sessions. Findings showed that 60.9% of the adolescents completing treatment no longer met DSM-IV criteria for MDD after treatment. In addition, comorbid anxiety, post-traumatic stress symptoms, and somatic symptoms were significantly reduced. At three-month follow-up, these results were maintained, and the percentage of adolescents that lost their MDD diagnoses increased even further, to 69.8%. The results of this brief trauma-focused intervention are promising and suggest that EMDR therapy can be both effective and safe for adolescents with mild to moderate MDD. Since this pilot study included only a small sample size and no control group, an RCT has been conducted to investigate whether EMDR therapy for adolescents with MDD is more effective in comparison to a waiting-list control condition (Paauw et al., 2023).

Additionally, two other EMDR studies with depressed adolescents have been conducted (Bae et al., 2008, case study; Tang et al., 2015, non-randomized controlled trial), with both showing remission of depressive symptoms within a small number of sessions (range = 3–7).

3.3.2 Behaviour Problems and Negative Self-Image

Three RCTs (Scheck et al., 1998; Soberman et al., 2002[4]; Wanders et al., 2008) have yielded mixed results for youth with behaviour problems and negative self-image, possibly due to the low number of EMDR sessions (range = 2–4). See Table 3.3 for further details.

Additional studies of high methodological quality with children and adolescents are warranted to determine the efficacy of EMDR in children with behavioural issues, conduct disorders, and negative self-image.

Table 3.3 Overview RCTs on EMDR for behavioural problems or self-image

Soberman et al., 2002	29	Boys 10–16 years with conduct problems in residential or day treatment, multiply traumatized population	CAU vs CAU + EMDR (3) CAU: n = 15 CAU + EMDR: n = 14	PTSD symptoms Behavioural problems Memory-related distress	IES-8 CROPS PROPS PRS BRS	CAU + EMDR > CAU: Significant reductions in memory-related distress (SUD) post-treatment. And significant reduction of problem behaviours at 2-month follow-up.
Wanders et al., 2008	26	Children 10–14	EMDR vs CBT	Self-image, behavioural problems, emotional problems	SPCC, PNG-C, Self-esteem scale, NOSI, Depression questionnaire for children, CBCL	EMDR: improvement in self-image and behavioural problems, not in emotional problems. CBT: improvement in self-image reported by parents/mentors, not in self-report; improvement in behavioural and emotional problems. EMDR > CBT for improvement in behavioural problems.
Scheck et al., 1998	60	Adolescents 16–25	EMDR vs Active Listening (AL)	Anxiety, depression, self-image	BDI, STAI, Penn Inventory for PTSD, IES, Tennessee Self Concept Scale	EMDR > AL, both effective, EMDR more effective in reduction PTSD, anxiety, depression, and negative self-image.

BDI (Beck et al., 1999); BRS (Butler & Lord, 2021); CBCL (Achenbach, 1991); CROPS (Greenwald & Rubin, 1999); Depression Questionnaire for Children—Dutch (De Wit, 1987); IES-8 (Horowitz, 1979); NOSI: Nijmeegse Ouderlijke Stress Index—Dutch (De Brock et al., 1992); Penn Inventory for PTSD (Hammarberg, 1992); PNG-C: Questionnaire Positive en Negative Thoughts in Children—Dutch (Bracke & Braet, 2000); PROPS (Greenwald & Rubin, 1999); PRS (Mooney et al., 2005); Self-Esteem Scale—Dutch (Wanders, 2004b); SPCC: Self-Perception Profile for Children (Harter, 1985); STAI (Spielberger, 1983); Tennessee Self Concept Scale (Marsh et al., 1988)

[4] The study by Sobermann is cited twice, because both PTSS and behavioural measures were included.

3.3.3 Somatic Symptoms

In the area of somatic symptoms, in an RCT Maroufi and colleagues (2016) compared one session of EMDR to a single neutral interview with 56 adolescent clients with acute pain after abdominal surgery. Compared to the control condition, adolescents receiving a single session of EMDR experienced a significant reduction in pain. Currently, an RCT is being conducted on EMDR in children aged 6–18 with sickle cell disease, persistent physical pain and pain interference (Nery et al., in prep.). Clients will be randomized to EMDR or a waiting-list control group, and assessments will be done pre- and post-treatment and at three months follow-up.

3.3.4 Anxiety Disorders

In the area of anxiety disorders, a meta-analysis of EMDR trials (adults and youth) for mental health conditions other than PTSD found evidence of efficacy, particularly in the area of phobias and test anxiety. However, further high-quality RCTs are needed before conclusions can be drawn (Cuijpers et al., 2020). More than 15 years ago, De Roos and De Jongh (2008) published a case series of four children (with a broad age range of 3–15 years) in the area of specific phobias. They all received EMDR therapy for near-choking experiences. After one or two sessions, children or their parents reported that their eating pattern had normalized and their weight had increased. The children felt more energetic, happier, less rebellious, and behaved more independently.

Concluding, the efficacy of EMDR therapy in children and adolescents with mental health problems beyond PTSD is supported by limited—but growing—results. Fortunately, a trauma-sensitive approach in mental health care (the AIP model) is increasingly gaining a foothold and evoking interest in research examining the efficacy of EMDR therapy for these conditions.

3.4 Future Directions

Researchers should design studies that meet the CONSORT criteria, with larger samples and longer-term follow-ups. They should add studies that assess the effectiveness of EMDR in PTSD following chronic trauma. Furthermore, there is a need for rigorous studies that involve dismantling multi-component interventions to identify core (i.e., effective) treatment elements and to determine who should be present in treatment (e.g., child only, child and parents). Additional challenges are determining the optimal time point and 'dose' to deliver treatment (Dorsey et al., 2017). Being able to ascertain what works best for whom (moderators), why, and how treatment exerts its effects (mediators) will require studies involving large samples, repeated assessment (including session-by-session during treatment), and multiple measures of treatment outcome. Cost-effectiveness should be explored in additional, well-conducted studies that examine the relative clinical- and cost-effectiveness for children and young people with PTSD, because findings at this point are inconsistent (Mavranezouli et al., 2020).

Other relevant questions to be examined by future researchers include the following (see also Beer et al., 2024): Beyond PTSD, what other symptoms or disorders in children can be effectively treated with EMDR therapy? How can EMDR be optimally embedded in treatment programmes offered as an adjunct to other therapies? What can we learn from children who do not respond to EMDR therapy? How can the involvement of parents/siblings be optimized in each phase of treatment?

Apart from research questions regarding the content, there are also issues concerning research design: What other study designs can be applied besides RCTs? RCTs are expensive for society, require a lot of time and effort, demand many participants for statistical power, and may not generate meaningful results generalizable to real-world practice relative to the efforts. Therefore, it seems plausible to consider other designs, such as the replicated SCEDs, within regular clinical practice. This design seems more efficient and provides a better understanding of what happens on different levels and in various phases of therapy. Hopefully, new researchers will continue to be practice-oriented so that their research findings, also in the future, will keep guiding clinicians to improved clinical practice.

3.5 Practical Recommendations

EMDR specialists should attract the interest of researchers and academic settings to EMDR. However, this is not easily realized, as most EMDR therapists do not work in university settings. Therefore, national associations' scientific committees should play a significant role, as these committees should represent the best-informed EMDR specialists in their countries. Reflection is needed on how these committees can stimulate the initiation of research projects in their country. See Beer (2018) for some practical recommendations for new researchers.

3.6 Concluding Remarks

This chapter aims to inform readers about the empirical status of EMDR and to help them educate their clients, referrers, trainees, and colleagues. Additionally, it might stimulate researchers to initiate new research projects and provide some helpful, practical recommendations and guidelines for realizing this. In the coming years, more research projects will follow which may contribute to supporting evidence for the effectiveness of EMDR, not only for the treatment of PTSD but also for a broader range of pathology resulting from inadequately processed memories of adverse or traumatic experiences. The qualification of EMDR as 'proven effective' and its adoption in the treatment guidelines for children and adolescents is crucial for clients to be treated with it, for therapists to apply it, and for relevant stakeholders and funders to finance those treatments.

4 Case Conceptualization

RENÉE BEER AND CARLIJN DE ROOS

4.1 Introduction

The concept of 'case conceptualization' originates from the cognitive behavioural therapy (CBT) field, and it is widely acknowledged that case conceptualizations or case formulations are fundamental to ('the cornerstone' of) psychological therapies (Santos, 2019). Case conceptualization is defined as a collaborative process between the therapist and the client to describe and explain the symptoms presented by the client.

Its primary function is to develop hypotheses about how symptoms or problems might have developed based on the client's learning experiences, how they might be currently maintained through (operant) reinforcement, and what is needed to reduce them. Based on these hypotheses, a therapy plan is developed which includes evidence-based interventions and techniques aimed at 'relieving client distress and building client resilience' (John & Segal, 2015; Kuyken et al., 2008, p. 3; Padesky, 2020).

Each therapeutic approach (e.g., cognitive behavioural, systemic, psychodynamic, client-centred) has its take on the purpose and process of case formulation. So, what does this imply for EMDR therapists who come from various therapeutic orientations? EMDR therapists have in common that they share the adaptive information processing (AIP) model as underpinning their EMDR therapy planning (Santos, 2019). Therefore, case conceptualization implies that relevant information is gathered for developing hypotheses about the possible relation between symptoms and maladaptively stored memories of crucial experiences, clarifying for both therapist and client (child and parents) how symptoms and memories might be related. Once this is clear, it becomes obvious why EMDR is implemented to reprocess relevant memories, and what effects can be expected.

The function of case conceptualization is to provide the client (child and parents) and the therapist with a shared understanding of the problems and a road map showing how they will collaborate and what they aim to achieve with EMDR. Figure 4.1 shows a format in which collected information and hypotheses could be summarized and arranged.

History taking and treatment planning for EMDR (phase 1 of EMDR therapy) can be differentiated from a more all-encompassing diagnostic phase, in which additional information is also gathered and analysed for case conceptualization, and from a broader treatment plan, in which EMDR is embedded. This more extensive diagnostic phase is not needed when the therapist expects, based on the information provided during intake, that EMDR

Renée Beer and Carlijn de Roos, *Case Conceptualization*. In: *Handbook of EMDR for Children and Adolescents*.
Edited by: Renée Beer and Carlijn de Roos, Oxford University Press.
DOI: 10.1093/oso/9780198918400.003.0004

1. Problems presented, DSM classification.
2. Relevant data from (trauma)history, diagnostic assessment, and family functioning.
3. Hypothesized relationship between current symptoms, past experiences, and perpetuating factors.
4. Selection of symptom(s) to be addressed and eligible paths for target selection.
5. Identification of targets: mental representations of past experiences/anticipated future catastrophes.
6. EMDR treatment plan comprising targets, sequence, and goals to be achieved using the standard protocol.

Figure 4.1 Format for EMDR Case Conceptualization.

therapy will be sufficient to adequately respond to the request for help and appropriately address the presented problems.

The case conceptualization for EMDR therapy specifies (a) which symptoms or symptom clusters will be treated, (b) which memories/mental representations seem to be related to the symptom or symptom cluster in such a way that (re)processing will result in symptom reduction, and (c) in what order memories will be addressed. The order of targets and the chosen search strategies can be adjusted at any point during treatment when indicated (Van Pelt et al., 2025).

However, children with complex post-traumatic stress disorder (CPTSD) have various symptoms (PTSD symptoms + emotion regulation problems + interpersonal problems + negative self-image) and multiple memories that could be related; thus, the relations between specific memories and symptoms are unclear. Therefore, in these cases, the first step is to identify and arrange the memories that belong together according to specified aspects (like period, type of event, or perpetrator) in the child's perception. Creating an overview of potentially relevant memories helps them and the therapist find their way more easily along the paths leading to target selection that will follow.

How are targets defined? Shapiro (2018) does this in several places: 'The therapeutic target is the disturbing memory as it is currently stored because the dysfunctional information has set the groundwork for the present pathology' (p. 39). However, except for a specific memory, a target can also be 'a dream image; a person; an actual, fantasized, or projected event; or some aspect of an experience, such as body sensation or thought' (p. 30); and, to conclude with a third citation: 'Appropriate targets for the EMDR processing session include any manifestation of the dysfunctional information (p. 73).

Memories of an event include images, cognitions, emotions, and body sensations, all of which are optional targets. This book uses the term 'target' to refer to complete memories or fantasies (worst-case scenarios) or the selected picture. The rationale for this choice (a focus on the visual component of memory representations) is that visual intrusions appear to be the most common modality of intrusive memories after trauma (Ehlers et al., 2002). Furthermore, Brewin and colleagues (2010) stressed the fact that involuntary images and visual memories are prominent in many types of psychopathologies. Additionally, experimental research on the efficacy of EMDR points to its effect on distressing images as a mediating variable. The impact of eye movements on distressing images, which has been tested in many studies, correlated with the reduction of PTSD or other conditions. Nearly 30 years ago Andrade and colleagues (1997) demonstrated that the vividness and emotiveness of distressing images are reduced by disrupting the function of the visuospatial sketchpad of working memory (see Chapter 1 of this book). Many studies confirmed these effects (e.g., Barrowcliff et al., 2004; De Jongh et al., 2013; Engelhard et al., 2010; Gunter & Bodner, 2008). On these grounds, the visual component of memory is seen as the best access to the maladaptively stored information of the disturbing memory. This applies to adults, and there is no reason to assume this might differ for children, although there is no research underpinning this: 'The image is only one manifestation of the disturbing information … the assessment phase delineates the most dominant manifestations of the incident (images, physical sensations, emotions, etc.) as the access points to the targeted information' (Shapiro, 2018, p. 125). The central role attributed to the visual component is evidenced by the question in the standard protocol: 'What is the most disturbing (or 'worst' for child) picture of the memory?' The subsequent questions in the assessment phase activate other manifestations of dysfunctional information (memory representations).

4.2 Familiar Methods for Target Planning

Several EMDR colleagues have described how target planning for children can be arranged (Adler-Tapia & Settle, 2023; Gomez, 2013; Greenwald, 1999; Tinker & Wilson, 1999).

Specific to working with children is that parents' information is included alongside the child's information. Therapists must know when this is appropriate and how to handle the provided information in the context of target planning. Information from parents is relevant if the child is unable to provide the necessary details.

Generally speaking, parents' information can be—but is not necessarily—included. In the group aged 16–18 years, it is usually not included, unless the adolescent or the therapist thinks their additional information might be relevant. It is included for the group aged 12–16 years, while it is considered the primary source of information for children aged under 12. The potential role of parents on each path for target selection is explicitly indicated in this chapter.

4.3 Paths for Target Selection

According to the AIP model, EMDR is an appropriate treatment for many psychopathologies resulting from maladaptively stored memories. These memories may relate to various types of events and result in problems in multiple ways. In search of ways to optimize the efficiency of EMDR therapy with different kinds of psychopathology, distinctive procedures for target selection have been developed by Dutch EMDR trainers, some of which have been published in the English language (e.g., Beer, 2019; De Jongh et al., 2010; Logie & De Jongh, 2016; Van der Vleugel et al., 2016). These procedures mark different paths the therapist can follow in search of the most relevant targets. We have inserted several adjustments on these paths to make them accessible—and traversable—for children, as was done with the standard protocol for children and adolescents (aged 4–18). The steps for children (and their parents) on these paths will be explained. The reader is referred to Van Pelt and colleagues (2025) for more specific information about the search strategies. The C&A versions are accessible digitally for therapists who have been trained, via this https://www.emdrchildandyouth.info. Figure 4.2 shows an overview of potential strategies.

4.3.1 Intrusion Path

The intrusion path regards the treatment of intrusions within the context of PTSD or other mental disorders.

- ***Intrusions***

An intrusion can be a manifestation of a non-clinical mental phenomenon that everybody experiences occasionally, such as bizarre, undesirable, and recurrent thoughts, images, or impulses that come and go. However, it can also be a manifestation of a clinical symptom, such as intrusive recurrent images, thoughts, or impulses that are unstoppable and that consume more and more time and energy (Brewer et al., 2020). Intrusive clinical symptoms are transdiagnostic phenomena, as they occur within the context of PTSD and also across many other mental health conditions, such as obsessive-compulsive disorder, eating disorders, psychosis, hypochondria, and social phobia.

- ***Intrusive symptoms in PTSD***

The classification of PTSD according to the DSM-5 requires that a person has at least one of the following symptoms defining criterion B (intrusive symptoms):

BOX 4.1 Intrusive symptoms according to DSM-5, Criterion B

- Recurrent, involuntary, and intrusive distressing memories of the trauma(s).
- Recurrent distressing dreams in which the content and/or the resulting affect are related to the trauma(s).
- Dissociative reactions (e.g., flashbacks) in which the individual feels or acts as if the trauma(s) is recurring.
- Intense or prolonged psychological distress at exposure to internal or external cues that symbolize or resemble an aspect of the trauma(s).
- Marked physiological reactions to internal or external cues that symbolize or resemble an aspect of the trauma(s).

The listed symptoms relate to both different manifestations of memories and reactions to these memories, which makes this criterion complex.[1] Brewin (2014) recommends simplifying the diagnosis of PTSD wherever possible and using more consistent terminology.

[1] Zeanah and Gleanson (2010) note that distress may not be present in the re-experiencing signs in preschool children. Chapter 2 lists additional deviations for young children (<6 years) in the symptoms mentioned in the DSM-5.

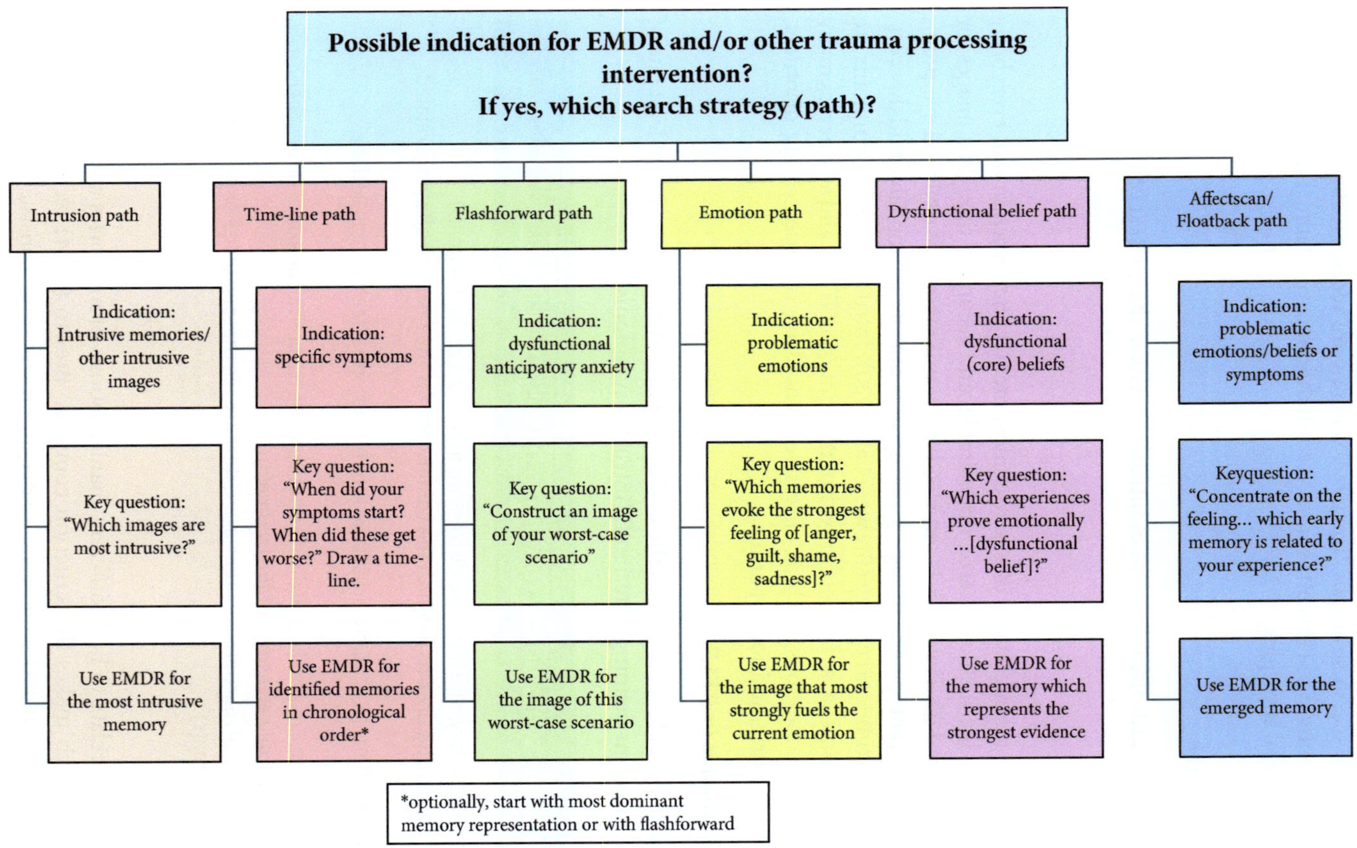

Figure 4.2 Flow chart.

To this end, Kvavilashvili (2014) proposed a taxonomy differentiating the critical differences between different kinds of memories: 'involuntary autobiographical memories' (an everyday phenomenon), 'intrusive memories' (involuntary memories with repeated and usually distressing content, associated with various psychological disorders), and 'flashbacks' (involuntary memories *involving re-experiencing distressing events in the present*, specific to PTSD). This is, in Brewin's view, a clear distinction implying that re-experiencing or reliving the event in the present distinguishes intrusive memories in PTSD from intrusive memories in other disorders (Brewin, 2015). It is essential to keep in mind, though, that re-experiences are always intrusive, but intrusions are not necessarily re-experiences. The last two groups of the listed intrusive symptoms in criterion B of the classification of PTSD (Box 4.1) are reactions (i.e., psychological distress or physiological responses) to internal stimuli (e.g., thoughts) or external stimuli (e.g., specific images, smells, sounds) that trigger the distressing memories. To summarize, within PTSD a spectrum of intrusive symptoms is possible, ranging from flashbacks to physiological and emotional reactions to distressing memories.

Intrusions are mainly sensory (visual, auditory, olfactory, bodily sensations) and come with various negative emotions. They predominantly relate to the event, while intrusive thoughts (guilt and shame) primarily relate to the period before and after, such as 'If I had not…', 'I wish I had…' (Van Minnen et al., 2005). To put it more precisely, intrusions often refer to the moment just *before* the traumatic event happened (like seeing the headlights of an approaching car), the so-called 'warning signals', being representations of the moments where the most significant cognitive and physiological changes took place and where adrenaline was released for the fight-flight-freeze response or shortly before the moment having the most critical emotional impact (i.e., when the meaning of the event became more traumatic) (Ehlers et al., 2002).

Typically, intrusions are the first symptoms clients want to eliminate because they are debilitating and significantly impact daily life. Moreover, they perpetuate other symptoms because the client tries to escape from (or avoid) the intrusions, thus avoiding potential triggers (such as, not going to sleep to prevent nightmares). Since eliminating these symptoms will relieve the client and motivate them to continue treatment, it is recommended to address intrusions first.

- ***Memories and intrusions in PTSD***

In PTSD, the intrusion path is straightforward when there are flashbacks and identified related events, such as nightmares of a car accident after having experienced this event. The SUD (subjective unity of disturbance) level of the intrusions determines the order of targets to be addressed. However, it becomes more complicated when the diagnostic phase has revealed that there are various traumatic events in the client's history from which the child might have intrusions (such as a long period of sexual abuse at home and being bullied in school). In those cases, the therapist collects the memories associated with intrusions, then ranks the intrusions according to the SUD level and addresses them in that order.

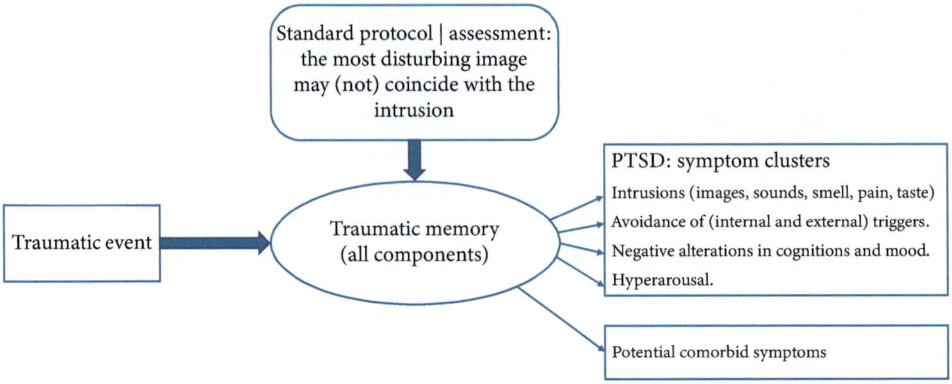

Figure 4.3 Standard protocol and intrusions.

Derived from Van Pelt et al. (2025)

In adults, intrusions usually refer to the events directly. In young children (< 6 years), contrarily, intrusions might also refer to the events indirectly (such as nightmares about monsters or ghosts).

The standard protocol addresses complete memories to be reprocessed. So, once the memory is identified, the most disturbing picture of the memory is determined in the assessment phase. The selected picture does not necessarily coincide with the symptom (intrusion); for example, the most disturbing picture of the memory could be 'seeing the headlights of the car coming' while the intrusive symptom is (visual flashbacks of) 'seeing her mother dead'.

Besides intrusive symptoms, there are additional symptom clusters in PTSD, such as avoidance behaviours (criterion C), changes in mood and cognition (criterion D), and hyperarousal (criterion E). The objective of EMDR is to reprocess all relevant memories that set the groundwork for the pathology. This implies that all potentially PTSD-related (intrusive and distressing) memories must be addressed to reduce all symptoms. Figure 4.3 shows the potential connections between the standard protocol, the memory of an event, and the symptoms.

- ***Intrusions beyond PTSD***

In other disorders beyond PTSD, the intrusions may relate to feared future fantasies (flashforwards)—'something terrible might happen'—like in obsessive-compulsive disorder, hypochondria, body dysmorphic disorder, eating disorder, separation anxiety, performance anxiety, and social anxiety. In these cases, the intrusion path seems less appropriate as the therapist can better explore the origin and development of the intrusions in these cases. If there are events in the past that might be relevant for understanding the development of these intrusions, then the timeline path could be suitable for identifying the appropriate events. However, when no relevant (learning) experiences are identified, or when they have been addressed already, it could be advisable to address these intrusions directly via the flashforward path because they perpetuate the existing pathology. Both paths will be explained hereafter, in Sections 4.3.2 and 4.3.3.

Generally, children can find relevant memories via the intrusion path without their parents' help. However, if a child cannot tell what is bothering them, parents may report that a child is troubled by nightmares or intrusions during the daytime. In those cases, the therapist can share this information with the child and await their reactions. Box 4.2 shows the steps for the intrusion path.

BOX 4.2 Steps for intrusion path

1. List intrusions and related memories.
2. Rank them according to SUD level.
3. Standard protocol for children and adolescents (4–18 years) on selected memory.

4.3.2 Timeline Path

The timeline path is eligible for treating specific symptoms—beyond the context of PTSD—that developed gradually over time after several consecutive experiences. The path is preeminently suitable for symptoms such as fears (avoidance and safety behaviours) that occur when confronted with neutral situations (such as being in class, riding a horse) or neutral objects (such as a car, a needle) that have become frightening after a 'learning history' of several experiences (being bullied in class, having fallen off a horse, car accident, painful injections). Besides fears, is the path suitable for other symptoms—such as gloomy moods, somatic symptoms, and eating problems—when there is an identifiable 'learning history'. The path starts with selecting the specific symptom the client wants to eliminate primarily, because of the dysfunction it causes. Subsequently, events are identified, after which the symptom began and subsequently exacerbated. The identified events are positioned on a timeline, and the memories of these events are desensitized using the standard protocol. The order may be chronological, based on the most substantial contribution to the onset or exacerbation of the selected symptom, or based on the highest SUD.

Reprocessing the selected memories on the timeline is insufficient when treating fears; the second and third prongs should follow if avoidance or safety behaviour remains. Potential present triggers must be neutralized if they exist, and preparation for the future must be explicitly involved (see Chapter 7). In these cases, EMDR should always be followed by exposure in vivo and homework assignments, teaching the child 'to prove the pudding by eating' it—that is, show that they dare to do again what they were avoiding or escaping from before.

The timeline path is inappropriate when multiple (series of) events have led to dysfunctional core beliefs that drive the symptoms. In such cases, chronology is irrelevant. Instead, the belief path might then be a more effective search strategy.

The parents can assist the child in searching for relevant past events by adding details and mentioning specific events. However, if the child says that the event a parent mentions is not important, or is unrelated to the symptoms, the therapist attunes to the child's words.

The same applies if the parents and the child have a different view on the development of the symptoms. If the child is under 12 years, the parents will always be invited to support them in this part of the strategy. Because the child cannot tell about events before age four, the therapist asks their parents if specific events happened during that period, especially those that might be related to occurred before the onset or exacerbation of the symptom(s). Box 4.3 shows the steps for the timeline path. See https://www.emdrchildandyouth.info for more detailed description.

BOX 4.3 Steps for timeline path

1. List presented symptoms.
2. Select the symptom to be treated first.
3. Identify with the child significant events for start and gradual exacerbation: timeline.
4. Select with child memories to be targeted and in what order.
5. Standard protocol for children and adolescents (4–18 years) addressing the identified memory.
6. Involve parents:
   - with children > 16 years old: depending on need and circumstances.
   - with children between 12–16 years old: mostly.
   - with children < 12 years of age: always, because the child cannot reflect sufficiently.

4.3.3 Flashforward Path

The effectiveness of desensitizing flashforwards is based on experimental findings, showing that vividness and emotional intensity of recurrent intrusive images (not only of past events but also of potential future catastrophes) can be reduced by taxing working memory using eye movements, (Engelhard et al., 2010; Logie & de Jongh, 2014).

The flashforward path is appropriate for the treatment of anticipatory anxiety, irrational fears provoked by intrusive fantasies of catastrophic events, and worst-case scenarios that might happen to the child in the future (for example, 'if I am in the classroom, I will vomit'), where the development (learning history) of the fear is not evident. The fear-related symptoms in this case (refusing to enter the classroom) are attempts to prevent what the child imagines (fears) from happening. The target image is the worst image of this nightmare or scenario: the so-called 'flashforward'. The imagery can be evoked by internal or external stimuli, such as thinking of the classroom (internal) or seeing the school building (external), or may arise spontaneously (in dreams). Though the content of the imagery relates to the future, the imagery is a present trigger activating anticipatory anxiety and fear-related symptoms (avoidance).

The flashforward path addresses irrational fears and anticipatory anxiety responses that persist after the memories of past events have been fully processed. However, the flashforward is processed directly when no relevant past events can be identified (for example, if the child is afraid of vomiting and being despised by her classmates because of this without ever having experienced vomiting or being treated negatively, or seeing this happen to someone else).

When the irrational fear is identified and no relevant events in the past are traceable, or past events have been dealt with already with the standard protocol for C&A (4–18), the child is asked to bring up in their mind what is the worst that could happen if they … (do something or confront something). The worst image of that scenario (the feared ultimate disaster) is the flashforward. The standard protocol is addressed to that image. The goal is to make the child realize that it is only an image in their mind that is frightening them.

The results of experimental findings with flashforwards (Engelhard et al., 2010; Logie & De Jongh, 2014) paved the way for EMDR to be implemented also for the treatment of disorders other than PTSD, such as obsessive-compulsive disorder (something terrible might happen if I do not …, therefore I have to …), separation anxiety (something horrible might happen to my parent or to me when we are separated; thus, my parents should not go anywhere without me), and social phobia (something terrible might happen when I … before the group, therefore I avoid …).

Parental help is needed only when the child cannot express their images or fantasies. Box 4.4 shows the steps for the flashforward path.

BOX 4.4 Steps for flashforward path

1. Identify feared future fantasy, ultimate flashforward.
2. Standard protocol for children and adolescents (4–18 years) on flash forward.

4.3.4 Emotion Path

The emotion path is appropriate for treating problematic emotions as core symptoms. 'Problematic emotions' are defined as those that are disproportionate to the occasion, dysfunctional, and more vigorous than those experienced by most people. Frequent problematic emotions are disgust, rage (blind, extreme anger), extraordinary shame, overwhelming sadness, and guilt. It is assumed that these 'problematic emotions' result from inadequately processed memories, that present situations trigger them, and that reprocessing these memories will reduce the dysregulation resulting from the problematic emotion.

When the 'problematic emotion' is identified, the therapist asks '*What memory evokes the strongest …* [mention the problematic emotion] *that bothers you so much in your daily life?*'

No adjustments seem necessary for children on this path, except the formulation of the question mentioned. Children from age six can answer this question, and parents can help verbalize the emotion only if the child cannot. Box 4.5 shows the steps for the emotion path.

BOX 4.5 Steps for emotion path

1. Identify problematic emotion.
2. Identify the memory that evokes the problematic emotion the strongest.
3. Standard protocol for children and adolescents (4–18 years) on identified memory.

4.3.5 Belief Path

The belief path is suitable for treating generalized symptoms and behaviour patterns driven by negative core beliefs. These core beliefs result from a multitude of adverse experiences. These patterns may entail generalized negative expectations (such as in social anxiety disorder), patterns of problematic behaviour (such as regular aggressive behaviour), or persistent negative affect or mood (such as permanent distrust or depression) driven by dysfunctional core beliefs about the self ('I am worthless') or others ('Others cannot be trusted'). The pathology in these cases usually does not result from several consecutive distinctive disruptive experiences but from a long period of smaller adverse events ('t-traumas'), or a combination of smaller and bigger adverse or traumatic events. The belief path is implemented to identify experiences that underlie the relevant negative core beliefs or associated assumptions, eliciting this persistent psychopathology. Knowledge of Beck's (2020) cognitive model for emotional disorders is required to understand this path. Because not everyone will be familiar with this model, the core details are provided in Box 4.6.

BOX 4.6 Summary of Beck's cognitive model (2020)

According to Beck's cognitive model, emotional disorders are mediated by dysfunctional beliefs. The model differentiates three levels of cognitive content.

Core beliefs are not just thoughts connected to specific situations but enduring beliefs (convictions) that are generalized (valid always and everywhere), absolute, and deeply rooted. Therefore, they are rigid and hard to modify. There is a great stock of past events—mostly starting early in life—that have formed negative dysfunctional beliefs about the self and others.

Examples: 'I am a failure'; 'Others will hurt you.'

Intermediate beliefs: these are guidelines for daily life derived from core beliefs. Intermediate beliefs are not generalized but conditional beliefs (if x, then y). Two kinds are differentiated: predictions and evaluations. Predictions are expectations regarding the effect of one's behaviour ('If I do x, then y will follow'). Evaluations regard the meaning that people attribute to their behaviour. ('If I do x, that means y'). Besides conditional beliefs, self-imposed precepts are derived from core beliefs. These are instructions to oneself on how to behave.

Examples:
Conditional-predictive: 'If I open up myself, others will reject me.'
Conditional-evaluative: 'If I cry, I am a wimp.'
Self-imposed precepts: 'Never make mistakes'; 'Always stay in control.'

Automatic negative thoughts are activated in specific situations and are related to what the person does and feels (the cognitive triangle: do, feel, think). They can relate to the self and the other; the negative cognition in the standard protocol falls in this category.

Example: 'I am a coward'; 'I am to blame for this.'

So, *core beliefs* will elicit behavioural and emotional reactions through *intermediate beliefs* (conditional beliefs and self-imposed precepts), which result in negative emotional and interactional experiences. The memories of these experiences, in turn, are stored as 'confirmation' of the core belief and increase its validity (i.e., its perceived credibility: 'You see, further proof that I am a piece of shit, or proof that everybody cheats you and nobody can be trusted').

Core beliefs are regarded as 'the driving force', that evokes the behavioural, emotional, and interactional problems. The goal of the belief path is to identify the memories that have substantially and significantly contributed to establishing and maintaining the selected core belief. In other words, it focuses on the crucial memories that keep the core belief alive.

The goal of this path is to identify the events or experiences that most convincingly 'prove' the validity (credibility) of the belief for the client, so that in the next treatment phase, 'the pieces of evidence' or the 'proofs' for the belief can be systematically discredited, one after the other. The 'Google-search strategy' (Shapiro & Laub, 2014) is utilized in this path. In computer terminology, the selected core or intermediate belief (assumption) is the *keyword*, and all potential relevant past events are '*hits*' on the World Wide Web. The client, with the support of the therapist, searches for the strongest '*hits*'. Memories of the experiences appearing at the top of the list seem to be the most crucial ones, and these 'proofs' are 'discredited', one at a time, successively, by reprocessing these memories with the standard protocol for children and adolescents (4–18 years).

The 'evidence' for the core or intermediate belief can be single experiences (like not being invited to a classmate's birthday party) or series of experiences repeated over and over during a specific period (like being regularly excluded for an extended period). The second type can be called an 'archive' (or a 'chapter'). In case of an archive, the next step on this path is the identification and selection of the experience that represents the archive (a prototypical experience), or the experience that supplies the most substantial evidence of all experiences in that archive (for example, in the archive 'father's continuously scolding and criticizing': that one time he did this after I came home with a bad report card). After having collected all relevant 'proofs,' a target memory is chosen to start with the standard protocol for children and adolescents (4–18 years). The criterion for choosing is how much a specific memory is currently experienced as a 'piece of evidence' for the validity of the core belief.

The belief path can be used when the presence of a dysfunctional core belief is evident, mostly with children from age 12. Between ages 6 and 12, children may already have dysfunctional core beliefs (like 'I am stupid') and negative (damaged) self-esteem. Still, due to their cognitive development, these beliefs are often not as crystallized as in adolescents.

With regard to the role of the parents in the belief path: the 'proofs' are often memories of events within the context of the relationship with one or both parents or siblings. Therefore, it is good that the child can look freely for relevant 'proofs'. The parents will be directly involved in the treatment later, after EMDR therapy, during the process of changing the core beliefs by having and arranging corrective experiences. Box 4.7 shows the steps for the belief path. See https://www.emdrchildandyouth.info for more detailed description.

BOX 4.7 Steps for belief path

1. Identify core or intermediate beliefs with the child. Select the most significant one.
2. Gather 'pieces of evidence'/'proofs' for the selected belief; single and archives.
3. Identify the strongest (most convincing) proof/piece of evidence related to the core/intermediate belief.
4. Standard protocol for children and adolescents (4–18 years) on selected proof (per memory). The strength of evidential value determines the order in which memories are reprocessed.

4.3.6 Affect Scan and Float Back

Affect scan and float back are both techniques that can be used independently or to support the emotion path (affect scan) or the belief path (float back). To differentiate these techniques (Hensley, 2020a), the *affect scan* is implemented when seeking the origin of a present problematic emotion of the child (like rage when being criticized), and the *float back* is implemented when looking for the presumably activated dysfunctional core belief, to understand the present problematic emotion. Both techniques are seldom used in treating children because the emotion and belief paths generally provide sufficient information. For more information about these techniques readers are referred to Van Pelt and colleagues (2025).

In both techniques, the client is asked to bring up a recent situation where the symptoms were evident or anticipated. This can be a situation where intense negative emotions flared up, undesirable behaviour or negative core beliefs were manifest, or where these could have occurred. The therapist then asks the child to concentrate on the memory of the recent event

BOX 4.8 Steps for affect scan

1. Select a recent, representative situation where the child reacted with the problematic emotion. The memory of this situation should still evoke a similar affective load, be characteristic of the child's problems, and presumably activate an (unknown) emotionally charged memory.
2. Let the child close their eyes and then direct their attention to the memory of that situation. Enhance the emotional intensity of the memory by focusing on sensory aspects.
3. Direct the attention to the emotions and have them named.
4. Ask for bodily reactions.
5. Let the child adopt a matching body posture and facial expression.
6. Ask the child to go back in time and look for a memory related to how they react now in the situation, as identified in step 1.
7. When a memory has been identified, continue with the standard protocol for children and adolescents (4–18 years).

BOX 4.9 Steps for float back

1. Select a recent, characteristic, specific problematic situation. The memory of this situation should still evoke affective load, be distinctive for the child's problems, and have presumably activated a particular core or intermediate belief.
2. Let the child close their eyes and then direct their attention to the memory of that situation. Enhance the emotional intensity of the memory by focusing on the related core (or intermediate) belief. The therapist can help by mentioning this belief.
3. Activate this memory by focusing on sensory aspects.
4. Direct the attention to emotions and have them named.
5. Ask for bodily reactions.
6. Let the child adopt a matching body posture and facial expression.
7. Let the child look for a memory related to this core (or intermediate) belief.
8. When a memory has been identified, continue with the standard protocol for children and adolescents (4–18 years).

and bring up accompanying thoughts and feelings. Next, the child is asked to open themselves for memories that come up, where these reactions were experienced intensely. Box 4.8 and 4.9 describe the steps for these techniques.

4.4 Concluding Remarks

This chapter clarifies the function of making case conceptualizations. It guides the process of creating individually tailored treatment plans by introducing potential search strategies for finding relevant targets for EMDR therapy. Van Pelt and colleagues (2025) describe these procedures more extensively. Therapists should implement EMDR as efficiently as possible to optimize its potential efficacy. Clear case conceptualizations and good collaboration with clients help accomplish this so that the standard protocol for children and adolescents aged 4–18 can do its job.

5 EMDR Indications

RENÉE BEER AND CARLIJN DE ROOS

5.1 Introduction

This chapter reviews the wide range of possible indications for EMDR therapy in children. Since there is a wide range, the therapist should be familiar with all of the options so that EMDR is used to its full potential in child and adolescent mental health care and its power is optimally utilized. Depending on the child's problems and the setting in which it will be treated, EMDR is suitable as a monotherapy or as an adjunct within a broader therapy package next to other interventions.

EMDR is indicated for children whose symptoms seem to be related to memories of adverse experiences stored with dysfunctional information. Most of the clinical research on EMDR has been conducted in adults and children aged 8–18 years diagnosed with post-traumatic stress disorder (PTSD) (Beer, 2018; De Jongh et al., 2024a; De Roos, 2021).

However, clinical experience with EMDR has demonstrated its effectiveness for a broader palette of psychopathology than only PTSD (Matthijssen et al., 2020). This should not be surprising as EMDR is a transdiagnostic therapy (Beer, 2024; Dominguez, 2023). Shapiro (2018, p. 40) says about the applicability of EMDR: 'While a wide variety of conditions are amenable to change, the specific diagnosis is less important than the appropriate targeting of the earlier experiences that are generating the client's dysfunctional symptoms, characteristics, and behaviours.'

In this chapter, we review the options for EMDR indications: for what (which symptoms or symptom clusters other than PTSD) and when (in what conditions), as well as when it is not yet indicated. In Chapters 13–24, guest authors will present how EMDR can be applied to several target groups that are frequently encountered in our child and adolescent mental health care systems.

5.2 Field of Indications

EMDR addresses problems that arise and persist due to memories of traumatic and adverse events which are stored with dysfunctional information carrying a negative emotional charge. The publication of a significant study on the consequences of 'adverse childhood experiences'

Renée Beer and Carlijn de Roos, *EMDR Indications*. In: *Handbook of EMDR for Children and Adolescents*.
Edited by: Renée Beer and Carlijn de Roos, Oxford University Press. © 2026, Oxford University Press. For the English edition.
DOI: 10.1093/oso/9780198918400.003.0005

(ACEs) (Felitti et al., 1998) brought to our attention the enormous impact these experiences can have on children's development and their mental and physical health in adulthood. ACEs are a risk factor for various adverse mental health outcomes, disruption of brain and nervous system maturation, attachment, and the development of negative cognitive schemas about the self, others, and the world (Bastien et al., 2020). In her first book, Shapiro (2001, pp. 42–43) wrote that EMDR seems applicable to the consequences of both big 'T' and small 't' events (meeting or not meeting the A criterion for events necessary to diagnose PTSD according to the DSM).

The adaptive information processing (AIP) model suggests that 'inadequately or unprocessed experiences are the basis of pathology across the clinical spectrum, and processed experiences are the basis of mental health' (Shapiro, 2018, p. 38). Based on this model, we could argue that EMDR therapy is indicated for children (as for adults) with any of the following three categories of symptoms:

1. Symptoms and symptom clusters, listed in the category trauma and stressor-related disorders (DSM-5), such as acute stress disorder (ASD) and PTSD, as well as other mental health conditions within this category.
2. Specific symptoms of other DSM-5 classifications related to 'T' or 't' events, beyond the category of trauma and stressor-related disorders.
3. Generalized symptoms, symptom clusters, and behavioural patterns, consequential to dysfunctional core beliefs and associated self-imposed precepts[1] resulting from 'T' and 't' events early in life.

5.2.1 Three Categories

- ***ASD, PTSD and other trauma- and stressor-related disorders (category 1)***

As discussed in Chapter 3, most research on the efficacy of EMDR has been conducted on PTSD. To our knowledge, there are far fewer publications about the effectiveness of EMDR in children with ASD and other trauma- and stressor-related disorders. Chapter 2 describes how symptoms of ASD and PTSD can manifest in children and what differentiates ASD from PTSD.

The question is: Should ASD be treated? How much time must have passed after an event before EMDR therapy can be impactful? Traumatic events do not always bring about trauma symptoms, and many symptoms resolve themselves (Alisic et al., 2014; Hiller et al., 2016). Nonetheless, we recommend considering EMDR as an early intervention in ASD as soon as debilitating symptoms have developed that are interfering with daily life, causing suffering in the child or their family members. Examples include severe sleeping problems that disrupt family dynamics, angry outbursts, and intense feelings of guilt. Rapid implementation of EMDR in these situations seems justified for the reduction of symptoms and suffering, even during the first month after an event when only ASD can be diagnosed and not PTSD.[2]

[1] The definition of core beliefs and self-imposed precepts can be found in Chapter 4.

[2] If there is 'dysfunctional blame' (i.e., the child wrongly believes that they are to blame for the outcome of an event), early use of EMDR is especially useful because targeting 'dysfunctional guilt' is simple and effective. This also applies to 'powerlessness': if a child is plagued by overwhelmingly intrusive images of what they have experienced, neutralizing these images can be achieved quickly, providing significant relief (Bronner et al., 2009).

In situations of war and natural disasters where masses of people are affected, EMDR is an option for early intervention to support standard processing of recent memories of events and prevent stagnated processing (Tarquino et al., 2016). In these circumstances, Recent Event—Protocols are used instead of the standard protocol because the various aspects of memories of recent events are not yet integrally linked (Jarero et al., 2011; Shapiro, 2018, p. 222; Shapiro & Laub, 2008).

The shorter the duration of symptoms, the lower the risk of secondary damage and the less the family will be affected by stress. Because children's psychosocial development may become obstructed by the symptoms (and by inadequately processed memories), prompt and effective interventions are even more urgent than in adults to prevent chronic psychopathology.

It is not difficult to identify target memories in children with ASD or PTSD. Typically, there are re-experiencing symptoms caused by memories that refer directly to the causative event (the aetiology of the symptom). The event may be categorized as 'Trauma (large T)' or 'trauma (small t)', according to Shapiro (2018). In younger children (< 6), however, the causative event is not always immediately evident. For example, if a child suffers from nightmares about monsters or ghosts, it is not immediately apparent which event this symptom refers to. The same applies if a child mainly shows avoidance- and hyperarousal symptoms but not re-experiencing symptoms. Therefore, with children (especially young children) one always needs information from the parents about what the child has experienced. See, for example, Case Study 5.1.

CASE STUDY 5.1 **Marc: PTSD**

Marc, aged five, was referred because of extreme hyperactivity, hyperarousal, aggressive behaviour towards other children, and occasional dreams about monsters. These symptoms began upon his entrance into kindergarten one year ago. He had experienced a gas explosion a year before that blew up the caravan in which he was playing a game with his brother. His parents suggest that there might be a connection between Marc's symptoms and this event. The most disturbing picture of his memory is seeing himself with scars on his shoulders and arms in a hospital after his wounds have been taken care of. When he thinks of or speaks about this picture, he immediately starts shivering.

It should be noted that children often do not show enough symptoms for a PTSD classification. Nonetheless, a consistent message throughout this book is that and why treatment is indicated, also for children with only partial (or sub-clinical) PTSD. Partial PTSD may manifest with comorbid symptoms/disorders.

The DSM-5 (2013) category 'psycho trauma- and stressor-related disorders' includes, besides ASD and PTSD, five additional disorders, all sharing the etiological criterion of one (or more) traumatic or stressful experience(s) meeting the A-criterion. Implementation of EMDR might also be indicated for the treatment of symptoms within these disorders. Generally, it will be implemented here as an adjunct element in treating the child, addressing disturbing memories that sustain specific symptoms.

Two of these additional disorders within this category—reactive attachment disorder and disinhibited social contact disorder—share a common aetiology: neglect and a lack of adequate care during childhood. However, the symptomatology associated with these disorders is different: the former involves an internalizing disorder with depressive symptoms and withdrawn behaviour, while the latter is characterized by disinhibition and externalizing behaviour.

Implementation of EMDR is less evident for disinhibited social contact disorder, especially at the beginning of treatment, because initially the child does not usually recognize any problems in themselves. It is mainly the parents who see problems (sometimes through information from professionals, like teachers) and are worried because of the child's behaviour.

The option of involving EMDR as an add-on in the treatment of children with reactive attachment disorder is largely unrecognized. Problematic attachment is regularly seen in children who have parents with psychiatric problems, in adopted and foster children, and in children of parents going through high-conflict divorces. These children, being troubled by attachment problems, typically exhibit a variety of behavioural or mood problems and sometimes have comorbid PTSD. Several therapy guidelines are available for children with attachment problems.[3] For this target group, EMDR could be indicated as an add-on intervention for reprocessing memories that typically cause distress to children. These memories often relate to experiences of, for example, being deprived of affection or attention by their parents, and may have been stored with the dysfunctional attribution that this was something they (the child) were responsible for.

Furthermore, children who are placed in foster or custodial care might be convinced that they are 'sent away' or 'disposed of' as a logical consequence of their own behaviour. EMDR can help them reprocess and reconsolidate these memories with a different (adaptive) meaning—namely, that the parent is responsible for their (parenting) behaviour, that this behaviour resulted from the parent's own problems, and that the child is not to blame. In other words, EMDR can help the child to feel 'discharged'. Wesselmann and colleagues (2014a) developed a programme (Integrative Attachment Trauma Protocol for Children [IATP-C]), which integrates EMDR with family therapy, especially for children who are chronically traumatized within their relationship with their attachment figures from an early age. This programme is presented in Chapter 21. Case Study 5.2 shows an example of a child with attachment problems.

[3] Common guidelines: https://www.jaacap.org/article/S0890-8567(16)31183-2/pdf; https://www.nice.org.uk/guidance/qs133;https://evidence.nihr.ac.uk/alert/which-attachment-interventions-are-supported-by-research/

CASE STUDY 5.2 Monica: Attachment trauma

Monica, age 14 and living in a foster home, has the following symptoms: she spends a lot of time alone in her room and interacts very little with the other children in the family or with her classmates at school. She does not bond with anyone. Monica remembers how her biological parents sometimes scolded her, especially her father. Her parents showed no interest in her, mostly leaving her to her own devices. It seemed to Monica that each of her classmates had a parent who always came to watch them, for instance, at swimming competitions or the primary school musicals. Her mother has been depressed for as long as Monica can remember. Monica's father left the family and her parents divorced when she was 10. When she was 13, she was 'disposed of', as she describes it. She was picked up at home and 'dumped' in a foster home. These experiences have led Monica to conclude that she is a worthless child.

A case like Monica's offers several possible entry points for EMDR. For example, her predominant feelings of loneliness and withdrawn behaviour could be linked to memories of specific experiences of her parents being absent during events that were important to her. However, these symptoms could also stem from core beliefs, such as 'I am worthless'. If she recognizes this core belief, potential targets for EMDR could be identified using the belief path. This case shows that, depending on the case conceptualization, different options are possible for finding relevant targets for EMDR with the search strategies described in Chapter 4.

- ***Specific symptoms of classifications, beyond trauma and stressor-related disorders (category 2)***

During intake and diagnostic screening, the therapist should always check if there is (subclinical) PTSD. When other mental health conditions are classified, EMDR is likewise indicated whenever there is (or seems to be) a link between symptoms and disturbing memories of adverse experiences. After all, EMDR has evolved from a desensitization technique to treat PTSD to a comprehensive psychotherapy approach that treats a broad range of clinical problems in a variety of contexts and with diverse populations (Laliotis et al., 2021). To illustrate the range of potential indications for EMDR in various classifications (DSM-5), Section 5.3 lists several disorders as examples where EMDR could be implemented as an add-on therapy,[4] such as anxiety disorders, mood disorders, somatic symptom disorders, conduct disorders, and eating disorders. Of course, EMDR could also be considered in the remaining disorders when the hypothesis is that the presenting symptoms are related to maladaptively stored memories.

An essential task for EMDR therapists is to always identify with the child, supported by the parents as needed, the relevant memories that have caused or now maintain the symptoms. Everyday negative experiences in children include being bullied for a long time, being

[4] Chapters 13–24 describe several target groups for whom EMDR could be effective to treat the consequences of (traumatic) experiences that parallel, underlie and/or exacerbate the symptoms caused by the primary disorders.

excluded because of symptoms related to a chronic psychiatric disorder (such as ADHD or autism), experiences resulting from a disability (such as mental retardation, hearing impairment, or a speech development disorder), physical or emotional neglect, and stress by being overburdened for a long period of time. For treating symptoms or symptom clusters resulting from these circumstances, EMDR can be considered an adjunctive intervention to evidence-based interventions for specific disorders.

- ***Generalized symptoms, symptom clusters, and behavioural patterns (category 3)***

The third area concerns persistent patterns of symptoms driven by dysfunctional core beliefs (about the self or others). This may relate to patterns with internalizing problems, such as depressive symptoms that can be traced back to negative beliefs about themselves—for example, 'I'm worthless', 'I don't matter', or 'I am a bad child'. Externalizing patterns, such as aggressive behaviours, often result from dysfunctional beliefs about others—for example, 'Others can't be trusted anyway' or 'Everyone will let you down'. In many cases, there are dysfunctional beliefs about both oneself and others. Such beliefs result from a multitude of negative experiences. If not treated, these persistent patterns may develop into personality disorders. The DSM-5 has eliminated the multi-axial system, leaving behind the differentiation between Axis 1 and Axis 2 categories. Mental health conditions, personality disorders, and medical conditions are now on a single axis (American Psychiatric Association, 2013).

5.3 Examples of Mental Health Conditions

EMDR can play a role in the treatment of several mental health conditions that occur frequently in children, in those cases where there is a (supposed) connection between the current symptom(s) and disturbing memories of events. In all cases, during intake and diagnostic screening the therapist checks if there is (sub-clinical) PTSD. Primarily, therapists should follow the available treatment guidelines for the specific disorder. EMDR can be included in the treatment plan if recommended treatments yield insufficient results and if there is a particular reason to assume that symptoms could be related to disturbing memories. Nonetheless, further research is needed to demonstrate the effectiveness of EMDR as a therapy for specific symptoms and disorders other than PTSD in children. The following subsections explain why EMDR might be indicated for several common mental health conditions, illustrating how broadly EMDR could be applied. This overview does not comprise all DSM-5 classifications. The message is that the therapist should always be alert, wondering whether the symptoms might be related to maladaptively stored memories.

5.3.1 Anxiety Disorders

Anxiety disorders are the most common psychiatric disorders in children. Several international guidelines are available, including Creswell and colleagues (2014) and Walter and colleagues (2020). The most widely investigated and recommended psychotherapeutic interventions for the treatment of anxiety disorders are cognitive behavioural therapy (CBT) procedures.

An indispensable element in any anxiety treatment is exposure to the feared situation or object and disconfirmation of the frightening expectation of what might happen—that is, to confront the client with the feared situation or object so that they can experience the realistic and not the fantasized (expected) outcome. Fears may be based on previous experiences and fantasies about what might happen in the worst-case scenario in the future if confronted with the situation or object (flashforward). These future fantasies may have arisen in response to past experiences, whether identifiable or not, and, as with memories, they can result in avoidance behaviours and suffering (Logie & De Jongh, 2014).

For treatment of all anxiety disorders, the therapist can work with the child to (a) look for specific experiences in their learning history, after which the fear started or worsened (timeline path) and (b) check if the child suffers from anxiety-/fear-inducing future fantasies about a disaster that is anticipated without specific relevant experiences in their past (flashforward path). The following anxiety disorders are common in children:

- *Separation anxiety disorder*: When separated, the child fears that something terrible will happen to either the parent or themselves.
- *Selective mutism*: The child cannot (is afraid to) speak in specific settings, but can talk in other settings.
- *Specific phobia*: The child fears confrontation with a particular situation or object because something terrible will happen (again).
- *Social anxiety*: The child has an intense, persistent fear of being watched and judged by others in a social situation.
- *Panic disorder*: The child has sudden and repeated panic attacks of overwhelming anxiety and fear without an apparent reason and anxiously anticipates the next attack.
- *Agoraphobia*: The child fears and avoids places or situations that might cause panic, where escape is not easy; therefore, they perceive these as dangerous.
- *Generalized anxiety disorder*: The child considers themselves unable to cope with all kinds of (non-specific) situations.

Case Study 5.3 shows what EMDR could do with a specific phobia.

CASE STUDY 5.3 **Roy: Choking phobia**

Eight-year-old Roy is afraid to eat various foodstuffs after having seen his big brother, Ronaldo, almost choke to death on a piece of baguette with melted cheese at the age of four. Ronaldo developed no symptoms after that incident; he coughed hard and recovered quickly. Roy, who stood by helplessly, has created a fear of eating anything like what his brother ate at the time. Roy no longer eats bread, cheese, yellow products, or melted substances. He avoids such food products for fear of choking. This fear intensified after Roy choked on a fishbone at age six.

How might Roy's phobia be addressed with EMDR? Using the timeline path, the therapist could identify two events related to the symptoms: witnessing his brother Ronaldo almost choke, and himself choking on a fishbone two years later. Perhaps additional relevant experiences could be added to the timeline. These can be addressed with the standard protocol. When the therapist discovers that Roy has also developed a frightening future fantasy—he sees himself hanging onto a chair, suffocated, with the whole family around him in a panic—the therapist can treat this flashforward with EMDR as well. After reprocessing all relevant memories and flashforwards, Roy will be prepared for the future so that he dares to eat everything again. After applying the mental video check and the future template (see Chapter 7), EMDR treatment is finished; further improvements could be achieved by CBT interventions (if needed). Roy must learn to eat different foods (again) and be confident that he can swallow by experiencing this. Exposure procedures and behaviour experiments (learning by doing) are added to this goal.

5.3.2 **Obsessive-Compulsive Disorder**

Obsessive-compulsive disorder used to be categorized as anxiety disorder but has been moved out of this category in the DSM-5, and has been regarded as a separate category since 2013. With this disorder, the child fears that something terrible will happen if they do (not) perform specific actions. The first-line treatment is exposure and response prevention or medication (SSRIs). EMDR can be considered if it is evident that the symptoms started (and/or exacerbated) after specific adverse experiences, or if the child has intrusive anticipation fears and is trying to prevent these from happening by the symptoms.

5.3.3 **Mood Disorders**

CBT is the recommended treatment for major depressive disorder in adolescents (NICE, 2019). However, effectiveness is limited, and high dropout and relapse rates are common (Weisz et al., 2006, 2017). Traumatic experiences often play a role in the onset or maintenance of depression (Paauw et al., 2019, 2023), which usually implies experiences with an interpersonal aspect, such as the loss of a loved one (by death or divorce), bullying, social exclusion, and humiliation. For the identification of depression-related targets, a combination of the timeline- and the belief paths may be used. If specific events can be identified that seem to underlie the onset or maintenance of the depression, the therapist can target these with EMDR. For children with depressive symptoms, EMDR can be added to therapy in the same way as in adults.

In a case like Laila's (see Case Study 5.4), EMDR can make an essential contribution to reducing depressive symptoms by creating space for the normal grieving process. EMDR could focus on the intrusive image of the memory (seeing her father hanging in the barn) and other images related to her dysfunctional guilt. Traumatic grief is blocking the normal grieving process, and therefore she remains feeling down and depressed; memories of any other events related to the start or worsening of her depressive symptoms can be looked for and may be identified.

CASE STUDY 5.4 **Laila: Depressive disorder**

Laila (aged 15) is referred for therapy because she worries a lot, feels down, procrastinates, and cannot concentrate in school since her father unexpectedly took his own life by hanging. No one had anticipated this. The father was occasionally depressed, but mostly he was in good spirits. He had been taking medication for years that kept his depressive disorder well under control (at least, so it seemed). Since her father's death, Laila sleeps badly and feels down and depressed. She withdraws to her room, shuts off contact with friends, and her appetite has decreased. She has barely cried over losing her father and is not sure what she feels or should feel about this. She procrastinates whenever possible and ruminates about questions like: Should I have paid better attention? Could I have prevented this?

5.3.4 **Somatic Symptom Disorder**

NICE provides many guidelines for conditions and diseases in children (https://www.nice.org.uk). However, an overarching guideline for somatic symptom disorder or persistent physical symptoms seems lacking; most evidence for the effectiveness of EMDR exists for clients with chronic pain (Matthijssen et al., 2020). There are few research studies in this area for youth (see Chapter 3).

EMDR is indicated when physical symptoms are maintained by unprocessed trauma or pain-related memories of events, such as an accident, sexual abuse, surgery, or previous overwhelming pain attacks. As always, during intake and diagnostic screening the therapist checks if there is (sub-clinical) PTSD. With the timeline path (see Chapter 4), pain-related emotionally distressing experiences are identified, after which the pain started and later exacerbated. Finally, the therapist checks for the presence of intrusive flashforwards (pain-related representations of future catastrophes). Through EMDR, the emotional distress of these memories and representations can be reduced or neutralized, improving the conditions for recovery of the physical symptoms (i.e., decreasing the symptoms' intensity, frequency, or duration). See Case Study 5.5.

CASE STUDY 5.5 **Ahmed: Somatic symptom disorder**

Ahmed (11) was referred because of severe headaches and fatigue. The headache started in fourth grade after a serious fall from his bicycle. He had a stabbing pain in his head and a mild concussion because of the fall. The headaches gradually increased further, and for six months he was also constantly tired. Although Ahmed used to be a fast learner, he needs to spend more and more time on his homework to keep up and sleeps more often during the day. A few weeks ago, he had a blackout at school, which made him panic. His parents attach great importance to good grades at school and urge Ahmed to do his homework well.

In Ahmed's case, the EMDR therapist could identify two relevant target memories: the fall from his bicycle, and the experience of the intense and overwhelming headache at school, which resulted in a blackout a few months later. It was clear that the unprocessed memories (PTSD and pain-related) were maintaining his headache. However, Ahmed's wish to make his parents proud of him by excelling at school was another factor hindering his recovery from the headache. The headache prevented him from excelling, so he would sit for hours doing extra homework to achieve this goal. The therapist explained to Ahmed and his parents what was going on by drawing a vicious circle with maintaining factors related to his headache. After this, EMDR therapy started and the traumatic memories maintaining his headache were reprocessed. At the same time, Ahmed and his parents were advised to install extra breaks to prevent overload and to improve conditions for further recovery.

5.3.5 Conduct Disorders

Guidelines report that conduct disorders (CDs) often involve comorbidity with ADHD, anxiety disorders, and mood disorders (Atkinson & Hollis, 2010). Also, the overlap between CDs and PTSD has been noted (Bernhard et al., 2018, p. 153): 'Studies with delinquent adolescents indicate a high rate of comorbidity between CD, trauma exposure and PTSD. In studies of incarcerated adolescents, up to 96% reported a history of trauma exposure, and up to 65% showed comorbid PTSD.' This implies that it is recommendable for EMDR C&A therapists working with this target group to draw attention to this in their setting and see if more trauma treatment is possible for these children because PTSD is hardly recognized.

Empirically tested CD treatments are parent training, CBT, and systemic treatments (Andrade et al., 2019; Matthys & Van de Glind, 2013). Interestingly, treatments for children who are diagnosed with a CD are usually primarily focused on increasing control of their behaviour. Attempts are made to influence the behaviour by attaching consequences to it. Unfortunately, less focus is directed towards the possible incentives eliciting this problematic behaviour. Children with CDs are engaged in many negative social experiences because of their disorder, which frequently damages their self-image further. Therefore, in children with CDs it is crucial in the diagnostic phase to screen for comorbid PTSD and to explore if specific memories might be identified that evoke or maintain the problematic behaviour. These may include memories of experiences that have further damaged the child's self-image, and the EMDR therapist should examine if EMDR might be indicated as part of the treatment.

CASE STUDY 5.6 **Boris: Conduct disorder**

Boris, 16, is the youngest of four children. He has a conduct disorder and has been obstinate and rebellious for some time. Recently his behaviour has become increasingly problematic, especially since an incident of violence between his parents. There were many years of domestic violence. It stopped after the parents received therapy for it one year ago, initiated after Boris's father had beaten his mother so severely that she had to be hospitalized.

Boris risks being expelled from school because of his offensive, cheeky, and rude behaviour. His grades are poor and he has concentration problems. He has a group of friends, several of whom have already been in trouble with the police. Boris is referred to therapy because he wants help. He has nightmares and intrusive images during the day of his parents arguing. His dreams frighten him; sometimes, he fantasizes that he is brutally attacking his father.

Case Study 5.6 shows several potential starting points for EMDR, such as Boris's intrusions and nightmares; these symptoms indicate that there might be comorbid (partial) PTSD. The therapist could also examine the extent to which his rebellious behaviour is driven by dysfunctional core beliefs about himself or others (belief path). If such beliefs can be identified, the therapist and Boris could look for memories of events that provide emotional 'evidence' for them (see Chapter 4).

5.3.6 **Eating Disorders**

International guidelines for the treatment of eating disorders distinguish several types of eating disorders (anorexia nervosa, bulimia nervosa, binge eating disorder, avoidant/restrictive food intake disorder) and mention recommended therapies for each of them (Couturier et al., 2020; Hay et al., 2014; Hilbert et al., 2017) Controlled studies reveal moderate results with considerable relapse rates (Berg et al., 2013; Datta et al., 2023).

The potential role of EMDR therapy as an add-on in a multidisciplinary and trauma-informed approach has been described by several authors (Beer in Luber (2019); Beer in Seubert & Virdi (2024); Rossi and colleagues (2024)). EMDR can be implemented for the treatment of, for example, specific fears related to eating-related situations or products, the urge to perform specific behaviours after eating (compensatory behaviour), negative self-image, negative body perception, and clinical perfectionism. See Case Study 5.7.

CASE STUDY 5.7 **Irina: Eating disorder**

Irina, a 16-year-old adolescent with anorexia nervosa, receives outpatient treatment at an eating disorder centre. In her view, the eating disorder started in 8th grade. Until then, she had always been a good learner and she had many friends. Suddenly, everything changed, which made her insecure. She was the first one in her class to get breasts, and her period started, leading to embarrassment about her body and gradually increasing social isolation. Several times, her classmates made remarks which embarrassed her. Everyone expected her to follow an academic track, but surprisingly she received different school advice. During her awkward school year in 8th grade, her mother also suffered a heart attack, from which she fortunately recovered well. The following months all family members were very stressed.
In Irina's experience, from 8th onwards everything in her life went downhill. She threw herself into dieting, hoping to gain control over her life (again) with a good figure and more connection with her peers.

In a case such as Irina's, there are several possible targets for EMDR, such as her memories of various events during grade 8 (remarks from classmates about her physical development, her mother's heart attack, specific incidents during the stressful period afterwards within the family, the school advice regarding her further education and everybody's reactions to it, poor grades, the feeling of not belonging anymore). Furthermore, Irina's frightening future fantasies about what will happen to her if her weight increases to a healthy level and her core belief ('I am inferior') and self-imposed precepts incite her to want control over all parts of her life and to excel.

All cases presented in this section illustrate this chapter's message: It is valuable for the therapist always to stay alert to whether symptoms might be related to maladaptively stored memories and whether reprocessing of these memories might lead to symptom reduction.

5.4 Relative Contraindications

Implementation of EMDR is an obvious choice when the psychopathology to be treated seems to be related to memories that are stored with dysfunctional information. However, sometimes, some preliminary work must precede EMDR to influence the child's living situation in such a way that trauma processing becomes possible and impactful. This is referred to as 'relative contraindications' instead of 'contraindications', meaning that the conditions must be improved to enable EMDR to be effective. If the therapist expects that EMDR cannot yet start, based on the presented information, it should be determined precisely what is needed before the start, to accomplish what, with which interventions, and how many sessions are expected to prepare the client for trauma treatment.

Usually, if the indication for EMDR is stated correctly, the child's functioning will improve after EMDR. Nevertheless, a temporary increase in symptoms may occur if, before treatment, the child was used to avoiding situations, feelings, or thoughts associated with memories such as those of abuse or maltreatment. Therefore, if several sessions are needed before all relevant memories have been reprocessed, while these memories are now no longer avoided, it makes sense that the child will temporarily be struggling. It is essential that the therapist explains (also to the parents) the expected course of the process, normalizes and clarifies possible temporary increases in symptoms (avoidance of the memories is no longer possible), and encourages the completion of therapy.

When there is no symptom reduction after EMDR, the conclusion may be, in hindsight, that symptoms were not related to the memories treated, apparently that indication for EMDR was perhaps not justified. Another possible explanation for this outcome may be that interfering factors such as avoidance behavior, played a role, so that there was insufficient 'room' for trauma processing. Sections 5.4.1 to 5.4.7 include a discussion of these issues.

5.4.1 Current Unsafety

The efficacy of EMDR therapy is impeded if the child is subjected to unsafe and distressing conditions in their current living situation. In such environments, a child must maintain high hyper-alertness to function. The survival mode is at odds with the attitude needed for trauma processing. The opposite is required: the child must dare to open themselves to thoughts, emotions, and physical situations associated with memories that led to their trauma symptoms.

Children living in sustained unsafety and distress cannot sufficiently distance themselves from their memories of these or similar situations, making it very difficult to modify the attributed meanings permanently; they cannot reflect on a mode other than survival. For complete trauma processing, it is essential that the memories concern past situations.

Offering EMDR in a currently unsafe or troubled situation suggests to the child that the symptoms can or should disappear, rather than that the situation needs to change. In such situations, for example, in cases of maltreatment, it is imperative that the therapist first ensures that adequate interventions are put in place to ensure the child's safety, such as 'Safety House' or 'Signs of Safety' (Turnell & Edwards, 2009). This may involve placing the child in an out-of-home setting, removal of the abusive family member from the home, or ensuring that there is a change in the behaviour of the (former) abuser. Once the child realizes that they no longer need to maintain a survival mode and that adults can also change situations, they will become receptive to trauma processing and the therapist can begin EMDR. If necessary, colleagues can provide parallel interventions to increase and monitor the child's safety during EMDR.

However, when a child's current situation remains relatively unsafe and the therapist knows that it will not improve despite efforts to optimize it, the therapist may decide to start EMDR. Its effects will be more limited in such circumstances than under optimal conditions, but providing some relief is better than offering nothing. At the very least, the distress resulting from inadequately stored memories of past events can be reduced. This may help the child better cope with the ongoing stressful living situation. After a few sessions, the therapist can assess whether continuing trauma therapy is appropriate. In such situations, the therapist should inform the child and parents that the symptoms may not disappear entirely because of the current stressful situation.

5.4.2 Insufficient Affect Tolerance

Children with trauma symptoms may have intense negative emotions because they are living with memories of overwhelming negative experiences. Trauma treatment is the first choice to calm those emotions. EMDR therapy requires the child to acknowledge and tolerate their feelings during treatment. Some children find admitting or focusing on strong emotions so frightening that they cannot or do not want to concentrate on the (initially negative) associations that arise during the EMDR process. If the child does not yet know how to deal with strong emotions and is used to applying escape strategies as soon as they arise, it is advisable first to teach the child strategies to deal with these emotions adequately in a limited number of sessions before beginning EMDR. Often, these children have never learned anything about feelings and do not recognize emotions in themselves or others. There are several ways to quickly teach children the skills they need. Numerous programmes and games are available (https://www.anagomez.org; https://www.sesamestreet.org). Subsequent trauma processing with EMDR will allow negative emotions to decrease further.

5.4.3 **Ongoing Legal Proceedings**

After reporting certain experiences, such as a traffic accident, interpersonal violence, or sexual abuse, the victim is likely to be questioned and cross-examined by both the police and others within the legal and judicial process. Until such interrogation is completed, EMDR should not be offered. Otherwise, the therapist may be accused of 'coaching' or 'leading' the victim, thus making the child's testimony less reliable, and this could have consequences for any legal proceedings. The objective of EMDR is symptom reduction by bringing memories of traumatic and other adverse life experiences to an adaptive resolution, which results in recalling the meaning of the event differently. The objective of legal proceedings is truth-telling. Each objective should be explained in full to both the child and their caregivers.

5.4.4 **Medical Conditions**

A medical condition where it is believed that stress may lead to an increase in physical symptoms, like a heart condition, asthma, or epilepsy, may make the parents or therapist question if applying EMDR is a responsible choice. The fear is that there is a risk that EMDR could cause a seizure in a child with epilepsy, for example, because of the high level of arousal associated with the treatment. In such situations, the therapist can explain that the child is already constantly experiencing a high degree of arousal because of the inadequately processed memories. Any (extra) increased arousal during the EMDR session will only occur briefly, mainly during the assessment of the memory (phase 3 of the standard protocol). During desensitization (phase 4 of the standard protocol), *distancing* from the memory takes place (Lee & Drummond, 2008). This implies that the extra arousal elicited by memory activation will decrease. For the peace of mind of the parents and the child, it is advisable to explain this beforehand and to consult with the child's GP or other medical specialists if required. Fear of high arousal is not a reason to omit or postpone EMDR.

Children who have suffered permanent brain damage due to an accident (non-congenital brain injury) might be referred with symptoms that may be related to the event from which this injury arose. Regularly, the question arises as to whether EMDR can be effective when such injuries are present: Can trauma processing be effectuated? The effect of the procedure depends on the amount of distress related to the unprocessed memory relative to other (maintaining) factors. The answer is that this cannot be determined in advance; it needs to be tested by applying EMDR.

5.4.5 **Substance Abuse: Alcohol, Drugs, Medication**

Adolescents may use sedatives or narcotics as a learned strategy to dampen or prevent emotions. For trauma processing to be effective, the adolescent must be able to tolerate relevant memories and associated emotions and stay in the process (not escape). This would be interrupted by recreational drug use. The therapist must explain that EMDR can only be successful if the adolescent agrees to abstinence as a condition of treatment under a binding agreement. See Markus and Hornsveld (2017) for detailed information on agreements that the therapist can make with an addicted adolescent regarding continuation or abstention of use.

Therapists using EMDR should be aware that the use of any medication that flattens emotional responses (benzodiazepines are best known in this regard) can harm therapy outcomes, as these drugs interfere with the activation and processing of memory material (Steenen et al., 2023). Here, it is recommended first to apply interventions aimed at reducing the intake of these medications and subsequently to start EMDR to maximize the effect of this treatment. If this proves impossible, then test sessions can be started to check whether EMDR can facilitate information processing. In this regard, one may consider adding a detox programme at the beginning of treatment. Conversely, medications used in connection with ADHD, such as Ritalin® and Concerta®, may have positive effects. Even more so, it is recommended to take ADHD medication before a session as it allows the child to be optimally focused during the session.

5.4.6 Secondary Gain

Trauma symptoms can also have positive consequences for the child, such as gaining certain privileges (e.g., being allowed to sleep in their parents' bed) or being able to escape unpleasant situations (e.g., not having to go to school, where the child must perform at a standard that they cannot live up to). These positive consequences are called secondary gains. If secondary gains play a role, it is imperative to insert interventions in addition to trauma treatment aimed at making these positive consequences redundant for the child. Such interventions may include psychoeducation or influencing parenting behaviours which (unintentionally) reinforce and maintain the child's unwanted behaviour.

5.4.7 Insufficient Expertise on the Part of the Therapist

It is recommended that therapists provide EMDR only to target groups for which they are sufficiently equipped to treat them with the appropriate expertise. Examples are children with intellectual disabilities, children with autism spectrum disorders, children with dissociative disorders, and children with vision or hearing problems. The therapist's expertise allows them to make sound assessments in the diagnostic phase about which part of the clients' problems may be attributed to unprocessed memories and which part to the underlying disorder or disability. In addition, the therapist should have the expertise to communicate adequately with the child.

5.5 Concluding Remarks

This chapter reviewed when (in what conditions) the application of EMDR is eligible and when not (yet) and for what kind of psychopathology. Children exposed to traumatic events are at risk of developing a variety of problems. For this reason, it is essential that, during intake, the therapist correctly identifies symptoms and relevant events (big 'T' and small 't') that the child has experienced. In doing so, the therapist should determine which of these events may be related to the symptoms because memories of these events may be inadequately processed. For this exploration, the search strategies described in Chapter 4 are helpful. If a relationship seems likely between the reported symptoms and memories of events, EMDR is indicated. Following the current treatment guidelines for the classified disorder(s) is always recommended as the first choice (if available). In international guidelines, EMDR is recommended only for the treatment of PTSD and not (yet) for other disorders. However, if (partial) PTSD is classified as a comorbid disorder, treatment should start with these symptoms, as treatment is short and effective. As with adults, EMDR can be used with children for an extensive range of symptoms and disorders. If the child is suffering, or if their development is stagnating, the application of EMDR is recommended as soon as possible to prevent further developmental stagnation and, with it, the possibility that the symptoms might develop into chronic psychopathology with an increased risk of comorbidity and re-victimization.

6 Parents and Families

RENÉE BEER AND CARLIJN DE ROOS

6.1 Introduction

EMDR therapy is focused on the individual. However, children always live in the context of a family: their biological family, a foster family, an adoptive family, or a family-replacement home.[1] With children, one should—in addition to the developmental psychological context—always take the child's family context into account because the reactions of family members mutually influence each other. Therefore, it can be desirable to involve family members directly in therapy in specific circumstances. Sometimes, this will concern only the parents/caregivers; at other times the siblings may be included, and at still other times only specific family members (a parent and a sister or brother). Parents are *always* involved in their child's therapy in some way: if the child is under 16 years old,[2] they should at least consent to the therapy. After informing them about the treatment plan, the therapist will ask them to give 'informed consent'. Furthermore, the therapist always needs relevant information from parents about their child's functioning.[3] The case conceptualization in each case should identify which family members must be actively involved in the therapy, in what capacity, and to achieve which goal(s).

The parents may have been directly traumatized by witnessing a traumatic event. They may have also been traumatized indirectly by learning that their child has experienced a traumatic event and by observing their child's reactions (Afzal et al., 2022; Wilcoxon et al., 2021). The child's traumatization may have occurred outside the family—for example, through medical interventions or an accident—or within the family—for instance, through abuse, violence, or neglect. Several studies have found an association between post-traumatic stress disorder (PTSD) in parents and similar symptoms in their children (Hiller et al., 2018; Trickey et al., 2012). Post-traumatic stress reactions in one or both parents were found to be an essential predictor for PTSD in children (Hiller et al., 2016; Silverstein et al., 2022).

[1] Family refers to the kind of family the child is currently living in.
[2] Or any other age criterion that may apply in the country of the therapist.
[3] Functioning includes developmental anamnesis, trauma history, complaints anamnesis, current psychosocial functioning, and relevant background data.

Renée Beer and Carlijn de Roos, *Parents and Families*. In: *Handbook of EMDR for Children and Adolescents*.
Edited by: Renée Beer and Carlijn de Roos, Oxford University Press.
DOI: 10.1093/oso/9780198918400.003.0006

However, the direction of this link is unclear (Bronner et al., 2006; Landolt et al., 2012). PTSD appears to be 'contagious', but who infects those in affected families remains a question (Afzal et al., 2022; Greene et al., 2023).

Conversely, a child can develop PTSD symptoms by seeing or experiencing PTSD reactions in their parents. Both situations are described as secondary traumatization (Dashorst et al., 2019; Dashorst et al., 2020). Because a correlation between parental and child reactions is evident in all cases, engaging parents is a *must* to maximize symptom reduction via EMDR, especially when the therapist has concrete indications that parent–child interactions reinforce PTSD symptoms in one another.

Including parents and other family members is not part of the EMDR standard procedure. Various views and practices that include the involvement of family members in the therapy of children have developed during clinical practice with EMDR, some of which are described in this book (Chapters 19–24). Shapiro and colleagues (2007) compiled a handbook on EMDR and family therapy that illustrates how the individual-oriented EMDR approach can be combined with techniques and interventions that involve more family members (the systemic approach).

In this chapter, we provide practice-based tools that can help therapists decide when to involve parents and other family members in therapy. We delve into the following questions:

- What questions are relevant in the diagnostic phase to identify systematically what is needed for which family members systematically?
- How can parents support their child during EMDR sessions and at home?
- When should parents be offered therapy for their problems, and what are the potential targets?
- How would therapy be best for the parents, and which therapist is best equipped to provide this if needed?
- What criteria should be used to decide whom to treat first?
- What points should be considered when involving the whole family in therapy?

6.2 Case Conceptualization and Roles for Parents

During the diagnostic phase, the therapist collects information to determine which family members should be involved in therapy. Table 6.1 provides an overview of helpful questions. Responses to these questions help therapists identify the impact of the traumatizing event(s) on the child, parents, and other family members and elucidate what is needed to achieve therapy goals, for whom, and what role(s) parents can play in the therapy.

The child may have experienced various situations, single or chronic, which may or may not have involved family members. Parents often suffer due to the fact that their child has experienced something nasty. After all, the parent could not protect the child from this event and the resulting misery. Cognitive processes (the meaning that parents assign to the event, as well as to their reactions to the event and their child's reactions), both peri-traumatic and

Table 6.1 Questions for case conceptualization

1	What happened?	Type of trauma: single or chronic; within or outside of the family
2	Who was affected by the event and how: directly or indirectly?	Child(ren), parents, other family members
3	Who developed symptoms?	Child(ren), parents, other family members
4	What are the symptoms of the affected child and—if relevant—the parents and other family members?	Cognitive, emotional, behavioural, or physical symptoms per individual
5	Is processing normal or has it stagnated?	Age-specific, transient reactions, or signs of stagnated processing in child, parents, or other family members
6	Which therapy goals for whom?	For child, parents, other family members
7	What is the goal for the presence or involvement of the parents or other family members in the child's therapy?	- Provide missing information (parents) - Enhance the feeling of safety, so that the child dares to start processing (parents) - Positive reinforcement of functional (new) behaviour (parents) - Enhance therapy efficacy by improvement of understanding the problematic behaviours (parents or family) - Improve interaction patterns (parents or family)

post-traumatic, influence their feelings of guilt and competence as parents. Being actively involved in their child's therapy—before, during, and after—helps to restore their sense of control and competence as parents. Involvement allows them to do more than passively wait to see if their child will recover through interventions provided by someone else.

The case conceptualization maps out how parents' reactions ultimately interfere with their child's recovery, and the treatment plan explicitly states how attention will be paid to influencing their reactions that may (inadvertently) contribute to maintaining the child's symptoms. These might be the parent's cognitive, emotional, and behavioural reactions. Parents may be so distressed that they first need to process their own trauma to be able to support their child during therapy, where they may be assigned various roles.

6.2.1 **Motivator**

Therapy success rates increase when parents clearly show their children that they trust the therapist and the therapy. This is particularly important with young children, who often assess the safety and trustworthiness of situations by observing their parents' reactions. Focusing on unpleasant memories usually evokes intense negative emotions and sensations in children initially, with the risk of premature disengagement. When a child exhibits avoidance reactions, the parent must take on the role of external motivator. Sometimes children need a push from their parents to keep going: for instance, by the parent saying 'You can do this!', 'This will help you!', or 'Just keep going, and soon you will feel better'. By providing such encouragement, parents can contribute to the continuity of therapy. In some cases, parents need precise instructions from the therapist on how to motivate their child to continue.

6.2.2 **Informant**

The therapist can involve the parents as informants during the diagnostic and therapeutic phases. During the diagnostic phase, they provide information about the child's past and present functioning: developmental anamnesis, symptom anamnesis, current psychosocial functioning, and background data. During the therapy phase, parents can pay attention to signals of change they observe in the child at home. They can record their observations on paper or digitally and give them to the therapist prior to the next session. These observations are necessary to establish the effects of EMDR (or its absence). The role of parents as informants is vital because children typically lack the capacity for self-reflection; they cannot signal or report changes in their *behaviour*. However, children are usually better able than their parents to self-report changes in *perception* (Strand et al., 2005). The ability to reflect increases as children grow older, and with adolescents there can be significant discrepancies between what they and their parents report. See Case Study 6.1.

CASE STUDY 6.1 **Annette**

A week after her first EMDR session, 14-year-old Annette says she has not noticed any changes in herself during the intervening days. Her mother, contrarily, reports that her daughter has become much more relaxed, reacting very differently from before to conflicts with peers (panicking less), that she sleeps better, that she grumbles less about nightmares, and that she has been in a happier mood over the past week. When the therapist asks what Annette thinks about the observations of her mother, she says these are just ordinary reactions: 'It's nothing special, that's why I didn't notice it.'

Parents' reports on observed changes between sessions are necessary for another reason: children show few facial 'emotional cues' during desensitization (Adler-Tapia & Sesttle, 2025; Tinker and Wilson, 1999). This makes it difficult for the therapist to assess to what extent information processing is taking place during the session and to what extent the physically felt distress is 'truly' dropping. Is the child saying 'SUD = 0' because they are no longer experiencing distress or because they want to be away from the therapist/therapy? The benchmark, of course, is whether there is a reduction of symptoms associated with the processed target memory in daily life. To determine whether the symptoms have reduced, and the therapy has been successful, the therapist relies (partly) on the parent(s) as informant(s).

6.2.3 Co-Therapist

Parents play an active role in the therapy of toddlers and older children with preverbal trauma, primarily if the storytelling method is used (see Chapter 8). In these situations, the therapist provides the therapy with one or both parents, who play an essential role as co-therapists.

6.2.4 Reinforcer

Problem behaviour can be evoked by distressing memories of negative experiences but be (partly) maintained by reinforcement patterns. For example, parents may attach positive consequences to problem behaviour, such as allowing the child to stay in the parent's bed if the child complains of having nightmares or allowing the child to miss school if the child says they are too frightened to go. Therapists should modify reinforcement patterns if parents keep reinforcing old dysfunctional problem behaviour and insufficiently or inadequately reinforce new functional behaviour. The therapist can give behavioural instructions to the parents *after* EMDR sessions with the child have taken place. An explanation of the process and of the needs of their child at that moment is often all that is required. See Case Study 6.2.

CASE STUDY 6.2 **Yassar**

Nine-year-old Yassar, who fled to the Netherlands with his family from a war zone 18 months earlier, no longer dares to go to sleep alone and suffers from nightmares about what the family experienced before the flight. Once the nightmares are effectively treated with EMDR, he is no longer afraid to sleep alone and sleeps peacefully. However, the family members (father, mother, two elder brothers, and two elder sisters) have become accustomed to taking turns sitting with Yassar every night until he falls asleep. This pattern needs to be broken by explaining to the family that their presence is no longer needed to reassure Yassar.

However, if problem behaviour creates more advantages than disadvantages, reinforcement patterns should be modified *before* EMDR. See Case Study 6.3.

CASE STUDY 6.3 **Dunya**

Sixteen-year-old Dunya is referred with PTSD after a rape. She is unsure whether to start EMDR therapy. Since the rape, she has a better connection with her mother, who paid little attention to her before. Dunya's mother had also been sexually abused and recognizes her daughter's symptoms. They both enjoy their mutual attention, and their satisfying good talks with each other about their experiences. Before the EMDR therapy starts, the therapist discusses with Dunya and her mother how they can maintain their good contact in other ways, even after Dunya will be symptom-free.

6.2.5 Witness

Parents can also observe their child's process and progress during EMDR by being present as witness. The therapist may invite them to take this role if the child indicates they would appreciate the parent staying in the room, provided the parent believes they can cope. Going through this experience together can be valuable for both the child and the parents: the child can derive support from the parents being close by, and the parents can better understand how the child has reacted to what they have experienced. Witnessing the recovery process after traumatization can strengthen feelings of compassion and closeness in the parents (see Chapters 21 and 22 in this book) and promote the attachment relationship between parent(s) and child.

6.3 Therapy for the Parents

It is essential during the diagnostic phase to identify whether psychological problems in the parents are manifested as well. This is relevant because parents may be so distressed by their problems (e.g., PTSD or depressive symptoms) that they can no longer function adequately as parents. Examples include inconsistent use of rules and boundaries and insufficient emotional support. A positive correlation has been established between not functioning well as a parent after adverse experiences in their youth (ACEs) and the emergence or persistence of behavioural problems in their child (Hanetz-Gamliel & Dollberg, 2022). It has also been demonstrated that EMDR therapy is less effective in children when parents are troubled by more severe symptoms (De Roos, 2021).

Research evaluating the effect of EMDR therapy on parents is emerging. The first randomized study of the impact of EMDR in traumatized parents of children with a metabolic disorder showed that four sessions of 90 minutes (spread over two half-day sessions) resulted in a significant reduction of post-traumatic stress symptoms, comorbid psychological complaints, and parental distress, compared with a waiting list group (Conijn et al., 2022). These improvements were found to be maintained at follow-up three months after therapy. Besides the reduction of PTSD symptoms, EMDR therapy for parents can focus on the desensitization of memories related to feelings of despair, anger, and powerlessness in parents who may doubt their parental competency. Such feelings may be evoked by their child's behaviour, triggering memories of their childhood experiences or of past situations where they felt incompetent as parents.

Answers to the following questions determine if and how EMDR therapy should be provided for the parents:

- What induces problems for the parent?
- Who should be treated first: The parent or the child? Or in parallel?
- Who should provide the therapy of the parent: The child's therapist, a colleague within the team, or a colleague from another team, or a peer institution?
- What will be the goals of therapy?

6.3.1 Causes or Triggers for the Parent's Problems

The manifestation of any parental problems may have been identified during the diagnostic phase. However, it may not be immediately apparent what factors induce these problems. Various events or circumstances can lead to dysregulated, inappropriate behaviours in parents. We mention four options. The parent may have been functioning well until an event occurred, after which the parent—as well as the child—developed post traumatic stress symptoms: for example, after an accident or a medical procedure on the child. A second option is that the parent's dysregulation results from the child's reactions to the event. These reactions may trigger inadequately processed memories of the parent's own traumatic experiences (e.g., abuse). A third option is that the parent had already, for an extended period, been displaying symptoms that are not related to the child's problems or the event(s) experienced (e.g., symptoms of a manic-depressive disorder or a borderline personality disorder). A fourth option is that inadequate parenting behaviour is not induced by disturbing memories but by a lack of relevant skills.

EMDR for the parent is indicated when their psychopathology, whether exacerbated by the event(s) or the child's reactions to it or not, interferes with the parent's capability to respond adequately to the needs of the traumatized child. However, a parent with pre-existing psychopathology will mostly need a longer and more comprehensive therapy programme than only EMDR.

6.3.2 Who Goes First?

When both the parents and the child have been traumatized by the same event (e.g., an accident), or when the parent's behaviour is driven by traumatic memories of experiences of their own (e.g., abuse during childhood) that are not adaptively processed, the question is who should receive EMDR therapy first to achieve the best results. Parents often nominate their child to be first because they fear that activating their own traumatic memories will make them emotionally or cognitively less available to their child. Therefore, they prefer to remain available to the child first so that they can provide support during the child's therapy. Once the child's healthy development is back on track, they dare to confront memories of their own traumatic experiences. Then the parents' therapy comes to the fore. Based on clinical practice experience, we recommend honouring the wish of the parents to centre therapy around the child. Most parents appear capable of making adequate choices and taking responsibility. Honouring their choice also strengthens their trust in the therapist and their sense of competence as a parent. Indeed, the child should be treated first to put their stalled development back on track. Delaying their therapy prolongs the burden of suffering for the child and the parents, and possibly causes (further) developmental delays.

The parents' therapy may run in parallel, if necessary, but cannot be a replacement for the child's treatment. After all, parents have sought help for their child because the child has trauma-related symptoms. There is currently no evidence that trauma symptoms in children resulting from inadequate processing can disappear if the therapy focuses exclusively on trauma treatment for their parents.

However, when a parent is no longer functioning well due to their own inadequately processed memories, it is most efficient to first provide therapy to the parents because the parent may be unable to provide the necessary emotional and cognitive support to the child during EMDR trauma processing (whether the standard protocol is applied or the storytelling method). Parents must be able to tolerate the confrontation with their child's memories during EMDR therapy or at least be able to give the child permission and space to start and complete EMDR.

6.3.3 Which Therapist?

We recommend using the criteria in Box 6.1 to decide who will provide the parents' therapy.

When using the storytelling method (see Chapter 8 of this book), the parent has an active role as a co-therapist: The writing of the story, describing the experiences of the child from the child's perspective ('through the eyes of the child'), touches the parents' memories. Therefore, the parent(s) may need to prepare for this by undergoing EMDR to adequately process their memories of the event(s) in the story (e.g., hospital admissions). For efficiency, it is recommended that the parent and the child be treated by the same therapist, if feasible, in the institution where the therapist works. The advantage is that the lines of communication will be short, and no time is lost waiting for the parents' therapy or exchange of information between therapists.

BOX 6.1 Selection criteria for the parents' therapist

- The severity of the parents' problems
  - Does the nature of the problems suggest a need for short or long-term therapy?
  - If long-term therapy is expected, referral to a colleague seems appropriate.
- The expertise of the child's therapist
  - Is the therapist trained and experienced in providing therapy to parents with these issues?
  - If not, referral to a colleague seems appropriate.
- The institution's scope and possibilities
  - Does the institution or practice accept adult clients, and is it financially feasible?
  - If not, referral to a colleague (other institution) seems appropriate.

6.3.4 Therapy Goals

Potential therapy goals for parents can be categorized into grades from less to more comprehensive. Gomez (2013) described three alternatives for the scope of therapy for parents metaphorically, as options for the 'cleaning operation'.

1. *Clearing the table*

The child receives EMDR therapy. Contact with the parent aims to support the child's therapy process through psychoeducation, enabling a better understanding of the child's reaction. If necessary, the parent receives instruction on better responding to the child's problematic behaviours.

The core is to instruct parents on how to support their children.

2. *Tidying up the room*

The child receives EMDR therapy. The parent's capacities are strengthened to regulate emotions better and apply the necessary parental skills. Emotion regulation work with parents is focused on increasing their capacities to both self- and co-regulate by teaching, for example, breathing exercises, yoga, and mindfulness exercises, using relational resources and Resource Development and Installation (RDI) to increase the parents' resources (Gomez, 2025)

The core goal is to enhance parents' capacities and resources for supporting their child.

3. *Cleaning up the house*

Both the child and the parent receive EMDR therapy individually. The parent processes their disturbing memories, which are activated repeatedly by the child's current behaviours. Multiple therapists can collaborate and exchange relevant information with the parent and child.

The core is therapy for the parent to improve their parenting behaviour, resulting in better support for the child.

In clinical practice, EMDR therapy is regularly offered to parents who exhibit harmful or inadequate parenting behaviours. The hypothesis is that their behaviours are provoked by their maladaptively stored memories of past events with the child or traumatic events from their childhood. Typically, this will involve short-term EMDR therapy (1–6 sessions), after which the treatment refocuses on the child. Obviously, the goals for the parents' therapy are consistent with the case conceptualization and with the parents' wishes.

6.4 Therapy for the Family

The therapist may prefer to have other family members observe the child's information processing besides the parents, if it is presumed that they can play a functional role (see Chapters 21 and 22 in this book). Often, family members have no idea what the child has experienced; they are mainly confronted with the resulting behavioural problems at home. Listening to the child's experiences and seeing the child process their experiences increases the likelihood of understanding and support within the family system. A family discussion can also promote understanding and support, but it is questionable whether its effects will be as profound. The aim of attending the EMDR process and of a family discussion is to promote family communication by expressing emotions and restoring structure and authority, which creates conditions for processing the event(s). However, if memories of the event(s) have led to dysfunctional interactions between family members, the involvement of family members is justified for another reason: improvement of family relationships. Strengthened family relationships improve the context for the child's recovery by creating better conditions for trauma processing.

When the traumatization is a consequence of chronic violence, abuse, or neglect within or outside the family, a combination of EMDR and systemic approaches is usually desirable. The objective, in addition to processing what has been experienced from each person's perspective, is to restore trust between family members and to improve the quality of living together (Fictorie et al., 2022; Lindstrom Johnson et al., 2019; Telman et al., 2016). Chapters 19–24 in this book describe different options for EMDR therapy in the context of families.

The priority of EMDR therapy for children is always individual trauma processing to enable the reduction of trauma symptoms and restart potentially stagnated development. This can be done in several ways if the therapist wants to involve the family because of problematic family relationships: family members are present as witnesses of the process of the child, or they share their experiences of a traumatizing event, or the therapist first works with the child separately and then consolidates the gains made by sharing the effects of this process with family members afterward.

Based on the case conceptualization, the therapist must make choices regarding parental and family involvement. The questions for family members in the diagnostic phase listed in Table 6.1 yield relevant information for the case conceptualization.

To summarize, the therapist can consider three options:

1. Therapy for the child, with parents supporting the child in one or more of the previously mentioned roles.
2. Therapy for the child and the parent(s), in which the parent(s) not only support the child but also undergo EMDR to support the child better. This involves processing parents' memories that hinder adequate parenting. If necessary, parenting competencies can also be enhanced with the help of interventions from other therapeutic models, such as trauma-focused cognitive behavioural therapy (Cohen et al., 2017) or non-violent resistance (Omer, 2021).
3. Therapy for the child involving the whole family. Witnessing each other's trauma processing is seen as essential for recovery (Morris & Silvestre, Chapter 22, this book).

6.5 Concluding Remarks

This chapter outlines considerations for making decisions about involving parents and other family members in EMDR therapy for children, and their potential roles in supporting the child, as well as the recovery process. Parents can contribute to the success of their child's treatment in many ways. Unfortunately, empirical grounds are as yet unavailable to guide us in deciding whom to involve and when. However, therapists can inform family members about the purpose of their potential involvement in the child's therapy and how they can contribute, either through active participation in the treatment or otherwise. The role of parents and other family members in EMDR is not protocolized. This chapter provides tools for constructing a treatment plan, in which the roles of parents and other family members are made explicit, as well as the desired goals to be pursued. Based on available knowledge, there are several roads leading to Rome, and more travel destinations are possible apart from Rome. There are no right or wrong choices, only more or less efficient ones.

Adjustments in EMDR Therapy and Standard Protocol for Children and Adolescents (4–18 years)

7

RENÉE BEER AND CARLIJN DE ROOS

7.1 Introduction

It is widely recognized that the severity of responses to trauma can vary and manifest in different ways depending on the developmental stage of the child. Expertise in developmental psychology is essential for both the diagnosis and the therapy. Therapists must conduct adequate diagnostic assessments to detect whether problems are related to memories of specific experiences, accurately interpret reactions during therapy, and apply the protocol appropriately. This chapter describes the necessary adjustments in the EMDR standard protocol to make it applicable to children and adolescents. Preferably, EMDR therapy is provided to children by psychologists, psychiatrists, or pedagogues who have knowledge and understanding of the following:

- Developmental psychological context to understand their reactions.
- Legal and systemic contexts to frame the problems identified.
- Neurobiological and cognitive development to understand the relevance of required adjustments in the standard protocol.
- Adjustments in the EMDR standard protocol tailored to the child, necessary to adequately apply EMDR to children in different developmental stages.
- Ways to involve parents optimally in supporting their child's therapy.

The chapter describes which areas of knowledge are relevant for the therapist (Section 7.2), why adjustments are necessary (Section 7.3), what adjustments are recommended in each phase of the standard protocol (Section 7.4), and how parents can practically be involved (Section 7.5).

7.2 Areas of Knowledge

The therapist needs expertise in three areas of knowledge to adequately provide EMDR therapy to a child or adolescent.

Renée Beer and Carlijn de Roos, *Adjustments in EMDR Therapy and Standard Protocol for Children and Adolescents (4–18 years).*
In: *Handbook of EMDR for Children and Adolescents.* Edited by: Renée Beer and Carlijn de Roos, Oxford University Press.
 DOI: 10.1093/oso/9780198918400.003.0007

7.2.1 Developmental Psychological Context

Reactions to traumatic events are age-specific (see Chapter 2) and can result in PTSD or other disorders. PTSD is not classified in many cases (not even partially), nor as a comorbid disorder next to one or more other mental health conditions or disorders (DSM-5). Nevertheless, EMDR can be indicated if symptoms seem to be related to inadequately processed memories. For this reason, developmental psychological knowledge is crucial for establishing accurate indications and adequately providing EMDR treatment tailored to the child's developmental stage.

7.2.2 Legal Context

Every C&A therapist should be aware of the relevant professional code and reporting requirements in their country. Knowledge of these is essential when confronted with (suspected) child abuse and contested divorces. Each country has its own codes, and the therapist should know how to respond if the safety of the child is at risk within the family setting, like with domestic violence. If the child is at risk of still being in a potentially ongoing dangerous situation, the therapist should endeavour to make the situation safer for the child. This endeavour might entail organizing a child protection order or an out-of-home placement before commencing therapy.

7.2.3 Systemic Context

Chapter 6 discusses the criteria for determining who should attend the sessions: only the child, only the parents, child and parents together, or the whole family. Additionally, it explains the roles parents can play in the therapy to support the child's process. In all cases, the therapist should be aware that a traumatized child always lives in a system—biological, foster, adoption family, residential care—and that significant others from the system that the child is living in must be involved in the therapy in the most efficient way.

In addition to these three areas of knowledge, the therapist should understand the rationale for protocol adjustments.

7.3 Rationale for Adjustments in the Protocol

Knowledge about neurobiological and cognitive development facilitates a better understanding of how children react at different developmental stages and why specific protocol adjustments are needed to enhance the effectiveness of EMDR therapy.

7.3.1 Neurobiological Development

Early stress and adverse experiences can have significant consequences for brain development on multiple levels, as Teicher and colleagues (2003) explained. Several structural and functional neurobiological implications have been identified, including reduced corpus callosum size; attenuated development of the left neocortex, hippocampus, and amygdala; enhanced electrical irritability in limbic structures; and reduced functional activity of the cerebellar vermis. These neurobiological implications may increase the risk of emerging psychiatric illness and behavioural dysfunction (Teicher et al., 2003). Additionally, alterations occur on the neuro-endocrinological level in the hypothalamic-pituitary-adrenal (HPA) axis. Although these early alterations in the stress response systems (i.e., altered cortisol secretion) are adaptive and might be beneficial for survival in the short term, they can become unnecessary and even maladaptive in a more benign environment later in development (Teicher et al., 2016). More specifically, they might hinder trauma-focused psychotherapy success (Zantvoord et al., 2019).

Repeated experiences of anxiety and fear may eventually become states of mind that are ingrained in the brain (Siegel, 2020). Several EMDR therapists and researchers have reflected on how brain development and emotion (dys)regulation may affect EMDR therapy (Gonzáles et al., 2017). According to the Adaptive Information Processing (AIP) model, memory networks, which result from interactions between the child and their environment, act as a lens through which the child views and organizes the reality around them (Gomez, 2013). Readers are referred to the work of Panksepp (2010), Porges (2022), Perry (2006), Siegel (2020), Schore (2001), and Teicher and colleagues (2003), among others, for a deeper understanding of how brain development impacts children's functioning. It is outside the scope of this chapter to delve into these theories in the level of detail required to do them justice. However, we review a few key points from the work of Panksepp (2010) because these findings are referred to in later chapters of this book.

Panksepp (2010) introduced the concept of affective neuroscience. Affective neuroscience is concerned with what happens in the brain at the neural level during the experience of emotions. This field of research aims to expand our knowledge about the mechanisms involved in the aetiology, maintenance, and therapy of depression, anxiety, and related emotional disorders. Affective neuroscience suggests that our perceptions of the present, our reactions to present reality, and our expectations for the future are influenced by how our past experiences have shaped our biological systems. Panksepp proposed that every mammal (including humans) has seven innate 'primary-process emotional systems', which are hardwired into the brain at a subcortical level and responsible for generating feelings and behaviours. Each system is associated with specific neural circuits and neurotransmitters in the brain and activated by specific stimuli or situations. Three of the neural systems described by Panksepp (2010) may have particular importance for the therapy of traumatized children, namely:

- Play
- Seeking
- Care

Play

Definition: Play is a system that generates playful interactions with others. Playing and having fun together strengthens joy and social bonds.

Playfulness is inhibited by negative emotions such as loneliness, anger, and anxiety, yet it acts as an antidote to these emotions. According to Panksepp, negative emotions and states of mind, like anxiety and depression, can be reduced by stimulating playfulness.

Seeking

Definition: Activation of this system leads to enthusiastic exploration and curiosity, accompanied by positive emotions such as happiness and optimistic anticipation.

Children who are being neglected, abandoned, or mistreated will eventually search for resources, and their feelings of helplessness and other negative emotions will become intensified if they do not find them. Seeking behaviour will stop, and negative emotions and moods will take over. Children who have reached this state benefit from therapeutic interventions that reactivate search behaviour, allowing them to regain access to positive experiences.

Care

Definition: The care system is one of the neural systems in the brain that generates or stimulates parental behaviour, such as attention to and nurturing of their child.

Chapter 20 discusses how therapists can mobilize these three biological systems in clinical practice as integral parts of EMDR therapy. The authors elaborate on how activating these three systems can promote attachment between parent and child. The authors also build on the work of Porges and Dana (2018), particularly the concept of 'social engagement': the parent and child establish a social bond (attachment) when they mutually experience security on a neural level.

7.3.2 Cognitive Development

Cognitive development includes not only thinking but also perception and imagination. Knowledge of this development leads to a better understanding of a child's symptoms and conceiving these as clues for the required protocol adjustments. In addition, this knowledge helps to see which cognitive skills a child may still need to learn, having failed to do so previously because of traumatization during that stage of their development.

Piaget (1970) was the first to describe children's cognitive development. Although his theory was criticized, the developmental stages and terms he defined remain influential (Barrouillet, 2015). He distinguished four stages in cognitive development:

- The sensorimotor stage (0–2 years): The child acts in response to sensory impressions, at first as a reflex, and then, at six months, starts to understand that an action can produce an effect.
- The preoperational stage (2–7 years, toddlers, and pre-schoolers): Initially, there is no 'object constancy'; a person/object[1] exists as long as it is visible. As soon as the child can

[1] Throughout this chapter, slash (/) means "or".

think symbolically, that is, they form a mental image of someone/something without seeing it, they can start to act by thinking instead of just reacting automatically to sensory impressions. Thinking is still limited to concrete experiences. Toddlers are still completely self-centred, while pre-schoolers begin to focus more on others. Toddlers develop an imagination and think in an animistic manner. They can use objects symbolically (e.g., a doll is a child, a stick is a car). A lot of energy goes into language acquisition as toddlers learn to think about concepts (i.e., they learn to imagine objects and events). Around the seventh year, the recognition of 'form constancy' develops (the amount of a substance does not change when its form changes), as does 'reversibility' (a house can be built from LEGO bricks, but so can a car after first taking the bricks for the house apart). There is no perception yet of how a sequence of events can lead to something. Only separate events are recognized.

- The concrete-operational stage (7–11 years, primary school age): the child learns to use 'concepts' and starts to see connections between different events: cause-and-effect relationships and processes are now perceived. Representations are still concrete: the child cannot yet deal with problems that are not visible. Thinking becomes less egocentric: putting oneself in the perspective of another becomes possible.
- The formal-operational stage (12–15 years, high school age): with the development of symbolic thinking, use of concepts, object constancy, and reversibility, the child can begin to form and juxtapose ideas independently. They can also handle abstract ideas, form hypotheses, and reason deductively. The child can think through and test different solutions to a problem.

According to Piaget (1970), children acquire new knowledge through exploration and (active) interaction with the environment. The child constantly adds new knowledge and builds on existing knowledge. Piaget believed that children actively process their experiences in line with their cognitive development, meaning how they structure and organize their thinking, and that their thinking changes as they mature. Piaget theorized that the order in which a child goes through thinking modes (mindsets) is genetically determined and fixed in the brain, and that each way of thinking follows its own logic. The mindset determines how the child deals with reality (i.e., how they think and act). The child constantly attunes incoming information to their way of thinking in an unconscious process. Piaget called this process of alignment 'adaptation', consisting of two mechanisms: assimilation and accommodation.

1. *Assimilation*: Adapting incoming information to the way of thinking and viewing information through the (limited) lens of the child's current way of thinking, as developed at that moment. If assimilation is successful, incoming information and thinking are in balance. According to Piaget's theory, information that cannot be assimilated because it no longer fits the child's way of thinking causes a 'cognitive conflict'. The child has then progressed a step ahead in development and is ready to adjust the structure of their thinking.
2. *Accommodation*: The child adjusts their thinking so that they regain a grip on reality and understand the world again.

Thus, according to Piaget, a child's brain develops by advancing through increasingly sophisticated, higher-level structures or ways of thinking.

Research has shown that children cannot learn everything at every age; however, subsequent studies have demonstrated that cognitive development can be influenced by focused attention and training (Verhulst, 2008). There are significant variations between children, influenced by their intelligence, motivation, and degree of training. There is general agreement that the development of perception follows a trajectory from understanding individual events to discovering cause-and-effect relationships of particular events; from egocentricity to the development of the ability to see another person's perspective; from external control by commandments and prohibitions that come from educators to internal control reflecting one's norms and values; from one-dimensional to multidimensional, nuanced feelings and judgements; and from concrete objects to abstract concepts (Nauta et al., 2011). To our knowledge, there are no precise empirically based indications for the age at which specific cognitive abilities are typically developed.

The above clarifies why *assessment* should be tailored to each child's developmental stage. Table 7.1 lists the skills that become available at each developmental stage and which elements can, therefore, be included in the assessment phase of the EMDR protocol for children and adolescents. Definition of developmental stage by age groups differs by country. Therefore, the ages mentioned in this book are indications.

Table 7.1 Milestones in cognitive development and standard protocol in children and adolescents 4–18 years

Development stage	Cognitive abilities	Assessment elements
Pre-schoolers 4–5	- can create inner images of an event - can link words to inner images - magical thinking - difficulty paying attention to more than one task at a time - troubleshooting by juxtaposing different options in mind not yet possible	- Picture + emotion + SUD + body location.
Primary school age 6–12	- can see cause and effect instead of magical thinking - can juxtapose different options - can see things from another person's perspective	- Picture + NC/PC/VOC + emotion + SUD + body location. - Between 6–8 years: NC + PC often (not always) possible.
Adolescents 13–18	- abstract thinking - testing of hypotheses and options - weighing factors - internal locus of control: awareness that individuals themselves can contribute to, prevent, and solve problems - challenge dysfunctional cognitions	- Picture + NC/PC/VOC + emotion + SUD + body location.

NC = negative cognition; PC = positive cognition; VOC = validity of cognition; SUD = subjective unity of disturbance.

7.4 **Protocol Adjustments**

The standard protocol for children and adolescents (C&A) aged 4–18 encompasses the regular phases, listed in Box 7.1.

BOX 7.1 **Eight phases of the EMDR standard protocol**

1. History taking, case conceptualization, and treatment planning
2. Preparation
3. Assessment
4. Desensitization
5. Installation
6. Body scan
7. Closure
8. Re-evaluation

EMDR therapy for children and adolescents is - as for adults - comprised of these phases of the standard protocol and a three-pronged approach to identify and reprocess (Laliotis et al., 2021; Shapiro, 2018):

a) Memories of relevant experiences from the past,

b) Present-day situations that elicit disturbance and maladaptive responses,

c) Anticipatory future scenarios that require adaptive responses.

For this reason, the standard protocol for C&A also includes the subsequent treatment phases, focusing on the present (b) and the future (c) after addressing relevant memories. Appendices 1 and 2 describe all steps and formulations for (b) and (c), making them easily accessible to the therapist. See https://www.emdrchildandyouth.info.

This section addresses recommendations for all phases of the standard protocol in a three-pronged approach relevant to children aged 4–18, beginning with an overview of general adjustments. See Box 7.2 below

BOX 7.2 **General adjustments throughout the eight phases**

Duration of sessions

Sessions with children are usually shorter than those with adolescents and adults because of their shorter attention span. Duration varies for different age groups.

4–5 years: 30 minutes for EMDR + 5 for introduction + 10 for after talk/play.
6–12 years: 45–60 minutes, the regular time for a session.

BOX 7.2 continued

13–18 years: 45–90 minutes, double sessions (90 minutes) in specific situations, but not standard.

Adolescents in intensive treatment and in research projects, 90-minute sessions.

Parent presence during sessions

Depending on the child's developmental stage and their wishes, one or both parents may be present during the sessions for support (for children 6–12 years). When working with the standard protocol in their presence, placing the parents outside of the child's field of vision may help the child stay concentrated on internal experiences and on the BLS/WMT. The presence of the parents, even if the child does not see them, increases the child's sense of safety, and their position prevents the child from signalling to the parent(s) to answer the therapist's questions.

In all cases, the therapist gives clear instructions to the parents regarding when they can or cannot speak.

Directive attitude

The therapist adopts a more directive approach with children and adolescents than with adults and assists more actively in the assessment phase, without taking over the initiative. By asking concrete, open-ended questions, the therapist continues to stimulate the child's concentration on the memory.

Visual support

The younger the child, the more visual support is needed for several steps of the protocol. This certainly applies to children aged eight years and younger. The EMDR standard protocol for children and adolescents (4–18 years) explicitly states which steps can be supported visually. The therapist can also support their verbal instruction with facial expressions and body language: for example, asking the child to rate their level of distress as a 10 (frown) or a 0 (neutral). See Chapter 15 for detailed information on support with visual aids, facial expressions, and body language.

7.4.1 Phase 1: History Taking, Case Conceptualization, and Treatment Planning

- ***Information sources***

Therapists must interrogate more sources of information when preparing for child therapy than for adult therapy. In addition to interviewing the child, the therapist always speaks with the parents and, in some instances—with the consent of the child and parents—also with a teacher or a mentor from school, and sometimes the referrer or the child's GP: in short, relevant others. The guideline for the treatment of PTSD from the National Institute of Clinical Excellence (NICE, 2018b) recommends that parents and their children be questioned in the diagnostic phase. We additionally recommend speaking with parents and children both jointly and separately if the child can accurately describe their symptoms. Speaking to parents separately is valuable because they may be concerned about symptoms that the child does not mention. Also, parents may be relieved to be allowed to speak freely about their worries and fears without the child being present. Parents are more reliable informants about the child's behaviour than the child because parents are better at noticing behaviour that the child might not be aware of.

Furthermore, a separate conversation allows parents to express their own reactions to the event(s). Based on the information provided by the parents, the therapist can assess if they also need (trauma) therapy. Speaking to the child separately is recommended when the child may want to hide specific details or negative emotions from the parents, either to spare them or to avoid certain emotions themselves (e.g., shame about sexual abuse). Young children may not yet be able to indicate how their behaviour changed in response to their traumatic experience(s), because of their limited level of cognitive development and limited reflectivity.

Additionally, it is beneficial to see the parents and child together, allowing the therapist to observe interaction patterns.

- ***Validated instruments***

It is recommended to use validated instruments whenever possible, in addition to intake interviews with parents and children, to map out the problems. This gives the therapist a more accurate picture of the symptomatology, allowing for an objective measurement and evaluation of the therapy results. For an overview of validated and reliable instruments, see: https://www.nctsn.org/treatments-and-practices/screening-and-assessment; https://www.nice.org.uk/guidance/ng116.

- ***Current child safety***

Besides defining the problems to be addressed, the therapist must assess the child's current level of safety and determine if additional interventions are necessary to improve it. This may be in addition to or prior to EMDR.

7.4.2 **Phase 2: Preparation**

During the preparation phase, the therapist ensures that the child and the parents get a clear understanding of what to expect, and what is expected of them, during EMDR therapy. This increases the likelihood that they will be receptive to treatment. The therapist provides psychoeducation about the child's post-traumatic stress reactions, the EMDR procedure, and what they can expect from trauma processing. A metaphor, like the 'chest of drawers', is helpful for explaining trauma processing (see Table 7.2). From https://www.emdrchildandyouth.info a visual overview can be downloaded showing 'EMDR step by step'.

For children under 12, the therapist can support the explanation of the EMDR procedure visually with pictograms (see also Table 13.2 and Figure 14.3) and introduce EMDR as an exercise or a game. Children are used to participating in exercises or games and typically adopt a cooperative attitude when EMDR is presented in this way. The therapist can also offer information leaflets to support their explanations of the procedure. See https://www.emdrchildandyouth.info for leaflets in several languages for children (up to 12 years), adolescents (up to 18 years), and parents. Several animations have been developed that may be helpful; see www.globalchildemdralliance.com.

Table 7.2 The 'chest of drawers' metaphor

	Think of your memory as a chest of drawers in your head. Each drawer holds a memory - what you saw, felt, and thought then, and what it makes you feel and think now. Good memories are neatly stored, so these drawers open and close easily. Some drawers with painful or scary memories are messy. These drawers are stuck open, and you keep bumping into them. Each time that happens, it hurts again. EMDR therapy helps tidy up these messy drawers, so they can close. The memory is still there, but now you can choose when to open and close the drawer.

- ***BLS/WMT***

The therapist introduces the child to the types of BLS/WMT that seem appropriate. The preferred type for this therapy component is eye movements because research in adults has shown that this provides the most distraction, reducing the vividness and emotionality of the memory most rapidly (Jeffries & Davis, 2013; Lee & Cuijpers, 2013; Van den Hout et al., 2011). It is recommended that a second type of BLS/WMT also be introduced to the child. This is to make it easier to eventually switch the type of BLS/WMT during desensitization if the therapist prefers to do so for any reason—for example, if the child needs more stimulation or stops making eye movements because their eyes start hurting or they get dizzy.

If eye movements are possible, the therapist offers them playfully to attract and hold their attention; for example, the therapist might draw a face on their finger for the child to follow with their eyes. Finger puppets or other objects the child finds attractive or exciting can also be utilized. The light bar is a good alternative for stimulating eye movements. Many children are thrilled by lights that change colour while moving back and forth. However, children with motor, vision, or concentration problems may have trouble performing eye movements. An alternative is tactile stimulation, such as drumming or tapping. The therapist drums their hands or taps alternatively left and right on the child's hands, or vice versa (i.e., the child taps), or introduces the butterfly hug (https://www.youtube.com/watch?v=zEDr-JJGn2Q) or buzzers. Auditory stimulation with clicks through headphones is an additional option. However, research has shown that auditory stimuli through headphones offer limited distraction. Therefore, this option is used only in exceptional cases (i.e., when working memory capacity seems limited or if a child is visually impaired). Another alternative is sensorimotor stimulation, such as making movements, like the V-step, or sitting on a bouncing ball. Different stimulations can be combined if a child needs more distraction to stay in the process (without being overwhelmed).

Eye movements are often too complicated for children under six. Therefore, therapists may choose tactile forms of BLS/WMT for this age group, such as 'tapping' or 'drumming'. Young children often take great pleasure in this task and see it as a game, which keeps them engaged longer.

Furthermore, various apps have been developed in recent years offering digital stimuli for eye movements.[2] These apps became more popular due to global restrictions on proximity during the Covid-19 pandemic. For children living in war zones who need EMDR therapy but cannot visit a therapist in person, these apps offer an essential solution. Most children have mobile devices, so with access to digital technology, they can receive EMDR therapy despite being physically separated from the therapist.

- ***Safe/Calm place***

If the child shows signs indicating that additional support is needed to feel safe or calm enough in the therapy room to be receptive to trauma reprocessing, the therapist may ask the child to imagine or draw a picture of a safe, calm, happy, or positive place (in war-affected countries it would not be appropriate to ask a child to come up with a safe place). The image of this place, along with the associated emotions and body sensations, is identified and then strengthened with EM⁺ for self-soothing (Adler-Tapia & Settle, 2025). The therapist can give the drawing to the child to practice with at home. The therapist can suggest that the child look at or think about the drawing several times a day (preferably at set times) and focus on the positive feelings the drawing evokes. In doing so, the therapist teaches the child that they can make themselves feel more at ease by focusing on something positive. This is a technique that the child can use at home whenever they feel unhappy. One option is always to include a safe place, as mentioned in the standard protocol; another option is to include it only when there are signs that additional support is needed.

- ***Stop signal***

Typically, during the preparation phase the therapist informs the child that they can give a 'stop' signal to take a break whenever they feel overwhelmed by their emotions, which have become too intense, too high, too big, or too unmanageable (Gomez, 2013). The stop signal is considered, just like the safe place, as a tool for helping the child move into memory reprocessing while feeling 'resourced and ready' (Adler-Tapia & Settle, 2025). If children are highly anxious about EMDR, it is valuable to increase their sense of self-control. However, these tools are not needed in all cases. By offering them, the therapist may give the implicit message that something is about to happen that might be too difficult for the child to tolerate. Instead of (or alongside) this tool, it could be more supporting and more empowering to explain the benefits of continuing the process using the metaphor of the tunnel when explaining the EMDR procedure:

> Leaving a train [or bus, or car—whatever the child is familiar with] in the middle of a tunnel is not reassuring or helpful. Instead, it may be terrifying. The best thing to do is to keep going as fast as possible because, at the end of every dark tunnel, there is always light … Besides, it is good to keep in mind that the worst thing about the experience was the experience, which was in the past and which you have survived. Memories are just remnants of our experience in the mind, and therapy will change these.

[2] Such as for example: www.remotemdr.com; www.moovd.nl; www.cloudemdr.com.

The therapist has several options to consider when introducing the tunnel metaphor in the preparation phase (regarding the inclusion of a stop signal and a safe place): If the child reacts neutrally, cooperatively, and curiously, continue with the activation and reprocessing of the memory during the subsequent phases of the EMDR protocol. When the tunnel metaphor and other psychoeducation prove insufficiently motivating, and the child is anxious and reluctant to cooperate, then teach a stop sign, a safe place, or both may be taught, or a use flashforward could be used to target anticipation anxiety for the EMDR treatment (disaster image).

- ***Cooperation of parents***

The therapist encourages the parents to cooperate by supporting their child. They are informed about *what* their child's therapy will entail, *why* therapy is done like it is done, and *how* they can support their child during treatment. Leaflets for parents are available in several languages at https://www.emdrchildandyouth.info.

A more extended preparation is needed for parents whose child has problems resulting from preverbal trauma. In these cases, EMDR therapy will be conducted with the storytelling method, where the traumatic memories of the child are activated with the help of a narrative from the parents. Then, the cooperation with the parents is more intense than when using the standard protocol. Chapter 8 describes the storytelling method in detail.

7.4.3 **Phase 3: Assessment**

The assessment phase aims to retrieve a specific memory from long-term memory and activate all components—visual, cognitive, emotional, and physical—while increasing arousal. To facilitate this process, the therapist provides more visual support than is typically done with adults, because children, depending on their developmental stage, are less adept at forming mental representations and communicating about their memories. Visual support is added when verbal instruction fails to elicit the desired memory activation or when feedback during assessment is insufficient to check if the memory is activated. Visual support creates a check for the therapist to ensure the child is concentrating on the memory and enhances the child's concentration.

Essential adjustments for children are made in the assessment phase. These adjustments concern the number of components of the memory that can be involved in the procedure (visual representation, cognitions, emotions, bodily sensations) and the wording of the questions. The younger the child, the more condensed the protocol is. Sometimes, parents must provide information to help the child describe the target memory.

- ***Activation of the memory***

Based on the case conceptualization, the therapist decides in each session, in agreement with the child and/or eventually the parents, which memory to address. The therapist asks the child to describe the memory like a movie in their mind: '*Please tell me briefly what happened, like a movie. What's important is how you remember it now, not exactly what happened then.*'

Figure 7.1 Film in head.

A memory is defined as what happened on that day. This one-day limitation is based on the notion that sleep affects memory consolidation and that memories are transferred from the hippocampus to the neocortex during sleep. This transfer is crucial for memory stability and retrieval over time (Wei et al., 2016). Sleep plays a vital role in memory processing, whereby recent experiences are replayed and gradually shifted from short-term storage in the hippocampus to long-term storage in the neocortex. For this reason, it seems reasonable to assume that what happened the next day is consolidated as another memory that could also need attention, but not necessarily so.

In specific cases where the memory cannot be accessed and activated sufficiently because the child is avoiding the confrontation with the memory, the therapist can ask the child or parents to bring an object to the session that represents the event and will activate the memory, such as a photo of the accident, a photo of the child in the hospital, or pictures of medical paraphernalia. If no pictures are available, the parent could use the internet or magazines to find images of a similar situation or another child of the same age in a similar situation. The therapist can also use perceptual cues (like sounds or smells) or body posture related to the event to trigger the memory. The memory must be accessed and activated before it can be changed.

- ***Picture/Image***

Generally, children develop the ability to form mental representations of memories and events between the ages of two and four. From about six years of age, they can communicate about it. From four years on, the therapist can use the question from the EMDR standard protocol for children and adolescents: '*What is the worst picture in your head of this …* [mention the concrete event, e.g., the car accident]?'

Figure 7.2 Pause the film: Worst picture.

The therapist lacks external tools to assess whether the child is concentrating on the traumatic memory, and if information processing is ongoing, if the child cannot create a mental image of the memory, or cannot sufficiently communicate about it. One option is to have the child draw a picture of the mental image, with help from parents or the therapist, as needed. An alternative is to help the child visualize the image by creating a representation of the event on a table using Playmobil or LEGO-type toys if the child is unable to draw because of a motor disability or because of resistance. By looking at this representation, the child can distinguish more clearly between the here-and-now and the past (distancing) during subsequent questions in the assessment phase.

- ***Cognitions***

Some children can recognize (negative and positive) cognitions by age six, while others develop this ability around age eight. The therapist has a directive attitude. If open-ended questions (like '*What makes this picture so disturbing for you now*'; '*What bad words (about yourself) go with the picture*'; '*What is your worst belief/thought with the picture*?') do not elicit a response, then the therapist can help the child by eventually limiting the options for cognitions.

For example, the therapist can elicit a negative cognition from the child by saying, '*Look at the picture and say to yourself: I am …* [NC1] … *Keep looking and say to yourself: I am … [NC2]. Which one disturbs you the most/is the most distressing/gives the worst/most yucky feelings now?*' The same directiveness can be applied to elicit a positive cognition by saying, '*Look at the picture; would you like to believe "I am normal"* … or rather "*I am strong*"?'

Figure 7.3 Positive cognition.

The therapist stops asking if the child cannot handle these questions. Continuing to ask questions could make the child feel 'stupid' or that they were doing something wrong. Instead, the therapist can suggest a positive cognition later in the installation phase.

- ***Emotion***

Children usually can identify basic feelings, such as sadness, anxiety, and anger. If a child is unable to do this, the therapist should accept more vague or general words that the child may come up with, such as 'rotten' or 'a bad feeling'. The therapist asks: '*Look at the picture/think of the image* (whatever is used) *and the words* … (NC), *what do you feel*?'

Figure 7.4 Feelings.

- ***Measuring VOC and SUD***

Visual support may be needed for measurements, such as indicating the validity of cognition (VOC), and the current subjective unity of disturbance (SUD) evoked by the image in the mind or drawing. Visual support is usually needed for children aged between four and eight years, and sometimes beyond this age range.

There are many ways to do this. The therapist must find a way to communicate with the child about the intensity of their level of distress (SUD).

Figure 7.5 SUD.

For example, the therapist can draw a line marked 0 through 10 and ask the child to draw a cross on the line indicating the level of distress that an image evokes or, likewise, the validity of a positive cognition related to an image on a scale of 1 to 7. Therapists can also use the SUD/VOC scales developed by Silverkit (www.silverkit.nl) and Ana Gomez (https://www.anagomez.org/product/emdr-suds-voc-collection/). For children under six, another simple way to measure the level of distress is to have the child indicate with their hands how much distress or 'yucky feeling' or 'unpleasantness' it causes if they look at a drawing of the memory or think of it. Hands placed wide apart means 'very unpleasant' and hands together means 'not unpleasant at all'. Case Study 7.1 illustrates the assessment phase.

CASE STUDY 7.1 **Ahmed: Assessment**

Seven-year-old Ahmed narrowly escaped a fire in his parents' house six months ago. His parents went out one evening, leaving him with his elder brother and a babysitter. While playing around, they knocked a candle to the floor. The carpets soon caught fire and in no time the fire had spread to the curtains. The babysitter took the boys outside and called the fire department, which arrived quickly; as a result, the fire damage was not too bad. Since then, Ahmed has been having nightmares. His parents cannot leave him alone at night and he is very anxious and irritable. The picture from his memory that is now most distressing, is seeing the candle on the ground just before the fire spreads and all three of them are nailed to the ground. He drew a picture of it at the therapist's request (below figure).

Ahmed: *I don't want to see this.* [Puts hand in front of his eyes and turns his head away.]

Therapist: Very well drawn, Ahmed.

Ahmed: *Don't know.* [Cries] *It's so scary ...*

Therapist: *Look at the drawing. What makes you feel bad the most right now? Does the drawing make you think 'I can't stand looking at it' ... or does the drawing make you think something bad about yourself, like for example 'I am stupid'?*

Ahmed: *I don't want this. I want to leave... I want to go home ...*

Therapist: *Are you saying that, when you look at the drawing now, you think mostly 'I can't stand to look at it'?*

Ahmed: [Nods]

Therapist: *You are doing very well, Ahmed. Soon after the EMDR, you will feel better, which is why we are moving on quickly. As you look at the drawing and you say I can't stand it, what feeling do you have now: scared, angry, or sad?*

Ahmed: *Scared and sad.*

Therapist: *Look at the drawing and say to yourself 'I can't stand looking at it'. How unpleasant is it now looking at the drawing, from zero to ten. Zero means not annoying at all and ten as annoying as it can be.*

Ahmed: *Ten.*

Therapist: *Where in your body do you feel that nasty feeling most strongly?*

Ahmed: *In my stomach and my eyes.*

7.4.4 Phase 4: Desensitization

- ***Visual support***

The therapist must ensure that drawings or arrangements of toys (if these were used during the assessment) do not remain visible during desensitization when free associations are requested. The therapist turns the drawing face down and, in principle, does not show it again when going back to target. The therapist shows the drawing again only if the child cannot mentally represent or communicate about it—typical for children younger than six. This way, the therapist can ensure that the child is not avoiding and is still focusing on the selected memory. If the therapist omits this, it is more difficult to interpret whether the child's memory is still activated and assess whether reprocessing is ongoing.

- ***Duration of sets***

Figure 7.6 Set.

Sets usually last slightly shorter than with adults (30–45 seconds). The younger the child, the shorter the sets: adolescents: 30 secs.; children 6–12 years: 20–30 secs.; children 4–6 years: 15–20 secs. There is no empirical evidence to determine the duration; instead, the therapist observes the child and adapts to what suits the child. It is a matter of attunement.

- ***Deep breath***

The therapist's questions after each set—'*What comes up? … What do you notice?*'—are preceded in the standard protocol by a standard instruction: '*Take a deep breath … let it go*'. This instruction aims to let the child calm down (ground) and reorient in the here-and-now before answering the questions. When used as a standard instruction, children might turn it into a game, 'blowing everything away'. Another outcome might be that it slows down their processing. An alternative option is to give this instruction selectively, only when the therapist notices high arousal during or after the set and is concerned that the child might be outside their window of tolerance. In such cases, this instruction serves an evident purpose.

Figure 7.7 What do you notice?

Table 7.3 Differences between adults and children during desensitization

Adults	Children
Abreactions likely	Abreactions unlikely
Rich associative connections	Few associative connections
Long channels	Short channels
Long sets of eye movements	Short sets of eye movements
Long sessions (60–90 minutes)	Short sessions (5–20 minutes)
Many emotional facial cues	Few emotional facial cues
Abstract language and thinking	Concrete language and thinking
Frequent use of metaphor	Little use of metaphor
Spiritual understandings	Spiritual understandings rare
Awareness of change	Less awareness of change

Source: Tinker and Wilson (1999).

- ***Processing***

The processing looks different in children than in adults. See Table 7.3 for a summary of the differences between adults and children during desensitization (Tinker & Wilson, 1999).

Emotional discharges (*abreactions*) rarely occur in children under age 12. We have no clear explanation for this. The younger the child, the less developed their neural network is. As a result, the associative chains and the flow of associations are usually shorter. The limited facial expression in children means that there will be few cues for therapists to assess whether the information processing is ongoing or complete. As children function cognitively at a lower level, their associations are usually more concrete, for example, after having experienced a car accident, toddlers may be more concerned about a dent in the car than about whether anyone was hurt or killed. Naturally, children with a concrete or associative thinking style will not include metaphors in their association chains.

- ***Back to target***

Typically, the therapist goes back to the target memory when memory reprocessing is not progressing: that is, if no new material emerges, or the child's associations remain repetitive without meaningful changes after several sets. The therapist asks '*Bring up the memory you are working on, as it is stored in your mind* ***now*** *... What do you notice/what comes up/what happens now? ... Go with that.*' This question aims to jump-start reprocessing.

The younger the child, the more precise the questions need to be to promote reprocessing, and help the therapist interpret how reprocessing proceeds. Therefore, several options can adjust the back to target for children, such as asking to bring up the selected (target) image instead of the memory, because this indicates more precisely what is expected—for example, *'Bring up the image, as it is **now**'* or *'Bring up the image of the memory you are working on, as it is stored **now**.'* Both align with what Shapiro (2018, p. 335) suggests about processing in children: 'The therapist should stay attuned to the child's level of tolerance for trauma processing and adjust accordingly.' With this optional adjustment ('Bring up the selected image as it is **now**'), the therapist stays attuned not to the level of tolerance but to the child's level of required coaching for trauma processing. We frequently see in clinical practice that the regular prompt to '*Bring up the memory . . .*' is too ambiguous for children.

Furthermore, in younger children their limited capacity to verbalize associations complicates assessing whether trauma processing is continuing or completed. For this reason, the therapist might want to check the SUD more often than in adults. This provides two benefits: (1) checking the SUD helps the therapist track progress, as processing in children can proceed very rapidly; (2) tracking progress reassures the child that they are progressing, which is encouraging.

To identify the specific point at which to restart the subsequent chain of associations, the therapist may ask which part (or element) of the memory (or target image or drawing) is most disturbing at that moment. This question, along with the child's response (focusing on the most disturbing part), may enhance the efficiency of the process(ing) because the child is coached in identifying what is causing the remaining disturbance. Focusing on that will reduce potential avoidance and speed up processing. Although no empirical evidence favours any of the options mentioned, they all seem helpful and feasible in clinical practice.

7.4.5 **Phase 5: Installation**

Installation is included (only) if cognitions have been established during the assessment phase (i.e., in children older than six). The therapist asks if the established PC still fits or if another one might fit better now. If the child prefers another one, the therapist must check if this new cognition is from the same domain as the NC because the installation process is, in fact, 'continued processing that is hypothesized to strengthen the client's new, more adaptive belief about themselves, making it more available for the future. Installing a positive belief about the self implies a cognitive restructuring' (Laliotis et al., 2021, p. 196). This can only be realized if the PC and NC are in the same domain or dimension: that is, if the old maladaptive belief is replaced by a more adaptive one.

7.4.6 **Phase 6: Body Scan**

The purpose of the body scan is to assess if any bodily disturbance arises when the child thinks of the original memory combined with the positive cognition. Shapiro (2018) states that the purpose is to check 'remaining disturbance'. One could argue that remaining disturbance is impossible when desensitization and installation are done correctly. However, because children often might have said SUD = 0 or VOC = 7 just to get rid of the procedure, the body scan gives them another opportunity to eliminate any remaining disturbance.

If no cognitions are identified during assessment, in children younger than age six, the therapist only checks whether an unpleasant feeling still emerges in the body when the child thinks of the memory or looks at the image/drawing. In children who have difficulty focusing their attention on the body or understanding the instructions to do so, the therapist should ask for information about any discomfort they might feel in the various parts of the body, especially those that were actively involved during the traumatic experience. Therapists can ask questions like '*When you think of the memory, does any unpleasant* (or "yucky" or "bad") *feeling come up anywhere in your body, like your head, chest, or stomach*?'

7.4.7 **Phase 7: Closure**

A positive closure provides an empowering ending to the EMDR session. It is added to the regular closure to ensure that the child always leaves the session with a positive feeling and satisfaction about what they have accomplished ('*What is the most valuable thing you discovered/learned about yourself today?*'). This question usually prompts the therapist or parents (if present) to give helpful suggestions to which the child can respond because children rarely spontaneously come up with an answer to this question or a positive sentence about themselves. Frequent statements include '*I am brave/tough/a hero.*' Incomplete sessions with children who have limited emotion regulation skills can be closed by the therapist asking the child to store away the memory in a storage box or container to be used again during the next session (see also Chapter 10). This allows the child to leave the session calmly. When a memory is processed (SUD = 0, VOC = 7), children under eight often like to visualize that a memory is 'done' by placing a cross through their drawing or its written title.

7.4.8 **Phase 8: Re-Evaluation**

The therapist gathers information about any changes in symptoms or behaviours that may have been noticed or observed between the sessions. Like in the diagnostic phase, it is essential to gather observations from the child and their parent(s). Because children have a limited awareness of change and a limited capacity for reflection and verbalization, the therapist usually gets less feedback from children than from parents about the effect of the EMDR sessions. Ultimately, the parents' observations are mostly the 'proof of the pudding.' Information from both sides is essential. See Case Study 7.2 for an example.

CASE STUDY 7.2 **Martina: Re-evaluation**

A week after an initial EMDR session, 14-year-old Martina says she did not notice any changes in herself during the intervening days. Her mother, on the other hand, reports that Martina reacted strongly during the first few days after therapy. She became angry at the slightest thing and scolded everyone and was irritable. After sleeping well for a few nights, she recovered and acted 'normal' again.

7.4.9 Second and Third Prongs

Re-evaluation occurs at the start of each session to establish what has been achieved. The outcome, combined with the case conceptualization, guides the next step(s). EMDR therapy, characterized by its three-pronged approach, does not end once the relevant etiologic memories have been processed (Laliotis et al., 2021; Shapiro, 2018).

Appendices 1 and 2 of the EMDR standard protocol for children and adolescents aged 4–18 describe how the following prongs can occur in children. They are included as appendices because the therapist should always verify whether these subsequent phases are necessary or beneficial; if so, having the required steps and formulations on hand is practical. However, if no further avoidance behaviours or anxious expectations remain after desensitization of the relevant memories and the child is functioning adequately, no additional targets need to be identified.

- ***Second prong: Flashforwards***

In the second prong, current situations and present triggers that maintain the symptoms (such as, avoidance behaviours or anxious unrealistic expectations) are addressed. Flashforwards are fantasies about terrible things (disasters) that might happen in the future. They are experienced in the present, may perpetuate the avoidance behaviour, and can, therefore, be understood as present triggers (Logie & De Jongh, 2014). Appendix 1 of the standard protocol for children and adolescents 4–18 years describes the steps for addressing flashforwards. The targets are frightening disaster images of anticipated, unrealistic future situations that the child suffers from in the present. For example, a girl aged 14 who was bitten on her leg by a dog remains afraid to walk on the street after having reprocessed all relevant memories related to the dog attack. She fears another attack, where she will be bitten on her face, and all over, by the dog. This worry is perpetuating her avoidance behaviour, and she suffers from intrusive images of this 'next dog attack'.

- ***Third prong: Mental video check/ future template***

Appendix 2 of the standard protocol for children and adolescents 4–18 years describes the steps for preparing the child for the future utilizing the mental video check and future template. These procedures are used after desensitization of the relevant memories and flashforwards, and are indicated when residual avoidance or safety behaviours exist. The goal of a mental video check (MVC) is to desensitize the remaining distress related to the neutral future situation; the goal of the future template (FT) is to instil the positive cognition '*I can handle doing this*' associated with the neutral future image. In this neutral future scenario (MVC) or image (FT), the child shows adequate behaviour.

Mental video check: The child is asked, with their eyes closed, to imagine going through a future neutral (formally anxiety-provoking) situation from beginning to end and check whether any cues are provoking disturbance and, therefore, might prevent the person from confronting the formerly frightening situation. The child is asked to open their eyes when they sense discomfort and then concentrate on the most disturbing cue. Next, one set of eye movements is performed (no associations are asked for). Thereafter, the child continues, in their imagination, to go through this future situation until they experience the next disturbance. Another set follows. This procedure continues until the child has reached the end of the future scenario and is repeated until the child can go through the imagined situation (movie) without opening their eyes or experiencing disturbance.

Future template: The child imagines the future situation with one image, and the positive cognition 'I can handle doing this' is installed. If the therapist thinks it might be helpful, they can invite the child to draw a picture of the desired future situation (a neutral picture with appropriate behaviour).

After these procedures, the child is or should be ready to practice in real-life situations. With homework assignments, the child can now test whether they have indeed overcome the remaining avoidance symptoms or safety behaviours. If symptoms persist, another intervention, such as in vivo exposure, may be indicated.

7.5 Logistics of Parental Meetings

This section addresses practical aspects of involving parents in their child's therapy, including what information needs to be exchanged and how best to organize the contacts with parents.

7.5.1 Information Exchange

The exchange of information between the therapist and parents is essential for monitoring the effects of EMDR. The therapist can only monitor the impact of EMDR between sessions at home based on the parents' observations of their child. This requires the parents to observe and report relevant changes carefully. These observations (besides the child's) help the therapist assess whether processing has been completed. This increases the chances of maximizing symptom reduction, encouraging positive behavioural changes, and achieving better emotional balance.

Parents often notice changes that differ from what their children notice. Both the parents and the child can email their observations to the therapist before the next session. If the child makes negative comments at home about the therapy and expresses a desire to stop, the parent should encourage the child to continue and, at the very least, adhere to the agreed-upon commitments. The parents are instructed by the therapist on both monitoring and motivating, if necessary.

However, the child or therapist may choose not to share information in certain situations. For example, the child may refuse to provide details to their parents about memories that they find shameful, such as those related to rape, or if the child has been traumatized by the behaviour of their parents, like in cases of violence, abuse, or neglect. In such instances, the therapist should check if the child is now safe and if anyone is putting emotional pressure on the child to keep the information confidential(preventing disclosure). A child's request not to inform their parents can put the therapist in a difficult position. Every country has specific rules for therapists, outlining their duties and any relevant prohibitions in such situations. Therapists should adhere to their national regulations. In careful consultation with the child, the therapist should decide what information will be shared with parents, and how it will be shared.

7.5.2 Organization of Parental Contacts

Parental contacts can be organized in various ways. At what point in the session and how often the therapist wants to speak with them depends on several factors: the age and problems of the child; the nature of the traumatization (interpersonal or not); parent–child relational issues that may perpetuate symptoms, such as insufficient emotional or cognitive support from the parents; and, finally, the working style of the therapist. The options per age group are as follows:

- ***Children up to and including 12 years of age***
  - For children aged 4–5, parents typically attend the therapy session (either in full or in part) to provide information and increase their sense of safety and cooperation.
  - For children aged 6–12, parents are (or can be) present in the therapy room at the beginning of the session (maximum 5–10 minutes) for a joint review of the past week, and at the end of the session (maximum 5–10 minutes) to hear from the therapist and child about what happened during the session and what changes might occur during the coming week. However, if one of the goals of trauma therapy is to improve the parent–child interaction, then the parent's presence in the room during the entire session may enhance understanding of what the child has experienced and encourage positive interaction between both.
  - The therapist may organize an extra session with the parents and child if discussing signals of emotional, social, or behavioural changes or changes in physical functioning requires more time and cannot be adequately addressed in each session.

- ***Adolescents aged 13 years and older***
  - Parents can inform the therapist about their observations between sessions in different ways: by being present at the beginning of the session (5–10 minutes), by telephone, or by emailing the therapist. This allows the therapist to reflect on the observed changes in the adolescent.
  - When the adolescent agrees to it, the therapist and the adolescent may inform the parents about details to be shared at the end of each session, or every few weeks. This can be done verbally if the parents are present, by email, or by telephone.
  - If the parents do not come along to the sessions or the adolescent is not living in the family home, and the adolescent agrees to it, the therapist can talk with the parents once every few weeks (with the adolescent present) to discuss identified changes.
  - If adolescents are unwilling to share details about what is being processed during EMDR, parents should be informed beforehand about what to expect from EMDR and what is expected from them. The therapist can explain to the parents that, with the consent of the adolescent, they will be informed about the results of EMDR at the end of treatment or at another agreed-upon moment. Parental understanding and support often increase when the adolescent explains their reasons for entering therapy to their parents. The therapist will encourage the adolescent to share (part of the) information with parents.

- ***All children and adolescents***
  - Therapists may also recommend that parents attend a session (as witnesses) to give them the best opportunity to understand and support their child during and after a session. This may be relevant if current problems in the parent–child interaction perpetuate the child's symptoms.

7.6 Concluding Remarks

This chapter addresses the necessary adjustments in the therapeutic approach to optimize the benefits of EMDR therapy for children and adolescents. It describes the expert knowledge required for therapists in several areas and how this translates into diagnosis, adjustments in the standard EMDR protocol, and therapy application. It also discusses managing parental involvement in their child's EMDR therapy.

EMDR Storytelling

Reprocessing Preverbal Traumatic Memories

8

CARLIJN DE ROOS AND RENÉE BEER

8.1 Introduction

Modifications to the standard protocol are created to make EMDR applicable to young children.[1] Lovett (1999, 2015) and Tinker and Wilson (1999) developed an approach in which a child's memory is activated via a story written by their parent.[2] This procedure, known as the 'storytelling method', has evolved in several countries through various EMDR child and adolescent trainers. The procedure is designed to reprocess preverbal emotionally charged 'memories'[3] of events that occurred when language was unavailable. Initially, it was developed for traumatized children younger than four years and adults with ID having the intellectual functional level of a young child. The EMDR storytelling method is a welcome addition to the limited therapy options for young children and those with ID because the procedure fits well with their associative thinking style and nonverbal way of expression and perception, which are characteristic of this developmental age. This is relevant because preverbal memories are not stored explicitly but implicitly, where the sensorimotor and emotional aspects of the memory predominate.

Positive results with the storytelling method are seen in clinical practice, culminating in awareness that traumatization before age four can lead to psychopathology later in life. Consequently, the use of the storytelling method has also been described as trauma therapy for children aged 4–18 years with preverbal trauma and adults with ID who function in that age range (De Roos & Beer, 2017). In addition, deployment of this method is possible for individuals with communication difficulties, such as deaf children and children with expressive language disorder and/or an inability to express themselves.

This chapter mainly reflects clinical experience. It describes the practical aspects of using the storytelling method as accurately as possible so that it can be implemented, further examined and refined.

[1] 'Child' or 'children' refers also to individuals with ID.

[2] 'Parent' refers to biological or foster parents, or significant other caregivers.

[3] By memory, we mean both explicit and implicit memory in young children, consisting mainly of sensory and emotional information.

Carlijn de Roos and Renée Beer, *EMDR Storytelling*. In: *Handbook of EMDR for Children and Adolescents*.
Edited by: Renée Beer and Carlijn de Roos, Oxford University Press.
DOI: 10.1093/oso/9780198918400.003.0008

8.2 Empirical Status

Scientific research on the effect of the EMDR storytelling method in traumatized babies and toddlers is limited, partly due to the lack of validated measures. However, research results are emerging. In a case study by Hensel (2009), which examined the effect of EMDR on children, only four of the 32 participants included were under four years of age. Results were reported for the entire age group (1.9–18 years). Consequently, no specific conclusions can be drawn for children younger than four. Nonetheless, various successful clinical applications of the storytelling method in children under four have been documented, showing that symptoms often reduced or resolved after treatment and developmental delays were rapidly corrected. (Adler-Tapia & Settle, 2017; Gomez, 2013; Logie et al., 2020; Lovett, 1999, 2015; Morris-Smith & Silvestre, 2014; Rathore, 2018; Swimm, 2018; Tinker & Wilson, 1999). In an exploratory pilot study, treatment data of 18 children aged 0 and 4 years were gathered to assess the effectiveness of a parent–child EMDR protocol (Went et al., 2024). This treatment combines various components: preparation, EMDR with the child and parents, EMDR for the parent (when needed), parent–child interaction sessions, and parental guidance sessions. Therapists scored PTSD symptom clusters based on the DC 0–5 criteria; all children lost their PTSD diagnosis after treatment.

In addition, single-case experimental designs (SCEDs) have also been conducted. Preliminary findings suggest that EMDR may be effective for this young age group. A pilot study on the feasibility and effectiveness of the EMDR storytelling method in infants and toddlers (n = 6, range 3–24 months) with trauma-related symptoms after medical trauma showed that four of six children had significantly reduced trauma-related symptoms after two sessions of EMDR; sessions for preparation and case conceptualization are not counted (Potharst et al., 2025). A replicated SCED study in children aged 4–8 years with PTSD (n = 9; mostly chronically traumatized in the preverbal phase) found that the application of the EMDR storytelling method combined with the standard protocol appeared effective (Olivier et al., 2022). After six sessions of treatment, 85.7% of these children no longer met the PTSD diagnosis. Furthermore, the severity of PTSD symptoms and emotional and behavioural problems decreased significantly. These positive results were maintained until the follow-up measurement three months later. As a follow-up, a replicated SCED study was conducted on 19 children aged 18 months to 8 years (De Roos et al., 2025). Most children had experienced chronic medical trauma besides domestic violence. After six one-hour sessions of EMDR, 79% lost their PTSD diagnosis. The child's PTSD symptoms and emotional and behavioural problems decreased significantly, as did parental stress. The reduction in PTSD symptoms was significant (very large effect) both for the group of 18-month to 4-year-olds (n = 10; story method only) and for the group of 4+ to 8-year-olds (n = 9; combination storytelling method and standard protocol). All children completed therapy (0% dropouts) without adverse effects. The percentage loss of PTSD diagnoses and other outcomes were maintained at follow-up three months after treatment. These results are promising because symptom reduction for this severely traumatized group was achieved after a brief EMDR treatment.

Study results in children and adults with ID were also positive (Mevissen et al., 2011, 2012; Hoogstad et al., 2024; also see Chapter 3). Randomized controlled studies are needed to enhance our knowledge about the effectiveness of the EMDR storytelling method.

8.3 Indication and Goals

The EMDR storytelling method is indicated if the therapist and the parents hypothesize that there is a link between the current symptoms and the memories of direct or indirect exposure to traumatic events about which the children or adults with ID are not able to communicate. Thus, the therapist needs the parent to formulate hypotheses about assumed connections between symptoms and memories. These may be memories of single and chronic traumatization. Sometimes, trauma treatment for parents is indicated before the child's treatment. This is the case if the parents' unprocessed memories are in the foreground or if the parent attempts to avoid confrontation with the child's memories. Both conditions would make it difficult for the parent to write the child's 'story' or support the child emotionally and cognitively during the EMDR sessions. Indication criteria for prior trauma treatment of the parents are described in Chapter 6.

The application of EMDR storytelling has four goals:

1) To promote the child's trauma processing;
2) To promote the parent's processing of memories related to their child's traumatic experiences;
3) To build the parent's confidence in their ability to fulfil their parental role (increase feelings of competence);
4) To improve the interaction between parent and child. Writing the child's story helps the parent to empathize with the child's perspective. By reading the child's story aloud, they share it with their child; as a result, the child feels more seen and heard, strengthening the attachment relationship.

8.4 Procedure

The storytelling procedure is described in Lovett's books *Small Wonders* (1999) and *Trauma-Attachment Tangle* (2015). Her creative descriptions and positive results inspired child and adolescent (C&A) therapists in many countries to apply this procedure. The EMDR storytelling method requires a more extensive preparation to identify and best describe the memories relevant to the child's symptoms, as compared to the standard protocol. Since children cannot recount preverbal negative experiences, identification, activation, and desensitization of their memories take place via the narrative. A fundamental point here is that the child's (supposedly perceived) experience of the event(s) is central to the story—not the parent's perception.

Four phases can be distinguished when applying the EMDR storytelling method:

1. History taking and case conceptualization (phase 1).
2. Preparation: Writing the story (phase 2).
3. Reprocessing: Activation, desensitization, installation, body scan, positive closure (phases 3, 4, 5, 6, 7).
4. (Re)evaluation (phase 8).

Compared to the standard protocol, the phases of the storytelling method are less distinguishable due to the integration in phase 3 of activation and desensitization of the memory, installation, body scan, and positive closure. As a result, the therapist has less guidance on when or how to intervene during phase 3. The following section presents points of interest for the different phases of the procedure.

8.4.1 History Taking and Case Conceptualization

During intake, the therapist gathers information about the child's symptoms, relevant traumatic events, current safety, the child's development, and the child's positive qualities. The therapist identifies the specific symptom-related experiences or events with the parent. These are usually events after which the symptoms have started or increased. For events that took place over a more extended period, such as in cases of domestic violence or physical abuse, it is often difficult to identify a specific event that is most strongly associated with the symptoms. In that case, the parents should describe a 'representative' event in the story ('Usually what happened was …'). The therapist lists these (presumably) symptom-related, specific, and representative events in chronological order and estimates, with the parents, which experiences seem most relevant from the child's perspective and—if many events—how these experiences can be grouped, for example type of events. Next, the parents and the therapist determine which events or experiences will be included in one story or several stories, and the order in which the stories are written and read. Clinical practice shows that a chronological order may be logical, but this is not always the best way to structure a story. When parents can provide an order, the therapist will follow the parent's lead. If they do not know, the therapist will propose an order.

8.4.2 Preparation

The therapist explains the procedure and guidelines for writing the story to the parents (Lovett, 2015).

- ***Structure of the story***

The story has three sections: a beginning, a middle section, and an ending. A positive beginning starts by describing a setting of safety, resources, and strengths. For example: *Robert lived in a house with his father and mother, and they greatly loved him. He was always cheerful and laughed a lot until Mum and Dad started hitting each other.*

Then comes the middle section, which zooms in on the traumatic experiences. This is where all the relevant details of the traumatic experiences emerge: what the child saw, heard, smelled, felt, or tasted (perceptual experiences), and the child's reaction to this (physical, emotional, and behavioural responses). The parents should include the 'hotspots' of the selected event(s) factually and as concretely as possible, with perceptual details.

The doctor put a tube in his nose while several hospital staff members held him. Tom was very shocked. It hurt, and he started screaming and kicking. Tom couldn't breathe properly. He wanted to remove the hose from his nose, but he couldn't because they had such a strong hold on him.

The parents can mention their reactions in the story to clarify them for the child. For example:

> *Mum and Dad found it very hard to see you in such pain. It made them sad. All those painful things had to happen to make you better. Mum and Dad love you and did not want any of that to happen. However, it had to be done.*

Sometimes, there is not enough information available to describe the 'trauma' in detail—for example, in the case of sexual abuse that took place out of the parents' sight, or in the case of an adopted child whose adoptive parents do not know precisely what the child experienced in their country of origin. When writing about the events, parents and therapists must limit themselves to describing the facts and should not include their assumptions or fantasies in the story. Therapists should adhere to their professional guidelines to avoid creating disinformation. When information is missing, parents can rely on the information at hand: how the child behaves now and how the symptoms have developed. From this information, the parents and therapist can distil the likely triggers (stimuli) that provoke adverse reactions in the here and now. For example, they may notice that the child reacts skittishly or stiffens when touched, or they may avoid eye contact and withdraw or become angry. Parents may incorporate such information into the story and interject that they do not know precisely what happened. For example:

> *We have noticed that you always flinch when we want to touch you. You withdraw your hand or turn away. We do not know exactly what you went through. However, we want you to know that it is ok and safe when we touch you. You do not need to be afraid now.*

The end of the story illustrates that the (imminent) danger of the past has disappeared and offers resolution and personal empowerment. It describes the positive aspects of the current situation in which the child's functioning and development are enhanced. It lists the resources the child has at their disposal, such as their positive qualities, described in combination with positive statements about the child. The child can use these resources to anticipate a future where they will function adequately and are ready to cope with potentially tense situations:

> *Mum and Dad live separately now and do not argue anymore. Tom is safe now and can play nicely again with his friends. He loves to laugh and cuddle. He knows he can go to Mum or Dad when he is sad. They can comfort and help him.*

Lovett (1999) instructs parents to write the story in the third person (i.e., about a boy or a girl) without explicitly mentioning the child's name. The underlying idea is that the child can decide whether they identify with the story's content. This more indirect approach should prevent the child from becoming overwhelmed by emotions and is consistent with how children in that age range are often addressed. In clinical practice, this 'indirect' approach usually appears unnecessary. Children enthusiastically note that the story, formulated in the third (neutral) person, is about them, and they point to themselves. We suggest letting parents choose the perspective from which they want to write/tell the story (he/she/you) and whether to mention the child's name (the little girl/little Wendy). They know their child best.

- ***The content: Event versus period***

Compared to the standard protocol, the storytelling method is like a 'hail of bullets' on the memory network, rather than a 'precision shot', because it is unclear beforehand which part of the narrative will evoke distress in the child. If a single event has been identified, the story covers the course of that event, including its consequences. However, the story most often relates to a period in which multiple events occurred, rather than a specific event, and may cover a more extended period of the child's life (e.g., two months or three years). The narrative may then capture specific events (if identified) and general experiences, and be divided into sections or chapters.

- ***The process of writing the story***

The parents write the story before the first EMDR session with the child. The story is preferably written by the person who is best informed about the traumatic event(s) and the child's development in response to the event(s). This is usually the parent who was present and clearly remembers the child's reactions. In principle, the story is written at home and not in the therapy room, so there is time and opportunity to gather information—for example, by looking at photos and any available medical records and psychologist's reports, or talking with each other and relatives. Relevant additional details are placed in the story. Parents often put off writing the story until the very last moment. They are usually reluctant to be confronted with the traumatic memory themselves because the memory also evokes distress in them—for example, if the parents watched helplessly as pain was inflicted on their child or the child was struggling to breathe.

If the parents are not available, the caretakers who have authority over the child (e.g., foster parents) may choose, in cooperation with the therapist, to write the story about the factual (known) events using information from significant others or official reports—for example, in the case of adopted or foster children. In such situations, extra caution is needed when selecting information to be included in the story. All possible efforts are made to involve the biological parents in writing and telling the story. At the very least, their agreement with the story's content is necessary.

- ***Therapist feedback***

Before starting therapy sessions with the child, the therapist checks the story's content with the parent(s). They review whether the story contains enough relevant perceptual details about the traumatic event to activate the child's memory and whether the story is written adequately from the child's perspective.

Feedback on the story can be given via email or in a separate session. If by email, the therapist asks parents to send the story before the first session with the child and review the story prior to using it. Experience shows that the positive beginning and end are usually well described. However, the appropriateness of the middle section is variable. Some parents describe the child's perceptual experiences in detail. In contrast, others describe it only in general terms or omit it, often because it is difficult for them to be confronted with their child's experiences. If necessary, the therapist gives suggestions for completing the missing information, following the procedure, and sticking to the facts. If required, the therapist may have an extra meeting with the parents to review the story and answer any questions about the planned therapy session with the child. The therapist can identify any omissions and explore whether these reflect avoidance by the parents (for example, if they are afraid of triggering their own traumatic memories). As needed, the therapist can help the parents complete the story, or the parents can do this upon returning home.

8.4.3 Reprocessing

Steps 3–7 of the standard protocol are integrated into the reprocessing phase of the storytelling method. Once the story is ready, the session with the child can start. Preferably, both parents will be present. The starting point is to actively involve the parents as much as possible. Being able to comfort and support the child adequately in the session increases the parents' sense of competence; an emotionally available parent is present, with a 'calm brain' for the child. This fosters a sense of security in the relationship and promotes emotion regulation (Struik, 2019b). The parents act as co-therapists during the storytelling method, collaborating with the therapist. Before this session, the therapist and the parent(s) have agreed on who will read the story aloud, who will observe the child's reaction, and what BLS/WMT will be used—in short, who does what, and what the considerations for doing so will be.

- ***Tasks***

Listening to the story (child) and reading aloud (parent) is aimed at activating the memory and identifying the current disturbing 'hot spots'. To this end, the therapist asks one of the parents to hold the (young) child on their lap. Usually, this concerns the parent who was closest during the event. Physical contact makes the child's bodily response more palpable during the EMDR procedure. Increasing physical arousal in the child indicates enhanced distress. This helps to identify moments in the story that are meaningful to the child now and may be related to the symptoms (stress reactions). This is felt by the parent and observed by the therapist.

If both parents are present, they choose who will read the story and who will observe; they discuss and agree on this beforehand. One takes the child on their lap, listens to the story, and observes the child's reaction. The other one reads aloud and observes the child's response also. If only one parent is present, they take the child on their lap and read the story aloud. The parent knows best where the possible 'hot spots' for the child may be and can thus read the story with appropriate intonation. At the same time, the parent pays attention to the child's reactions. The therapist reads the story aloud only in cases where the parent cannot.

- ***Choice/type of BLS/WMT***

Eye movement activities are usually not feasible for toddlers and babies. For children under four years of age, the therapist or parent 'taps' the child's knees, lower legs, feet, or hands or uses buzzers. It is essential to offer the distraction playfully, such as with a hand puppet, to attract and hold the child's attention. Auditory stimuli, such as clicks through headphones, are used rarely: Research in adults shows that clicks put only limited strain on working memory, and headphones are impractical in this group because they can easily fall off when the child moves.

Research on the function of BLS/WMT in (young) children is lacking, and it is not evident whether working memory theory can be conceived as an explanatory model to understand symptom reduction in children as it is in adults. The orienting-response model (see Chapter 1) might adequately explain the effects seen in clinical practice in young children. The predictable stimuli (taps) elicit a relaxation response, after which symptom reduction can occur. Lovett (1999, p. 17) suggests that EMDR could be viewed 'as an extension of natural soothing methods that parents use daily'.

- ***Memory activation***

The storytelling method is adjusted to the child's emotional regulation skills, with less emphasis on creating maximal arousal, compared to the standard protocol. Nonetheless, the goal of both procedures is identical: to activate and desensitize the memory as completely as possible to achieve complete symptom reduction. If the child has passive language comprehension, listening to the story read aloud by the parent is usually enough to activate the child's memory. However, should activation through the story not succeed—if the child is still not involved, or there is suboptimal activation—then the therapist can increase the level of disturbance by using trauma-relevant material or specific trauma-related cues: for example, pictures of a hospitalization or tangible material, such as a spit bowl, pills, or plaster, or a visual representation depicting the traumatic situation using dolls. Sounds, smells, tastes, sensations (by touching involved body parts), and body positions related to the traumatic event (e.g., lying down) can also be used to enhance the activation of the memory network.

When the memory is activated, the child may become increasingly agitated while listening to the story. They may start to react more strongly by stiffening, struggling to get off the lap, screaming, or kicking. Although this may look intense to the observer, it permits the therapist and the parents to recognize that the child's memory has been triggered. Parents often indicate that this reaction corresponds to the child's response during the traumatic event and the current behaviour at home.

- ***Desensitization***

Once the child's attention has been drawn to the story and the memory has been activated, trauma processing proceeds runs, as in the standard protocol. The therapist and the parents follow what happens and focus on the associations. The therapist may facilitate the reprocessing by verbalizing the child's observed responses to help them recognize and understand their feelings. The therapist can say, for example, 'You are scared, angry, sad, or confused' to encourage the child to focus on their feelings and bodily sensations. Therapists might ask children who can describe or point to the part of their body where they feel the sensations: 'What do you feel, and where is that feeling in your body?'

The therapist's additional intervention is only necessary if the process is blocked or blocking is imminent. Some parents read quickly through the most challenging parts of the story—for example, at the point in the story where the child is suffocating, alone, or in unbearable pain. The reason may be that this part of the story is difficult for the parents to hear, and they want to avoid stimulating intense emotion in the child and possibly also in themselves. The therapist can intervene and make the child focus on the painful details by instructing the parents to pause the reading and observe how the child is reacting or to repeat the pertinent section again, but more slowly. This creates space for the child to feel and respond, allowing the parents and the therapist to observe the child's reaction.

Continuous BLS/WMT: The therapist or the parent keeps tapping/drumming throughout the reading of the story to avoid the child becoming overwhelmed with intense emotions or sensations. Children have limited emotion regulation skills, so they might stop cooperating if they become overwhelmed. The therapist may do the tapping themselves, which enables them to adjust the process, such as speeding up the taps when intense emotions or sensations arise. The same applies to the use of buzzers. However, clinical experience shows that trauma processing also runs well when parents do the tapping— for example, during online treatment or when the child does not tolerate tapping by the therapist. Letting parents tap increases their feelings of competence and strengthens the child's sense of safety.

Estimating the optimal speed for the tapping is difficult: slow, fast, or alternating. This dilemma is related to the dual purpose of the procedure: activation of the relevant memories and reduction of the associated arousal. It is conceivable that maximum BLS/WMT would hinder listening to the story, resulting in limited activation of the relevant memory. By comparison, the therapist does not offer BLS/WMT during the assessment phase in the standard protocol. However, during storytelling, it is vital to provide enough BLS/WMT to prevent the child from becoming emotionally overwhelmed by high arousal. Increasing BLS/WMT can also help keep the child's attention focused on the story (see Case Study 8.1). Remember that processing is only possible when the child is within the 'window of tolerance' (Ogden & Minton, 2000). Research is needed to identify the optimal speed and whether differences in

CASE STUDY 8.1 **Jordan**

Shortly after his father starts reading the story, one-year-old Jordan suddenly falls asleep on his mother's lap. He wakes up, and his father restarts the story, but again, Jordan falls asleep. As a result, the (re)processing is hampered. The therapist taps Jordan faster in different places on his little body; he remains awake and listens, and the father can read the complete story during the session. Jordan seems to be more relaxed afterward.

speed are helpful. Thus far, we should rely primarily on the therapist's intuition to determine the speed of the BLS/WMT. The case study below illustrates the relevance of careful attuning.

- ***Sharing observations***

After the complete story has been read aloud, the therapist and parent(s) share their observations. Together, they try to interpret the child's reactions (e.g., freeze, fight, flight) to the story in the context of trauma processing. During this evaluation, the child may play, do something else, or stay on the parent's lap. It is recommended that trauma-relevant toys be available in the room so the child can play with them. Observation of the child's activities often reveals an immediate effect of the EMDR session. For instance, the child may spontaneously play out a different, often more positive, course of the selected event (post-traumatic play), or they may suddenly speak more clearly or move more smoothly. All these phenomena indicate that reprocessing and development have been initiated. After seeing their child's reaction in the session, parents often say that it helped them to better understand what the child went through during the traumatic event or the lingering effects that bother the child.

Three helpful questions to evaluate the EMDR session are:

1. Has the memory been sufficiently activated?

This can be inferred from the parents' and therapist's observations. Often, parents remark that they recognized their child's physical, emotional, and behavioural reactions during the session, which they also saw at the time of the traumatic event. For example, '*That is curious, how odd, that's how she held her arm then, too.*'

2. Is the affective load of the memory(s) reduced, and is the child more relaxed?

This can be inferred from a visible decrease in bodily tension. Parents feel this relaxation, especially if the child leans against them while sitting on their lap. Relaxation is often visible to the therapist—for example, when the child adopts a different posture. Other signs of relaxation are getting hungry, falling asleep, and having to pee or defecate. Note that these reactions can also be a form of avoidance behaviour if they occur at the beginning of the session. Once the traumatic memory has been reprocessed, rapprochement between parent and child is possible (again). This is regularly immediately visible in the therapy room when children turn towards their parents and experience, for the first time in a long time, how they can 'connect in relaxation'.

3. How did the parents experience the process?

The therapist invites parents to share how they perceived actively contributing to their child's recovery. Witnessing their child's reactions is impressive. A father whose son was maltreated by a robber in the house while he was at work said:

> *Because I heard what happened and saw his reactions to the story, I now understand better what he went through. It's scary to see how much he was in agony and how he tried to fight his way out, but it does bring me a step closer to my child.*

At the session's closure, the therapist instructs the parents to record daily observations.

8.4.4 Re-Evaluation

The parents' observations, shared by email or phone before or at the start of the next session, are essential for monitoring the course of symptoms. The therapist uses these observations to estimate, together with the parents, which memory (or aspect of it) continues to agitate the child so they can determine what should be targeted in the session.

How often the same story needs to be repeated—or repeated with different emphases—is decided by assessing the remaining distress generated by the story. Parents can usually detect whether their child becomes agitated when the story is repeated or whether they only participate out of 'politeness'. When the child can listen to the story calmly, no longer shows any stress reaction, or has lost interest in the story, there is no need for repetition. At this point, the reported symptoms may diminish or disappear if the trauma processing is completed. The standard protocol offers several tools for estimating the 'completeness' of the (trauma) processing (i.e., SUD and VOC). However, these process checks are not necessarily incorporated into the storytelling method. Children as young as three can indicate with their hands how disturbing it still is to hear the story or think about it (not disturbing to very disturbing). Interpreting their responses is tricky, as young children sometimes point randomly with their hands.

A decrease in symptoms indicates that trauma reprocessing is ongoing or even completed. Especially when a child is chronically traumatized, it is not expected that the symptoms will disappear or diminish after a single session. Stories can encompass long periods and may comprise several 'main parts' and 'hot spots', all of which need to be read and processed carefully; this takes several sessions. Treatment is completed when the symptoms have disappeared and the therapist and the parents assess that the child's reactions have normalized. For example, it is expected that a child would be sad when processing the sudden death of a parent. Sadness could indicate that the grieving process has started and that further EMDR sessions to support processing would not be needed.

8.5 Effects

Parents typically report that therapy with the EMDR storytelling method (as with the standard protocol) results in a decrease in their child's post-traumatic stress reactions and a catch-up in psychosocial, motor, or language development, and sometimes a physical growth spurt as well. The EMDR storytelling method also has a positive effect on parents. Firstly, writing the story and reading it aloud helps parents organize their memory material, which enhances the natural completion of their trauma reprocessing. Secondly, their sense of competency as a parent increases.

Clinical practice shows that trauma-related symptoms can sometimes reappear in the form of re-experiences, anxiety, or increased irritability when a child enters a new developmental phase, even if therapy for previous traumas was completed with good results and no new traumatic events have occurred since. This might occur if certain aspects of the traumatic memory have not been processed yet and are now being triggered. For example, the child may encounter new situations in school where rough physical contact happens, which may trigger memories of medical trauma where a child was held against their will. Secondly, the child might re-evaluate the 'old' traumatic memory because they have received new information or acquired new cognitive skills, such as time awareness or logical reasoning. See, for example, the case of Emma (Case Study 8.2).

CASE STUDY 8.2 Emma

At the age of two, Emma witnessed the stabbing death of her mother by her father. After successful treatment at the age of three, she got intrusive symptoms of re-experiencing seeing the stabbing when she was eight years old. Due to her cognitive development, she developed the capacity for logical reasoning (see Chapter 6). She now worries about what she should have done to prevent the murder.

The extent of memory processing may be inversely related to the likelihood of a relapse. No objective criteria exist to test whether activation and desensitization have been completed. Therefore, it cannot (yet) be predicted which children are likely to develop symptoms in a subsequent development phase related to a previously treated memory. When parents report a return of the child's symptoms, therapists should be aware of a possible relationship between the symptoms and previously treated traumatic experience(s). A limited number of EMDR sessions is usually sufficient to reduce the symptoms again.

8.6 EMDR Storytelling and Standard Protocol Combined

A combination of the EMDR storytelling method and the standard protocol is indicated for children aged 4–18 years or for adults with ID and functioning within this age range when it is hypothesized that symptoms are related to preverbal experiences. Using the storytelling method combined with the EMDR standard protocol is advantageous for this group because of their limited ability to articulate emotional, physical, or cognitive reactions while applying the standard protocol. This allows the therapist to follow the client's associations and facilitates an evaluation of the trauma reprocessing. It is hypothesized that integrating the two procedures increases chances for optimal activation and desensitization of the emotionally charged memory network and, consequently, increases the likelihood of symptom reduction.

When using both procedures, the storytelling method's purpose is more limited than using it as a *stand-alone* procedure. When using the combination, the parent's story replaces the description of the memory by the child in the assessment phase of the standard protocol, where the therapist asks the client to describe the negative memory as if it were a film. A slight modification in the standard protocol is needed for optimal alignment with the storytelling method. Instead of the first sentence in the instruction of the assessment phase ('Please look at the memory/movie and choose the picture that is the most disturbing one to look at right now'), the therapist says,

> *You have just heard the story. Which part of this story is the most disturbing for you now? What is the worst picture for you now? Make a drawing of it [depending on age]. What do you see in this picture?*

Subsequently, the therapist continues with the regular questions of the assessment phase (NC, PC, VOC, emotion, SUD, body location). The therapist matches the standard protocol to the child's level of functioning. So, for a five-year-old or adult with ID functioning at this age, the therapist uses the adjustments for pre-schoolers and has the target image drawn (see standard protocol for children and adolescents).

The combined procedure (storytelling method + standard protocol) does not require adding BLS/WMT when the parent reads the story because the story replaces the child's memory description in the assessment phase of the standard protocol. A BLS/WMT is not needed then because the purpose of the assessment phase is to create optimal arousal; therefore, no dual attention is required yet. During the desensitization phase of the standard protocol, however, the therapist ensures optimal speed of the BLS/WMT, preferably via eye movements, as is usual in the standard protocol.

8.7 Concluding Remarks

This chapter has described tools and specific points of interest for using the EMDR storytelling method as procedure for symptoms of preverbal trauma in children or adults with ID. We hope that this chapter will encourage therapists to treat clients with preverbal trauma more readily and more often. We trust that research on the effectiveness of the EMDR storytelling method will reveal whether the clinically observed positive results can be objectified. Research into the optimal workload or speed of BLS is desirable to improve the procedure and enhance trauma reprocessing in the various age groups.

Interweaves

9

RENÉE BEER AND CARLIJN DE ROOS

9.1 Introduction

According to the adaptive information processing (AIP) model, the EMDR procedure promotes a physiological state that facilitates adaptive information processing, resulting in integration of memories. Integration requires a change in the assignment of meaning. This process can stagnate due to various factors. Stagnation occurs when the child shuts off from the process because of either being overwhelmed by emotions or fearing that this might happen (blocking), or when the shift from dysfunctional to functional meaning-making does not occur, therefore resulting in circling between dysfunctional associations (looping). This chapter reviews signals that may indicate that processing is blocked or stuck, potential causes for this, what type of intervention is appropriate to restart processing, and when to intervene. Interventions to resolve stagnation are called 'interweaves': 'The therapist initiates interweaves through questions or instructions that elicit thought, actions, affect, and/or imagery' (Shapiro, 2018, p. 256).

Because interweaves do not always focus on *cognitive* information, we refer to *interweaves* rather than *cognitive interweaves* in this chapter. Interweaves can be categorized based on different variables, such as:[1]

- Goal: What should be achieved by the interweave
- Theme: Substantive theme on which the processing gets stuck
- Information channel: Aspect of information on which the processing gets stuck
- Type of interweave: Type of suggestion, instruction, or question for the interweave.

All interweaves share the same goal: to promote adaptive information processing. This chapter provides an overview of potential interweaves using the above-mentioned criteria. The goal is to provide guidance to therapists for the selection of suitable interweaves in specific situations. The challenge for the therapist is to know when to use which interweave, and how to assess whether an interweave should be used or whether it might be better to not intervene, and instead trust the process.

The most empowering effect is to be expected from allowing associations and new insights to emerge spontaneously (Shapiro, 2018).

[1] See also Adler-Tapia and Settle (2008), Gilson and Kaplan (2000), and Gomez (2013).

Renée Beer and Carlijn de Roos, *Interweaves*. In: *Handbook of EMDR for Children and Adolescents*.
Edited by: Renée Beer and Carlijn de Roos, Oxford University Press.
DOI: 10.1093/oso/9780198918400.003.0009

9.2 Blocked Processing

According to the AIP model (Shapiro, 2018), trauma-related information is stored in neural networks in state-specific form with dysfunctional meaning. During EMDR, a connection is established between networks of functional and dysfunctional information, which allows assimilation of functional information and integration of the memory by adaptive information processing. However, if that connection fails to occur, an interweave can be initiated during desensitization to help establish that connection. This concerns not only provoking thoughts, but also making other functional information—of any kind—accessible or adding new information that is needed for a different perspective on the experienced event, all of which allows the adaptive information processing to continue.

The purpose of EMDR is assimilation and integration of functional information. During desensitization, a metaphorical train travels from one station to the next. If the train is blocked because of a stuck switch or the absence of a piece of track, the therapist deploys an interweave to reroute or construct the rails in such a way that the train can continue rolling down the track.

This allows relevant neural networks of functional and dysfunctional information to become interconnected. Shapiro (2018, p. 256) said that interweaves are 'statements that weave together the appropriate neuro networks and associations'.

The more networks of dysfunctional information there are and the more dysregulated the child is, the greater the likelihood of blocked processing during desensitization, since the child is more likely to go outside their window of tolerance and enter a state of hyper- or hypo-arousal (Gomez, 2013). Chapter 10 describes optional interventions to prevent or remedy this.

9.2.1 Signs of Stagnation

There are two ways in which stagnation can manifest itself: blocking or looping. Blocking means a general blocking of information processing. This can be caused intentionally by the child, or it can happen to the child. Looping is a specific variant of blocked processing in which stagnation occurs at the level of meaning-making, whereby the child keeps circling around in associations without moving forward.

Blocking can be deliberate, to a greater or lesser extent. Children who consciously block the process by shutting themselves off from it usually do so to prevent or stop being overwhelmed by negative emotions. By blocking, the child (momentarily) calms down and feels in control of the situation or themselves. The motive is thus usually (active) avoidance of something negative that the child fears and feels unable to cope with. Avoidance can also be a reflex, rather than deliberate, resulting in dissociation.
Blocking may be present if the following reactions are observed:

- The child is restless and wants to do something else.
- The child refuses to continue.
- The child becomes extremely sleepy or even falls asleep.

- The child shows other dissociative reactions.
- The child edits their associations.
- The child hops from one memory to another.
- The child makes repeatedly statements such as: 'I can't do this', 'I don't want this', 'Nothing comes up', 'I don't know'.

Looping is recognized by substantive reactions:

- The child repeats approximately identical answers two or three times to what comes up, with no shift in meaning from dysfunctional to functional.
- SUD remains stuck at the same level when going back-to-target.

9.2.2 Causes of Stagnation

Several causes are possible for the varying degrees of intentional occurrence of stagnation. Blocking:

- Fear or shame of strong emotions and/or physical sensations.
- Lack of resources to stay within the window of tolerance.

Looping:

- Missing knowledge.
- Present knowledge is inaccessible.
- Dysfunctional (underlying) beliefs ('big boys don't cry').

9.2.3 Removal of Stagnation

When noticing blocked processing during desensitization, the therapist should first ask themselves if perhaps the necessary conditions for information processing are missing. Two categories of conditions are relevant:

- *Contextual conditions*: Is there sufficient safety in the home situation? Are there any interfering stressors in the current living situation that could obstruct the child from being able to focus on the process?
- *Procedural conditions*: Does the child understand what is expected of them? Does the child want treatment themselves or do they attend due to pressure from their parents? Is the selected target image currently the most disturbing one or was it the most disturbing image at the time of the event? Has the correct negative cognition been selected for optimal activation of the memory/target image? Is the therapist applying the procedure properly?

If all these conditions are met but blocking occurs nonetheless, the therapist can first try to unblock adaptive information processing with the procedural interventions described in Table 9.1.

Table 9.1 Procedural interventions

What	*When or how*
Repeat the instruction	When the therapist assumes that the child does not know or understand what to do, it is useful to repeat the instruction and reiterate that anything that comes to mind is good. This can be done with, for example, one or more of the following phrases. – *Just wait and see what is coming to your mind, you don't have to tell me everything.* – *Just watch where you notice a change: in your thoughts, feelings, or in your body.* – *Perhaps thoughts come to mind that don't seem related to this, but feel free to tell those too.* When the therapist assumes that the child understands but is afraid to verbalize their reactions out of shame: – *If you do feel, think, or notice something, but don't want to say what it is, that's totally okay. Just tell me so. Everything you say is right, you can't say anything wrong.*
Offer more BLS/WMT	When the therapist assumes the child is blocking out of fear of being overwhelmed by sensations or emotions, the therapist can add BLS/WMT. This can be done by speeding up the lights/hand movements in front of the eyes, or by utilizing additional tasks simultaneously (visual, tactile, auditory), or by changing the distracting task. For example, the therapist can ask the child to tap the hands of the therapist instead of the therapist tapping the child; motor activity is more distracting as it requires more concentration.
Back to target more frequently	When the child gives the same reactions repeatedly without 'moving forward', the therapist can go back to target more frequently. Repeatedly focusing on what is causing the remaining disturbance will restart the processing to go further down the track.
Direct attention to other information channels (aspects)	When the child seems stuck in one information channel without reporting any changes, a little push can be adequate to help the child move further. A characteristic feature of EMDR is that during desensitization the child is given space to follow their own track ('go with the flow'), where all information aspects (channels) can come up during the stream of associations. Some children report mainly physical reactions, others associate with emotions or new insights, still others react by describing images, switching freely between the different aspects of information (channels). Change is a sign of ongoing processing. The therapist intervenes only when information processing stagnates. When the child remains stuck in a particular 'information channel', the therapist can direct the attention to other 'channels'.
	If a child lingers on cognitive associations (like 'I'm failing', 'I'm not doing well', 'I'm being a dick','I screwed up again', and so on) and shifting is not happening, the therapist can ask about visual, emotional, or physical aspects of the associations which the child is reporting, such as: – *What images come to mind?* – *What else strikes you?* – *What do you feel now ... [emotion]? And where do you feel. that ... [emotion] in your body?* When lingering on negative bodily sensations, such as pain, the therapist may ask: – *What do you think about that?* (directing attention to another information channel) – *What do you feel in other places in your body?* (directing attention to another place)

What	*When or how*
Utilize installed resource	When the child does not dare to continue out of fear of not to be able to handle whatever will come up, the therapist can ask: – *What is it like when you take your ... [e.g., self-confidence] with you?*

If these procedural interventions do not help smooth the process, then interweaves can be considered. Interweaves are preferably short, well-timed, open-ended questions or suggestions, that promote progress in adaptive processing, while interfering as little as possible (Van Pelt et al., 2025). Interweaves can be classified according to different variables: goal, theme, information channel, and type of question/suggestion. The following paragraphs will clarify these and offer examples of possible interweaves (Sections 9.3–9.6). Figure 9.1 provides a visual overview *including the variables that will be discussed in the annex.*

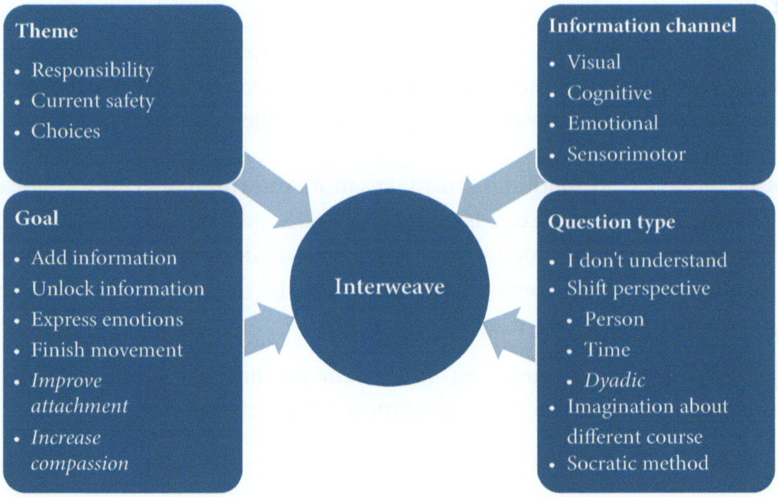

Figure 9.1 Overview of options for developing or selecting an interweave.

9.3 **Goal**

A potential goal for interweaves is to complete missing information or to make existing information more accessible, so that the child's perspective of what they have experienced can change (Van Pelt et al., 2025).

An additional goal for interweaves with children may be to strengthen the child's relationship with an attachment figure or with themselves, changing the child's—and the parent's—perspective on what the child has experienced. Interweaves with this goal, developed by Wesselmann and colleagues (described in Beer & De Roos, 2017b), are integrated in this chapter as an Annex. The original chapter is summarized and the goal of this type of interweaves (*dyadic interweaves*) are referred to as '*improve attachment*' and '*increase compassion*'.

- ***Completing missing information***

If the child lacks relevant information, the therapist should provide this missing information. Psychoeducation can be given by means of a fairy tale (for younger children) or a metaphor or an analogy (for older children), and can be relevant if, for example, psychiatric problems are a factor in one or both parents, which has prevented the child from receiving what they need. Below is an example of psychoeducation from Gomez (2013, p. 205).

> Some parents have a wound in their head or heart. Because of that wound, parents may do or say things that hurt another person, especially their own children. Sometimes because of that wound, parents cannot make their child feel how much they love them and then a child may start thinking there is something wrong with them. Remember well that it is not a child's job to take care of his parent's wound. Only the parent himself can do that and make sure it heals. Also remember that it is not a child's fault if what a parent says or does hurts the child. The child cannot do anything about it. This does not mean that that parent is bad; it does mean that the parent has a wound in his heart. Children have the right to protect themselves from the wounds in their parents' hearts.

Completing missing information usually takes more time than offering a single sentence, suggestion, or question. Therefore, it is questionable whether it is appropriate to do this as an interweave; the provision of such information is better done at another time (e.g., at the beginning of a session). Later, during desensitization, the therapist can then return to the information provided with a question:

- '*Then you didn't know what was going on. What do you* ***now*** *know about ...?*' [e.g., the illness/mental state/circumstances of father/mother/perpetrator], or
- '*What have you learned about...?*'

- ***Making existing information accessible***

Often the required information is present but not accessible. To determine the nature of the necessary (cognitive) information that the child cannot access, the therapist can use the themes described by Shapiro (2018). These are explained in the Section 9.4.

9.4 Theme

Shapiro (2018) learned from her experiences with adults with early childhood traumatization that three stages can be distinguished in the process of adaptive information processing:

- adequate allocation of responsibility
- experiencing current safety
- new choices for the future

Based on her observations, she suggested that in cases of early childhood trauma, clients should be helped to reach the subsequent stages by using interweaves, so that in a proactive form of EMDR one stays as close as possible to the spontaneous course of the process. The classification into these three themes, related to the stages, is also described by other authors and appears equally applicable for children (Adler-Tapia and Settle, 2008; Gomez, 2013). This is Shapiro's (2018, p. 260) explanation of the stages, or plateaus, of processing:

> The initial objectives are to help clients 1) recognize and attribute appropriate responsibility, and 2) discard the guilt and self-blame that have undercut their sense of self-esteem and self-efficacy. Once these clinical goals have been achieved, it is easier for clients to recognize that they are no longer threatened and are able to take safe choices in both the present and the future.

For children, there is an added dimension to this. Many children in therapy were traumatized by maltreatment from parents/caregivers. These children often have an inadequate attribution of responsibility for what happened. If violence, neglect, or abuse has played a role, it is complicated for a child to attribute responsibility to the parent/caregiver, because the child still has a dependency relationship with this adult and does not yet have the necessary physical and emotional distance that an adult clients usually has with their perpetrator. Because of loyalty to their parents/caregivers, children would therefore rather be 'bad' with 'good parents' than 'good' with 'bad parents' (Gomez, 2013). The therapist should take this loyalty conflict into account when applying EMDR to children who have been traumatized by the behaviour of their parents. The theme of responsibility is less likely to play a role in children who were damaged by other types of events than interpersonal traumatization (see Chapter 2 of this book). The following are examples of interweaves by theme (which parallels stage): responsibility, safety, and choice.

- ***Responsibility***

Stagnation within this theme manifests as lingering shame, guilt, and/or self-blame about past situations or behaviour. The aim of interweaves here is to help the child place responsibility where it belongs—namely, with the aggressor and not with themselves.

Examples of interweaves

- *Who did it?*
- *How old were you? And how old was the person who maltreated you?*
- *Who was stronger?*
- *Who should be ashamed?*

- ***Safety***

Stagnation at this level occurs when the child does not become sufficiently aware during desensitization that the danger is over. This is manifested by the child remaining in a state of high physical arousal and fear. The aim of interweaves in such situations is to help the child recognize the difference between then and now, to realize that they are no longer in danger, and to feel that they are safe(er) now.

Examples of interweaves

- *Where is [the perpetrator]* ***now****? Can they hurt you now?*
- *Take a good look around you. Where are you* ***now****?*
- *It wasn't safe* ***then****. How safe is it* ***now****?*
- ***Did*** it [the negative outcome that could have taken place] *actually happen? And* ***did*** *you* [die, drown, crash, another dramatic outcome]?
- *How did it end? How did it go further?*

Children remain partly dependent on adults for their current safety. Thus, knowing that the danger has passed is not always enough for them to feel safe in the here and now. Interweaves that indirectly increase feelings of safety are interweaves that help the child to be aware that support is possible (possibly with psychoeducation) and that the child has the ability to ask for support (Gomez, 2013, p. 206). It is the job of parents to ensure that their child is safe (psychoeducation). Therapists can help them meet this responsibility by informing them of help that is available.

Other examples

- *What did you need* ***then****? Who could give you that* ***now****?*
- *What do you need* ***right now****? Who can/will help you with that?*
- *Who can you trust* ***now****?*
- *Who can you ask for protection* ***now****?*

- ***Choice***

Stagnation at this level can occur if the child is not sufficiently aware that they are free to choose to behave differently now. Children who are ambivalent about behavioural change, who believe they cannot change their own behaviour, or who are not yet sure if they want to change their behaviour are not sufficiently aware that they have a choice. The aim of the interweaves for such children is to help them realize that they can make their own decision to behave differently, and that they now have choices that they did not have before (at the time of the traumatization).

Examples of interweaves

- *What options do you have* ***now****?*
- *What can you do (differently)* ***now****?*
- *What would you like to do* ***now****?*
- *What can you say/what would you like to say now? Whose decision would it be if you choose to do that?*
- *Whose choice would it be?*

9.5 **Information Channel**

Adaptive processing should result in assimilation of all aspects of the memory representation. The interweaves mentioned in Section 9.4 are initiated to establish a connection between functional and dysfunctional information networks. However, other aspects of information besides cognitive factors can also be chosen as focal points for the interweave: 'looping reveals itself when ... the same emotions, sensations, images, and so forth, are recurring in successive sets' Shapiro (2018, p. 171).

In this section, we discuss interweaves that target emotions or sensorimotor information.

- ***Emotions***

If processing is stuck because of withheld or inadequately expressed emotions, the therapist may consider interweaves that elicit imagery, enabling the child to express these emotions. The goal is to promote connection between functional and dysfunctional information so that the emotional aspect of the memory representation becomes less overwhelming and thus more accessible. An interweave is initiated through questions or instructions that elicit 'thoughts, actions, **affect** and/or imagery' to jump-start blocked processing (Shapiro, 2018, p. 256).

This situation should be distinguished from blocking, where the child consciously shuts off from the process to avoid further confrontation with traumatic memory material (see Section 9.2.1). Here, the child does try to move forward, but 'the switch of the train track needs to be converted' so that the child can move forward.

Interweaves focused on emotions aim to create a situation in which the child allows themselves to feel more emotions and/or express them. Adaptive processing can get blocked by 'stuck' emotions, where something unpleasant has happened in the past or something positive has been lacking (like abuse or neglect) and the child has not (sufficiently) expressed the related emotions. Assistance in expressing them now may then be needed.

For finding appropriate interweaves here, the proposed division into levels of processing—responsibility, safety, and choice—is helpful. Based on the associations mentioned, the therapist knows whether the child has attributed responsibility to the right person, and whether the child realizes that the current situation is safe. If the child is not there yet, the therapist can help the child reach this stage (of processing) with interweaves described earlier (Section 9.4). If the child then realizes that they no longer need to be afraid to express their emotions, the therapist can use direct questions ('*What do you feel with that?*') to help the child focus their attention on their emotions: allowing them, naming them, and expressing them. Behind the fear may be other emotions, such as anger, sadness, and possibly disgust. These emotions may come to mind in subsequent associations. If the therapist presumes that there are hidden emotions that are not being acknowledged, the question '*What else are you feeling?*' can help the child to become aware of them and to express them.

In cases of stagnation during this process, interweaves can be considered. With interweaves and/or imagery with rescripting, the therapist can encourage the child to imagine a possible different course, allowing emotions to be acknowledged and expressed. For example, if adaptive processing stagnates in a child who has been a victim of actions (or neglect thereof) by other/others, and who has already recognized the emotions they are feeling now (e.g., anger and sadness), the therapist could ask:

- '*What did you need then?*' (e.g., support, comfort, protection, attention)
- '*What would you like to make clear to him/her/them?*' (e.g., that I am angry)
- '*How would you like to make that clear?*' (e.g., say, make them feel, show)
- '*Okay, just do it /make it clear*' (e.g., say, show, express your feelings)

Therapists can use these questions to help the child to access the excess emotions of that time and express them to the other person. These interweaves will only be effective if the child can think of what they needed to get protection from or what they had/would have wanted to do or say to an aggressor/perpetrator.

Recognizing and expressing emotions can also be promoted with interactive interweaves. Here, the therapist stimulates adaptive processing via indirect questions to the child. An interaction is initiated between child and parent or an internal dialogue between child and self (inner-child interweave). The therapist directs their question to the child through the parent or the inner child. This strategy is appropriate when the therapist wants to promote adaptive processing by creating positive imagery or a positive experience on the spot in the context of closeness and comfort, allowing the child to dare to feel and acknowledge more emotions. This not only brings about a change of perception of the memory, but also a deepening of the current affective relationship with the parent/caregiver.

Wesselmann and colleagues (2017c) have developed an extensive repertoire of interweaves of this type. See Annex to this chapter for dyadic (interactive) interweaves developed by Wesselmann and colleagues. Gomez (2013) describes several examples of interactive interweaves that are appropriate when a child has been damaged by parental behaviour (e.g., neglect).

If the parent who was involved in that situation—whether as perpetrator, bystander, or observer—is present in the session, they can validate the child's feelings and apologize.

- ***Sensorimotor information***

If symptoms arose after an event in which a physical action or movement was not completed or an impulse was not even executed at all, the interrupted or unexecuted action may be 'frozen' in memory—for example, after an accident or a fight (Adler-Tapia & Settle, 2008; Ogden et al., 2006). If a physical sensation or other symptom seems to represent an inhibited movement and the processing is blocked, the therapist can instruct the child to make the body do what it wanted to do at the time—namely, complete the movement or action. The goal of an interweave that addresses sensory information is to complete or perform a movement or action, thereby setting the processing in motion again. In the words of Shapiro (2018, p. 256), 'The clinician initiates interweaves … that elicit thoughts, action, affect and/or imagery'.

In the case of a child with chronic (pain) symptoms as a result of a car accident who sits stiffly on the seat during the desensitization phase (as if the car is now approaching again), and so remains stuck in a 'freezing response', the therapist can suggest 'Let your body do what it would have liked to do, just complete the movement' (e.g., huddle, brace yourself). Or, for a child who was beaten up and remains in a 'frozen' body position with clenched fists during desensitization, 'What movement does your body want to make now?'

9.6 Question Type

The overall goal of an interweave is to maximize the effect on information processing with as little intrusion as possible. The specific goal is to unlock present information or add new information, so that functional information networks are connected to dysfunctional ones. Any short (preferably open-ended) question or suggestion that can deblock blocked processing is suitable. The trick is to ask the right question at the right time. Below, we have ordered the question types suggested by various authors (Adler-Tapia & Settle, 2008; Shapiro, 2018) by purpose of the interweave and theme within the processing.

To supplement missing knowledge, the therapist does not ask a question, but provides information. This can be done at the beginning of a session. Subsequently the therapist can, however, in case of any stagnation during desensitization, ask 'What do you know now about . . .?'

The question types that are suitable for making present knowledge accessible across all themes, including responsibility, safety, and choice, are presented in Table 9.2, with examples for each.

Table 9.2 Examples of question types[a]

I don't understand Use if looping on the theme of responsibility (i.e., the child continues to wrongly assign blame to themselves for the event): C: *I should have stopped him.* T: *I don't understand ... What made you not do that?*
Shift to another perspective (person) Use if looping on theme of responsibility: C: *It's my own fault; I have been so stupid.* T: *If it had happened to your best friend/mother/father, what would you think about them?* or T: *If you asked [hero, helper] whose fault it was, what would they say?*
Shift to another perspective (time) Use when looping on the themes of safety and choice: C: *It was always misery and always will be.* T: *What's different now?* C: *I was always powerless and could never talk to anyone about it.* T: *Who could you ask for help now?*
Imagination of different course of events Use when open-ended questions do not get the process moving (such as: *What would you like to ask or say or do to ... now?*), then consider more directive questions or suggestions. C (abused by father): *So stupid that I let all of this happen.* T: *Suppose you had offered more resistance. What would have happened?* **Let's pretend** Use when a child knows what he would have wanted to do but did not/could not. C: *Then it would have only gotten worse ... I couldn't stop him. I never dared to say anything.* T: *Let's pretend that you dare to do it/say something now. What would want to do or tell him now?* C: ....(wait until the child brings up something) T: *Imagine that you are doing it*

Continued

Table 9.2 *Continued*

The Socratic Method[b] Sometimes a series of easily answered questions is used to lead the child to a logical conclusion (Shapiro, 2018, p. 272). These are needed to unlock existing knowledge or bring about a different perspective. When the processing has not yet restarted after one question, then the therapist gives it another try by asking another (or even more) question(s). The questions are formulated in such a way that a changed view emerges from the child rather than being provided by the therapist. This approach characterizes the Socratic method: a strategy to influence the outcome or perspectives through a series of questions that do not add substantive information, but rather stimulate the child to reflect on their position so that they will reconsider their underlying thinking patterns or assumptions. The question types mentioned earlier, aimed at making existing knowledge accessible or re-evaluating it, are basically Socratic questions, as they stimulate reflection on expressed or unspoken assumption(s). As with the Socratic method, is the aim of an interweave to stimulate a process in the child, leading them to come to a different understanding on their own.

Sources: Adler-Tapia & Settle, 2008; Shapiro, 2018

[a] The table only indicates examples of interweaves, substantiative responses, and when they seem appropriate. Standard questions/instructions before and after sets are excluded.

[b] In a Socratic dialogue, one asks questions to (1) clarify and explicit the assumption(s) of the child; (2) test for tenability; and (3) check whether the child still finds the assumption tenable or not, to make them realize that their assumption may not be tenable.

9.7 Designing or Selecting an Interweave

The therapist can sometimes make a rough estimate in advance of where processing might get blocked during the desensitization phase, and develop an idea of what interweaves would be useful if so. Although the therapist can only select or design an effective interweave once stagnation has occurred and it is clear why, the following questions are helpful in this global orientation in advance:

- What could be the goal for an interweave: complete missing knowledge or make present knowledge accessible, allow emotions to be vented, perform an unfinished or unperformed action or movement, improve attachment, or increase compassion?
- On what theme (stage of processing) might it get stuck: responsibility, safety, or choice?
- What role could parents play? How could they be prepared: for it, if needed?
- Which question type would be appropriate?

This cannot always be estimated in advance. The more clearly the therapist has defined the goal of the interweave, the easier it is to select or design an appropriate interweave.

9.8 Concluding Remarks

The therapist can select or design interweaves based on different variables or focal points. It is not predetermined what makes an interweave effective. An interweave proves to be effective if it restarts the processing. That is the goal of every interweave. Because so many interweaves are possible, the therapist may be tempted to use too many, too quickly, and too often. The best approach is to intervene as little and as briefly as possible. The guiding principle remains to deploy an interweave only when (1) processing is blocked or blocking is imminent and (2) there is a hypothesis as to what information is inaccessible or missing, so that it is clear what is needed to jump-start blocked processing.

Figure 9.1 provides an overview of optional focal points for selecting or designing an interweave, including those discussed in the annex *written in italics*.

ANNEX

Interweaves for Children with Attachment Trauma

Developed By Debra Wesselmann, Stefanie Armstrong, and Cathy Schweitzer[2]

A prerequisite for benefiting from EMDR is the ability to: access traumatic memories without becoming overwhelmed or dissociating; access information relative to the event; reflect; express inner thoughts and emotions.

Children with a history of chronic abuse, repetitive loss experiences, and inadequate nurturing and emotional support have not developed the ability to observe, express, or control their emotions. They also lack adequate and relevant information to help them make sense of their traumatic experiences with adaptive meaning.

Therefore, involving one or both parents in the treatment of children with attachment trauma increases the chances of successful EMDR. When parents are coached to connect physically and emotionally with their child, the child's sense of safety and security increases. Bonding with supportive parents enables children to access emotions and process traumatic memories. Parents who are present during EMDR—as their child describes their memories, thoughts, and feelings—get a better understanding of their child and can better empathize with what their child has experienced. The therapist encourages parents to be supportive—for example, by encouraging the child to sit as close to the parent as is comfortable for them so that they can feel a sense of connection during the session.

This strengthens the child's sense of connection and comfort in dealing with their memories. Most children with attachment trauma suffered emotional or even physical deprivation in early childhood, resulting in poor storage of adaptive information. This, in turn, reduces their ability to observe and verbalize their inner states or to process information compared to their more well-nurtured peers. Two types of interweaves are effective for emotionally or physically deprived children—inner-child and dyadic parent–child interweaves—giving parents the opportunity to meet previously unmet needs for protection and affection while providing adaptive information to enable trauma processing.

The therapist teaches the parents to understand and see the child's behaviour through the lens of the AIP model. As they begin to better understand how their child's behaviour is related to trauma triggers and negative beliefs, they become more empathic and patient with their child.

[2] An abridged account of a chapter previously published in Beer & De Roos, 2017b.

- **The concept of the inner child**

The therapist introduces the concept of the inner child to make the traumatized child aware of their more vulnerable emotional state and to help the child realize that certain feelings are rooted in a younger, wounded part of themself. This approach encourages traumatized children to be compassionate towards themselves for what happened to them earlier in life. The therapist explains the concept using Matryoshka dolls. As the child takes the Matryoshka dolls apart and puts them back together, the therapist provides psychoeducation for the child and their parents.

- **Inner-child interweaves**

Inner-child interweaves invite the child or parents to engage in some kind of dialogue with or about the inner child. Some of these interweaves stimulate positive imagery to provide security or affection for the inner child. This type of interweave is appropriate when the child seems stuck in the perspectives of their younger ego. Encouraging the child to address the younger ego state from the more mature ego state promotes a shift to the more mature viewpoint, strengthening the more mature state and calming the younger child ego state. The interweaves promote neurobiological integration by helping children to keep one foot in the present and one in the past, giving them more compassion for the younger, traumatized part of themselves.

- **Dyadic parent-child interweaves**

Dyadic parent–child interweaves involve stimulating parents to give the child affection, an image, or certain information when the child gets stuck at some point in the desensitization phase. Dyadic interweaves validate the parent's role as educator, protector, and expert in the child's eyes and strengthens feelings of trust and connection.

Examples of Interweaves

The following are examples of interweaves for different purposes. For each purpose, interweaves are classified as general, inner-child, or dyadic parent–child interweaves.

Self-Reflection and Expression of Inner Experiences

To the therapist's standard question after a set, '*What is happening now?*', children with poor self-reflexive ability usually reply '*I don't know*' or '*Nothing*'. In most cases, this does not mean that they have no emotions, images, or thoughts; rather, the child is simply unable to observe and describe their inner experience.

The dyadic parent–child interweaves in Table 9.3 allow parents to help their child with self-expression while showing compassion to the child.

Table 9.3 Examples of interweaves

General	*Thoughts are not good or bad, they are just there. Focus on the memory again. What is the first thing that comes to mind?* *I will go through the eye movements one more time. When you notice something like a feeling, a thought, an image, or whatever, you give me a sign, please. OK?*
Inner child	*Think about the inner, or younger, you that lives in your heart. What do you think your inner child might be feeling right now?*
Dyadic	*Mum,[a] if this had happened to you when you were young, what would you feel now?* *Mum, as you listen to and watch your child, what do you think your child is noticing and feeling inside right now?*

[a] Mum/Dad if both are present.

Table 9.4 Support to feel emotion

Dyadic	*You can feel everything right now, because you are here with your Mum [and Dad] and me, and we all care about you.* *I feel sad right now. Mum, do you feel sad too?* *Mum, what's going on in your heart right now?* *Mum, now that you know what happened to your child and now that we know how much you care about them, can you tell us how you feel at this point?* *Mum, what would you like your child to know right now about your determination to help them get better?*

Support to Dare to Feel Emotions

If the child's facial expression or body posture suggests that they are trying to avoid or suppress emotions, the dyadic interweaves in Table 9.4 can be considered. These are statements that invite parents to show non-verbal affection and compassion. The compassionate interweaves give the child the confidence to let their emotions come to the surface by helping them to experience the love and support of their parents.

Self-Regulation

Coaching children in mindful awareness and self-regulation helps them experience their feelings during EMDR without dissociating or shutting down. Dyadic interweaves emphasize that parents are knowledgeable and trusted caregivers. They can be used before a set of EM^+, or as a part of coaching, during a set. Examples of general and dyadic interweaves are given in Table 9.5.

Table 9.5 General and dyadic interweaves

General	*Don't forget that feeling these emotions helps you get better. You can have these feelings and still be okay.* *Feelings come and go like waves, washing up on the shore and then drifting back to the sea.*
Dyadic	*Mum, are you okay with your child having these feelings?* *Mum, what do you want your child to know about their feelings?* *You can have these feelings and feel also your parents' arms around your shoulders, supporting you.* *You can have these feelings and know that you are safe and will get through it, because your Mum is here with you.*

Shame and Self-Blame

A child who is preoccupied with shame may be overwhelmed and therefore mute and unable to express their feelings. The therapist needs to be emotionally attuned to the child's facial expressions and body posture to recognize when the child is feeling shame. Some children will ask 'Why did this happen?' This is their way of asking, 'What did I do wrong?' Dyadic interweaves provide an opportunity for parents to provide adaptive information and compassion that will help the child release the shame and feel closer to the parent. See the examples in Table 9.6.

Belonging, Being Loved, and Self-Esteem

An appropriate time for using the interweaves described in Table 9.7 is when feelings of alienation or worthlessness inhibit children. Dyadic and inner-child interweaves

Table 9.6 The inner child plus dyadic interweaves

Inner child	*Ask the child inside you 'why', and then tell me please what you hear from that child.*
Inner Child	*Is this question about why or what you did wrong coming from your big self or from the young child inside you? How can you respond to the questions of the young child inside you?*
Inner child/Dyadic	*Your inner child seems to blame themselves for what happened.*
Dyadic	*Mum, Dad, do you think your child is responsible for what happened?*
Dyadic	*What do you want the inner child to know about your child right now?*
Dyadic	*Mum/Dad, is there anything your child may have done that makes them deserve what happened?* *Mum/Dad, do bad things sometimes happen to good people?*

Table 9.7 Interweaves to overcome feelings of alienation and low self-esteem

Inner child (I)	*What would your big self say about this to your younger self inside?* *What does your big self want your younger self to know right now?* *What would you say to your younger brother or sister if this happened to them? Say this now to your younger self.* *What can you do for your little self, inside you right now?*
Inner child/Dyadic	*Mum, what do you want your child's inner child to know right now?* *Mum, what would you like to do right now for that little child?*
Dyadic	*Mum, what do you know to be true about your child?* *Mum, what would you want your child to know about your feelings for him or her right now?* *Mum, when you are angry, do you then no longer love your child?* *Mum, is there anything your child could do that would make you stop loving him/her?* *Mum, what characteristics of your child do you most enjoy?*
	Mum, I think the little one believes they are not good enough. Can you look at the little one through the eyes of the bigger child, and tell them how you feel about them?

help children address these feelings, which are rooted in attachment trauma in early childhood.

Empowerment

Children, by definition, are dependent on others for their development and unable to defend themselves. When adults process childhood trauma, they do so with one foot in adulthood and one foot in childhood. Through desensitization and reprocessing, adults can merge the child's perspective of powerlessness and helplessness with the current truth that they are now older, smarter, wiser, and have more resources at their disposal. When children process trauma, they have one foot in the past and one in the present, but both feet are still small and young. Empowerment interweaves help children connect their own feelings of strength with the feelings of safety and protection they get from the stronger adults in their lives. The interweaves in Table 9.8 are useful when a child is going round in circles or is stuck in feelings of helplessness or powerlessness during the desensitization phase. The therapist encourages the use of imagination and provides tangible materials, such as drawing supplies, a sandbox, and small toys or figures.

When children can trust their parents to protect and care for them, they are strengthened by this relationship. The dyadic interweave in Table 9.9 offers parents the opportunity to 'go back in time' and rescue the child using their imagination, thus creating a new, positive network of memories that includes feelings of security and protection.

The dyadic interweave shown in Table 9.10 provides another opportunity for parents to protect their child and support the child's ability to express themselves.

Table 9.8 Helping a child to feel protected

General	*Can you show me the image that is stuck in your mind using the drawing tools/sandbox and toys? Imagine that you could travel back in time to that day with a protector. Who would you want that protector to be and what would you want them to bring? Can you show in the drawing/sandbox how the protector would help? Now you get to change the image in the drawing/sandbox however you wish.* *[Wait for the child to think about these questions and respond.]* [......Child's response......] *Now you have permission to change the image in your mind.*

Table 9.9 Changing memories

Dyadic	*Mum, Dad, if you could travel back in a time machine to the time of that event, what would you have done?* *Some parents need additional guidance such as:* *What would you have done to protect the little one so this would not have happened?* *What would you do to nurture the little one?*

Table 9.10 Self expression

Dyadic	*Mum, Dad, if you could say something to the person that hurt your child, what would you say?* *This interweave can be enforced by saying to the child:* *With your parents standing beside you and protecting you, what would you like to say to that person today?*

Distinction Between Past and Present

Among other things, dissociative processes can give the child the impression that past traumatic experiences and the associated emotions and sensations are persistent and real. EMDR is an effective method for integrating adaptive information about current safety with stored memories from the past. However, dissociative processes are a hindrance during EMDR, leading children to become stuck in the past, experiencing traumatic events as if they are occurring today.

The therapist explains: 'Trauma is stored in a part of the brain that doesn't understand the passage of time, leaving children confused and anxious.' Concrete, practical interweaves using props can be very powerful (see the examples in Table 9.11).

Table 9.11 Using props

General	*Show the child a pair of shoes:* *This is how small your feet were when you went through this event. Let's compare the size of your feet, then and now.* *Show the child a ruler or hold your hand at a certain height:* *This is how small you were then. Stand up and let's see how big you are now.* *Draw a timeline on a piece of paper:* *Let's draw a line for each birthday. Then let's draw an arrow at the age that this happened. Then we will draw a second arrow at the age you are now.* *How is this mum different from your first mum?* *How is this home different from your first home?*
Dyadic	*Mum, Dad, how will you try to make sure that your child will never experience such unpleasant things again?*

Conclusion

Parental presence during EMDR and the use of dyadic parent–child interweaves to strengthen the parents' role as experts and caregivers further enhances the feelings of closeness of both parents and children. These types of cognitive interweaves promote self-awareness, emotion regulation, empowerment, and internalization of new, adaptive information.

Stress Regulation

10

RENÉE BEER AND CARLIJN DE ROOS

10.1 Introduction

Severe and prolonged traumatization can result in a chronically deregulated stress system. The consequences of experiencing potentially traumatic events are determined by various factors besides the nature and frequency of the events. EMDR therapists should be able to assess what stress management skills are needed to improve stress regulation in a child with a chronically deregulated stress system. These competencies enable therapists to ensure that children with deregulated stress systems can benefit optimally from EMDR.

The chapter is organized as follows: Section 10.2 explores the role of stress regulation in the context of trauma treatment and reviews various prevailing views on this issue. Section 10.3 provides insights into the terminology related to stress (regulation), the factors influencing the development of stress regulation skills, and the goals of interventions to improve these skills. Section 10.4 provides an overview of interventions and techniques for different treatment phases.

10.2 Stabilization Debate

This chapter focuses on children who are not covered by international treatment guidelines for PTSD because they cannot (yet) adequately handle the confrontation with their traumatic memories (Phelps et al., 2022). These children present a wide variety of problems—in addition to, or instead of, symptoms of PTSD—which are often unrecognized as trauma-related. Research among foster children has revealed that severely traumatized children who are placed in out-of-home facilities after being subjected to abusive parenting practices have a range of symptom profiles. The predominant symptoms were related to emotions, behaviour, peer relationships, attention, and hyperactivity (Jonkman et al., 2013). These symptom profiles meet the ICD-11 Criteria (World Health Organization, 2019) criteria for complex PTSD (CPTSD). However, CPTSD is not included in the DSM-5 (American Psychiatric Association, 2013). Chapter 2 of this book explains the reasons for this. Several researchers have since shown that the ICD-11 detects with this classification children who are traumatized multiple (by different types of events) and chronically (by a single type of events

Renée Beer and Carlijn de Roos, *Stress Regulation*. In: *Handbook of EMDR for Children and Adolescents*.
Edited by: Renée Beer and Carlijn de Roos, Oxford University Press. © 2026, Oxford University Press. For the English edition.
DOI: 10.1093/oso/9780198918400.003.0010

repeatedly) and have more functional limitations than children with PTSD alone (Brewin et al., 2017; Haselgruber et al., 2020; Sachser et al., 2017b). Some of these children do, and others do not, exhibit sufficient symptoms to qualify them for the classification of PTSD. They usually receive other classifications or diagnoses because they show other, more prominent symptoms. As a result, they are denied trauma therapy unfairly (Martin et al., 2021; Nestgaard Rød & Schmidt, 2021).

A consensus document of the International Society for Traumatic Stress Studies (Cloitre et al., 2012) and a guideline from the European Society for Trauma and Dissociation (Potgieter-Marks et al., 2015) recommend phase-based therapy, consisting of a stabilization phase, a trauma processing phase, and an integration phase. The first guideline applies to adults who struggle with dysregulation on multiple fronts (cognitive, emotional, physiological, neurobiological, behavioural, relational, and focused attention) in addition to PTSD, and the second to children with dissociative symptoms and dissociative disorders. There is an ongoing debate in the trauma field about the (un)desirability of a stabilization phase before trauma processing (Corrigan et al., 2020; De Jongh et al., 2016; Dyer & Corrigan, 2021). This debate centres around divergent views on what is possible versus what is necessary. Our view is that trauma treatment should always start as soon as possible, since this can reduce symptoms, alleviate suffering, and prevent further developmental stagnation and re-victimization. Research on adults has shown that direct trauma treatment (without a stabilization phase) is feasible, safe, and accepted (Oprel et al., 2021; Van Vliet et al., 2021). Additional research on children has to establish evidence-based criteria for determining if and when interventions before trauma processing are indicated. Future guidelines should define more precisely what needs to be achieved if a pre-trauma processing phase is implemented, as well as whether alternative or additional interventions are required. This phase is referred to as the stabilization phase because it intends to achieve psychosocial stabilization of the individual. We advocate for re-framing the term as 'preparatory phase' because in this phase, all interventions are aimed at preparing the individual for trauma processing[1] (see also the Preface of this book). The interventions listed for a preparatory phase focus on any of the following goals for the child: increasing the safety of their environment, improving emotion regulation skills (recognition and expression of emotions), increasing impulse control, strengthening the child's coping skills, strengthening parenting skills, mobilizing support figures, and expanding communication skills within the family (Blaustein & Kinniburgh, 2018; Cloitre et al., 2022; Cohen et al., 2016; Knipschild et al., 2023; Struik, 2019b). The intended psychosocial stabilization of the individual is achieved by trauma treatment and by working towards any of the goals mentioned above, which are considered relevant.

Future research will reveal which of these intentions are a prerequisite for trauma processing and for which groups of children additional interventions are needed to achieve readiness for trauma processing. The published literature and clinical experience regarding the requirements for trauma processing suggest that children need to be able and willing

[1] The preparatory phase is to be distinguished from the preparation phase (phase 2 standard protocol).

to turn their attention inward, have access to their emotions, and be able to dwell on them. To some degree, the child must also be capable of stress regulation, aided by acquired skills and knowledge. For the time being, we recommend following the treatment guidelines for PTSD and employing a preparatory phase based on the individual case conceptualization. Some children may quickly exceed the limits of their window of tolerance. They might not know how to return within the limits, either independently or with the help of others. In this chapter, we describe techniques for teaching these children to improve their stress regulation, enabling them to stay within or return to their window of tolerance. In doing so, we hope to fill the EMDR therapist's toolbox, making trauma therapy possible for a group of children who cannot begin or complete EMDR without these tools. See Chapter 12 for additional techniques and interventions to prepare the child and their family system for trauma processing.

Sometimes, the therapist must accept that the context for therapy cannot be made better than it is: 'good enough stability' (Kliethermes & Wamser, 2012). In these cases, the techniques discussed in this chapter mainly contribute to child empowerment by improving their stress regulation skills.

10.3 Stress

There are numerous misunderstandings about the term 'stress', like there are about 'trauma'. Several everyday terms related to stress and stress regulation are clarified below in Section 10.3.1.

10.3.1 Terminology

- ***Trauma and stress***

The term 'post-traumatic stress disorder' illustrates the close relationship between the concepts of 'stress' and 'trauma'. An event or situation that causes stress is a 'stressor', and the reaction is a 'stress response' or 'stress reaction'. Both the source of stress and the stress response are often mistakenly referred to as 'stress' (Van der Ploeg, 2013). Stress, like trauma, refers to an internal condition. Trauma means there is an internal psychological 'wound' due to directly or indirectly experiencing a traumatic event. Stress means that someone experiences overload due to a perceived imbalance between carrying capacity and carrying a burden (load); therefore, they feel off-balance, insecure, anxious, sad, or angry. This emotional state is accompanied by physical reactions, such as a stomachache, headache, or dizziness due to physiological dysregulation (Van der Ploeg, 2013). The physiological responses associated with stress, such as accelerated heart rate, increased blood pressure, pupil enlargement, tear production, sweating, and alertness, are referred to as states of 'arousal'. Stress and arousal are two overlapping terms that must be differentiated. Arousal refers to the physiological response to a stressor, whereas stress refers to the emotional state of being off-balance, combined with physiological dysregulation, occurring when arousal level is too high.

Perry explains the function of physiological responses to stress: 'Whereas the physiology of the arousal response is to optimize fight or flight, the physiology of dissociation is to help us rest, refuel, survive injury, and tolerate pain' (Perry & Winfrey, 2023).

Stressors range from mild to severe and include experiences other than just traumatic ones, often involving a child's ordinary life experiences, such as their parents splitting up, moving house, changing schools, and the death of a loved one. Traumatic experiences such as rape, almost drowning, and physical assault are examples of life-threatening stressors.

Stress can be perceived as negative (distress), but also as positive (eustress). The relationship between the degree of perceived stress and the quality of functioning or performance is distributed normally. A moderate level of stress is usually experienced as a challenge: at too low a level, the challenge is lacking, and at too high a level, the challenge becomes a threat, preventing one from performing well. Toxic stress refers to chronic stress that emotionally impacts children to the extent that their brain development is hindered (Holman, 2018).

Appraisal and coping

In response to stress, strategies are utilized to maintain or restore balance (*coping*). The choice of a strategy is preceded by an assessment process called 'appraisal' by Lazarus (1993). An appraisal assesses the situation (How dangerous is it?) and one's (in)ability to tackle the situation (What can I do? How competent am I?). A young child looks at the facial expression of their parent or attachment figure to appraise an unfamiliar situation, using 'social referencing' to assess whether a situation is dangerous (Aktar et al., 2013). If the person the child depends on for social referencing looks frightened or startled, the child infers that the situation is dangerous and they will seek protection. In contrast, if the attachment person's facial expression is reassuring, the child will explore the situation. As children age, they gain the ability to assess situations themselves.

Coping is the application of cognitive and behavioural strategies to control the emotions, cognitions, and behaviours resulting from stressful events or situations (stressors). Children learn coping skills primarily in their families. They will better cope with stress and become more resilient as they develop and gain more adequate coping strategies.

Resilience

Resilience is another important concept related to stress. It refers to the ability to overcome problems and recover from setbacks. There are several definitions of resilience, and it is the subject of much research (Brom et al., 2009; Masten & Barnes, 2018). It is of great benefit to children that we seek ways to promote resilience, to make them more resilient to stressors, help them develop fewer symptoms, treat symptoms, and promote mental health in general (Zolkoski et al., 2012; Chmitorz et al., 2018). Layne and colleagues (2009, p. 30) define resilience as 'The capacity to initiate previously applied, effective adaptive processes to reduce tension, which has arisen as a result of exposure to stressors, and thereby efficiently restore balance or adaptive functioning within a given psychosocial area, following a temporary disturbance'. Resilience can be understood as the ability to adopt adequate coping strategies to reduce distress. How does resilience develop? Several studies have shown that it has a biological basis and develops through an interactive process between predisposition and the environment (Brom et al., 2009; Van der Ploeg, 2013).

10.3.2 Stress Regulation

Stress regulation refers to the ability to regulate the level of stress in such a way that behavioural or emotional problems do not occur. Stress regulation and resilience result from interactive processes between various factors, which therapists should examine during the diagnostic phase.

- ***Predisposing factors***
  - **(Neuro)biology**

The degree of emotional sensitivity to stressors varies among children; some are affected much more quickly than others. The stress response results from several interacting processes in the nervous system and the brain. Hormones and neurotransmitters (cortisol, adrenaline, noradrenaline) communicate signals and activate neurological networks. Three systems are involved: (1) the limbic system (amygdala, hippocampus, and hypothalamus), which controls emotions and detects danger; (2) the hypothalamic-pituitary-adrenal (HPA) axis, which helps us respond appropriately to stress or danger by releasing adrenaline when danger is imminent and cortisol when the threat has passed; (3) the prefrontal cortex, which controls cognitive processes (Van der Ploeg, 2013). People with stress-related mental health issues often have a dysregulated HPA axis, resulting in decreased cortisol production, which explains the prolonged alarm response typical of PTSD (Rothschild, 2000).

Neurotransmitters and hormones are not measured in the regular diagnostic phase. Nonetheless, the therapist can explore how a child copes with stress through questions and validated instruments (if available in the therapist's country).

- ***Environmental factors***
  - **Adverse life experiences**

There is a chance that the stress system will become chronically deregulated when a child faces many stressors due to adverse or traumatic experiences, especially with high frequency over a long period. The stress system no longer recovers but remains in a permanent alarm state. The child may then react with permanent hyperarousal or an opposite state of deregulation: The child seems untouchable and numb, no longer recognizes danger, and no longer makes efforts to evade danger by bringing themselves to safety (Knipschild et al., 2024). Consequently, it is relevant that therapists, during the diagnostic phase, explore the events the child has experienced and how the child reacted to them.

- **Attachment patterns**

In the context of assessing (disrupted) stress regulation, it is helpful for the therapist also to evaluate the type of attachment pattern present (De Wolff et al., 2015; Naveed et al., 2020):

- Secure attachment: the parent is sufficiently responsive to the child.

- Insecure attachment: the parent is insufficiently responsive to the child.
    - Ambivalent/Resistant: parental behavioural response is unpredictable.
    - Anxious/Avoidant: parental behaviour is consistently insensitive, so the child stops seeking support and appealing to the parent out of fear of rejection.
- Disorganized: parents are a source of threat by frightening the child due to incomprehensible and unpredictable behaviour; no clear attachment pattern forms; the child seems confused when the parent approaches and exhibits contradictory behaviour and emotions.

Attachment patterns merit attention during the diagnostic phase because they indicate the extent to which the child will be capable of stress regulation independently or with the help of the parent/caregiver. The *Guideline on Problematic Attachment* (De Wolff et al., 2015) describes the relationship between parent/child attachment and stress regulation:

> When a child has established a secure attachment relationship, the child's stress and anxiety are 'buffered' by the parent or caregiver, so the child is not overwhelmed by their own emotions. Children with attachment problems experience continuous stress and helplessness, which is not 'buffered' by a secure attachment figure, as happens with securely attached children.

- **Parenting styles**

Parenting styles influence attachment patterns. Therefore, observing and evaluating the parenting style in the diagnostic phase makes sense. Three styles can be differentiated: sensitive, overreacting, and neglecting.

Children whose parents respond sensitively and appropriately to their needs learn to experience their environment as safe and secure. Such parenting styles encourage the child to express their needs for warmth, food, drink, nurturing, and the like, trusting that the parent will try to meet them. Children learn that if they find themselves outside the limits of their 'window of tolerance', the parents' responses will guide them back within those limits. This parenting style is usually accompanied by secure attachment.

In contrast, parents with an overreacting parenting style show and teach their children that if they become aroused, their parents will also become aroused. The parent overreacts and over-controls in response to the child's behaviour (if the child expresses worries about being bullied, the parent threatens to beat up those children to defend their child). The stress reaction of the parent keeps the child outside their window of tolerance, if they have already arrived there, and may even push them further away. Parents and children reinforce each other's reactions, being trapped in a negative spiral. As a result, the child does not learn to perceive the environment as safe and will not communicate their need for reassurance or to be soothed by the parent. Children can calm themselves down only if they have learned to do this from (calm) parents or others.

Parents with a neglectful parenting style often do not respond to their children's needs because they are either not sensitive to them or they notice them but do not know how to respond. These parents usually need all their attention and energy to regulate their own stress levels, leaving the child's needs unmet.

In summary, predispositional and environmental factors combined determine how a child learns to regulate stress. Children acquire this skill primarily from their parents and significant others. Children of parents with overreacting or neglectful parenting styles lack examples of how to calm down when stressed. As a result, their stress response system becomes permanently overturned like an overly sensitive thermostat: even the slightest stimulus provokes a fight-or-flight reaction; their *window of tolerance* is small.

10.3.3 Goals

Stress regulation techniques have specific indications and goals; they can be relevant at each stage of phase-based trauma treatment (preparatory phase, trauma processing phase, and integration phase).

Since the preparatory phase aims to facilitate trauma processing, interventions in this phase serve to enhance the child's sense of self-efficacy. This can be achieved by improving their stress regulation. Increased self-efficacy helps to reduce the child's and the family members' fears that the child will respond to stress by damaging themselves (auto-mutilation) or others.

Children who have never learned to deal with emotions (feeling, knowing, acknowledging, recognizing, and expressing them) should be differentiated from children who have learned this but have deliberately closed off access to their emotions because they fear being overwhelmed. Both groups can benefit from interventions that help them identify and tolerate emotions, which prepare them for trauma processing.

The goal of stress regulation techniques in the trauma processing phase is to facilitate EMDR and reduce the risk of blocked processing because the child is dissociating, decompensating, or stopping the treatment prematurely.

Finally, since the integration phase aims to implement new behaviour, the techniques used in this phase teach how to adequately handle the (eventual) associated in daily practice stress. We omit a presentation of methods for this phase as that is beyond the scope of this book. EMDR focuses on the middle phase and prepares for daily practice only by imagination in the third prong.

10.4 Interventions and Techniques

This section provides an overview of interventions and techniques for the preparatory phase, before the start of EMDR (Section 10.4.1) and for the trauma processing phase, during EMDR (Section 10.4.2). When discussing the treatment plan, we recommend clarifying to children and their parents that trauma processing will ultimately result in reduced stress levels, even if the stress level may temporarily rise during treatment.

10.4.1 Interventions for the Preparatory Phase

There are no empirically validated criteria for the prerequisites of trauma processing. Based on the information in Section 10.3, a key criterion could be that the child is capable of stress regulation with the support of parents, other members of their social network, or

Table 10.1 Questions to determine if interventions are needed before trauma processing (preparatory phase)

Categories	Questions
Family	Can parents provide adequate security for the child? Can parents provide sufficient structure to the family?
Social	Does the child have potential support figures outside of the family? Is the child able to ask for emotional support from others?
Individual	Can the child self-soothe when distressed?

independently. This section gives an overview of questions that therapists can ask themselves when unsure if a direct start of trauma processing is possible. Three categories appear to be relevant: (1) family functioning, (2) social functioning of the child outside of the family, and (3) individual functioning of the child. See Table 10.1.

One or two 'key questions' are proposed for each category. If these cannot be answered 'positively enough', interventions could be considered to prepare the child for EMDR. The goals for these interventions are formulated preferably in 'SMART'[2] terms. To ensure readiness for a rapid start of EMDR and to optimize efficiency, the therapist should describe explicitly in the case conceptualization (a) which must be enhanced, (b) for what reason and (c) how many sessions will be reserved to achieve this.

- ***1. Family functioning***
  - *Clarification of the questions (Table 10.1)*

Parents should (be able to) take responsibility for a sufficiently structured family environment, providing safety, and protecting children from harm. If there is a history of violence or neglect in the family, parents should acknowledge their actions and be able to guarantee that this danger has passed. They should also be able to coach their child in stress regulation.

- *Interventions*

Several interventions qualify for increasing safety, improving the family environment, or enhancing parenting skills, thereby promoting adequate structure. They have been tested to different degrees. Information about these programmes can be found on relevant country-specific websites. For example, Signs of Safety (SoS, Turnell & Edwards, 1999); Parent-Child Interaction Training (PCIT; Abrahamse et al., 2012; Eyberg et al., 2008); Parent Management Training Oregon (PMTO: https://www.generationpmto.org); and Functional Family Therapy (FFT: Alexander et al., 2000).

Inpatient treatment in a family psychiatric setting is indicated when parents cannot (yet) take responsibility for creating a safe climate after prior abuse or severe neglect, but are willing to learn the needed skills. In this treatment setting, the family is admitted, and the

[2] Requirements for 'SMART' goal formulation: Specific, Measurable, Achievable, Relevant, and Time-Bound (Bowman et al., 2015).

parents learn to enhance safety for their children. They also acquire pedagogical (and other) skills to establish a daily routine and address psychosocial problems. If parents are not willing to participate in such therapy, out-of-home placement of the child should be considered.

- ***2. Social functioning outside the family***
  - *Clarification of the questions (Table 10.1)*:

People in the immediate environment should be available for the child to turn to for emotional support during trauma processing. If this cannot be the parents or other family members, then extended family members, peers, or other adults should be able to step in. The child should have the required skills to seek support from others.

  - *Interventions*

If there are no support figures, the child should get help to expand a social safety net. In addition, interventions aimed at strengthening social and problem-solving skills are suitable. Numerous interventions based on cognitive and learning-theoretical principles and methods have been developed and experimentally tested. These can be found through relevant websites, such as

https://www.twinkl.nl/resource/resource-pack-social-skills-interventions-t-p-2490 and https://childdevelopment.com.au/areas-of-concern/play-and-social-skills/social-skills/.

- ***3. Functioning of the child individually***
  - *Clarification of the question (Table 10.1)*:

The child should be able to calm themselves and manage their stress sufficiently to respect agreements about stopping (self-)damaging behaviour during the treatment period., .

  - *Interventions*

Severely traumatized children with severe behavioural problems who do not yet have access to their traumatic memories, refuse to confront them, or have insufficient stress regulation skills, may lack motivation or show resistance to therapy. Several programmes are available to help these children become motivated; these programmes have been empirically tested to varying degrees. Examples include MASTR protocol (Greenwald, 2013b); STAIR-A (Cloitre et al., 2022; Knipschild et al., 2023); Attachment, Self-Regulation, and Competencies (Blaustein & Kinniburgh, 2015); and the Sleeping Dogs method (Struik, 2019b; see also Chapter 12 of this book).

10.4.2 Techniques for the Trauma Processing Phase

This subsection discusses techniques to consider when distress is imminent or present during EMDR. These child-friendly 'EMDR-related'[3] techniques either ease confrontation with relevant memories (in the assessment phase) or prevent/stop blocked processing (in the desensitization phase). Some empower the child by activating positive memory networks, while others do so by reducing fear or stress. All interventions widen the child's 'window of

[3] EMDR-related' because also appealing to memory networks or BLS/WMT

tolerance'. Some are optional for different phases. Several of them can also be used at home to shield the child against disturbing mental representations, help them handle daily situations, or make them feel better. All of them serve as extra tools in the therapist's toolbox if the regular procedure does not suffice. Table 10.2 provides an overview and indicates in which treatment phase they are applicable.

The line between the first and second columns is broken because the techniques listed in the first column can also be used during the preparation phase. A guiding principle for optimal EMDR results is that once the assessment of a specific memory has begun (phase 3), the process should preferably not be interrupted by additional interventions. For each intervention, we describe the indication, goal, and procedure.

- ***During organizing memories (phase 1)***

If the child experiences excessive stress (distress) at the start of EMDR treatment, the following interventions can be considered to enhance self-efficacy and empowerment. Some of these techniques also enhance the ability to handle specific daily situations.

Table 10.2 EMDR-related techniques during EMDR indications and *goals*

During sorting memories	During preparation or start assessment	During desensitization
DISTANCING (wall, framing, container) Fear of being overwhelmed by memory representations > *sense of mastery*	**FLASHFORWARD** Fear for what might happen to them during EMDR > *stress reduction*	**EXTRA WMT** (Imminent) distress > *stress-reduction, keep processing*
RDI Insufficient self-efficacy or support for specific daily situations> *empowerment*	**RDI** Insufficient self-efficacy to cope with EMDR > *empowerment*	**INSTALLED RESOURCE** (Imminent) blocking > *empowerment, prevent blocking*
OTHER RESOURCES Insufficient self-efficacy or support for specific situations > *empowerment, support*	**POSITIVE PLACE** Distress > *stress-reduction, comfort*	**RESISTANCE AS TARGET** Actual (complete) blocking > *resolve blocking*
	CIPOS Fear of being overwhelmed by memory obstructs assessment > *sense of mastery*	**INTERWEAVES** Looping > *resolve looping*
	ANTICIPATE DISSOCIATION Dissociative reactions are expected > *enhance self-efficacy*	**DEALING WITH DISSOCIATION** *Dissociative reactions* > *stress-reduction, keep processing*

- *Distancing Techniques*

Three distancing techniques are mentioned that may increase the child's sense of self-control, allowing them to stay receptive to their feelings and continue EMDR. These techniques can be implemented during the arrangement of memories (phase 1) and during the preparation phase (phase 2). They can also help the child deal better with identified challenging daily situations.

- *The Wall*

Indication: The wall is helpful for children who have been traumatized by interpersonal violence, like being bullied by children or assaulted by adults for a long time, making them feel unsafe and anxious when confronted with memories of this aggression, and also in daily life when being around other children or adults (Greenwald, 2013b).

Goal: To increase the child's sense of safety (control) so that they can continue (1) to confront the memories, (2) to process without blocking, and (3) to cope better in daily life without avoidance behaviour.

Procedure:

1. The therapist asks the child to imagine a wall between themself and the target image.
2. The therapist then zooms in on the wall by asking questions about it, such as what kind of material it is made of, how high it is, how thick it is, how hard it is, what they want to add to the wall so that no one from the other side can reach them, and what else is needed to help them feel safe on their side of the wall.
3. The therapist asks the child to draw the wall if that seems helpful. The raising and lowering of the wall is practiced a few times during the session: '*Now think of this situation where the wall could help you and where you can raise the wall whenever and how you want. When the wall has done its job, and you feel better, you can lower it again ...*'
4. The therapist recommends that the child practice raising and lowering this wall at home three times a day so that they learn to use it whenever needed. The child can apply this technique in everyday life. It is essential to check that the wall works for the child. If it does not, the therapist asks the child how to make it work.

Figure 10.1 shows a drawing of a wall.

- *Framing*

Indication: Framing is an option when intrusive images trouble the child. Dagmar Eckers (2010), a C&A EMDR trainer from Germany, developed this technique based on a notion from hypnotherapy: 'Paying more attention to the frame accompanies the disappearance of the picture's content and meaning'.

Goal: To give the child a sense of mastery by teaching the ability to manipulate troubling images. This will help the child increase the distance between memories and the here-and-now.

Procedure: The therapist has several blank sheets with frames of different sizes, drawn on it. The therapist explains the purpose of the intervention: '*I'm going to teach you how to control the nasty pictures in your head. I will show you how to make them smaller so they do not get in your way so much.*'

Figure 10.1 Drawing of a wall by an 8-year-old girl.

1. The therapist asks the child to describe the worst picture of the annoying situation and then to project it on an A4-sized blank sheet with a frame, which the therapist holds in front of the child as if it were a screen.
2. *'Look here—I have a sheet of paper. When I come closer to you with the sheet* [approach the child slowly from some distance], *you say: Stop! when you can see the picture in the frame, okay?' Stop at the distance where the child says stop and stay there.*
3. *'When you see the picture in the frame, how disturbing does it feel now between 0 and 10, when 0 means "no disturbance at all" and 10 "the worst you can imagine"?'*
4. The therapist holds a sheet with a smaller frame and has the child project the same image onto it.
5. The therapist repeats this until the child can no longer project the picture into the frame because it has become too small (after about five repetitions). The therapist asks every time: '*Can you still see the picture within the frame?*'
6. If no: *'You have made the picture very tiny. If you can put that tiny picture in a place where it can stay locked away, what would you favour—a box, a bag, or anything else?'* The older child can think of an imaginary box/bag. Younger children may prefer tangible objects they can choose from, like a metal or wooden box.

7. *'Now put it there! And where do you want to place this …* [whatever the child has chosen]? *Perhaps into a safety box that only you can open?'* The child might want to draw a picture of the safety box.
8. When the picture is locked away: *'Now you know that the nasty picture is in a safety box, how disturbing does it feel from 0–10?'*
9. The therapist explains to the child that they can do the same at home between sessions when bothered by distressing mental images: *'You did very well with this nasty picture. Let us see how you get along with your picture next week. You can do the same with other nasty images in your head.'*

The paper's size can also be used as a frame instead of drawn frames on the sheet. The sheet is then double-folded each time.

- *Container*

Indication: The container metaphor can be helpful when negative feelings, sensations, or thoughts have been activated by sorting the memories or later phases. The therapist can use this metaphor to help the child to 'leave behind' in the therapy room everything they do not want to think of at home. The container is beneficial at the closure of any EMDR session in which many negative associations or feelings have surfaced.

Goal: To highlight the child's sense of staying in control. This metaphor enables the child to feel calm when they leave the office, be confident they can continue next time, and not get overwhelmed by mental representations between sessions. Greenwald (2013b) has described this metaphor.

Procedure: The therapist asks questions like 'What does the container look like? What kind of material is it made of? How can you lock it? Who keeps the key? Where should we place it …?'

Figure 10.2 shows the drawing of a container.

Figure 10.2 Drawing of a container by a 7-year-old.

– *Resource Development and Installation (RDI)*

RDI is a protocolized intervention (Korn & Leeds, 2002) that aims to increase emotional self-regulation, adaptive behaviour, and a sense of mastery by providing tools for changing affect states (Shapiro, 2018).

Indication: This intervention can be considered when the therapist assumes the child may need activated (installed) resources during desensitization or in identified specific daily life situations.

Goal: To prevent blocking in EMDR or to improve coping with specific daily life situations by use of resources.

Procedure: Relevant traits, such as self-confidence, courage, or perseverance, are activated using positive memory networks. The child learns to recall the mobilized and installed resource with an anchor (hand gesture). A C&A version of the RDI protocol has been developed. The modifications pertain to the formulation of the questions, the potential addition of fantasy figures, and parents' commitment. If the child cannot recall a specific event where they successfully utilized the selected trait, they may choose fantasy figures or role models with the required qualities or skills (Adler-Tapia & Settle, 2008). See www.emdrchildandyouth.info for a C&A version of the RDI protocol.

– *Other resources*

Indication: For some children, the RDI protocol is not empowering enough, or the steps are too abstract. In these cases, alternative, more concrete resources are required.

Goal: To introduce helpful concrete resources, including objects or persons, that evoke positive physical sensations and feelings in the child, helping them feel competent to cope better with an identified problematic situation (stressor).

Procedure: They can bring a support figure (parents, role model) or an object (doll, cuddly toy, stress ball, stone, mascot) in fantasy or reality to the session —a so-called 'transitional object'. Another option is brainstorming together to find helpful phrases (positive phrases such as 'I am confident', or 'People like me', or 'I am smart') written on a card, which they carry with them.

- ***During preparation or start assessment (phase 2 or start 3)***

– *Flashforward*

Indication: If during the preparation phase (phase 2) the child shows or expresses fear of what might happen to them during and due to EMDR treatment.

Goal: For the child to calm down by realizing that only their fantasy induces this fear ('It is just my imagination').

Procedure: The therapist asks for the worst disaster fantasy: '*What is the worst thing that could happen if you engage in EMDR?*'; '*What is the nastiest image in your mind of what would happen in the worst-case scenario*?'

If a child has expressed fear of feeling an emotion: '*What is the worst thing that could happen if you would feel/ angry/sad/desperate/afraid* [whatever is applicable]?'

Once the flashforward has been identified, this target can be treated using the standard protocol; see Appendix I in the standard protocol

- *RDI*

Indication: If, during the preparation phase, the child expresses doubts about being able to cope with something they expect to happen during and due to the EMDR process.

Goal: For the child to get self-confidence that they will be able to cope with what they expect.

Procedure: See RDI protocol-C&A version.

- *Positive/safe place*

In 'the positive place'—often called 'the safe place'—the therapist asks the child to imagine a place that brings positive feelings and associations, whether it is real or imaginary. Sadly, many children around the world do not have a 'safe place', but instead they should have a 'positive place' that evokes happy and comforting feelings. Every child should have access to a 'positive place', which is why we prefer this term.

Indication: This intervention can be helpful for children who are reluctant to work with their traumatic memories, because they have a lot of negative intrusive symptoms.

Goal: To give the child a tool that helps them feel better.

Procedure: The therapist invites the child to draw their positive place when they expect that the child cannot imagine this without a drawing or when positive associations and feelings are most powerfully evoked with a drawing. Next, the therapist draws attention to this place by asking the child questions that engage their senses: *'What do you see? What sounds do you hear? What does it smell like? What do you feel? Where do you sense that most strongly?'*

The therapist then encourages the child to let positive associations arise through concentration and imagination. The positive place is introduced as an intervention that the child can apply at home to calm themselves when bothered by disturbing images or feelings caused by mental representations.

- *Constant Installation of Present Orientation and Safety*

Knipe (2010) developed the Constant Installation of Present Orientation and Safety (CIPOS) protocol, which Eckers (2010) adapted for children.

Indication: This protocol can be used when the child has an intense fear of being confronted with their memories and is vulnerable to responding with blocking or dissociative reactions, or if this fierce fear is related to a specific memory (which makes the assessment phase for this memory impossible).

Goal: To enable a child to remain within—or return to—their 'window of tolerance' during the assessment phase, with dual attention: 'one foot in the past and one foot in the present'.

Procedure: To achieve this, the therapist arranges gradual exposure to an image of a highly intrusive and distressing memory of a past event that evokes negative feelings, alternating this with orienting the child to the present safety and evoking positive feelings. The child's attention is drawn to seeing positive images (such as what they can see in the room that they like, the drawing of their positive place), an activity (like tossing something back and forth), or answering questions (such as 'How many pens do you see?', 'What is blue in this room?', 'What is good about being here?'). The child learns to tolerate the image of a negative memory through repeated exposure, experiencing a decrease in distress (evoking a *sense of mastery*). The therapist explains the procedure and then follows three steps:

1. Establish a baseline response to an image of a memory with a negative affective load.
2. Direct attention to the present situation and safety, evoking positive feelings and sensations.
3. Alternate steps 1 and 2 until the child can confront the negative image; at this point, the assessment phase can be started or continued.

Three rounds of these steps are usually sufficient. See the www.emdrchildandyouth.info for more detailed information.

- *Anticipating potential dissociative reactions*

Indication: When it is expected that dissociative reactions may occur during desensitization, based on the information gathered during the diagnostic phase, the therapist explains dissociation and agrees with the child on how they will handle this when it occurs.

Goal: For the child and the therapist to know how to move on if processing gets stuck.

Procedure: The essential intervention is to reconnect with the child and increase awareness of the distinction between 'here and now' and 'then and there' (i.e., the activated memory of the past situation). This distinction can be emphasized by asking questions (taxing working memory), by touching (if allowed and agreed upon beforehand), or by requiring motor activity (engaging the prefrontal cortex). All potential interventions aim to refocus on the here and now.

- ***During desensitization (phase 4)***
  - *Extra WMT*

Indication: The therapist assumes or observes (imminent) distress in the child.

Goal: To keep the child within the window of tolerance.

Procedure: The most effective stress regulation technique during desensitization is to continue and increase WMT, so the child remains focused on the BLS/WMT and does not shut off from the inner process nor gets stuck in a state of *mindless emoting* (i.e., immersion in emotional experience with little self-reflection, Chamberlin (2019)). Guiding the child through 'the tunnel' as quickly as possible with dual attention is the most effective way to keep moving forward (see Chapter 7 for the metaphor explaining what happens during desensitization).

- *Implementation of installed resources*

Indication: Blocking is imminent (or is happening) because the child exceeds the upper or lower limit of their window of tolerance and, therefore, shuts off from the process.

Goal: To keep the child in the process of processing or return to it.

Procedure: The therapist's first option is to implement installed resources: for example, '*Take your self-confidence* [or other installed trait] *with you … Have you got that? Now continue …*' In addition, the presence of a parent (or a pet) can be a calming or empowering resource for children. Besides support figures, support objects can also be helpful.

– *Resistance as a target*

Indication: The child experiences the urge (wish) to avoid continued processing and actively blocks the process. This emotional state can be conceived as a target (Knipe, 2009).

Goal: To get the child back on track and move on (i.e., solve ambivalence and reduce resistance).

Procedure: The therapist asks, '*What's good about stopping/avoiding continuation*?' Next, the therapist asks the child to indicate the felt level of urge to avoid on a scale from 0–10 and where in the body this is felt, '*Where in your body do you feel that the strongest*?' Subsequently, sets with BLS/WMT are added. This way, the therapist invites the child to mentalize and verbalize their ambivalent feelings and motives. After several sets, the urge (wish) to avoid will be reduced as information processing always moves towards adaptive resolution. When the urge has been reduced to around 3 (Knipe, 2009, p. 55), adaptive reprocessing can follow by continuing the desensitization phase, which is usually enlightening for children who can do this. The therapist can implement this intervention if it seems useful and understandable for the child.

– *Interweaves*

Indication: Looping.
Goal: To resolve looping.
Procedure: Chapter 9 discusses various types of interweaves.

– *Dealing with dissociation*

Indication: Dissociation is imminent or present.
Goal: Reduction of distress so processing can continue.
Procedure: When dissociation happens (signals are observed, such as numbness, staring, frozen body posture), the therapist gives reassuring comments: '*You are not there anymore; you are here with me; nothing can happen here; you are safe now.*'

The therapist must stay calm: '*Just notice what you feel or that you feel nothing maybe … That is okay … This is a normal reaction to what was happening to you then. Just notice and follow what comes up now.*'

When the therapist loses contact with the child entirely: '*I notice that you do not react to what I am saying … Take the time you need, and let me know when we can continue.*'

The prefrontal cortex can be engaged by asking the child to stand up, hold their hands (if touching is allowed), or allow them to hold yours and continue standing. The intervention continues until the child fully realizes they are no longer in that past situation. Then, desensitization can continue.

Altogether, several auxiliary interventions are possible in different treatment phases. The common goal is to prevent (or stop) blocked processing by increasing the child's self-confidence in working with mental representations of traumatic experiences. These interventions empower or calm the child by activating positive networks, reducing anxiety, and increasing self-control.

10.5 Concluding Remarks

This chapter reviews various interventions for improving stress regulation before or during EMDR. These interventions expand the therapist's toolkit. Therapists with a well-stocked toolbox are better prepared to work with severely deregulated children who have limited stress regulation skills. Developing competence in stress regulation is empowering for children. This empowerment helps increase the success rate of EMDR and enhances the child's resilience.

Group Protocols 11

RENÉE BEER AND CARLIJN DE ROOS

11.1 Introduction

EMDR is an individual-oriented therapy. However, since 1997 group protocols have been developed to address situations that affect masses of children and adults, with insufficient numbers of mental health workers available to meet the resulting needs. This gap was the rationale for developing group protocols designed to enable mental health workers to alleviate the distress among multiple individuals simultaneously. Over time, several group protocols have been empirically evaluated to varying extents. Robinson and Kaptan (2024) edited a handbook on EMDR group therapy intended to be used in regular EMDR training programmes to give information about group protocols supplementary to the standard protocol. Kaptan and colleagues (2021) conducted a systematic review involving 22 randomized and non-randomized trials (n = 1.739 people) focusing on EMDR group interventions. Both publications were primary resources for building this chapter. Trauma treatment can be complex and complicated. Harm can be done if the treatment is applied inadequately (Robinson & Kaptan, 2024, p. 17). Some group protocols require fully trained EMDR therapists as providers because trauma material is addressed directly; other protocols do not because trauma memories are not activated directly.

Group protocols can be considered in the following situations, as large populations are being affected.

Pandemics, like COVID-19, affect people worldwide. COVID-19 caused developmental delays and social isolation in children due to lost schooling and reduced opportunities for psychosocial growth. A systematic review assessing the mental health impact of COVID-19 indicated an increase in depressive and anxious symptoms, a high prevalence of COVID-19-related fears, and a decline in mental health among children and adolescents resulting from the pandemic control measures (Samji et al., 2022). Furthermore, natural and man-made disasters often lead to environmental losses, loss (death) of loved ones, displacement of families, property damage, and physical injuries (Robinson & Kaptan, 2024). These and additional consequences of direct and indirect exposure to traumatic events may cause PTSD or other trauma-related conditions, like depression, anxiety, (traumatic) grief, conduct disorder, and substance misuse, in thousands of adults and children. In war-affected countries, these effects are aggravated by ongoing threats and parental psychopathology during and after the war (Bürgin et al., 2022).

Renée Beer and Carlijn de Roos, *Group Protocols*. In: *Handbook of EMDR for Children and Adolescents*.
Edited by: Renée Beer and Carlijn de Roos, Oxford University Press. © 2026, Oxford University Press. For the English edition.
DOI: 10.1093/oso/9780198918400.003.0011

Several barriers to delivering interventions to the affected population can be identified. Natural disasters often strike countries with underdeveloped mental health services, leaving the available mental health workers feeling overwhelmed and powerless to meet the high demand. In addition to operational issues, insufficient emergency workers are available for the number of affected people in these situations. In war-affected countries, various additional barriers hinder the provision and receipt of assistance for mental health problems, alongside the quantitative gap (Danese et al., 2024). These barriers include structural obstacles, such as disruption of infrastructures (transport systems, family networks, and support systems); cultural barriers, like fear of being stigmatized when seeking psychological help; and psychological barriers, such as avoidance of engaging with mental health services due to feelings of shame, guilt, or distrust towards adults.

As a potential solution to help overcome some of these key barriers, many digital mental health interventions have emerged. However, there are also limitations to consider in these interventions' development and implementation phases. Because the World Psychiatry Association's Commission on the Future of Psychiatry has designated digital psychiatry a key priority for improving global mental health in the next decade, Danese and colleagues (2024) conducted a scoping review, mapping and analysing the evidence base of available digital, individual- and group-oriented interventions for children and adolescents affected by war. This review revealed that the evidence base for these interventions is only minimal (Danese et al., 2024). Digital EMDR applications for individuals and groups have made significant advancements since the onset of COVID-19. While preliminary evidence supports its efficacy for both children and adults (Karadag et al., 2021; Lenferink et al., 2020; Perri et al., 2021; Streichuk et al., 2023), further robust research is necessary to determine its effectiveness and identify specific considerations for the optimal implementation of digital EMDR (and other interventions) for children and adolescents.

Several systematic reviews and meta-analyses have evaluated the effectiveness of various non-digital, individual- or group-oriented psychosocial interventions, revealing that EMDR and group interventions are effective in these situations. Brown and colleagues (2017) found that psychosocial interventions, including EMDR, for children affected by man-made and natural disasters yielded similar effect sizes regardless of the type of disaster. The conclusion was that group treatments could be cost effective, as they seem to yield similar effect sizes in fewer sessions than individual treatments with more sessions. Considering the growing number of minor refugees, short-term treatments reaching many children and adolescents simultaneously could be beneficial. Davis and colleagues (2023), in a systematic review and meta-analysis of 42 studies ($n = 5.998$) describing group-based interventions (EMDR not included), concluded that group interventions were effective in reducing PTSD. These interventions were delivered in highly complex and resource-scarce settings to children and adolescents exposed to war/conflict, natural disasters, or abuse. However, given the high prevalence of depression and anxiety in this population, Pfefferbaum and colleagues (2019) suggest, based on their findings in a meta-analysis of studies examining youth mass trauma intervention effects on depression and anxiety relative to natural recovery, that trauma-focused interventions may need to be supplemented with specific components addressing depression and/or anxiety. Relevant in this respect are the findings of Xie and colleagues

(2024) who, in a network meta-analysis of various psychological interventions provided to children and adolescents following exposure to natural or man-made disasters, encompassing 26 studies (n = 4.331), including EMDR, concluded that EMDR most effectively reduced PTSD and depression. In Chapter 2 of this book, it was clarified that untreated PTSD in youth is a risk factor for developing adult psychopathology. Thus, based on the findings of these studies, it seems reasonable to consider implementing evidence-based EMDR group interventions in these situations.

Shapiro (2014) emphasized the urgency of providing EMDR after both natural and man-made disasters all over the world. She stated that 'unprocessed memories have contributed to generations of ongoing violence fueled by distrust, anger, pain, fear, and hypervigilance inherent in traumatization. Intergenerational effects include a lack of bonding and disrupted attachment due to the anger, depression, anxiety, and fear associated with the disorder.' (Shapiro, 2014, p. 184). In response to this appeal, many nonprofit EMDR humanitarian assistance programmes have been established in the US and European countries (now called 'trauma aid') to offer pro bono services to people suffering from trauma following these disasters. EMDR clinicians have travelled to affected countries not only to provide EMDR therapy but also to offer and develop other interventions as required.

Carrière (2014) advocated launching an ambitious global trauma-therapy plan, stating that

> EMDR offers a potentially scalable intervention that combines effectiveness, efficiency, affordability, and acceptability—essential preconditions. It has the potential to transform trauma *from* a lifelong destructive burden, as it is for most victims, *into* a transitory, treatable affliction in conflict zones and 'normal' everyday settings. Given their enormous magnitude and devastating consequences, traumas should be regarded as a mental health challenge we now resolve to take on as a top priority ... Addressing it would greatly benefit the millions who suffer from mental health issues. (Carrière, 2014, p. 193)

This handbook would be incomplete without a chapter on group protocols that differentiates between EMDR protocols, which should be provided by trained EMDR therapists (because traumatic memories are activated), versus EMDR-derived interventions, which (para)professionals and volunteers can deliver.

11.2 Levels of Interventions

This section clarifies the distinct categories of EMDR interventions as formulated by the EMDR Council of Scholars (Laliotis et al., 2021), the different levels of interventions needed in emergencies proposed by the Inter-Agency Standing Committee (IASC)—'the multilevel intervention pyramid for mental health and psychosocial support' (IASC, 2006; Snider & Hijazi, 2020)—and how both are connected.

Laliotis and colleagues (2021) described three categories of EMDR interventions. Below is a shortened and slightly adapted version of their proposed text for this.

Categories of EMDR Therapy

1. EMDR Psychotherapy

Comprehensive application of EMDR therapy, addressing the complete clinical picture, incorporating EMDR treatment protocols and EMDR-derived techniques as part of a comprehensive treatment plan.

2. EMDR Treatment Protocols

Application of protocols designed to treat specific disorders or symptoms for individuals or groups, as stand-alone interventions or as components of more comprehensive psychotherapy.

3. EMDR-Derived Techniques

Truncated procedures using core elements of EMDR Psychotherapy, applied either as a stand-alone intervention or as a supplement to EMDR psychotherapy.

The Inter-Agency Standing Committee (IASC, 2006), United Nations' forum for ensuring a coherent, unified, and rapid response to global emergencies, proposed a multilevel intervention pyramid indicating four levels of intervention for mental health and psychosocial support in emergencies, differentiating between levels of needs, including (1) provision of essential (basic) services and security, (2) community and family support, (3) focused non-specialized support, and (4) specialized support. All layers of the pyramid are essential and should be implemented concurrently according to the needs of the individuals. Psychosocial support and mental health interventions for war-affected children should be multisystemic, multilevel, targeted towards the child's needs (from basic physical needs upwards), and be trauma-informed and resilience-oriented (Bürgin et al., 2022).

One could argue that specialized evidence-based treatments for individuals with DSM-5 classifications are represented in layer 4; focused individual or group treatments for specific symptoms are in layer 3; interventions to support individuals, families, and the community belong in layer 2; and various basic non-EMDR- related interventions and services are in layer 1.

Figure 11.1 combines the distinct categories of EMDR and the pyramid layers. EMDR individual psychotherapy is positioned at the top of the pyramid, in layer 4. EMDR group

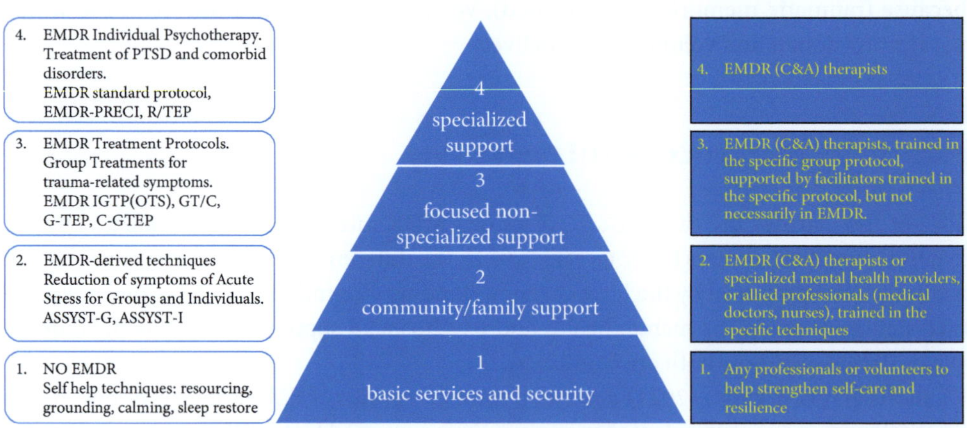

Figure 11.1 EMDR integrated in a pyramid of interventions for mental health and support in emergencies.

treatment protocols belong in layer 3. The EMDR-derived interventions for assisted stabilization belong in layer 2. The types of interventions/protocols are mapped on the left side of the pyramid, and the right side shows the providers' requirements. All protocols mentioned are described generally or in detail in Sections 11.3–11.5.

11.3 Group Protocols

Several group protocols have been developed independently in different parts of the world. Ignacio Jarero and Lucina Artigas (2008), living in Mexico (Latin America), where natural disasters such as hurricanes and other natural phenomena regularly strike, developed the EMDR Integrative Group Treatment Protocol (EMDR-IGTP) in 1998 and later adaptations of this protocol, such as the EMDR-IGTP for Ongoing Traumatic Stress (EMDR-IGTP-OTS) and EMDR-Protocol for Recent Critical Incidents and Ongoing Stress (EMDR-PRECI). These protocols have also been used and studied with children and adolescents. Korkmazlar (2024) independently designed an additional Group Protocol for Children (GP/C) in Turkey, where earthquakes often occur. GP/C has similarities with the EMDR-IGTP. Both use the eight phases of the EMDR standard protocol. However, the content of the meeting, preparation, installation, and closure phases in GP/C deviate from EMDR-IGTP, and are adapted to the traumatic event and the developmental level of the participating children.

Shapiro and Laub (2014), who reside in Israel, a region that is continuously plagued by man-made disasters like wars and terrorism, developed the Group Traumatic Episode Protocol (G-TEP), which is an adaptation to a group setting of the Recent Traumatic Episode Protocol (R-TEP; Shapiro, 2012; Shapiro & Laub, 2014). This protocol is used and studied on adults (but not on children) with acute trauma shortly after the event (Korkmazlar et al., 2020). Gomez (2024) developed a version of G-TEP for children: the C-GTEP.

All protocols aim to facilitate the processing of memories related to traumatic events or episodes. For a better understanding of the differences among these group protocols, two additional concepts need clarification:

- ***EMDR Early Intervention (EEI)***

Francine Shapiro postulated that memories associated with recent events might require a different approach than those related to non-recent events, conceptualizing memories associated with recent events as having insufficient time for memory consolidation and thus demanding adapted interventions (Luber & Shapiro, 2009). Therefore, various protocols have been developed to reprocess memories related to recent events. Shapiro recommended a narrow focus on the disturbing image, to which the therapist returns frequently, each time checking the SUDs level, limiting associations.

- ***Traumatic Episode versus Traumatic Event***

The EMDR standard protocol addresses the memory of a single event. However, several group protocols for recent events (EMDR-IGTP-OTS and G-TEP) address the memories of an extended period instead of a single event because they are applied in ongoing traumatic stress situations, whereby many traumatic events occur continuously over several periods, like during a war or life-changing events with ongoing consequences conceptualized as continuous trauma. The episode is defined as the time just before the onset of the events until the present (Shapiro & Laub, 2014).

In addition to protocols designed to alleviate trauma-related symptoms by reprocessing memories of traumatic events, there are EMDR-derived interventions aimed at reducing symptoms of acute stress resulting from ongoing traumatic stress situations. These interventions were developed by Jarero and Artigas (Jarero & Artigas, 2018; Jarero et al., 2019), who named these ASSYST (**A**cute **S**tress **Sy**ndrome **St**abilization) treatment intervention procedures. These interventions can be delivered to groups (ASSYST-G) or individuals (ASSYST-I) and focus on regulating the person's Autonomic nervous system activation by reducing or eliminating the activation level caused by the sensory, emotional, or physiological components of intrusive pathogenic memories of adverse experiences. These interventions aim to achieve optimal levels of nervous system activation, reduce the production of stress hormones (see also Chapter 10), facilitate the AIP system to process the information adaptively, and thus mitigate acute traumatic stress.

EMDR (C&A) therapists, specialized mental health providers, and allied professionals (medical doctors, nurses) trained in the specific procedure can provide these procedures as traumatic memories are not fully reprocessed like in the EMDR standard protocol. In the ASSYST treatment interventions, only the most prominent memory component (e.g., smell, sound, image) is targeted, and the reprocessing phase is limited to returning to this targeted component after each set of BLS/WMT. Thus, no association channels are opened, keeping the client and the reprocessing contained. These interventions can be administered within the first hours (critical care), days (rapid response), or the first three months following an adverse event. They are categorized as early interventions and can be provided individually, in groups, in person, or online. They bridge the gap between psychological first aid and individual EMDR or any other evidence-based individual therapy.

Robinson and Kaptan (2024) provide specific details on every protocol. Conversely, this chapter is narrowed to protocols concentrating on children and adolescents. Four group protocols are used and studied with children. For an overview, see Table 11.1. Their empirical evidence is detailed in Section 11.4.

Table 11.1 EMDR group protocols used with C&A

Name of protocol	Developers
1. EMDR **I**ntegrative **G**roup **T**reatment **P**rotocol (EMDR-**IGTP**)	Jarero and Artigas
2. EMDR **I**ntegrative **G**roup **T**reatment **P**rotocol for **O**ngoing **T**raumatic **S**tress (EMDR-**IGTP-OTS**)	Jarero and Artigas
3. EMDR **G**roup **P**rotocol for **C**hildren (EMDR **GP/C**)	Korkmazlar
4. EMDR **C**hild-**G**roup **T**raumatic **E**pisode **P**rotocol (EMDR **C-GTEP**)	Gomez

11.4 Group Protocols for Children and Adolescents

11.4.1 The EMDR Integrative Group Treatment Protocol (EMDR-IGTP)

EMDR-IGTP is an EEI protocol that combines the eight phases of the standard protocol with self-administered BLS/WMT (the butterfly hug) to administer individual EMDR therapy in a group setting. This protocol is administered by an EMDR therapist specifically trained in this protocol, supported by a team of EMDR clinicians or non-specialized mental health providers called the 'emotional protection team' (EPT). The application of the protocol takes an average of 60 minutes. Usually, there is one group session. A recommended ratio of 5 children per mental health professional indicates that one team of 5 clinicians can treat 100 children in 4 hours. Several elements of this approach help to reduce potential barriers to receiving treatment (see Section 11.1). Creating a narrative of the experience is not required. It is assumed that instead of mentally visualizing the memory (or the worst part), representing it by a drawing or symbol is less intrusive. Emojis with numbers show different SUD levels, and the children are asked to write the corresponding number on their picture to indicate how much disturbance they are experiencing. After sets of BLS/WMT with the butterfly hug they are asked to draw whatever comes up and rate the SUD level. The process is repeated until there are four pictures. Instead of the installation phase, the children draw an image representing their real future vision without forcing a positive outcome, along with a word or phrase. Subsequently, the last drawing of their future vision, the word/phrase, and the butterfly hug are combined. Finally, a body scan is implemented to reprocess any remnants of disturbing material held somatically, and the session is concluded with a self-soothing exercise (Jarero & Artigas, 2012).

11.4.2 The EMDR Integrative Group Treatment Protocol Adapted for Ongoing Traumatic Stress (IGTP-OTS)

The EMDR-IGTP has been adapted for adolescents (ages 13–17) and adults living in situations with ongoing traumatic stress (EMDR-IGTP-OTS), where there was no post-trauma period of safety for traumatic memory consolidation. Participants work on their traumatic material individually in a group format, as in the EMDR-IGTP. They express themselves through drawing; notice changes in thoughts, emotions, and body sensations; and rate their level of distress utilizing the SUD scale. The butterfly hug is used as a self-administered BLS/WMT. Six sessions are recommended for optimal results. The difference with EMDR-IGTP is the type of memories that can be addressed. The EMDR-IGTP-OTS addresses distressing memories of experiences in their current situation and anticipated future worst-case scenarios. It is designed to identify and target prolonged adverse experiences that have happened recently and might continue for an extended period.

11.4.3 Group Protocol for Children (GP/C)

Korkmazlar started developing this protocol after an earthquake in Turkey in 1999, which affected 20 million people. The protocol evolved over the subsequent years. It was developed alongside Jarero's protocols. Several studies examined its application to children affected by earthquakes, mining accidents, war, and COVID-19 (Korkmazlar, 2024). The goal is to help children integrate and reconsolidate their traumatic memories, feel safe and stable, use their resources, express their feelings, and make sense of their traumatic experiences. Alternatively, it is an EMDR early intervention (EEI) to prevent PTSD, delivered as soon as possible after the traumatic event. It can be applied to children ages 6–18, and to younger ones (4–6) if accompanied by a caregiver. The groups can contain 2–14 children. It is a single-session treatment, taking around three hours, wherein all eight phases are implemented (Korkmazlar, 2020). The therapists are EMDR C&A therapists with field experience and are ready to cooperate with officials and key people in the field.

Several protocol phases are tailored to the type of trauma and the community since every disaster or traumatic event is as unique as each individual:

- During the preparation phase, therapists select appropriate warming-up, grounding, stabilization, and resource exercises tailored to the children's developmental level.
- During the desensitization phase, children are encouraged to draw each traumatic image on separate pieces of paper and then flip the papers over to prevent them from repeatedly confronting the traumatic memory. Depending on the child's preference, the BLS/WMT consists of either the butterfly hug or self-administered knee tapping.
- During the installation phase, a therapeutic story based on Lovett's principles (1999), is utilized to mitigate the further adverse effects of trauma. The therapist prepares this story for the group, customizing it to the traumatic event, the AIP, the EMDR principles, and the children's developmental level. The story is designed to help children articulate and understand their traumatic memories.

11.4.4 Child-Group Traumatic Episode Protocol (C-GTEP): The Journey of the Butterfly

Gomez (2024) developed a child version of G-TEP during the mental health crisis resulting from COVID-19 in 2020, called C-GTEP. Therapists in more than 30 countries have been trained to use C-GTEP, and clinical practice shows it is effective and efficient in reducing symptoms and stabilizing the child's functioning. It is meant for children (ages 4–12) with low or moderate symptomatology, sufficient access to resources, and the capacity to shift emotional states. It can be applied as a stand-alone or as part of an extensive group treatment. A trained EMDR therapist provides the protocol with the assistance of paraprofessionals. The treatment takes 1–4 sessions of 60 minutes. The metaphor of the butterfly's journey (transforming from caterpillar to butterfly) is used to bring hope and transformation for the future.

G-TEP and C-GTEP address the entire traumatic episode, conceived as a continuum from the original incident to the present and anticipated future concerns (Shapiro & Laub, 2014), encompassing the event itself, its aftermath, and how its effects may extend into the future. C-GTEP has three delivery formats: (1) the workbook and book (the story of the journey of the butterfly); (2) C-GTEP on the ground utilizing movement-based BLS/WMT, offering the most significant structure for scaling up and using it with larger groups; and (3) C-GTEP using the sand tray.

The memories related to the traumatic episode are activated by drawings or representative figures when possible. Children are guided to focus on the points of disturbance (PODs)—which can be any disturbing part related to the memory of the episode, such as images, feelings, sensations, sounds, or thoughts—while engaging in multiple sets of BLS/WMT to reduce its impact (SUD level). While the ideal goal is to minimize the disturbance to zero, the primary aim is to decrease it enough to alleviate the child's distress and enhance their regulation and stability. Children are welcome to share their resources if they choose, while trauma-related material remains private (i.e., is not shared) to prevent vicarious traumatization. C-GTEP can also be used with groups of individual children who have experienced different types of trauma.

There are several differences between EMDR-IGTP (and GT/C) versus G-TEP (and C-GTEP). The target is different: the memory of an 'event' in EMDR-IGTP and GT/C versus a memory of an 'episode' in G-TEP and C-GTEP. G-TEP/C-GTEP works in a gradual way gradually addressing the PODs (the disturbing parts of the memories of the episode). Additionally, it incorporates multiple resources, including a relational resource (a team of helpers), the four elements (earth, air, water, light), a positive memory, positive meta-perceptions, and positive beliefs.

11.5 Evidence Base for the Protocols for Children

Kaptan and colleagues (2021) examined all studies that evaluated the efficacy of group protocols and mapped their findings. We extracted the protocols applied to children and adolescents. See Table 11.2.

Six studies have examined IGTP with children (Adúriz et al., 2009; Brennstuhl et al., 2019; Jarero et al., 2008; Maslovaric et al., 2017; Perilli et al., 2019; Trentini et al., 2018). These studies consistently demonstrated significant reductions in PTSD symptoms, with the effects maintained at follow-up. The follow-up period varied across studies (range 1–12 months).

Three studies examined the effectiveness of IGTP-OTS in children (Molero et al., 2019; Osorio et al., 2018; Smyth-Dent et al., 2019). These studies reported significant reductions in symptoms of PTSD, depression, and anxiety, with sustained results at 3-month follow-ups.

Gomez, who developed C-GTEP, studied the effectiveness, and the results of this study will be published soon. The effectiveness of GP/C was examined in several studies (see Korkmazlar, 2024 for an overview), demonstrating that this protocol efficiently resulted in a significant reduction of symptoms of PTSD. The protocol was evaluated under varied conditions, including children impacted by an earthquake, parental loss resulting from a mine explosion, being a refugee after having experienced a war situation, COVID-19, and wildfires.

Taken together, Kaptan and colleagues (2021) conclude that evidence is emerging that the studied group protocols contribute to significantly reduced PTSD symptoms and, in some studies, improvements in symptoms of depression and anxiety. The advantages of group protocols are that more individuals can be reached in less time. Because participants do not have to share their memories, there is a reduction of fears around confidentiality, stigma,

Table 11.2 Overview of the four protocols for group therapy with C&A and their empirical findings

Protocol	Authors	N	Ages	Sessions	Outcome measures PTSD Depression Anxiety	Follow up In month's	Traumatic events	Control group
IGTP	Jarero et al., 2008	16	6–12	6	X	3	Parental loss in mine explosion	-
	Adúriz et al., 2009	126	7–17	1	X	3	Flood	-
	Maslovaric et al., 2017	116	13–20	3	X	3	Earthquake	-
	Trentini et al., 2018	332	5–13	3	X X X	unclear	Earthquake	-
	Brennstuhl et al., 2019	36	12–13	3	X	3	Terrorist attack	-
	Perilli et al., 2019	14	8–17	3	X	No f.u. due to mobility of refugees	Living in a refugee camp after escape from war	-
IGTP-OTS	Osorio et al., 2018	23	13–22	6	X X X	3	Having cancer	-
	Molero et al., 2019	184	13–17	3	X X X	3	Life as a refugee, not living in a refugee camp	waitlist
	Smyth-Dent et al., 2019	48	12–17	6	X X X	1	Life as refugee, living in a refugee camp	-
C-GTEP	Gomez et al., in prep	?	4–12	?	?	?	?	
GT/C	Korkmazlar, 2020	66	6–13	1	X	12	Victim of natural or human-made disaster	waitlist

Source: Kaptan et al. (2021). Copied with permission.

and shame around asking for help. The group setting creates a sense of belonging, and group interactions promote emotional support. Being a group member eases the integration of positive cognitions, like 'I am normal' and 'my reactions are normal reactions to abnormal events'.

Limitations of the included studies are that many participating children did not meet the full criteria for PTSD or another clinical diagnosis, and that a control group was lacking in most studies. Therefore, it cannot be concluded that the protocols are effective in reducing PTSD, depression, or anxiety in clinically diagnosed populations. Future research projects should have more robust study designs, larger sample sizes, control groups, extended follow-up periods, and more similar validated tools to improve study comparability (Beer, 2018). More understanding is needed regarding the role of group interactions in treatment effectiveness, cost effectiveness, and the factors that moderate or mediate outcomes (Kaptan et al., 2021).

For more detailed information on these and other EMDR group protocols and EMDR-derived interventions, we refer the reader to Robinson and Kaptan (2024).

11.6 Concluding Remarks

Group protocols can be differentiated between protocols for EMDR treatment in groups and EMDR-derived interventions in groups. Research with several group protocols has shown promising results in reducing symptoms of PTSD and, in some studies, depression symptoms. However, further research is warranted to establish empirical evidence for the specific goals per protocol (such as reduction of acute stress, trauma-related symptoms, PTSD, trauma-related depression, and anxiety). It is clear that scaling up EMDR is required in particular situations to bridge the gap between available therapists for providing evidence-based therapy (layer 4 in the pyramid)—like EMDR or TF-CBT—and the number of children and adolescents who need evidence-based individual therapy after collective trauma on a (inter) national scale. The number of traumatized children needing interventions on all levels of the pyramid in these situations is enormous. For time- and cost efficiency, it is essential to preserve transparency about what needs to be done by specialized EMDR therapists versus mental health workers or volunteers to accomplish which goals. Clear criteria are required to indicate which children need what type of intervention, enabling optimal allocation of resources (i.e., money and (wo)manpower). Evidence-based protocols for EMDR group interventions can be appropriate and efficient in situations where children face collective trauma.[1]

[1] Thanks to Ignacio Nacho Jarero and Nicolle Mainthow for their valuable comments on the text.

PART II

EMDR for C&A with Specific Psychopathologies

Preparation and Treatment

Preparing Resistant Children for EMDR with the Sleeping Dogs Method

12

ARIANNE STRUIK

12.1 Introduction

EMDR therapy requires a child to identify and be willing and able to talk about their traumatic memories. When a child is not able to do that, it is often said that it is best to wait until they are ready, out of fear of 'waking up sleeping dogs' and destabilizing the child. However, unprocessed trauma can impact and damage all areas of development (Felitti et al., 1998; Schore, 2019). Therefore, it is important to prioritize preparing these children to be able to talk about their traumatic memories, engage in EMDR therapy, and 'wake up the sleeping dogs', over offering non-directive therapies (Cohen et al., 2010). The Sleeping Dogs method can be used to prepare children to engage in EMDR therapy (phase 1 and 2) and complete it (phase 3–8), and to structure interventions in the integration phase after EMDR therapy is finished (Struik, 2019b). The Sleeping Dogs method can also be used when EMDR therapy did not work, symptoms have increased, or the child dropped out. The Sleeping Dogs method was developed in 2010 and is described in *Treating chronically traumatized children: The Sleeping Dogs method* (Struik, 2019b), with Danish and Dutch translations (Struik, 2019a, 2021a). This chapter provides a summary of what the Sleeping Dogs method entails and when and for which children it can be used.

12.2 Target Group

The Sleeping Dogs method can be used with children with chronic trauma who refuse to engage in EMDR therapy, are unwilling or unable to talk about their traumatic memories, say they cannot remember the traumatic events, or when the caregivers or professionals worry about the risk of worsening of symptoms, such as sexualized and aggressive behaviour, dissociation, suicidality, self-harm, and substance abuse. The 'sleeping dogs' metaphor refers to traumatic memories that children refuse to or cannot discuss; by waking up the 'sleeping dogs', traumatic memories become accessible and treatable. Children with so-called 'sleeping dogs' have usually been chronically traumatized by behaviour of their biological parents/caregivers or were not protected by them, grew up in war conditions, were adopted, or have experienced chronic medical trauma. The Sleeping Dogs method can be used with children

Arianne Struik, *Preparing Resistant Children for EMDR with the Sleeping Dogs Method*. In: *Handbook of EMDR for Children and Adolescents*. Edited by: Renée Beer and Carlijn de Roos, Oxford University Press. © 2026, Oxford University Press. For the English edition. DOI: 10.1093/oso/9780198918400.003.0012

from about the age of two years, when they are able to actively refuse to talk about traumatic memories, and with children or adults with an intellectual disability. Sleeping Dogs is only used when EMDR therapy is not (yet) possible. If techniques such as Flash Forward, CIPOS, RDI, or Flash can engage the child and support them to complete EMDR, Sleeping Dogs is unnecessary.

12.3 Empirical Evidence

The Sleeping Dogs method was piloted in a study in the Netherlands. Participants were 14 children, aged 3–9 years (M = 5.1), refusing to participate in EMDR therapy. All were living in residential care (n = 12) or with foster families (n = 2) and were considered stuck cases because of their severe problems. With the treatment package of 'Sleeping Dogs plus EMDR therapy' all children completed EMDR therapy.

In 2020, a consortium of organizations in the Netherlands began data collection for a multi-centre study on the effect (pre-post treatment) of a combination of the Sleeping Dogs method plus EMDR therapy in children placed in youth care institutions. These youth care institutions have implemented Sleeping Dogs as part of the treatment programme in (semi-) residential and foster care. With this study, the consortium hopes to demonstrate the effectiveness of the method to engage children in EMDR and to improve it where necessary. In 2022, the consortium also launched a qualitative study into the experiences of children whose EMDR treatment was completed using the Sleeping Dogs method and their clinicians who used Sleeping Dogs. The results of this study will be published in 2026. Several factors complicate research in this target group, such as case management decisions, unexpected transfers of the child to a different residential unit or foster home, psychiatric hospitalization, suicide, and imprisonment of a parent. Also, obtaining permission for the child to participate in the study from parents with an intellectual disability, psychiatric problems, or from child protection services can be challenging.

A similar method to Sleeping Dogs is motivation-adaptive skills-trauma resolution therapy (MASTR), developed by Greenwald (2002). MASTR is an individual treatment programme for traumatized children with severe behavioural problems that is designed to overcome their resistance to EMDR therapy. MASTR was shown to be effective in a study of 42 traumatized children with behavioural problems who initially refused EMDR. Only two children refused EMDR after MASTR treatment (Farkas et al., 2010). Greenwald (2009) recommends adding systemic interventions to individual programmes, which is one of the critical elements of Sleeping Dogs.

A group of researchers has questioned the need for stabilization prior to EMDR therapy, based on the lack of research supporting the need for this (De Jongh et al., 2016). They argue that clients do not need stabilization, though this assumption is not supported by research. For most children stabilization prior to EMDR therapy is not needed, and would lead to unnecessary delays and prolonged suffering. However, it is evident that children who refuse to talk about their memories, or who say they don't remember anything, need preparation to engage them in EMDR therapy. Sleeping Dogs is used for those children, and only when it is impossible to start reprocessing of traumatic memories (phase 3 and 4). As soon as the child is willing and able to do so—that is, has so-called 'awake dogs'—traumatic memories should be processed in order to reduce symptoms as soon as possible.

12.4 Sleeping Dogs Method: Goal and Key Principles

12.4.1 Goal

The goal of the Sleeping Dogs method is to engage the child in an evidence-based trauma treatment, such as EMDR therapy, as soon as possible, support the child in completing EMDR, and improve the child's development in all areas. The Sleeping Dogs method starts by assessing the child's situation, their network, and the possible reasons why the child is unwilling or unable to talk about their traumatic memories (i.e., their barriers). Based on the barriers, a customized treatment plan of interventions is offered to remove them. The interventions can be done by the EMDR therapist but also by others, such as a foster care worker, family counsellor, residential caregiver, child protection case manager, or people from the child's network. Preparation for EMDR therapy with Sleeping Dogs can take a few weeks, but could take months or even a year. The Sleeping Dogs plan also provides interventions to support the child in completing EMDR, and describes post-EMDR interventions to address trauma-related developmental delays.

12.4.2 Key Principles

The Sleeping Dogs method is based on the principles of the self-determination theory (Deci & Ryan, 2002), which states that intrinsic motivation is determined by fulfilling three basic human needs: autonomy, competence, and connection. Thus, interventions within the Sleeping Dogs method focus on increasing the child's sense of autonomy, competence, and connection, as well as on empowerment and increasing the child's resilience and sense of control. Psychoeducation provides knowledge, allowing children to feel more competent in making their own decisions about their treatment. The child feels more connected by improving their relationships with their network, family, and caregivers. Many barriers involve the biological family, including parents who abused or neglected the child, for whom the term 'perpetrator-parent' is used for convenience in the rest of this chapter. Providing that it is safe to do so, these parents need to be involved in the child's treatment to overcome barriers and motivate the child. Even for children who are no longer living with their biological parents, it is important to involve their biological parents. Sleeping Dogs also uses active involvement and collaboration with child protection services to help motivate the child and remove potential barriers by, for example, reconsidering case management decisions about contact with biological parents or discussing the possible consequences of disclosures the child may make. The relational environment is the most important mediator of therapeutic change (Perry & Dobson, 2013). Resistance to trauma treatment can be reduced by keeping the number of therapy sessions to a minimum. This limits the therapist's ability to build the therapeutic relationship, which is compensated by collaborating with the child's support network. Key figures who already have a relationship with the child participate in treatment by, for example, attending live or online sessions, or making a narrative or video message. They learn to use Sleeping Dogs interventions that explain daily life situations to the child—for example, about the relationship between traumatic memories and their symptoms. This way, treatment takes place indirectly through the key figures in the network without the need to see the therapist.

12.5 Sleeping Dogs Method: Procedure

12.5.1 Before Trauma Processing

When the case conceptualization suggests that the child could benefit from EMDR therapy, but they are unwilling or unable to engage, the clinician fills in the Sleeping Dogs tool (see https://www.ariannestruik.com/wp-content/uploads/2023/10/9780367076146_E-resource-1-Barrier-Tool-colour.pdf). The tool consists of a case summary/Sleeping Dogs case conceptualization (1), barrier form (2), and action plan (3), which are explained in the following subsections. Worksheets can be used to support interventions (see https://www.ariannestruik.com/wp-content/uploads/2022/02/6_worksheets.pdf).

Sleeping Dogs Case Conceptualization

The EMDR case conceptualization clarifies the presumed relationship between the child's symptoms and distressing traumatic memories, and the factors presumably maintaining the symptoms. In many of the 'typical' Sleeping Dogs cases, so much has happened that it is difficult to get an overview. The Sleeping Dogs case conceptualization is used to provide clinicians with that overview. It describes the child's symptoms, the potential traumatic memories, and whether the traumatic memory is a sleeping dog (SD), which means that the child cannot start processing with EMDR, or an 'awake dog' (AD), which means that the child can process this memory. The child can also have 'preverbal dogs' (PD), referring to traumatic memories of events experienced at an early age (preverbal phase) of which they have no conscious memory.[1] The Sleeping Dogs clinician draws a timeline of the traumatic events and the caregivers with whom the child has lived in sequential order—such as first father and mother, then mother, then mother and stepfather—to visually support the overview. As many barriers are related to the child's family network and family members are important to resolve barriers, the Sleeping Dogs clinician describes important things about the child's network in keywords. Noah's example illustrates this process.

[1] See Chapter 8 for treatment of children with symptoms due to preverbal trauma.

CASE STUDY 12.1 Noah

Eleven-year-old Noah is aggressive at home and at school. He has no friends, seems lonely, and often says that no one loves him. Noah experienced domestic violence between his parents until he was five years old. During the last argument, his father was locked out by his mother. He shouted at Noah to open the door, but Noah froze and did nothing. The police took his father and Noah has not seen him since. His mother says his father doesn't care about him. Noah lives with his mother, stepfather, and half-brother. His mother has PTSD, and she dissociates when Noah is aggressive. She often says that he will turn out just like his aggressive father. The school recommends EMDR therapy. At the initial consult, the therapist explains EMDR to Noah, but he refuses to participate or talk about his memories. The therapist fills out the Sleeping Dogs Case Conceptualization, concluding that his traumatic memories of domestic violence are SDs for which he needs preparation to engage him in EMDR processing (phases 3 and 4).

Barrier Form

On the barrier form, the Sleeping Dogs clinician notes the child's SDs, the negative cognitions the child might have in relation to these memories, and the positive cognition the child needs to shift to in order to reduce symptoms. The clinician fills in whether the child passes the motivation check—meaning that they want to engage in EMDR—and passes the nutshell check—meaning that they are able to make an overview of their traumatic memories with the therapist without becoming too overwhelmed and dysregulated. If the child has failed one or both checks, the child has SDs and the clinician forms hypotheses about potential barriers based on the child's symptoms, the timeline, and information about the child's family network.

These children are often called 'unmotivated' or 'resistant to treatment'; however, this wrongly assumes that the child makes a conscious choice. The child's barriers to EMDR therapy are usually caused by a combination of their current circumstances and their traumatic experiences. A review on resistance in chronically traumatized children suggests the following underlying factors: unsafety; too many problems in daily life; lack of support and connection; difficulties in feeling, tolerating, and regulating emotions; and negative trauma-related cognitions about themself, others, and the world (Struik et al., 2017). The conclusion from this review, combined with many years of clinical experience with the target group, contributed to formulating the 19 barriers in the Sleeping Dogs tool. The Sleeping Dogs clinician and other involved professionals form hypotheses about potential barriers for these traumatic memories (SDs) by completing 19 yes/no questions on the barrier form in the Sleeping Dog method tool. The clinician also identified barriers for Noah.

CASE STUDY 12.2 **Noah continued: Part 2**

The Sleeping Dogs clinician assumes that the last fight between Noah's biological father and his mother is Noah's most important SD, and that he has started to think negatively about himself and feel guilty about what happened. If, during trauma processing, he could make the shift to 'It's not my fault/I forgive myself/I'm ok', then he would start to feel better about himself and his anger would reduce. But he absolutely does not want to talk about it. The Sleeping Dogs clinician tries to think from Noah's perspective and forms the hypothesis that Noah does not want to talk about his memories because he feels guilty about not helping his father (if he had opened the door, his parents might still be together). Maybe he does not want to say negative things about his father because he thinks that would make his father not want to see him. Noah may also be protecting his mother by not talking about the domestic violence and making sure that she does not dissociate, but he does not have anyone else to talk to.

It is often said that a child is too unstable and cannot participate in EMDR therapy when, for example, they don't have a stable placement or attachment figure, their daily life is chaotic, the collaboration with their parents or network is problematic, or the child struggles to manage emotions and is aggressive, suicidal, or self-harming. However, if a child has awake dogs, wants to process their memories with EMDR therapy (motivation check), and is able to do so (nutshell check), there is no reason to postpone EMDR therapy. If in doubt, the barriers can be checked to assess whether it is likely for any to arise during EMDR therapy.

Action Plan

If the child's parents or legal guardians and the care team agree that EMDR is necessary, the Sleeping Dogs clinician makes a plan to remove the child's barriers. Sometimes this requires a great deal of psychoeducation about treatment for parents, legal guardians, caregivers, and other professionals to agree. The Sleeping Dogs interventions can be conducted by the Sleeping Dogs clinician or in collaboration with other professionals or people from the network. The action plan describes examples of interventions, but other methods—for example, signs of safety (Turnell & Edwards, 1999; Turnell & Essex, 2006), non violence resistance (Omer, 2004), and integrative attachment trauma protocol for children (IATP-C) (Wesselmann et al., 2018)—can also be used to address barriers. The Sleeping Dogs clinician periodically evaluates the plan until all barriers are removed or the child is willing and able to commence EMDR therapy.

Some children agree to engage in EMDR therapy without a full understanding of what it means or under a parent's or caregiver's pressure. This increases the likelihood that they will drop out, so the therapist should confirm that the child is sufficiently and intrinsically motivated and understands the benefits of EMDR therapy (motivation check). Noah's example illustrates how barriers can be removed.

CASE STUDY 12.3 **Noah continued: Part 3**

Noah's mother thinks EMDR therapy could be an option for her son, but wonders if he even remembers what happened as he never talks about it. She consents after several conversations, in which Noah's stepfather is involved, about the harmful effects of unresolved trauma. However, she worries that Noah's EMDR therapy will trigger her own traumatic memories and aggravate her PTSD and dissociation.

The Sleeping Dogs clinician explains to her that in order to remove Noah's barriers, it is important to contact Noah's father. It takes some time before she agrees and the therapist receives the father's contact details through a grandmother, an aunt, and an ex-girlfriend. The father has been released from prison and has done therapy. He is very happy to hear from his son. In a video message for Noah, prepared with the Sleeping Dogs clinician, he gives Noah permission to talk about the violence, which addresses a barrier. He explains that the violence was not Noah's fault and that he is not angry that Noah had not opened the door, which addresses another barrier. He explains that he has thought about Noah every day but found it difficult to contact him and so kept putting it off, but that he would really like to re-establish contact. The Sleeping Dogs clinician first watches the father's video message with Noah's mother. Initially it is very distressing for her, but gradually this confrontation reduces her fear of Noah's father. Together, they watch the video message with Noah. Noah is very relieved and tells his mother that for six years he had believed that his father was still angry with him and blamed him for the divorce. This barrier is now removed. Noah consents to engage in EMDR therapy but he is very concerned that his mother will not be able to handle it, which forms another barrier. Noah's mother introduces his grandfather as a support figure. Granddad discusses with Noah that he will take him to therapy to shield his mother from becoming overwhelmed. The grandfather tells Noah that he can talk to him about the arguments between his parents if he wants to, which removes that barrier. Noah agrees with the plan and indicates in the motivation check that he would like to be less angry.

After passing the motivation check, EMDR therapy phase 3 can start. The EMDR therapist checks whether the child is able to make a brief overview of their traumatic memories—list them 'in a nutshell', so to speak—while staying within their window of tolerance (nutshell check). Based on this list of memories, the EMDR therapist determines the order in which memory clusters are to be addressed. Many of these children mention not only traumatic memories of past experiences but also distressing current circumstances, such as being rejected by a mother who has a borderline personality disorder, having a father in prison, or being a foster child. Of course, EMDR therapy cannot change these difficult circumstances; the child must learn to deal with them. It is important to be aware of this distinction when selecting distressing memories for EMDR.

CASE STUDY 12.4 Noah continued: Part 4

Noah makes an overview of the traumatic memories that are still distressing. He passes the nutshell check and is ready to activate and desensitize his memories with EMDR.

The following section describes common barriers and interventions to overcome them.

Barriers and solutions: Some examples

Many children have SDs because they fear the consequences of discussing their memories with others. They may struggle with a secret, fearing that they will be removed from the home or that they or their parents will have to go to jail if the secret becomes known. They are usually not aware of the child protection caseworker already knowing about, for example, domestic violence or a parent's alcohol abuse. This barrier can be removed by mapping out with the child protection caseworker, police, and parents what the actual consequences could be and then sharing this information with the child.

Another barrier may be that the child is afraid that their parents will get angry if they talk about their traumatic memories, they don't know if the parent approves of them talking about their traumatic memories in therapy. The parents may have threatened the child. The Sleeping Dogs clinician can discuss this barrier with the parents and try to get their permission. The parent(s) can then give the child explicit permission, in the presence of the Sleeping Dogs clinician, to talk about their traumatic memories. If this is a barrier but there is no contact with a parent for an extended period (for example, because they are in prison, hospitalized or not in communication with the family), their Sleeping Dogs clinician can try to contact the parent. A powerful way to remove this barrier can be to have the parent express a message for the child in the form of a video, letter, or conversation, encouraging the child to talk about their memories and engage in EMDR.

Another common barrier is that children are taking care of their parents—for example, if the whole family has experienced traumatic events. The child doesn't want to engage in EMDR because they are afraid the mother will dissociate or get upset, or their father will get angry again. They have no one to talk to about their experiences, are afraid of their own anger and sadness, and therefore prefer to forget or pretend it didn't happen. To remove this barrier, the parent can learn to improve self-regulation, so they can support the child during EMDR with a calm brain. If this is too difficult, the parent can set up a compensation plan by, for example, asking a grandparent with a calm brain to support the child and take them to therapy. They can buy a notebook in which the child can write down questions for the parent, so that the parent is not overwhelmed by questions and can prepare the answer with the therapist first. Parents can explain to the child that although it may upset them, they still want the child to do EMDR, and then explain the plan they have made to make that work.

Finally, the most common barrier is that the child cannot make the cognitive shift during the desensitization phase in EMDR therapy. The child stays loyal to the parent and cannot believe they are not responsible for the trauma, because they are afraid of the parent's rejection if they were to blame them for the trauma. EMDR is based on the AIP model, which assumes that clients do have adaptive information such as 'it's not my fault', but that this information is temporarily unavailable. Interweaves can be used to link dysfunctional information to adaptive information. However, many children with SDs actually don't have this adaptive information, and therefore they don't want to start EMDR, or the processing gets stuck, and they cannot let go of the dysfunctional cognition (belief) that the event was their fault. They feel ashamed, they hate themselves, they think they should have done things differently, but they can't change the past. Thinking about it is unbearable because there is no way out. Sleeping Dogs clinicians can challenge the child's cognitions and beliefs, but this is usually not enough to prepare them to make the shift during EMDR. Removing this barrier usually requires the perpetrator-parent to acknowledge the child's innocence and provide them with an explanation about why they have hurt the child as an alternative to it being the child's fault. Parents can explain this in conversation with their child, in a video message, in a letter, or in a more elaborate story illustrated with drawings (trauma healing story). In the box an example of a page out of the traumahealing story for ten-year-old Tanya who was removed from her mother after neglect and abuse, but did not want to talk about that and feels responsible for her mother's wellbeing.

BOX 12.1 Trauma healing story

'Mum drank a lot of alcohol because she had a lot of bad memories that she wanted to forget. When mothers drink a lot of alcohol, they can't think straight and forget to buy food or take their child to school.'

This allows the child to let go of their own explanation ('it was my fault') without fear of the parent rejecting them and later, during the desensitization phase in EMDR, make the cognitive shift to the PC 'Its not my fault'.

In addition to these common barriers, many of these children do not know how they can benefit from EMDR therapy and they don't have intrinsic motivation. This problem can be solved by having the network motivate and encourage the child. The therapist can provide psychoeducation to the child and their network about how unprocessed memories can cause a variety of problems, such as aggressive behaviour, dissociation, flashbacks, attachment problems, sexualized behaviour, submission, and freezing responses, and how EMDR can help to reduce these problems. The child can learn skills to increase self-control over trauma-related emotional responses. The child can practice these at home with the network's support.

12.5.2 During Trauma Processing

Trauma processing is a difficult phase for many children as they work through feelings of loneliness, guilt, and shame. The therapist or Sleeping Dogs clinician makes a plan with the network to support the children and ensure they engage in EMDR and complete their treatment. This plan focuses, firstly, on maintaining a sense of connection before, during, and after the sessions; secondly, on providing enough distraction before and after the sessions; and, thirdly, on promoting physical activity after the sessions to increase the sense of control and reduce disturbance in the body.

For example before the EMDR session, someone from the network can bring the child to the session, send a supportive text message, or call the child. Parents who cannot attend sessions (e.g., are in detention or in hospital) can support the child by making a supportive video message. The child can watch these before the EMDR sessions. During the session, the child can, for example, bring the family dog, wear dad's jumper with his smell, bring grandma's photo, wear mum's special bracelet. A support figure could sit in the session and, for instance, tap the child on their back if needed. People from their network could tell the child they will pray for them during the session. The EMDR therapist can remind the child of these things when they are struggling and about to give up. After the session, people from their network could visit, go boxing, biking, or swimming with the child, have a meal together, or watch an engaging movie. Noah's therapist plans an intensive EMDR week.

CASE STUDY 12.5 **Noah continued: Part 5**

The therapist decides to plan the EMDR sessions on five consecutive days. During this week, Noah's grandfather stays at their house with mum. He attends therapy with Noah while Noah's stepfather and half-brother stay with Noah's grandmother. At the start of the session, the therapist and Noah watch the video of Noah's father encouraging him and saying he is proud of him. Noah's guinea pig sits on his lap, and he is wearing his stepfather's leather jacket. During EMDR, the therapist repeatedly reminds Noah that his grandfather is waiting for him and that his mother and father will be proud of him. After the therapy sessions, his grandfather goes for a 20 km bike ride with Noah. When they return home, Noah, his grandfather, and his mother watch an exciting TV show that Noah has chosen and they eat dinner in front of the TV, which is not allowed normally. After the week of EMDR sessions, Noah sleeps better, feels calmer, and is no longer aggressive.

12.5.3 After Trauma Processing

After processing traumatic memories with EMDR therapy, chronically traumatized children usually feel a lot better now their traumatic memories may have been processed. However, they still struggle with the broader impact of chronic traumatization such as developmental delays, lack of skills, and their difficult circumstances. The Sleeping Dogs tool supports the clinician in making a customized plan of interventions to improve the child's circumstances and functioning to a level where trauma-focused treatment is no longer needed. Themes that can be addressed in this phase include school and learning problems, family contact arrangements, confrontation or re-connecting with a perpetrator-parent, improving attachment relationships, and skills training. Noah also needed support in the integration phase.

CASE STUDY 12.6 **Noah continued: Part 6**

After several conversations with Noah's mother, supervised contact between Noah and his father starts. Noah motivates his mother to engage in EMDR therapy for herself. Parenting support helps Noah's mother and stepfather to set more boundaries, to support Noah in the contact with his father. Noah is diagnosed with ADHD and receives extra guidance at school for his learning difficulties. He takes up kickboxing and participates in social skills training.

12.6 Return to Preparation

Clinical practice shows that in chronically traumatized children the processing of traumatic memories can take place in layers. Children may indicate that they no longer have distressing traumatic memories and complete EMDR therapy, but after several months the symptoms may return or other symptoms may arise. As they become more sensitive and connect more to themselves and others, and they experiment with new behaviours, other aspects of the same memory or new memories can suddenly become distressing. These memories can be processed with EMDR therapy again. If these memories are causing symptoms but the child is unwilling or able to process them, barriers are again analysed and a plan is again made to remove the barriers.

12.7 Concluding Remarks

The Sleeping Dogs method is a treatment for chronically traumatized children who need EMDR treatment but are unable or unwilling to engage. When all other treatment options have failed, the Sleeping Dogs method can be used to find ways to engage these children in EMDR therapy as soon as possible and support them to complete it. Results from pilot studies and clinical practice are promising; however, more research is needed. As EMDR therapists, we are also responsible for making evidence-based treatment available to children who are difficult to engage.

EMDR for Children with ADHD

13

ARIANE TJEENK-KALFF,
TIRTSA EHRLICH,
AND ANNEKE EENHOORN

13.1 Introduction

Attention deficit/hyperactivity disorder (ADHD) is one of the most common psychiatric disorders diagnosed in children (4–12 years old) and adolescents (12–18 years old). This chapter describes the potential of EMDR for these age groups, collectively referred to as children. ADHD is characterized by difficulty regulating attention, hyperactivity, and impulsivity, which can lead to many negative and potentially traumatic experiences, as well as other problems during a child's development. These behaviours regularly irritate those around them, causing them to experience more conflict, rejection, and bullying than their healthy peers, and they are often underachievers. This puts them at high risk of developing post-traumatic stress disorder (PTSD), other trauma-related conditions, and a negative self-image. Traumatic experiences, in turn, can exacerbate ADHD behaviours, such as worsening hyperactivity. This chapter describes points for attention and recommendations, based on clinical practice, for treating trauma-related symptoms in this target group with EMDR.

13.2 Target Group

13.2.1 Clinical Presentation

ADHD in children can be identified by a pattern of inattention with or without hyperactivity and impulsivity (American Psychiatric Association, 2013). If these behaviours are observed in two or more settings (for example, home and school) before 12 years of age, ADHD is diagnosed. Three types of ADHD have been described.

- **Predominantly hyperactive-impulsive:** mostly hyperactive and impulsive, such as difficulty sitting still and/or talking a lot; behaviour is often disturbing to their environment.
- **Predominantly inattentive:** difficulty in maintaining attention: for example, easily distracted by external and/or internal stimuli, very associative, forgetful, and/or chaotic, with the result that things often fail, and not hyperactive-impulsive—or to a lesser extent.
- **Combined:** inattentive, hyperactive, and impulsive.

Ariane Tjeenk-Kalff, Tirtsa Ehrlich, and Anneke Eenhoorn, *EMDR for Children with ADHD*. In: *Handbook of EMDR for Children and Adolescents.* Edited by: Renée Beer and Carlijn de Roos, Oxford University Press. © 2026, Oxford University Press. For the English edition. DOI: 10.1093/oso/9780198918400.003.0013

In the remainder of this chapter, ADHD refers to all types of attention deficit disorder, including the predominantly inattentive type, which in practice is commonly referred to as ADD.

The combined type is most common, followed by ADD. A distinction is made according to the severity of the characteristics and the degree of impaired functioning, ranging from mild to moderate to severe. The clinical presentation changes with age and varies from person to person: hyperactivity and impulsivity are more prominent under the age of 12, while for those over 12, problems with attention, planning, and organization are most common. Children with ADHD often have problems with executive function, including timing and motivation (Sonuga-Barke et al., 2010). This leads to many difficulties in daily life, which will be discussed in more detail later in this chapter.

13.2.2 Prevalence and Comorbidity

ADHD occurs in all countries and cultures and is often accompanied by other (psychiatric) problems. In recent decades, the prevalence of ADHD in children and adolescents has remained constant (5% on average; Faraone et al., 2021). Reliable data on the prevalence of PTSD in children with ADHD does not appear in the scientific literature. It is conceivable that PTSD and ADHD may coexist, and that the symptoms of each condition overlap and reinforce the other. In a study of Unver and Karakaya (2019), 22% of children and adolescents with PTSD also met the criteria for ADHD. In our clinical practice we often see children with ADHD and comorbid PTSD, and ADHD characteristics remain even after treatment for PTSD. Therefore, it is recommendable that children who present with ADHD and PTSD should be treated for PTSD first and evaluated afterwards for ADHD behaviours.

13.2.3 Origin

ADHD is considered a multifactorial disorder involving multiple biological, psychological, and social factors (Faraone et al., 2021). Genetic inheritance appears to be an important risk factor that increases susceptibility for developing ADHD by creating a vulnerable brain. Social, cultural, and societal factors play an additional role, such as deprivation, stress, infection, poverty, and trauma, as do sleeping problems and the many stimuli and pressures of modern society on children. Symptoms may manifest earlier and more strongly in children growing up in an environment without structure and with a lot of stimuli than in children growing up in a structured, predictable environment. Additionally, problems in executive functions and motivation, among others, are often seen as underlying explanations for ADHD.

13.2.4 Executive Functions

Executive functions have been described by Barkley (2012) as self-control or self-regulation of behaviours, thoughts, and emotions to achieve goals. Barkley theorized that the prefrontal cortex controls these functions. In children with ADHD, these control functions are thought to develop later and to a lesser extent than in healthy individuals. This causes problems for the child and the people around them. Children with ADHD have difficulty being purposeful in new and complex situations and are at greater risk of encountering problematic situations, both at home and at school. They can be impulsive and violent. They lack self-calming abilities, so they depend on others to calm them. They are forgetful and have a poor ability to judge the passage of time or predict the duration of activities, so they cannot plan well. They are often overexcited and have intense sensations that guide their actions. If they stub one of their toes, they react like all 10 toes have been pulled off. They lack inner speech to reassure themselves. Therefore, they need outside guidance to calm themselves. In short, children with ADHD are more likely to have problems planning and organizing their behaviour and regulating their emotions.

13.2.5 Motivation

In addition to the executive function problems mentioned, motivation problems are also seen. It is often wrongly assumed that children with ADHD are not motivated to perform a variety of tasks. Motivation has been extensively studied in children with ADHD, in part to explore the theory that ADHD is caused by impaired executive functions (Dovis et al., 2012; Luman et al., 2020; Van der Oord & Tripp, 2020). Children with ADHD find it difficult to motivate themselves (intrinsic motivation) and have a strong preference for immediate over delayed rewards. Dovis and colleagues (2012) showed that rewards (extrinsic motivation) can lead to some improvement in performance on a working memory task, but to a lesser degree than in children without ADHD. It was concluded that problems in task persistence in ADHD result from motivational deficits. This deficit makes it difficult for these children to keep themselves motivated to perform well. Especially with tasks that are dull and monotonous, they depend heavily on motivation from their environment. They are often told 'you can do it, if you just try harder', which, instead of motivating the child, makes them believe that they are incapable and makes them feel gloomy instead of motivated.

13.2.6 Consequences

Children with ADHD are at risk of developing secondary problems because of their ADHD behaviour. A recent review concludes that ADHD is associated with severe restrictions and suffering (Faraone et al., 2021). For instance, due to their concentration problems combined with their impulsive, hyperactive behaviour, and the negative reactions from others that this invokes, they are at an increased risk of developing a negative self-image and/or fear of failure. Also, concentration problems can lead to lower school performance or even school dropout. Comments such as 'Stop that', 'Shut up already', and 'Pay attention' reinforce the feeling that they are constantly failing. Remarks such as 'If you make an effort, you can do it' or 'Try harder' and being laughed at by their peers can all contribute to their belief that they are incapable of doing anything right.

ADHD children are also at increased risk of social problems, such as bullying or even exclusion. Due to their hyperactive and impulsive behaviours, they may provoke irritation in others and miss social cues, causing them to lose a sense of connection, which isolates them and increases the likelihood of creating or reinforcing negative core beliefs.

Some children with ADHD are accident prone. Because of their impulsiveness and absentmindedness, they fail to see danger, resulting in large or small accidents (e.g., falling from a tree or from a bicycle, getting involved in traffic accidents). Some are also clumsy and subject to falls or bumping into things. Adolescents with ADHD can end up in dangerous situations because they exhibit more risky behaviour (Dekkers et al., 2016). They may also be more likely to engage in aggressive behaviour resulting from their hyperactivity and impulsivity.

Some children with ADHD are also slower in motor skills, with a less developed ability to have an overview in game situations. As a result, they often become less quickly chosen for sports and games events and are sometimes even excluded, resulting in negative core beliefs (such as 'I can't do anything right'). Finally, there is a greater chance of family problems due to negative interaction patterns between the parents and the child or relationship problems between the parents. There is an above average chance of relationship problems and divorce in families where there is a child with ADHD. The many arguments that include the child may cause them to think that they are to blame for all the family problems. In addition, there is a high probability that one of the parents also has ADHD, which is an obvious risk factor for partner violence and domestic violence (Buitelaar & Ferdinand, 2013). It is well accepted that these secondary problems can lead to the comorbid disorders mentioned above, especially if treatment is not provided.

13.3 Rationale for EMDR

The guideline treatment for ADHD varies depending on the age of the child and the degree of any additional behavioural problems (NICE, 2018a). It is common for children with ADHD to have experienced traumatic events and they are, therefore, more likely to have PTSD than their peers without ADHD (Faraone et al., 2021). Post-traumatic stress reactions may in turn exacerbate ADHD symptoms, as increased stress levels can exacerbate existing psychological symptoms in anyone. EMDR and other evidence-based trauma treatments can be considered for treating PTSD in children with ADHD. PTSD is always the first focus in treatment, in alignment with the guideline for treatment of PTSD. This also applies if ADHD might be a comorbid disorder. In those cases, it is more reliable to assess whether ADHD symptoms remain after trauma treatment. EMDR is also recommended in cases where PTSD symptoms are related to experiences resulting from the child's ADHD-related behaviours (secondary problems).

Furthermore, the child may have developed negative core beliefs about the self, resulting from negative social experiences related to their ADHD/ADD. With the belief path (see Chapter 4), 'pieces of evidence' ('proofs') can be sought for these core beliefs. Examples of regularly occurring negative core beliefs include:

- 'I am stupid': They do poorly in school or have problems completing tasks, or are often told 'Just sit still' or 'Try harder; I know you can do it'.
- 'I'm a loser': They have been bullied a lot or often get into arguments.
- 'I'm a failure': Their hyperactivity and forgetfulness (appointments, things) cause constant conflicts with their parents.

- 'I'm a klutz': They are frequently involved in accidents due to their unruly behaviour—for example, after recklessly starting fires or using a scooter.

13.4 Empirical Evidence

Although there is considerable clinical experience of using EMDR in children with ADHD, very few research studies have appeared in the scientific literature so far. A recent case report describes EMDR treatment of a 12-year-old with ADHD and a history of multiple traumatic experiences and behavioural problems, all of which may have been due both to PTSD and to ADHD. EMDR treatment resulted in a reduction of emotional regulation problems and an improvement of the executive functions (Guidetti et al., 2023). Curiosity for the potential effects of EMDR in children with ADHD has increased due to the emerging hypotheses on the mechanism of action of EMDR, specifically the hypothesis that EMDR might derive its effect from taxing working memory load (Gunter & Bodner, 2008; Van den Hout & Engelhard, 2012). An intriguing question to test would be if the efficacy of EMDR deviates for children with ADHD, who have low working memory capacity and problems with attention (Kofler et al., 2008; Martinussen et al., 2005). One could wonder whether it relates to working memory specifically, or attention processes more generally, and how the two are functionally related.

Although working memory and attention can be distinguished conceptually (theoretically), it is extremely difficult to distinguish between them in experimental research. This distinction is less important for explaining the clinical outcome of EMDR. However, if we can better understand the mechanisms of action that produce a therapeutic result (in other words, how EMDR works here) in children with ADHD—who have attention problems and a working memory with limited capacity—then we could gain important insights into the relationship between attention and working memory.

If the theory that EMDR works by taxing working memory during recall is correct, then one might expect EMDR to yield faster results in children with ADHD than in children without ADHD, because their working memory becomes taxed more quickly due to their more limited working memory capacity (Dovis et al., 2012). On the other hand, the (sustained) attention problems of children with ADHD could interfere with the entire processing process, leading to a longer total treatment duration to achieve a therapeutic benefit than in children without ADHD. Shorter sessions will be needed because children with ADHD cannot focus and concentrate for extended periods (Faraone et al., 2021). This makes results difficult to interpret. Nevertheless, such research could provide valuable information.

A lot of clinical experience has been built with the application of EMDR in children with ADHD; however, there are hardly any publications on the subject. Adler-Tapia and Settle (2012) note that their experience shows that EMDR can help process unpleasant social experiences that have led to increased anxiety and hyperactivity. We had similar experiences, leading to corresponding conclusions. In clinical practice, we see a difference between children with ADHD and those with ADD. The former benefit from as few external stimuli as possible during the assessment to maximize focus and raise arousal, while the second group may need more external prompts (such as 'focus again' and 'here we go') to avoid straying.

The experience of the authors is that most children with ADHD or ADD need extra BLS/WMT during desensitization despite presumed weaker working memory capacity because of their distractibility.

These observations are only clinical impressions and speculations. Experimental research should tell us whether—and, if so, what—modifications are needed for children with ADHD/ADD to maximize the effectiveness of EMDR.

13.5 Points of Consideration for EMDR Therapy

This section describes points of consideration and recommendations for EMDR therapy in children of different ages with ADHD. After discussing some general points, we go through the protocol steps and provide suggestions for preventing or minimizing problems posed by this target group's behaviours.

13.5.1 General Recommendations

The standard protocol for children and adolescents can be used in children with ADHD with comorbid PTSD once the relevant traumatic memories have been identified. When the post-traumatic stress symptoms subside after EMDR treatment, the child may become less hyperactive and more attentive, resulting in less rejection from those around them. After trauma treatment, symptoms that can only be attributed to ADHD become apparent, and standard ADHD treatment, such as medication, can be considered if indicated and not already started. Relevant symptom-related memories are searched by using one or more of the available search strategies (see Chapter 4).

- ***Promoting continuity and planning***

Problems with executive function in children with ADHD can make regular meetings and consistent processes a challenge. Some recommendations to counteract this are:

- Provide a low-stimulation treatment room with as little background noise as possible so that the child is not easily distracted.
- Set a fixed time and send reminders via WhatsApp, email, or text. This is reassuring for any child but is especially recommended for the target group of children and their parents, who often suffer from attention problems themselves. There is a high chance that one of the parents also has ADHD (Faraone et al., 2021), and their forgetfulness and planning problems may lead to missed appointments.
- Schedule more and shorter sessions. Given their limited attention span, limit treatment sessions to a maximum of 30–40 minutes, especially for children younger than 8 years old. Even adolescents can lose their concentration after 40 minutes.
- Keep the child attentive by getting them moving. Consider EM^{+}, such as throwing a ball, making specific repetitive movements like V-steps, playing with the buzzers, and/or allowing walking and moving around while making eye movements.

- Sometimes, encouragement or re-explanation of the process is needed at the beginning of each session, leaving less time for EMDR. Especially with complex problems, the child will not always receive a perceived reward with a positive outcome (SUD = 0) or an immediate reduction in symptoms. This can make it challenging to keep the child motivated. For this reason some children may need more sessions. A good explanation of the concept of processing combined with a reward schedule can help (see examples of reward cards in Appendices 13.1 and 13.2).

- ***Medication***

- For children who are about to switch to taking medication for ADHD, it is advisable to start EMDR treatment only once the child's medication has been appropriately adjusted. However, it is not always necessary to wait, especially if the adjustment of their medication will take a long time. The child and their parents should be made aware that the child must take their medication before their sessions. This will optimize the child's ability to concentrate. If necessary, agree on a plan to help the child adhere to their medication schedule.
- Therapists should be aware of a possible rebound effect at the end of the day in children taking short-acting medication. ADHD symptoms may temporarily return in an intensified form, making late afternoon sessions undesirable. Sessions at the end of the day are also unfit for children who are not taking ADHD medication, as their ability to concentrate will be reduced after a day at school.

13.6 Recommendations per Protocol Phase

13.6.1 Diagnostics and Case Conceptualization (Phase 1)

Various search strategies are possible to identify and select appropriate targets for the symptom to be treated (see Chapter 4).

13.6.2 Preparation (Phase 2)

- ***Reinforce motivation***

If necessary, insert interventions to motivate and engage. A reward scheme can help encourage the child during treatment (see Appendices 13.1 and 13.2). We have found that children with ADHD seem to be quicker than other children to say that something is okay to hasten the end of activities that they find boring or that take too long. The therapist should emphasize to the child that they must be honest to achieve the best results.

Motivational interviewing techniques increase compliance and motivation for treatment in adolescents with ADHD (Boyer et al., 2013). Adolescents procrastinate, show avoidance behaviour, and are not very motivated to change their behaviour, and especially not to undergo treatment for it. Setting clear and concrete goals helps to increase the child's motivation. A recommendation is for the therapist to elaborate on the potential benefits of achieving the goals of EMDR for the young person, who should write them down and refer to them regularly. See an example of this in Case Study 13.1.

CASE STUDY 13.1 Enhancing motivation

Therapist: *Is this memory still disturbing for you now?*

Client: *It's not bad now, it's long gone from my mind.*
[Mother smiles and shakes her head.]

Therapist: *I can imagine you putting it away.*

Client: *I don't, I just think about other things.*

Therapist: *Many children do that, but we know that children who just put away unpleasant memories/images continue to suffer from them anyway.*

Client: *Yes, if it comes back, I get very angry. It's just behind a door somewhere.*

Therapist: *Then I want to ask you to open the door and see why this memory/image is still so bad for you now.*

Client: [Sighs] *This is so exhausting!*

Therapist: *It is. Do you remember what we had agreed with Mum for when we finished today?* [Points to reward schedule.]

Client: *Okay, I'm going to try.*

- ***Structure the treatment in advance***

It can be helpful for the therapist to compile a list of rules for the client (Table 13.1).

The therapist can also prepare a written overview of the phases of the EMDR protocol with picto's (Table 13.2).

If desired, this can be combined it with a reward programme. See Appendices 13.1 and 13.2 at the end of the chapter.

Items in Table 13.2 can be ticked off as they are completed. If necessary, a portion of the process can be hidden if it might be too much information for the child at once.
Additionally, cards visualizing SUD and VOC and potential resources can be helpful (see, for example, www.silverkit.nl or https://www.anagomez.org/shop/).

If EMDR is provided online, it is vital to make precise arrangements. For example, online sessions should be conducted on desktop computers, not laptops or tablets, so the child cannot

Table 13.1 EMDR rules for children with ADHD

Ages 12 years and younger	Ages 13–18 years
Go to the toilet beforehand Drink afterwards No chatting during eye movement Stand up at the agreed signal	Turn off mobile phone during session Catch-up before the start of EMDR No stories or discussion during eye movements

Table 13.2 Phases of the EMDR protocol with picto's

Phase	Picto's
Explain EMDR	
Describe the traumatizing event	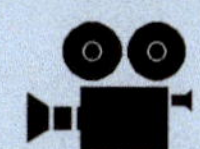
Identify the image	
Examine why this image is still so disturbing/unpleasant	
Use EM^{+} (eye movements, light bar, buzzers, etc.) Start EM^{+}	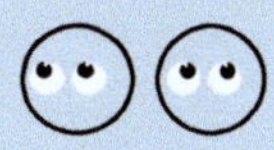
Check if there is still disturbance	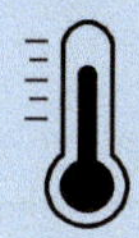
If there is still disturbance remaining, continue and repeat	X...X...X...X...X...X
When there is no more disturbance, link positive thoughts or words to the memory	
Body scan and positive closure	

walk around with the screen. Agree with parents that the child should not be disturbed by family members and that they will have gone to the toilet and had a meal beforehand.

- ***Explaining EMDR***

The general explanation of the procedure is the same for children with and without ADHD. However, there are some differences in emphasis.

Because children with ADHD lose attention quickly, they must understand that concentration is the key to eliminating distressing memories. For example, after explaining the chest of drawers analogy (see Chapter 7), the therapist might say 'You need to concentrate very hard because the drawer needs to be completely tidied up for EMDR to work as well as it can. It may bother you if a bit of clutter is left behind.' If the child is becoming distracted, bring their attention back to the task.

Children with ADHD have a poor sense of the passage of time. So, therapists should emphasize that the objective is to deal with what is happening here and now, not what happened during the experience. It is also helpful for the therapist to point out that the target memory or image may become blurred or change throughout therapy and that the child does not need to hold on to the original image. The therapist might illustrate this by saying 'You know how your screen can get blurry while you are playing a game if you don't have a good internet connection? That is what will happen to this memory.' The therapist will often have to repeat this because children with ADHD find this concept difficult to understand or they may forget this point. The impulsiveness of children with ADHD and their tendency to create associations means that negative feelings are likely to arise during therapy. The child should be reassured that these associations are not harmful and can help the process. Therapists should not be distracted if the child makes nonsensical comments during the session. Instead, the therapist should maintain the structure of the session. See Case Study 13.2 for an example.

CASE STUDY 13.2 **Marc: Keeping on task**

Marc listens attentively while the therapist explains how the light bar works. Marc enjoys trying this out and takes a moment to follow the lights.

Marc: *I can just keep looking in the middle because then I can also see that* [Marc points to the right side] *and that* [Marc points to the left side].

The therapist then tells Marc that he is supposed to move his eyes back and forth, following the lights.

13.6.3 Assessment (Phase 3)

The therapist needs to be more directive with this target group than with other children to keep up the momentum. Because they tend to be hyperactive and impulsive, children with ADHD have difficulty staying in their seats or being silent. They may make all sorts of inappropriate and out-of-context comments. It is best to minimize this by remaining directive. The therapist must remind them of the rules that were already agreed upon. The children may respond to everything they see or hear in the room or correct everything the therapist says. For example, because of their associative tendency, when searching for the negative cognition (NC) they will often want to elaborate on why a particular event was so unpleasant.

Recommendations: Put irrelevant information aside; tell them you will return to it later and continue with the protocol questions. Redirect their attention to the questions needed for the assessment each time. See Case Study 13.3. Drawing a picture of the target image, especially for children with ADHD, can help them to stay focused.

CASE STUDY 13.3 Looking for negative cognition

Client: *I don't know what you mean by your question ... It's awful because now I'm thinking about it again. I had gotten it completely out of my head. Now my head is starting to feel all weird because of your questions and I feel like I'm being totally rewound to what happened then and it's bad, I don't want that. Can't we do something else? I know something else we can talk about.*

The therapist briefly repeats an earlier explanation of why they are doing this and continues with the next question in the protocol.

Therapist: *Is it that you can't stand looking at that picture now from the chair you are sitting on now?*

Client: *Yes, exactly! I can't handle it.*

13.6.4 Desensitization (Phase 4)

The pace of the EM+ should sometimes be adjusted (lowered or raised) according to the speed of information processing. Dual attention should be maintained: Attention must simultaneously focus on the triggered memory and the WMT. The therapist should observe the client's ability to keep pace and adjust as needed.

Recommendations: The therapist supports the client's concentration by regularly reminding them to keep following their finger or the light and motivating them by complimenting them.

Because they are adept at making associations, children with ADHD may mention other memories during desensitization. At back to target, therapists should check whether the child is still making associations related to the identified target. See Case Study 13.4.

CASE STUDY 13.4 Bob: Back to target

Bob is an 8-year-old boy with ADHD. When going back to target, the SUD has dropped to 1. When asked 'What makes it still 1'?, Bob replies 'I don't know'. The therapist asks Bob to think of the original memory as it is in his mind, now.

Bob: [Sighs] *I don't even remember when my birthday date is ... that's hard enough. This is even harder. So, I can't deal with this at all.*

Therapist: *Bob, you are doing very well. When you go back to the original memory, what do you notice now? What do you remember about the memory we began with?*

Bob: [Squeezes his eyes shut and presses his hands against his temples.]
Then we must be very quiet ... well, now I can see that again ... and it still feels a bit unpleasant.

Therapist: *What makes it still so unpleasant?*

Bob: *The teacher's nasty voice.*

Therapist: *Okay. Just concentrate on that and move on.*

Frequently, back to target fails because the child thinks of several memories simultaneously, including irrelevant ones. Perhaps this is because their thinking is so associative.

Recommendations: Repeatedly refer to the target: 'Think of the memory that we started with, what do you notice now?' If the child cannot describe what they feel and they say 'something', then encourage them to focus on that 'something'.

They might be dreading the sessions because they must sit still, and the same happens every session. The treatment process can be tedious to them, especially if the results are not immediately visible or noticeable (the SUD does not drop immediately, or their symptoms do not diminish quickly). For this reason, it is good to keep them motivated ('Well done, you are doing well, just keep going') or remind them about their reward card. Concentration can also be improved by alternating distracting tasks/BLS or offering different tasks simultaneously: eye movements, buzzers, or having them tap themselves. The therapist can also combine eye and motor movements, like V-step (see Chapter 7). The light bar also provides good opportunities for additional WMT. Most children find light bars exciting, which increases their motivation for treatment. As an extra task, they can be asked to name the colours of the lights on the light bar. Sometimes, creativity is vital to maintain an optimal working memory load and to maintain attention. Case Study 13.5 provides an example of how this can be done.

CASE STUDY 13.5 A creative solution for optimizing working memory load

Therapist: *When I say roses, you say tulips. And when I say tulips, you say roses.*

Client: *Okay.*

Therapist: *Roses, roses.*

Client: *Tulips, tulips.*

Therapist: *Tulips, roses, tulips, roses.*

Client: *Roses, tulips, roses, tulips.*

To make it even more difficult (and to increase working memory load), the therapist asks Bob to sing a melody using the words roses and tulips, changing the tempo and intonation.

13.6.5 Installation and Body Scan (Phases 5 and 6)

The therapist must remain directive and maintain the pace of the process, even during the installation of the positive cognition (PC) and body scan.

13.6.6 Closing the Sessions (Phase 7)

It is customary at the end of the session to instruct the parents to let the child calm down first and take some time off. Since treatment has usually been an intense experience, it is good if parents can ensure that their child does not receive too much stimulation afterwards.

In children with ADHD, many stimuli lead to hyperactivity. Ask the child and the parents to monitor and record responses in a diary. This helps to channel the flow of thoughts and reactions. Especially with parents of children (up to 12 years), it is good to fully explain the importance of this, as the children themselves will soon forget. Parents can, for instance, leave a notebook ready at the front door as a reminder when they get home.

13.7 Case Studies

13.7.1 Children (4–12 Years)

The main concerns for young children are their physical restlessness and impulsiveness. These characteristics require the therapist to maintain a directive attitude, adhere to the steps of the protocol, ensure a consistent pace, minimize external stimuli, and retain the child's attention. Visualization of the protocol steps (see Table 13.2) and rewards can help provide guidance. See Case Study 13.6 for an example.

CASE STUDY 13.6 **Bob: A directive approach**

Bob is an 8-year-old boy with ADHD who has been medicated for some time. He angers easily and has frequent conflicts with other children. Lately, he has been saying things like 'I don't want to go to school anymore because I get blamed for everything.' His mother says he suffers from extreme fear of failure. He is often anxious at night, and he sleeps badly. He denies having problems. His mother has witnessed his behaviour and says that he appears to get scared and angry when his teacher or a classmate corrects him. After some questioning, it becomes clear that there have been various events that have caused him to no longer want to go to school and he quickly loses his temper (swearing, rudeness). These reactions cause him additional problems: he is sad at home.

Therapist: *Together we will find out which memories have caused you to become afraid of going to school now. After which event did this start and after which events did it get worse?*

The therapist and Bob search for the relevant events and put them on a timeline. Bob's mother is present during this session. The therapist and Bob ask her to provide missing information where necessary. They put the memories they found on the timeline to create an overview.

Therapist: *Look at the timeline, we have come a long way in sorting it out.*

Bob: All this talking only makes my head very busy right now and I don't want to think about this exactly, because then I only get sad. I really don't remember anything, and I also have all these other things in my head. Every time I want to say something, I suddenly think of something else, and I forget what I wanted to say.

Therapist: Yes, that's how it goes in your head, which is a bit full. Do you know what I find so clever about you now? That you are thinking so incredibly hard to make this overview together with me. We have already made super progress! I think you've already earned a nice sticker! You may choose one.

Then Bob and the therapist choose the memory after which, according to Bob, his fear of school started. He had been told to leave the classroom after being falsely accused of something. The target image is 'I see the teacher saying to me, "Leave the classroom and stand in the corridor", when I had not done anything at all. I see myself waiting in the hallway, even though I didn't know what to say.' While reading the protocol's instructions, Bob looks at the pictures of the protocol's steps which gives him guidance. Nevertheless, he is easily distracted: he laughs and keeps making comments, such as 'I'm already thinking of something', when he hears that all sorts of feelings and thoughts can come to mind as part of the process.

During assessment, Bob's thoughts constantly return to the past, how bad it was then, and he finds it difficult to look at the drawing from the perspective of the present. He also frequently wants to get up from his chair and walk around. The therapist remains patient and asks him nicely but firmly each time to return to his chair. The desensitization goes well, and after the first session the SUD related to this memory is 0.

During the next session, another memory is selected from the timeline (bullying on the bus to school: a boy points a ball gun at him, SUD = 10). When going back to target, the SUD is reduced to 6:

Bob: *It has moved backwards a bit, that ball gun, but it is not all gone yet.*

Therapist: *Okay, we continue ... What comes to your mind?*

Bob: *That gun.* [He follows the moving lights of the lightbar with his eyes.] *How many times are we going to do this with the lights and the eyes?*

Therapist: *Just keep going.*

Bob: [The lights stop] *It's a pity that the light bar is not round because that would be much harder.*

Therapist: *What do you notice now?*

Bob: *I don't know, I can't concentrate on anything.*

Therapist: *You're doing super well! Look again at the memory as it is now. What comes up?*

Bob: *That feeling that I can't do it ... no, that I'm mad at that boy with the gun.*

Therapist: *Okay, good. Concentrate on that and move on.*

The session ends at SUD = 1. The session is concluded with the positive statement 'I'm the best'. Treatment is concluded after five sessions. Bob dares to go to school again. He would like to learn to respond calmly when he is wrongly accused of something.

It is also essential to be mindful that intense emotional discharges can occur during treatment. A good example is found in Case Study 13.7.

CASE STUDY 13.7 **Milan: Dealing with intense emotions**

Milan is an 11-year-old sporty boy who has been known to suffer from ADHD for some time and plays football at a high level. His dream is to become a professional footballer. On the way to a football training, for which he leaves in a hurry because he did not have all his stuff ready in time, he is hit by a car. He is seriously injured and has to recuperate for several months. His physical recovery is reasonable but not optimal, which means he can no longer play football at a high level. He is very frustrated by this and his angry moods become disproportionate. He can no longer concentrate at school and is very busy.

Milan is referred to our clinic because of behavioural problems and concentration problems. In addition to ADHD, partial PTSD is diagnosed and EMDR is indicated. It soon becomes clear that his anger is directed at the driver who continued driving after the accident, meaning the family was unable to file a claim for damages. His worst image is the driver who drives away. He cannot properly describe what the image looks like, because he does not have a clear picture in his head. He draws a picture of a head with an empty face in it.

NC: I can't stand thinking about this picture.

During the desensitization, Milan becomes mercilessly angry. He gives his school bag a mighty kick, sending it flying across the room. The therapist offers a longer set with even faster eye movements, after which the tension (SUD) decreases significantly and eventually drops completely to 0. Milan goes home exhausted, but relieved.

A week later, Milan says that he doesn't understand why he feels different now, but that he now feels better about himself. He says that he is still angry with the driver, but that he would now like to meet him and calmly tell him how he ruined the life of a future professional football player. At school he becomes slightly less distracted and his angry moods are greatly reduced.

13.7.2 Adolescents (13–18 Years)

Adolescents often have several relevant target memories, especially if they were diagnosed with AD(H)D at a later age. In this case, they have had frustrating experiences for a long time because their problem had not been recognized and a diagnosis had not yet been made. This often creates damage to one's self-image. Relevant evidence (memories) can be sought through the core belief path. The intrusion or timeline path may also be useful if intrusive mental representations or specific symptoms are involved. Compared to children younger than 12, adolescents show less physical agitation during the session, but associations can make them agitated. With this age group, one should also remain alert to problems with motivation. Using adequate rewards can help. It is also sensible to repeatedly reassure the young person that all associations are welcome, as they will be more worried than younger children about making mistakes. They may be fortunate to have a gift for associative thinking because it can benefit them in EMDR. Indeed, this treatment is designed to allow associations to emerge and simply to follow them. Case Study 13.8 illustrates this.

CASE STUDY 13.8 **Lotte: 'Nothing goes well'**

Lotte is 17 years old and was recently diagnosed with ADD. This is a huge relief for her. Finally, there is an explanation for everything that has gone wrong in her life. Lotte had a series of negative experiences related to ADD throughout her childhood. She struggled a lot at school and was often told she was lazy, when in fact she tried very hard. She has two older sisters who do not have ADD and got through their schooling very easily. This makes Lotte feel stupid compared to them. Her parents and other family members have said regularly that she should become more like her sisters.

Lotte suffers from fear of failure and has also become socially anxious. Her symptoms are instigated by her negative core beliefs: 'I am not good enough' and 'I am stupid'.

Using the belief path, relevant 'evidence' for her core beliefs is sought. Lotte panics at the start of assessment of a specific memory. She is afraid that she will not be able to concentrate properly or that she will be distracted by unrelated thoughts. The therapist reassures her and emphasizes that all associations and reactions are allowed and that no comments will be considered wrong. Throughout the treatment, the therapist maintains a fast pace with short breaks between sets, during which Lotte occasionally has to be slowed down when answering the question 'What comes to mind?', as she tends to elaborate enormously. Otherwise, the treatment runs smoothly and is successfully completed. After six sessions, four memories are desensitized. Her social anxiety has decreased, and she has gained a more positive self-image. Lotte knew before the treatment that she was neither stupid nor a failure, but after the six sessions of EMDR she really felt that way too.

13.8 Concluding Remarks

Clinical experience shows that EMDR can produce good results in children and adolescents with ADHD. During the diagnostic phase, it is crucial to be mindful of general traumatic experiences, as well as specifically ADHD-related negative social experiences, that may have caused secondary problems, such as anxiety, depression, and low self-esteem (with underlying negative core beliefs).

EMDR is indicated in cases of full, partial, and comorbid PTSD or other trauma symptoms that result from negative ADHD-related experiences. Because post-traumatic stress reactions can increase the characteristic irritability of children with ADHD, EMDR will reduce the stimulus sensitivity, subsequently improving emotion regulation and overall functioning. EMDR treatment of children with ADHD requires a lot of creativity, patience, and perseverance—just as their upbringing by their parents and teachers requires that. So, continuous motivation, encouragement, and additional structuring of the treatment process are recommended. Rewards can also increase motivation for EMDR, provided they are carefully chosen in agreement with the child and their parents. It is recommended to set aside time during the preparation phase for determining adequate rewards and concrete treatment goals and to consider the gains that can be made from treatment explicitly.

As of this writing, there is little scientific research describing the effects of trauma treatment with EMDR in children with ADHD, but the impression from clinical practice is that EMDR works equally well in children with ADHD and in those without ADHD. Research into attentional processes and WMT in this target group might contribute to knowledge about and understanding of the supposed working mechanism of EMDR.

Appendix 13.1: Example of a Reward Card

- After each session, a smiley face is drawn or a sticker is placed on the card.
- The child qualifies for a reward after a pre-agreed number of sessions. For some children, it is best to offer a reward immediately after each session—for example, something sweet or an activity.
- A diploma may be awarded at the end of the treatment.

This reward card belongs to: ______________________________

Session 1		
Session 2		
Session 3		After three sessions, [name] may choose from the following rewards: - go to bed half an hour later - choose what to eat - watch a movie together
Session 4		
Session 5		
Session 6		

Appendix 13.2: Example of a Reward Card

This reward card belongs to: ______________________________

Why do I need treatment and what will the treatment do for me?	
Afterwards I will (for example)	**Check what applies to you**
Be less restless in my head	
Be able to concentrate better, so I will finish homework faster and sleep better	
Feel better	
My parents will nag me less that I have to do something	
Be hassled less by other kids	
Cross off each session after completion and make an appointment for a big reward when the treatment is completed	
Session 1	
Session 2	
Session 3	
Session 4	
Session 5	

After completing all the EMDR sessions I may ______________________________
(e.g., buy a new Play Station game)

EMDR for Children and Adolescents with Autism

14

ESTHER LEUNING AND PETRA SPUIJBROEK

14.1 Introduction

Care providers working in child and adolescent (C&A) psychiatry, youth welfare services, and schools are becoming more adept at recognizing and supporting children with autism (autism spectrum disorder/ASD). This makes it possible to identify problems faced by parents of children with ASD quickly and to initiate early therapy. However, it is not always easy for therapists to use EMDR with children in this target group when there is comorbid PTSD. There are several reasons for this: the symptoms of PTSD may not be recognized, EMDR in children with ASD proceeds differently than therapists are accustomed to, and the communication problems of children with ASD can complicate therapy.

This chapter describes the characteristics of children with autism and the consequences for therapy with EMDR. The aim is to provide therapists with the information and tools needed to make trauma therapy more accessible to this target group. We review how to recognize and qualify these children's problems, summarize related findings from scientific research, present a rationale for EMDR in children with ASD, and review the indication criteria. We discuss points of interest and suggestions for optimizing the use of the EMDR standard protocol for children and adolescents in this target group. The chapter concludes with a summary of the characteristics discussed, potential complicating factors for EMDR therapy, and possible solutions.

14.2 The Target Group

14.2.1 Definition

The prevalence of autism is currently estimated at 1–3% of the population (Hoeberichts et al., 2022), with autism occurring three to four times more often in boys than in girls (Baio et al., 2018; Loomes et al., 2017). Fifty per cent of those with ASD have an intelligence quotient (IQ) below 70. Although the cause of autism is not well defined, it is generally assumed that the disorder results from an interaction between a genetic predisposition, environmental

Esther Leuning and Petra Spuijbroek, *EMDR for Children and Adolescents with Autism*. In: *Handbook of EMDR for Children and Adolescents*. Edited by: Renée Beer and Carlijn de Roos, Oxford University Press. © 2026, Oxford University Press. For the English edition. DOI: 10.1093/oso/9780198918400.003.0014

risk factors, and social factors (Lai et al., 2014; Schaefer 2016). A biopsychosocial model has, therefore, been proposed as an explanatory model (De Bildt et al., 2021).

The heritability component of autism is between 60% and 90% in identical twins and between 10% and 30% in fraternal twins. It is plausible that hundreds of genes contribute to the aetiology of ASD (Gilman et al., 2011) which, in combination with various environmental factors, increase the risk of developing ASD, particularly when exposure occurs during the prenatal period (Croen et al., 2005; Gidaya et al., 2016; Ornoy et al., 2015; Raz et al., 2015; Volk et al., 2013). Older parental age correlates with an increased risk of autism (Idring et al., 2014). Other associations continue to be discovered: for example, the total brain volume of children with autism is significantly larger, especially in the first four years of life, after which there is a growth arrest that is not seen in normal brain development (Rommelse et al., 2011; Staal et al., 2016).

The range of manifestations of autism is enormous. Many people associate ASD with an image of a hand waving, swaying, mentally retarded boy who does not make eye contact and can hardly speak or is mute. The character in the film *Rain Man* will also be familiar to many: he is very good at maths but seems 'naive and stupid' when dealing with other things, which constantly gets him into trouble. This leads to funny situations in the film, but in the real lives of children with autism and their parents, it is usually less humorous.

The DSM-5 (American Psychiatric Association, 2013) replaced the distinction between different forms of autism, as given in the DSM-IV-TR (American Psychiatric Association, 2000), and now describes a 'spectrum from less to more severe impairments' and refers to autism spectrum disorders (ASD). This spectrum is classified as a neurodevelopmental disorder with the following diagnostic criteria:

A. Deficits in social communication and social interaction.
B. Restricted, repetitive patterns of behaviour, interests, or activities; hypo- or hyper-reactivity to sensory stimuli.
C. Impairments are present in early childhood.
D. Substantial impairments in all areas of daily life.
E. The impairments cannot be better explained by intellectual disability or global developmental delay.

For the characteristics listed in criteria A and B, the level of severity is distinguished according to the amount of support and assistance the person needs:

1. Needs support.
2. Needs substantial support.
3. Needs very substantial support.

14.2.2 Behavioural Characteristics

No biological marker has yet been found for autism, so diagnosis is based on behavioural char acteristics. Box 14.1 provides an overview of the behavioural traits mentioned in the DSM-5.

BOX 14.1 Features of ASD according to DSM-5: Behavioural traits

A. **Persistent deficits in social communication and social interaction**

1. Deficits in social and/or emotional reciprocity, including reduced sharing of interests or affect, limitations in spoken language, failure to initiate/sustain conversation
2. Deficits in non-verbal communication, including eye contact, facial expression, body posture and gestures
3. Deficits in maintaining relationships, including lack of fantasy play, no interest in peers

B. **Limited, repetitive patterns of behaviour, interests, or activities**

1. Stereotypic or repetitive motor movements, use of objects or speech, including fluttering, echolalia
2. Stubborn adherence to routines or ritualized patterns of verbal or non-verbal behaviour (e.g., rigid patterns of thinking and difficulty with change)
3. Very limited and fixed interests or preoccupations
4. Hypo or hyper-reactivity to sensory stimuli, including negative reactions to specific sounds and textures, excessive smelling of objects, or visual fascination with lights or movement

Mounting evidence from scientific research suggests that problems in information processing are responsible for the behaviours described in Box 14.1. Studies of cognitions in children and adults with autism show that they are less able to process and integrate information than people without autism. This results in a lack of overview, leading to misunderstandings of the world around them and impaired social interactions (Brundson & Happé, 2014). Information processing difficulties consist of:

- Deficits in executive functioning (EF): difficulties in planning, organizing, and switching, resulting in loss of information.
- Lack of central coherence (CC): the inability to monitor and categorize a multitude of information, combined with an over-focus on details, resulting in an inability to see the bigger picture.
- Lack of theory of mind (ToM): a limited ability to empathize and to see things from another person's perspective, also known as 'difficulty mentalizing'.

The scientific literature emphasizes peculiarities in the way various parts of the brain work together and their connectivity in people with ASD. For example, several studies show that the functional connectivity of cortical areas is reduced (underconnectivity) in autistic people compared to non-autistic people, leading to difficulties in processing complex information (Just et al., 2004; Kana et al., 2011). The working memory of people with autism is also smaller than in people without autism. Therefore, people with autism cannot 'scale up' when greater demands are placed on their working memory

(Rahko et al., 2016; Wang et al., 2017). It has also been shown that there is less connectivity between perceptual and memory regions in children with autism. This leads to difficulties in processing sensory information.

Van den Hout and Engelhard (2012), in their study on working memory load, concluded that a reduced emotional response to a memory image does not occur when the working memory load is too low or too high. An impression from clinical practice is that the working memory of people with autism is likely to be overloaded sooner than in people without autism and that this prevents processing from taking place. This would explain why eye movements as a working memory taxing task often must be offered slower to these children, and this would also explain why eye movements can be too complex, to such a degree that switching to another BLS/WMT is needed. Features of information processing in autism that require adaptation of the standard EMDR protocol for children and adolescents are listed in Box 14.2.

BOX 14.2 Additional features of ASD in information processing

1. Delayed information processing
2. Rapid overload of working memory
3. Problems with central coherence
4. Dysregulation due to overstimulation
5. Difficulty generalizing

Source: de Bildt et al. (2021); Rommelse et al. (2011); Staal et al. (2016).

14.2.3 Comorbidity

Autism is accompanied by mental retardation in about 50% of cases and epilepsy in about 30% of cases. Other common somatic comorbidities in autism include visual and auditory impairments and autoimmune diseases. There is also a higher risk of obesity, which is associated with an increased risk of diabetes and cardiovascular disease (Muskens et al., 2017). In terms of psychiatric comorbidity, ADHD, Tourette syndrome, anxiety disorders, behavioural disorders, and depression are common (Mutluer et al., 2022; Staal, 2016). Trauma- and stressor-related problems and gender dysphoria are also relatively common in autism (Leef et al., 2019).

Research on autism and comorbid trauma-related symptoms is still in its infancy. The prevalence of traumatic stress and PTSD in the population and the effects of potential traumatic events on people with autism are yet to be confirmed. It is generally believed that children with autism have a higher risk of encountering unpleasant life events (Peterson et al., 2019).

Mehtar and Mukaddes (2011) conducted an initial study of the effects of traumatic events on children with ASD and comorbid PTSD in a population of 69 children and adolescents aged 6–18 years. Over 56% (40) of them also had an intellectual disability; 26% of them had experienced one or more traumatic events, such as sexual abuse, maltreatment, or witnessing or being a victim of a disaster or violence, and 66% of those 26% met the criteria for PTSD. Behavioural changes that emerged following these events were measured using a semi-structured questionnaire (Trauma Symptom Investigation Form in Autism Spectrum Disorder, TIF-ASD) developed by Mehtar and Mukaddes, which was completed by the parents of the studied group members. The results showed that the experience of trauma was associated with reduced social skills, communication skills, and self-reliance. Stereotypical autistic behaviours increased, as did levels of aggression, distractibility, sleep problems, hyperactivity, irritability, and self-harm.

There is disagreement in the scientific community about the effects of traumatic events on autistic people. Some believe that people with autism may be more susceptible to traumatic stress reactions because of their difficulties with language comprehension and information processing, deficits in emotion regulation, and more social isolation. Others hypothesize that autistic people may be less susceptible to developing traumatic stress symptoms because of differences in social perceptions and difficulties in describing emotional events, which may lead them to experience and/or interpret events differently (Brenner et al., 2018).

14.3 Empirical Research

The first case reports describing therapy for children with autism and PTSD appeared between 2006 and 2014 (King, 2010a, 2010b; Kosatka & Ona, 2014). Case studies showed that both trauma-focused cognitive behavioural therapy (TF-CBT) and EMDR can be used in clients with autism. Earl and colleagues (2017) mention some focal points for the application of TF-CBT which are very similar to the focal points described in Section 14.5 for EMDR therapy.

A first study on the effectiveness of EMDR therapy in 21 adult clients with autism and (partial) PTSD was conducted by Lobrecht-van Buuren and colleagues (2019). The therapy consisted of eight sessions of EMDR for PTSD symptoms in addition to treatment as usual consisting of guidance with daily life problems. After EMDR, the severity of both the PTSD symptoms and the severity of autism traits were found to have decreased. The author concluded that EMDR can be an effective therapy for adult clients with autism and PTSD. The reduction in autism traits was attributed to reduction in stress and anxiety.

Building on the work of Lobrecht-van Buuren and colleagues (2019), Leuning and colleagues (2023) investigated whether EMDR could reduce autism symptoms in 21 autistic adolescents (aged 12–19) who did not have PTSD, but lived under conditions of daily stress and turmoil. After 10 sessions of EMDR on stress and turmoil situations, these adolescents were found to have significantly less stress symptoms and fewer autism symptoms, as measured by the parent-reported Social Responsiveness Scale (SRS), when the baseline scores were compared with the follow-up scores at three months after treatment.

This application (EMDR aimed at stress reduction in everyday stressful situations) may be a welcome addition to the few existing therapeutic options for this target group.

14.4 Rationale for EMDR

The EMDR procedure has several features that fit well with the disorder-related needs of children with ASD and with the general therapy guidelines for these children (Subramanyam et al., 2019).

- A structured protocol: After a few repetitions, the child learns exactly how the sessions go. This predictability increases the child's sense of security. The protocol provides opportunities for the child to exercise control throughout events in several places.
- The therapeutic procedure places only limited demands on the child's verbal abilities.
- The child's associations are accepted ('Anything that comes to mind is right'), so the child does not need to be afraid of making mistakes. As a result, the therapeutic process will not stagnate because of the autistic child's anxiety.
- The EMDR standard protocol for children and adolescents up to 18 years can be tailored by making step-by-step adjustments for different chronological and or social-emotional ages—an advantage for children with autism who have discordant profiles.

14.5 Points of Consideration for EMDR Therapy

This section describes recommended adaptations relating to indication criteria (Section 14.5.1), per autism characteristic (Section 14.5.2), and per phase of the standard protocol for children and adolescents up to 18 years of age (Section 14.5.3).

14.5.1 Indication Criteria

The indication criteria for children with autism are the same as those for other children and no specific (deviating) instruments are used to screen for or diagnose PTSD in this target group. Indication becomes complicated if the severity of autism prevents adequate contact between the child and the therapist. For such cases it is important to recruit an assistant for the therapy sessions: either a parent or caregiver who can 'read' the child. This is an adaptation that is also used when treating young children and adults with intellectual disabilities with EMDR (Mevissen & De Jongh., 2010; Mevissen et al., 2011; see Chapter 16).

- ***Diagnostic overshadowing***

In the diagnostic phase, it is important to differentiate between symptoms attributable to autism and symptoms attributable to PTSD. The risk of 'diagnostic overshadowing', in which symptoms are classified as due to autism and not identified as PTSD, occurs both in children with autism and in children with intellectual disabilities. For example, if a child does not tolerate being touched this might be attributable to autism or to PTSD. Due to 'overshadowing', the PTSD diagnosis can be missed if the symptom is wrongly attributed to autism.

- ***To treat or not to treat?***

In the past, many therapists and psychiatrists working with autistic people (children and adults) believed that providing a structured environment for clients with comorbidities was the most important therapeutic goal. The underlying assumption was that an appropriate environment was important for maintaining emotional balance and reducing the risk of emotional disturbance. Interventions such as psychotherapy were seen as potentially emotionally disruptive, and therefore 'risky', ruling out EMDR. However, in recent years case histories have convinced therapists of the opposite: often clients (adults and children) with autism themselves insist on confronting 'old ghosts' and are highly motivated for therapy (Barol & Seubert, 2010; King, 2010a, b; Mevissen & Jongh, 2010; Mevissen et al., 2011). Therapy often leads to unexpected developmental and functional gains.

- ***What level of development?***

Limitations in communicative and social skills, possibly in combination with a general or partial developmental delay, result in disparities between the functional level and chronological age of children with autism. Therapists must determine which adaptations of the EMDR protocol for children and adolescents aged up to 18 best suit each child's abilities.

14.5.2 Autism Characteristics

- ***Limitations in social communication and interaction***

(Characteristics A.1 and A.2 in Box 14.1)

- ***Involving a significant other in therapy***

The support of a significant other, such as a parent or caregiver, is needed to facilitate communication between therapist and child when the communication and social interaction skills of the child are limited. Their role is to interpret the child's reactions for the therapist and 'translate' the therapist's comments, questions, and instructions for the child. See Case Study 14.1 for an example.

CASE STUDY 14.1 Peter: Facilitate communication between therapist and child

Peter, age 11, says that his grandfather has died. While explaining this he loses track of the story and panics. The therapist tries to reassure him, but Peter does not want to continue because he is 'afraid that the story he is telling is not correct'. At this point, his father is asked to join the session. He listens to the story to supplement details as necessary. The only detail that needs to be added is where grandpa was during his hospitalization and during the visiting hours. If the father can provide this detail (which to other people may seem unimportant), Peter can continue the rest of the session on his own. Peter's father is very impressed by the details his son manages to remember. Peter's mode of narration illustrates how he perceives the world: in loose detail.

The EMDR storytelling method (see Chapter 8) can also be used for children with little verbalizing ability.

- ***Limitations in verbal and non-verbal communication***

(Characteristics A.1, A.2 in Box 14.1)

- Verbal communication

Therapists can be led astray by taking a child's language literally. See Case Study 14.2 for an example.

CASE STUDY 14.2 **Rosalie: Trauma masked by a verbal communication style**

Rosalie, age 14, had been assaulted. Discussing the event did not evoke any distress. 'It happened in July 2018 and now it's February 2019, so it's over and we don't need to talk about it,' she said. However, it was reported that she was having nightmares, flashbacks, and behavioural changes and was avoiding social situations. The therapist and Rosalie's mother explained to her that events from the past can still hurt and cause nightmares and flashbacks. Rosalie's trauma symptoms were reduced.

Even if the language used by children with autism seems clear and coherent, misunderstandings can arise. Therapists should mirror the child's use of language and confirm their understanding of what a child means by keywords or statements.

- Non-verbal communication

The therapist's ability to detect and understand a child with autism's non-verbal communication can be constrained by characteristics typical of autistic people: facial expression and body language can be absent or in conflict with what the person is saying. As a result, the therapist may receive little feedback from the EMDR process, making it difficult to assess whether information processing is taking place. See Case Study 14.3 for an example of non-verbal cues.

CASE STUDY 14.3 Ruben: Non-verbal communication

Ruben, age 9, has been diagnosed with autism and is highly intelligent. During desensitization, the therapist asked him repeatedly what came up. Each time Ruben was questioned, he was very slow to respond and all he did was frown, shrug his shoulders, and utter 'hmmm'. The therapist noticed that Ruben's shoulders lowered and the frown on his face slowly disappeared during desensitization. These non-verbal cues were the only indication that information was being processed. When the SUD reached 0 and the VOC was 7, Ruben opened his eyes and smiled radiantly.

If there is no (non-)verbal feedback during a session, the session's effect must be inferred from whether there has been a reduction in symptoms. It is not uncommon for there to be no detectable therapeutic response during sessions with children with autism even though the SUD may have subsided by the next session. In such situations, it is advisable to just follow the protocol.

- ***Deficits in maintaining relationships, including a lack of fantasy (play)***

(See characteristic A.3 in Box 14.1)

- ***Inability to use imagination***

It is challenging for many children with autism to make a mental representation. A lack of imagination and imaginative ability is one of the most prominent characteristics of autism. This inability may imply that memories are not visually represented in the mind or that it is not possible to create a still image or a drawing of the memory. As a solution for allowing activation of the memory, the therapist can ask the child to bring pictures to their sessions: for example, a photograph of a person associated with the bad event or someone similar, a picture of the child at the age of the event, or pictures from a magazine that evoke associations with the event. Also, the therapist can draw a picture, following the child's instructions. Case Study 14.4 describes the stimulation of memories in a child with limited imaginative ability.

CASE STUDY 14.4 Romy: Limited imaginative ability

Romy, age 10, does not have a mental image that can evoke the distress she feels when she thinks about the death of her guinea pig. The guinea pig was in bed with her. She fell asleep on it and accidentally squashed it. Because she was asleep when this occurred, she cannot imagine or create a picture of it, so the emotional charge of what happened cannot be evoked. By using pictures of her guinea pig and having her mother tell her what the guinea pig looked like when it was dead, combined with a picture of herself of that age, a collage of her feelings is made. By looking at this collage, Romy feels the necessary distress and the memory can be further activated and reprocessed.

Another solution to the limitations posed by a lack of imaginative ability is to ask about other sensory perceptions: 'What do you hear, what do you smell, what do you feel on your skin when you think about that event now?' The therapist then asks the child to draw what they see when they think about these other sensations to create a visual representation of the event. It is sometimes helpful to practise making and remembering mental representations with autistic clients before starting EMDR therapy.

- *Limited, repetitive patterns of behaviour, interests, and activities*

(See characteristics B, Box 14.1)

- Preoccupations

One of the main features of autism is stereotypy (B1), including stubborn adherence to routines or ritualized patterns of verbal or non-verbal behaviour—for example, rigid patterns of thinking and difficulty with change (B2); and very restricted fixed interests: for example, being abnormally intense or focused (B3). These behaviours make it difficult to assess what is the most relevant aspect of an event to a child with autism. This may be related to the abnormal perception and stimulus processing, which can influence all phases of EMDR therapy. Case Study 14.5 is an example of a preoccupation with numbers.

CASE STUDY 14.5 **Kevin: Preoccupied with numbers**

Kevin, aged 13, has a preoccupation with numbers. When Kevin and his father are seriously injured in a car accident, Kevin indicates that the upturned number plate with the snapped speed limit sign (see arrow in Figure 14.1) is the most disturbing image of the accident.

Figure 14.1 Broken hectometre post.

The tendency to fixate on things makes children with autism susceptible to fixating on, for example, the EMDR light bar, the therapist's fingers moving back and forth, or the 'buzzers' (giving tactile stimulation). As a result, the child cannot focus on both internal changes and external stimuli, so processing becomes impossible. A preoccupation with numbers can complicate defining SUD and VOC values because the child wants to score too precisely. See Case Study 14.6.

CASE STUDY 14.6 **Donovan: A tendency to fixate**

The SUD in a boy with autism is 7.775. The therapist's instruction to mention only one decimal point eventually leads him to accept the 'new' rule and this allows the process of therapy to continue.

Sometimes, the child will ask whether the SUD can drop to 0. They may point out that 'If the event in question was so unpleasant and awful, it can never be 0 and will remain at 0.2'. To avoid such discussions and prevent potential blocked processing, the therapist may measure the disturbance associated with an event in a more global sense by asking only if the disturbance has increased or decreased. The therapist could ask, for example, 'Can you indicate on the sheet with smileys whether it is more disturbing, equally disturbing, or less disturbing than before?'

Typical preoccupations of children with autism can interfere with EMDR. A recommended way to counter this is to agree with them on boundaries of time, place, or number of repetitions, preferably during preparation; for example, a boundary is to decide when attention will and will not be paid to the fascinating object or the repetitive action. Depending on the preoccupation, the therapist and child can agree on how many actions the child may do and/or the amount of time they can spend on it. Preoccupations can occur spontaneously during assessment and desensitization. If that happens, the therapist should pause the process and insert an instruction, like in Case Study 14.7.

CASE STUDY 14.7 **Georgio: Setting limits to keep the process going**

Therapist: *Okay, you may now turn the device [with the clicks or buzzers, or the light bar] on and off by yourself three more times and then we will continue working on the memory using it.* (number limit)

Or

Therapist: *We will discuss whether the exact number of the final disturbance score is 0 or 0.5 during the final minutes of therapy. For now, we will continue our work.* (time limit)

Or

Therapist: *This therapy room is used for working with the light bar for eye movements. The room next door is used for talking about other things. We go there when we are done in this room.* (place limit)

- ***Rigidity***

(See characteristics B2 and B3 in Box 14.1)

Rigid ideas and attitudes can inhibit therapy motivation and interfere with adaptive processing; for example, if the child adamantly takes the view 'I can't handle this therapy' or 'It won't work once again'.

Cognitive strategies, such as challenging thoughts or a Socratic approach to change beliefs, are rarely effective with this target group. Rigidity can block the EMDR process in all phases. It takes creativity, persistence, and humour to break through this rigidity.

- ***Hypo- or hyper-reactivity to sensory stimulation***

(See characteristic B4 in Box 14.1)

Children with autism may have reduced or enhanced sensitivity (hypo- or hypersensitivity) to certain sensations. This may manifest as hypersensitivity to light or sound, intolerance of being touched, or high sensitivity to certain smells or tastes. This has implications for the choice of distraction task during the desensitization phase of the EMDR protocol. Children with autism often report that eye movements make them dizzy or that the light from the light bar is too bright. Research shows that eye movements are the most effective distractive task (Van den Hout & Engelhart, 2012). Therefore, this task should be used whenever possible. Clinical experience with these children shows that the lightbar is usually more accessible to follow than the therapist's fingers because it requires less social interaction between the child and the therapist. However, it is essential for these children that the therapist does not sit behind the lightbar but rather to the side of it, so that the child does not meet the therapist's gaze when trying to follow the light bar. For many of them, dual attention is impossible. Sometimes, slowing down the eye movements can be enough to enable them to accomplish this dual task. When a child is hypersensitive to sensory stimuli, their working memory becomes so overburdened that processing cannot occur. In such cases, letting the child get used to the EM⁺ first can be helpful. This can be practiced by having the child view a photograph that is not disturbing before starting the desensitization phase. Tapping as a distraction task is unsuitable if a child cannot tolerate touch. This can play a role both during the standard protocol and during storytelling. In the case of a young child, sometimes a parent or a hand puppet or soft toy may be tolerated for tapping on certain parts of the body. Case Study 14.8 provides an example.

CASE STUDY 14.8 **Romy: Hyper-reactivitity to touch**

Romy is a retarded girl with autism whose guinea pig died after she lay down on top of the animal in her sleep. Since this incident, she has had huge temper tantrums and is constantly angry with her stepfather. This is because he did not honour their agreement that the guinea pig could only be in bed with her when her mother was watching to make sure everything was all right. Romy always takes her two new guinea pigs with her to therapy appointments.

It is impossible to get her to make eye movements during storytelling. She keeps looking away and gets distracted by everything, pacing and leaving the room when the distress gets too high. She takes off her headphones. She removes the buzzers from her pocket and socks. Romy is only able to remain seated and concentrate on the story if she is allowed to hold her guinea pigs on her lap. The therapist decides to have Romy gently tap the guinea pigs on her lap with her left and her right hand.

- ***Virtual reality***

A BLS/WMT using virtual reality (VR) technology has recently become available for EMDR therapy. The VR glasses can be configured to project a therapy room. The client tracks a ball that moves back and forth in the virtual room with their eyes as a BLS/WMT during EMDR therapy. An advantage of VR glasses is that they can enable children with autism to focus entirely on processing the traumatic memory without being distracted by non-verbal and socio-emotional cues from the therapist. The client hears only the therapist's voice, giving instructions that can prevent or reduce overstimulation.

- ***Problems with information processing***

(See characteristics in Box 14.2)

Delayed information processing is a characteristic of autism: Long reflection times are needed before answers come to questions. Therapists need to give children with autism an explicit time frame to formulate responses. Therapists can also structure their questions to facilitate a response, such as offering the child a choice between two possible answers: For example, 'Is it very or only a little disturbing to think about this picture'?

The phenomenon of delayed information processing, with no decrease of SUD during the session but in between sessions, seems to occur more often in the autism group. Therapists should arrange accessibility to the clients between sessions, as intense emotional reactions can happen in the home environment within a few days of a session. This is recommended to prevent the child with autism or their parents or caregivers from panicking or losing motivation due to unexpected and intense reactions.

Because of the delayed information processing, it might be expected that sessions would take longer than with non-autistic people. However, experience shows that long sessions are mostly not feasible. Shorter sessions of 30 minutes (or even less) are the rule rather than the exception. This benefits children who tire easily because they must do many things they find difficult at once, such as imagining things, focusing on sensations in their bodies, and communicating about them.

- ***Rapid overload of working memory***

(See characteristic 2, Box 14.2)

As mentioned in the chapter introduction, people with autism have deficits in working memory function. Suggestions on how to deal with these are described in Section 14.5.2: section 'Hypo- or Hyper-reactivity to Sensory Stimulation'.

- ***Problems with central coherence***

(See characteristic 3, Box 14.2)

Children with autism take longer than other children to get an overview of a situation, and they can easily become lost in the details. This problem can be addressed by the therapist having a clear plan, being directive, and providing the child with visual information telling (showing) what will happen, in what order, when, and why. The therapist should define which memories will be worked on, in what order, how, and why, ensure uniformity of the process from session to session, and explain the process similarly at the start of each session.

When a lifeline (see Section 14.5.3: 'Case Conceptualization') is made with a child, including the unpleasant events that require therapy and the pleasant things in their life can be essential. The advantage of this is that positive experiences in the child's life can be referred to at various times during therapy.

- ***Dysregulation due to overstimulation***

(See characteristic 4, Box 14.2)

These children's problems with processing information can lead to intense overstimulation or dysregulation when confronted with stressful information. This can lead to an 'autistic meltdown' (emotional outbursts) or an 'autistic shutdown' (withdrawal and unresponsiveness). This can happen during and between EMDR sessions, at home or school. Participation in EMDR sessions by a significant other who knows the child can help to monitor the child's emotions and alert the therapist if problem behaviours emerge or increase between sessions—for example, self-mutilation, bed-wetting, or nightmares. If this occurs, the client should receive training in emotion regulation skills before continuing with EMDR therapy. Experience shows that decisions about this should be made together with the child and their parents or caregivers. Often, the child will choose to continue therapy, even if this leads to a temporary increase in dysregulation, if they are convinced that the therapy will eventually lead to a reduction in their symptoms. The child's desire, combined with the support available from their environment, usually leads to the continuation of EMDR therapy, sometimes after a break. See Case Study 14.9 for an example of the importance of support for children.

CASE STUDY 14.9 **Simon: Support from adults can be important**

Simon, age 12, witnesses his brother being thrown onto an ice rink by a group of boys. He draws a picture of himself next to his brother, crying (Figure 14.2). Simon tries to attract the attention of some adults, but no one responds to him. He bursts into tears while explaining this to the therapist. His father asks to stop the session for a moment because Simon is crying so much that he cannot be understood. But Simon says he wants to continue. His memories then turn out to be about being abandoned by adults at important moments. Simon's father remains present in the therapy room throughout the session and is actively involved in the desensitization process by doing the tapping. The aim is to restore Simon's trust in the adults around him. This proved effective. Simon asked his father for support more often after that.

Figure 14.2 Scuffle at the ice rink.

When dysregulation occurs during a session, the parent or caregiver may be able to suggest a means to calm the child so that therapy can continue. Extra sessions during holidays, taking a day off from school, or transferring certain tasks may be solutions. Relief in one area (less pressure from school) frequently leads to increased coping capacity, allowing the therapy to be continued.

Various programmes are available that teach and train the child how to regulate their emotions better—for example, TF-CBT (Cohen et al., 2017), STAIR-A, (Guidiño et al., 2017), the Sleeping Dogs method (Struik, 2019b; see Chapter 12)—so that trauma therapy can be resumed afterward.

- ***Problems with generalization***

(See characteristic 5, Box 14.2)

Children with autism commonly lack the problem-solving skills, creativity, and imagination needed to find appropriate solutions and apply them in everyday life. They do not readily recognize that what they learn in one situation can also be used in other conditions. For example, a child may learn not to be afraid of being bullied at school, but they will not transfer this learning to the sports club or other places outside of school. Therapists must clearly explain that new skills are transferable to different settings. This can be reinforced by using role play to practice new skills.

14.5.3 Per Phase of the Protocol

The following are the points to consider for each phase of therapy.

- ***Case conceptualization***

It can be helpful to create a visual overview or lifeline covering the main events in the client's life in the order in which they occurred. The onset and severity of their trauma symptoms can be superimposed on this visual overview. Their lack of 'central coherence' makes it difficult to indicate the progression of a symptom's severity over time. Therefore, they are asked to assign a global (current) SUD.

The lifeline can be looked at repeatedly as therapy progresses, helping them to keep track of their progress. For children without autism, therapy often starts by reprocessing the memory that gives the highest disturbance (SUD). For children with autism, however, it is recommended to first practice with memories having a low SUD until the child becomes familiar with the protocol, gains confidence in its operation, and possibly becomes less frightened by the emotions that may be evoked.

- ***Preparation***

  – Explanation of the therapy

It is important to explain EMDR to the parents and the child well in advance of therapy. In an initial meeting, the therapist explains the procedure and asks the parents and child if they have any questions. Because children with ASD have difficulty extrapolating the information they receive to their situation, the therapist must explain the process of EMDR in a manner that enables the child to identify with it. This can be achieved by emphasizing the connection between traumatic experiences (events) and the child's symptoms. On the internet, a lot of material can be found for psychoeducation.

  – Pictograms

Due to verbal communication limitations, a visual representation of the EMDR procedure can be helpful. Figure 14.3 provides an example.

The sequential steps of the therapy are shown in pictograms: tell the movie of the memory of an event, pause on a picture, determine the type and level of emotion caused by looking at it, deploy the chosen EM^{+} (taps, eye movements via light board, taps, buzzers, eye movements via the hand, eye movements via light board), determine the emotion again, and finish. The pictograms are used every time.

Pictograms have also been developed for children with ADHD (see Chapter 13). The therapist's choice of pictograms will depend on what is expected to be most easily understood by the child.

  – Resource development and installation (RDI)

The RDI protocol is usually implemented to help children learn to cope with difficult situations through mobilizing reliance on one of their traits as a resource, such as perseverance or self-confidence. The problematic situation may involve confronting the traumatic memory during therapy. Resource installation requires abstract thinking, which can be difficult for children with ASD. In the RDI protocol the child needs to recall a situation when the resource enabled them to handle that situation well and imagine themselves using it to

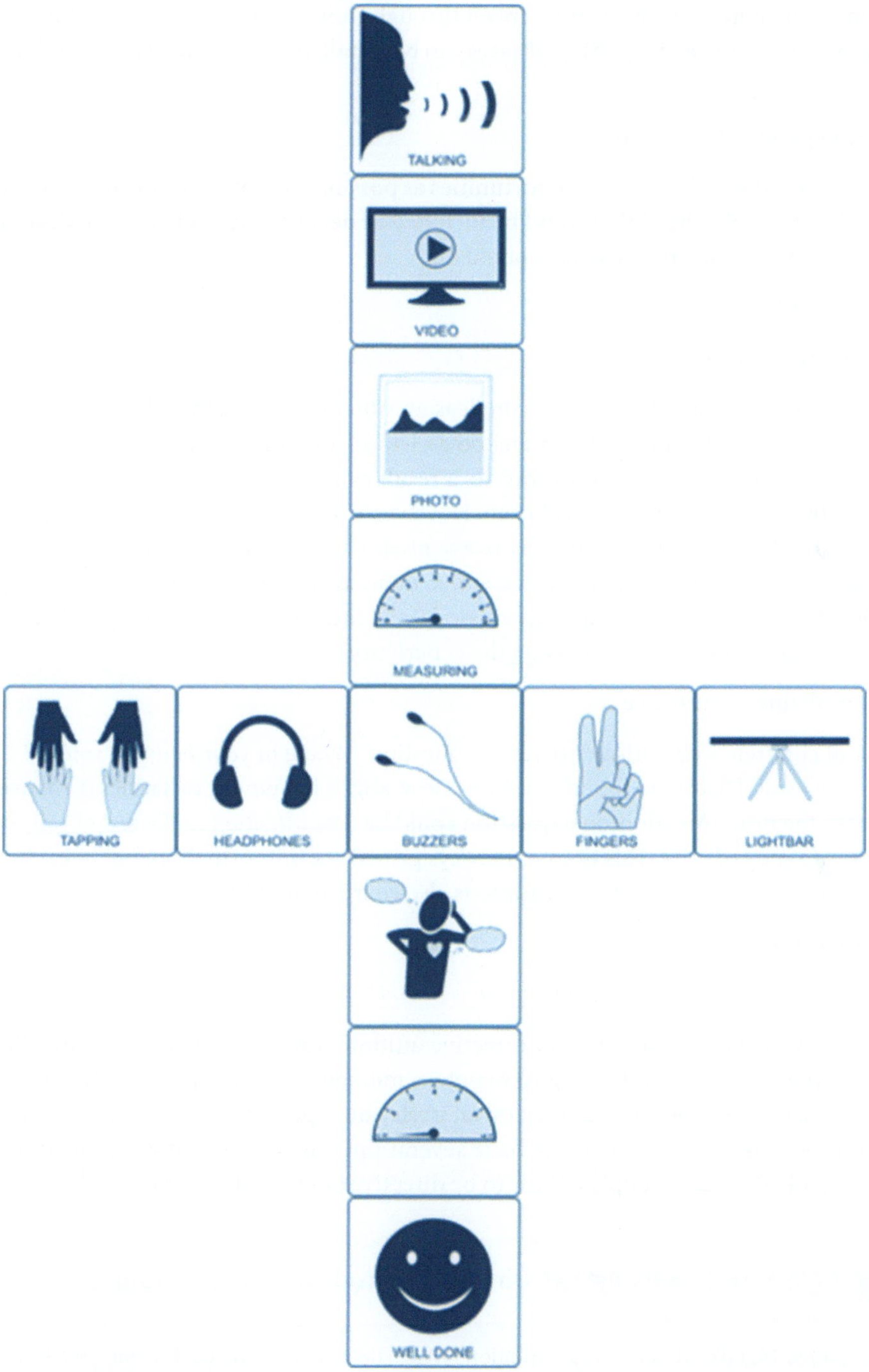

Figure 14.3 Pictograms.

overcome a current problem, so as to 'travel through time'. For many children with autism, this is too difficult. Instead, uplifting phrases can be installed: *'I can do it', 'I am brave', 'I have done difficult things before'*.

- Strengthen sense of control

It is vital to give the child as many opportunities as possible to feel a sense of control over the process. For example, the child should be included in deciding which issues are dealt with, and when and how long they will be worked on.

- ***Assessment***

  - Domain choice

Children with autism often experience unpleasant situations where they do not understand what is happening. This makes them feel powerless at the time and when they think back on it. Being bullied is an example of this. As a result, when focusing on a selected memory, the 'powerlessness' domain is often chosen. However, exploring if the relevant negative cognition might also lie in other domains is essential. Children with autism usually cannot describe nuances, although they can recognize nuances suggested by therapists. The guilt and self-esteem domains are frequently missed if the therapist does not provide them as an option. This can inhibit fully processing the experience.

  - Localizing disturbance

Almost all children with autism answer the question *'Where in your body do you feel that?'* with 'In my head'. Disturbance and emotions (fear, anger, happiness, or sadness) are usually felt only in the head. An additional question could be *'Pay attention to the rest of your body; where else do you feel this?'* This does not always provide new information, but it teaches the children to become more aware of sensations elsewhere in their bodies.

- ***Desensitization***

  - Directive attitude from the therapist

Therapists must show a guiding and directive attitude during desensitization by offering limited response options and trying to maintain momentum in the process. The goal is to prevent the child from becoming stuck on an irrelevant aspect of a memory. If this happens and the process stagnates, therapists have several options for regaining momentum. See Case Study 14.10 for an example of how to be directive but not take over control.

CASE STUDY 14.10 **Ashraf: Directive attitude from the therapist**

Ashraf, aged 14, talks about various situations where he has been bullied, but each time the events get mixed up. He associates on the colour of the clothes of the bully and the other children who were involved. As a result, he loses the thread of his story. The therapist lays three sheets of paper on the table in front of Ashraf, and labels them: Bullying situation 1;

Bullying situation 2; Bullying situation 3. When Ashraf continues his story of being bulled and it is unclear for the therapist which situation he is referring to, he asks Ashraf to indicate to which number it belongs. When during desensitization an association comes up that belongs to one of the other situations (not the one they are working on) the therapist writes the association on one of the other papers and then points Ashraf back to the situation they are working on. This way they manage to desensitize situation 1 until SUD = 0.

- ***Mental video check***

A mental video check is implemented when there is still avoidance behaviour after all relevant memories have been reprocessed (see Chapter 7). The child goes through an imaginary future situation with adequate behaviour (no avoidance) and opens his eyes as soon as disturbance is experienced. Children with autism can usually do this and follow a sequence of imaginary steps describing a future event that still makes them nervous. For example, if a therapist talks a child with autism through the process of returning to school after a long break ('You will get up in the morning, eat your breakfast, then you will pack your things for school and walk to school with your mother and your sister'), the child will be able to show the therapist at which points in the process they expect to become nervous. Such a 'mental video check' is an ideal way to help children with autism mentally prepare for an event that might otherwise overwhelm them and make them anxious. VR glasses can also help by allowing the child to see a school visit in the glasses, in a way compensating for the autistic child's lack of imagination.

- ***Future template***

The limited imaginative capacity of children with autism implies that creating an image of a future situation may be too difficult for them. Therapists can help them develop an image of a future situation which is neutral or reflects the child's everyday reality by asking the child to draw a picture of this anticipated situation and then install the statement 'I can handle it' (regular installation procedure). If the child cannot make a drawing, the therapist can role play the future situation with the child while linking the role play to the positive statement 'I can handle it'. Role play can help to make abstract situations concrete, enabling the child to experience what a future situation might be like and helping them to feel empowered.

See Case Study 14.11 for an example of role play.

CASE STUDY 14.11 **Vince: Role play**

Vince, age 8, is being bullied. Children touch him and then shout, 'Yucky! Vince has an infection!' They then wipe their hands cross another child's hands who in turn says same thing. The therapist re-enacts this with Vince. Vince says, 'I can handle it'.

- ***Closure***
  - Closing the session

A traumatic memory that has not yet been completely neutralized to SUD = 0 by the end of a session should be set aside with care. If not, the child might leave the session in an aroused emotional state, incapable of regulating their emotional and physical tension. Together with the child, the therapist may devise an effective way to put the traumatic memory aside, to be addressed again at a future session, by literally putting the material used in a session in a box and storing it. The lifeline can also be used to put the traumatic experience in perspective; the memory is placed on the line between positive memories, with less disturbance than before the session.

  - Closing therapy

It is helpful to visualize the results of therapy when the process comes to an end. This can be done by having the child check off all the adverse events that were treated on their lifeline or by shredding the drawings and pictures used. It can be good to involve significant others and let them know what has been achieved, remembering that the child often cannot articulate this themselves. A tangible reminder (a homemade drawing or an image from the internet symbolizing that the child is doing better) can help them to visualize what has been achieved.

14.6 Concluding Remarks

Table 14.1 provides an overview of ASD features, resulting complications, and suggested solutions to optimize the use of EMDR in children and adolescents with autism.[1]

Table 14.1 EMDR in autistic children and adolescents: Complications and solutions

ASD characteristics	Complications	Solutions
A: Persistent deficit in social communication and social interaction (see Box 14.1)		
1. Deficient social-emotional reciprocity	Child does not understand the therapist's explanations	- Read EMDR information together - Use pictograms - Involve parent/ caregiver in sessions
Reduced sharing of emotions	Child does not give information about the internal process	- Parent/caregiver interprets child's body language and answers - Therapist settles for less information - Therapist offers range of responses

[1] Thanks to all the children whose drawings we were allowed to use.
Pictograms: M. Zeldenrust, Freelance multimedia developer, The Hague: mischka@mmmz.nl.

ASD characteristics	Complications	Solutions
Not taking initiative, not able to set limits	Child does not give a signal to stop when overstimulated	- Ask at regular pre-set intervals if the child can continue or stop - Draw the child's attention on how to stop the device (e.g., lightbar or buzzers) or agree a stop signal - Ask the parent/caregiver how to detect fatigue or overstimulation
2. Deficiencies in non-verbal communication: – Eye contact – Facial expression – Body posture – Gestures	Therapist does not understand the child's body language	- Take time to learn the child's non-verbal communication - Be alert to non-verbal signals and understand their meanings (voice inflection, facial expressions) - Ask parent or caregiver for the meaning of signals
3. Deficiencies in developing relationships		
- inability to use imagination	- Child unable to imagine what EMDR is after explanation	- Demonstrate use of EMDR on a minor event of daily stress SUD < 4
	- Child cannot form a mental picture	- Use photos from the internet to represent events - Construct picture of event using a collage of photos, comics, drawings from parent/carer/therapist
	- Child unable to make a future template	- Role play for future template - Make images representing the future experience with desired/adequate behaviour and have the child say 'I can handle it' - Ego-strengthening statements and flash cards
B: Limited, repetitive patterns of behaviour, interests, or activities (see Box 14.1)		
1. Stereotypic or repetitive movements, use of objects or speech	– Inability to sit still	- Choose BLS/WMT that do not interfere with stereotypical movements (e.g., buzzer in trouser pocket when child is rocking)

continued

Table 14.1 *continued*

ASD characteristics	Complications	Solutions
	– motor movements, like rocking, prevent client paying attention to BLS/WMT	– choose more distracting task (e.g., hand or finger puppets, or let the child do the tapping)
Echolalia—or Peculiar or repetitive use of language	Echolalia hinders the EMDR process	Validate the child's attempt to communicate
2. Persistent adherence to non-functional routines or patterns, rituals, and thoughts	Inability to let go interfering thoughts	– Write or draw interfering thoughts, then have the child rip them up – Use soap bubbles to represent the interfering thoughts, and let them splash apart
	Need to control the process	– Delegate control to child for choosing distracting task order of targets, duration of desensitization – Let the child use a remote control to use stop, pause and play button
3. Very limited fixed interests	Unable to focus on processing	– Practice looking at a picture – Train the amount of time to focus
	Fascination with equipment which prevents or disturbs processing	– Set limits for preoccupations in time, place, number – Agree how long preoccupations will be allowed – Choose distraction suitable for the preoccupation
	Process stagnates because child focuses on SUD and VOC values	– Indicate values with smileys instead of numbers – Avoid dialogue during desensitization – Round off numbers
4. Hypo- or hyper-reactivity to sensory stimuli	Inability to perform eye movement	– Sort out cause, such as background, speed, too many distractions – Reduce speed of WMT/BLS – Change distracting task: buzzers, taps, headphones with taps – Do not sit behind the light bar, but to the side – Use VR (virtual reality) glasses with quiet background
	Head is described as the place where tension is felt	– Ask where else tension may be felt in the body

ASD characteristics	Complications	Solutions
C: Problems of information processing (see Box14.2)		
1. Delayed information processing	Inability to follow BLS/WMT	- Slow down distracting stimulus - Try different BLS/WMT
	Slow response to the question 'What comes up?'	Allow sufficient time for verbal reactions
	Delayed therapeutic effect of EMDR	- Explain the delayed effects of EMDR to child and parents/carer - Accessibility of therapist for child and parents between sessions
2. Rapid overload of working memory	Difficulty with simultaneous eye movements and concentrating on internal process	- See also B4 - Let child practice with EM+ - Try leaving EM+ on or off when asking 'What comes to mind?'
3. Problems with central coherence	Inability to take an overview	- Make visual overview of symptoms, events, and current disturbance (SUD) in a lifeline - Select from lifeline which symptoms and targets are subject of the session - Let the child put a cross through the treated targets of the lifeline, at the end of the session
	Unsure where one is in the process, what is being dealt with	- Start and end each session in the same way: review lifeline
	Back to target fails, no recall	- Give some verbal cues - If available, show drawing of event
4. Dysregulation due to overstimulation	Can focus on EMDR process only for short time	- Substitute one session with two shorter sessions each week - Shorter desensitization phases
	Overwhelmed by stimuli and associations	- Increase child's sense of control - Increase predictability - Let parent/caregiver signal when it becomes too much for the child - Consider alternative trauma treatment method (e.g., TF-CBT)
	Overwhelming fear in response to memories	- Pendulating: Alternate concentration on memory image and safe place

continued

Table 14.1 *continued*

ASD characteristics	Complications	Solutions
5. Weakness generalizing	Unable to transfer what has been learned to analogous situations	- Explain explicitly that other situations/places are safe again - Use mental video check - Use role play and review situations that have become less unpleasant after role play - Visit places where child still feels distress and reduce it through exposure in vivo
	Distress develops in similar situations	Practise butterfly hugs at home and in other situations that cause distress

EMDR for Deaf and Hard-of-Hearing Children and Children with Developmental Language Disorder

15

LIEKE DOORNKATE, JEANTINE JANSE,
AND GERARDA JEANNETTE WIETEN

15.1 Introduction

This chapter aims to make EMDR accessible to deaf and hard-of-hearing (DHH) children and children with a developmental language disorder (DLD).[1] We hope to contribute to this by providing education on the relevant aspects of these disorders and by giving recommendations for adequate therapy for these target groups. The EMDR protocol is ideally suited for DHH and DLD children with trauma-related symptoms because of its focus on visually and sensorially stored information, making it appropriate for children who have problems with verbal communication. Therapists working with other target groups for whom therapy is impractical because of the level of their verbal communication skills—such as young children who have no abstract language, children with intellectual disabilities, or children who are not treated in their mother tongue—can also benefit from the recommendations given in this chapter.

15.2 Target Group

The target group consists of two populations: DHH and DLD children. The global prevalence of children in both populations is as follows: 5% of the world's population has a hearing loss of 35 decibels (dB) or more (World Health Organization, 2023); 1.7% of children worldwide are born deaf with a hearing loss greater than 40 dB, but only 0.5% of children born in high-income countries are born deaf (World Health Organization, 2012). DLD is present in approximately 7% of 5-year-olds (Leonard, 2014). Children of both populations will be featured based on characteristics, the importance of language for their social-emotional development, and psychopathology per group.

[1] This Chapter contains many outdated references or references written in Dutch. The reason is that more recent alternatives are lacking, as are references in English.

Lieke Doornkate, Jeantine Janse, and Gerarda Jeannette Wieten, *EMDR for Deaf and Hard-of-Hearing Children and Children with Developmental Language Disorder*. In: *Handbook of EMDR for Children and Adolescents*. Edited by: Renée Beer and Carlijn de Roos, Oxford University Press.
DOI: 10.1093/oso/9780198918400.003.0015

15.2.1 DHH Children

- ***Characteristics***

There are different types and degrees of deafness.

- Early deafness: born deaf or became deaf before the age of three. These children cannot hear spoken language and usually acquire language with difficulty. They communicate through sign language.
- Late deafness: initially acquire spoken language, then face a gradual decline in hearing due to factors such as chronic ear infections or inherited traits that force them to adjust psychologically and socially. Their loss influences their perspectives on life.
- Event-related deafness: for example, due to an accident, meningitis, or side effects of medicine, from which they experience acute stress.
- Hearing impaired (HI): hear more than deaf children, which allows them to function better in society. However, the amount of effort they must expend to achieve the same level of functioning as their hearing peers often remains hidden.

- ***Language and social-emotional development***

Because the degree of hearing loss has a significant impact on language and social-emotional development, we distinguish two subgroups within the DHH group: deaf and HI children.

- *Deaf Children*

Hearing children learn much about social manners, social relationships, coping skills, and forms of interaction through a continuous flow of auditory information. Deaf children have no natural access to this. They only receive what is offered in their visual field or explicitly communicated. As a result, knowledge on various topics can be lacking, and there are significant differences between these children regarding the knowledge they acquire: 'funds of information gaps' (Pollard et al., 2009). They also receive less specific feedback from parents (Rieffe, 2015). These factors, combined with reduced opportunities to learn from social interactions, may result in deaf children being less socially skilled and more insecure than their hearing peers. This may affect social learning and the development of knowledge about their own emotions (Broekhof et al., 2021; Eichengreen et al., 2023; Ketelaar et al., 2015). Tsou and colleagues (2021) found that DHH children with low social-emotional competence exhibited more externalizing behaviours.

Sign language is the preferred means of language and information acquisition for these children. Only 40% of information is acquired by watching the mouth of speakers who articulate their words well; the remaining 60% is lost (Sleiffer, 2013). Research by Giezen (2011) shows that DHH children acquire information faster if presented in sign and spoken language. However, sign language is usually not available. As a result, these children are regularly excluded from (family) communication, leading to them feeling excluded (Kouwenberg, 2013). The deaf child may interpret this as a personal rejection. The feeling of not fitting in and not belonging affects the deaf child's identity formation and self-perception.

Growing up with deaf peers in a deaf cultural context is perceived to be a protective factor. An alternative option to make language more accessible to DHH children is a cochlear implant (CI). Today, 90–95% of deaf babies receive a CI between 10 and 12 months of age, which improves language acquisition (Faes, 2018; Verbist, 2010). Possibly as a result of this, the current generations of deaf babies suffer less from knowledge deprivation or funds of information gaps. Research by Rieffe and colleagues (2009) showed that DHH children with a CI are as skilled as their hearing peers in identifying emotions but are less likely to be able to come up with a strategy to resolve conflicts and to feel less angry or sad. This study clarifies that while a CI contributes to language acquisition, it does not eliminate all social-emotional difficulties.

– *Hearing Impaired Children*

Language acquisition appears to be easier for HI children than for deaf children, but parents seem to provide less language to HI children than they do to their hearing peers. Dirks and colleagues (2020) found that parents of HI children used shorter sentences, described fewer emotions and cognitions, and asked their HI children fewer questions. Increased dB loss correlated with lowered levels of language supply. As a result, the HI children in this study had fewer words and concepts with which to express themselves, affecting their social-emotional development.

Because HI children usually grow up in a hearing environment and their disability is not easily noticed, their behaviour is frequently attributed to a personality trait or social or cognitive inability.

Another feature to consider is that HI children primarily focus on a speaker's mouth rather than their eyes, which can be misinterpreted. They often ask 'What?', which may be considered rude, and an inability to listen is frequently mistaken for not wanting to hear. They may feel they cannot keep up because they do not fully understand what is being said. Or, they may joke about something they thought they heard only to realize from people's surprised reactions that they have misunderstood what was said. These phenomena can lead to social isolation or exclusion. HI children develop a range of strategies to appear 'normal', such as disguising that they have not understood something, or they may monopolize conversations to control them.

Because of all this, HI children often feel that the world takes little account of their disability. It is often difficult for those around them to understand that someone who speaks normally has not heard what is being said. The frustration this causes can lead to negative core beliefs, such as 'I am not worthwhile' or 'I am worthless'.

- ***Psychopathology***

A lack of appropriate language provision has significant consequences for the development of a child's social-emotional skills, which in turn affects the emergence of possible psychopathology. Studies of psychopathology in DHH children show higher scores for depressive symptoms and behavioural problems compared to psychopathology in hearing peers (Kouwenberg, 2013; Theunissen et al., 2011; Van Gent 2012). Schild and Dalenberg (2012) found that a group of deaf adults from the general population was more likely to have experienced traumatic events: for example, traffic accidents (75.9%), the unexpected death of a loved one (74.7%), physical abuse (72.2%), natural disasters (67.1%), and sexual abuse (women 53.3% and men 44.1%). These extremely high rates could be explained by information deprivation making them extra vulnerable (Schild & Dalenberg, 2012). Ohre and colleagues (2015) found that amongst their psychiatric deaf clients, 71% of traumatizing events occurred before the age of 16.

In addition, an essential factor is that DHH children find the periods before, during, and after regular 'life events'(like hospitalization or parental separation) more challenging to deal with, and they communicate less about these than their hearing peers. For example, parents may suddenly notice more angry or regressive behaviour in their young deaf child. Still, due to communication barriers, they have less insight into how this may be related to the experience of a traumatic event. Not being able to properly support their child reduces the chances of healthy coping. Deaf adolescents' awareness that their social opportunities are more limited than those of their hearing peers can damage their self-image or lead to other symptoms.

Research on the specific responses of DHH children to traumatic experiences is unfortunately lacking. In clinical practice, DHH children often present with diffuse symptoms, the most prominent being behavioural problems, aggression-regulation problems, concentration problems, and hyperarousal. It is usually challenging to determine whether these problems are deafness-related or trauma-related. Symptoms of avoidance and hyperarousal were found in studies of PTSD in deaf adults by Schild and Dalenberg (2012) and Anderson (2017).

In conclusion, the DHH target group has a higher risk of experiencing a traumatic event and developing some form of psychopathology in response to it.

15.2.2 DLD Children

- ***Characteristics***

A DLD is not caused by hearing problems, too little or poor language exposure, or multilingualism. A DLD is a neurobiological developmental disorder of genetic origin. There are wide variations in the nature of the disorder and the severity of the impairment. A child with DLD remains affected, to a greater or lesser extent, throughout their life.

Children with DLD have problems processing language, understanding language, or expressing themselves in language. Language is divided into three categories: form, content, and use.

- Language form (phonology, syntax, morphology): intelligibility, sentence structure, word conjugations, and inflections.
- Language content (semantics): word meaning and expression of a connection or relationship (for example, cause-and-effect relationships).
- Language use (pragmatics): the application of language in everyday communication. How does the child convey their message, for example, to resolve something or express

feelings? Are their words connected to the topic? Do they take into consideration the other person's prior knowledge? Do they provide enough context for the other person to understand?

Children with DLD have difficulties in one or more of these categories (Gerrits et al., 2017). Language processing encompasses distinguishing sounds, then recognizing words in them, and linking meaning to words. The sequence of words in a sentence then indicates the intention. This process happens automatically and in a fraction of a second in our common language. When something goes wrong somewhere in that process—and sometimes at multiple points, as in children with DLD—it leads to misunderstanding, delays in interaction (as processing is more complex), and the risk of miscommunication.

Because problems are present from birth—that is, from the start of language acquisition—these problems affect various areas of development. Other processes in the brain are also affected in DLD. Children with DLD often have issues with neurocognitive functions, such as auditory perception, (working) memory, attention, planning, inhibition, cognitive flexibility, and executive functions. These functions are essential in setting goals, planning and performing tasks, and evaluating behaviour (Hermans et al., 2021).

- ***Language and social-emotional development***

Inner speech, by which we direct ourselves and give words to what we think and feel, is also impaired (Isarin et al., 2017; Kapa et al., 2021). This means that it is difficult for children with DLD to put words to the thoughts and feelings they perceive or expect in themselves and others (theory of mind). As their inner language is less well deployed to express and direct themselves and to comprehend what they or others are feeling or experiencing, social-emotional development also proceeds differently (Vissers, 2020).

Children with DLD have difficulty describing their feelings and have fewer words to express their emotions. Recognizing and understanding emotions in others is equally difficult, especially when emotions need to be labelled and assigned to a person or situation (Rieffe & Wiefferink, 2017).

Language is also a means of acquiring knowledge and skills, even from non-verbal communication. Difficult or limited social contact leads to less practice and, thus, less knowledge about social interaction and understanding: after all, the linguistic explanation is missing or may not be understood. Children with DLD between the ages of 9 and 16 have an increased risk of psychosocial problems, especially if they are less good at recognizing, understanding, and regulating emotions (Van den Bedem, 2023).

Others often underestimate problems with language comprehension because it is primarily a process that occurs internally, invisible to the outside world. For example, word-finding difficulties, not properly defining or not quickly understanding words, and poor understanding of synonyms, multiple meanings, or which word games are appropriate for a given social setting are often not recognized as such. An impaired ability to provide adequate information about important events and to tell a coherent story can result in miscommunication, misunderstanding, and frustration. Children with DLD frequently face impatience and misunderstanding, which fuels a chronic sense of powerlessness and inability

(Isarin, 2013). This can lead to externalizing behaviours, such as anger or aggression. In contrast, the internalizing DLD child also has difficulty expressing their feelings and experiences, but is more likely to withdraw, possibly resulting in gloom or depression. Both externalizing and internalizing behaviour can lead to a damaged self-image and negative core beliefs about oneself.

- ***Psychopathology***

Longitudinal research in children and adolescents with DLD shows that language difficulties and psychological problems often go hand in hand (Clegg et al., 2005; Boerma et al., 2023). Several studies of children and adolescents with DLD report more internalizing problems, such as depressive symptoms, social anxiety, and psychosomatic symptoms, and more externalizing problems, such as hyperactivity and tantrums, than in non-DLD peers (Lindsay, 2012; van den Bedem et al., 2018a). They also experience more social problems, such as being excluded or bullied, and have lower-quality friendships (Van den Bedem et al., 2018b; Angels Esteller-Cano et al., 2022). In daily life, DLD is a barrier to independence and social functioning.

The problems in children with DLD are also often diffuse and PTSD symptoms might easily be missed because parents and therapists may be lost in the variety of symptoms that also may be related to language problems or other problems.

15.3 Empirical Evidence

Descriptions of the psychotherapeutic treatment of DHH and DLD groups are still scarce and focus mainly on the preconditions for therapy—for example, the provision of therapy in sign language, knowledge of the deaf cultural context, protection of privacy due to the small community, and the use of deaf role models (Anderson et al., 2016; Bishop, 2013; Glickman, 2009; Leigh, 2010). At the time of writing, there is no scientific support for the effectiveness of trauma treatment for these client groups. Similarly, empirical evidence to validate the use of EMDR therapy with DHH and DLD groups is not yet available in the scientific literature. However, clinical experience with EMDR has been positive.

15.4 Points to Consider for EMDR Therapy

This chapter provides an initial impetus for recommendations concerning EMDR therapy for these target groups, including points to consider for communication during the application of the EMDR standard protocol with children and adolescents aged 4–18. The protocol gives children something to hold on to because of the structure and predictability of the steps. This structure provides a sense of security to all children struggling with anxiety. This aspect of the protocol is precious for DHH and DLD children because their language difficulties imply that they are less able to meet expectations from their environment and have a greater-than-average need for clarity and predictability. Another advantage of the protocol is that terms and questions are often repeated for DHH and DLD children.

Another strong point is that therapists can stay close to the child's experience. Children can follow their internal process and communicate about it in their language (to a greater or lesser extent). A well-attuned therapist is vital to facilitate and guide this process.

Parental involvement in therapy can be crucial. They can relay facts and events during the intake phase so that information from the child can be better understood and interpreted. Furthermore, during the therapeutic process they are the eyes and ears, so to speak, who provide additional information or feedback from the home situation about the course and effects of the therapy. Parents see how the child reacts at home, whereas the child is not always aware of these reactions and, as mentioned above, has difficulty reflecting and expressing themselves. Of course, the autonomy of the child or young person is paramount.

15.4.1 General

- ***Attitude and sensitivity of the therapist***

Working with the target groups described in this chapter requires an exploratory, nonjudgemental, and welcoming attitude. Glickman (2009) emphasizes the importance of equality and modesty on the therapist's part. He also encourages elegantly matching the child's knowledge, frame of reference, and skills. Good attunement to the child's language comprehension, language use, and level of communication is also essential.

- ***Working with a sign language interpreter***

Sign language skills are essential for therapists working with DHH children. Therapists who do not have this skill at their disposal should be aware that communication in both directions will be heavily compromised. Although some DHH children can cope quite well with spoken language, this is not always sufficient for them and is, therefore, not the most desirable language during therapy. If necessary, the therapist can use a sign language interpreter trained in the child's first language. Good cooperation between the therapist and the interpreter will improve the working relationship in the therapy room. The therapist can instruct the interpreter in advance about the goal, working method, and expected reactions during EMDR and agree with the interpreter on how to relay subtle signals to the therapist (for example, the child's subtle facial expressions indicate that they do not understand the question). Open questions used during the start of the session can sometimes unintentionally become closed questions when translated into sign language.

This example illustrates that the therapist and the interpreter need to be well attuned to each other to initiate the EMDR process and keep it going. While using an interpreter can enrich and facilitate communication, this example also illustrates that the presence of an interpreter can be confusing (see Case Study 15.1 Part 1).

CASE STUDY 15.1 (PART 1) **Eva: Working with sign language**

The therapist asks Eva *'How did it go after your first EMDR session?'*

The interpreter signs to Eva: *First time EMDR good?*

Eva replies *'Yes, good'*.

Using open questions, as in the following example, can yield more meaningful feedback.

The therapist says *'We have had our first EMDR session'*.

The interpreter signs to Eva *'First time EMDR has happened'*, while pointing to where they were in the room during the session.

Eva nods and looks nervous.

The therapist asks 'After?'

The interpreter looks inquisitively at another point in the room and signs 'After?'

The therapist then asks *'How did you feel afterwards, Eva?'*

The interpreter signs *'How are you feeling now?'*

Eva replies *'Very tired and a little sad. But relieved'*.

- ***Picking up non-verbal cues***

When working with an interpreter, hearing therapists tend to focus mainly on verbal information from the child. However, it is worth paying close attention to the child during the EMDR therapy so that non-verbal cues are also noticed. Gestures, sounds, and movements can be subtle or more intense and noticeable. In either case, it is important to appreciate and interpret these forms of expression as intended. The therapist should be sensitive to the message of the non-verbal signals given by the child. These signals can have different meanings: misunderstanding, shame, anger, fear, and insecurity. Verbalizing the signals that are detected can strengthen the working relationship. It is recommended to use non-verbal signals to complement verbal communication and to pay special attention to the child's apparent physical sensations.

The therapist should keep in mind that these children need to see the therapist's face to communicate. The visual flow of information, which is so important for them, can be hindered if the therapist looks away, writes, or talks at the same time, or if the child cannot see the therapist's mouth because it is hidden by a hand or piece of paper.

Some children develop a distorted view of reality because the information they receive is limited due to deafness or, in the case of DLD, because of limitations in language, thought structure, and information processing. They can be unfamiliar with certain concepts or abstract language; they may take concepts literally and might need to gain the level of knowledge and skills that would be expected of them for their age. Therefore, therapists need to present concepts in concrete rather than abstract terms, use short sentences, and check that the child and the therapist are communicating about the same topic.

The therapist should provide clarity and an overview to give the child a grip on the process and the conversation. Intermediate steps can be added if the therapist gets the impression that the child is 'lost'—for example, if the therapist notices that a child cannot distinguish well between emotions. The therapist can expand the child's knowledge of emotions through an exercise using cards with pictograms representing various emotions, such as disappointment or anger. Visual support of verbal language with body language or the symbolic use of objects can help to concretize concepts. For example, hiding a drawing of an unpleasant event under a book and looking away can clarify the meaning of avoidance.

15.4.2 Per Phase of the Protocol

- ***Diagnostics and case conceptualization (phase 1)***

DHH and DLD children often have an extensive (health)care network around them, consisting of medical, speech therapeutical, remedial, and pedagogical professionals. In clinical practice, a diagnosis of PTSD is often overlooked despite the availability of different professional perspectives. The diagnosis of DHH and DLD children is frequently complicated by the difficulty of determining how behavioural problems relate to speech- and language-related issues. Are depressive symptoms the result of traumatization in social situations or a lack of social skills? Is the child able to self-report what is going on or what is bothering them? Is there a possible comorbid autism spectrum disorder?

Because these children have difficulties in verbalizing their experiences, they might not report traumatic events even though they still suffer from the effects of it. Research indicates that they potentially have experienced many traumatic events. This implies that parents and professionals have an important role to play. Using the Child and Adolescent Trauma Screener (CATS) (Sachser et al., 2017a) can be the start of formulating hypotheses about a possible relationship between symptoms and experienced events.

However, a lack of communicative skills in the therapist may hamper the recognition of PTSD as non-verbal cues are missed. When using questionnaires, we regularly encounter the limited language skills of DHH and DLD children. They sometimes tend to fill in questionnaires in a manner they believe is socially desirable, or they may not understand the expressions used in the questionnaires.

- *Parent and family factors*

It is essential to correctly identify child factors, and parental and family factors, that may influence current symptoms. Parents who have a child with DHH or DLD often face a long process before a diagnosis is made and therapy is offered and implemented. This is often a complicated process in which parents face emotional, medical, practical, and social challenges. They might have PTSD symptoms themselves. In addition, it is often difficult to adequately guide the child through the different stages of development while remaining attuned to both the child's limitations and their potential.

Egberts (2015) describes the complex relationship that parents have with a disabled child and the lack of adequate models of 'good parenting'. This combination has consequences for the attachment relationship, adaptations in communication, the parents' natural parenting style, and the other (hearing) family members. Other influential factors are parental frustration with rearing a disabled child and sibling jealousy arising from the extra attention for the disabled child.

A genetic component may also play a role in DLD, as one or both of the parents may also have a DLD.

Zaitman-Zait (2015) reported that parents of DHH children experience increased stress not only because they have difficulty communicating with their DHH child, but also because they are concerned about their child's language skills, behaviour, and social-emotional competence. Deaf and DLD children must deal with psychological, social, and systemic problems, which makes them vulnerable to the development of psychological symptoms. As a result, they have a reduced ability to recognize or respond appropriately to danger, which increases the likelihood of further traumatization (Beer & De Roos, 2017a).

In conclusion, we advise clinicians to have a trauma-sensitive approach to DHH/DLD children and their parents. PTSD symptoms can be easily missed due to a lack of verbalizing traumatic events and misinterpretation of symptoms. Questionnaires might not reveal PTSD symptoms due to language difficulties.

- ***Preparation (phase 2)***

During the diagnostic phase, the therapist will have gained an impression of the child's knowledge of concepts, emotional skills, and language abilities. During the preparation phase, the therapist will get a more precise picture of the materials or strategies that are likely to suit this specific child.

– *Psychoeducation*

Because DHH children are prone to information gaps (see Section 15.2.1) and because DLD children have difficulties processing linguistic information, psychoeducation about trauma reactions, avoidance behaviour, and the coping process is recommended. In each session, therapists might have to repeatedly remind the children and their parents about what they have learned to keep the topics alive. Psychoeducation is best given with visual support; consider using body language or objects: for example, opening a jar with unpleasant feelings and shaking it empty, after which the child is no longer bothered by these feelings when thinking about the memory.

It is helpful to ask DHH/DLD children what they know about the event they experienced and its possible consequences so that the therapist can fill in any missing information. For example, consider providing information about air turbulence to a child who fears flying after a traumatic flying experience. The therapist can refer to this later, if necessary, during desensitization in the form of an interweave: 'What do you know about turbulence?'

– *Resources*

DHH and DLD children are often dismissive of their positive traits because of their negative self-image. Positive resources are usually installed during preparation to be available for use during desensitization. These can be used as cognitive interweaves during looping. It is striking that the physical RDI anchor (see Chapter 10) offers these children much support. Drawing the anchor can serve as an additional visual reminder to recall the resource (see Figure 15.1).

Figure 15.1 Drawing of an RDI representing boldness made by Dewi (15 years old).

- *Expressions and gestures*

The therapist can use facial expressions and gestures to support their verbal explanation of what will happen during an EMDR session. For example, the therapist can express visually unpleasant experiences and what should be done about them by miming pushing away unpleasant emotions while grimacing with disgust. This can help DHH and DLD children understand better than just a verbal explanation can. However, this approach must be nuanced, as an expression that is too childish can evoke resistance. The previously mentioned attitude of equality and modesty (Glickman, 2009) is indispensable here. Building the child's trust in the therapist is essential in this phase, as the therapist must act as their translator and guide.

Doornkate (2008) reported that adult DHH clients show with body language and facial expressions what they are experiencing during desensitization, like an uncontrolled shout and a distraught face to express distress and terror, or the physical portrayal of experiences. During preparation, the therapist explains to the child that intense emotions may surface during the desensitization phase, which is perfectly fine, and they may express, verbally and non-verbally, within certain limits. It is recommended that concrete examples be given to indicate which behaviours are allowed and which are not. This preparation is relevant for both therapist and child, because during the desensitization phase DHH and DLD children may express their emotions more vehemently than the therapist is used to with hearing children.

Another critical issue to be aware of is the potential presence of tinnitus (hearing a high-pitched squeal or booming sound). Experience shows that this target group can suffer from tinnitus, especially during assessment and desensitization, because of the child's increased arousal. Therapists should be alert to this and, if required, explain it to the child and normalize it, so that it does not cause unnecessary additional distress, anxiety, or avoidance behaviour.

- *Communication options*

The text of the EMDR protocol for children and adolescents is adapted to age level. For children with DLD, the protocol text will need to be adapted to the level that best suits the child. The language and the amount of information can cause problems due to difficulty in (quickly) understanding words or sentences, mentalization, and weak (working) memory. So, verbal information is remembered laboriously. Therefore, it is advisable to provide information in simplified language and, if necessary, give children time to practice using the words, allow them to experience the meaning of the words, demonstrate the meaning to them, or show or draw examples of the meaning. The steps in the sessions can be visualized so that the child gains and maintains a better insight into the course of what will happen. See Chapters 13 and 14: the tools mentioned there for visualization can be used for this target group as well.

- *Choice of BLW/WMT*

The choice of the most appropriate BLS/WMT for DHH and DLD children requires extra attention because sometimes it may be challenging to find the task and the speed that best matches the child's working memory capacity and maintain optimal conditions for dual attention.

In cases of comorbidity, such as epilepsy, Ménière's disease, or vision problems, eye movements may be too taxing as a BLS/WMT, or may induce (fear of) an epilepsy or dizziness attack. In these situations, tapping or a butterfly hug can be a suitable alternative.

- ***Assessment (phase 3)***

  - *Describing the memory*

In the standard protocol for children and adolescents, children are instructed to narrate their memory like a movie. In children with DHH and DLD, misunderstandings about the 'movie metaphor' sometimes arise. See Case Study 15.1 part 2 for an example of using this technique.

CASE STUDY 15.1 (PART 2) **Eva: Using the movie metaphor**

The therapist asks '*Eva, can you describe what happened as if it were a film; not exactly what happened but how it is now in your mind*'.

Eva looks confused and ask '*A real film?*'

The therapist says '*No, not a real film*' and points to her head. '*You know that memory you can't forget?*'

Eva nods affirmatively.

The therapist asks *'What does the film of that memory look like?'*

Eva says *'Oh, yes!'*, with a look of comprehension in her eyes.

The therapist responds *'Yes, that film'*; she moves her hands from her head and holds them in front of her face, so it looks like she is looking at a cinema screen, and asks *'Can you tell me about it, Eva?'* (See images below.)

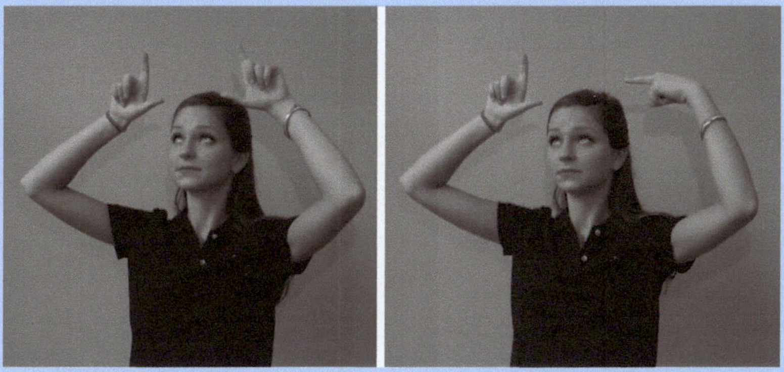

Annoying images in your head *That film.... Can you tell me about it?*

This approach works best if the therapist first lets the child narrate the memory of the event, and only afterwards mentions that it is like a movie (visualizing if necessary), from which the child chooses the image that causes the most disturbance right now.

Some children think mainly in images in their mind but need help to relate essential information about time, location, and people. Children with DLD have problems with time awareness, which can result in multiple memories being jumbled up together.

Sometimes it may be unclear to the therapist who played a role in the memory (images), and who did what. One way to clarify this is to draw the memory or illustrate it with puppets. Sign language can also be used effectively, as the people involved in the memory can be placed in space through gestures. The child can point to that place when talking about a particular person. This method also works for therapists who are not fluent in sign language. An example, showing that a boy hit a girl, appears in Figure 15.2.

It can be difficult to convey who said what in a traumatic memory. The images in Figure 15.3 illustrate that, by turning one's shoulders and head, it is clear what person A (the girl) is saying or doing (threatening). If one turns one's shoulders and head the other way, what person B (the boy) is saying, feeling, or doing (afraid) is clear.

Some DHH children, and particularly DLD children, describe their memories in an illogical and muddled way because they have difficulty translating chronology into language. Visualizing time with the hands can clarify chronological sequences during events. The left hand represents the story's starting point (1) (Figure 15.4). The right hand moves horizontally from the left hand to the right and the endpoint (2).

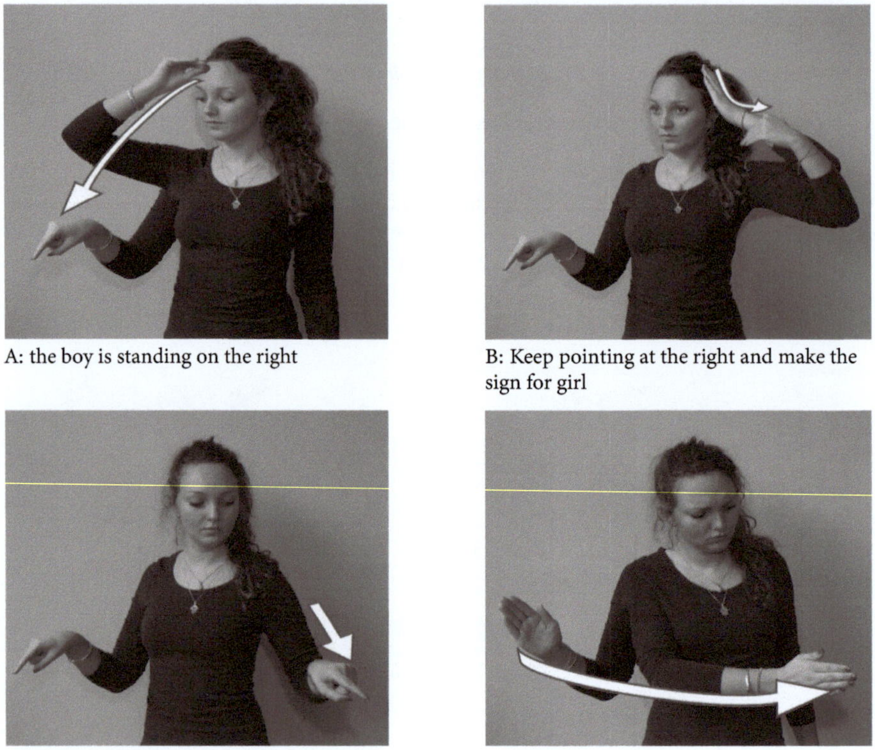

A: the boy is standing on the right

B: Keep pointing at the right and make the sign for girl

C: placing the girl on the left while pointing to the boy on the right

D: the boy hits the girl

Figure 15.2 Gestures can illustrate a sequence of events and who was involved.

Events can be designated as having occurred at points in the intermediate area. If a child cannot clarify the chronology to the therapist, an alternative is to ask the child to depict the memory as a series of drawings (see Figure 15.5). A sequence or chronology automatically emerges from this series of successive images.

– *The target image*

Identifying the target image involves the therapist asking which image is causing the most distress currently. 'Currently' can be defined as the current date or the child's current age. The difference in time between now and when the event occurred can be clarified by placing the target image in space relative to the current date or the child's current age. A drawing or play materials, such as Playmobil or LEGO dolls, can help visualize the target image. Once the target image is established, the dolls can be placed in the correct arrangement on a sheet of paper (Figure 15.6).

Another point that can confuse target selection is the concept of distress or disturbance, which may not be understood or may be taken literally by the child. The therapist's facial

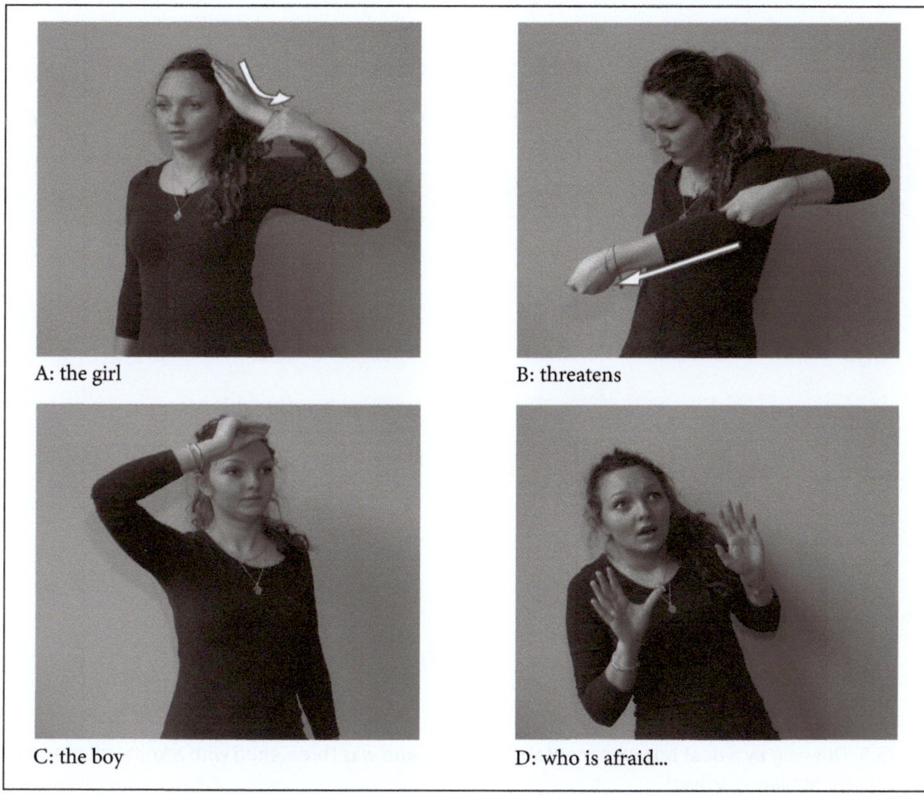

Figure 15.3 Gestures illustrating who was involved and what happened.

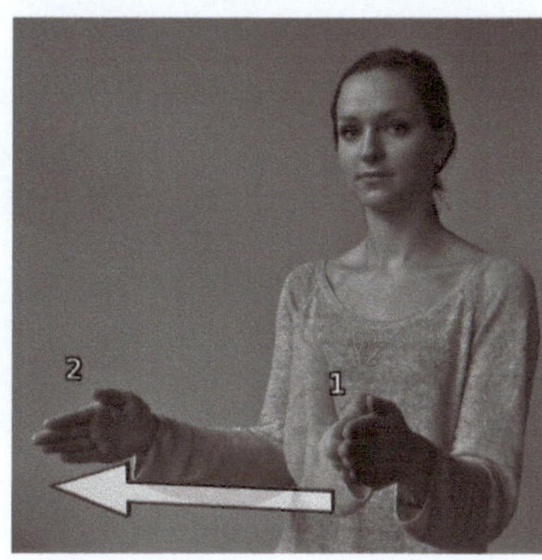

Figure 15.4 Gestures can illustrate a chronological sequence of events.

expressions and body language can support the explanation. For example, they could shrug their shoulders and look anxiously at the target image being pointed out.

If the target selection involves choosing between different disturbing images, these images can be hung in the room like paintings. The child can then indicate their choice by using facial expressions to indicate the degree of distress invoked by each image.

Figure 15.5 Drawing by a deaf boy with mental disabilities who was threatened with a knife, after which police and an ambulance arrived.

Figure 15.6 Target image of a child being trampled by a horse.

– *Negative cognition*

The child's language difficulties can complicate identification of the negative cognition (NC). Sometimes, the arrangement of the puppets used to depict the target image can simplify the identification of the NC. The trick is to balance finding an appropriate NC and showing respect and patience for the child's language difficulties. Sometimes, it is necessary to ask some additional questions: '*You, today, 14 years old* [point to now], *looking at the girl, that's you, at 8 years old* [point to another place]. *What do you think of her today* [point from now to the other place]?' At this point, it helps to repeat the child's response and add *'Oh, you think she* [point to spot of eight years] *is stupid. What do you* [point to now] *think is stupid about her* [point to spot of eight years]?' Sometimes, a suggestion can help because the child knows the right word but can't put it to good use, '*So is she in danger*?'. This is how one can work, step by step, towards a suitable NC.

Children with DLD often have great difficulty with questions that require reflection. They also have difficulties remembering, naming, and expressing the NC from within themselves. Help cards with an NC domain written on each can be helpful. Experience shows that children with DLD can often recognize the most suitable NC if several options are proposed to them in this fashion.

If the child cannot clearly distinguish the difference between the present and the past, puppets can be added to the set-up to help them visualize the difference (a 'now-puppet' and a 'then-puppet', Figure 15.7). An example is given in Case Study 15.1 part 3.

Figure 15.7 The child looks at the target image from the present time.

CASE STUDY 15.1 (PART 3) **Eva: The therapist deciphers the traumatic event**

The therapist points to the 'now' puppet and says '*This puppet is you now, Eva*'.
Eva nods.

The therapist asks '*What does she* [pointing to the "now" puppet] *think of her?*' The therapist points to the arrangement of puppets.

Eva looks frightened and responds '*She thinks she is scary*'.

The therapist pays attention to Eva's reactions rather than her word choice and asks '*What is scary?*'

Eva says '*Horse on girl scary and pain*'.

The therapist points to the 'now' puppet and says '*Okay, she sees that she* [pointing to the "then" puppet] *is in pain. What about that makes you anxious now?*'

Eva looks disgusted, says '*Doesn't want to*', and turns the 'now' puppet face down.

The therapist points at the 'now' puppet. '*So now you think I don't want to look at it?*' The therapist looks from the 'now' puppet to the 'then' puppet.

Eva answers '*Yes*'.

The therapist points to the 'now' puppet and asks '*Are you the same as her?*'

'*Yes*', says Eva.

The NC can be depicted visually if the child cannot verbalize the NC but can express it through facial expressions and body language. For example, the NC 'I am lazy' is portrayed by the child's shoulders and arms drooping, looking down, and mouth hanging open slightly.

– *Positive cognition*

Once the child has found or possibly depicted the NC, the therapist and the child look for a similar positive cognition (PC). The PC should be depicted by the child, with help from the therapist, only as needed (read how this happened for Eva in Case Study 15.1 part 4).

CASE STUDY 15.1 (PART 4) **Eva: Replacing negative cognitions with positive cognitions**

'*Eva, look at that picture,*' says the therapist. '*What would you rather believe about yourself instead of…?*' The therapist portrays the visual NC by slumping in her chair and opening their mouth slightly.

'*I don't understand,*' says Eva, looking a bit bewildered.

'*Okay Eva,*' says the therapist, motioning with her hands as though pushing something aside. '*We'll park that question for now. What is positive and better than fat?* Not quite the other extreme, but more positive on the line from fat to thin?'

'*Don't know,*' says Eva.

The therapist says '*Slim?*'

A look of recognition comes across Eva's face. '*Yes, yes!*'

The therapist looks questioningly at Eva. '*White?*'

'*Black,*' says Eva.

'*Yes, very good. Dirty?*' asks the therapist.

'*Clean,*' replies Eva.

'Yes, good. And now, back to the other picture.' The therapist slumps again in her chair, portraying the NC. *'What would you rather believe about yourself instead of ...?'*

Eva sits up straight with her chest out, face tilted up, and raises her eyebrows.

'Okay, good! You'd like to look like this picture today,' says the therapist and shows Eva a picture of a child looking proud and confident. *'You would like to think: I am strong?'*

'Yes, absolutely,' replies Eva.

- *Validity of the PC*

Facial expressions indicate the difference between 1 and 7 when inquiring about validity. At a VOC of 1, the therapist shakes her head no, frowns, and puts her shoulders down and back. At a VOC of 7, the therapist nods yes and raises her eyebrows and shoulders. She then asks the child to point out where they are on the scale. The VOC scale also provides visual support.

- *Emotion*

If the child has already shown limited recognition of emotions or has limited words for them during intake and preparation, images or pictograms of facial expressions representing the four basic emotions can be used.

- *Level of disturbance*

Indicating the level of disturbance with the hands, as is familiar with young children, does not work well with DHH children. Perhaps this is because deaf children, partly because of sign language, are used to indicating with their hands signs where a starting point and ending point are. Children with DLD need other, more concrete tools to indicate the level of disturbance as well. Some children of both groups can use numbers on a meter, while others prefer a scale with facial images. It is important to be alert to appropriate and shared meaning. When, for example, the facial image at SUD = 0 shows a happy face instead of a neutral face, this can cause a misinterpretation and, therefore, misunderstanding.

- ***Desensitization (phase 4)***

  - *Asking for associations*

A signing therapist must be alert to grammatical aspects of sign language when translating the protocol into sign language. Doornkate (2008) noted that the question 'What comes to mind?' can refer to different experiences. If one gestures this question at the head, one is usually asking about thoughts. The focus is on emotional associations if the gesture is made in front of the chest. And when gestured in front of the stomach, the focus is on physical associations. For children with DLD, the formulation '*What comes to your mind*?' is too abstract and therefore unclear. This can be resolved by explaining and illustrating with examples the variation of potential associations they might get of what they think, see, or feel, and emphasizing that any reaction is okay.

DHH and DLD children respond non-verbally during desensitization through body language and facial expressions. Therefore, processing usually goes well. If the therapist isn't sure whether the child is still within a window of tolerance, back-to-target can be used to check.

Avoidance reactions during desensitization can also manifest, for instance, by the child looking away. In these situations, it is sometimes helpful to refer to previous explanations about avoidance reactions. If the child needs more security, the parent can take a role (for example, by sitting closer), or a support figure can be given an imaginary place ('this cuddly toy is your sweet dog for now'). A previously installed resource with the RDI protocol can also support starting or continuing the desensitization process.

- *Interweaves*

Interweaves adapted to age, perception, and form of communication can be applied in the usual way, and often work surprisingly well. An example is a child who cannot explain to their angry father how frightening his facial expressions are. As a cognitive interweave, the therapist could suggest using an imaginary mirror to show the father how scary he looks to the child. See an example of using a cognitive interweave in Case Study 15.2.

CASE STUDY 15.2 **Marie: Using a cognitive interweave**

Marie looks anxious and says '*Daddy scary face*'.

The therapist encourages the client, '*Go on*'. (Set)

Marie looks frightened; her shoulders are down. She repeats her complaint (looping) and says '*Scary face won't go away.*'

'*Does Daddy see that Marie is scared by his expression?*' asks the therapist (introduction of an interweave).

Marie shakes her head and says '*no*'.

The therapist asks '*How can Marie explain that to Daddy?*'

'*With a mirror?*' suggests Marie.

'*Can you take a mirror and hold it in front of his face so that Daddy can see himself? Okay, just concentrate, Marie,*' says the therapist (set introduced). '*What happens?*'

'*Daddy is startled by his scary face,*' says Marie, with her shoulders down, and she sighs.

- *Resources*

The inclusion of meaningful objects, such as mascots (cuddly toys) or pictures, can increase the child's sense of safety or confidence that they can stay within the window of tolerance or return to it. Physical cues (anchors) or body postures mobilized during RDI can also be used when there is a threat of blocking.

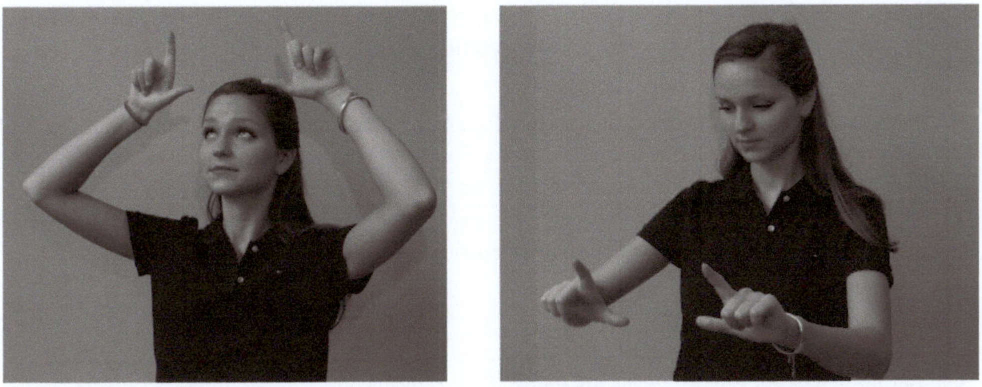

Figure 15.8 *'The disturbing image in your mind.'* *'Look at the mental image. How disturbing is it now?'*

- *Back to target*

Back to target in the standard protocol for children and adolescents refers to the target as it is now stored in the child's mind. The therapist makes the sign of a picture near the head, pulling it down so that it can be looked at (Figure 15.8). If the child does not understand the sign, using play materials to represent the target may be helpful.

- ***Installation (phase 5)***

When installing the PC, a depicted PC can be expressed through body language and facial expressions. The child sits in the posture that matches the PC, after which the sets are offered until the PC is installed and the VOC is 7.

- ***Body scan (phase 6)***

The body scan requires no extra attention or adjustment.

- ***Positive closure (phase 7)***

Like other children, DHH and DLD children may find it difficult to assess themselves positively at the end of a session. An intervention, as described below, can help. The therapist can strengthen the empowering effect of positive closure by asking the child to depict the chosen statement. See an example in Case Study 15.3.

- ***Subsequent treatment phases***

- *Flashforward*

When explaining flashforward, the therapist can point to the image in the mind (see Figure 15.8). The disaster image terrifies the child, although what they see has not 'really happened'. This can be easily clarified in sign language. For DLD children, an explanation of the concept of a 'disaster fantasy' is very important. Once the therapist and the child have established a word for this together, it is important to not vary this word to avoid confusion.

CASE STUDY 15.3 **Max: An EMDR session closes on a positive note**

The therapist makes a gesture of grasping something and pushing it to the side, and says *'The EMDR session is over'*.

The client nods.

The therapist points to the thing that had been pushed aside and asks *'If your friend had done this, what would you think of them?'*

The client responds *'That they are very smart!'*

'Can you say that about yourself?' asks the therapist.

The client responds with an expression of understanding. *'Yes, that's right! Yes, I am smart!'*

'Okay, tell yourself that you are smart,' says the therapist, 'and sit like someone who is handsome'.

- *Mental video check*

The therapist works together with the child to determine which situations (related to the treated memory) the child still avoids or anticipates with a lot of anxiety and therefore need imaginary exposure. For DLD and DHH children with limited working memory, it can help to break down the experience of confronting the situation into smaller fragments. This creates a positive learning experience. Instructions for the assignment should preferably be short and clear (see Chapter 16).

Some children prefer not to close their eyes, especially if the memory makes them very anxious or if they are completely deaf. In these cases, the mental video check can also be done with their eyes open and staring at a fixed point with the therapist sitting (diagonally) across from the child.

- *Future template*

Typically, young children are encouraged to draw a picture of the future template. Even with older DHH and DLD children, visualizing the future template by drawing or using play materials can help to evoke a picture of the future with the desired behaviour.

15.5 **Concluding Remarks**

In clinical practice, PTSD and other trauma-related symptoms appear to be common in DHH and DLD children. These symptoms require trauma therapy. Unfortunately, empirical data on the prevalence of these symptoms and therapy outcomes are lacking. The experience of EMDR therapists in clinical practice shows that EMDR is usually successful in this target group and can generate impressive results.

With the recommendations mentioned in this chapter, EMDR therapy can be applied to these children. The main recommendation is to be alert to their specific mode of communicating and information processing (in DLD children) and to use and activate the different sensory modalities during EMDR therapy. Examples include visualization through drawings, dolls, and other play materials and using sign language.

The great advantage of EMDR for this target group is that the children can follow their associations in a way that accords best with their own language, way of thinking, and experience. This allows them to stay close to their authentic experiences. Communication problems—which they usually experience frequently in contact with others—are less pronounced. Of course, a good match with the communication level and age is essential. This target group requires a specific approach from the therapist, namely an extra focus on non-verbal aspects of communication, a culturally sensitive approach, and providing additional clarity, overview, and guidance during the use of the EMDR protocol. The efforts and patience of therapists are often richly rewarded with symptom reduction and elimination of developmental stagnation. EMDR therapy yields gains in self-esteem and increased coping capacity. Thus, EMDR can make a substantial contribution to the reduction of trauma symptoms and an improved quality of life for these challenged target groups.

16 EMDR for Children and Adults with Intellectual Disabilities

LIESBETH MEVISSEN

16.1 Introduction

The diagnosis of trauma-related problems in people with intellectual disabilities (ID) is often overlooked, for several reasons:

- Until a few decades ago, it was not recognized that people with ID can suffer from various forms of psychopathology, including PTSD.
- Many disruptive or abnormal behaviours that could be attributed to trauma are often misdiagnosed as symptoms of ID or other mental health problems (diagnostic overshadowing).
- Until recently, validated tools for measuring PTSD in this target group were lacking, resulting in insufficient recognition of PTSD.
- Therapy protocols for PTSD that have a strong verbal component are inappropriate for people with ID.

The body of research into the effects of traumatic experiences and the therapy for trauma-related symptoms in people with ID has grown in recent years, contributing to an increased awareness of trauma in ID clients. The importance of proper diagnosis and therapy for trauma in ID is particularly important because, compared to the average individual, people with ID are exposed to a greater number of potentially traumatic events and have more difficulty processing trauma (Mason-Roberts et al., 2018).

EMDR therapy is an eminently suitable form of therapy for people with ID because of its non-verbal nature and its applicability regardless of level of functioning. EMDR is even suitable for people with severe ID (Barol & Seubert, 2010; Hoogstad et al., 2024; Mevissen et al., 2012;). Because the level of functioning of people with ID is less than that of children without ID, the standard EMDR protocol for children and adolescents up to the age of 18 is 'by definition' appropriate for children and adults with ID. The recommendations in this chapter apply to people with ID regardless of their chronological age.

Liesbeth Mevissen, *EMDR for Children and Adults with Intellectual Disabilities*. In: *Handbook of EMDR for Children and Adolescents*. Edited by: Renée Beer and Carlijn de Roos, Oxford University Press. © 2026, Oxford University Press. For the English edition. DOI: 10.1093/oso/9780198918400.003.0016

16.2 **Target Group**[1]

An ID is a condition that affects both the ability to learn and the ability to function independently. IDs refer to developmental deficits rather than developmental disorders or psychopathology. Development follows normal patterns, but at a slower pace, so development lags the chronological age and stops earlier. Various terms for ID have been used: mentally handicapped, mentally retarded, mentally weak, or retarded. It is now common to speak of 'people with intellectual disabilities'. A summary definition is found in Box 16.1.

BOX 16.1 **DSM-5-TR definition of intellectual disability**

An intellectual disability (an intellectual developmental disorder) begins during the developmental period, with impairments in both intellectual and adaptive functioning in the conceptual, social, and practical domains. The following three criteria must be fulfilled:

- Deficits in intellectual functions (such as reasoning, problem-solving, planning, abstract thinking, judgement, schooling, and experiential learning) that have been confirmed by both a clinical assessment and an individualized, standardized intelligence test.
- Deficits in adaptive functioning that result in the person's inability to meet developmental and sociocultural standards of personal independence and social responsibility. Without ongoing support, deficits in adaptive functioning limit functioning in one or more aspects of daily life, including communication, participation in social life, school or work functioning, and personal independence at home or in the immediate social environment.
- The deficits in intellectual functions and adaptability begin during the developmental period.

There are four levels (severity) of ID: mild, moderate, severe, and profound. Previously, the DSM assigned an IQ range to each level. The DSM-5-TR no longer does this, but emphasizes the impact of cognitive impairment on daily functioning and distinguishes severity levels in terms of adaptive functioning in the following three domains:

- conceptual skills, such as the ability to read write and count.
- social skills, such as communicating; being able to empathize with what others think, feel, and mean; and solving social problems.
- practical skills, such as personal care, being able to perform tasks around the house, and using public transport.

Currently, an IQ score of about 70 and below is considered indicative of ID.

Source: American Psychiatric Association, 2022.

In research and practice, ID severity levels are commonly associated with the following IQ ranges:

[1] Most studies on EMDR in persons with mild ID included participants with Borderline Intellectual Functioning (BIF, IQ 71-85 and deficits in adaptive functioning). See chapter 3 in this book. The key points and adaptations for persons with mild ID also apply to those with BIF.

- Mild: IQ 51–70;
- Moderate: IQ 36–50;
- Severe: IQ 21–35;
- Profound: IQ ≤ 20.

Roughly speaking, we can divide people with ID into two categories:

- Mild ID (IQ 51–70);
- More severe impairments (IQ ≤ 50).

Validated prevalence figures are not available. Approximately 1% of the total world population has an intellectual disability. Severe intellectual disability is estimated to occur in 6 in 1,000 people (APA, DSM-5-TR, 2022).

16.3 Rationale for EMDR

EMDR is relevant for this target group because people with ID are more likely than people without ID to be exposed to potentially traumatizing events within their family and following placement in residential care facilities. Moreover, they are less able to process traumatizing events due to their limited cognitive and adaptive abilities, and therefore have a higher risk of developing trauma-related symptoms in response to these events.

Because EMDR is applicable regardless of the nature of the events (traumatic or adverse) and regardless of the level of communication skills, EMDR seems ideally suited for people with ID.

16.3.1 Traumatizing Events

The following are examples of the types of potentially traumatizing events that people with ID may experience.

Within the family, children with ID often experience violence or are victims of physical and emotional neglect. In fact, many children with ID who have behavioural problems come from families with numerous additional problems, such as material deprivation, psychiatric illness, substance abuse or addiction, and/or divorced parents (Vervoort et al., 2021). Often, more than one child in a family, and one or even both parents, will have ID. Because of their disabilities, children with ID are often less accepted or even rejected by peers, and are vulnerable to bullying and sexual abuse. In addition, children with ID who have been placed in institutions are at risk of experiencing traumatic events, such as being the target of aggression, sexual abuse, or punitive therapy. Residential care facilities, where staff turnover is high, provide few opportunities for these children to form secure attachments. The risk of experiencing upsetting negative events may accumulate and persist into adulthood. Parents with ID are more likely to have harsh parenting styles and to perpetuate trauma in the lives of their children, whose safety may be compromised. This can lead to threatened or actual out-of-home placement and cycles of intergenerational transmission of trauma. Adults with ID who can work are often bullied, abused, or excluded in the workplace.

People with more severe ID are more likely to have specific genetic disorders associated with physical abnormalities or pathologies, such as epilepsy. They are at risk of being traumatized by radical medical examinations and therapies. More than one in three people with Down syndrome undergoes major surgery early in life (Valkenburg, 2012). People with ID and epilepsy suffer from traumatizing epileptic seizures and distressing medical examinations (Rodenburg et al., 2009). Swallowing problems are also common in people with more severe ID, which can be very frightening. When they are together with their peers in residential or day-care settings, they may be targets of aggression (Hoogstad et al., in press).

16.3.2 Increased Vulnerability

People with ID have more problems with information processing than others do. Several characteristics of the disability are responsible for this:

- Weak working memory;
- Low attention span;
- Difficulty distinguishing between main and secondary issues;
- Limited problem-solving abilities;
- Difficulty with processing verbal and social information and poor behavioural regulation.

In persons with ID, developmental deficits often remain unrecognized until primary school. School curricula can be overwhelming and may lead to behavioural problems at home and at school (verbal and physical aggression), anxiety, withdrawn behaviour, or passivity. An exception is the relatively small proportion of persons with more severe ID, where the prevalence of organic-cerebral problems is higher. For example, autistic spectrum disorders (ASD) and epilepsy are more common in this group. The combination of cognitive impairment and ASD-related fragmented perception obviously makes it more difficult for these individuals to process traumatic experiences.

Sensory hypersensitivity increases vulnerability to trauma. Because of this sensitivity, seemingly minor unpleasant events—such as the unexpected sound of a balloon bursting, physical pain or vomiting during a bout of flu, unpleasant images on TV, or unpleasant stories—can trigger trauma-related symptoms. In addition, their limited understanding of what is happening to them and around them plays a role, and sharing their experiences is made difficult by communication limitations. Because of their limited independence, their reliance on others is also a factor: others are not always aware of the trauma triggers and therefore cannot always respond appropriately.

16.4 Empirical Evidence for EMDR in the Target Group

Since 1994, EMDR has tentatively made its entry into counselling for people with intellectual disabilities, as reflected in the scientific literature, with several case reports on the application of EMDR in children and adults with ID. Controlled studies on the effectiveness of EMDR in people with ID did not appear until 2017. An overview of these publications is included in Chapter 3. In summary, there is increasing scientific support for the applicability, safety, and effectiveness of EMDR in children and adults with ID, including individuals with severe ID (Hoogstad, 2024).

16.5 Points to Consider for EMDR in Intellectual Disability

16.5.1 General

With the standard protocol for children and adolescents, wherein adjustments are inserted to make it applicable for children, EMDR is a highly appropriate and relevant method of therapy for this very vulnerable target group because it can be used to treat a wide range of psychopathology that can arise from unprocessed events, and it can be applied to all levels of functioning. The effects in clinical practice are often impressive, as in the case of Mitchell (see Case Study 16.1).

CASE STUDY 16.1 Mitchell: Symptoms of trauma not recognized for years

Mitchell has mild ID (IQ 61). He was placed in a residential care home four years ago because of unmanageable, aggressive behaviour, which was mainly attributed to ASD. Mitchell heard little voices that prompted him to behave aggressively. This particularly affected him when he went to visit his mother. He would break things and hit his brother. Consequently, he visited only rarely, and under the constant supervision of an attendant. Both Mitchell and his mother suffered from this situation.

The voices appeared to have been wrongly diagnosed as psychotic experiences, fitting the picture of an ASD, subtype multicomplex developmental disorder (McDD) (De Bruin et al., 2007; Van der Gaag, 2009). The boy had been taking antipsychotics for years. It was discovered that his behaviour was related to re-experiencing the trauma of witnessing domestic violence on several occasions at a young age. His aggression was triggered at home by his brother's comments and in the residential facility when fellow group members argued. After five sessions of treatment with EMDR, the voices and aggressive moods disappeared, allowing Mitchell to return home without any problems. The use of antipsychotics was completely phased out after the EMDR treatment.

The application of EMDR in children and adults with ID does not differ fundamentally from the approach with other children. Therapists should be familiar with the arsenal of tools and techniques that are suitable in EMDR therapy for children in general. The main consideration when implementing the standard protocol is to tailor the application to the limitations of the person with ID. Section 16.5.2 explains how to adapt the protocol, per phase, in response to these limitations. Throughout the therapeutic process, the therapist should assume a directive attitude, as is recommended with all young children.

- ***Communication***

Verbal information and materials appropriate for the developmental age of the individual are needed to explain post-traumatic stress disorder symptoms and the purpose and process of EMDR therapy. Professionals who work with people with ID must be able to communicate simply and concretely; Box 16.2 lists some tips. These professionals are trained to repeatedly check whether they have correctly understood what the person with ID has said. However, this is undesirable during EMDR. For therapists who have become experts in this approach over the years, it is a challenge not to summarize every sentence the person says while applying EMDR, but instead to keep the person focused on the memory.

Communication is most effective if the therapist takes the points summarized in Box 16.2 into account.

BOX 16.2 Tips for communicating with people with ID

- Adjust the pace of speaking
- Leave time for thinking
- Summarize what the child or adult has said and confirm that you have understood correctly
- Ask the client to summarize what you have said or repeat for them the essence of what you have said
- Speak in short sentences and use simple words
- Give one message at a time
- Avoid abstract concepts
- Support spoken language with pictures or objects, or the demonstration of actions
- Make metaphors concrete and visual
- Interact with adult clients in an equal, non-childish way

- ***Involving significant others as co-therapists***

People with ID differ significantly from those without ID in being highly and persistently dependent on others. It is therefore necessary to involve parents or caregivers in therapy—preferably their parents (or relatives if the parents are no longer able to do so), even if the person with ID lives in an institution. They can then actively contribute to recovery and possible family reintegration. During preparation, the therapist assesses the ability of the parents or relatives to adequately cooperate. They may have experienced numerous upsetting events with their child (Hoogstad et al., 2025). Sometimes, the parents or relatives are unwilling or unable to play a role in the therapy. In this case, a trusted caregiver can take on the role of co-therapist.

- ***Trauma therapy for parents?***

Parents of a child or adult with ID may have experienced numerous profound events, such as life-threatening complications during the child's birth, multiple hospitalizations of their child, epileptic seizures, and severe behavioural problems such as food refusal, self-mutilation, and verbal and physical aggression. The parents may have been convicted by ignorant outsiders as incapable of managing their child, sometimes resulting in the placement of their child in residential care. They might then be confronted with the shocking experiences that their child is encountering in said institution, such as peer aggression, a coercive and punitive regime, neglect, or abuse. Parents who are faced with diagnosis of their child as intellectually disabled may experience a profound sense of loss that they need to process. They may also suffer from memories of events unrelated to their disabled child, such as a car accident or childhood abuse. As a result of these traumatic experiences, the parents may have developed post-traumatic stress reactions, which could affect their ability to parent, while their child makes very strong demands on them. The parents and the child may become trapped in an exhausting spiral of negativity, eventually making residential care inevitable. Because parental reactions can interfere with the child's recovery process, it is important for the therapist to assess whether and for what purpose trauma therapy is indicated for the parent (Mevissen et al., 2020b; see also Case Study 16.2).

CASE STUDY 16.2 **Peter: Benefits of additional parental trauma treatment**

Peter is a 10-year-old boy with Down syndrome and severe ID (see also Mevissen et al., 2012). He had regular tantrums and refused to eat solid food. There was no medical reason for his eating problems. However, there was clear evidence of preverbal medical trauma. Peter underwent major surgery for a congenital heart defect at 4 months of age. Tube feeding was stopped upon his return home from hospital. Since then, encouraging Peter to eat has been a constant struggle. At the age of three, he was admitted to a clinic for children with eating disorders where his eating improved. He returned home after one year, where the eating problems resurfaced.

At intake, it became clear that Peter's mother was traumatized. Her memories of giving birth to a son with a disability, his life-threatening operation, the struggle to get him to eat, and his placement in residential care were treated with EMDR over four sessions. Peter's father asked for treatment himself when he saw her recovery. The same events had also traumatized him. After five sessions, he felt relieved and more positive about life. Their relationship with their disabled son, and with one another, improved. The atmosphere at home became more positive. It was then possible to begin work on Peter's traumatic memories, which included his surgery, his struggles with eating, and the separation from his parents when he was admitted to the eating clinic. After three sessions of EMDR, Peter's angry outbursts disappeared and his self-reliance increased. With the help of practical, educational family counselling, the parents were able to permanently change his ingrained dysfunctional eating patterns in a short space of time. At a follow-up meeting two years later, Peter's eating behaviour appeared to have remained normal and the other improvements had been maintained.

- ***Trauma therapy for other family members?***

Therapists should also be alert to signs indicating that other family members might have been traumatized. For example, they may have been victims of or have witnessed physical aggression by their disabled brother or sister, or have been confronted with (stories of) unpleasant examinations or therapies their sibling has undergone. They may have seen distress in their parents, or they may have felt shame when peers compared their family unfavourably to a 'normal' family. The parents may have unintentionally deprived their other children of attention due to the demands of their child with ID. It is important that any damage to siblings is repaired through individual therapy for family members or via family therapy. This applies equally to loved ones of adults with ID—for example, their partner, children, and parents.

Choosing the Right Protocol

When it is clear which negative experience(s) should be addressed and the child or adult lacks the verbal skills to recount the relevant memories, the therapist, with the support of the parent or caregiver, will use the storytelling method. The storytelling method (alone or in combination with the standard protocol) can be crucial, if relevant (symptom-related) memories cannot be activated with the standard protocol alone.

16.5.2 Recommendations for Each Phase of the Therapy

- ***Diagnostics and case conceptualization (phase 1)***

In recent years, research has improved the understanding of the consequences of severe negative experiences in people with ID. Wigham and colleagues (2011) developed the Lancaster and Northgate Trauma Scales (LANTS) to measure the effects of stressful and traumatic events in adults with mild or moderate ID. Since 2018, for individuals with mild ID a diagnostic tool has been available online and free of charge in the Netherlands (DITS-LVB; Mevissen et al., 2018). An English version of this protocol for mild ID and a second for severe ID are in preparation. With this clinical interview, a DSM-5 PTSD classification can be validly and reliably established in children and adults with mild ID (Mevissen et al., 2014, 2016, 2020a; Versluis et al., 2025). A wide range of profound negative events (both 'big T' and 'small t' traumas) and associated post-traumatic stress symptoms can be assessed in both children and adults using this tool.

ID clients who have a long history of traumatic events that began in early childhood present a diagnostic challenge to therapists. They must determine if behavioural problems are symptoms of PTSD or are due to an organic-cerebral condition, such as problems in stimulus processing that lead to increased irritability and overlap with PTSD symptoms. EMDR can be used as both a diagnostic and a therapeutic tool in such cases, ensuring that appropriate therapy is initiated. EMDR can act as a diagnostic tool because abnormalities in contact, communication, regulation of emotions, and stimulus processing are detected during an EMDR procedure. If this occurs, differential diagnostic research can then be used to diagnose any other psychological disorder, such as ADHD or ASD (see Case Study 16.3).

CASE STUDY 16.3 **Monique: EMDR as a diagnostic tool**

Monique is 8 years old. She has mild ID and cerebral palsy. Her parents were at their wit's end due to Monique's continual panic attacks and extreme possessiveness. In her first six years of life, Monique underwent numerous surgeries, each time accompanied by episodes of severe panic. Because traumatization had begun in the preverbal phase, it seemed a logical first step to use the EMDR storytelling method. Contrary to expectations, no behavioural changes were evident during treatment. During the sessions, her rigidity in thinking and behaviour, as well as her peculiar and one-sided way of communicating, became increasingly noticeable. With the help of diagnostic research, an ASD was diagnosed. The parents adjusted their approach accordingly and Monique started functioning better.

- ***Preparation (phase 2)***

  – Estimate the developmental level

In addition to diagnostic data, it is advisable to find out in advance which age adaptations in the child and adolescent protocol best match the client's intellectual abilities. To what extent can the child or adult recall and describe a memory (an image); draw a picture if verbalization is too difficult; verbalize thoughts, feelings, and physical sensations; and use numbers or gestures to indicate the degree of distress or credibility of a belief?

  – Explain memory reprocessing

The well-known metaphor of a 'chest of drawers' (see Chapter 7) can be used to explain the reprocessing of traumatic memories. The therapist can visually support this metaphor with a drawing or picture of a chest of drawers, where the drawers are named after the memories. The use of a 'real' toy chest, in which the drawers are filled with drawings or objects symbolizing memories, can also be used.

  – Choice of BLS/WMT

The limited working memory capacity of people with ID (Trezise et al., 2014; Van der Molen et al., 2007) has implications for choosing an appropriate type of BLS/WMT. For example, making eye movements may be too demanding, leaving no room for memory processing. People with Down syndrome are at a relatively high risk of overburden, as there is evidence that they have particularly limited working memory (Walker et al., 2011). For people with severe developmental delay, such as very young children, eye movements are sometimes simply not feasible and may not necessarily be the best type of BLS/WMT for this target group. If eye movements prove impractical, a tactile or auditory task, buzzers, or taps through headphones can be used. If the child suddenly refuses to continue during desensitization, it may be necessary to change the task. In short, the therapist needs to be flexible, have a range of alternatives available, and be prepared to switch if necessary.

- ***Assessment (phase 3)***
  - Target memory/image

Because cognition is impaired in ID, memory activation needs to be supported. This is often done using pictures or drawings. Children with additional problems, such as visual impairment or ASD, require non-visual memory stimulation, such as auditory or olfactory cues, for example, to provide the necessary emotional charge. Case Study 16.4 Part 1 describes memory activation for a child with a visual impairment that was compensated for by an enhanced auditory ability; therefore, auditory stimuli were used to activate his memory.

CASE STUDY 16.4 **Marnix: Part 1: Following the standard protocol is not a matter of course**

Marnix, 16 years old (intellectual developmental age 7 years), suffered a brain injury at birth. He has epilepsy, is paralysed on one side, and, because of brain damage, he is visually impaired. Five years ago, Marnix was told that his best friend was involved in a crash at a railway crossing. He avoided talking about this event because he would become overwhelmed by intense emotions.

An excerpt from the assessments phase:

Therapist: *Marnix, you have just told us how you remember the accident. What do you see when you think about the worst part of the accident?* (The literal text of the protocol is too complicated, and asking Marnix to draw the target image is not possible, because of his motor impairment).

Marnix: *The sound of the train on the track.*
Marnix leans forward, drops the buzzers on the floor, and holds his hands in front of himself, then puts his head on the table and starts crying very loudly. Because of his intense emotional reaction, the expectation that he will not calm down quickly, and his demonstrated difficulty in following instructions, the therapist decides to start desensitization immediately and pushes the buzzers back into Marnix's hands.

Therapist: *Just hold them in your hands and feel how they vibrate. Just let the sadness come.*

- Directive attitude in identifying negative and positive cognition (NC/PC)

Usually, an NC/PC combination can be determined with the help of the therapist after the target image has been established. This part of the assessment phase is the most problematic aspect of preparing children and adults with ID for EMDR because it involves a reliance on cognitive skills. Therefore, it is important that the therapist is directive and keeps the questions very simple.

– Control and Safety

If an NC can be identified, it is often in the 'control' domain. Depending on the nature of the event, the client may also feel in danger when looking at a drawing or image of the worst part of the memory. Often, it is mainly the negative emotions and physical sensations that bother children and adults with ID. Therefore, it is important to avoid a discussion that would cause an unwanted decrease in the emotional charge of the target image. This can be avoided by presenting the image to the client and asking if looking at it causes any disturbance or distress.

For example, show the client the drawing and ask *'You can't stand looking at the drawing, can you? Does it make you angry or scared or sad?'* This phase can be simplified by delaying the choice of a PC (also in the domains of 'danger', 'self-esteem', and 'guilt') until the installation phase, when the therapist can propose an appropriate PC.

– Self-esteem and guilt

Damage in the domain of self-esteem is common in people with mild ID. This is not surprising considering that they are often confronted with their limitations and with being different from their social contacts. If an NC proves difficult to verbalize, the therapist can offer suggestions, as one would do with younger children. For example, show the client the drawing or picture and ask *'What do you think about yourself now? Do you think "I am a loser" or "I am worthless"?'* Or, show them the drawing and ask *'Which makes you feel the worst: "I am a loser" or "I am not worthwhile"?'* They may also be wrongly convinced that they are to blame for what has happened because they have difficulty assessing social situations.

– Visual support SUD/VOC

Visual support for measuring SUD and VOC is always recommended. The tools developed for this purpose for other children are also suitable for people with ID.

- ***Desensitization (phase 4)***

Usually, the EM+ are stopped after about 30 seconds, the client is asked what comes to mind, and then the next set of stimuli follow immediately after their answer. This part of the protocol must be adapted for persons with ID because responses tend to come with a delay, as they need more time to complete the processes that are needed before they can respond:

- They must focus their attention on the therapist;
- They must absorb and understand the instruction;
- And then they must focus on the inner process.

These cognitive processes can demand so much capacity from working memory that the process stagnates. This can be addressed by reducing the demand for cognitive action. For example, by extending the sets, the frequency of having to answer questions that appeal to inner reflections regarding thoughts, feelings, and sensations can be reduced. Furthermore, negative thoughts, feelings, and sensations can be difficult to deal with. Therapists are advised to have pictures available of positive traits to be used as an interweave. The therapist can point to these when negative associations are difficult to tolerate and say '*Go on, you can manage this, you are strong*', '*You have guts*', or '*You have the courage to send that person away*'.

- ***Installation and body scan (phases 5 and 6)***

The installation phase should not begin until the level of disturbance (SUD) in response to the target memory is completely zero. Effective questioning and careful observation are important because people with ID tend to give socially desirable responses because they want to give what they think is the 'right' answer, or they don't understand what is being asked of them.

If the establishment of a PC was postponed (see 'Control and Safety', above), the therapist can be directive and provide a PC themselves during this phase. If no visual representation (image) of the memory was established during phase 3, focusing, installation, and body scan take place in this phase, coupled with the alternative chosen aspect of the memory representation. In Marnix's case, an auditory cue was chosen—namely, the sound of the railway tracks (see Case Study 16.4 Part 2).

CASE STUDY 16.4 **Marnix: Part 2**

Therapist: *... and if you think about the sound of the train again now and you say to yourself 'I can stand it', how true does that feel now?*

Marnix: [replies immediately] *I can stand it.*

Therapist: *You can totally stand it?*

Marnix: *Yes, then of course I will think for a while: yes, um, why does this have to happen?*

Therapist: *Now, when you think, why does this have to happen, do you get another bad feeling?*

Marnix: [Immediately and very clearly shakes his head no.]

Therapist installs 'I can totally handle it' at VOC = 7.

A directive attitude from the therapist is also important during the body scan. If the child or adult can no longer recall the original image or drawing, the therapist can show it to them and say '*If you look at the drawing and say* [PC], *are there any unpleasant feelings* [in your stomach] *now*' or '*If you look at the drawing and say* [PC], *do you feel completely okay* [in your head] *now*?' Step by step, attention can be explicitly focused on the body parts where distress was noticeable or named during the previous phases.

- ***Positive closure (phase 7)***

If the client does not comment on their experiences during this session, the therapist can describe what they observed. For example, the therapist might say *'How clever of you that you dared to think about the unpleasant event again and again. Think about how clever you are* [allow about half a minute for this]. *Do you notice anything else positive*?' Read Case Study 16.4 Part 3 to see how it went for Marnix.

CASE STUDY 16.4 **Marnix: Part 3**

Therapist: *Looking back, what is the most positive thing you have discovered about yourself, here, in the past hour?*

Marnix: [Takes a moment] *I didn't expect this to cheer me up so much.*

Therapist: *Okay. And what does that tell you about yourself?*

Marnix: *What do you mean?*

Therapist: *What good did it do you.*

Marnix: *It showed me that I can get through this.*

Therapist: *Okay. You're a go-getter! Think about that. That's very good of you though! You're a real go-getter!*

Marnix: [Smiles broadly].

Therapist: *Does anything else positive come to mind?*

Marnix: [Still smiling] *No, just that!*

- ***Re-evaluation (phase 8)***

During the next session, the EMDR procedure is completed. If the entire memory is processed but residual symptoms remain, the protocol is repeated on other relevant memories. People with ID may have a range of unprocessed experiences of failure, despite support from their family circle or caregiver. In Case Study 16.4 Part 4 is shown how a second important unprocessed memory could be traced in Marnix.

CASE STUDY 16.4 **Marnix: Part 4**

Marnix remained an insecure adolescent who did not dare to stand up for himself, even after he processed his best friend's accident. He could not cope with other traumatic events on his own. So, together with his parents, we created a story that dealt with his disabilities and their unpleasant consequences. He had vivid memories of epileptic seizures and the horrified faces of loved ones when the epileptic seizure ended, and this had damaged his self-image. He became remarkably calmer, less easily agitated, and more able to stand his ground after these memories were treated. An unexpected improvement was that Marnix's seizures became less frequent and less severe, and he recovered faster after a seizure.

- Flash forward (after symptom-related memories are neutralized)

People with ID can also have 'disaster images' (future fantasies) that drive anxiety and avoidance behaviour. These images or fantasies can be desensitized with the flashforward procedure. Also, the therapist's language here should match the person's abilities and the other constraints associated with their ID.

- Mental video check (MVC)

The MVC is a helpful next step towards (improved) functional behaviour in a specific situation for people with ID. The regular instruction (see Chapter 6) to create a future movie and walk through it is too complicated for people with ID because several instructions for consecutive steps are given simultaneously (see Case Study 16.1). Instead, each step of the procedure (performing desired behaviour in the situation) should be explained and performed one after another. At first, the therapist creates, with the client, the scenario (movie) of the future situation. In some cases, each scene/fragment is visualized using pictures, like in a comic strip; in other cases, each scene is verbalized by the therapist and/or the child. Next, the client is instructed to think of or look at one scene and answer the therapist's question. The therapist asks '*Do you feel any disturbance*?' If yes, say '*Notice what gives you disturbance*' and offer one regular set of BLS/WMT. The client looks at or thinks of the next scene, and the therapist asks again '*do you feel any disturbance*?'. This continues to the end of the future movie, and then this procedure is repeated until going through the entire scenario (movie/comic strip) no longer causes any distress. So:

1. Creation of scenario.
2. Step-by-step think of/look at one element/picture of the scenario.
3. Answer the question of the therapist.
4. Think of/look at next element/picture, etc.

- Future template

The future template is also an important step in the protocol for people with ID. It promotes appropriate behaviour in situations previously experienced with anxiety and avoidance behaviour. It is important to be aware of what the client understands, to be directive, and to provide visual support using a drawing and/or the VOC card as needed.

After the MVC is completed, the future template typically involves the client drawing a representative picture of the future situation where adequate behaviour is shown. This can be simplified for ID clients. The therapist can say '*You can now play the whole movie/comic strip quietly in your head. Can you actually do this* [name the desired behaviour] *in real life now?*' Then ask the client to indicate the degree of credibility (validity) of their reply using visual support. For example: 1 = 'I don't believe at all that I can [name the desired behaviour]' and 7 = 'I totally believe that I can [name the desired behaviour]'. Then, install as for the normal installation procedure.

16.6 Concluding Remarks

People with ID are particularly vulnerable to encountering traumatic events and to developing symptoms afterwards. The likelihood of this is increased by lower levels of development, additional disabilities, and low levels of support from the individual's environment. When traumatic events have been experienced, post-traumatic stress reactions often remain unrecognized. Instead, symptoms of PTSD are attributed to the ID or additional disorders. As a result, post-traumatic stress symptoms are usually not treated in this target group.

Clinical experience and scientific research show that EMDR is applicable, safe, and effective for people with mild ID. Scientific research into PTSD and EMDR therapy in people with more severe ID is still in its infancy. Results are promising. Knowledge gained from the use of EMDR in children without intellectual disabilities and the strategies developed for them can be applied to children and adults with ID, even those with severe intellectual disabilities. Specific additional impairments, such as autism or sensory and physical disabilities, often require additional adjustments to the EMDR protocol.

ID involves lifelong dependence on others. Symptoms should therefore always be considered in the context of the client's environment. Parents of children with ID may have been traumatized by what they have experienced with their child, or by other events in their own history. If this is the case, EMDR may be indicated for the parents, even if their child is already an adult. EMDR therapy can help them feel more able to cope with their challenging parenting role. If the person with ID lives in an institution, it is important to involve parents or relatives, as well as caregivers, in the therapy for optimal results. A common misconception is that there is a high chance that people with ID may relapse after successful therapy. Clinical practice has shown that, as in people without ID, once a memory file has been 'repaired', the changes are permanent. Of course, symptoms may reappear in response to new traumatic events. It is important that scientific research continues to explore the possibilities for use of EMDR, as promising therapy, in this target group. And, as far as possible, let us use all the knowledge and experience that has been gained with EMDR in people without ID to treat symptoms of trauma in people with ID.

EMDR in Children and Adolescents with a Dissociative Disorder

17

KIRSTEN HAUBER AND ARIANNE STRUIK

17.1 Introduction

This chapter describes EMDR therapy as part of the treatment for children and adolescents[1] diagnosed with one of the five dissociative disorders described in the DSM 5: dissociative identity disorder, dissociative amnesia, depersonalization (or derealization) disorder, other specified dissociative disorders, and unspecified dissociative disorders (for a detailed description, see AKWA, 2020). Dissociation is a disruption, interruption, and/or discontinuity of the normal, subjective integration of behaviour, memory, identity, consciousness, emotion, perception, body representation, and motor control (American Psychiatric Association, 2013). A dissociative disorder involves a personality that consists of a system of multiple, distinct survival strategies which developed in response to an unsafe environment and associated internal conflicts. This identity fragmentation is characterized by two or more distinct personality states. A personality state includes a marked discontinuity in self-perception and sense of self-control, accompanied by associated changes in affect, behaviour, consciousness, memory, perception, cognition, and/or sensorimotor functioning which leads to a lack of coordination and coherence within the personality (AKWA, 2020).

A large proportion of children diagnosed with dissociative disorder have experienced sexual abuse, maltreatment, and emotional neglect within the family (Kate et al., 2021), leading to attachment problems in addition to dissociation (Waters, 2016). Processing traumatic memories is an important part of treatment, but it is not sufficient to treat the disorder. Treatment also requires focusing on the attachment issues these children always have (Cronin et al., 2014).

With some modifications, EMDR therapy can be used to process traumatic memories. However, there are several difficulties that are likely to occur. Many children with dissociative disorders seem to have (temporary or partial) amnesia for (parts or aspects of) their traumatic memories. One moment they can talk about something, but at a later moment only certain information in the memory network may be accessible; children say they do not remember anything; or they display conversion symptoms, suddenly cannot talk, or do not feel anything. By processing associated traumatic memories, EMDR aims to resolve the

[1] Hereafter referred to as children, unless specific information is given about the child or an adolescent.

Kirsten Hauber and Arianne Struik, *EMDR in Children and Adolescents with a Dissociative Disorder*. In: *Handbook of EMDR for Children and Adolescents.* Edited by: Renée Beer and Carlijn de Roos, Oxford University Press. © 2026, Oxford University Press. For the English edition. DOI: 10.1093/oso/9780198918400.003.0017

internal conflict that led to the identity fragmentation. Trauma processing can be blocked for various reasons, making it necessary for the child to maintain the identity fragmentation. It is important to understand that identity fragmentation is a survival mechanism: a solution for a strong internal conflict between incompatible feelings and tasks, appropriate in a threatening situation but becoming dysfunctional when the child's circumstances have become safe. The child can perceive a therapist who confronts and pressures them to open up too soon, before the child has a way out of the internal conflicts, as a 'perpetrator'. This can lead to an increase in symptoms, such as functional neurological symptoms and conversion, suicidal behaviour, self-harm, anxiety, and aggressive behaviour both during and after an EMDR session. This chapter provides guidance on how to reduce the risk of this occurring. It is important to acquire the best possible insights into the severity and nature of the child's disorder before starting EMDR, and to consider what interventions are needed prior to and during EMDR.

17.2 Clinical Presentation

17.2.1 Children

Children with dissociative disorder have PTSD symptoms and severe attachment problems, making them behave alternately distant and avoidant or affectionate and clingy. The child's presentation fluctuates during treatment. As identity fragmentation decreases, PTSD symptoms usually increase. Functioning (in all areas) is highly variable, and caregivers say 'The child has two faces' or 'He has a devil or a monster in him'. What they have learned in school and other skills may suddenly disappear; regressive or strange behaviour may occur (e.g., crawling and barking like a dog). They may exhibit sub-assertive, pleasing, and over-adaptive behaviour, along with violent outbursts and (sadistically) hurting others or animals. They may express their anger in a passive-aggressive way by secretly breaking, defacing, or stealing things. They can display sexualized behaviours or 'somatoform dissociation', such as functional neurological and conversion symptoms or pseudo-epileptic seizures (Struik, 2019b; Waters, 2016). Most have memory loss, to a greater or lesser extent, for traumatic memories as well as for everyday things, both negative and positive. The child's amnesia can be perceived as lying. Pedagogical strategies are ineffective. The child may become intensely sad because they believe they have been wrongly accused of bad behaviour for which they are convinced they are not responsible. Certain behaviours can sometimes disappear for months, then suddenly occur again. The clinical presentation described above can be observed as early as toddlerhood. Simone's case illustrates this presentation.

CASE STUDY 17.1 **Simone**

Four-year-old Simone regularly becomes so aggressive that she attacks her foster parents and destroys everything around her. She then asks for a hug as if nothing has happened. At first, she denies her aggressive behaviour, but after her foster parents insist on an apology, she usually says 'Just kidding, sorry'. Pedagogical advice has not lead to change and her foster parents are desperate. After three sessions of EMDR therapy, her aggressive behaviour has increased, and she has encopresis and smears poo. She is then diagnosed with dissociative disorder.

17.2.2 Adolescents

The clinical presentation of dissociative disorders is different in adolescents than in children, because in adolescents the fragmentation of identity is usually further developed and the phobia for the separate personality states has become much greater (Silberg, 2013). This phobia for the individual personality states (and especially the emotional states) helps to suppress intense feelings and memories so that the adolescent can cope with everyday life (Van der Hart et al., 2010). However, supressing these creates psychological problems, such as selective mutism, self-harm, suicidality, eating problems and, increasingly, amnesia in daily life. The important developmental tasks of developing an identity and separating from primary caregivers are especially difficult when one of the parents is a perpetrator of abuse. An adolescent needs a certain level of actual and perceived safety in their relationship with their parents to be able to stand up to them. The expression of anger, resisting their parents' wishes, and expressing one's opinion—all of which are appropriate as an adolescent develops—often increase the likelihood of maltreatment for these adolescents. This leads to an increase in amnesia and the adolescent's fear of their individual personality states, often accompanied by acting-out behaviour, such as violence, self-harm, and suicidality. In addition, PTSD symptoms, such as re-experiencing, avoidance, and conversion symptoms, interfere with everyday life. Other developmental tasks, such as progressing in their education, graduation, forming friendships, and developing sexuality, suffer.

17.3 Explanatory Models

There are different views on the causes and mechanisms underlying the onset of dissociative disorders (Boyer et al., 2022; Mangiulli et al., 2021). According to the DSM-5, dissociative disorders are a form of defence, created because of having to survive chronic maltreatment, abuse, and/or neglect as a child (i.e., a form of coping). The sociocognitive explanatory model, on the other hand, questions whether there is a direct causal relationship between trauma and dissociative symptoms (Lynn et al., 2022). This model assumes that dissociative symptoms and disorders emerge under the influence of media, suggestive techniques of therapists, sleep problems, and broader sociocultural expectations. This model is not supported by research findings (Dimitrova, 2020), and, in practice, we see toddlers, pre-schoolers, and primary-school children with dissociative disorders where the influence of media or suggestive therapists has been ruled out and the disorders cannot be explained by the sociocognitive model.

The theory of a 'meta-memory deficit' (Marsh et al., 2021) suggests that the different personality states of people with dissociative disorder in principle have access to the full memory network, but to survive and continue to function, they have erected an amnestic barrier. Marsh and colleagues (2021) and Dimitrova et al. (2024) support this theory by research in adults showing evidence that memory transfer occurs. This contradicts the perception of many clients with a dissociative disorder (and the beliefs of some therapists), but is consistent with clinical practice, in which we see children with alternating amnesia for or access to different personality states, traumatic memories, and everyday events.

The structural dissociation model assumes that there are two types of distinct personality states within the individual: emotional states and apparently normal states, also called 'parts with internal conflicts' due to incompatible feelings and tasks resulting from trauma (Van der Hart et al., 2010). The extent to which parts are developed is divided into three stages: primary, secondary, and tertiary structural dissociation.

Another commonly used theory is the Ego-state theory, a psychodynamic approach which assumes that internal conflicts between distinct personality states (so-called ego states) are based on trauma and cause unwanted behaviours and thoughts. The boundaries between ego states are permeable (more or less), and with dissociative states (or parts) these boundaries have become extremely rigid and impermeable (Forgash & Knipe, 2012; Watkins & Watkins, 1997). (For an overview of theoretical models, see Waters, 2016; for the ESTD guideline, see Potgieter Marks et al., 2015, https://estd.org)

There is insufficient research to be conclusive about explanatory models, but available research findings provide support for the hypothesis that traumatic experiences form a basis for the development of dissociative disorders (Dimitrova et al., 2020; Kate et al., 2021) and for the theory of structural dissociation (Brand, et al., 2012; Reinders et al., 2018; Schlumpf et al., 2013; Vissia et al., 2016). This theory provides a good framework for understanding and treating these children, and in this chapter unprocessed early childhood traumatic experiences are considered the main cause of dissociative disorders (AKWA, 2020).

17.4 Empirical Evidence

Both assessment and EMDR treatment for this target group are still experimental (Woolard et al., 2024). The literature on assessment and treatment outcomes consists mainly of successful case reports (Gomez, 2013; Hauber, 2009; Perry and Szalavitz, 2007; Silberg, 2013; Struik, 2019b; Struik, 2021b; Waters, 2016; Wieland, 2015). EMDR is included as part of treatment in the ISSTD and ESTD guidelines (ISSTD, 2003; Potgieter Marks et al., 2015). There is consensus in the field about using a phased treatment model as standard care, but there are major disagreements on the extent to which stabilization is a goal and on the required length of a stabilization phase. The Sleeping Dogs method (see Chapter 12) provides criteria for assessment and structuring of what is needed as preparation for EMDR.

17.5 Rationale for EMDR

Outpatient, individual psychotherapy focused on integration of the identity fragmentation is the first-choice treatment. Treatment consists of interventions aimed at improving attachment and systemic interactions, reducing disruptive systemic factors, and processing traumatic memories with EMDR. We believe it is important to start EMDR as soon as possible because of the negative impact of identity fragmentation on all areas of development. Integration of personality states leads to symptom reduction and promotes restoration of normal development (Potgieter Marks et al., 2015). This was also the case for Sophie.

CASE STUDY 17.2 **Sofie**

Sofie (16 years old) is admitted to a psychiatric ward with suicidal behaviour and aggressive self-harm, of which she often has no recollection. She discloses to one of the nurses that her recently deceased father sexually abused her for one year when she was six. In a family therapy session Sofie tells her mother about the abuse. With the disclosure of her secret, and her mother's supportive response, she starts with EMDR. Her suicidality and severe self-harm rapidly decrease and Sofie returns home with a safety plan. She continues EMDR treatment on an outpatient basis.

17.6 Points to consider for EMDR Treatment

The following paragraphs describe general keypoints for treatment followed by keypoints in preparation, reprocessing and integration.

17.6.1 General

- ***Phases alternate***

Treatment consists of a preparatory phase,[2] trauma processing (with EMDR), and integration, which may alternate. With the reduction of dissociation, memories that were previously inaccessible due to identity fragmentation become accessible (see Case Study 17.1: Simone). Clinical practice shows that a memory can also be processed in layers, meaning that amnesia is gradually lifted. The same memory is processed several times, with a different aspect of the memory causing the distress each time.

- ***The child is one person***

Children with a dissociative disorder perceive the world differently. A child may be confronted with the consequences of their behaviour (e.g., breaking furniture), while being adamant they did not do that. These children may believe that separate personality states (or parts) are other people or ghosts and have a strong tendency to maintain identity fragmentation. After all, they have survived by pretending it did not happen to them. Giving up the identity fragmentation means facing reality, and that is very scary. When they say they

[2] This phase is typically referred to as the stabilization phase, but, as explained in the Preface, the term 'preparatory phase' is advocated and used in this book for this phase.

have not done or said something, they are not lying; they don't remember. However, even when the child does not remember, they need to be held accountable for their behaviour. Because of identity fragmentation, the child's feelings are stronger and purer; it is more difficult to withstand the avoidance and tempting to go along with the child's perception that there is more than one person. However, that means going along with the phobic avoidance of reality and reinforcing identity fragmentation. The therapist should, therefore, always adopt an integrative treatment approach and treat and address the child as one person with one personality, even if the child does not recognize or feel this way about themselves. The individual personality states (or parts) may think differently and remember different aspects of situations, but this can be normalized by the therapist, who explains that all human beings have different ideas about things that can cause internal conflicts.

As a coping strategy, children with dissociative disorders have divided the different sides of intolerable internal conflicts into separate personality states/parts. In treatment, the child should not get rid of these states or parts, but integrate them as parts of themselves with associated memories and difficult (positive and negative) feelings and behaviours. The DSM-5 uses the term 'identities or distinct personality states', instead of parts as more integrative terminology. In line with the DSM-5, we therefore suggest refraining from using the term 'parts', and in this chapter we use 'states' as the main term. When simpler language is necessary due to the child's developmental level, the child's states can be addressed as 'parts of you'.

- ***Working with individual personality states/parts***

There is still no consensus in the field about working on collaboration between the separate personality states (or parts) within a child, or the extent to which that is needed. Some therapists spend dozens of sessions mapping out the child's inner world and promoting collaboration between the separate personality states (or parts)—sometimes by directly working with the child's separate personality states (or parts)—and installing, for example, safe places for all separate personality states (or parts). Other therapists (Potgieter Marks et al., 2015; Silberg, 2013; Struik, 2019a) believe this mapping and working with different states (or parts) can reinforce and maintain identity fragmentation. We believe working with personality states (or parts) should be kept to a minimum pending empirical evidence and consensus on the most desirable (effective) approach.

- ***Transference and countertransference***

Due to the intense and conflicting emotions, transference and countertransference when working with these children are usually strong, and the longer the therapeutic relationship lasts, the stronger these phenomena become. Behaviour such as saying '*Therapy is boring*' or responding with '*I don't know*' to all questions can sabotage or block progress, and therapists can feel powerlessness, out of their depth, like they are a failure, or even resentful or disgusted. Therapists can also have strong nurturing feelings, especially if the child is young or has states (or parts) that feel and behave young. However, a therapist who takes over responsibility from the child or caregivers risks promoting regression and maintaining identity fragmentation. Instead of the therapist fulfilling the child's need for nurture and care, they can try to arrange an attachment figure in real life (see Chapter 12, barrier 1b). Older children and teenagers who have missed out on so much nurturing have the difficult task of facing reality and learning to take care of themselves, and of grieving what they will never have instead of maintaining the fantasy that others will take care of them. This requires a therapist who can reflect on and resist the countertransference, and who maintains strict boundaries in the relationship and around contact outside sessions. The strong transference phenomenon can also lead to conflict within the treatment team or network around the child, as the different states (or parts) can transfer conflicting feelings and needs. It is important that the therapist and the treatment team reflect on these feelings and phenomena and discuss them as a part of supervision.

17.6.2 Preparatory Phase

To be able to commence phases 3 and 4 of the EMDR protocol, the child must have access to the traumatic memories, be motivated to process them, be able to stay present while processing, and be aware of a way out of their internal conflicts. The therapist prepares the child and their network to reduce the risk of blockages during the therapy process. In the following paragraphs, we briefly describe points to consider for the preparatory phase by using the structure of the Sleeping Dogs method (see Chapter 12). A wide range of useful interventions for these children can be used in addition to the Sleeping Dogs method structure, as described by Gomez (2013), Silberg (2013), Sinason and Potgieter Marks (2022), Struik (2022), Waters (2016), and Wieland (2015).

- ***Motivation***

Dissociation offers these children a quick, short-term solution by reducing distress and temporarily easing children's trauma symptoms, and thus motivating these children and their caregivers, family, and care team for trauma treatment can be difficult, especially since trauma symptoms may initially increase when dissociation reduces. The child, their parents and their carers can be reluctant or opposed to trauma treatment, and repeated psychoeducation about the long-term adverse effects of identity fragmentation is therefore important. The child, their support team, and their parents can be reassured with a plan for how to deal with a possible worsening of symptoms. In Tom's case psychoeducation was helpful.

CASE STUDY 17.3 Tom

A demonstration using Matryoshka dolls helped 10-year-old Tom understand the strange things that were happening to him. His mother regularly accused him of getting angry and kicking her, but he had no recollection of this. Previously, he had kept denying that he had done these things. Now, he began to understand that although he did not remember kicking his mother, there was a part of him (the smaller Matryoshka doll inside him), that held on to his old anger and kicked his mother. He started to remember more of his behaviour, but also had more nightmares and flashbacks about sexual abuse. He became motivated for EMDR.

- ***Keeping focus***

The chaos of the problems and severe symptoms of these children can make it difficult to determine the treatment focus and stay on track. Starting phases 3 and 4 as soon as possible and processing traumatic memories is the main goal. Therefore, treatment focuses on the root of the problem that led to the structural dissociation, the internal conflicts, and helping the child to find a solution and a way to resolve these.

Children with dissociative disorder grow up in unsafe circumstances in which they have strong feelings of fear, anger, and sadness towards the person harming them (often their parents), but are afraid of being rejected by them when they express these feelings. This creates internal conflict, guilt, and shame, which are temporarily resolved through identity fragmentation and detachment. However, after circumstances change (i.e., become safe), the identity fragmentation creates problems for daily life, attachment, and emotion regulation. The child's state of holding strong feelings of unsafety, guilt, and shame then prevent them from connecting with others. Therefore, the focus is on preparing the adaptive information. This reduces shame and increases feelings of self-worth and connection needed to resolve the internal conflicts during EMDR. That was very helpful for Annabel.

CASE STUDY 17.4 **Annabel**

Annabel, aged 17, often consented to having sex with her stepfather because he threatened to abuse her little brother otherwise. She feels it was her fault and considers herself a whore, but she can also see her intentions were good as she did it to protect her brother. Discussing this internal conflict creates more self-compassion, making processing of these memories with EMDR possible.

- ***Safety***

Therapists need to be mindful of ongoing physical or sexual abuse because these children have amnesia for events and strong loyalty to the perpetrator(s). Many children (and adults) don't disclose ongoing abuse out of fear of the consequences or because they have been threatened by the perpetrator, especially in cases of organized sexual abuse and assault. Signs of the children trying to keep secrets can be often replying 'I don't know', not answering, hitting themselves on the head, complaining about headaches, or being unable to speak.

Even when things are safe, individual personality states (or parts) may be 'living in the past', so to speak, causing the child to perceive the abuse and threats as ongoing when they are not. Personality states (or parts) oriented in the past may threaten the child's other personality states (or parts) in the form of voices the child hears or threatening notes the child sends to themselves that are perceived as external threats.

Clinical practice shows that structural dissociation often runs in the family, with a parent or grandparent also having a dissociative disorder. In such situations, the child's identity fragmentation may be a way of coping with their parent's different states (or parts) (Liotti, 2009). The child can then only safely integrate their states (or parts) when they no longer need to cope with the parent's behaviours.

- ***Too many problems in daily life***

For young children, problems in daily life often don't form a barrier to engaging in EMDR. But for adolescents, suicidal behaviour, self-harm, restricted eating, aggressive or sexualized behaviour, or substance misuse can create barriers which need to be addressed. For some adolescents, improving school attendance, daily life functioning, and social relationships may be necessary to increase their motivation and resources. When the family circumstances are very unsafe, they may first need to become more emotionally independent, to be able to explore their traumatic experiences and feelings.

Switching between separate personality states (or parts) often results in problematic behaviour in everyday life. The child can learn skills to increase control over the switching between states of dissociation, using psychoeducation, such as the window of tolerance, by keeping a diary or learning interventions such as the Here and now exercise (Struik, 2019b), the back of the head scale (Knipe, 2018), the safe place, and the safe deposit box or container (see Struik, 2019b).

The round-table intervention (Fraser, 1991) is a commonly used technique, in which the child imagines a conference table at which all the individual personality states (or parts) are seated. They collaborate to come up with solutions for problems in daily life or for the EMDR process. Personality states (or parts) that are reluctant to participate can sit behind a one-way screen. We believe this technique should be used with caution so as not to strengthen identity fragmentation or to increase internal conflict by gathering states (or parts) around the table too early in the process, resulting in an increase of symptoms.

- ***Insufficient support/attachment***

Dissociation occurs when the child cannot use the attachment figure to co-regulate them. The dissociation and amnesia for the traumatic memories will reduce only if the child feels connected and co-regulated enough to deal with the overwhelming feelings and sensations. If the child does not have an attachment figure, it is very difficult to reduce the amnesia for traumatic memories and to prevent dissociation during EMDR. If possible and safe, the child's parents are the preferred attachment figures, otherwise alternative attachment figures (preferably family members or former foster parents) can be considered. With older adolescents, if necessary, peers, residential counsellors, or teachers can take on that role temporarily. However, it is important to keep working on finding at least one attachment figure in the network as a prerequisite for starting trauma treatment. This is important for the adolescent's well-being and future, and certainly also for the therapist's well-being.

- ***Insufficient emotion regulation***

Improving emotion regulation is often seen as a necessary part of preparation, but we believe learning this is not always needed. The child's ability to tolerate distress also increases when the child feels more connected and co-regulated, as described in the previous section. When the child does not feel supported by the attachment figure, they will have to regulate their emotions themselves. This limits their window of tolerance and increases the chance of dissociation during the EMDR process. It may be then necessary to teach emotion regulation skills before initiating phases 3 and 4 of the EMDR protocol.

- ***Unable to make the cognitive shift***

Most children with a dissociative disorder have experienced abuse by one or both of their parents or within their family. They love their parent(s) and are dependent on them, but also feel angry with them or fear them. They are afraid of being rejected and losing their connection with their parent if they feel those feelings and resolve this internal conflict by storing memories and feelings in separate personality states (or parts). This enables them to stay loyal to the perpetrator (usually one or both parents) who they are dependent on. Identity fragmentation is mainly caused by the child's inability to reconcile their positive feelings and desires towards the perpetrator with the abusive actions they commit. Guilt, self-hatred, and loyalty to the perpetrator are persistent because the child wants to maintain the relationship and does not want to risk rejection from the perpetrator.

During EMDR the child needs to make a cognitive shift from the NC to the PC by using the adaptive information that becomes available during the process. The AIP model (Shapiro, 2018) assumes everyone has adaptive information; however, these children often don't. They have been told their whole life that they are evil and truly believe that. To enable them to make the cognitive shift they first need to receive adaptive information, which can be provided by the therapist or by the child's own network.

Making the cognitive shift from the NC to the PC can be challenging if part of the child feels like they are younger and living in the past and is convinced that the abuse or maltreatment is still happening. That state (or part) has amnesia for the present time and needs adaptive information about the here and now. They can make a list of things reminding them that the abuse is over and that they are safe now—for example, writing how old they are and/or where they live now; they can also bring objects, such a photo of their current caregivers, or make a playlist with new 'safe' music.

Instead of being afraid to allow anger towards the perpetrator, they can also be afraid to 'allow' themselves to feel longing for the parent that harmed them'. By providing psychoeducation and validating and discussing how to manage these feelings, the child can be prepared. This can also be helpful to prepare a way out for 'moral injuries'—for example, things the child has done to others or harm the child failed to prevent, or the child's 'bad behaviour'.

- ***Overview of traumatic memories and preparation (phases 1 and 2)***

To assess readiness for EMDR (trauma processing), the child is asked to make an overview of their traumatic memories. If the child can do this while staying within their window of tolerance and not dissociating or becoming dysregulated, they are ready. As different identity states (or parts) may store different (fragments of) memories, some memories may be missing at phase 1 (history taking). The therapist explains that, over time, many children remember new things or have memories or secrets they didn't want to talk about. They explain that the child can always add new memories to the overview. Together with the child, the therapist arranges the memories into clusters or on a timeline, and then determines the order in which clusters are processed with the following parameters: the chronology of memories, correlation with symptoms, level of SUDs, type of trauma (such as relational trauma or not), preverbal or verbal trauma, cognitive domain, and the child's preference. The child and the therapist actively plan this together to increase the child's sense of control. However, the therapist decides the order of processing as they can oversee the consequences. Since individual personality states (or parts) of the child function at different developmental levels, the therapist adapts their language and uses visualization, if needed.

- ***Recovered memories***

In the trauma field there has been debate around the danger of 'recovered memories' in this target group. However, this debate centres around the use of these memories as evidence in the context of a police investigation aimed at convicting an alleged perpetrator. That is separate to the context in which therapists are working; therapists are aiming to promote symptom relief and the child's well-being. There is no reason for not using these memories in that context. Firstly, the assumption is that the memories of these children have not been recovered but have become accessible. Secondly, for the application (and even efficacy) of EMDR it is irrelevant whether an event took place in the way the child describes it. Moreover, some of these children have been drugged or misled by the perpetrator, which makes the process of distinguishing facts difficult. The goal of EMDR treatment is not to determine the accuracy of the memory, but to reduce symptoms resulting from a memory, a representation, or a fantasy (flash forward) in whichever way it is stored in the child's memory.

17.6.3 Memory Reprocessing

- ***Assessment (phase 3)***

During the assessment phase, dissociation may occur, often accompanied by immobilization (inability to move). Techniques described in Chapter 10 can be used to prevent or stop this. Instructing the child to move their body before starting phase 3, such as by sitting on a wobble cushion, standing on a balance board, or tapping themselves, makes it more difficult to dissociate. These children may struggle to verbalize details of the traumatic experience and therefore say '*I don't know*'. Drawing, writing, or using objects instead of talking can make it easier to activate the memory; the details of the target image remain (at first) unknown to (blind to) the therapist. The child can also choose a symbolic image: for example, a microwave oven as a symbol for the time when an adolescent was neglected and abused, and she had to cook for herself and her little sister (using a microwave oven) because their mother was depressed and in bed.

These children may not be able to answer all questions in the assessment phase, or name the emotion or location of the disturbance in their body, because they struggle with feeling, tolerating, and recognizing emotions or because different personality states (or parts) answer differently. The purpose of the questions in phase 3 is to activate the memory, but since the distress level often is already at the maximum at the start, these questions can remain unanswered. Moving as quickly as possible to the desensitization phase, where WMT is added, makes it easier for the child to stay within their window of tolerance.

- ***Desensitization (phase 4)***

1. Preventing dissociation

As their brain cannot properly distinguish between then and now, high working-memory load is often needed to reduce the risk of being overwhelmed by emotions and sensations. These children can usually multitask amazingly well. To keep the child oriented in the here and now, BLS/WMT is offered in relatively short sets using extra working-memory load. During the sets, the therapist may encourage the child, emphasizing the distinction between then and now and making the child feel connected to the therapist—for example, by saying *'Let that old anger come out; good, this is all old sadness and old pain. Let it come out, then you can let go of it!'* If the process moves towards an association chain for which there is no way out, the therapist either directs the attention of the child to a specific distressing aspect, such as the perpetrators eyes, or goes 'back to target'. Three alternative ways to prevent dissociation are described in points 2, 3, and 4 below.

2. Creating a sense of connection

During desensitization, the child re-experiences intense feelings of loneliness associated with the memory. It is important that the child feels connected at the same time, to co-regulate their distress and provide the adaptive information they need to shift. The presence of an attachment figure, a support figure, a pet, a transitional object, a specific song or music, or photos of (new) attachment figures can increase their feeling of connection and therefore facilitate the EMDR process. The therapist provides a lot of verbal and non-verbal support during a set. Rosa's case illustrates how this can work out.

CASE STUDY 17.5 **Rosa**

Rosa (16 years old) became very suicidal during and after the previous EMDR session, and refused to continue EMDR. Together, Rosa and her parents came up with a plan to allow their dog to attend and sit on her lap, so she could pet it during EMDR. It was also agreed that Rosa's mother would take care of her after the sessions and spend the following days with her. They planned what to do if Rosa became suicidal again. This comprehensive preparation and planning made Rosa feel connected and valued, and she decided to continue with EMDR. The SUD reduced quickly, and she was no longer suicidal.

3. Handling abreactions

In clinical practice, these children seem to have more intense physical and sensory sensations at re-experiencing (such as pain, taste, smell), possibly because their memories are stored in a fragmented way. This makes the implementation of high-taxing and modality-specific distractive tasks (Matthijssen et al., 2017) especially important because it can promote processing, such as smelling perfume when they have a yucky smell as association, eating a sour or strong-tasting candy when reporting a bad taste, clapping when hearing a sound, et cetera. Often, physical and emotional aspects of the memory predominate because personality states (or parts) feel younger. Therefore, in clinical practice non-verbal associations (abreactions) are common, such as choking or gagging, shaking leg(s), jerking of the neck, or a sexually abused child spreading their legs in an uncomfortable position. Interweaves like finishing or making the movement that the body could not make at the time (pushing the imaginary perpetrator away, or getting up from the chair and walking out of the therapy room) makes adaptive information available. The child can also be instructed to take deep breaths with the therapist while the therapist says *'You couldn't breathe then, and it may feel the same now, but it's just a memory. You can breathe freely now.'* Anger that is stuck and re-experienced can be expressed physically by having the child hit a punching bag, hit a chair with pool noodles or kick a kick-pad, while visualizing doing that to the perpetrator in the memory.

4. Keeping distress levels within the window of tolerance

Children may indicate, during desensitization, that they feel nothing or want to leave. They may also loop, block, or dissociate and stop responding as if they are in a trance, looking through you with a glassy stare. This indicates that the child is outside their window of tolerance and processing will no longer take place. The EMDR procedure is thus interrupted for a few minutes for here-and-now exercises (Silberg, 2013, pp. 129–147; Struik, 2019b, pp. 142–143). The desensitization then continues with a back to target. It is important to reflect on what happened at the end of the session. A plan for how to avoid this in the next session is made—for example, with more working-memory taxation, more bodily movement to continue to feel and experience being in the here-and-now and looking back to the past, or other ways for the child to feel more connected.

5. Using interweaves

The therapist frequently implements interweaves to prevent or resolve looping, besides pre-installed resources, like strength or self-confidence, to resolve blocking (see Chapter 9 on interweaves). Despite preparation, allowing and expressing anger at the perpetrator during desensitization can be difficult for these children. They are very loyal to the perpetrator and/or fear or condemn their anger. The following interweaves can be used to encourage children:

- *'If the big Renee could step into the picture to help the little Renee, what would you want to say to the perpetrator? ... Imagine saying that.'*
- *'If the big Renee could step into the picture to help the little Renee, what would you want to do to the perpetrator? ... Imagine doing that.'*

- *'If the big Renee could step into the picture, what would you want to say to the little Renee? ... Imagine saying that.'*
- *'What does the little Renee need now? ... Just step into the picture and imagine doing that* [provided it is positive, like giving a hug or taking them out of the picture].'

When using these interweaves, be mindful that the perpetrator is usually one of the parents, whom this child is angry with for their behaviour but also feels love for. It is important to time interweaves well, using Shapiro's stages or plateaus of processing (see Chapter 9). Anger at the perpetrator can be expressed only when the child has stopped blaming themself, and feels that the event is over and the current situation is safe. If the adaptive information has been prepared with the child (e.g., through a message from the perpetrator-parent), then this can be referenced.

6. Managing re-enactment and (counter)transference

Re-enactment (Draijer & Nicolai, 2020) occurs frequently during desensitization. The child unconsciously recreates the same aspects of the trauma in relationships with others, as is the case for 14-year-old Kay. See Case Study 17.6.

CASE STUDY 17.6 **Kay**

Kay's mother had previously prostituted her and rewarded her cooperation with extra pocket money. Kay was now refusing to come to EMDR sessions. The residential caregivers made a reward system for Kay, which the therapist was unaware of. They gave Kay extra pocket money after participating in sessions, unintentionally re-enacting the traumatic experiences from the past. After the EMDR session, Kay became nauseated with disgust at herself and threw up in the plants outside the room. She saw herself as, yet again, taking money for something she did not want to do. In Kay's mind this was confirmation that she was a disgusting person and that the abuse was her own choice.

Because of the strong (counter)transference, the child's pain, fear, and grief can be intense for the therapist. This can cause doubt: 'Am I doing the right things with EMDR?' A helpful thought can be that these children have experienced and survived the event already, and they are now just processing their memories. Rather than having them sit alone with these memories every day, they can now share their memories with you, the therapist.

Developing self-compassion usually takes longer with this target group as their guilt and shame are deeply rooted. This requires many interweaves and a lot of patience. If a child persistently maintains one aspect of the trauma or one point of view—for example, '*I am bad*' or '*I want to die*'—be mindful that there is always ambivalence and ask the child '*Is there also a part of you that has other memories or doesn't want to die?*'

Therapists need to tolerate the strong feelings of 'wanting to care' for the child, as the child needs to be loved and cared for by their attachment figure until they can care for their own 'little self'. Therapists need to be mindful not to become impatient and regard the slow progress or ongoing amnesia for the trauma memories as avoidance. This can cause a re-enactment of earlier situations, with the impatient and irritated therapist unintentionally and unconsciously behaving like the perpetrator, pressuring and frightening the child. This behaviour reinforces the child's powerlessness, resulting in re-traumatization.

7. Back to preparation phase

If interventions to get the processing back on track do not help, the therapist should go back to the preparation phase to identify the barriers and plan the interventions needed (by using the Sleeping Dogs method; see Chapter 12). Common barriers are fear of the possible consequences if they talk about what happened or disclose a secret, insufficient support, or lack of adaptive information. If the process is stuck, listening carefully to what these children say, trusting them, and letting them take charge is essential. After all, they know what they need or can tell you in the next session. Usually, they have already said it somehow. They need to be listened to properly.

8. After the sessions

In consultation with the child and their caregivers, a concrete plan is made regarding what to do after the session. As they relive strong feelings of loneliness, old bodily sensations, and immobilization, moving their body and feeling connected can help as they are essential ingredients to differentiate past from present. Aggressive behaviour, sexualized behaviours, self-harm, or suicidality may suddenly occur or increase after the sessions because memories have been activated and identity fragmentation reduces. This may cause panic with caregivers or school staff wanting to pause treatment when it is necessary to continue. Therapists should explain to the child's caregiver team what to expect and how to interpret the changes. When the child's memories no longer create distress, shame is reduced, and the child's feeling of self-worth increases, then their longing for connection and contact with family and peers increases. It is important to plan for this and discuss what needs to be in place to meet the child's needs after completing EMDR, such as child protection services changing contact arrangements with a parent.

17.6.4 **Integration**

By processing their memories, the child realizes that these are past experiences rather than current circumstances, and that their memories are about their own history: their feelings and thoughts are not those of another person. This means that identity fragmentation is no longer necessary. The child needs to acquire skills to regulate distress so that dissociation (their former manner of coping) becomes redundant. Separate personality states (or parts) usually integrate spontaneously in children. In this phase, the child grieves about what happened and what they will never have. Children sometimes say that EMDR did not help and that the unpleasant memories are not gone. Usually, EMDR has helped to neutralize and integrate the memories, but children find it difficult to accept what happened to them.

In clinical practice, we find that in adolescents, all personality states (or parts) rarely integrate spontaneously. EMDR treatment of adolescents takes longer, partly because adolescents need to fulfil developmental milestones, such as studying to graduate. Another reason could be that, in part, adolescents may prefer to preserve their fragmented identity because they remain dependent on the person(s) who harmed them. In the integration phase of treatment, it is important for adolescents to focus on developing their personality. After all, many adolescents with dissociative disorder remain stuck in the developmental phase in which the traumatization took place. Intimacy, sexuality, having fun, autonomy, assertiveness, setting boundaries, and developing a more positive body image are important topics in sessions. Mental video checks, future templates, and behavioural experiments can be used again to reduce avoidance behaviours, try out new things, and challenge themselves.

Lastly, support may be needed to integrate past and present in children who kept their worlds separate due to dissociation. Systemic sessions with family, and contact with biological parents, grandparents, uncles/aunts, and siblings, as well as perpetrators, can help the child realize that the event(s) really happened to them, and, more importantly, that it is over now and happened in the past. These conversations aim to make a new history so that the child can connect their memories from the past with new memories. This worked out really well for Jody.

CASE STUDY 17.7 **Jody**

After a conversation with an older brother who had abused her in the first four years of her life, 8-year-old Jody said 'He is much smaller than I thought. I'm not afraid of him at all now.' The therapist then organized a series of separate sessions with her other siblings. After each meeting, Jody functioned in a more integrated way.

Renewing contact or confrontation with family members the child has not seen for a long time can also trigger dissociated memories or aspects of them. This should be welcomed as an opportunity to process further with EMDR.

17.7 **Concluding Remarks**

EMDR therapy is a suitable treatment for processing traumatic memories in children with dissociative disorder, if embedded in a phased treatment and offered at the right time. EMDR can also have temporary negative effects: Children can be overwhelmed by a multitude of simultaneously triggered memories or by remembering things for which there was previous amnesia. This may temporarily increase their symptoms and cause them or their caregivers to (want to) terminate their treatment prematurely. They may also become confused or panicked if memories suddenly come back for which there was amnesia, increasing the child's resistance to continue with EMDR. Identity fragmentation is a protective mechanism or survival strategy that a child has used until then, with good reason. They can only let go of that strategy when they no longer need that protection to survive. To ensure their strategy is not removed prematurely it is important to first carefully assess whether, and which kind of, preparation is needed before starting EMDR. This chapter presents not a protocol, but a guideline on how to set up treatment that fits the child, their caregivers, and their network. Treating this target group requires a creative interplay in which the child, their caregivers, and the therapist search together for ways to process traumatic memories safely. When the therapist continuously respects and discusses the child's needs and boundaries, and reflects on the therapeutic relationship and its boundaries, this will provide the child with a corrective emotional experience of connection.

18 EMDR in Adolescents with Borderline Personality Disorder

STEVEN MEIJER, AGAATH KOUDSTAAL, AND LAURIAN HAFKEMEIJER

18.1 Introduction

Adolescents with borderline personality disorder (BPD) often have a life history of traumatic and other intrusive experiences. A poor self-image and distrust of others often appear early in development. They are also highly emotional and impulsive. The combination of these characteristics can lead to major problems in many areas of life, providing a constant supply of new negative learning experiences. Adolescents with BPD try to maintain emotional stability through (self-)destructive behaviour. This chapter discusses points for attention for all phases of EMDR therapy in adolescents with BPD and comorbid PTSD and/or other trauma-related symptoms. It describes how the therapist can prepare for and implement EMDR. In addition, it describes target-group-specific features that can interfere with trauma processing and how to overcome these barriers. It also explains how EMDR therapy can be integrated into a comprehensive therapeutic framework. There are many similarities between the presentation of BPD symptomatology and the principles of therapy in adolescents and adults. This chapter focuses on working with adolescents.

18.2 Target Group

Maladaptive patterns of thought and behaviour that cause high levels of suffering are characteristic of personality disorders. The classification 'personality disorder' in the DSM-5 (American Psychiatric Association, 2013) indicates the severity of the problem and, combined with a descriptive diagnosis, also guides its therapy. This is especially true for BPD: An absence of therapy is known to result in even more severe and enduring problems that cannot and should not be ignored, and for which several effective therapies have now been developed.

The DSM-5 reserves the classification of BPD in adolescents under 18 years of age for individuals with interfering problems in emotion regulation and impulse control that have been present for at least one year and which cannot be explained by another symptom disorder or life stage alone. The National Institute of Clinical Excellence (NICE, 2023, https://www.nice.org.uk/guidance/qs88) recommends not using concealing language (e.g., 'adolescents

Steven Meijer, Agaath Koudstaal, and Laurian Hafkemeijer, *EMDR in Adolescents with Borderline Personality Disorder*.
In: *Handbook of EMDR for Children and Adolescents.* Edited by: Renée Beer and Carlijn de Roos, Oxford University Press.
 DOI: 10.1093/oso/9780198918400.003.0018

Table 18.1 Characteristics of borderline personality disorder

Areas of Disruption	DSM-5 Criteria
Relationships	(1) try frantically to avoid being—or perceived to be—abandoned (2) a pattern of unstable and intense interpersonal relationships, characterized by shifts between excessive idealization and belittling
Identity	(3) marked and persistent instability of self-image or self-esteem (7) chronic feeling of emptiness
Behaviour	(4) (other) impulsive behaviour (5) recurrent suicidal behaviour and threat of suicidality and/or self-harm
Emotions	(6) affect-lability due to marked reactivity of mood (8) inadequate, intense anger or difficulty controlling angerdissociative phenomena
Cognitions	(9) transient stress-related paranoid ideas

Sources: DSM-5 (American Psychiatric Association, 2013) and Linehan (1993). The criteria are numbered as per the DSM-5.

with threatened personality development'), but classifying adolescents as BPD only if the DSM-5 criteria are met. For this reason, in this chapter we refer to adolescents 'with BPD' rather than adolescents with 'characteristics of BPD' if the criteria are met. However, the advice discussed in this chapter also applies to adolescents who do not have a complete BPD image (BPD classification according to DSM-5), but in whom the underlying dynamics are recognizable: we refer to these individuals as 'adolescents with subclinical BPD'.

The DSM-5 specifies BPD in individuals with the symptoms described in Table 18.1 (right-hand column) which, according to Linehan (1993), can be clustered into five areas of dysregulation (left-hand column). An automatism has often developed in these individuals as an attempt to prevent dysregulation by suppressing emotions as much as possible: They 'over-control' their emotional experiences. Because the influx of intense emotions is often large, their overall baseline tension (arousal level) rises. This leaves them primed to react to even small things with a violent emotional outburst accompanied by impulsive, self-destructive behaviour. At such times, there is 'under-control': The adolescent cannot sufficiently control their behaviour and the disruption becomes more pronounced in the long term. Both over- and under-control (and the sudden switch between the two) can make therapy—and thus EMDR—difficult.

18.3 **Therapy Options**

The reader is referred to the (international) guidelines for personality disorders for an overview of effective specialist therapies for this target group, such as schema-focused therapy (SFT), dialectical behaviour therapy (DBT), and mentalization-based therapy (MBT). The National Institute for Health and Care Excellence (NICE) guideline concludes that adolescents with (sub-clinical) BPD should also be able to receive the recommended therapies (NICE, 2023). The American Academy of Child and Adolescent Psychiatry (APA) (2011) lists DBT and MBT as proven effective therapies for adolescents: https://www.aacap.org/AACAP/Families_and_Youth/Facts_for_Families/FFF-Guide/Borderline_Personality_Disorder_Young_People-127.aspx

Whether the adolescent follows a specialist treatment programme (like DBT or MBT) or not, some general factors are always important with this target group (Hutsebaut et al., 2020):

- It is essential to involve parents and/or significant others intensively in the therapeutic process, as well as in the preparation of the therapy plan.
- It is also important to establish and maintain a good working relationship. In adolescents with BPD, this requires extra investment. The therapeutic process must take place within the context of a clear and predictable structure, and with a clear framework of agreements regarding accessibility, mutual expectations, and responsibilities. Adolescents with BPD often have difficulty trusting others and themselves, which creates extra challenges in the therapeutic relationship. Therefore, when disruptions in the relationship occur, it is important to (1) notice and bring these up, (2) validate the adolescent's perception, (3) acknowledge one's own part in the communication, (4) offer an alternative perspective, and (5) check back with the client regarding whether the relationship has been restored (Hutsebaut et al., 2020). Finally, it is important for therapists to feel embedded in a team that helps to them to align in a productive way with the adolescent and the system so that they can be effective (Hutsebaut et al., 2020).

18.4 Empirical Evidence for EMDR

Increasingly, research in adults shows the added value of EMDR in addition to other therapies for BPD, such as SFT, DBT, and MBT. A study by Slotema and colleagues (2019) found that EMDR had positive effects not only on PTSD, but also on dissociative symptoms and insomnia. A recent meta-analysis (Slotema et al., 2020) of results obtained in people with BPD and PTSD also showed that trauma therapy led not only to a decrease in PTSD but also to a decrease in BPD symptoms. Another study showed that brief, intensive, trauma-focused therapy with EMDR and prolonged exposure (PE) (Kolthof et al., 2022) led to a decrease in PTSD, and in BPD symptoms too. People with a personality disorder who did not meet the criteria for PTSD also appeared to benefit from EMDR therapy (Hafkemeijer et al., 2020).

Several studies show that adding PTSD therapies to usual interventions (such as DBT and MBT) also adds value. Harned and colleagues (2018) found that the addition of PE enhanced the effects of DBT and prevented relapse. Not only did quality of life improve significantly compared to DBT alone, but behaviours characteristic to the borderline disorder, such as suicidality and self-harm, also decreased. In addition, trauma-related beliefs (negative beliefs associated with having experienced trauma, such as interpersonal distrust) changed, possibly explaining better social adjustment.

We conclude that research shows that EMDR therapy is effective in (adult) clients with BPD to reduce PTSD symptoms, emotional dysregulation (such as dissociation), and insomnia. EMDR therapy does not appear to lead to serious complications, such as increase in suicidal behaviour or hospital admissions; EMDR thus appears to be a safe therapy in this target group. A study by Barnicot and colleagues (2012) showed that BPD clients with higher severity of symptoms may have greater potential to benefit from therapy. Also, for clients with another type of personality disorder, initial research shows promising results, and follow-up research is in progress (Hofman et al., 2022).

Results of research on the effects of trauma therapy specifically in adolescents with BPD are not yet available. However, experiences in clinical practice are in line with research findings obtained in adults. Based on this, and combined with the fact that the history and clinical presentation in adolescents with BPD do not differ fundamentally from those of adults, we assume that trauma therapy in adolescents with BPD will be especially beneficial compared to a (specialized) BPD treatment alone.

18.5 Rationale for EMDR

At least one type of early childhood trauma, such as abuse or neglect, is reported by 97% of those diagnosed with BPD (Slotema et al., 2018). Their backgrounds are often characterized by unstable parenting situations, emotional neglect, sexual or physical abuse, and parental psychopathology (Porter et al., 2020). There are also often negative experiences outside the family, such as lack of connection with peers and frequent bullying experiences (Antila et al., 2017). Although additional research is needed, EMDR seems to make a valuable contribution to therapy for adolescents with BPD for the following reasons.

Studies show that prolonged and severe traumatization, especially in childhood, can lead to an inability or a reduced ability to control and modulate emotions (Braquehais et al., 2010): this is the characteristic problem of people with BPD. PTSD clients are reported to have BPD comorbidity ranging from 37–68% (Heffernan & Cloitre, 2000; Zlotnick et al., 2002) and, conversely, among BPD clients 25–58% are diagnosed with comorbid PTSD (Golier et al., 2003; Harned et al., 2010; Zanarini et al., 1998). These figures are not surprising as the life history of many people with BPD is marked by traumatic experiences. Adults with BPD appear to respond as well to trauma therapy as people with other types of personality disorder (Slotema et al., 2019).

18.6 Points to Consider for EMDR

18.6.1 General

- ***Indications***

EMDR therapy is indicated, as with other children and adolescents, when unprocessed traumatic experiences give rise to symptoms.

There are three categories of symptoms for which EMDR is indicated in people with BPD:

(a) PTSD or another diagnosed trauma-related disorder caused by events (not) fulfilling the A-criterion of the DSM-5 (see Chapter 2, Section 2.4.3 of this book).

(b) 'Masked' trauma-related disorder—that is, a trauma-related disorder that is hidden by inadequate coping behaviour, such as self-harming behaviour and suicidality, so that the behaviour or disorder is not immediately recognizable as trauma-related.

(c) Symptom clusters (e.g., 'fear of abandonment') driven by dysfunctional beliefs concerning distrust, guilt, and self-esteem.

This chapter will mainly focus on (a) and (b); (c) will be discussed only briefly.

In general, behaviours such as self-harm, suicidality, and other impulsive behaviours are not reasons to postpone trauma therapy (Slotema et al., 2020). If there is a trauma-related disorder (including PTSD), it is preferable to start EMDR as soon as possible, even if there is not yet (complete) control over the (self-)destructive behaviour, because one can expect that treatment of PTSD will result in reduction of dysregulation. In our experience, this also applies to a 'masked trauma-related disorder'. Although not an official diagnosis, this can be seen as 'masked' trauma-related problems because the flashbacks characteristic of PTSD are not clearly visible and are thus 'masked' by the problem behaviour.

The (self-)destructive behaviour is either an automatic, reflexive response to an activated memory of an event (respondent behaviour) or a purposeful, consciously chosen response to prevent the activation of a traumatic memory/negative mental representation, or to reduce or avoid its impact (operant behaviour).

In an automatic response, the aggressive behaviour is driven by the intense emotion (anger) generated (in Mo's case) by the socio-therapist's touch (trigger), which activates the traumatic memory. In many cases, the adolescent and/or people in their environment are not aware that a memory plays a role in behaviour.

See Case Study 18.1 for an example of an automatic response (respondent behaviour).

CASE STUDY 18.1 Mo: An automatic reaction

Therapist: *That was quite an intense tussle that you had with the socio-therapist ... what happens to you in situations like that?*

Mo: *I then get a sort of haze in front of my eyes and then I totally freak out ...*

Therapist: *When did you get that haze?*

Mo: *It was the way he looked at me, as if I am 'nothing', anger began to boil inside me ... and when he put his hand on my shoulder, the light went out.*

Therapist: *The light went out ...?*

Mo: *I struck out wildly ... he has to get away ... from me ... not again ...*

Therapist: *Not again?*

Mo: *Not another guy touching me. That has happened enough already ... it will never happen again.*

Therapist: It seems like you were in a situation that happened in the past and that you can't keep then and now apart?

Mo: Yes ...

See Case Study 18.2 for an example of a purposeful, chosen response (operant behaviour).

CASE STUDY 18.2 Leontine: An example of a purposeful, chosen response

Therapist: *If I understand correctly, the trigger for drinking is quite often a bad feeling. Describe that feeling.*

Leontine: *Yes, it's a kind of, yes, ... nasty, nauseous feeling, it makes me disgusted with him, my boyfriend, ... but also with myself ... he should get his paws off me right away ... then I can't stand it.*

Therapist: *Disgust, then?*

Leontine: *Yes ...*

Therapist: *And then ...?*

Leontine: *When my boyfriend is away, I go drinking.*

Therapist: *What happens just before you decide to drink?*

Leontine: *That rotten feeling comes over me, it gets completely stuck in my body. I keep getting nauseous.*

Therapist: *Is that a recognizable feeling for you that you can link to certain memories?*

Leontine: *What do you mean?*

Therapist: *Are there memories from the past that cause this feeling of disgust when you think of them?*

Leontine: *Well, it happens when I think about what my father did to me, but I'm kind of done with that now, I thought.*

Therapist: *That rotten feeling, how's that, after drinking?*

Leontine: *It's gone, then I'm nice and numb ... sometimes I also drink when he—my boyfriend—is there ... after half a bottle, he can quietly go about his business. Then I'm fine with anything.*

In both situations (automatic and consciously chosen response), the problem behaviour is driven by memories that have not been properly processed. EMDR can make a valuable contribution to therapy for both types of reactions because after processing the triggered memories, the emotional dysregulation will decrease.

- ***Timing***

It is advisable to consider implementation of EMDR right from the start of BPD treatment. The factors listed below may help you to decide whether to apply a more extensive preparation phase before starting EMDR:

1. *Current stress*: The question to be answered is whether the self-destructive behaviour is mainly related to traumatic memories or mainly to current sources of distress, such as family tensions, conflicts with peers, or problems at school. If the latter predominates, it is better to initially focus therapy towards reducing sources of distress and increasing skills aimed at better problem solving, emotion regulation, and impulse control. In cases where the adolescent is still traumatized in a home situation (e.g., domestic violence still ongoing), systemic interventions are indicated before starting EMDR to increase safety. When violent incidents have occurred within the system, but the parents/caretakers are able to guide the adolescent in coping, restoring contact with parents/caretakers is given priority. The therapist can play a guiding role in this.
2. *Environmental reinforcement of self-destructive behaviour*: If the self-destructive behaviour is unintentionally reinforced (e.g., by little attention from the environment to painful emotions, versus a lot of attention to suicidal actions), communication with significant others should be improved before starting EMDR by teaching the significant others to pay attention to painful emotions at an earlier stage. At the same time, the adolescent should learn not to delay a request for help.
3. *Coachability*: A third consideration is whether an adolescent in crisis is willing to be coached by the therapist or others. When this is the case, self-control does not need to be fully adequate to start EMDR. Others can then help the adolescent, if necessary, to cope with any disruption in a non-self-destructive way. This requires careful assessment of the willingness to be coached.
4. *Affect tolerance*: A fourth consideration is whether the adolescent can allow their emotional experience to some extent or has some affect tolerance. In adolescents with over-control (i.e., excessive pushing away of emotions), this can hinder the EMDR process. Over-control makes it difficult to experience the emotional charge associated with a memory and to allow and follow associations during desensitization. For EMDR therapy to succeed, the adolescent must first learn to (re)acknowledge their thoughts and emotions to some extent and allow themselves to feel. Making space for the emotional experience and acknowledging its functionality with the help of psychoeducation, among other approaches, provides a fertile ground for this (De Bruin et al., 2013; Linehan, 1993). Behavioural experiments which enable the adolescent to learn that emotions do not lead to 'disasters' can also be of value here.

18.6.2 Specific Points per Treatment Phase

Table 18.2 shows four treatment phases for which we provide recommendations regarding treatment of BPD clients. Where relevant, we discuss how to deal with under-control and

Table 18.2 Sequence for EMDR therapy Preparation for EMDR

Increase motivation and commitment, by:
- Psychoeducation
- Predicting 'side effects'
- Involvement of parents and/or other network members
- Creation of a crisis-alert plan

1. Implementation of the Standard Protocol
   - Specific guidelines for the eight phases and the second and third prong
2. Registration and evaluation
3. Perception of self and others
   - Beliefs related to interpersonal distrust
   - Beliefs related to self-esteem

over-control issues (i.e. rapid and intense dysregulation combined with impulsive behaviour versus issues relating the suppression of emotional experience), both of which can hamper and complicate initiation of the therapeutic process.

1. Preparation for EMDR (Table 18.2)

- ***Increasing motivation and commitment***

Sustained commitment to therapy is usually as crucial as it is complicated. Because of their highly volatile emotions and impulsivity, this target group can be fully motivated for therapy at one moment and adamantly opposed to it the next. Therefore, when preparing, it is important to give the adolescent the necessary information to make an informed choice about commencing EMDR. Doing so in an interactive (and Socratic[1]) manner can be useful, with the therapist acting as a coach to let the adolescent opt for therapy based on both feeling and reason. Setting realistic expectations for the outcome of EMDR is important. The therapist should explain to the client that although they have some severe issues to deal with, EMDR will produce results at the same rate that it does for less severe problems.

- ***Psychoeducation***

When explaining what is expected of the adolescent during therapy, the therapist should realize that these adolescents often tend to avoid unpleasant memories because they fear far-reaching disruption (and becoming suicidal (again), for example). Maintaining strong control over their feelings has become a way of sustaining themselves, whereas therapy requires them to dwell on painful memories. They avoid and suppress painful feelings whenever possible, often leaving them feeling 'empty', while occasionally 'the bomb' explodes. Because processing requires a non-avoidant attitude, the therapist must explain the importance of focusing attention on an unpleasant memory. For an example, see Case Study 18.3 for an explanation of how a therapist explained this to a client, Karen.

[1] See Chapter 9, Section 9.6 for an explanation of the Socratic method.

CASE STUDY 18.3 **Karen: Understanding the value of facing unpleasant memories**

Karen: *When I think about what happened at my foster parents' house, I get really angry.*

Therapist: *I'm going to ask you to think about it anyway ... In fact, when we start EMDR, I'm going to ask you how you remember it now and what still bothers you most about it now. All those unpleasant experiences are like open wounds. That's why they bother you so much. You can try to not look at it, but if that would have worked, you wouldn't be sitting here. Right?*

Karen: *Yes, that's true.*

Therapist: *It is natural to try not to think about situations that make you feel very angry, sad, or scared. Sometimes this works for a while, but unfortunately only temporarily. Do you recognize that?*

Karen: *Yes.*

Therapist: *Processing is done by thinking about it, and experiencing the emotions that come to mind, and at the same time doing something else, namely following the lights of the lightbar [or: my fingers] with your eyes. That, in short, is how EMDR works. You will notice that emotions are like waves: they come, and they go. Once we have done this with several memories, your symptoms will subside. The beauty of EMDR is that you don't have to dwell on the unpleasant images for very long during therapy. You focus your attention on them for just a while, then I distract you again with eye movements, and you just follow the reactions that come to mind.*

When explaining the concept of processing to this target group, it should be emphasized that reactions in the process cannot be wrong. These adolescents often have little confidence in the validity of their own reactions and therefore look for 'the right one' or hold back because they are afraid of doing something wrong or saying something stupid. The therapist will have to convey (implicitly and explicitly) that everything that comes up is appropriate.

- ***Predicting 'side effects'***

Adolescents are usually afraid of having to surrender to the therapy at the start of EMDR. They fear the possibility that they will not respond well to therapy, so a good explanation and clear reassurance are very important. It helps to explain that (i) based on scientific research, there is no reason to believe that severe dysregulation will be a consequence of the therapy, and (ii) negative effects may occur temporarily after EMDR sessions, such as intense negative feelings or moods. These effects may frighten the adolescent, causing them to worry that 'out of habit' they will, for instance, turn to substance abuse and/or self-harm. The risk of this happening should be discussed with the adolescent, and their concerns reduced by explaining that the temporary intense negative feelings should be viewed as a normal and short-term part of trauma processing.

Adolescents may experience more symptoms when the memory is activated during EMDR therapy, causing them to think that EMDR is making everything worse. As a result, they can feel more vulnerable than they did before EMDR. Therapists should anticipate this and ask the adolescent to think about the planned therapy and make a list of what the benefits of therapy might be in the long term. Here, a useful analogy can be that of a ball that you try to keep under water. This takes a lot of energy and succeeds only temporarily and briefly: occasionally, the ball shoots up anyway. The therapist could say 'It is precisely by letting the ball float and following it with your eyes that you lose less strength and are less caught off guard by unexpected movements of the ball.'

- ***Involvement of parents and/or other network members***

Parents also need sufficient information about the expected course of therapy to be able to adequately support their child by showing understanding, trust, and emotional closeness, adapted to the child. It is essential that parents also commit to the therapy and know what to do in case of mounting distress. Offering comfort and other forms of emotional closeness is an essential part of this. The therapist must assess beforehand how capable the parents or other members of the network are to offer support, and how skilled the adolescent is in effectively asking for support and closeness. These adolescents often have grown-ups in their environment who do not have sufficient understanding. Problematic interaction with the environment is often a major contributor to disruption. For them, it is not a given that interaction with loved ones will suddenly become more supportive and safer. Parents often need targeted interventions to help them to (re)connect with their child and their emotional needs, and the adolescent needs help to share more and ask for care in a healthy way.

- ***Creating a crisis-alert plan***

Before starting EMDR, the therapist draws up a plan with the adolescent that indicates what to do in case of (impending) loss of control between sessions. This plan describes:

(i) What the adolescent can do to distract from negative emotions like agitation, panic, feelings of loss of control, or anger;

(ii) How to calm themselves down;

(iii) Who can help from their network;

(iv) How to get in touch with their therapist or aid agencies for coaching.

This plan describes which skills the adolescent can use themselves and what parents and others from their network—such as friends, teachers, and family—can do. The adolescent determines which behaviour is supportive in a crisis and acts as their own case manager: they, together with their therapist, explain to their parents (and possibly to others in their network) what is needed from them and what the adolescent will do in a crisis. Agreements about this are reached and noted. This plan also describes the role of the EMDR therapist. In adolescents with BPD, EMDR therapy is often embedded in a broader therapy context. It is good to discuss in advance which therapist does what: Who monitors the (self-)destructive behaviour (e.g., via a registration form; see Appendix 18.1), who helps the adolescent and the family handle problems in daily life, and who does what in case of a crisis. Precisely anticipating high-running emotions and crises helps to maintain sufficient support and facilitates the continuation of EMDR therapy.

Telephone consultations can often be an important means of breaking (self-)destructive patterns in adolescents with BPD. This defines the availability of the therapist to make contact and coach the adolescent by phone in the case of a crisis. Also, a voucher could be arranged for an overnight stay in an appropriate facility, where the adolescent will be admitted, without an admission interview, for relief from a negative spiral.

In the case of adolescents with over-control behaviours, the therapist may be tempted to dwell less on the likelihood of dysregulation during preparation because emotion is less visible. However, therapists must keep in mind that adolescents with BPD often have a strong fear of losing control of their emotions. This fear is often based on previous experiences when they became completely emotionally dysregulated. As they gain experience with perceiving their emotions, the balance may shift to the opposite direction, to the extent that they become emotionally dysregulated, resulting in a crisis. A possibility for explaining EMDR therapy is to draw the two extremes—emotional dysregulation versus emotional over-control—on a seesaw, with the seesaw swinging either one way or the other, until gradually, after a lot of wobbling back and forth, a balance emerges. Sometimes EMDR can also be helpful to reduce anxiety about disruption by reprocessing memories of previous disruption, including, for example, previous suicide attempts. This can be followed up by processing a flash forward on the fear of disrupting again by EMDR.

2. Implementation of the Standard Protocol (Table 18.2)

Below are points of interest in the eight phases of the EMDR standard protocol.

- ***Arrangement of memory material (phase 1)***

The search strategies for identifying and organizing target memories are described in Chapter 4 of this book. The step-by-step plan used in the studies on the effect of EMDR in people with personality disorder (De Jongh & Hafkemeijer, 2024; De Jongh et al., 2024b) has been partly inspiring, and some aspects of it have been implemented.

Although adolescents with BPD are often victims of chronic traumatization, this does not mean that they still necessarily suffer from all the individual experiences and that these all need to be reprocessed. Often, there are only a few events that they re-experience.

Usually, the starting point of EMDR therapy is the treatment of post-traumatic stress symptoms, of which flashbacks are predominant. The search strategy for finding the most relevant targets in this case is the 'intrusion path' (see Chapter 4, this book). Following a global inventory of the entire traumatic history including the archives, the therapist invites the adolescent to describe globally the (three) most disruptive flashbacks, without discussing them in detail to avoid disruption. These may include memories of events that meet the A-criterion as well as those that do not, and these are ordered according to the degree of disruption they cause in everyday life. In principle, the most disturbing and disruptive re-experience is addressed first, as this leads to a large and rapid SUD decrease with the greatest chance of symptom reduction.

It is important for the therapist to know whether the selected flashbacks relate to similar experiences (i.e., experiences that fall within the same 'archive') or not. This information helps the therapist to best influence the EMDR process and set limits for the adolescent as necessary. Targeting similar experiences that share the same archive (e.g., sexual abuse) is likely to activate the other traumatic memories of sexual abuse. Therapy can then result in a roughly simultaneous decrease of other similar, activated memories, with a lot of material being processed at the same time.

If, instead, the targeted flashback also might activate experiences from different archives (e.g., sexual abuse and neglect and unpleasant experiences in counselling), it is better to prevent this by applying limitations or boundaries—not to circumvent the risk of disruption following the session, but to prevent the accumulation of too much traumatic material needing to be processed at the same time, leading to blocked processing.

A better solution to this problem is to deploy a 'precision bombardment'. The boundary of the field to be bombarded can be set using the 'stop rule': when the adolescent notices that the associations fall outside the agreed archive, the adolescent will give the stop sign, signalling to the therapist to give the instruction 'back to target'.

After successful treatment of flashbacks, the memories that are associated with the adolescent's main symptom or symptom clusters (such as self-harming behaviour, including suicidality) are selected. The therapist and the adolescent discuss the function of their problem behaviours. The essence of this discussion is to help the adolescent understand that this behaviour serves to help them avoid, reduce, or eliminate negative feelings (such as intense sadness, guilt, shame, or anger) relating to an activated memory. It is important to define which memory is involved in the problem behaviour. The therapist therefore asks the adolescent to describe their thoughts/feelings just before they initiate the problem behaviour (such as self-mutilation). A therapist helps a client begin to understand their behaviour in Case Study 18.4.

CASE STUDY 18.4 Max: Understanding his own behaviour

Therapist: *I want to ask you to go back to the moment just before you started cutting yourself: Where were you?*

Max: *I was in the bathroom with the razor at the ready.*

Therapist: *I want to ask you to go back to that moment: You are in the bathroom again. You feel a strong urge to cut yourself. Tell me what you felt just before you started cutting.*

Max: *I felt bad through and through. I felt such a strong need to hurt and punish myself…*

Therapist: *Which memory or memories, giving you that feeling of being thoroughly bad, were evoked in that moment?*

Max: *That I just let it happen, that I didn't stop it. I should've bitten him, kicked that bastard in his crotch, but I just let it happen.*

Therapist: *What do you mean? What are you talking about now?*

Max: *The abuse.*

Therapist: *Thinking about that made you want to start hurting yourself ...*

Max: *Yes, I think so ... It went to the back of my mind, but that's what came up.*

- ***Preparation (phase 2)***

In the preparation phase, information is again given about the procedure, the expected effects, and how to deal with them. Alongside this, the rationale for EMDR including the explanation and demonstration of the WMT (s) are again discussed.

- ***Assessment (phase 3)***

At this stage, very few problems are to be expected in adolescents with under-control behaviour, provided the therapist can keep therapy moving at a good pace. A slow pace can result in no emotional charge arising or the charge that has arisen 'cooling down'. An advantage with this target group is that if their emotions are activated, the risk of 'cooling down' is not very high. Clinical practice experience is that assessment—if done correctly—will usually lead directly to high levels of disturbance (SUD). In adolescents with over-control, however, the situation is different. They often need to be encouraged to focus on the target (memory or image) and to adopt the perspective that they will ultimately suffer less by allowing their emotions and the related emotional charge to arise.

- ***Desensitization (phase 4)***

Perhaps contrary to what one might expect, desensitization also usually proceeds without major problems, especially if the adolescent is well prepared. Several signs may indicate problems in information processing related to under- or over-control. Below are some first points of attention for possible blockages in the case of under-control, and then for the case of over-control.

  - *Resolving blockages when under-controlled*

Adolescents, especially those with under-control, may linger in a state of violent emotionality. Transient violent emotional dysregulation is not problematic; 'infinite' continuous emotional flooding (mindless emoting) is. This is usually evident through a lack of variation in associations. This intense emotionality can lead to a blockage in information processing, through, for example, remaining 'stuck' in reliving an event without becoming aware that the event is over. Sometimes this dysregulation is not visible. For instance, the adolescent may seem calm while processing but otherwise resorts to cutting themselves or pinching themselves until they bleed to regulate their distress. Various techniques are available for therapists to guide an adolescent who is mindlessly emoting to stay in or return to processing. This is done with the same techniques used to counter or stop dissociation, such as administering strong sensory stimulation.

– *Increasing working memory load*

A consistently high level of working memory load is one way of keeping an adolescent within their 'window of tolerance'. This can usually prevent emotional dysregulation. When intense emotional reactions occur, it makes sense to increase the working memory load even further. For instance, the therapist can increase or vary the speed during eye movements. It is also possible to add another task for working memory load to eye movements, such as tapping, counting, and/or having the adolescent do some mental arithmetic, so that information processing can continue more effectively. Possibly more importantly, the therapist should continue to provide strong support by remaining calm and maintaining confidence in the process. A discussion between therapist and client beforehand about what to expect in therapy and how to deal with it helps to create a calm atmosphere for both parties—for example, by making agreements about touching if an adolescent no longer follows instructions or lies down on the floor. Agreements can be made in advance to continue the working memory load or initiate an active balancing exercise (e.g., jumping from one leg to the other) when attention level drops. It is good to remember that these adolescents are used to an environment that co-dysregulates in response to their intense emotions. A therapist who remains involved and calm provides a good context for them to notice that intense emotions can be endured and are also of value in the process of processing.

– *Brief moment of rest*

If it seems that the adolescent has transgressed the limits of their window of tolerance, the therapist can build in a moment of rest before going back to target. This provides an opportunity to get the process back on track. This can be done by asking the adolescent to take one or a few deep breaths, having a short distracting conversation, or giving an assignment that draws the adolescent's attention to the here and now. Then, via back to target, the desensitization process is continued. However, care must be taken to ensure that these interruptions do not lead to avoidance or that the adolescent wrongly concludes that they cannot handle the therapy.

– *Stop rule*

Sometimes associations arise that are related to other traumatic experiences. As a rule, this is beneficial because these experiences can be taken along in the adaptive processing. When therapy started with the most upsetting flashback, one would not expect the adolescent to suddenly recall experiences with even more emotional charge. In exceptional cases, it can be agreed to leave certain memories 'untouched' for a while—for instance, if an adolescent really doesn't dare to start yet and first wants to gain some confidence in the procedure. In this case, the therapist instructs the adolescent to give a stop signal in case these memory(s) are activated anyway. If the adolescent gives the stop signal, the therapist goes back to target.

– *Looping*

Processing has become stuck when the adolescent remains entangled in dysfunctional meaning-making (looping): for example, 'I am in danger; it is my fault'. If this occurs, familiar cognitive interweaves can be used so that more functional information becomes available, such as 'How did it end?', 'Are you safe now?', and 'Who actually bears responsibility?' Cognitive interweaves require immediate improvisation by the therapist, who must notice what theme is involved and come up with a sharp question that will elicit a functional response. Experience from clinical practice shows that this approach is not always successful, even with very experienced and quick-thinking therapists. However, failing to come up with an effective interweave is no disaster. If looping occurs and the therapist cannot come up with a good interweave, the following steps are proposed.

After ending the EMDR part of the session (clearly distinguishing the next step from being a part of the standard protocol), the therapist and the adolescent can identify and explore the meaning behind their dysfunctional thinking, with the therapist directing a Socratic dialogue. The adolescent is encouraged to find arguments against their belief (e.g., the sexual abuse was my fault) and list these arguments in an adapted 'thought record'. The adolescent can bring this list to their next EMDR session. If looping occurs, the therapist can ask 'Who is guilty?' and if the adolescent says 'He is!' the therapist can ask 'Because?' and the adolescent can then read one of the arguments from their thought list. This exchange concludes with the therapist instructing the client to 'concentrate on that!' Then there is no need to interrupt the process.

- *Imagery and Rescripting possibly in combination with Resource Development and Installation*

Sometimes the interweaves and thought records are not enough and more work is needed to get or keep the EMDR process on track. In this case, imagery and rescripting (ImRs) can be used as an extended interweave. ImRs is a technique aimed at changing the memory representation of a traumatic experience. The original script of the traumatizing event is actively rewritten, so to speak, and given a different course and an alternative, more positive ending. A theme is selected from the original script from the point at which the adolescent becomes 'stuck' during processing. The original event will then be actively modified. For example, if the theme is 'powerlessness', the therapist introduces 'control'. The adolescent is asked to imagine what they would have done in the original situation if they had been in full control. When necessary, the alternative script (as in cognitive interweave) can be prepared and written down, so that it can be read in case the adolescent cannot immediately recall the alternative outcome. See Case Study 18.5 part 1 for an example.

CASE STUDY 18.5 **Luke: Part 1**

Therapist: *It seems that the process gets stuck every time you see your father in front of you, wanting to do something to you.*

Luke: *Yes, when that image comes to mind, I freeze totally and can't do anything. It is then also very difficult for me to stay with it.*

Therapist: *Yes, I can see that. That's why I want to prepare something with you that we can use later while we are doing EMDR. I want to ask you to imagine how you would want the situation to end if you had all the power in the world.*

Luke: *I would want to push him off me and scold him. Beat him and kick him until he lays on the floor and can't get up. And then I would like to tell him what I think ...*

Therapist: *Very good, write down what you've just said, what you would like to do ...*

[Luke writes.]

Therapist: *Is there more?*

If the therapist sees that the processing gets stuck and decides to implement this intervention, they will pause the desensitization, propose this method, and then work with the adolescent to prepare the new script. The preparation is not complete until this story is fully written down. The therapist then asks the adolescent to read the whole story out loud again, to check whether it is sufficiently powerful. The therapist subsequently instructs the adolescent; see Case Study 18.5 part 2.

CASE STUDY 18.5 **Luke: Part 2**

Therapist: *... Okay, fine ... We'll start EMDR again soon. It is to be expected that processing will get stuck again at the point where you feel the strongest sense of powerlessness. I am going to ask you then to think about the other ending, which you have just prepared. Think about what you have written down and then tell me what you would want to do in that situation ... Is the intention clear? If it is not, I will let you read it out loud.*

EMDR is then resumed. When the process stagnates again and the powerlessness is experienced strongly, the therapist starts reading aloud the rewritten story as a kind of extended cognitive interweave, as in Case Study 18.5 part 3.

CASE STUDY 18.5 **Luke: Part 3**

Therapist: *What's coming to mind?*

Luke: *I can't do anything, I can't do anything, what should I do?*

Therapist: *Think deeply about what you will do differently now. You have all the power in the world, think of how you will make it turn out differently.*

Luke: *I want to punch and kick him ...*

Therapist: *Imagine doing that ... and focus on that ...*

In many cases, this facilitates the restarting of the process. However, if the adolescent fails to imagine the powerful action, a helper can be involved. A 'helper' is preferably a real, known person who could support the adolescent in coping with the traumatic situations by being given a role in the new script. This helper could be a close friend, the therapist, or an idol. This helper can encourage the adolescent to carry out the intended action or (often initially) demonstrate the intended action, as illustrated in Case Study 18.5 part 4:

CASE STUDY 18.5 **Luke: Part 4**

Therapist: *What have you thought about doing?*

Luke: *I know what I want to do but I can't do it.*

Therapist: *Who can help you do what you're not able to do yourself?*

Luke: *My best friend, John.*

Therapist: *Imagine him in this situation, let him hit and kick. See it in front of you concentrate on that ...* [Set]

[Afterwards Luke will, in his imagination, perform the action himself.]

Therapist: *What's coming to mind?*

Luke: *I can see John kicking him and punching him.*

Therapist: *Okay, he invites you to join in. You have all the power in the world, imagine joining forces, and concentrate on that.* [Set]

Therapist: *What's on your mind?*

Luke: *Together we hit and kick him.*

Therapist: *Keep going.* [Set]

Therapist: *What are you thinking?*

Luke: *He is bleeding, and he wants to run away.*

Therapist: *Focus on that.*

In Case Study 18.5 part 5, resource development and installation (RDI) has been inserted, which illustrates the closing part.

CASE STUDY 18.5 **Luke: Part 5**

Therapist: *Now, bring up that capacity of strength in yourself by saying to yourself, I can take on the world. Take that powerful stance and put on a face that best expresses that strength. And stay with that!*

[Luke concentrates on this without applying eye movements.]

Therapist: *Great! I'll take a picture of how you look now, and I'll email it to you. I want you to practice adopting this facial expression and body posture every day in front of the mirror at home, so that you can increasingly evoke the feeling that comes with power. At the next EMDR session we will use this when the powerlessness overwhelms you. I am then going to help you to harness that power.*

Before the next session, the adolescent should have practiced the RDI daily at home. First, it is discussed how practicing bringing up 'strength' went at home, and the therapist asks the adolescent to evoke this ability with the corresponding body posture. If the adolescent can evoke 'strength' well, the EMDR starts. Next, a sign or word can be agreed with which the ability can be quickly evoked. In this case, balling the right fist or saying/thinking a word that illustrates strength (e.g., 'power'). Only when the process gets stuck is the adolescent helped to invoke the resource (see Case Study 18.5 part 6).

CASE STUDY 18.5 **Luke: Part 6**

Therapist: *What is coming to mind?*

Luke: *I see his face in front of me again. He's going to do it, I can't move.*

Therapist: *What would you do if you had all the power in the world?*

Luke: *I don't know, I cannot think of anything.*

Therapist: *Okay ... remember what we practiced. Adopt the attitude of someone who has all the power in the world. Say to yourself 'I can take on the world' and have the corresponding expression. Yes, good, feel the power flowing inside you. Go back to what just came up. What would you do if you had all the power in the world, make those fists ... think: power!*

Luke: *I would punch him in the mouth ...*

Therapist: *Focus on that!*

The therapist may also choose to select matching music that further activates the ability of strength (Korrelboom et al., 2011). The adolescent can play that music during the eye movements. The music not only provides a distraction and thus complements the eye movements, it is also 'empowering'.

– *Resolving blockages in case of over-control during desensitization*

For adolescents with over-control, one may choose to use less working memory load, so that more emotional charge is felt. The therapist could also insert RDI focused on daring to experience emotions. Courage or self-confidence could then be relevant traits. The RDI protocol is used for mobilizing relevant traits or abilities.

During desensitization, the therapist should be alert to under-arousal. Brief accompanying phrases during the set or during back to target—such as 'Just look closely' (encourage zooming in) or 'Just let it/feel it'—can help prevent under-arousal, when the adolescent mentions a feeling as an association. In Case Study 18.6 part 1, Demi learns to focus attention (about sadness and anger) on her (underlying) feelings.

CASE STUDY 18.6 **Demi: Part 1—Focusing on underlying feelings**

Therapist: *How disturbing is it to look at that picture?*
Demi: *A '5'.*
Therapist: *Why is it disturbing you so much?*
Demi: *The anger.*
Therapist: *What part of that picture evokes the anger?* [Set]
Therapist: *What comes to mind?*
Demi: *Sadness.* [Set]
Therapist: *What comes to mind?*
Demi: *I don't want this.*
Therapist: *You don't want what?*
Demi: *That sadness.*
Therapist: *Just focus on the sadness.* [Set]

During desensitization, adolescents with over-control often do not express their primary reaction or association; instead, they attempt to make this primary reaction disappear. This can take the form of self-blame, commands to themselves, or attempts at avoidance, such as 'I shouldn't feel this', 'Why can't I be a robot?', 'I don't grant him the pleasure of this affecting my life so much', 'Why did I let this happen?'. The EMDR therapist directs the attention to the primary immediate emotional response to break through avoidance. See Case Study 18.6 part 2.

CASE STUDY 18.6 **Demi: Part 2—Breaking through avoidance**

Therapist: *What comes to mind?*
Demi: *I don't want this to rule my life. I want to leave.*
Therapist: *What exactly did you feel before you wanted to leave?*
Demi: *Anger.*

Therapist: *Okay, focus on that.* [Set]

Therapist: *What comes to mind?*

Demi: *Why can't I put it away?*

Therapist: *What do you want to put away?*

Demi: *That dirty feeling.*

Therapist: *Okay. Focus on that.* [Set]

- ***Installation (phase 5) and body scan (phase 6)***

In the installation phase, the positive cognition (PC) is installed until the highest level of validity (credibility) is reached (VOC = 7). A body scan is then performed to check whether the image combined with the PC evokes any disturbance. As with all adolescents, it is advisable to give the adolescent time to properly feel if there is any distress evoked in the body by this combination.

- ***Positive closure and conclusion of session (phase 7)***

Positive closure can be difficult in adolescents with low self-esteem. Some coaching is usually needed. See an example of closing a session in Case Study 18.7.

CASE STUDY 18.7 Amara: Closing a session

Therapist: *What is the most positive thing you learned about yourself because of this session?*

Amara: *I wouldn't know ... In my opinion, it went lousy ... I still feel as bad as at the beginning.*

Therapist: *Was it awful?*

Amara: *Yes, awful.*

Therapist: *Did you make it through?*

Amara: *Yes, with a lot of effort.*

Therapist: *What do you call someone who endures tough things?*

Amara: *Err ... a go-getter?*

Therapist: *Yes, that's what you are! Focus on that.*

It is wise to allow ample time (about 10 minutes) to wrap up the session. Besides the usual wrap-up interventions, such as positive closure, you can take a moment to reflect on further plans for the day to help the adolescent make the transition to everyday reality. It is not recommended to discuss at this point what, if anything, happened in the session, as this easily increases distress again. It is better to spend the last few minutes on a more light-hearted topic that the adolescent enjoys talking about, such as music or fun activities.

- ***Re-evaluation (phase 8)***

No specific areas of concern.

- ***Second and third prongs***

If all relevant memories have been desensitized and there are still avoidance and/or safety behaviours or fears of future situations, then a flashforward can be implemented, followed by a mental video check combined with a future template.

By doing this, the therapist increases the chances that the adolescent will dare to face a given situation. Motivation to implement the new behaviour and jointly devising appropriate behavioural experiments can be a useful next step.

3. Registration and Evaluation (Table 18.2)

When progress has been made in reprocessing (neutralizing) memories, the therapist checks whether this has reduced the symptoms. The expectation is that in addition to PTSD symptoms, such as suffering from intrusions and hypervigilance, for example, there is also a reduction in self-mutilative and suicidal behaviour. This improvement should become visible in the course of the symptom registrations (see Figure 18.1 for a sample form).

If the symptoms worsen, the therapist will work with the adolescent on how to deal with distress in a non-destructive way. It is wise to consider beforehand whether this is a task for the EMDR therapist or another therapist. Sometimes it makes sense to include a joint session with the family. This allows for sharing concerns, the crisis awareness plan can be adjusted, and the necessary explanations given so that sufficient trust in the therapeutic process is maintained.

Figure 18.1 Card: Daily registrations

Name:					Date:		
	M	T	W	T	F	S	S
Feeling of despair or panic (0–5)							
Urge to self-damage (Yes/No)							
Implemented self-determination (Yes/No)							
Suicidal thoughts (0–5)							
Suicidal behaviour (Yes/No)							
Space for other relevant items							
Skills used from crisis plan (which)							

4. Perception of Self and Others (Table 18.2)

Sometimes there are no further explicit PTSD symptoms, but the adolescent continues EMDR to reprocess memories of experiences that are strongly associated with negative core beliefs about themself or others that drive residual symptom clusters. People with personality disorders are particularly prone to suffering greatly from deeply held beliefs such as 'I'm worthless', 'I can't do anything', and/or 'Everyone will discard me sooner or later' (Beck et al., 2015).

- ***Beliefs related to 'interpersonal distrust'***

Interpersonal distrust can lead to alienating behaviour alternating with clinging behaviour arising from idealizing other people (for example, the therapist). This may create the appearance that there is no interpersonal distrust. These adolescents' relationships with others are often much more ambivalent than they may initially appear. Spaans and Van Meekeren (2000) aptly characterized this ambivalence as 'Hold me, but don't touch me!', 'I hate you, but don't leave me!', 'I decide for myself, but you are responsible!' Interpersonal distrust is mostly expressed in the (core) belief 'Others cannot be trusted'. Such a belief could perhaps be expressed more specifically, for example as 'Men cannot be trusted'. The therapist's task is to identify contradictions and then help the adolescent identify the belief within a chosen theme that is most strongly related to the problem.

- ***Beliefs related to 'self-esteem'***

It is preferable to address the theme of self-esteem only after the theme of interpersonal distrust has been completed. Then there is more space to dwell on themes such as self-esteem, for example, within the therapeutic relationship. Three aspects of self-esteem can be distinguished: general value ('I am worthless'), competence ('I can't do anything right'), and appearance ('I'm ugly'). Each belief involves specific learning experiences. It is therefore important to ask the right questions to identify the most relevant beliefs so that one gets as close to the core as possible. For the application of the belief path, see Chapter 4 in this book.

18.7 Concluding Remarks

This chapter provides recommendations for applying EMDR therapy in adolescents with BPD and comorbid PTSD and/or other trauma-related symptoms. It also discusses possible approaches to treat characteristic symptom clusters, which are driven by perceptions of the self and others. Accumulating research in this field shows that this target group can benefit from EMDR therapy. We describe how the therapist can deal with adolescents with under-control and/or over-control behaviour in the different phases of EMDR therapy. The credo is 'prevention is better than cure'. By identifying potential problems during the preparation for EMDR therapy, before they occur, and agreeing on an approach with those involved, one can prevent complications, keep calm as a therapist, and optimize the commitment of the adolescent.

PART III

EMDR in Specific Settings

Preparation and Treatment of the System

EMDR for Adolescents in the Forensic Mental Health System

19

MIRJAM HEINEMANS, JACQUELINE VAN BAAR, AND THIMO VAN DER POL

My destiny is to be a criminal. How can I do good when all the good is taken away from me, when my good will is pushed through a pile of shit? They say you will fall on your face many times, and the trick is to get up again. But what do I stand on if there is no ground and no way to get anywhere? What is the point of standing in a bottomless pit? So, I struggle with doing good, because the bad keeps me in chains. I have an incredibly strong feeling that one of these days I'm going to do something stupid, but I don't know what it will be. The only things in my mind are hatred, anger, killing, and hurting people.

Quote from a letter written by Noval, an adolescent aged 17 years, to his therapist.

19.1 Introduction

Forensic youth mental health services, also known as adolescent forensic psychiatry services, focus on adolescents (12–25 years old) with mental health problems who have been involved in one or more police intervention(s) and/or court appearances for criminal behaviour. It is only since the early 2000s that attention has been drawn to the fact that adolescents in forensic psychiatry services have undergone traumatic experiences earlier in their lives, with research into the relationship between behaviour and traumatic experiences (Bernhard et al., 2018). Their offending behaviour often appears to be more or less directly related to these traumatic events (Malvaso et al., 2022). Although there is a paucity of good research on the relationship between behaviour and traumatic experiences, clinical practice shows that EMDR yields positive outcomes in this target group by reducing the number of trauma-related symptoms and offences.

This chapter deals with the application of EMDR in adolescents receiving treatment in inpatient closed forensic settings or in outpatient mental health care. It includes a description of the target group and information on the results of regular EMDR treatment. Issues requiring special attention for these adolescents in the preparation for and the implementation of EMDR treatment are discussed.

Mirjam Heinemans, Jacqueline van Baar, and Thimo van der Pol, *EMDR for Adolescents in the Forensic Mental Health System*.
In: *Handbook of EMDR for Children and Adolescents*. Edited by: Renée Beer and Carlijn de Roos, Oxford University Press.
 DOI: 10.1093/oso/9780198918400.003.0019

19.2 Target Group

In this section we provide a picture of delinquent behaviour, the psychopathology of delinquent adolescents, the prevalence of behavioural disorders in delinquent adolescents, and characteristics of the families of these young people.

19.2.1 Criminal Behaviour

Criminal behaviour is a collective term for various types of behaviour that are punishable by law and can therefore lead to a fine or punishment. The age of criminal responsibility, meaning the age under which a person cannot be arrested or charged with a crime, differs internationally. The age of criminal responsibility is 14 in most European countries, except England and Wales (10), the Netherlands and Scotland (12), and Luxembourg and Portugal (16). However, children below 10 years of age can be criminally prosecuted in some states in the USA, Africa, and India (Souverein et al., 2019).

Offences can be divided into three main categories. Violent offences include acts where physical or psychological violence is used or threatened, such as assault, robbery, rape, murder, and manslaughter. Property offences concern acts directed at obtaining, damaging, or unlawfully interfering with someone else's property, such as theft, shoplifting, burglary, fraud, and embezzlement. Other offences cover acts that do not fit into the previous two categories. Examples are vandalism and the possession of weapons.

Although juvenile crime is a major social problem, there has been a decline in juvenile crime in most Western countries in recent decades (Harrendorf, 2018; Tonry, 2014). However, this decline must be interpreted with caution, as some serious crimes, such as violent assaults, have increased in some countries. There appears to be a relationship between violent crime and the rise in popularity of drill rap, a subgenre of hip-hop known for its dark, aggressive beats and lyrics about street culture, violence, and survival, and the widespread use of social media where (criminal) peers challenge each other directly (Pinkney, 2018).

19.2.2 Psychopathology

Adolescents in forensic care generally meet the DSM-5 (American Psychiatric Association, 2013) criteria for having a norm-breaking conduct disorder or an oppositional defiant disorder. Conduct disorder is characterized by the repetitive and persistent violation of the basic rights of others. Oppositional defiant behaviour disorder, while involving hostile behaviour, does not involve wilful violation of the rights of others.

Conduct disorder is referred to as 'transgressive behaviour disorder'. In the case of oppositional defiant disorder, the DSM-5 classifies the disorder according to severity: mild, moderate, or severe. Adolescents in forensic care often also suffer from other mental disorders, such as dysthymic disorder, anxiety disorder, (complex) post-traumatic stress disorder, attention deficit/hyperactivity disorder, reactive attachment disorder, substance abuse, autism spectrum disorder, intellectual disability, and sometimes psychotic disorder. So, the adolescent is usually struggling with a variety of mental health symptoms. They feel, and often are, misunderstood. They are irritable and hyper-alert to (perceived) danger. Their aggressive behaviour provokes disapproving reactions from others, which reinforces their already negative view of themselves and others. In secondary school, teachers—as authority figures—trigger this hyper-alertness because their reactions activate the adolescent's memories of previous negative experiences with authority figures. The adolescent responds to these activated memories with aversion to school activities, truancy, changing schools, and dropping out of school. If left untreated, these adolescents often develop personality disorders, such as borderline personality disorder.

Delinquent adolescents can be characterized as 'avoiders' (Protic, 2020). They compensate for feelings of displeasure with bravado and narcissistic behaviour to avoid experiencing negative feelings, such as pain of rejection and/or loneliness. This strategy to make life bearable is often maintained for years. Delinquent adolescents consider their occasional outbursts of aggression, contact with the police and courts, 'nagging' from adults at school, and some inner turmoil as part of life. This ingrained strategy for avoiding psychological pain makes it difficult to motivate these adolescents to change their behaviours. They often seem to have a complete lack of understanding of their problems.

19.2.3 Prevalence

Boys suffer from conduct disorders more often than girls, and this is especially true for norm-traversing conduct disorder. Among adolescents in detention, the prevalence of both disorders is high (Beaudry et al., 2020).

The association between conduct disorders and trauma-related symptoms has not been robustly studied. Malvaso and colleagues (2022) found that 89% of delinquent adolescents had experienced traumatic events, mostly associated with conduct disorders and addiction. Becker and Kerig (2011) concluded that 95% of their sample (of 83 incarcerated boys aged 12–17 years) had experienced traumatic events, 20% met the criteria for PTSD, and the severity of their trauma-related symptoms had a positive correlation with the severity of their behavioural problems.

19.2.4 Family Characteristics

Adolescents are at greater risk of developing behavioural problems if their parents have mental health problems (Van Santfoort et al., 2015). Furthermore, the risk of delinquent behaviour is increased in children exposed to an accumulation of high-risk socioeconomic factors (Felitti et al., 2019), such as low income, low levels of education, single parent families, children of teenage mothers, migrant backgrounds, and substance abuse. These children are about as likely as are maltreated children to develop a pattern of insecure and disorganized attachment relationships (Cyr et al., 2010). Many adolescents in forensic care come from a family in which insecure attachment styles have been a feature for generations. Insecurely attached children often have parents who, because of their own problems, are not sufficiently available to their children. These children continue to try to attach to their parents in the hope of receiving care and love. When this is not forthcoming, they are forced to suppress their own feelings and needs. This results in stress and hinders healthy emotional development. Over time, it becomes increasingly difficult for them to properly interpret other people's behaviour and to function adequately in social situations. They develop a limited mentalizing ability, meaning they have difficulties understanding their own behaviour and that of others (Knapen et al., 2020). This makes them vulnerable to experiencing relational trauma.

Most parents of these children suffer themselves from a lack of mentalizing ability and therefore have difficulty understanding their children's behaviour. They do not recognize the mild transgressions of their growing children as developmentally appropriate and, therefore, feel powerless and resort to disproportionately harsh punishment. Parents and adolescents become embroiled in mutual accusations and become unable to communicate constructively. If the adolescent subsequently encounters the police and the courts, the parents are so shocked that they can no longer bring themselves to acknowledge and trust their child for things that are going well. This drives the adolescent to seek refuge in their peer group, with like-minded young people, where they find recognition and a sense of belonging. Typically, adolescents from this target group seek refuge in a cocoon of friendships with similar 'rejected' young people. Together, the members of this group easily engage in transgressive behaviour towards society.

19.3 Regular Treatments and Empirical Evidence

Many types of interventions have been developed in the United States over recent decades to reduce delinquent behaviour among young people. Following the Columbine High School shooting deaths in 1999 in the United States, funds became available for research on and development of effective treatment programmes. This gave a major boost to the development of expertise for the treatment of delinquent young people.

Several meta-analyses of studies on the effectiveness of these interventions have since been published. Litschge, Vaughn, and McCrea (2010) published an important overview paper which reviewed 26 meta-analyses published between 1980 and 2007 (a total of almost 2,000 studies). In almost all studies, treatment effects were compared for their effectiveness in reducing antisocial or externalizing behaviour, sometimes complemented by a reduction of internalizing behaviour and/or substance abuse, and improvement of coping skills. The authors distinguished five groups of intervention types from their meta-analysis: The effect sizes found (mean and range of 'Cohen's d') are listed in brackets, where $d = 0.2$ represents a small effect, $d = 0.5$ represents an average effect, and $d = 0.8$ represents a large effect:

- *(Cognitive) behavioural therapy*, both individual and group ($d = 0.49$, ranging from 0.04 to 1.15). This includes interventions such as aggression-regulation training, rational emotive therapy, behaviour modification, and parent behavioural therapy (behavioural parent training).
- *Group therapy* ($d = 0.26$, ranging from 0.10 to 0.31). Includes all interventions in which the group process is considered a central and crucial therapeutic ingredient.

- *Family therapy* (d = 0.41, ranging from −0.15 to 1.06). This includes different types of systemic therapies, including partner-relationship therapies and parent–child training.
- *Multimodal therapy* (d = 0.47, ranging from −0.24 to 1.13). These interventions consist of combinations of individual and systemic interventions, including functional family therapy (FFT; Sexton & Alexander, 2002), multi-systemic therapy (MST; Borduin Henggeler, 1990), and multidimensional family therapy (MDFT; Liddle, 2001).
- *Other interventions* (d = 0.13, ranging from −0.07 to 0.84).

The effectiveness of the studied interventions varied widely. The authors concluded that the following factors determine the effectiveness of an intervention for behavioural problems:

1. *Group composition*: Interventions in which adolescents are treated as a group of antisocial peers yielded poorer results than treatment among prosocial peers.
2. *Focus on skills*: Training (diverse) skills is more important than talking.
3. *Focus on parents*: Family interventions focusing on parents' parenting skills are more effective than family interventions focusing on the antisocial behaviour.

In the early 2000s, interventions for adolescents with behavioural problems that had been shown to be reasonably effective were further elaborated. The initial focus was mainly on variants of individual cognitive therapy, such as individual-focused aggression-regulation therapy. Although these techniques produced a reasonable reduction of aggressive behaviour and other behavioural problems, they needed to be embedded in a wider range of treatments to be beneficial. The reason for this was that factors perpetuating problematic behaviour—particularly family influences and criminogenic factors such as relationships with friends and acquaintances, drug use, lack of work or education, and housing problems—were insufficiently addressed by these interventions. For this reason, systemic treatment programmes were implemented and further developed, including MST, MDFT, and FFT.

Although these therapies differ slightly in content, they share similarities (van der Pol et al., 2019). They all focus on increasing the adolescent's motivation for treatment, redirecting negative family interaction patterns towards more positive mutual involvement, reducing risk factors for delinquent behaviour (for example, substance abuse), and increasing factors that prevent delinquent behaviour, such as the development and maintenance of 'good' friendships and promoting academic achievement. In short, these therapies reflect the Risk Need Responsivity (RNR) model of Bonta and Andrews (2007), supplemented by the Good Lives Model (GLM) of Ward and Brown (2004). An international trend is the use of interventions, initially developed for adults with personality disorders for adolescents with behavioural problems. Examples include dialectical behaviour therapy (DBT) and schema-focused therapy, both of which have been shown to be effective in reducing borderline personality problems in adults. Although clinical experience is positive, there is a lack of controlled research on the effects of these interventions in adolescents in the target group. Virtual reality therapies and other wearables (apps and health watches, with or without physiological measurements) have also been used more recently. These aim to improve interoceptive awareness so that the wearers learn not to lose control of their emotions (for example, become less likely to get angry). This teaches them to better control negative behaviour. It is a promising development, but research into the effectiveness of these forms of treatment for adolescents is still in its infancy (Ter Harmsel et al., 2021, 2023).

19.4 Rationale for EMDR

The treatments referred to in the previous section focus primarily on the behavioural problems of the adolescent and on family interactions. Because of the high prevalence of PTSD among adolescents in forensic care and its assumed association with delinquent behaviour, trauma treatment has been offered in recent years (Bernhard et al., 2018). Little research has been done so far on the effects of trauma treatment (EMDR or TF-CBT) on behavioural problems in adolescents in forensic care. Soberman and colleagues (2002) investigated the effects of EMDR in 29 boys with severe conduct disorders aged 10–16 years. Treatment as usual (TAU)—treatment in a residential setting with many different interventions—was compared with TAU plus three EMDR sessions. Two significant differences were found: Treatment plus EMDR led to a greater decrease of emotional charge of trauma-related memories at post-treatment measurement. Parents reported also a greater decrease in problem behaviour (reported by the parents) of the adolescent at follow-up.

EMDR offers three specific advantages for these adolescents over other forms of trauma treatment:

- less dependence on communication skills;
- the possibility to retain control in the process to a certain degree, something that adolescents in this developmental phase and with these problems crave;
- the freedom to decide what (not) to tell the therapist during the inventory of memories and during treatment.

19.5 Preparatory Phase

Clinical practice shows that the chances of successful outcomes from EMDR treatment are higher in this target group if a preparatory phase has been included. This allows for a working relationship to be built with all family members and with the adolescent separately.

19.5.1 Family Preparation

It is important to motivate the family for treatment from the first contact at intake. The adolescents do NOT come voluntarily, and they do not have a specific request for help. They are often afraid that treatment will make them vulnerable.

Intake and introduction should not begin with questionnaires and a developmental history, or with exploration of symptoms and offending behaviour. This tends to increase resistance to and fear of treatment. Besides, questionnaires are only of use if the adolescent is motivated to complete them honestly. Therefore, performing the diagnosis gradually and mainly through a series of interviews is preferable. Of course, if diagnostic information is lacking it may be helpful to use diagnostic instruments and screen for PTSD at a later stage, assuming the adolescent is then motivated to collaborate. The working relationship with the adolescent must be established, and the system must be sufficiently supportive to get meaningful responses. Adolescents usually become habitual ('professional') avoiders. Additionally, questionnaires are aimed at people who can read well, which is not always the case with this target group.

Therapists work primarily on restoring constructive communication and trust within the family during the preparatory phase. The aim is to create a new narrative in which everyone is forgiven. Good intentions are emphasized: 'Doing the wrong things for the right reasons'. Attention is paid to interpersonal traumatic experiences gained within or outside the family. Recognition is given to the mutually caused damage, and remedial moments are created. This acknowledges the consequences of traumatic experiences and the need for trauma treatment.

Through this process, the family is given opportunities to deal with conflicts in new ways and to prevent them. This reduces stress, which (re)activates mentalizing abilities. This in turn benefits attachment relationships in the family. Family preparation usually requires 5 to 10 sessions. It is preferable to use the same therapist for both the family and the individual therapy. The issues discussed in the family sessions can then be responded to immediately. New developments in EMDR therapy, involving working with a rotating team of therapists across the course of treatment, could be counterproductive for this target group, as these adolescents have low problem awareness and an embedded, persistent distrust of others. We illustrate the different phases of EMDR treatment with Noval, starting with his intake in Case Study 19.1.

CASE STUDY 19.1 **Noval-Intake**

Noval (17 years old) was reported for violent street robbery. There have been aggressive outbursts at home and at school, moodiness, smoking marijuana, excessive alcohol consumption, no friends, school absenteeism, and insomnia. He lives with his brother (20 years old) and his grandparents, the parents of his Moroccan father who died when Noval was two years old. His Dutch mother remarried a Pakistani man when Noval was two and has not been seen since she moved to Pakistan with her husband.

During a few family sessions the topic of how fate shaped the family history is discussed. Noval's Moroccan grandparents were forced to become parents again at a time when they were grieving the loss of their son and daughter-in-law. This was particularly difficult because they were living in a (Dutch) culture in which they had always felt like strangers. The grandparents have raised their grandchildren with love since they came to live with them, but Noval's behaviours, which are normal for his development age, such as the need for more autonomy, experimentation, and freedom, combined with his development problems (violent robbery, etc.), worried them.

Noval's grandfather, fearing the loss of his grandchild to the outside world, has so far ruled with a very harsh hand. He has already lost one son and now sees Noval drifting further and further away from him. Noval's grandfather has previously attacked his grandson with belts and an iron, but now that Noval is older he has begun to hit back and intimidate his grandfather, especially verbally. After four family sessions, the violent confrontations between the grandfather and Noval have diminished. After another four sessions, the family members have a good understanding of what caused the grandfather's behaviour. His behaviour was the result of the great pressure he feels to raise his deceased son's child as well as possible and his feeling of powerlessness as Noval enters a developmental stage where he wants to be more autonomous. All family members understand the connection between Noval's rebellious behaviour and the traumatic early loss of his parents. They understand that Noval's anger has kept him afloat until now and that he is afraid of sinking into depression if he begins to feel his grief through trauma treatment.

It was decided that Noval would start treatment with EMDR.

If family treatment gets stuck during the preparatory phase and produces insufficient results because of ongoing trauma (for example, in the case of physical or emotional abuse within the family), the therapist can consider (temporary) out-of-home placement in consultation with a probation officer or a social worker. In these situations, family sessions are continued with changed pace or frequency of the sessions. The goal in such cases is to keep on building good family relationships.

19.5.2 Preparation with the Adolescent

Preparation with the adolescent aims to create or ensure the preconditions for trauma processing and to mentally prepare the adolescent for it. Desirable conditions are that they have a permanent place of residence, a daytime activity, and supportive relationships.

The realization of these conditions is worked on in this phase.

During the preparatory phase with the adolescent, it is essential that the therapist adequately connects and builds contact. The aim is for the therapist to be in tune with the developmental phase of the adolescent while maintaining the necessary distance. This may involve, for example, showing genuine interest in their choice of music, watching video games with them, and trying to understand their world, whilst admitting with humour that because they are 'old', they do not really 'get it'.

A risk may be that the therapist does not tune in enough to understand the adolescent's perspective. If this happens, the therapist may appear like an authority figure to the adolescent, causing them to rebel. Conversely, if the treatment relationship becomes too amicable, this can lead to avoidance of complex topics. The adolescent needs to understand better the relationship between their memories, how they function in daily life, and the pain and problems they cause.

In clinical practice, the therapist must constantly build a relationship with the adolescent on a foundation of patience, security, and trust. Patience is needed because it takes time to get them motivated. The therapist fosters trust by, among other things, always commenting during the treatment on the good in the adolescent and acknowledging that their life has been difficult so far. The therapist creates security by being transparent in word and deed, and by explaining professional codes if necessary. Making minimal demands on the client and good accessibility with home visits if necessary—also outside of office hours, if possible—help to build opportunities for contact.

Providing information to the family and the school during interim evaluations is always done in coordination with or in the presence of the young person. The family and the school are kept informed about the course of the treatment process. The people in the young person's environment are thus better able to support them, or at least show understanding, and they can be confident that people are talking with them and not about them. If a solid working relationship is established, as well as trust in the therapist, it becomes possible to discuss dysfunctional behaviour and shameful situations. The therapist gives psychoeducation on fight, freeze, and flight reactions in response to (perceived) danger after trauma. This can include the therapist and the adolescent watching, for example, Siegel's explanation (YouTube: https://www.youtube.com/watch?v=gm9CIJ74Oxw) of his Hand Model of the Brain (2018). In addition to this, the metaphor of the backpack helps:

> *You have a heavy burden to carry with you, like an overfilled backpack. It works best to deal with the traumatic experiences which came into the backpack most recently, and to work back in time from there. This is going to be a positive experience for you. The backpack will feel a little lighter from the beginning and will become even lighter the farther we go. We are going to empty that coverbackpack completely so the things that are deep down in that backpack, the worst 'shit', will soon no longer be hanging like lead weights on your back.*

The role of drugs, sex, or delinquent behaviour is also discussed as a means of dampening unpleasant feelings (like fear and anger) that arise from traumatic memories. The disabling effect of choices and behaviours, like dropping out of school and conflict, are also discussed. A start is made on helping the adolescent learn to recognize and regulate emotions better and to choose alternative behaviours. If necessary, the therapist supports the client's motivation to take prescribed medication, such as Ritalin.

Because of the fear of negative emotions, such as anger, shame, and guilt, that may accompany confronting their memories, these adolescents often resort to various forms of avoidance. The therapist encourages them to start trauma processing as soon as the preconditions are sufficiently met and they are ready to confront the traumatic memory.

In summary, in preparation for EMDR therapy, negative interaction patterns are replaced with positive and supportive family interactions. In addition, the therapist establishes a good working relationship with the adolescent separately, so motivation for entering trauma therapy results.

19.6 Points to Consider for EMDR Therapy

The following points require attention for the success of EMDR therapy for the target group.

19.6.1 Diagnostics and Case Conceptualization (Phase 1)

EMDR therapy with this target group can only be initiated after working with the adolescent and the family on the goals described in Section 19.5. As a result, the adolescent's symptoms will already be known. Only additional screening and diagnostic testing (PTSD and others) takes place in this phase, if necessary, to determine what EMDR will be used for. Usually, these adolescents have severe symptoms of PTSD along with behavioural disorders and other comorbidities. The therapist will have already explained the relationship between traumatic events and current symptoms during preparation but, if necessary, this relationship is explained again in this phase:

> *Because of all the violence you have experienced, you are now constantly in a state of high alert. You are in a fighting mood during the day and in your bed at night, which makes you sleep badly! Just like a soldier who lived in wartime had to pay attention even in his sleep at night, because there was constant danger. When that soldier is safe at home again, they can let go of that fighting attitude, but it doesn't always happen right away ... That is why we use trauma treatment, so the noise from old memories will disappear, and danger alarms will stop, so you can sleep better and feel better again.*

Most adolescents in this target group have endured a multitude of negative experiences. Therapists can ask the adolescent to make a sort of inventory of memories by grouping them based on their similarity (clusters). This inventory is used as an overview for the client and therapist during treatment. Below you see the search strategy used for Noval in Case Study 19.2.

CASE STUDY 19.2 Noval—Part 2. Searching target.

The therapist explains: *'Think of your brain as a computer screen where unsolicited "pop-ups" appear when you open certain sites (memories). For example, if you think of your grandfather, annoying pop-ups appear in your mind, just like on your computer. These pop-ups are disturbing. Just write down the pop-ups that generate the strongest disturbance right now. You don't have to write down details of the event; a key word or short sentence will do. Important is that you know which situation it concerns. We first need to get an overview of the sites where those pop-ups appear, and then which pop-ups appear most often.'*

Noval records five clusters of memories: grandfather, father, mother, school, and outside on the street. All clusters contain various events that are still distressing; some of them generate intrusions.

The ranking of clustered memories can be arranged in different ways. A point to keep in mind is that the most recent traumatic experiences are usually more accessible and vivid in this target group (see Box 19.2). By treating these first, one increases the young person's willingness to be open to treatment of earlier traumatic experiences afterwards. If the memories cause a lot of suffering because they generate nightmares and/or flashbacks (intrusions), it is recommended that the therapist ranks the intrusive memories according to the degree to which they cause distress or disturbance. EMDR is preferably focused on reducing intrusive memories first, as they cause a lot of suffering. These can lead to a quick SUD reduction and, therefore, symptom reduction.

After the relevant memories linked to PTSD symptoms have been reprocessed, the therapist can organize the remaining memories with the adolescent according to the extent to which they drive specific residual symptoms. By using the timeline path and the belief path (see Chapter 4), relevant memories can be identified that either drive particular symptoms, such as fear of fire (timeline path) or that have led to symptoms that can be explained from a negative core belief (Van Pelt et al., in prep).

With the belief path, the therapist looks for memories of events that (still) instinctively 'provide evidence' for specific negative core beliefs, such as 'no one can be trusted' and 'I am bad/worthless/not worthwhile'. Such beliefs are frequently seen in this target group. Most have damaged self-esteem because of numerous negative social experiences. This search strategy is used to treat symptoms resulting from negative core beliefs, such as gloominess, avoiding peers or smoking marijuana. Usually, several search strategies are needed in the treatment of these adolescents to treat all symptoms adequately.

19.6.2 **Preparation (Phase 2)**

If the therapist considers it valuable, the resource development and installation (RDI) Protocol can be used during the preparation phase to strengthen resources so the adolescent feels better equipped to dare to stay focused during EMDR (without avoidance). These adolescents often choose 'self-confidence' and 'perseverance' to maintain and/or strengthen their sense of control. It can also be helpful to create a safe (positive) place to help the client remain calm during the arrangement of the memory material.

Manfield's concept of dyadic resourcing (see Rosoff, 2019) can be useful when working with severely attachment-disordered adolescents. This allows them to experiment with secure attachment figures in their imagination. See Case Study 19.3. The therapist invites the adolescent to choose a (publicly known) figure with whom they would feel secure and to imagine the extent to which they would be comforted by that person (see Noval).

CASE STUDY 19.3 **Noval—Dyadic resourcing**

The therapist asks Noval to choose a character from a film or book with whom he would feel safe. Noval chooses a father figure from a Japanese cartoon. The therapist asks him to imagine what it would be like if this father figure could sit next to him and offer support. Through guided imagery, in which all senses are activated (*'what do you smell, what do you hear?'*, etc.), Noval eventually experiences a positive relationship with this imaginary father figure and positive feelings. These are strengthened by incorporating a set of slow eye movements or calm butterfly hugs.

19.6.3 **Assessment (Phase 3)**

Clinical experience shows that the target group usually describes their target image only globally, not providing details. When establishing the target image, the adolescent is given the choice of whether to describe the image aloud or, if they prefer, only to keep it in mind. Often, activation of the memory evokes intense emotions, and therefore they cannot manage to tell the story well. They have never talked about it before and often find it embarrassing to recall the event and put the images into words.

An advantage of EMDR is that clients do not have to describe their mental images in detail if they do not want to or cannot do so. The therapist should encourage the client to focus on the mental image and its painful details during the assessment phase. This is needed to activate the memory and get the desensitization process going optimally.

19.6.4 **Desensitization (Phase 4)**

Interweaves are regularly necessary with this target group: looping and blocking are common (see Chapter 9). Often, particular interweaves are appropriate, aimed at the imaginary expression of anger or directing their attention to emotions beneath the anger, such as sadness. When processing memories of traumatic early childhood events, the chain of associations often leads to the theme of powerlessness. In such situations, the therapist can ask the adolescent how they might want to use the knowledge and wisdom they gained in this phase, and what they would like to do or say. See below an illustration of the desensitization of Noval, Case Study 19.4.

CASE STUDY 19.4 **Noval—Desensitization**

Target image: He sees that his grandfather, who has laid him on his stomach, is on top of him and has tied his hands and feet together, while beating him. Noval is 7 years old at the time.

The negative cognition is 'I am powerless' and he feels scared and sad. The SUD score is 10: Noval feels it in his heart and gets tears in his eyes.

Noval: *I don't understand why a grandpa would do such a thing to a child. I hate him. Am so angry ... still. I couldn't do anything. Am so angry.*

Therapist: *What would you like to do now with that anger at your grandfather?*

Example of an interweave:

Noval: *I would like to hit him myself.*

He begins to sob and closes his eyes.

Therapist: *Noval, open your eyes and follow my fingers. You are here with me now, you are safe* [said emphatically].

Noval: [calms down slightly] *I don't understand how you can do such a thing to a child.*

Back to target: 'the furious look in grandpa's eyes'.

Noval: *I think now of another time ... I must have been singing to amuse myself. I wasn't allowed to go outside and there was nothing in the house to play with. Grandpa was changing clothes to go to the coffee house with his friends. I annoyed him so much that he suddenly ran up to me and beat me up. I didn't know what to do. I hit him back. I had to do something. Grandpa then said I was very bad because I hit my own grandfather.* [Noval cries.]

Therapist: *What did you need then?*

Another interweave:

Noval: *Someone to be there for me.*

Therapist: *Who can be there for you now and offer what you need?*

Noval: *My girlfriend, but I don't know...She can comfort me when I feel bad...I am often so bad to her...I don't know if I deserve that love.*

Therapist: *Okay, that little boy back then needs a comforting arm. What would you like to say to little Noval now and what would you like to do for him?*

Noval: *Give him a hug.*

Therapist: *Go ahead. Can you do that?*

Noval: [Nods 'yes'].

Therapist: *How does it feel to you to comfort this child?*

Noval: *It feels good.* [Sobbing.]

Therapist: *And how does it feel for the child?*

Noval: *Good.*

In this case, the memory of a specific situation could be reprocessed by using an interweave, focusing on imaginary expression of anger and the emotion underneath the anger (sadness), comforting oneself.

19.6.5 Concluding Incomplete Sessions (Phase 7)

For the installation of the positive cognition and body scan, there are no specific points for consideration in this target group. Given the slower SUD decreases due to looping/blocking during desensitization, incomplete sessions occur regularly. If the SUD is not 0 at the end of a session, the therapist asks the adolescent to close their eyes, store the memory in an imaginary box or container, and close it. This allows the adolescent to 'leave' the memory with the therapist. Careful closure of the session and imaginary storing or leaving the memory behind is necessary for the adolescent to leave the session with a sense of control. See below the closure of an incomplete session for Noval, Case Study 19.5.

CASE STUDY 19.5 **Noval—Concluding an incomplete session**

Therapist: *Okay Noval, you've worked very hard, we'll end it like this. What is the best thing you learned about yourself today? ... How would you describe people who do this sort of thing?*

Noval: *Tough.*

Therapist: Say to yourself: 'I am tough' and sit in a tough pose. Concentrate for 10 seconds. Does anything positive come to mind?

Noval: [Shakes his head 'no'.]

The therapist asks Noval what he is going to do next. He says he would prefer to go home to light up a joint, but he is supposed to go to his internship. The therapist recommends that he goes to his internship.

Therapist: *Shall we agree on something, Noval? Shall we leave the memory here in an imaginary safe, for which only you have the key and code? Then it will stay here in this room, and you can bring it out again next time. We'll continue our work together next time.*

Noval: *Okay.*

19.6.6 Accessibility Between Sessions (General)

Good accessibility for any questions between sessions and carefully connecting to the adolescent's perceptions are important. The therapist needs to keep the treatment goals firmly in place and not be distracted by the noise and turmoil that characterizes this challenging target group—for example, in the case of recidivism.

19.7 Concluding Remarks

This chapter aims to promote the identification of PTSD and other trauma-related symptoms in adolescents in forensic mental health services, who are usually diagnosed with conduct disorder or oppositional defiant disorder. Trauma treatment in these adolescents is almost always indicated, given the large number of unprocessed traumatic experiences they have. This chapter highlights the importance of starting evidence-based trauma treatment, such as EMDR, as soon as possible after a preparatory phase with the family and the adolescent. Together with the adolescent, the therapist identifies symptom-related memories of traumatic experiences and helps the adolescent understand how these memories are related to their symptoms.

After treating PTSD, treatment focuses on reducing the remaining specific symptoms and negative core beliefs. The damaged self-image can be transformed into a more neutral self-image with the help of EMDR, after which the adolescent can have positive experiences and build a more positive self-image. When these adolescents progress into adulthood untreated, a personality disorder is almost always present, to the extent that they are unable to make positive and sustainable choices in all areas of their lives (relationships, work).

When intrusive and disturbing memories no longer haunt the adolescent, the likelihood of improved emotional regulation increases. As a result, contact with people in their environment becomes less conflicted, restoring healthy and positive social development. The threatening negative spiral of rejection by parents, 'healthy' peers, school, work, and social institutions can thus be broken.

An essential addition to the standard EMDR protocol is that, in principle, EMDR treatment for this target group takes place after extensive preparation of the adolescent and their family. This chapter describes why this specific addition is essential and what relevant points of attention have emerged in clinical practice. Because the adolescent is still in the environment (the family) in which they suffered traumatic experiences, attention must be paid to ensuring safety in the family and a more positive family dynamic. Arrangements are made to deal with current conflicts to minimize the likelihood of new negative experiences in the family. If necessary, relevant skills are taught during preparation. Individual preparation is essential to build a working relationship between the therapist and the adolescent and to create a better understanding of the relationship between memories and their current behaviour.

Adolescents from this target group often seem to be without hope, but at the same time appear to be powerful, and their behaviour can be changed. The treatment process with this target group is a long and often challenging journey, involving a lot of trial and error. The therapist must climb the mountain together with the client. The therapist acts as guide and sherpa. Once they reach the top of the mountain, they can take off their backpacks and see that new vistas are revealed.

20 EMDR in Children

A Dyadic Approach With Playful Interventions

ESTIE BAR SADE AND BARBARA WIZANSKY

20.1 Introduction

The dyadic approach to trauma processing in young children proposed here offers a psychotherapeutic treatment model anchored in the Eye Movement Desensitization and Reprocessing (EMDR) protocol and the attachment relationship. The efficacy of EMDR therapy in treating child and adolescent issues arising from violence, physical illness, or other adverse experiences has been well documented (Banoğlu & Korkmazlar, 2022; Manzoni et al., 2021). However, empirical and clinical evidence for the efficacy of EMDR therapy in addressing the consequences of early attachment trauma is lacking. The Dyadic Playful EMDR therapy model that is presented here provides clinical tools for evaluating and repairing relational impairments within the caretaker–child dyad, as well as treating current symptoms associated with early relational trauma.

The focus is on children under the age of eight (and eventually older children with early attachment trauma), who are living under ongoing war stress, with immigration or refugee status, or who have suffered long-term attachment trauma due to medical conditions. There is evidence demonstrating the effectiveness of EMDR in these populations (Fleming, 2012; Diehle et al., 2014; Meentken et al., 2020; Olivier et al., 2022). The Dyadic Playful EMDR therapy model emphasizes the relational aspects of the treatment.

Attachment literature, when integrated with EMDR literature, underscores the importance of the therapeutic relationship (Dworkin, 2005; Hase & Brisch, 2022). Attachment-focused EMDR (AF-EMDR) in adults involves utilizing the classic EMDR framework with an added focus on attachment repair (Parnell, 2013; Civilotti et al., 2019). When treating young children, the relationship focus shifts directly to the present caregiver–child dyad, where there is still an opportunity for the reconsolidation of traumatic memories and relationship repair. In the presented model, the therapist evaluates the dyad during the initial phases of the protocol, identifying experiences of either the parent or the child that may have disturbed the relationship, and their influence on forming developmental infrastructures. These implicit disturbance patterns are conceived as sources of ongoing dysregulation for both parent and child, often leading directly to the present symptoms. The therapist aims to identify and repair attachment disturbances within the therapeutic setting.

The literature describing EMDR in young children provides only a few case studies involving parent–child attachment interventions (Wesselman et al., 2012; Gomez, 2013; Wizansky

Estie Bar Sade and Barbara Wizansky, *EMDR in Children*. In: *Handbook of EMDR for Children and Adolescents*.
Edited by: Renée Beer and Carlijn de Roos, Oxford University Press.
DOI: 10.1093/oso/9780198918400.003.0020

& Bar-Sadeh, 2021; Van der Hoeven et al., 2023a). The EMDR Dyadic Playful therapy model presented here attempts to fill this gap.

20.2 The Attachment Relationship

Attachment theory elaborates an innate system, activated through the child's relationship with the attachment figure and influenced by the caregiver's state of mind (Main et al., 2011). The theory highlights the role of early mother–infant interactions in regulating present emotions and their impact on the infant's future schema for viewing themselves and others. In essence, the early mother–child relationship is a major factor in defining early development. Ideally, cycles of distress are followed by calming, affect-regulating interactions, which can reduce activation and distress caused by repeated experiences of negative emotion, amplify and intensify positive emotion, and pave the way for healthy relational development. This process facilitates an integrated self-organization (Lyons-Ruth & Jacovobitz, 2008; Beebe et al., 2010). Particularly relevant are studies analysing videotaped interactions between mothers and infants after the 2001 bombing of the World Trade Center, which highlighted the children's acutely sensitive reactions to the mother's shock, distress, and mourning following the traumatic loss of a husband and father (Beebe et al., 2012; Bigelow et al., 2018; De Palma et al., 2023).

Child–caregiver interactions in both past and present, and the role of those interactions in enhancing a child's ability to recover from a traumatic event, are closely related. This understanding has led to the development of various treatment models based on close observation of the interaction between caregiver and child (Beebe & Lachman, 2014; Wesselman et al., 2014a; Wizansky & Bar Sade, 2021). In line with these theoretical and practical models, we assume that early trauma treatment requires a focus on the parent–child interaction, particularly on the caregiver's ability to respond sensitively to distress. Therefore, the Dyadic Playful EMDR model provides concrete assistance to the EMDR therapist in maintaining this focus.

20.3 EMDR with Attachment Trauma

Attachment trauma arising from early disruptions or adverse experiences in the caregiver–child relationship can significantly impact brain development and emotional regulation (Schore & Schore, 2014). Attachment, as defined by Bowlby (1969), is a deep and enduring emotional bond that connects one person to another across time and space. Attachment trauma occurs when this bond is disrupted or when the child experiences significant ongoing negative interactions with their caregivers. Emerging research in neuroscience and developmental psychology provides insights into the way in which early adverse experiences can affect brain structure and function, leading to difficulties in emotional regulation, relationship formation, and cognitive development. Direct interventions encouraging affective attunement and reflective dialogue not only help regulate the child's immediate emotional responses, but also foster brain connectivity in the prefrontal cortex, which may influence future development. (Bakermans-Kranenburg et al., 2003).

Van der Kolk and colleagues (2021) conclude that the integration of EMDR and attachment-based therapy offers a powerful and effective treatment for complex trauma in children. They emphasize the importance of a holistic approach that addresses both the traumatic experiences and the relational disruptions caused by trauma. EMDR addresses the reprocessing of traumatic memories, while attachment-based interventions work on repairing and strengthening relational dynamics. The integration of these therapeutic modalities highlights the need for clinicians to directly involve caregivers in the treatment process as the immediate agents for change in the child's emotional and relational functioning.

Artigas and Lehnung (2020) also emphasize the developmental aspect of the therapeutic process and offer an additional dimension: the importance of play as a child's natural, safe mode of expression. The work of O'Shea and Porges (2020), describing the integrative treatment of a 10-year-old boy and his parents for attachment trauma, illustrates this approach. Playful dyadic activities, encouraging positive interactions and co-regulation, are used throughout the treatment. Further evidence demonstrates that play-based interventions with positive caregiver involvement promote emotional regulation and cognitive development (Blaustein & Kinniburgh, 2018).

In summary, in line with the findings emerging from research in developmental neuroscience, the therapeutic model presented in this chapter aims to promote secure attachment through playful attunement and reflective dialogue, which help regulate the child's emotional responses and foster brain connectivity in the prefrontal cortex.

20.3.1 Dyadic Focus and the Attachment Relationship

Figure 20.1 supports the therapist in assessing the strength of the dyad and exploring possible areas where the attachment relationship failed to support the child's development, in the past or the present. Careful tracking of attachment interactions allows informed decision-making about what is needed for parent and child to find safety in the relationship. It guides therapists in assessing if the parent can:

Notice the child's emotional needs (attunement)

Empathize and invite emotional contact (emotional communication)

Contain and calm the child when over-activated (corrective reaction)

Support the child's feelings while setting boundaries (affect regulation)

Provide consistent and coherent information (coherent narrative)

The attachment relationship is not only a potential source of trauma, but also a significant source of strength or resources (Kinniburgh et al., 2005; Schore & Schore, 2014; Siegel, 2012). Beginning with the initial interview, the therapist focuses on identifying and reinforcing resources, characteristics, or activities that promote positivity, regulate intense negative emotions, and enhance positive ones. These strengths are bolstered and integrated throughout the EMDR protocol by creating experiences of joy and fun.

Attunement	Emotional communication	Corrective response	Affect modulation	Coherent narrative
Parents' response to the child's needs? Can parent identify child's emotional needs? Can parent calm child when they gets out of his window of tolerance?	Quality of non-verbal communication, is there constant exchange of body contact and body language, of vocal tone and timber, of eye contact and the transaction of basic feelings? Do feelings resonate, is there a range of emotional expression synchronicity, are there reciprocal transitions? Can parent contain the distress level of the child and his own?	When attunements is broken, can the caregiver invite the child to become engaged in comforting emotional transactions? Can the caregiver maintain the 'adult role' and give the necessary lacking information? Take proper responsibility and help child regulate?	Source of physiological organization. Helping the child whenever they are out of their window of tolerance). Encouragement\Sup port strategies Caregiver as a role model of affect modulation.	Helpful in comprehension of child's self and others.

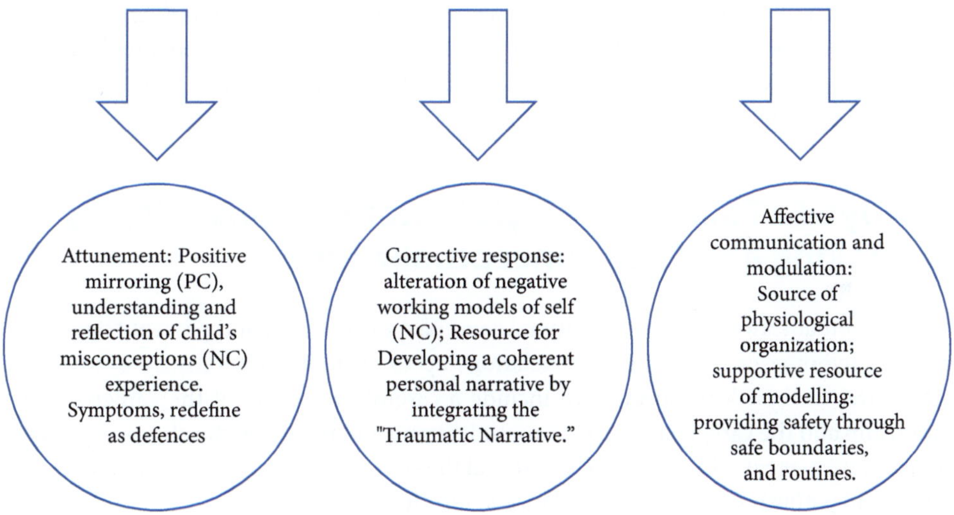

Figure 20.1 Elements of a positive attachment relationship.

20.3.2 Playfulness

The word 'playfulness' in the proposed model does not refer to using toys but to fostering a state of mind and an attitude that creates an atmosphere of safety. It involves experiences of curiosity, wonder, physical contact, and fun. The literature on Thera-play supports the effectiveness of this approach in therapy (Eruyar & Vostanis, 2020; Hiles Howard et al., 2018; Weaver et al., 2021).

Neurobiological research underscores the significance of playfulness and joy within the parent–child dyad, and their role in conveying safety. The work of Panksepp and Porges is particularly relevant in this regard. Their research highlights the activation of innate emotional systems that facilitate healthy development. Panksepp (2009) describes how activating the 'search system' enables the child to access calming signals and new experiences. Porges' research describes a process in which the autonomic nervous system (ANS) detects safety signals within relationships from birth, communicated through facial expressions, tone of voice, and muscle movement (Porges, 2022).

Throughout EMDR therapy, the therapist widens their treatment lens to include a close evaluation of the caregiver–child interaction, in separate meetings with parents and in dyadic sessions: noticing, eliciting, and reinforcing individual strengths and positive safety interactions. The emphasis on playfulness allows the therapist to introduce verbal and non-verbal pleasurable interventions if there is a break in communication.

Taken all together, attachment trauma treated with the Dyadic Playful EMDR model looks like this: In history taking (phase 1), relationship elements are evaluated (Figure 20.1) and reparative playful interactions are integrated into dyadic sessions, paving the way for trauma processing within the eight phases of the EMDR protocol. In the preparation phase with the dyad (phase 2), interventions are designed to encourage dyadic experiences of safety and joy. Parents are helped to identify their difficulties in attaching to their child and are encouraged to understand and identify with their child's state of mind, creating a safe space in the relationship. Corrective experiences are gradually incorporated into the interaction, allowing the identification and processing of early traumatic experiences with phases 3 and 4 of the protocol.

20.4 Dyadic Focus and Playful Interventions: History Taking and Case Conceptualization

Case conceptualization aims to identify relevant past experiences and present triggers and formulate hypotheses regarding their relationship to current symptoms. A dyadic focus expands the therapist's perspective to include a careful evaluation of the caregiver–child relationship and the caregiver's capacity to understand and reflect on the child's experience, both past and present. This approach can reveal the sources and maintenance of current difficulties and pathways to strengthen relational resources.

A dyadic focus broadens perspectives by:

a. Including a historical inventory of disruptions in the attachment relationship that may relate to the current problem. (e.g., medical trauma, separation, family issues).
b. Evaluating the parent's ability to understand and reflect on the child's experience.
c. Providing psychoeducation to explain developmental and psychological factors contributing to disruptions.
d. Integrating the therapist's understanding of symptoms and triggers within the context of the dyad.

e. Selecting relevant target memories and the order of processing these targets in collaboration with the parent and child. The therapist focuses on eliciting resources and identifying positive attachment cues and experiences during the first interview. The questions presented in Figure 20.2 help in assessing both the parent's and the child's perspectives.

The therapist reinforces and creates signals of safety and love, directing attention to physical sensations, emotions, and, if appropriate, cognitions. Some examples:

The therapist might say to a child, 'Can you choose a special, pleasant spot where mommy can touch you when you are sad? Maybe on your forehead? Or maybe right on the side of your face? Mommy, can you touch your child in this special, chosen spot? Where can you feel that good feeling in your body?'

The therapist might say to a mother, 'Can you tell [child's name] what you were most proud of this past week? Did you find time for an extra hug? If the answer is no, maybe you could do it now?'

The therapist directs the child's attention to positive feelings and sensations by gently tapping the child's knees, toes, hands, or shoulders. Parents may also be encouraged to anchor their positive sensations with EM^{+}. This approach aligns with Porges' model, which theorizes that safety requires unique cues for the nervous system. According to this model, safety

Questions to elicit resources	**Questions to identify positive attachment cues and experiences**
○ What can your child do well? ○ What makes you proud of your child? ○ When do you particularly enjoy being with your child?	○ How could you soothe your child when they were a baby? ○ What type of soothing was most effective? ○ How did your child respond to being sung to? What were their favourite songs or rhymes? ○ Did you have a pet name for your child? What was it? ○ Did your child have a special blanket or stuffed animal to hold?
Questions to assess the parent's capacity for mentalization of the child's experience	**Questions for the child**
○ How do you think your child felt during the traumatic event? ○ If they could have expressed their feelings, what might they have said? ○ If your child could express themselves now, what would they say about themselves?	○ What are you good at? ○ What makes you happy ○ When have you been brave ○ Who do you like to be with? ○ What are you most afraid of ○ What makes you most angry? ○ What makes you most sad? ○ What would you like to be different?

Figure 20.2 Questions for the first interview.

cues are accessed through reciprocal social interactions that dampen defensive responses. These cues are optimized by environmental and bodily signals (Linden, 2015).

20.5 Dyadic Focus and Playful Interventions: Examples and Case Studies

Figure 20.3 shows what the parents (can) do in all phases to maintain the dyadic focus.

This section provides examples of playful interventions with a dyadic focus for various EMDR phases (Section 20.5.1); two case studies (Section 20.5.2) illustrate these interventions and this model: Lee (Case Study 20.1) and Gili (Case Study 20.2).

20.5.1 Examples of Dyadic Playful Interventions

Light-hearted, playful interventions are implemented as needed to continuously enhance the sense of safety in the relationship. They are grouped in EMDR phases.

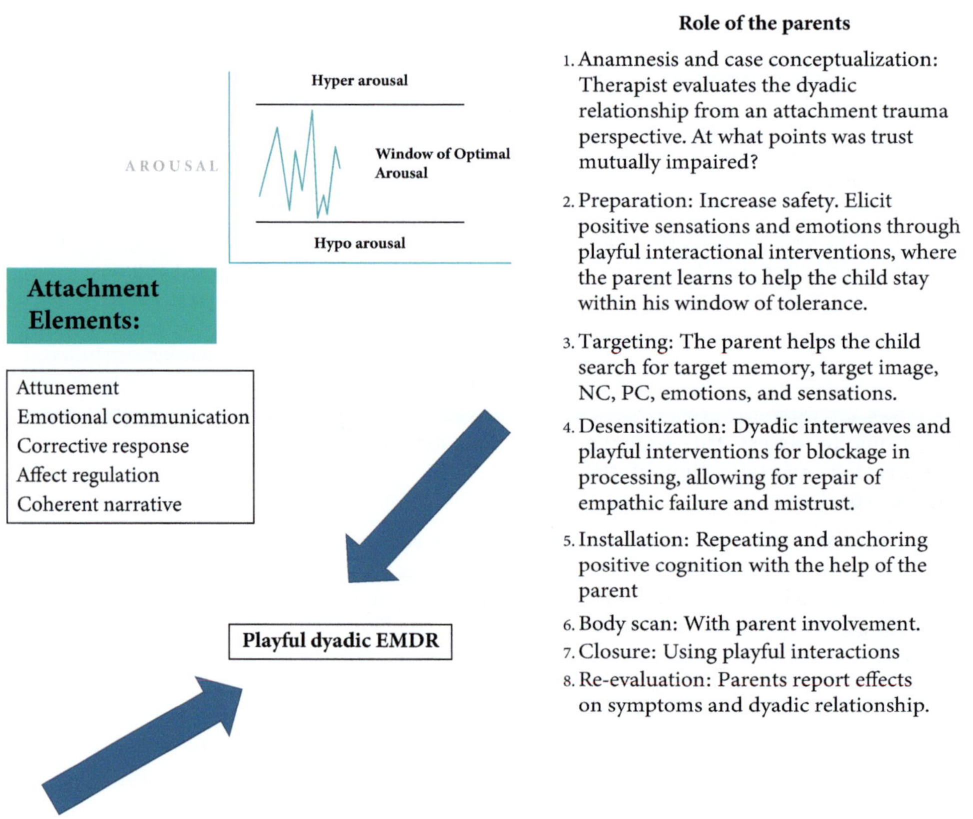

Figure 20.3 Dyadic focus through all phases.

- *Phase 1: History Taking*

BOX 20.1 Games for Phase 1

I. Fears Buster Game

Objective:
Normalize fears, strengthen coping skills through affect modulation, and encourage an empathetic response.

Description:
Parents and children take turns naming scary things. The parent guesses the intensity of each fear for the child on a scale from 0 to 10. The child confirms or refutes the parent's guess. When the parent guesses correctly, they share a story of handling a similar fear, such as a siren alarm or night-time fears.

- *Phase 2: Preparation*

BOX 20.2 Games for Phase 2

II. Looking Without Laughing Game

Objective:
Enhance emotional contact and attunement between parent and child.

Description:
Parent and child sit facing each other. They take turns making happy, sad, or angry faces for the other to imitate. The goal is to maintain eye contact and avoid laughing. If someone laughs, the turn switches. The therapist asks the child how it felt to play with the parent and where they noticed this pleasant feeling in their body. The therapist taps gently on the child's knees, toes, or shoulders to focus on the positive sensation, reinforcing it. The same can be done for the parent.

III. Getting Closer Game

Objectives:
Enhance parent–child bond: Strengthen the emotional connection and trust between the parent and child.

Description:
A set of picture cards with prompts or emotions is required (can be handmade or printed).

1. Introduction:

The therapist explains the purpose of the game to the parent and child, emphasizing the goal. The parent and child sit comfortably facing each other in a relaxed environment, free from distractions.

continued

BOX 20.2 *Continued*

2. Choosing the Cards:

A deck of picture cards is placed between the parent and child. The cards can include images that represent various prompts or emotions, such as a happy face, a sad face, a heart (for love), a star (for pride).

3. Taking Turns:

The parent and the child take turns drawing a card and showing the picture to the other person, asking 'What makes you happy/sad/do you love most of being together/makes you proud?' At the end of the activity, they choose one thing that evoked positive feelings and sensations and the memory related to it is activated and installed with EM^{+}.

IV. Pretending to Become Enraged Game

Objective:
Help parents manage and regulate their child's anger (affect regulation).

Description:
The child is instructed to pretend they are angry and express it as they would at home, such as by shouting or stomping. The parent is asked to help the child calm down in a novel way. The therapist suggests strategies to the parent, such as placing a hand on the child's shoulder, asking the child to go running to release anger, or offering a hug. The therapist monitors and provides feedback. If the child responds positively, the therapist reinforces this by having the parent tap the child's knees to remember the good feeling. Roles can also be switched if more flexibility is needed. The parent is directed to pretend anger while the child helps calm down.

V. Simon Says Game

Objective:
The parent develops capabilities in using corrective responses to encourage the child to follow instructions and highlight positive listening skills.

Description:
Parent and child take turns following commands in a game of Simon Says (such as Simon says to stand still while counting to 10, to take a deep breath and then blow it out, to shake your body like a boiled spaghetti strand, and then stand stiff like an uncooked one). The therapist highlights the child's ability to follow directions well, asking the parent to acknowledge and praise this skill. The parent is encouraged to praise the child for being a good listener, reinforcing this positive behaviour.

VI. Master of Storms Game

Objective:
To help parents and children manage dysregulation and restore calm (affect modulation).

Description:
The therapist explains that every emotional storm has a peak, which eventually dissipates. Parents are guided to help the child calm down by counting backwards, clapping, or finding other soothing strategies. If the child does not calm down, the therapist asks the child to suggest ways to calm the storm. The therapist and parent acknowledge the child's role as the 'master of storms' and tap to reinforce the calming experience.

VII. Let's Pretend Game

Objective:
Address and reframe unmet needs from earlier childhood experiences in a supportive and imaginative context. Provide a safe space for the child and parent to create and explore scenarios that fulfil these needs collaboratively. Strengthen the parent–child bond through shared creative problem-solving and role play.

Description:
Parent and child role play a scene where the child acts the 'younger child' of the age that the trauma occurred. Parent is asked to role play how he would have provided the 'younger child' with all of his unmet needs: comfort, protection, safety, self-worth—needs that weren't provided at the earlier traumatic period of his life. Once parent is playing his role child is asked how it feels for him at the present moment. If a positive reaction is evoked the therapist adds EM^{+}.

VIII. Frightening the Fears Game

Objective:
Help the child address and manage fears. Provide a supportive and imaginative context for the child to practice coping strategies. Strengthen the parent–child bond through collaborative problem-solving and role play.

Description:
Explain to the child and the parent(s) that they are going to play a game where the child will be a brave explorer facing his fears. Help parents reassure the child that they will be their support throughout the adventure. Begin by imagining a situation where the brave explorer faces something that might be frightening or may evoke anger. For example, the explorer might need to venture into a 'dark forest' or explore a 'mysterious cave' where they encounter something that causes fear.

Exploring the Fear:
As the brave explorer (the child) is encountering the 'fear' (e.g., a shadowy figure or strange noise), the parent helps the child by reassuring them that they are safe and supported. Ask the child how their explorer character feels and what they might do to handle their fear. For example: 'What does our brave explorer do when they see the shadow? How can they make it less scary?'

Coping Strategies:
The therapist introduces and practices, with the parent and the child, coping strategies within the adventure. For instance, they may pretend that the explorer has a magical 'courage

continued

BOX 20.2 *Continued*

shield' or a 'glow stick' that helps them feel safe. The parent encourages the child to use these strategies as part of the game. For example, they might hold a flashlight (or a toy) to feel braver or imagine using deep breathing to calm themselves. Once the child imagines or practices a coping strategy and feels calmer, the imaginary scene of coping and accompanied feelings are reinforced with EM^{+}.

IX. Role Reversal

Objective:
To help both parent and child understand and empathize with each other's perspectives during moments of anger or frustration, improve communication and emotional regulation, and strengthen the parent–child bond.

Description:
Explain to parent and child that they are going to play a game where they switch roles to understand each other's feelings better. Emphasize that this game is about learning and empathy, not about blaming.

Create a scenario where a common situation of anger or frustration occurs. For example, the child is upset because they can't have a toy they want, or parent is frustrated due to a messy room. Let them act out the situation where one person is experiencing a meltdown or loss of temper. The 'child' in this role might express frustration or anger, while the 'parent' responds to their behaviour.

Playing Out the Scenario:
Start by having the 'child' act out a meltdown or angry outburst in the role of the parent. For example, if the scenario is a messy room, the child might express frustration about not being able to find something. The 'parent' (playing the role of the child) should respond to the behaviour and try to handle the situation as they would if they were actually the child. For example, they might try to calm the 'angry child' and offer comfort or solutions.

Switching Roles:
After playing out the scenario from one perspective, switch roles. Now, the parent acts out a meltdown or loss of temper, while the child plays the role of the parent. Use the same or a different scenario.

X. Going Through Stormy Water Game

Objective:
Support the child in engaging with and processing of rough emotional moments (affect modulation and empathic communication).

Description:
The therapist asks the parent how they support the child through tough times.

The parent might suggest holding hands, whispering reassurances, or singing together.

The therapist encourages the parent to check with the child regarding what support they need at that moment. They explore if the suggested support helps the child and provide BLS if necessary. It is an in vivo activity where the parent is asked to notice if the child calms down. The present calm state is reinforced with EM$^+$

- *Phase 5: Installation*

BOX 20.3 Games for Phase 5

XI. Bravery Courage Dance

Objective:
Celebrate the child's bravery and reinforce positive self-image (reinforcement of positive self-concept).

Description:
When the child has successfully processed their experiences, the therapist asks to describe their positive feelings, such as 'I am brave'.

If the child struggles, the parent affirms their efforts with statements such as 'You are brave' or 'You handle scary things well'.

The therapist suggests a victory dance where parent and child create a celebratory dance, tapping themselves or each other, or stomping around the room.

- *Phase 8: Closure*

BOX 20.4 Games for Phase 8

XII. Postures Game

Objective:
Anchor the feeling of overcoming challenges and experiencing strength or relief (anchoring positive feelings).

Description:
The therapist asks parent and child to choose a movement or position that represents overcoming challenges or feeling strong. They hold this posture while tapping the butterfly hug, while the therapist guides them to notice the associated body sensations and emotions.

20.5.2 **Case Studies**

CASE STUDY 20.1 **Lee**

- ***Introduction and phase 1***

Lee, a 6-year-old boy, was referred for EMDR therapy in preparation for a tonsillectomy. Lee had a longstanding fear of doctors. His mother's primary coping mechanism was avoidance. The tonsillectomy was essential, but Lee and his mother were overwhelmed with panic. During the initial phase of therapy, the therapist discovered that Lee had spent two months in an incubator following his premature birth. His mother had felt frightened, helpless, and unable to protect her child. An exploration of the mother's experience in that period revealed a connection between her anxiety and her continuing difficulty setting safe boundaries for Lee.

A close look at the mother–child relationship

Lee's mother speaks openly about her son's achievements. She expresses pride in his reading abilities and enthusiastically recounts his role as a lion in a school play while Lee smiles proudly. When asked about how she calmed him as an infant, she begins to cry, saying *'I had four other children to care for and I was so weak and tired. When he cried, I never even tried to comfort him. Something froze inside me.'* Her voice, body language, and words convey deep distress.

Lee can also recognize his own capabilities, such as competence and bravery, but he is resolute about his intense fear of doctors. He expresses a desire to be unafraid, like his brother, but he reacts immediately to any mention of medical treatment as if he is in danger. His body stiffens, he stamps his foot, and says *'That's just the way I am. I'm not going. No one can change my mind. No one can force me to go.'*

Processing a mother's birth trauma

Gradually, Lee's mother's paralysing feelings of guilt for not having cared adequately for him give way to a positive cognition of confidence in her capabilities and she is able to believe and to say *'I take good care of Lee. I have the strength to support Lee when he's afraid.'*

Establishing Lee's triggers and targets for processing

Past: *Early medical experiences*

Present: *Current fear of doctors*

Future: *Upcoming doctor visit and tonsillectomy*

- ***Phase 2***

The preparation phase is augmented by distancing activities and playful interventions, such as the Let's Pretend game (See VII in Figure 20.5).

The therapist asks Lee to draw the fear he feels. Lee draws a picture of a baby hugging himself, labelling it Dear Little Baby Lee (Figure 20.4). When the therapist asks him to describe his drawing, Lee stiffens and fixes his attention on the ceiling.

Figure 20.4 Dear Little Baby Lee (drawing 1).

The therapist introduces an intervention that involves the re-enactment of previously experienced events, using the Let's Pretend game to allow Lee's mother to provide a different, more supportive reaction than she had in the past (a corrective response).

The therapist says to Lee: *'Let's have a pretend play about your picture, Lee. This can be the stage. Lee, can you pretend you're the baby in the picture? Mum, you can be the baby's mother and speak as a mother would to her baby. What kind of voice would this baby have? Lee, you need to talk with a baby voice and pretend to be afraid. Can you feel the baby's fear in your tummy or in your chest?'*

The therapist instructs Lee's mother: *'You are the baby's mother. Every time baby Lee cries and tells you how he is feeling, you can do whatever you think will help baby Lee calm down.'*

The therapist is active throughout the process, encouraging both mother and child to focus on their feelings and body sensations, thus strengthening positive neural networks (Porges, 2022).

Initially, Lee feels awkward as he and his mother play the Let's Pretend game. Lee pretends to cry, but soon he allows himself to cry louder and louder. Mother and son laugh. Lee's mother cradles and kisses him, and Lee contentedly murmurs *'ga, ga, ga'*, followed by more laughter and cuddling from his mother.

As both mother and son move within their window of tolerance, the therapist compliments their teamwork by saying *'You make a great team*. Baby Lee let his mummy know how he felt, and his pretend mummy was able to calm him down.'

The therapist asks Lee and his mother to perform butterfly hugs to consolidate that good, safe, calm feeling, saying *'Concentrate on the nice feelings in your body. What do you feel and where do you feel it?'* (see Figure 20.5).

If Lee had objected to playing the baby in the Let's Pretend game, the therapist could have suggested that the mother play the baby and that Lee assume the role of the mother. The laughter and fun generated by this role reversal would convey the safety of a positive relational experience (see IX in Figure 20.5).

Figure 20.5 Now I am strong (drawing 2).

Reflection on the Let's Pretend game: It is versatile and can be used in various scenarios where the dyadic relationship is blocked by either the child's or the parent's strong defensive reactions to stress, such as tantrums, stubborn shutdowns, parental helplessness, or the child's panic. During the game, the therapist may offer gentle suggestions, such as *'I wonder what would happen if Mom put her arm around you, or let's see, I wonder what would happen if she just said "I love you"?'*

Addressing fears through another playful intervention: Frightening the Fears game (see VIII in Figure 20.5)

In a subsequent session, Lee reveals that he doesn't like going to bed because he often thinks about the needles that the nurse had used and 'other scary stuff'. The therapist notes that Lee glanced at his mother when he mentioned 'other scary stuff', yet the mother did not respond to his fear.

The therapist turns to Lee's mother and asks, *'Lee's scary things include needles and other stuff. I wonder what the other scary stuff could be?'*

The therapist asks Lee and his mother to sit opposite each other and hold hands. They are invited to shout types of scary things. Lee's mother shouts *'Dinosaurs!'* and Lee shouts *'Monsters and huge lions!'* They are encouraged to brainstorm ways to make the scary things less scary, exploring solutions like chasing them away, spraying them with magic disappearing powder, et cetera.

Eventually, Lee suggests *'We can just shut the door and say "stay outside; you are not allowed to come in".'* Lee's mother agrees. Together, they use this solution with each scary thing, including the nurse's needles.

The therapist asks *'Mom, can you tell Lee that you'll always be there, ready to take care of scary things together?'*

- *Phases 3 and 4: Processing trauma, preparing for future events*

Lee and his mother are ready to move to processing traumatic memories and future events, using storytelling techniques (Lovett, 2015; Wesselman et al., 2014a). The rationale for using storytelling combined with the standard protocol is as follows: the preverbal memories are 'feeding memories' to unresolved relational issues. The therapeutic process first addresses these 'feeding memories' through a relational narrative. Only then are conscious memories and present triggers processed with the standard protocol.

Targets to be processed by Lee: with the help of the therapist, Lee's mother constructs a narrative to help Lee process his initial trauma from the incubator, as well as future challenges. The narrative includes the following components:

1. Processing the initial incubator trauma: Lee's early medical experiences were processed in a safe and supportive manner, reinforcing that *'You were strong and you did well and all went well. Now, it is all over and you are safe. Now you are better, and mommy is here to help you when you're afraid.'*
2. Anticipating necessary trips to the doctor: Present and upcoming medical visits are described, again reinforcing him how well he is doing this, helping Lee to anticipate and cope with future events from a place of strength.
3. Preparing for future hospital visits: Preparation for the tonsillectomy, reinforcing Lee's own strength and the support he will receive from his mother.

With his mother's support, Lee can face memories of his previous doctor's visits and the upcoming tonsillectomy without significant distress.

CASE STUDY 20.2 **Gili**

- ***Introduction and Phase 1***

Gili, a 6-year-old girl, exhibits behavioural problems at home and at school, including defiance, violent temper tantrums, and avoidance behaviours. Gili's therapy demonstrates the eight phases of EMDR therapy in a child-focused, dyadic, and playful context. The approach integrates the structured phases of EMDR with creative, interactive interventions to address emotional and behavioural challenges, enhance parent–child relationships, and facilitate trauma processing.

Gili's family lives in a conflict zone where frequent rocket threats have become a way of life. Initial evaluations suggest possible ASD or anxiety disorder. However, dyadic evaluation revealed a close connection between her father's untreated PTSD during Gili's infancy and her present behavioural issues.

The therapist assesses the attachment relationship between Gili and her father.

Because her father's PTSD had caused him to avoid emotional and physical closeness, Gili was left feeling unsafe, unprotected, and fearful. Despite his eventual therapy for PTSD symptoms with EMDR, her father struggles with guilt and fear that he may have harmed his daughter.

During the therapist's relationship evaluation, she asks *'What was Gili like as a baby? What were her favourite songs? What did you like to do together? How did you calm her when she was distressed?'*

Her father's discomfort with his inability to answer these questions reflects his emotional distance from Gili during her early years. The therapist explores the connection between his avoidant behaviours and Gili's current symptoms.

The first dyadic session

In the therapy room, Gili avoids eye contact with her father and plays independently. When she needs help, she demands it angrily. Her father responds with either cynicism or withdrawal, lacking the ability to comfort her physically or emotionally.

- *Phase 2: Preparation*

Therapy progresses to psycho education, playful interventions (the Getting Closer game; see III in Figure 20.5) and processing Gili's father's trauma.

The therapist educates Gili's father about the potential link between his daughter's problems and his past trauma-related behaviours. He agrees to process his attachment trauma to increase his sensitivity to Gili's needs, which involves processing his fear.

He recalls being afraid to touch or even look at his infant daughter, fearing he would harm her. Through processing, he moved to a PC of 'I can trust myself to be in control and love my daughter.'

In light of the therapist's observation that Gili seemed to prefer solitary play, combined with her father's distant behaviour, the therapist proposes a game that will help them connect physically and emotionally.

The therapist asks Gili's father '*Can you tell Gili why you are here*?' He responds '*Because I want us to be closer. If we could become closer, maybe I could help her stop being so angry with everyone*.'

The therapist suggests a game in which they move towards each other from opposite sides of the room, counting, stopping when uncomfortable and then trying again, getting a little closer each time. The therapist encourages them to look into each other's eyes and do a butterfly hug.

The therapist says, '*What a great team you are. You counted to 10. I wonder if you can get to 15?*' The therapist notices that Gili tends to break eye contact and act silly when her anxiety increases. To address this, she suggests to Gili's father '*Perhaps you could ask Gili to hold your hands as she gets closer*?'

Gili's father's increasing comfort in his role creates space for his daughter to remain connected. The therapist observes Gili's interest waning and whispers '*I bet Daddy has an idea to make the Getting Closer game even more fun*.'

Gili's father looks at her and says '*I bet we can get to 100 together*.'

As the sessions progress, father and daughter engage in more face-to-face games. They take turns imitating each other's sad, happy, or angry faces, making each other laugh. The therapist grounds each experience by focusing attention on Gili's and her father's physical sensations to reinforce their feelings of pleasure. Gili learns to perform the butterfly hug, and her father gently taps Gili's knees to soothe her. (An alternative game could be the Looking without Laughing game; see II in Figure 20.5.)

Gili and her father were introduced to further playful interventions that correlate with EMDR phases to continue evoking positive emotions, managing symptoms of the damaged relationship, and repairing it. The goal of these interventions was to create safe interactions, feeling safe being close to each other, whereby partners can relate, communicate, and maintain physical and emotional closeness. To dampen the child's automatic reactions of anger and opposition, the game created a new schema: '*I can feel safe being with you*'.

- Games and role reversals: Continued playful interactions, such as making funny faces and playing role reversal games, allowed Gili to continue expressing her emotions safely and build positive experiences with her father.
- Installing positive emotions: The therapist used the butterfly hug to anchor positive feelings, reinforcing the new, secure attachment.

- *Phase 3–8*

When the father tells the story, the therapist taps gently, helping the father when necessary (Gomez, 2013; Lovett, 2015; Wesselman et al., 2014b). A constant transition from negative to positive thoughts (e.g., I am/I am not protected) becomes an intrinsic part of the story. Gili continues to draw as the story unfolds.

Gili was able to process relevant memories for her symptoms—her inability to soothe, detachment from her father, over-clinging to her mother, separation anxiety from the past, and school and family problems from the present—and she was prepared for the future. Furthermore, the symptoms that were caused by her memories disappeared.

A review of Gili's case

Gili's initial case conceptualization suggested a significant connection between her present symptoms and early attachment problems with her father. Thus, treatment planning aimed at first repairing the attachment bond in the present before processing past trauma. Gili learned to regulate her emotions and build trust through playful dyadic interventions, while her father gained confidence in his ability to be emotionally available and supportive. As he played with his daughter, Gili's father developed the needed skills to provide emotional support. Gili's past trauma and behavioural issues could then be addressed and processed.

- *Dyadic EMDR processing during phases 3 and 4.* Storytelling with a Dyadic Focus: The therapist guides Gili's mother and father in the creation of a story to describe their caregiver–child experience of attachment trauma. Gili's father shares the story of Gili and his trauma. The therapist helps him to verbalize, in language Gili can understand, his fright and the reason he distanced himself from her when she was a baby, and to identify and verbalize Gili's experience while reiterating his current commitment to being a loving and present father.

Managing the Parent–Child Interaction

Gili's father sits opposite her as he tells the story, while her mother sits close by. Gili chooses to draw during the storytelling, allowing for non-verbal processing and expression of emotions.

The final phases of the standard protocol are also conducted with the dyad. Therapy continues in a pleasurable, safe atmosphere when they arrive for the next session. Using a light, fun approach, the parent and child work together to ground a PC, do a body check, and go home with ideas for healing games.

When they next arrive, the therapist continues to focus on maintaining a pleasurable, safe atmosphere.

The therapist helps when necessary. For example, she says 'Mommy took care of you, but you might have felt very alone when Daddy wouldn't even look at you.'

Gili's father is helped to craft reparative interventions. For example, Gili's father says, 'Daddy takes good care of you now. He loves to look at you, hug you, and play with you.'

The angry man drawing (Figure 20.6) represents Gili's preverbal memories of her father during his angry episodes. Drawing allows her to externalize her fear and process her feelings of vulnerability and abandonment.

Figure 20.6 Mr Angry Man (drawing 3).

Figure 20.7 shows Gili processing her own anger and helplessness (present triggers) and connecting to the feeling that Dad is helping her to calm down. She no longer feels alone; the therapist added to the text in purple present triggers with harsh feelings.

Continued playful interaction

- Games and role reversals: Continued playful interactions such as 'making funny faces' and role reversal games allowed Gili to continue expressing her emotions safely and build positive experiences with her father (see IX in Figure 20.5).

Figure 20.7 Daddy helps me control Mr Angry Man' (drawing 4).

Figure 20.8 shows a positive experience of being with her father and family, and a new positive statement emerges: *'Even when I am angry, I can remember the good things; I can handle my anger.'*

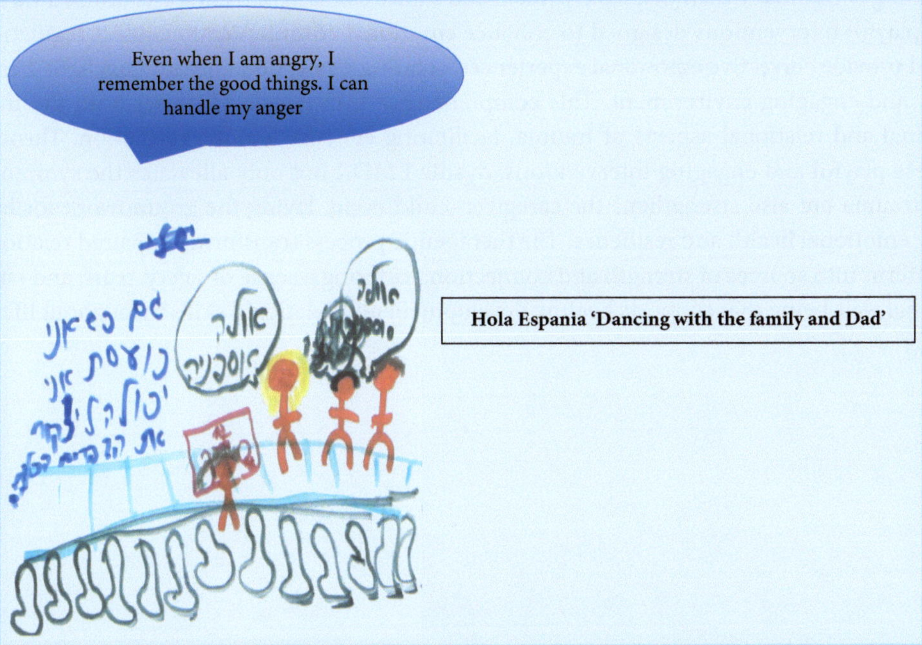

Figure 20.8 New positive statement emerges (drawing 5).

- Installing positive emotions: The therapist used the butterfly hug to anchor positive feelings, reinforcing the new, secure attachment.

Gili then processed school and family problems in both the present and future.
Gili's initial case conceptualization viewed the connection between her present symptoms and early attachment problems with her father as significant. Thus, treatment planning aimed first at repairing the attachment bond in the present before processing past trauma. Gili learned to regulate her emotions and build trust through playful dyadic interventions, while her father gained confidence in his ability to be emotionally available and supportive. As he played with his daughter, Gili's father developed the needed skills to provide emotional support. Gili's past trauma and present behavioural issues could then be addressed and processed.

20.6 Concluding Remarks

EMDR Dyadic Playful therapy offers a dynamic and engaging approach for young children to develop emotional regulation skills and coping strategies. It facilitates the successful processing of traumatic memories and present and future challenges. Therapists utilize a variety of playful interventions designed to enhance emotional communication, affect regulation, and provide corrective emotional experiences, creating a safe, non-threatening, light-hearted, and engaging environment. This comprehensive framework addresses both the individual and relational aspects of trauma, facilitating effective trauma resolution. Through these playful and engaging interventions, dyadic EMDR not only alleviates the symptoms of trauma but also strengthens the caregiver–child bond, laying the groundwork for lasting emotional health and resilience. The therapeutic process transforms impaired relational patterns into sources of strength and connection, fostering a sense of safety, trust, and emotional well-being that supports healthy development and relational skills throughout life.

Integrative Attachment Trauma Protocol for Children

21

DEBRA WESSELMANN, IRMA HEIN, AND NATHALIE SCHLATTMANN

21.1 Introduction

Integrative Attachment Trauma Protocol for Children (IATP-C: Wesselmann, 2025a, 2025b; in Dutch: Integratieve Gehechtheidsbevorderende Traumabehandeling voor Kinderen (IGT-K), Schlattmann et al., 2023) has been developed for children who are chronically traumatized at a young age within the relationship with a parent or caregiver. As a result of traumatizing experiences, these children struggle with a broad spectrum of trauma-related symptoms. The IATP-C is for children for whom regular evidence-based trauma therapy or traditional family therapy is predicted to be unsuccessful due to their behavioural challenges or for children and families with whom these methods have failed. Often, these children suffer from extreme fears resulting in avoidance behaviour and rapid emotional dysregulation combined with problematic family relations. The IATP-C addresses four domains of symptoms: post-traumatic stress symptoms, attachment problems, behavioural problems, and difficulties with emotion regulation. This chapter describes the target population for the IATP-C, followed by an overview of evidence-based treatment options for this group. Because none of these evidence-based treatments is designed to treat trauma and attachment problems within the same protocol, this new treatment model was developed. Then, we introduce the IATP-C model, which has three treatment stages in which a family therapist and an EMDR practitioner collaborate. Illustrated with vignettes, the systemic and EMDR techniques within each stage are described, as well as creative and playful adaptations within the EMDR standard protocol for children and adolescents for this specific group of chronically traumatized children.The research on the IATP-C model so far is summarized.

21.2 Target Group

Having multiple interpersonal traumatic experiences at a young age is common. Approximately one in seven children in the United States (Centers for Disease Control, 2023) has experienced some form of abuse or neglect. This can permanently affect the child's neurobiological system (Teicher & Samson, 2016) and result in a broad spectrum of psychopathology, including problems in psychosocial functioning, such as post-traumatic stress

Debra Wesselmann, Irma Hein, and Nathalie Schlattmann, *Integrative Attachment Trauma Protocol for Children*. In: *Handbook of EMDR for Children and Adolescents*. Edited by: Renée Beer and Carlijn de Roos, Oxford University Press.
 DOI: 10.1093/oso/9780198918400.003.0021

disorder (PTSD), anxiety disorders, depression, attachment problems, behavioural problems, and difficulty with emotion regulation. Problems in their relationships with family members and others are frequently observed. Difficulties can manifest in diverse areas, such as social contact, play, and physical functioning (such as eating, sleeping, potty training, muscle tone, and alertness). Van der Kolk (2005) proposed a formal diagnosis (developmental trauma disorder) for children suffering from pervasive developmental and functional symptoms deemed as occurring after early neglect and abuse. The proposed diagnosis was not included in the DSM-5 (American Psychiatric Association, 2013) due to insufficient empirical evidence. However, further studies have supported indications for the validity of this diagnosis (e.g., Spinazzola et al., 2018, 2021). Because the complex presentation of symptoms and problems is related to a large number of maladaptively stored memories of adverse and traumatic events, the symptoms do not get resolved without therapeutic support (Shapiro, 2018).

21.3 Treatment Options

The treatment options for PTSD in children of seven years and older which have proven to be effective are trauma-focused cognitive behavioural therapy (TF-CBT) and EMDR therapy (Bisson et al., 2019; NICE, 2018b). However, some of the children impacted by trauma-related problems are not yet receptive to trauma processing, as shown in clinical practice. These children appear to have a strong need for restoration of communication and trust within their family before trauma treatment. The Sleeping Dogs method (Struik, 2021a; Chapter 12 in this book) provides tools for promoting the conditions necessary to enable trauma treatment.

Problematic attachment can be addressed through the parents to whom the child is (somewhat) attached. Interventions are used with the goal of improving the quality of the attachment relationship (increasing the child's felt sense of trust and security) by helping parents become more sensitive and responsive to their child.

For children aged 0 to 7, potentially effective interventions in promoting attachment relationships include Video Feedback Interventions to Promote Positive Parenting and Sensitive Discipline (VIPP-SD; Juffer et al., 2016), Parent-Child Interaction Therapy (PCIT; Abrahamse et al., 2016; Zisser & Eyberg, 2010), and Child-Parent Psychotherapy (CPP; Guild et al., 2021; Lieberman et al., 2005).

For children over age 7, evidence for the potential efficacy of Differentiation and Phase Therapy is supported by initial research (Putman et al., 2020). Follow-up research has been initiated (De Wolff et al., 2020). The effectiveness of other interventions for improving attachment security in older children has not been studied sufficiently (De Wolff et al., 2020). There is consensus that providing support for parents improves parents' sensitivity towards their children (De Wolff et al., 2020). Where appropriate, parents are referred for help with their own stress or mental health issues. Psychoeducation for parents with video recordings and discussion of parent–child interactions can improve parents' sensitivity towards and understanding of their children. The Basic Trust method (Polderman et al., 2011) incorporates these elements, and there is initial evidence for its efficacy (Zeegers et al., 2020). Modified Interaction Guidance (MIG; McDonough, 2000) has shown favourable results for disruptive parenting behaviour (Madigan et al., 2006). Family-oriented systemic treatment like a Narrative Approach (Vermeire, 2023; White & Epston, 1990) and attachment-based family therapy, also known as Dyadic Developmental Psychotherapy (Hughes et al., 2015), are not yet evidence-based.

None of the above-mentioned treatment options effectively address the traumatic experiences. Therefore, an integration of models and techniques and a multidisciplinary approach was sought to treat the group of children who experienced early childhood interpersonal traumatization resulting in problems related to trust and attachment security, reactivity to present triggers, avoidance of participation in treatment, and frequent, severe emotional and behavioural dysregulation.

21.4 Rationale for the IATP-C

Obstacles to the treatment of these children often include ongoing problems with family relationships and mistrust, dysregulation, and behaviours that are difficult to manage, even within the therapy sessions. Furthermore, they may be unwilling to address traumatic or adverse events due to the associated anxiety (see Box 21.1). For these children, the first treatment stages are used for trauma treatment preparation. Interventions are implemented that focus on increasing safety, enhancing attachment security, improving emotion regulation, improving understanding and motivation for treatment, and helping the children become comfortable articulating feelings and experiences.

BOX 21.1 Gwen and Melissa

Gwen, age 7, was brought to therapy by her foster parents, who were her grandparents, after Video Feedback Interventions to Promote Positive Parenting and Sensitive Discipline (VIPP-SD: Juffer et al., 2016) and Trauma-Focused Cognitive Behavioural Therapy (TF-CBT: Cohen et al., 2017) had failed. Gwen has lived with her grandparents since she was 4 years old because both biological parents were incarcerated for drug- and child-abuse-related offences at that time. Gwen argued and had aggressive episodes throughout the day. She refused to stay in bed at night. The grandparents were called to school regularly due to Gwen's behaviours.

Melissa, age 14, has severe PTSD symptoms. She has a terrible history of being bullied in school, and her mother had an episode of severe psychosis when Melissa was 1 and again when she was 4 years of age. The relationship with her father appears warm and secure, but she shows signs of an insecure attachment pattern with her mother. She avoids talking about her traumas in therapy. Therefore, TF-CBT and EMDR are likely to fail.

For this group of children, the IATP-C treatment model was developed (Wesselmann, 2025a; Schlattmann et al., 2023). This new model applies an integrative approach wherein family therapy and EMDR therapy are combined, including EMDR-related methods for preparation and attachment. The IATP-C is implemented within a multidisciplinary team and addresses the specific needs of children who have experienced attachment trauma and for whom traditional evidence-based trauma treatments failed or are likely to fail.

21.5 Overview of the Treatment Model

In the IATP-C model, two therapists work closely together: a family therapist and an EMDR therapist. They have separate roles and tasks. Generally, the family therapist does the preliminary work, preparing the child and parent(s) for EMDR work. In addition, the family therapist supports the parents throughout the entire treatment. The EMDR therapist provides EMDR therapy for trauma processing and uses EMDR-related interventions to strengthen attachment security and self-regulation skills. Good communication and collaboration between therapists increase the effectiveness and efficiency of treatment. Therefore, both therapists meet regularly to discuss the process and content of their sessions.

The IATP-C model consists of three stages:

1) Psychoeducation for parents.
2) Providing adaptive information to the children and their parents, plus stimulating activities that increase children's sense of security in attachment and capacity for regulation.
3) Trauma processing for the children, often with the supportive presence of their parents.

These stages are described below, including the tasks for both therapists in each stage.

21.5.1 IATP-C—Stage 1: Parent Psychoeducation

Children's inadequately processed memories of early abuse and neglect are easily activated by the actions or words of their parents, leading to dysregulation, defiance, or aggressive behaviours. Parents, in turn, become stressed. They often don't understand their children's behaviours and react with anger, reinforcing the children's mistrust and fear.

Stage 1 involves family therapy sessions, working with the parents on 'integrative parenting strategies'. In the first sessions, the parents and family therapist get to know each other and find a way to work together. The family therapist explains in detail the treatment model and its elements and provides psychoeducation about trauma and attachment. This is supported by the book *Attachment trauma in children: Integrative strategies for parents, 2nd Edition* (Wesselmann, 2025b). Integrative parenting teaches sensitive, attuned parenting responses to challenging behaviours designed to help children develop greater attachment security and a calmer, more integrated brain and nervous system.

The parent work is crucial for improving family relationships because it allows parents to vent about the daily challenges of parenting their child, receive validation and emotional support from the therapist, and gain information about the upbringing of a chronically traumatized child. Putting much effort into the therapeutic relationship with parents promotes a positive collaboration with them and enhances the chance of treatment success. The family therapist should create a nonjudgemental, warm atmosphere that allows parents to 'open up' and share their feelings honestly. This is called the *reflective dialogue* within the 'Circle of Security' parents' intervention (Marvin et al., 2002), in which the parent feels heard, understood, and supported by the therapist. In turn, the parent can begin to offer emotional support to their child in a similar way. Through these reflective dialogues, the child can develop more positive mental representations of the parent. These sessions lay the foundation for cooperation between parents and therapists (see Box 21.2).

BOX 21.2 **Anthony**

Anthony's adoptive mother came in, expressing anger and frustration over an incident in which 14-year-old Anthony had stolen her car keys, locked himself in her car, and camped there. The therapist listened carefully and attuned to the mother's feelings in a way that helped the mother calm down and reflect upon the incident. The following week, she reported successfully discussing the incident with her son. By remaining calm and encouraging him to 'open up', she found out he had been afraid she wouldn't let him come in when he was late for curfew. He had locked himself in the car to make sure that he had a place to sleep that was warm and safe.

21.5.2 IATP-C—Stage 2: Attachment and Regulation

This treatment stage includes family therapy sessions and EMDR therapy sessions. The child and parent(s) attend all sessions together. Parents are present during treatment to learn how to create a safe environment for the child so that the child can learn to 'open up' (Gomez-Perales, 2015).

- ***Family therapist's tasks***

The family therapist continues to work with the parents, helping them gain a better understanding of the impact of the traumatic history of the child on their behaviour. The family therapist gives psychoeducation to help the child and the parents to better understand how trauma is stored and how the associated cognitions and affects are repeatedly triggered and affect the child's behaviour. The family therapist also provides the child and their parents with self-regulation exercises and adaptive information, such as the 'jobs of moms and dads' (see Box 21.3 below), to increase the child's capacity to utilize EMDR for trauma processing later.

BOX 21.3 **Bethany**

At age 10, Bethany had tantrums each time her foster parents reminded her to brush her teeth or shower. By exploring the thoughts and feelings triggered by the parents' reminders, the therapist discovered Bethany's dysfunctional thought: 'My mom and dad are mean and

continued

BOX 21.3 *continued*

make me do stupid things.' They also discovered that Bethany did not have to brush her teeth or take regular showers in her biological home, from which she had been removed at age 4 due to neglect. Therefore, she was not used to mums and dads telling her to do these things. The family therapist conducted a 'jobs of mums and dads' activity, designed to help the child understand the intentions behind their parents' actions and words, including 'keeping their children safe', 'helping their children stay healthy', and 'learning skills they will need when they are grown-ups'. This information was entirely new for Bethany and helped her understand that her parents' intentions came from a place of love and concern for her well-being.

The family therapist introduces the concept of 'the little child inside' and helps the child and the parents understand many problem behaviours as misguided coping behaviours associated with a younger child state that is activated by present triggers (Arntz et al., 2021). Furthermore, the family therapist employs therapeutic techniques to help the child become aware of their memories of past experiences and the accompanying thoughts and emotions that influence their choices for behaviour in current situations. Together with the family therapist, the parent(s) and the child identify traumatic memories, negative cognitions, and current triggers. This so-called 'detective work' lays the foundation for the EMDR sessions, allowing the EMDR therapist to move efficiently into the reprocessing phases.

- ***EMDR therapist's tasks***

The EMDR therapist starts to work with the parents and the child and gets to know them. Next, the therapist creates a visual overview of the child's life with a timeline[1] (=EMDR phase 1: History taking and treatment planning). Preferably, both parents and child are present. Still, the therapist can also conduct (some of) the history taking without the child present if the child's tolerance for addressing traumatic events is low. With the help of the child and their parents, the therapist adds positive events, major traumatic events, and other interruptions in the attachment relationships to the timeline.

Within the IATP-C stage 2, the EMDR therapist implements EMDR phase 2 preparation activities, like the standard safe place, regular resource development and installation with the RDI protocol (Korn & Leeds, 2002; Leeds, 2009), and additional resourcing techniques specific to the IATP-C protocol for enhancing positive representations within the child with assistance from parents. These IATP-C-specific EMDR preparation activities include Attachment Resource Development (ARD) for deepening trust and attachment security and Self-regulation RDI (S-RDI) for strengthening the capacity to self-regulate (Schlattmann et al., 2023; Wesselmann, 2025a). During these preparation activities, Shapiro (2018, pp. 246–250) recommends slow, short sets of alternating stimulation, which are generally addressed

[1] This timeline should not be confused with the timeline that is used in one of the paths for target selection: the so-called timeline path. See Chapter 4, RB & CR.

as 'slow BLS' or, in some countries, as 'mild working memory taxation' (WMT).The slow, short sets of BLS are clinically observed to have a relaxing effect while supporting focused attention. The EMDR therapist provides the BLS/WMT the child prefers, chosen from all regular and alternative options, including rocking the child, tapping a doll, or giving child-specific tasks such as rolling a ball or toy car.

Traditional RDI

Traditional RDI involves elements of the EMDR procedure to strengthen internal qualities with the help of an activated positive memory; if the child has no positive, relevant memory, a role model or a symbol associated with the desired quality is identified. Within the IATP-C, emphasis is given to a resource activity that strengthens the child's 'most mature' or 'big kid' state through memories of experiences in which the child felt 'big' or 'competent'. The parent may be prompted to help the child recall these positive moments (Wesselmann, 2025a). The therapist follows the usual RDI protocol and assists the child with noticing the body posture and internal feelings associated with the mature state before applying slow BLS (EM+) to deepen the positive affect. Positive memories may include situations in which the child effectively self-calmed or solved a problem.

Standard installation of an imaginary safe place, as described by Shapiro (2018), can encourage a relaxation response. The child can be encouraged to use a place from their imagination, or from movies or books, and most children enjoy using a sand tray, art materials, or images on a computer or in a book.

Attachment Resource Development

ARD is a specific form of resource development that involves activities in which the therapist creates experiences of closeness and security in the session between the child and parent and then deepens the positive affect through slow BLS (Wesselmann, 2013, 2025a; Wesselmann & Shapiro, 2013; Wesselmann et al., 2012, 2017a, 2017b, 2018). ARD activities, including 'messages of love', 'cord of love', and 'safety for the smaller one', are best conducted with the child and each parent one at a time. Some parents will be able to spontaneously give the appropriate answers, while others need to be well prepared by the therapist for these activities.

The ARD 'messages of love' activity is initiated by prompting the parent to provide a positive view of the child and evidence of love and connection. For example, the therapist might ask '*What positive qualities do you enjoy in your child?*', '*What do you remember about the first time you laid eyes on your child?*', or '*What are your future hopes and dreams for your relationship with your child?*' When the parent responds positively, the child's associated positive emotions are deepened with the slow BLS.

The ARD 'cord of love' (or 'magical cord of love', depending upon developmental age) is implemented by prompting the child to picture the loving connection between child and parent as a beautiful cord or string of light connecting them from heart to heart. The child's positive emotions are deepened with slow BLS (See Box 21.4).

BOX 21.4 Latasha

Latasha (8 years old) experienced anxiety every night and wanted her mother to sleep with her. When prompted, she described the magical cord of love between her heart and her mother's heart as being glittery red. The therapist suggested that Latasha draw a picture of the cord between her mother's heart and her heart running from their bedroom to her bedroom during the night. At the direction of the EMDR therapist, Latasha sat on her mother's lap while her mother swayed her side-to-side, and the therapist also tapped on Latasha's legs. At the same time, Latasha looked at the picture and listened to her mother describing how she was sending Latasha her love through the beautiful connecting cord all night long, even when they were in different beds and even when they were asleep. In the next session, the cord of love activity was repeated with the father, and Latasha drew a yellow and blue bubble cord connecting her heart with her father's heart.

After the family therapist has introduced the concept of 'the little one inside', the EMDR therapist can start with fun activities to reinforce safety for the 'little child on the inside' by playing out what the parent might be doing for the smaller child in a playful role play. For example, the child may be invited to 'play baby' on the parent's lap, along with rocking or sucking on a lollipop (as a pretend bottle), instructing the parent to attune to the child's cues. Additionally, the child may be encouraged to draw a picture of the 'little child on the inside' being cared for by the parents 'in a safe place inside the child's heart'. The parents can describe ways in which they would nurture the 'little child on the inside'. Slow BLS is applied to deepen the child's observed positive affect (Lovett, 2015; Wesselmann, 2025a). The therapist carefully reinforces the child's mature state with the previously reinforced mature state exercise before the child leaves the session.

The parent should be prepared ahead of time on how to provide positive emotional support during all activities. The attachment resource activities may leave the child anxious about losing the newfound closeness with the parent, and therefore the parent is encouraged to continue providing experiences of comfort and closeness after the session as well.

Self-Regulation Development and Installation

As the child develops greater self-confidence and capacity to trust through RDI, ARD, and the exercises in the family therapy sessions, self-regulation development and installation (S-RDI) activities are initiated to deepen the child's awareness of and capacity for managing their internal state. The EMDR therapist utilizes small moments of dysregulation to coach the child with self-regulation tools provided by the family therapist to help the child shift to a calm state. The EMDR therapist encourages the child to notice the affect shift and deepens the awareness with slow BLS (Wesselmann, 2025a; Wesselmann et al., 2015).

The S-RDI activity 'talking to the brain' can be conducted after the family therapist teaches the child the concept of the feeling brain (right brain) and the thinking brain (left brain). The EMDR therapist can invite the child to a role play in which the therapist plays the feeling brain, and the child plays the thinking brain (with the help of the parent, as needed).

BOX 21.5 Jimmy

Jimmy (11 years old) did not wish to stop playing his computer game on his mobile phone when his father and the therapist were ready to start the session. The therapist used this as a good starting point for the 'talking to the brain' activity. The therapist tried to play her role of the feeling brain so that Jimmy felt his frustration about having to finish his game was understood. Jimmy and his father tried different thinking brain sentences to calm the feeling brain, such as 'It's okay, this therapy session won't take long, and in the car going home I can play again' and 'Better not to make a big fuss; I can think about Dad's promise to go to McDonald's after the session.' The therapist adds a slow, short set of BLS and states '*Notice what your thinking brain tells you*.'

Speaking as the feeling brain, the therapist makes negative statements. The child responds with helpful statements, speaking as the thinking brain. The EMDR therapist encourages the child to notice the affect shift and deepens awareness with slow BLS (see Box 21.5).

21.5.3 IATP-C—Stage 3: Trauma Processing

As in stage 2, the child and parent(s) attend all family therapy and EMDR therapy sessions. Trauma processing through EMDR is initiated. Therapists must usually incorporate creative and playful adjustments, as well as additional interweaves during the EMDR standard protocol.

- ***Family therapist's tasks***

The family therapist implements exercises focusing on parents' and children's interpersonal and problem-solving skills. Furthermore, adaptive information is provided as needed, and the child is coached in awareness and expressing thoughts and feelings. Although identification of past traumatic experiences and present triggers would be considered an EMDR phase 1 activity (history taking and treatment planning), the willingness of this population to talk about past traumas and present triggers develops gradually. Therefore, the family therapist continues gently assisting the parent with co-regulation of the child, helping the child build trust with the parents and learn to express internal thoughts and feelings through stage 3. One family therapy exercise, the dominoes activity (as described in Box 21.6), helps both parents and children reflect upon their triggers, thoughts, feelings, and actions related to a small conflict and identify skills that could lead to a better outcome in the future. As self-reflection and trust improve, the child's defences typically will lessen. Hence, the child becomes ready to share more openly regarding present triggers and memories, which are critical targets for EMDR reprocessing.

- ***EMDR therapist's tasks***

The EMDR therapist focuses on reprocessing the identified, relevant, symptom-related memories of traumatic experiences with EMDR therapy. EMDR preparation phase activities (RDI, S-RDI, and ARD) are repeated whenever necessary. The EMDR therapist targets

BOX 21.6 Jonathan

One family therapy exercise is the 'dominoes activity': The family therapist sets up an arrangement of dominoes and demonstrates with these how one quickly knocks over the next and then the rest. Using a whiteboard or sticky notes on the wall, the therapist, parent(s), and child figure out the dominoes that led up to a recent upset in the home. For example, Jonathan (9 years old) had an aggressive outburst before going to school. The mother identified the first domino involved, suggesting that Jonathan wear something 'nice' for picture day at school. Jonathan admitted that the second domino was his thought that his photograph would turn out ugly and that other children would make fun of him. His mother was surprised, as she had no idea that he had such a worry. She realized she contributed to the dominoes by becoming frustrated with his sullen mood and raising her voice. Jonathan admitted that he felt hurt and angry at his mother's tone. The family therapist helped Jonathan and his mother re-enact the morning and remove their dominoes using new skills. The mother practiced attuning to Jonathan's worries and Jonathan practiced communicating his feelings more directly. When Jonathan and his mother saw the EMDR therapist, she helped Jonathan reduce his distress and negative beliefs related to picture day at school by targeting and reprocessing this present trigger with EMDR.

current triggering situations (for example, asking the child to complete a chore) and traumatic memories. Often, it is difficult to devote the entire session to processing. The therapist makes creative adjustments when children have difficulty sitting still and concentrating, are dysregulated quickly, or lack adaptive information. The EMDR therapist involves parental emotional support as well as a variety of tools, including drawings, stuffed animals, and various types of interweaves, to help children effectively reprocess their traumatic memories.

21.6 Points of Consideration for the EMDR Component in IATP-C

21.6.1 Involvement of the Parent During the EMDR Therapy Sessions

At least one parent is invited to accompany the child in the session during EMDR reprocessing to provide emotional support. The parent's presence also increases the parent's empathy and compassion for what the child has experienced. It may be more appropriate to implement EMDR reprocessing without parents present in the case of trauma reprocessing that will trigger the parent and for adolescents with a desire for autonomy. In this case, the parent may be invited to leave an encouraging note or send a text or a supportive video for the child or adolescent to watch prior to the session (Struik, 2021a, p. 154). The EMDR therapist can improve the quality of the parents' support by explaining how EMDR works and their role. The parents are educated on when not to interfere and when to offer help; for example, they may be asked to help provide BLS/WMT and to respond to prompts from the therapist in the form of interweave questions (Schlattmann et al., 2023; Chapter 9 of this book; Wesselmann, 2025a).

21.6.2 Storytelling Method

Many children with a history of attachment trauma are highly avoidant of talking about the trauma and are very confused by the events in their lives. For these cases, Lovett (1999, 2015, p. 169) recommends writing a therapeutic narrative, with input from parents, to give children a developmentally appropriate explanation with adaptive information necessary for making sense of the events. A therapeutic story, as designed by Lovett (1999, 2015), can be written collaboratively by the EMDR therapist, with input from the parent(s), in a concise manner in the third-person, and sometimes with input from the child.[2] The family therapist may become involved in the writing of the story if the family therapist is EMDR trained. The story is written using known facts to help organize the significant events of the child's life into proper sequence and to highlight helpful information. Schlattmann and colleagues (2023) describe clinical experiences with focusing the story on the traumatic events and negative beliefs that are most directly related to the child's current problems and triggers. BLS/WMT is applied throughout the story's reading, and the therapist observes the child closely for any activation to determine points in the story that need to be targeted and reprocessed later with the EMDR standard protocol for children and adolescents.

21.6.3 Processing of Present Triggers

The child with attachment trauma may be triggered by everyday interactions with parents, siblings, teachers, or peers due to mistrust and negative interpretations regarding the intentions of others (Wesselmann, 2025a; Schlattmann et al., 2023) In IATP-C the current triggers are processed before addressing associated traumatic memories. Triggers may be identified during family therapy sessions. The child may be instructed to 'Place the old memories in a container', such as a desk drawer in the therapist's office, before targeting and processing the recent triggers. Triggers for processing may include being told 'no', being asked to complete homework or another task, or noticing irritation on the face of an adult. The target image (the triggering situation) is identified, along with a negative cognition (NC), such as 'My parent is trying to hurt me', and a preferred positive cognition (PC), such as 'My parent wants the best for me'. These NC and PC examples deviate from the standard formulations of cognitions, which are self-referencing because children with attachment trauma often resonate more strongly with beliefs that reference parents or others. Validity of cognition (VOC), emotion, subjective units of distress (SUD), and body sensation are identified through child-friendly methods, such as pointing to numbers on a number line and choosing emotions from a deck of feelings cards. The triggering situation is processed with fast BLS/WMT until the SUD is reduced and the PC feels true (Shapiro, 2018; Wesselmann, 2025a).

21.6.4 Interweaves

Cognitive interweaves are brief suggestions, statements, or questions that assist clients during EMDR reprocessing when they are stuck or looping due to a lack of adaptive information

[2] This procedure deviates from what is described in Chapter 8. Various deviations have been evolved from the original procedure as proposed by Lovett, RB & CR.

or developmental deficits (Shapiro, 2018). In the IATP-C model, different categories of interweaves are implemented. The most frequently used categories are interweaves that orient the child to the present, interweaves that empower the child, and informational interweaves. Next to providing interweaves directly to the child, in IATP-C the interweaves can also be applied in a dyadic way, referred to as either 'dyadic' or 'interactional interweaves'. Using dyadic interweaves offers a way to direct parents to provide reassurance, connection, or adaptive information between sets. Involving parents in interweaves strengthens the child's sense of their parents as protective and trustworthy (Wesselmann, 2025a, Wesselmann et al., 2017a; see also Chapter 9 of this book).

Interweaves that orient to the present help the child separate the past from the present, as the sense of time in these children is relatively weak. Examples of time orienting interweaves include '*How is the present situation different from the past?*', '*What size shoes do you wear now? What was your shoe size back then?*', and '*Who keeps you safe today?*'

Dyadic interweaves to empower the child with the parent's help include '*Mom, what would you like to tell the little one on the inside about this?*' A dyadic informational interweave might be '*Dad, how would you soothe a crying baby and find out what is wrong?*' This interweave moves the child's attention to adaptive information that the child received in stage 2 during the family therapy exercise about the cycle of trust. See Chapter 9 of this book for more examples.

21.6.5 Adaptations to the Standard Protocol for Children and Adolescents

Drawing materials, a sand tray, or other play objects such as dolls and stuffed animals may be used to help the child 'show' images or feelings related to the memory to access the components of the memory during the assessment phase in a child-friendly manner, especially with children who might otherwise struggle to stay focused. Throughout EMDR desensitization and reprocessing, the child may be invited to continue 'showing' rather than telling what they are experiencing.

Other playful ways are used to engage the child in EMDR therapy, such as the EMDR 'station technique' of Gomez (2013), in which seven 'stations' in the room or on the table are created playfully. At station one, the child finds an image of a movie screen. At station two, the child finds paper and pencils to draw the picture; at station three, the child can fill in thought bubbles to help find the NC, and so forth.

Playful methods for BLS/WMT help keep the child engaged during EMDR processing. These include electronic tactile buzzers, hand-clapping games, pounding a drum, stomping or shaking maracas or another type of rattle, holding one in each hand.

With most children for whom the IATC-P protocol is used, it is difficult to adhere strictly to the protocol as they so quickly start avoiding or becoming dysregulated. When the memory is activated, the therapist sometimes must skip some elements in the assessment phase and start the desensitization phase. For children who have difficulty describing the whole memory or articulating their associations, the folded paper method of Lovett (2015) can be used: The therapist uses a folded paper and asks the child to draw the picture in the first box (if possible, with the NC, the emotion, and the SUD). After some sets with BLS/WMT, the therapist asks the child to draw the picture of how it looks now in the second box, et cetera, until the SUD is 0 and a more positive image can be drawn in the last box. Gomez (2013, p.197) asks avoidant children to tell her about three pictures: (1) The most disturbing, (2) the least disturbing, and (3) the one 'that stands out about the difficult thing that happened to you'. In the IATP-C this creates the option to start with (2) or (3) if starting with (1) is still too difficult.

21.7 Research Using this Model

The IATP-C has been researched by its developers in the United States and a research group in the Netherlands (see Table 21.1). A case study with a 12-year-old child with a history of interpersonal trauma and reactive attachment disorder was carried out in the United States by Wesselmann and colleagues (2012). Measures indicated that externalizing behaviours, attachment problems, and traumatic stress symptoms were improved following 6 months of IATP-C treatment, and this was maintained at 3 and 6 months post-treatment.

Table 21.1 IATP-C treatment effects

Author	N	Age	Treatment length/number sessions	Target symptoms	Significant results
Wesselmann et al. (2012)	1	12	6 months, 24 family therapy, 24 EMDR therapy sessions	Externalizing behaviours, PTSD, attachment problems	Measures indicated improved target symptoms following treatment completion. Follow-up measures 3 and 6 months after treatment was completed showed gains were maintained.
Wesselmann et al., 2018	23	7–12	Duration ranged from 6 to 24 months. Ave. 12.7 months/ ave. 45 EMDR, 45 family therapy sessions	Externalizing behaviours, PTSD, attachment problems	At group level, measures indicated improved target symptoms following treatment completion. Follow-up measures were returned by 15 families 3 months after treatment showing gains were maintained.
Van der Hoeven et al., 2023	8	6–12	9 months/ave. 28 EMDR, 28 family therapy sessions	Behavioural problems, PTSD, attachment problems, emotion dysregulation	At group level, measures indicated improved target symptoms following treatment completion.

The second study (Wesselmann et al., 2018), carried out by the same researchers, was a case series study of 23 children between 7 and 12 years of age, living in permanent adoptive placements, with a history of neglect and abuse. On a group level, measures indicated that externalizing behaviours, attachment problems, and traumatic stress symptoms were improved following an average of 12.7 months of IATP-C treatment (duration ranged from 6 months to 2 years). Treatment gains were maintained 3 months post-treatment for the 15 families who returned for follow-up measures. Despite the notable strengths of the study, its limitations include small sample size, lack of a control group, and lack of assessment for fidelity.

A third study was performed in the Netherlands by Van der Hoeven and colleagues (2023). It involved a single-case experimental design (SCED) with randomized baseline periods. The study sample consisted of 15 children with a background of child abuse and neglect residing in a permanent placement. Eight cases completed all treatment sessions and all weekly measurements within the narrow time frame of the study, without interruption by external circumstances, so they were suitable for analysis. All except one participant showed improvement in one or more symptoms. At the group level, there was evidence of improvement in attachment, behavioural, and emotional problems, mostly with large effect sizes.

A fourth study was performed with the same population as the third study, also by Van der Hoeven and colleagues (2024). Still, a larger group of participants (n = 12) could be included in these analyses (all children who completed the treatment could be included in this analytical method). This study aimed to investigate whether the attachment style and core cluster PTSD symptoms act as moderators for the treatment outcomes of the IATP-C. Results showed that children with a disorganized attachment style had more severe trauma-related symptoms in addition to PTSD. The IATP-C appeared to be more effective in successfully treating children with a non-disorganized attachment style, particularly those with a non-disorganized attachment style and re-experiencing as core cluster PTSD symptoms.

In conclusion, preliminary studies with the IATP-C model show promising results. However, more extensive, in-depth studies with innovative analytic methods are needed to determine the effectiveness of the IATP-C model. Further exploration into child and parent characteristics associated with optimal treatment length and positive and negative treatment effects is required.

21.8 Concluding Remarks

The IATP-C is designed to help children with a history of attachment trauma who present with obstacles to traditional treatment, including avoidance, disruptive behaviours, lack of cooperation, and difficulty verbalizing their internal state. During the IATP-C stage 1, psychoeducation helps parents interpret the child's behaviours through the attachment and trauma lens and respond with more attunement and emotional support. During the IATP-C stage 2, the family therapist works on self-regulation, the quality of attachment, and the identification of triggers, beliefs, and relevant traumatic events. The collaborating EMDR therapist assists through resource work: strengthening skills and positive affect, and deepening trust and connection between the child and the parent(s). During IATP-C stage 3, the family therapist provides support as needed to the EMDR therapist, whose task is to process present triggers and earlier traumatic events. The IATP-C allows children with a history of chronic trauma to move towards healthier functioning in their families, in their school life, and in their peer relationships.

22 EMDR and Family Therapy with Families Following Child Abuse

JOANNE MORRIS-SMITH AND MICHEL SILVESTRE

22.1 Introduction

For this chapter, child abuse is defined as 'witnessing or being a victim of domestic violence, emotional or physical neglect, sexual abuse, and emotional or physical maltreatment, which occurs in the context of a relationship of responsibility, trust or power, leading to actual or potential harm to the child's health, development or dignity' (World Health Organization, 2022).

Readers will be familiar with the work of Felitti and colleagues (1998), who identified the relationship between childhood abuse and household dysfunction as one of the leading causes of death in adults. Norman and colleagues (2014) conducted a meta-analysis of 124 studies of the effects of non-sexual child abuse on the mental and physical health of victims in Western Europe, North America, Australia, and New Zealand. They found statistically significant links between physical or emotional violence and neglect and depressive disorders, drug use, suicide attempts, and risk-taking sexual behaviour: 80% of child abuse appeared to be perpetrated by parents or parental guardians.

Several Dutch prevalence studies conducted over a period of 12 years have consistently shown that 25–37 out of 1,000 children (i.e., 3%) have experienced some form of child abuse (Fictorie et al., 2022). In nearly 50% of cases, this involved violence within the family. Domestic violence increases parental stress and correlates with higher post-traumatic stress in children. Since trauma treatments have appeared to be less effective in treating symptoms following family violence than following other types of traumatic events (Ehring et al., 2014), it seems justifiable to conclude that domestic violence specifically, and child abuse in general, is a complex form of traumatization with a potentially significant impact on children.

22.2 Relevance of EMDR for Abused Children

Abused children can find it challenging to describe their experiences, especially when the abuse started at a very young age. Also, the child may have developed dissociative processes that make verbalizing what happened to them difficult. EMDR therapy is ideally suited for

Joanne Morris-Smith and Michel Silvestre, *EMDR and Family Therapy with Families Following Child Abuse*. In: *Handbook of EMDR for Children and Adolescents.* Edited by: Renée Beer and Carlijn de Roos, Oxford University Press. © 2026, Oxford University Press. For the English edition. DOI: 10.1093/oso/9780198918400.003.0022

abused children because it allows them to process their traumatic memories through sensory and emotional associations. EMDR therapy is also helpful for this group because feelings of humiliation and shame, inherent in abuse, are implicitly processed during the desensitization phase.

The AIP model describes stimulating memory processing and promoting associational connections between sensory, emotional, and cognitive networks, using BLS/WMT to unblock stuck information processing. The research by Pagani and colleagues (2012) provides neurophysiological support for the AIP model by making connections between these networks. Therefore, EMDR therapy might be particularly relevant for abused children.

22.3 Empirical Support

Research on the effectiveness of EMDR for children with PTSD after having experienced abuse is steadily growing. The efficacy of EMDR has been demonstrated in children exposed to sexual abuse (Jaberghaderi et al., 2004), domestic violence (Jaberghaderi et al., 2019), and a mixture of sexual and/or physical violence (Jiménez et al., 2020). All studies found a significant effect on post-traumatic symptoms, including reduced comorbidity, such as behavioural symptoms (Jaberghaderi et al., 2004), anxiety, and depressive symptoms (Jiménez et al., 2020). Diehle and colleagues (2014) evaluated the effectiveness of EMDR in children who had experienced single or multiple and varied types of traumatic events (interpersonal and non-interpersonal). The results were positive, but because statistical analysis was done on the whole group of participants the results of this study cannot be generalized to children exposed to child abuse only. However, the study showed the effectiveness of EMDR in reducing the severity of PTSD symptoms.

22.4 Rationale for Combining EMDR and Family Therapy

The family context is essential when treating abused children and affects how EMDR can be used. Many families in which child abuse occurs are characterized by a dysfunctional family hierarchy, inappropriate boundaries between subsystems, attachment disorders, emotional instability, a poor capacity for mentalization, and a narrow window of tolerance (Morris-Smith & Silvestre, 2014).

Norman and colleagues (2014) show that poverty, mental health problems, low educational achievement, alcohol and drug abuse, being abused as a child, family breakdown, and witnessing domestic violence are all significant risk factors for parents to abuse their children. Following this finding, they suggest that evidence-based *systemic* interventions aimed at improving parenting strategies and family functioning may be more effective and less expensive than attempts to treat only the extensive harmful effects of child abuse in adulthood.

In clinical practice, integrating EMDR and family therapy (EMDR-FT) appears to improve the therapeutic outcome for abused children. This integrative approach has been reported in the literature since 2007 (Shapiro et al., 2007; Field & Cottrell, 2011; Morris-Smith & Silvestre, 2014; Silvestre & Tarquinio, 2022). Combining these is essential for this group, as the individual child's and family's problems can be addressed and their needs can be met optimally.

22.5 Contraindications for EMDR- FT

There are several contraindications to the use of EMDR-FT. It cannot be done if there is insufficient current safety in a family because domestic violence is ongoing. Furthermore, EMDR-FT could be problematic in extremely chaotic families with severe adult mental health disorders. EMDR-FT is also contraindicated if parents are unwilling or unable to cooperate. Finally, EMDR-FT is not possible when children are trapped in unresolvable, 'frozen' family situations, where no changes are possible and where parents do not take responsibility for their past behaviour. In these cases, children may exhibit dissociative behaviours that have a protective function and help them survive in the present. The child must maintain the attachment relationship regardless of the inappropriate content in the relationship. The child has no choice but to dissociate from the inappropriate content generated by this attachment relationship to maintain it (Goldsmith et al., 2004; Kate et al., 2021). In these situations, the therapist should focus first on interventions for the child, developing resources, building on the child's strengths and coping skills, and increasing safety for the child. Next, attention can shift to treatment for the parents. Only in a later phase can interventions be considered that stimulate improvement of the parent–child interaction.

22.6 Points of Consideration for EMDR-FT

22.6.1 History Taking (Diagnostic Assessment)

Usually, with EMDR-FT the whole family is invited to the initial assessment interview. This gives the therapist an idea of the family context and allows them to assess safety, family dynamics, quality of attachment, and available resources. On this basis, the therapist can formulate a treatment plan, thinking multidimensionally at the child and family levels to address not only the family narrative and dynamics but also the child's functioning and symptoms.

- ***Family narrative***

The family narrative is constructed following the initial assessment interview, and all family members contribute. The family members can tell and draw what has happened. The family narrative is the family members' story about what happened. The parents' contribution is not about what they may have objectively experienced in their childhood, but rather about what sense they have made of these experiences currently and how this affects their behaviours as parents in their interactions with their children (Delage, 2008). Children can contribute to the family narrative either verbally or in re-enactment through their play and behaviours during the family's construction of the narrative. Their contribution can help identify potential targets for EMDR therapy; for example, a very young child played joylessly and repetitively with the water in the sink in the room while his siblings and parents talked about what happened when their boat capsized.

The therapist pays attention to discrepancies between the explicit content of the family members' stories and the implicit emotional content observed in their non-verbal interactions. The therapist elicits a more congruent narrative by making the observed discrepancies explicit. A further consideration is whether there is incongruence between the family message and the child's understanding, given their developmental level and emotional needs. Incongruities in the non-verbal communication between family members may indicate that incorrect information is being given or something is being hidden.

- ***Safety: Risk assessment***

Abused children are among the most vulnerable in our society. The safety of the child and family is of the highest priority. A risk assessment of the family is essential to establish whether the violence in the family is ongoing, in which case it must STOP before EMDR-FT can be considered.

If domestic violence has occurred, work with the family only begins after the perpetrator has been removed from the family or has undertaken the necessary work to allow amelioration to become possible. The perpetrator needs to have taken responsibility for their behaviour and to show empathy towards the victim's suffering before any work could be possible with the couple before considering it with the children.

Relevant questions are:

- What degree of safety is guaranteed for the child within the family context?
- What legal action may (still) be necessary?

The therapist must assess how safe the relationships are for the child and what is needed to increase safety. This is done by looking at (among other things) the quality of the boundaries between the different subsystems. The quality of attachment is a crucial element. The therapist must examine the family's daily attachment rituals and routines (mealtimes, playtimes, bathtimes, and bedtimes) to determine whether the parent/caregiver can provide sufficient holding and containment for the child in the real world.

Various difficulties can occur in the family system, particularly with parents who are unable to protect their children from violence and who themselves struggle with attachment problems. Sometimes, parents' behaviour is so inappropriate and inadequate that the child must be removed from the home and transferred to a safer environment (other family members, foster care, or residential setting) before trauma treatment for the child can be considered.

The risk assessment of behaviours of these children must also be explored, as many may be experimenting with (illegal) drugs and alcohol as a form of self-medication. Some have suicidal ideation or undertake suicide attempts; many also self-harm or take other dangerous risks. These may be ways to escape the pain caused by traumatic memories.

With these families, there is an increased chance of missed appointments and continued experiences of events in daily life that need attention and disrupt therapy. The therapist should consider these factors, and an assessment of the treatability of both the child and the family system must be made.

- ***Family dynamics and hierarchy***

The therapist identifies the nature of the family dynamics and family hierarchy. They use questions such as the following:

- What roles do the different members play in the family?
- Who is/are the perpetrator(s), and who is/are the victim(s)?
- Is the parent–child hierarchy adequate or disrupted?
- Are the parents acting as parents?

- ***Individual symptoms and behaviours***

In addition to family-level assessment, the functioning of the individual child is evaluated. Many abused children exhibit dissociative symptoms, such as depersonalization, poor sense of time, and a lack of integration of their sense of self, and they are often reported as lying as they do not remember what they did in dissociative states. Using the adolescent dissociative experiences scale (A-DES) (Putnam, 1997) as a semi-structured interview rather than a screening questionnaire helps identify dissociative symptoms and allows the exploration of qualitative information. Any developmental delays should also be determined. Creating a trauma and developmental timeline can help identify where the trauma may have disrupted the development. For this, see Morris-Smith and Silvestre (2014).

22.6.2 Treatment Planning

Once safety is established and the therapist has formed an idea of family functioning, they can determine who needs standard individual EMDR therapy and what is needed to restore and heal family dynamics using the stabilization techniques, narrative, and daily family attachment rituals described in Morris-Smith and Silvestre (2014).

Figure 22.1 illustrates the potential treatment duration for integrated EMDR-FT treatment. The duration of treatment depends on the degree of traumatization, the severity of attachment problems, and the nature of the family structure. The more impersonal (outside of the family) the trauma, the less impact it will have on family functioning. If a family member perpetrates the violence, more aspects of the family's functioning will be disrupted.

Other relevant factors affecting the duration of the treatment (moderators) include vulnerability due to temperament, age at traumatization onset, chronicity, and nature of traumatization (Morris-Smith & Silvestre, 2014). Information about these moderators is collected during the initial assessment and serves as a guide for the treatment plan.

The therapist can decide whether:

- *Integrated* treatment plans (EMDR-FT) can be applied because the family is intact enough, enabling the therapist to work flexibly with the family, the parents, and the child, interweaving these different elements as therapy progresses.

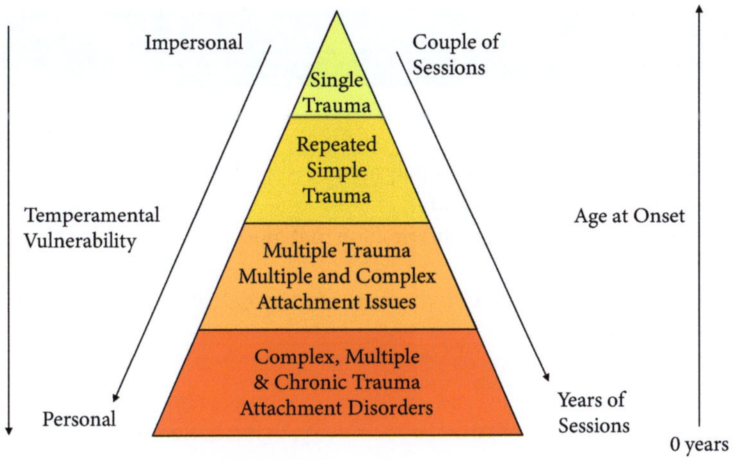

Figure 22.1 Treatment duration using EMDR-FT.

- *Parallel* treatment plans are needed for the parents and the child.
- *Separate* treatment plans are needed for each member of the family before future family interventions can be considered.

With abused children, an ongoing question is whether a parent/caregiver should be present during the child's EMDR sessions. The prerequisite is that the parents can regulate and manage their feelings to contain, adjust, validate, and support the child's reactions in therapy. Sometimes, one or both parents must first undergo trauma treatment to become emotionally stable enough to be able to stay within their window of tolerance at home and during the child's sessions.

Discussed below in Box 22.1 are points of interest that apply to treatment in all cases where child abuse has occurred, both within and outside the family.

The above points apply to all situations. The case examples below illustrate the difference between maltreatment by someone outside the family (Section 22.6.3) or by a family member (Section 22.6.4).

22.6.3 Abuse by Someone Outside of the Family

If an outsider committed the abuse, all family members are victims, to a greater or lesser extent. Relationships within the family may also be disturbed, and the goals for treatment with EMDR-FT are:

- Restoration of the quality of attachment (parents–children).
- Respect for each other's integrity and separate identities.
- Increase the parents' ability to manage and regulate affect in the family.
- Restoration of the family dynamics (boundaries, daily attachment rituals, communication skills…).

BOX 22.1 Points of consideration

1. Family secrets:
   - How much does the therapist ask family members to share?
   - When is it too much or inappropriate?
   - What is the minimum amount of information that must be shared to start a healing process?
   - Is it safe to share, or is it dangerous because of potential retribution or further domestic violence?
2. Creation of a family narrative:
   - Can a family narrative be constructed collectively, or is it better to hear the members separately?
   - Is the content of the shared information appropriate to the child's developmental level?
   - If the parents seem unable to create a narrative that is understandable to the child, it is the therapist's responsibility to protect the child from inappropriate information and see the parents separately first to help them develop a more appropriate narrative.
3. Parental reactions:
   - The more the parents suffer from their post-traumatic stress reactions, the less they will be able to support their child emotionally unless this is addressed first.
   - It may be necessary to involve additional therapists to offer individual therapy to different family members in more complex situations.

Using an EMDR-FT approach, the therapist can administer individual EMDR therapy to process memories of the abuse, both for the abused child and their siblings, together or separately. See Case study Jenny as an example of how this might work.

CASE STUDY 22.1 Jenny: Part 1—EMDR-FT for abuse outside the family

Jenny (aged 4 years) lives with her father (41 years old), mother (36 years old), and two sisters (8 and 11 years old). She was referred by social services after the parents reported to the police sexual abuse of their child over a 4-month period committed by a male friend of the family. Jenny developed secondary enuresis, refused to go to school anymore, had nightmares about wolves, and no longer wanted to sleep alone in her room.

In the first session, the entire family was seen to assess the impact of the trauma and family functioning. This traumatic experience had left them all in a state of shock and paralysis. The therapist determined that the family narrative could be jointly constructed by the family members because there was a healthy family structure and secure attachment patterns. All family members were invited to share what had happened.

They were asked to jointly draw the family's story on three large sheets of paper:

1. What the family was like before the sexual abuse on the first piece of paper.
2. What the bad man did (sexual abuse) on the second.
3. What happened after that to the family on the third drawing.

During the session, the family gradually began to relax and share information. See below the continuation with Jenny and her family.

CASE STUDY 22.1 **Jenny: Part 2**

A second family session followed two weeks later to obtain information about what had changed since the first session. During that session, the therapist also arranged a separate appointment with the parents to assess the impact Jenny's sexual abuse had had on their relationship with each other. In addition, they assessed the parents' ability to regulate their own emotions and adequately handle their children's problem behaviour.

With these first two sessions, the family's natural coping process was initiated through the construction of the family narrative, which improved the communication and support between them. As a result, Jenny's enuresis began to decrease and her anxieties diminished. When parents can establish a congruent family narrative together with the children in a family session there is often an improvement in the child's behaviour. This intervention seemed to initiate improvement in the child's emotion regulation and behaviour.

During the third session, Jenny received EMDR therapy (EMDR standard protocol for children and adolescents adapted to her developmental level) in the presence of the family members. The first target image was 'What the bad man did to me' (she pulled a face and clutched the lower part of her tummy). Jenny sat on her mother's lap, between her father and two sisters, who witnessed the EMDR session. At the end of the session, all family members were asked to share what they understood from it and how they felt about it. Then they practiced together imagining their own safe place, which was installed with the butterfly hug.

In two subsequent sessions, EMDR was applied to her two sisters: one at a time, but in the presence of all family members, because their own memories of their sister's sexual abuse had been activated. They felt guilty and sad because they had not helped Jenny. In addition, they blamed Jenny for them losing a good friend (namely, the perpetrator's daughter). Applying EMDR in the presence of parents and siblings aims to strengthen parents' ability to support their children emotionally to increase family resilience.

In a subsequent family session, Jenny spontaneously asked her parents *'Why did you let me go to that bad man's house?'* Jenny's mother explained how sorry she was for not noticing earlier and that sometimes parents don't know everything. Her father confirmed this.

By the 10th session of EMDR-FT, all of Jenny's symptoms had disappeared, as had the other two children's apparent problems; all the children were doing well. However, the parents turned out to be very sad and requested to be seen together, without the children. The fact that their daughter had been sexually abused had created a distance between them, kept them from having intimate relations, and put pressure on them. They saw separation as the only possible solution. Three additional EMDR-FT sessions with the couple were held. The first two targeted the individual impact of their daughter's abuse on each of them processed in the presence of the other, and the third session was a couple's session that worked on repairing the relationship. This healed both the individual and relational wounds. The total therapy lasted 13 sessions, given bi-weekly.

22.6.4 **Abuse by a Family Member**

If a family member has committed the abuse, the existing family rules and structures suffer a severe blow, and the prospects of the family to continue as a functional unit are limited. Family cohesion and coherence either collapse and become chaos, with individuals stuck in their survival mode, or rigidity occurs, with no movement. Since there is one (or more) perpetrator(s) within the family and there are often multiple family members affected as victims or witnesses of the violence/abuse, the disruption is more severe than with abuse by a perpetrator outside the family.

Therefore, in this situation, we distinguish more treatment aims with EMDR-FT for the remaining family (without the perpetrator):

- Safety for the child and the remaining family.
- Restoration of the quality of attachment.
- Respect for each other's integrity.
- Restoration of a congruent family hierarchy with adequate boundaries for responsibilities, power, and control.
- Trauma treatment for the child and other family members who are victims.
- Building and restoring a positive self-image and self-esteem.
- Catching up on the developmental delays of all children.

The following Case Study 22.2 is an example of chaotic family functioning caused by parental psychopathology, leading to chronic domestic violence, both physical and emotional.

CASE STUDY 22.2 **Pauline: Part 1—EMDR-FT for abuse by a family member**

Her father's domestic violence had begun when Pauline was a toddler. She regularly saw her mother being beaten and her father physically and emotionally abusing her. Her parents separated when she was 11, but the father maintained great power and control over the family afterwards. He still came into the house regularly, disregarding social rules and boundaries, forcibly imposing on the family members what they should do, and occasionally using violence towards the mother and the daughters. The first step was to gain a restraining order to stop this and prevent the father from coming anywhere near the home to ensure safety.

Pauline (age 16) lived with her mother and sister, Elisabeth (age 18), at the time of referral. The family hierarchy was dysfunctional and the boundaries of the ex-couple were unclear; the parents had behaved unpredictably. Pauline had a long history of various problems: speech/language problems, separation anxiety, frequent violent emotional outbursts, self-destructive thoughts and behaviours, concentration problems, fear of failure at school, and several failed school placements. She had been unruly since the age of 10, used drugs, self-harmed regularly, and had run away from home several times. Recently, she had become reclusive; she was afraid to be alone and only felt safe in the presence of her mother or sister. Over the past six years, she had received many other diagnoses, including generalized anxiety disorder, antisocial disorder, and depression. In the past, these had been treated with several different therapies, with minimal improvement.

At the time of referral, Pauline was put on antidepressants and had regular appointments with a psychiatrist. Her mother had to bring her to the sessions and stay near her all of the time. The attachment was anxious-ambivalent and there was an enmeshed relationship with occasional role reversal. When mother was overwhelmed by her own emotions, she behaved like a needy child rather than a parent. Occasionally she would go against Pauline or tell her she was exaggerating. There was no coherent family narrative. Gathering information for the family narrative in the assessment phase led to excessive tension at home afterwards. Individual therapy was indicated for both sisters to process their traumatic experiences of father/partner abuse. Because of the symbiotic relationship Pauline had with her mother, her presence was required during her daughter's EMDR sessions. After five joint sessions, it appeared possible to separate Pauline from her mother before the start of a session. She agreed to allow her mother to simultaneously see the other therapist in an adjoining room with a one-way mirror so that she could see her mother sitting there while she underwent therapy.

The target memories initially chosen and addressed with Pauline were:

- Being brought to school and forcibly separated from her mother when she was 5 years old.
- Being locked in a room at school in a panic along with a teacher when she was 7 years old.
- Sitting at home alone at age 12, believing her mother was dead after she had been beaten unconscious. See the continuation below here.

CASE STUDY 22.2 **Pauline: Part 2**

Memories addressed in later sessions included specific incidents of physical, emotional, and verbal abuse by the father. While processing the physical abuse, Pauline often cringed and re-experienced pain in various parts of her body; she also felt cold and hungry. She then processed memories of incidents related to her mother's depression, such as times when her mother had taken unacceptable risks. For example, she sometimes ran away from her two daughters when in bad shape.

As individual EMDR therapy progressed for Pauline and her mother, their relationship improved, and their bonding became more secure. Pauline began to realize that she could make her own choices and that what had happened to her was not normal. She developed a greater sense of herself as a separate individual with a life of her own.

These two clinical cases, as examples, highlight how EMDR-FT works to heal individual and family wounds. In the first case, all family members were victims of the perpetrator's abuse of Jenny. The integrated approach could restore the healthy family dynamics. In the second example, the family's integrity was shattered; however, it was still possible to heal the remaining family victims using EMDR-FT.

22.7 Points of Consideration for the EMDR Therapy

This section highlights some clinical points of consideration during the application of the standard protocol for children and adolescents with abused children after phase 1.

- ***Preparation (phase 2)***

  – **Sense of safety and security**

Attention must be paid to the *window of treatment opportunity.* This is determined by the degree to which the family and child are ready to start treatment. Additional measures may be needed to increase the sense of safety (in the real world) and security (within the relationships in the family) before family members can confront the negative memories. The therapist needs to attune to the child, help them to develop trust in the therapeutic relationship, and realize that they are safe in the here and now. The child needs to know that they are not alone in the process, and the therapist will make the journey with them through the traumatic memories. The child also needs to learn that what has happened to them has happened to other children as well, so they can realize that they are not alone in having experienced this.

  – **Empowering activities**

Many abused children lack adequate internal resources and have a negative self-image and a severe lack of self-esteem. Many of them have an external 'locus of control' and feel powerless, voiceless, and worthless. For this reason, finding empowering activities that the child can perform independently, if desired, is crucial to offer some sense of achievement, control, and hope. Examples include horseback riding, judo, athletics, fishing, cooking, and individual drama lessons. These activities can give them positive feelings about themselves and their bodies by giving them a sense of control over a situation and respect from others.

- **Medication**

Many abused children have comorbid conditions besides PTSD, particularly severe depression and/or severe anxiety disorders. For these, a psychiatrist can prescribe medication. The medication should preferably start during the preparation phase (or earlier) so that the child is well-adjusted before the processing begins and can proceed optimally.

- **Increasing emotion regulation and impulse control**

If dissociation is presented as a symptom of PTSD, the start of the desensitization phase can be destabilizing and lead to a temporary increase of symptoms as previously unintegrated memories become accessible. In clinical practice, it is observed that some children self-harm within a couple of days of starting desensitization. Therefore, in the preparation phase, discussing with the child how to cope with overwhelming images or emotions and how to use resources is essential. At this stage, the therapist should also make it clear to the child that the trauma treatment can, at times, be a painful and challenging journey, but that the therapist will be there to guide and help them and build resources to help. A good explanation and normalization of dissociative symptoms is also essential: Dissociation is a protective mechanism from the past, which enabled them to survive and take care of themselves when they were overwhelmed by what happened.

- ***Assessment (phase 3)***

- **Target selection**

In clinical practice, if there is dissociation, it may be an option to start with memories of recent events and then work backwards in time so that the dissociated material can be gradually activated and integrated; this can be a gentler approach. Although no specific research has been conducted yet, we recommend this approach.

In addition, the therapist should keep in mind, during target selection, that mundane things may trigger memories of traumatizing events and need targeting.

In a few cases, the child may completely shut down and become mute when thinking about what happened. If establishing a target image proves impossible because the child can neither get a picture in their mind nor draw it, the therapist may ask the child to think of what happened without giving a detailed description and to notice what they are feeling and where they are feeling it. Usually, during processing, they become more communicative. In most cases, asking all relevant questions during the assessment phase is possible. Negative cognitions that come up frequently are 'I am bad', 'I am worthless', 'It is my fault', 'I am helpless', and 'I do not deserve to live'.

- ***Desensitization (phase 4)***

Therapists need to be mindful that, generally, during desensitization of one traumatic event or aspects of it, the next one will arise. However, given the young age at which a lot of abuse occurs, sometimes associations need to be prompted by asking when the SUDS reach zero: *'Can you remember another time when you thought this … or felt this … or had that same sensation …?'* This promotes 'associative chaining' (Tinker & Wilson, 1999, p. 202).

Given the young age at which much abuse occurs, the therapist can check if the desensitization process is ongoing by paying attention to non-verbal cues, including changes in body language, and by simply asking the child if things come up or change. A precise description of what happens during the sets is not required as long as the processing continues. The information processing leads to a reduction of abuse-related feelings and sensations. Over time, as emotions and sensations of the traumatic memory are integrated, the children may spontaneously begin to articulate negative cognitions. They start to connect words for their experiences as the information process becomes more cognitively linked. The therapist must allow the material to flow naturally.

- **Interweaves**

If the processing is blocked, the therapist should initially provide more distraction to counterbalance a potentially overwhelming flood of emotions or sensations or dissociative block. In case of looping, other interweaves may also be needed. Educational interweaves (psychoeducation) can help make the incomprehensible understandable: for example, *'Do you know that adults are not allowed to hurt children?'*; *'How small were you when you were 3 years old?'*

Abused children often have sensory triggers that activate the traumatic memories of the abuse and that can come up as associations—for example, sensations of hunger and thirst or pain sensations and unpleasant smells. The therapist should anticipate these potential associations and possible countermeasures to prevent the processing from stalling. A glass of water or juice, a snack, aromatic oils or scented sticks, and a soft toy or blanket, for example, can help the child by allowing them to experience an alternative and corrective pleasant sensation.

- **Unfinished physical actions**

During desensitization, the child may also experience a desire to make movements that could not be fully executed during the traumatic experience. For example, the legs may shake violently because they had wanted to run away but could not. The therapist may then ask the child to notice this sensation and what comes up, then start some EM^+, asking the child to indicate when something changes. The child must know that the change can be a thought, a feeling, or a sensation. The EM^+ continues as usual until the child indicates something has changed or until the therapist notices a non-verbal change.

- **EM^+**

Traumatic memories of abuse may be stored as sensory or sensorimotor memories because of the young age at which the abuse mainly occurred. A tactile distracting task, such as tapping or hitting a large, soft, thick cushion, can help when working with these. Hitting as hard as they want can help them experience that they are now more in control and that feelings such as anger, sadness, or shame can be felt and expressed because it is now safe to do so. As the child's processing matures up to its current developmental level during the desensitization, the therapist may switch to eye movements to accommodate the more advanced processing.

- ***Installation and body scan (phases 5 and 6)***

These phases differ little in implementation from what we experience when using the EMDR standard protocol with non-abused children and adolescents. There are no specific areas of concern.

- ***Closure (phase 7)***

Regularly, sessions will end incomplete (SUD > 0) given the long-term nature of the work needed with severe PTSD and comorbidities. Therefore, the therapist must take enough time at the end of each session to allow the child to calm down so that they can transition to daily life with sufficient resilience. For closure, the therapist should set aside at least 10 minutes. It is essential that the child feels contained, grounded, and in control before leaving the treatment room, and that they are accompanied by a trusted person when leaving the building.

- ***Re-evaluation (phase 8)***

At the beginning of each session, the therapist asks the child and the parents about observed changes.

When EMDR therapy is completed with abused children, it is vital to check whether developmental delays that may have occurred because of the trauma have been resolved. The therapist is proactive in recognizing any delays that persist and promotes development by recommending any necessary interventions for the next developmental step. Clinical experience shows that after EMDR therapy is concluded, developmental catch-up often spontaneously occurs, and physical growth may even occur.

22.8 Concluding Remarks

For the treatment of abused children with PTSD plus comorbid symptoms, we recommend integrating individual EMDR therapy with a family therapy approach (EMDR-FT). This requires the therapist to have knowledge and expertise in several areas: namely, individual trauma treatment, family dynamics, recognition and treatment of disturbed attachment patterns, and skills to deal with dissociative symptoms and behaviours. Therapists must be careful not to get outside their window of tolerance because of the information they face when working with abused children and adults. In this regard, supervision, peer review (intervision), team meetings, or in-service training can be helpful. As a rule of thumb, the more complex the psychopathology, the more contextual the approach must be to promote healthy development from within this context. By involving the family system in the trauma treatment and making the implicit explicit, the therapist helps the dysfunctional family to develop a healthier family narrative. This integrated approach creates favourable conditions for processing the traumatic memories and enables the child to take new steps towards a healthier future.

23 EMDR in Refugee Families

Custom Work

TRUDY MOOREN*

23.1 Introduction

This chapter deals with the implementation of EMDR therapy combined with family-focused interventions in refugee families. Refugee children are—more than other children—dependent on their parents, and in addition to their own trauma and stressor-related symptoms, they also suffer greatly from those of their parents (De Haene & Rousseau, 2020). This chapter describes the characteristics of refugee families and the empirical evidence for EMDR therapy and family interventions in this population. The indication of EMDR therapy for the child, separately or combined with family-focused interventions, is discussed with associated concerns, illustrated by the experiences of Fatma and her family (see Case Study 23.1 part 1).

CASE STUDY 23.1 Fatma: Part 1—An Introduction to Fatma and her family (Syrian refugees)

Fatma is a 12-year-old girl from Syria. She fled to the Netherlands with her parents, grandmother, and her brothers (aged 2 and 8). Over two years ago, while still in Syria, a series of problematic contacts with police culminated in a raid on their home and the rape of Fatma's mother, who was heavily pregnant at the time. Fatma and her little brother witnessed this, as did Fatma's father and grandmother. Fatma's grandfather was killed in a bombing raid when Fatma was 10 years old.

Fatma is a kind and helpful girl who is very committed to her family. She takes care of her little brothers, and runs the family life together with her grandmother. She is ambitious, a diligent student, and performs well in school.

The family received a Dutch residence permit after a 1.5 year stay in a centre for asylum seekers. They moved to their 'own' home and have a stable future perspective for the first time. At this point, Fatma revealed that she suffers greatly from memories of the violent

* This chapter is a revision of an earlier version, written with Jelly van Essen. Thanks to Annemariek Sepers, who provided comments on this version.

Trudy Mooren, *EMDR in Refugee Families*. In: *Handbook of EMDR for Children and Adolescents*. Edited by: Renée Beer and Carlijn de Roos, Oxford University Press. © 2026, Oxford University Press. For the English edition.
DOI: 10.1093/oso/9780198918400.003.0023

events she witnessed during the raid on their home in Syria. She has nightmares about it, is fearful of falling asleep, is often irritable and afraid of men in the street, especially those in uniform. She prefers to stay at home. She has no contact with friends outside of school and she does not belong to any clubs.

23.2 Characteristics of Refugee Families

Fatma's story illustrates several of the characteristics of refugee families, which will be described in this section: consequences of traumatization, traumatization of multiple family members, burdened parenthood, and current stress.

23.2.1 Consequences of Traumatization

Since World War II, not as many children worldwide have been forced to leave their homes to seek safety outside their countries' borders as in recent years (UNHCR, 2025). A significant proportion of these children are at risk of endangered psychosocial development resulting from their traumatic experiences (Kien et al., 2019). They suffer not only from exposure to traumatic events but also from long-term stressful living conditions (Fazel et al., 2012; Reed et al., 2012; Scharpf et al., 2021). In the period before (forced) migration, stressful events related to war occur, such as bombings, confrontations with dead and wounded bodies, loss of their homes and familiar surroundings, homelessness, hunger, or extreme poverty. The escape and the period immediately afterwards cause a lot of distress. This is followed by further distress as the family typically endures years of asylum processing and constant moves between different asylum centres (see also Lustig et al., 2004).

These cumulative changes are stressful for family members, who must constantly readjust to unstable circumstances in a new country (Van Essen & Bala, 2007). However, these pressures can lead to greater family cohesion and a strengthened problem-solving ability. Parents often go out of their way to find safe havens for their children (Henley & Robinson, 2011). Although the literature on refugee families' adaptation to stressful circumstances is still sparse, available publications highlight the importance of harnessing the strength present within the family to support recovery. Restoring resilience is thus an essential element in providing support to refugee families (Weine et al., 2014).

Regardless of the potential available social support and adequate coping strategies, psychological problems are more prevalent among refugee children and adolescents than among their native peers (Kien et al., 2019). In a review of 47 studies among refugee children, Kien and colleagues (2019) found evidence of post-traumatic stress disorder (PTSD) in between 19% and 52.7% of those studied. This prevalence is higher than in non-refugee children (Alisic et al., 2014), and, in terms of number and nature, PTSD symptoms are more severe and varied in refugee children (Fazel et al., 2012). In addition to PTSD, comorbid psychological and physical symptoms are seen, such as depression, anxiety, grief reactions, externalizing behaviour, hyperactivity, bed-wetting and/or trouser-wetting, and impaired school performance (Henley & Robinson, 2011; Kien et al., 2019; Pacione et al., 2013; Rousseau & Drapeau, 2003).

23.2.2 Traumatization of Multiple Family Members

In the refugee population, it is common that several family members are traumatized independently or by being joint victims of the same situation of violence, or that they were forced to watch powerlessly as relatives were assaulted, as was the case with Fatma. Witnessing violence is often at least as traumatizing as experiencing it in person and can result in PTSD (American Psychiatric Association, 2013; Howard, 2021; Mollica et al., 1992). Family members whose circumstances are equivalent during the traumatizing events form distinct memories, which may persist and result in symptoms. In the case of Fatma's father, his inability to protect his family members was the most distressing aspect of his memory. For Fatma, hearing her grandmother cry and plead was the most distressing aspect because she had never experienced her grandmother so powerless before. For Fatma's mother, the most horrifying aspect that still haunted her was that her pregnancy left her extremely vulnerable, combined with her fear at the time that her unborn child had been endangered. It was unclear if and what memories Fatma's 8-year-old brother had of the events. He had never been asked, and both parents hoped he had forgotten much of what happened. For Fatma's grandmother, the anxious expectation (in retrospect) that they could have all been killed—as had happened to her husband before—was most distressing and terrifying. Although all family members experienced the same event(s), for each of them individually, different memories, or a different aspect of the same memory, may still distress them today.

Processing of memories is quite often hampered in refugee families by taboos around talking about memories of events because of shame or fear. Parents experience their children's questions about such events as painful, and the children's questions may evoke reactions in the parent that can be frightening for the children. Parents who are themselves too anxious to talk about the traumatic experiences can hardly help their children talk about it. This is how family secrets arise: Children know that something terrible happened but do not dare to ask questions about it. This mechanism ('conspiracy of silence') also played a role in many families immediately after World War II (Danieli, 1998). What is not told can be as meaningful as what is told. The gaps are filled in with fantasies that are sometimes worse than the reality. For example, a girl left behind in her country of origin misses her sister. Her mother knows that the sister was murdered but does not want to tell the girl to spare her enormous grief. Because the girl does not know exactly where her sister is, she fears she could also disappear. Parents sometimes assume their child has forgotten the unpleasant event(s) they witnessed because they never speak about it, as with Fatma's little brother. Generally, it is good for their children's well-being if parents can talk about traumatic experiences in a sensitive, age-appropriate way (Sloover et al., 2024).

23.2.3 Burdened Parenthood

A secure attachment relationship is indispensable for children to develop confidence, independence, and self-esteem. Parents who have been traumatized and suffer from ongoing distress may have difficulty raising their children due to the symptoms of their distress. For example, a common symptom in traumatized parents is a reduced sensitivity to what children need. This increases the risk that the parent–child relationship will become problematic (Mooren et al., 2023; Van Ee et al., 2012). Several terms have been coined to describe the symptoms that children develop in response to their parents' trauma symptoms: secondary traumatization, indirect traumatization, and inter- or transgenerational traumatization.

Many studies have now demonstrated the critical role that refugee parents play in the psychological health of their children (Scharpf et al., 2021). PTSD in the parent has been found to be associated with mental health problems (internalizing and externalizing symptoms) in children (Scharpf et al., 2021).

In addition to reduced sensitivity, there is often increased irritability (hyperarousal) and re-experiencing in parents. We regularly see signs of emotional neglect and psychological and/or physical abuse of children in refugee families, which seem to result from the parents' post-traumatic stress reactions (e.g., a hot temper). The traumatic event (war) is reflected in the family. Environmental factors such as unemployment, poverty, and lack of resources increase parental stress and reduce the likelihood of a safe family environment for the children involved (Bryant et al., 2018; Scheeringa & Zeanah, 2001; Sim et al., 2018).

23.2.4 Current Stress

Staying in an asylum seekers' centre, many moves between different centres, uncertainty about the future due to lengthy asylum procedures, and contact with lawyers and national and international judicial institutions are all distressing. Even once a residence permit has been obtained, numerous administrative procedures persist before peace of mind can come. Refugees must be constantly alert to ensure they follow all necessary procedures and complete all the supporting paperwork. Frequently, children help their parents fulfil these requirements as they often speak the host country's language better. They may read the mail before their parents do, and in this way a child may perhaps learn that their mother was raped or discover other shocking events were experienced by their parents. Persistent insecurity in the country of residence or negative news from the country of origin keeps reactivating memories of traumatic experiences.

Families can find themselves caught in a vicious circle: The parents' symptoms, such as irritability and re-experiencing, result in being less available to the child, and the parent(s) feel guilty about this. The parenting problems and current stress further exhaust the parents and hamper them from processing their own traumatic memories. Building a new life and lacking social support can cause a lot of stress in the family. This perpetuates the symptoms, and thus the parent–child relationship deteriorates further (Scharpf et al., 2021; Timshel et al., 2017; Van Essen & Bala, 2007).

When current stress is predominant, such as during a protracted asylum procedure or imminent deportation, recognition of these current distressing circumstances is essential, as is the promotion of stress regulation and coping. Current stress leads to hyper-alertness; as a result, the brain does not fully calm down, which can lead to stagnation in the processing of traumatic experiences. Parents may attribute all problems to current events and lose sight of other causes. Understanding the current issues, practical support, and psychoeducation can help parents understand that memories of previous traumatic experiences partly cause their reactions. This understanding motivates them to engage in EMDR treatment so that post-traumatic stress symptoms can be reduced. This creates more space to handle the other problems better, and improves emotional availability between family members.

23.3 Empirical Evidence

Studies on the effectiveness of both individual and family-focused interventions for refugees are scarce at present, although they are increasing (Pacione et al., 2013; Velu et al., 2022). This applies especially to research on children and adolescents within this group.

Randomized research in refugee populations is complex for several reasons. Culturally diverse backgrounds primarily need standardized instruments; cultural and linguistic differences mean that answers to these tests often need to be revised. High mobility due to frequent transfers (between residential centres) also hinders participation in research. Distrust towards research(ers) and research resources may play a role. Having to fill in questionnaires about traumatic experiences or having to answer questions about migration may remind refugees of interrogations that they experienced during detentions or asylum applications.

23.3.1 Individual-Oriented Interventions

The following interventions have been investigated for effectiveness for individual refugees with post-traumatic stress symptoms: trauma-focused cognitive behavioural therapy (TF-CBT), EMDR therapy, narrative exposure therapy (NET), interpersonal therapy (IPT), and problem management plus (PM+) (De Graaff et al., 2023; Morina et al., 2016; Murray et al., 2010; Nocon et al., 2017; Pacione et al., 2013; Velu et al., 2022). Some of these interventions, such as PM+ and EMDR, are also offered in group form.

Furthermore, there are interventions that focus on strengthening abilities for coping with stress through programmes in schools, or through creative expression (Sullivan & Simonson, 2016). Finally, there are interventions that focus on improving family interactions (Van Es et al., 2021).

Overall, studies using more robust methodologies are needed to reach sound conclusions. For example, positive findings have been reported for TF-CBT (Ehntholt et al., 2005) and for EMDR (Oras et al., 2004; Wadaa et al., 2010). However, these were non-randomized trials with modest effect sizes (Nocon et al., 2017).

Lempertz and colleagues (2020) examined the effect of EMDR as an intervention, with a pre-post design, in 10 pre-schoolers and found that the children became less anxious after intervention and at follow-up. Molero and colleagues (2019) used EMDR as a group treatment with a large group of refugee adolescents in Spain (n = 184), and found significant reduction of symptoms of PTSD, anxiety, and depression after treatment and at follow-up. Finally, Kaptan and colleagues (2022) offered EMDR embedded in an online group programme for refugee parents in the UK. They examined feasibility in a small sample (n = 14) and concluded that parents who suffered from traumatic stress symptoms showed symptom reduction and were satisfied with the programme.

Another trauma-focused individual-oriented intervention which was designed specifically for refugees is NET (KIDNET for children; Neuner et al., 2008). Two RCTs and a pre-post study of effectiveness in high-income countries have been conducted. A significant reduction in PTSD symptoms was found for KIDNET compared with TAU (Peltonen &

Kangaslampi, 2019) or waiting list (Ruf et al., 2010). Said and King (2020) found decreases in PTSD symptoms after KIDNET treatment in a pre-post comparison in a small number of unaccompanied refugees (n = 3). Van Es and colleagues (2023) reported a decrease in trauma-related symptoms in unaccompanied refugee minors who were offered an 8-session KIDNET-EMDR treatment, whereas no improvement in depressive symptoms was found.

23.3.2 Family-Oriented Interventions

Many family-oriented interventions have been conducted in refugee families; some have been reviewed, evaluating their effectiveness in refugee populations. Three types of interventions were described: parent groups, family groups, and home visits. Although it is generally thought that these are all potentially effective interventions that promote the psychological health of family members and family processes, as yet too little systematic research has been conducted on them to conclude effectiveness (Bunn et al., 2022).

23.4 Rational for EMDR +/– Family-Oriented Interventions

Individual treatment may be sufficient for therapy in children from refugee families if there are no psychological problems in other family members and the parents can sufficiently support the child in their treatment. In such cases, the parents are still involved in their child's treatment, as is usual in trauma treatment. However, many refugee children come from families where several family members have trauma-related psychological problems or where secondary issues have arisen in the parent–child relationship or family functioning. In these situations, individual-oriented treatment would be insufficient. Instead, a combination of individual- and family-oriented treatment is indicated (Bardin et al., 2007; Mooren et al., 2023). In the case of combined treatment, it is crucial to determine which interventions are needed, the relationship between individual and family-oriented interventions, and the order in which they should be offered. Thorough diagnostic research is required in such cases.

23.5 Points to Consider at Indications

Preferably, referral of refugee children and families starts with an intake with the whole family, where individual trauma-related and other problems of both parents and children are identified. A family survey also takes place to explore family problems, the parent–child and partner relationship, possible family secrets, and current living conditions. It is important to identify and record the family's strengths for the treatment as well as exploring the problematic consequences for individuals and families. The intake and the family survey can be supplemented with questionnaires and/or standardized observations regarding symptoms, problems, and quality of relationships of parents with children, between partners, and between the entire family. Several instruments are available for this purpose (Stratton & Low, 2020).

Table 23.1 Questions for intake and indication

What have family members experienced (individually and collectively)?
Which family members show post-traumatic stress reactions and/or other symptoms?
How do these symptoms affect the current functioning of parents and family?
What are the strengths and sources of strength within the family?
What changes are desired/what is the request for help?
What interventions are indicated, for whom, and which are feasible for parents and children?
What are the barriers to trauma processing (e.g., family secrets, domestic violence, current stress)?
Are sufficient conditions present conducive for trauma processing (e.g., safety; can parents provide sufficient support)?

The questions in Table 23.1 can be helpful in deciding which family members could benefit from trauma treatment and whether family interventions are also needed.

Based on the intakes of parent and child, the family survey, and the answers to the questions in Table 23.1, the therapist draws up a treatment plan with a combination of interventions. Child trauma treatment can be provided before, after, or simultaneously with individual treatment of the parent(s) or family treatment. The combination of trauma treatments is tailor-made; there is no fixed sequence of interventions. Two treatment options will be clarified and illustrated: individual treatment only and individual treatment combined with family treatment.

23.5.1 Individual Trauma Treatment of Parent or Child Only

If there are severe post-traumatic stress symptoms, individual trauma treatment for each family member individually is indicated, aimed at processing the traumatic memories. EMDR therapy is ideally suited for this. After all, it has proven effective for PTSD, and it requires relatively little verbalization of experiences and is thus less dependent on language skills than other trauma treatments for children (e.g., KIDNET). In clinical practice, the EMDR standard protocol usually turns out to be quite feasible with this population. Sometimes, however, the questions asked during the assessment phase are too complicated. It is recommended that this phase be completed smoothly. Therefore, sometimes it may be wise to skip the assessment of cognitions related to memory and focus directly on other aspects of memory representation (target).

When only the child is traumatized, and the parents are not (or not to the extent that effective parenting is hindered), then treatment of the child alone is often sufficient. Parents get advice on how to deal with their child's traumatic stress symptoms and how to support them. Here, one might consider involving a parent as a witness in EMDR therapy (Aelen, 2008). The aim is for the child to feel heard and seen, as they may have felt great loneliness since the traumatic experience(s) (see Case Study 23.2).

CASE STUDY 23.2 **Mohamed: EMDR therapy for managing fearful memories**

Mohamed (9 years old) receives EMDR therapy for the nightmares and fears he has been having following the explosions that destroyed his family home and killed his neighbour's little boy. His parents suffer from this themselves, but try to shelter Mohamed from their own problems and worries. They would like Mohamed to be a carefree child and are cooperating with EMDR therapy for him. He finds it very difficult to talk about his emotionally charged memories. He asks his mother to join in the EMDR sessions to help him to talk about his memories. Together, they recount what happened. His mother no longer needs to be there when his memory is focused. Before the target image is established, Mohamed's mother returns to the waiting room. After eight sessions, Mohamed's fears have subsided considerably, and he sleeps well again.

23.5.2 **Individual Treatment Combined with Family Treatment**

When several family members (parents and children) are traumatized, it may be necessary to provide family treatment in addition to individual therapy for each traumatized family member. Psychoeducation on the impact of a family member's symptoms on the other family members and parenthood should be provided. This should involve a joint discussion on the history and the traumatizing events experienced, and what consequences and meaning these have had on their (family) life. Attention is also paid to current problems and their impact on the family. Sometimes, family discussions are not possible—for instance, because family members have such severe psychological symptoms that active and constructive participation is not feasible. In such cases, psychoeducation on the impact of the symptoms on parenthood and family functioning can also be offered within a parent's individual therapy (i.e., system therapy with an individual).

Psychoeducation is mostly about primary and secondary traumatization:

Parents and children may have symptoms because of unpleasant events or experiences they have been through. Children can also suffer when parents pay less attention to their children because they have problems of their own. In treatment, we want to help both children and parents deal with their problems and help the parent become a good father or mother again.

Family treatment goals may include sharing experiences, promoting mutual support, improving interpersonal relationships and parenting, and reducing (traumatic) stress-related symptoms in family members. Family treatment also aims to remove barriers to individual EMDR therapy, such as the existence of family secrets or lack of parental support. Moreover, individual EMDR for parents or children may result in improved communication in the family because talking about traumatic experiences became possible or less distressing (see Case Study 23.1 Part 2).

CASE STUDY 23.1 **Fatma: Part 2—Fatma and her family begin EMDR therapy**

Fatma and her parents receive combined therapy composed of individual EMDR therapy for Fatma and her mother and family therapy. The family starts with three sessions of psychoeducation covering the primary and secondary effects of the traumatic experiences. The therapist explains that Fatma suffers from memories of the attack and seems to take over parental duties out of concern for her mother. This has not allowed Fatma to pay sufficient attention to her own emotions.

Fatma is treated with EMDR targeted at her memory of the attack. The target image that evokes the most distress is the image in which she sees her mother being raped. The desensitization process is difficult. The SUD does not subside, and she indicates at 'back to target' that she feels a lot of grief for her mother and worries about her so much that she cannot concentrate on this process. She asks if her mother can be helped. The therapist decides to take a break from Fatma's therapy and treat Fatma's mother with EMDR so that she can function better in her current daily life. After five sessions, the mother is freed from her stressful memories to the extent that she is more available to the children again. She gives explicit permission to her daughter to process her own memories in the EMDR sessions. It becomes apparent that the most destressing part of Fatma's memories was that there was nothing she could do to help her mother. This makes her unable to tolerate the image. After discussing this with Fatma and her mother, EMDR with Fatma is restarted and is successfully completed after four sessions.

23.6 **Points to Consider for Optimization of EMDR**

Sometimes, the refugee's background, descent from another culture, and current developments within and outside of the family require extra attention. This section discusses some specific issues to consider.

If there is domestic violence or imminent eviction, more time may be needed before EMDR therapy can start, or interventions by social work organizations may get priority to guarantee safety in the household or arrange for reimbursement of travel costs.

EMDR requires a thorough explanation and justification, for the children and for their parents. Sufficient time must be allocated for this, and an interpreter should be arranged as needed.

The EMDR standard protocol is adequate for treating refugees, although the therapist should limit the use of abstract language. It is also essential to keep up the pace, especially during the assessment phase when establishing negative and positive cognition.

Refugee families are more thrown upon themselves than families who have not migrated due to the absence of their extended families and their limited social support networks. Migration experiences and the desire to adapt often entail strong loyalties among the family members. In addition, children usually master the host-country language faster than their parents. This can change their position in the family and increase parents' dependence on their children. These acculturation processes, combined with different views on illness and treatment of children and their feelings of loyalty, can make it difficult for refugee children to speak up for themselves and draw attention to their problems. Parents often only raise the alarm very late, and then, moreover, it takes longer in many cases to motivate parents to consent to treatment for their child.

- **Cooperation and parental consent**

Parents may be reluctant to have their children treated because of their own traumatic experiences. Family secrets, wanting to forget, wanting to avoid a confrontation with their own problems, or the assumption that children will grow out of it by themselves can all play important roles in this.

It is sometimes difficult for parents to tolerate a child talking to someone outside the family about their own experiences or problems in the family. This can trigger memories in parents and exacerbate their own PTSD symptoms, leaving the parent unable to offer the child sufficient support during EMDR therapy. It also reinforces the feeling of failing as a parent, and they may feel guilty about their child's symptoms. Furthermore, it is difficult for parents when the child asks questions about family secrets that the parent is not prepared to discuss. Comorbid psychological problems, especially depressive symptoms, can also make parental support during EMDR difficult.

If a parent refuses to give consent for their child to undergo EMDR therapy, the therapist should provide additional information about the relevance of trauma treatment in children and provide psychoeducation. If a parent is ultimately unwilling or unable to cooperate in the child's treatment, the parent's trauma treatment takes priority so as to make EMDR possible for the child.

- **Dealing with family secrets**

Many refugee families have secrets due to their experiences of war and violence. For example, a female family member may be a victim of sexual violence, but they are not allowed to talk about it. No one says a word about it, and thus not all family members know that this happened. In treatment, it is essential to pay explicit attention to this. This does not always mean sharing their secrets. Discussing the consequences of secrets is often more critical, especially with children. In a family conversation, a comment could be:

> Things have happened in your family that are difficult for all of you, that's why Dad is sometimes angry, or Mum [or sibling's name] is sometimes sad. They will get help, so they no longer have to be angry or sad. Then you won't have to worry about them anymore either.

The existence of family secrets or the impact of family secrets on the family is discussed, if possible, before the start of EMDR to prevent the child from having conflicts of loyalty towards the parents.

- **Using an interpreter**

Due to language problems, it can be difficult to involve a refugee parent in the EMDR treatment of their child. Sometimes no one in the family speaks the language of the therapist.

Using an interpreter then becomes essential, and can also be a relief. The disadvantages of working with an interpreter are the indirect communication (resulting in a different quality of contact), the delay (not being able to respond immediately to what a child or parent says), as well as the risk of misunderstandings due to incorrect translation. Therefore, it is recommended always to give prior explanation and instructions about the nature and purpose of the EMDR treatment. In addition, it is good to work with the same interpreter for all sessions. Some interpreters are already well-informed and familiar with EMDR. They can then translate almost simultaneously, which promotes good pacing and retention of concentration and attention to the memories.

23.7 Points to Consider for EMDR Combined with Family Interventions

- **Restoration of safety**

When, there is domestic violence or neglect resulting from post-traumatic stress symptoms of a parent, measures are needed to ensure the safety of children. In addition to informing local child protection agencies and discussing any concerns with parents, it may be useful to involve people in the family's environment (their social network).

- **Creating a shared narrative**

Because of the different experiences of family members, an essential part of family treatment is the creation of a shared family narrative—verbally, but also through visual material (Schouten et al., 2015). Such a narrative aims to bring back continuity and connection within the family history, which has maybe been fractured by traumatic experiences, forced separations, flight, and other current problems. It is possible to discuss with parents what they will tell their children and how. For example, a father who has seen his son beheaded can get help on how to speak about this to other family members without (re)traumatizing them. Sometimes, experiences may have too significant an impact when they are expressed. For example, a Muslim woman may risk being disowned if she reveals to her husband that she was raped. For this woman, it is essential that she is aware that not all needs to be disclosed.

Creating the family narrative can be started during family discussions before the EMDR. It is usually only after the trauma treatments (of the child and parents) are completed that the family members, using a shared narrative, can try to repair the fractures in their history and focus on the future once again.

- **Restoration of resilience and positive experiences**

Highlighting positive experiences for the individual, but also for the family, is essential. Trauma treatment will be complex without each other's support, care, and joint positive experiences (see also De Haene & Rousseau, 2020). A ritual around a shared positive experience can support the process of individual trauma treatment. When all family members have severe symptoms and no one talks to each other anymore because it quickly turns into arguments, the therapist can encourage having a meal together in the evening and asking about each other's positive experiences of that day. This brings some lightness back into the family. During treatment, when parents are desperate because they are convinced that the experience(s) of war have damaged their children forever, the therapist can refer to these daily positive moments. This gives parents renewed faith in their ability to become good parents. Shared positive experiences and restoring resilience are essential before, during, and after the EMDR treatment.

- **Optimal attunement**

EMDR therapy and family intervention can be carried out by different practitioners, who should ensure good mutual alignment. The aim of treatment is always to reduce the problems of family members and to promote interactions within the family so that they can (again) support each other better and have more fun together. At the same time, it can be quite a task for a family with young children, for example, to come to appointments on location. Alignment on the frequency, number, and duration of individual trauma-focused sessions and family-focused meetings is essential.

23.8 Concluding Remarks

This chapter has described the embedding of EMDR therapy in the systemic treatment of refugee families, many of whom have gone through a series of traumatic experiences and developed symptoms. Trauma treatment using EMDR helps refugee children and their parents to be less troubled by their memories, resulting in symptom reduction. The standard protocol requires no adjustments. However, the preparation for the procedure requires more time than usual, mostly in terms of motivating parents and children and increasing the involvement of the parent(s) in the procedure. Furthermore, in clinical practice a combination of individual treatment and family treatment appears to be effective for traumatized families. Treatment aimed at processing the traumatic memories is necessary not only to reduce psychological symptoms in parent(s) and child, but also as a prelude to positive meaning-making. A better understanding of all the positive changes that occurred within a short period helps children and their families to make a new start. This chapter has described how EMDR can play a role for this group of vulnerable children and families. Many families are finding their way in societies that are new to them. The children and parents we see in clinical practice usually make a deep impression on us because of their resilience. The challenge is, therefore, to make the EMDR therapy as effective as possible to match this resilience, which has already brought the family so far.

24 EMDR in an Inpatient Setting

KINGS (Kid IN Good System)

CAROLINE PLOEG, HENRIËT SCHOLTS, LYSBERT ZEINSTRA, AND FEMY WANDERS

24.1 Introduction

Accare is an institution[1] for child and adolescent (C&A) psychiatry with outpatient, day-clinic, and inpatient facilities. Within the inpatient facility, a phased treatment model has been developed for children with severe behavioural problems and their parents, consisting of a combination of several evidence-based interventions. The development of this treatment model was initiated in 2008 because of a gap in the provision of services for this target group. Children with severe behavioural problems were often placed in a children's group in an inpatient setting for long periods, during which they had little or no contact with their parents. Parents were exhausted and withdrawn, making it difficult to involve them constructively in their child's treatment at the clinic. Treatment teams were also exhausted, and key figures around the families acted out of powerlessness. What should have been *treatment* in the clinic often became an extended *stay* in the clinic. With 'survival behaviour' we refer to persistent, maladaptive coping strategies such as aggression, avoidance, and distrust that the children developed to protect themselves in unsafe environments. They displayed this behaviour while living together in a group with other children who also had severe behavioural problems, which tended to reinforce rather than reduce such behaviour. Child protection services were frequently involved, and many of the children had either already been placed under a court order (family supervision order) or this was imposed during their time in the clinic.

In most cases, the children could not return home after their long-term stay, so they often ended up in a foster family or another institution. The KINGS treatment model (an acronym for Kid IN Good System) emerged from this 'state' of C&A psychiatry. KINGS aims to reduce post-traumatic stress disorder (PTSD) symptoms in children and parents, increase pedagogical skills in parents, and improve parent–child relationships (Ploeg & Wanders-Mulder, 2019). The ultimate goal of KINGS is for each child to grow up in a good, healthy system.

[1] Based in the Netherlands.

Caroline Ploeg, Henriët Scholts, Lysbert Zeinstra, and Femy Wanders, *EMDR in an Inpatient Setting*. In: *Handbook of EMDR for Children and Adolescents*. Edited by: Renée Beer and Carlijn de Roos, Oxford University Press. © 2026, Oxford University Press. For the English edition. DOI: 10.1093/oso/9780198918400.003.0024

In this chapter, we will first review the characteristics of the KINGS target group in Section 24.2, and then describe the structure and content of the KINGS treatment model in Section 24.3. A detailed case study will illustrate how the model is applied in practice. The Section 24.4 presents empirical evidence for the use of KINGS. This is followed by the Section 24.5, highlighting essential points of interest regarding the implementation of EMDR and imaginal exposure (IE) within KINGS and the treatment setting.

24.2 The Target Group

The target group of KINGS consists of families with multiple and complex problems (Bodden & Deković, 2016; Tausendfreund et al., 2016). A recent qualitative content analysis of case information on the characteristics of KINGS families shows that they experience problems simultaneously in several of the following areas:

1. child factors (e.g., behaviour, emotions);
2. parent factors (e.g., behaviour, emotions);
3. parenting (e.g., inadequate or inconsistent parenting strategies, pedagogical powerlessness);
4. family functioning (e.g., low levels of cohesion and organization, and high levels of communication and relationship problems);
5. contextual factors (e.g., problems at school or work, financial problems);
6. social network problems (e.g., disrupted or absent social network, conflicts), and
7. problems with family support services (e.g., long history of family support services).

The problems are intergenerational, and both children and their parents have been exposed from an early age to profoundly disturbing interpersonal events, such as domestic violence, neglect, sexual abuse, and peer (physical or emotional) violence (Zeinstra et al., 2024).

Parents' unprocessed traumatic experiences can have a significant impact on their parenting, their emotional availability, and, thus, their children's well-being (Van Ee et al., 2016). A longitudinal study showed that 'parental PTSD' is a risk factor for insecure attachment, and, in turn, insecure attachment increases children's vulnerability to PTSD (Bosquet Enlow et al., 2014). The close connection between parental trauma and insecure attachment emphasizes the importance of treating parent and child together, focusing on PTSD symptoms of both parent(s) and child, the attachment relationship between parent(s) and child, strengthening sensitive parenting, and improving emotion regulation in both parent(s) and child. In doing so, the KINGS model offers a distinctive and innovative approach to helping families with chronic, pervasive, and intergenerational problems that are considered difficult to solve (Barth et al., 2024; Zeinstra et al., 2024).

CASE STUDY 24.1 **James: PTSD in Parent and Child**

James is a 9-year-old boy who lives with his mother in a deprived neighbourhood. They are referred by a C&A psychiatric outpatient clinic. An outside family therapist has been visiting the family's home for some time and has initiated the referral. James's biological father left before he was born and has not been in the picture since. James's mother has never had good contact with her own parents and has not seen them for years, having been emotionally neglected and abused by them. She was also sexually abused when she was a child by a foster parent. She has had several relationships throughout her adulthood, all of which could be described as violent. She has been physically and emotionally abused by her ex-partners and has been forced into prostitution, which has involved several serious violent sexual attacks. Her social network is very limited; the only social contact she currently has is with a neighbour. Her symptoms include flashbacks, re-experiencing, sleep disturbance, depression, suicidality, and fear of being around others. James and his mother had moved five times, with James having to change school each time. At the time of the report, James was no longer attending school due to suspension. His time at school has been characterized by constant conflicts between James and his classmates and with teachers. His teachers indicate that James is often involved in playground fights, he does not follow instructions and goes completely his own way, and he displays defiant, aggressive, and threatening behaviour (e.g., tripping others, throwing things and squeezing other people's throats).

24.3 The KINGS Treatment Model

24.3.1 Structure

The KINGS treatment consists of three phases—preparation, treatment, and integration—each lasting 1 to 3 weeks on average (see figure 24.1). An inpatient treatment's average duration is 8 weeks. The parent goes through the same phases as the child but is one phase ahead each time. The reason for this is so that the parent can support the child during their treatment, as the parent's trauma treatment—EMDR+IE[2] (imaginary exposure)—allows them to respond from a calmer brain. The duration of each phase varies by family and family member. The parent and child move to the next phase when the directing therapist, family therapist(s), and parent assess that the step to the next phase can be taken. A detailed mapping of the practice elements that clinicians apply within and across these phases is available in Zeinstra et al. (2025), including their intensity, mode of delivery, target recipients, and their alignment with family treatment goals.

[2] Imaginary exposure means repeated exposure to a memory. The patient is asked to bring up a traumatic memory and describe it in a vivid and detailed manner.

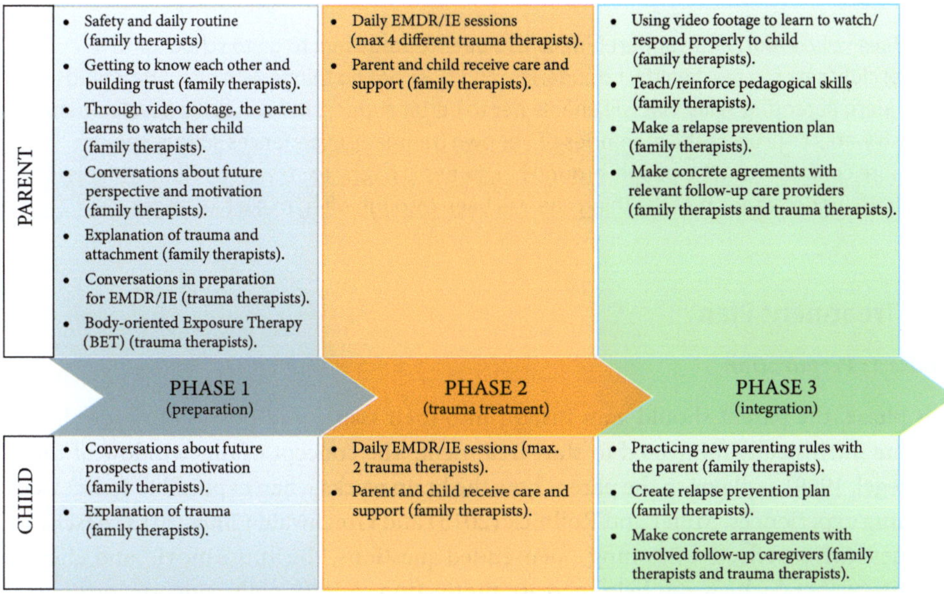

Figure 24.1 Schematic representation of KINGS treatment phases.

- ***Before admission***

An orientation meeting is held before admission. Meeting attendees include the parent, the child, other family members, and the referrer. A family therapist and the directing therapist are present from the clinic. During the orientation meeting, the practitioners maintain a non-judgemental, respectful, transparent, and sincere attitude, which is characteristic of KINGS treatment. They listen to the family members with compassion and with a trauma-sensitive attitude. This allows family members to feel heard, understood, and recognized. The clinicians convey that it is logical for the family to be in the current situation, given their history and the resulting beliefs and behavioural strategies they have developed. During the orientation interview, the clinicians also explain what the treatment will be like and that the KINGS practitioners want to actively cooperate with the family members, the referring agency, and the current care providers. A condition for admission is that the regular care provider is ready to take over treatment again after discharge from admission. If all parties agree that treatment is indicated, the parent decides whether (or not) to undergo KINGS treatment.

CASE STUDY 24.1 **James: Part 2**

After the orientation interview, James's mother understands that her son's behavioural problems are largely driven by the unpleasant experiences he has had. She also understands that because of her past, she reacts and thinks in a certain way. She understands that because of this she does not respond appropriately to her son. For example, she argues with James a lot, does not comfort and support him, does not encourage him to go to school or to a (sports) club, sets too few healthy boundaries, and does not do things with him. She would like to learn parenting skills that will enable her to better support her son in his development. She also wants to process the memories of her own traumatic experiences so that she can gain more confidence in the people around her. James is happy to stay at the clinic with his mother. He understands that the things he has been through often make him angry.

24.3.2 Treatment Plan

- ***Phase 1: Preparation***

In this phase, the parent should gain insight into their issues and possibilities for change to become intrinsically motivated to start treatment. The concept of the 'window of tolerance' (Siegel, 1999) explains to the parent how the brain works when exposed to (perceived) threatening experiences. Miller and Rollnick (2013) and Greenwald (2009, 2013) described techniques such as reflective listening, open-ended questions, 'the future movie', and 'choices have consequences' which can help increase motivation. Additionally, video recordings of family interactions are made. The recordings allow the parent to look objectively at their child's behaviour and to notice positive interactions (which previously went unnoticed due to excessive distress).

Body-oriented exposure therapy (BET) is also part of phase 1. Each parent is offered 1.5 hours of BET four times a week. BET is a group training that teaches participants how to focus attention on the body (stress reactions in the body) and connect with the body in a positive and pleasurable way. It teaches the parent to use their body better to set boundaries, make choices, and regulate emotions. It is a good preparation for EMDR+IE, because during BET the parent discovers that allowing physical sensations and emotions does not lead to a catastrophic event.

Using the diagnostic tools, the Clinician-Administered PTSD Scale for DSM-5 (CAPS; Boeschoten et al., 2014; Weathers et al., 2013), or the Diagnostic Interview Trauma and Stressors for individuals with mild intellectual impairment (DITS-LVB; Mevissen et al., 2018a), the parent's traumatic experiences and symptoms are identified. The therapist and the parent, in collaboration, make a signalling plan to clarify what the parent and the environment can do if the tension builds.

CASE STUDY 24.1 James: Part 3—The Therapist Helps James's Mother to Discover her Role

During the first two weeks of admission, James and his mother establish a healthy daily routine. A family therapist works with them to develop a daily schedule. This includes set times for getting up and going to bed, set mealtimes, appointments with trauma therapists (as part of case conceptualization), and other appointments and activities in between. The family therapist is often with James and his mother. The mother has many questions about trauma and the therapy that awaits them, which the family therapist answers. He is also sensitive to the mother's positive parenting behaviour towards her son, which he reinforces. The family therapist shows video footage taken earlier to James's mother, who is pleasantly surprised when she sees herself on video for the first time. She says that she feels that it is crazy to hear herself, but she is very happy to see that James often looks at her questioningly and seems to be waiting for a response from her. She says it has never occurred to her that her son wants or expects anything from her. She has now had four sessions with a trauma therapist who has taught her about attachment, trauma, and trauma processing. She has also had to answer many questions and talk a lot. The trauma therapist drew up a plan for EMDR/IE, which he presented to her. A signalling plan was also drawn up, which tells her what she will do when she feels depressed or suicidal. This allows the trauma therapist to ensure that James receives the right care at the time of his mother's EMDR/IE. For example, when she is having a hard time, she can lie down on her bed for a while and listen to music, while the family therapist stays close to James.

- ***Phase 2: Trauma treatment***

The parent begins EMDR/IE (usually in week 3) and remains at the clinic with the child during this phase. Each day, the parent usually receives at least two EMDR/IE sessions, each lasting an hour and a half. Several trauma therapists (up to four) work with the same parent to ensure the therapy progresses. This phase of the parent receiving EMDR/IE lasts up to three weeks. As soon as the parent is almost finished with EMDR/IE, the parent and their child have established a good daily routine, and the parent can support the child emotionally, the child also starts EMDR/IE.

CASE STUDY 24.1 **James: Part 4—EMDR for a Mother that Ultimately Helps her Child**

Halfway through the second week of admission, James's mother reports that she is experiencing more peace and is getting used to the new daily routine. It is agreed during the weekly assessment that she will start EMDR/IE after the weekend. As she is now moving into her second phase (trauma therapy), it is time for James to start his phase 1 (preparation). The mother's EMDR/IE has now started and begins with a repeat explanation of trauma processing and what reactions, if any, she can expect during and after the EMDR/IE sessions. The trauma therapists work from the case conceptualization prepared earlier. She receives EMDR/IE every day for a week and a half. The first week of therapy is very difficult for her. She has little space and energy outside the sessions to pay attention to her son or herself. The family therapists look after James and do many activities with him during this week. At one point the mother indicates that she wants to leave. The family therapist talks to her at length, particularly about why she is undergoing therapy. In the end, she says she wants to continue the therapy to give her son a better life.

After a week and a half of EMDR/IE, she notices more peace and order in her mind. She also feels more inner strength. She dares to go out a bit more and takes the initiative in social interactions. She reports that these social interactions are positive. She sleeps better and no longer suffers from flashbacks and re-experiencing.

- ***Phase 3: Integration***

In addition to learning parenting skills, generalization and transfer of what has been learned to the home situation occurs in the integration phase. In this final phase, the parent should be able to emotionally support the child, who is still receiving EMDR/IE. The parent now knows from their own experience what EMDR/IE involves and is therefore better able to understand what their child is going through and how they can support them. The parent receives the necessary support from the trauma therapist. In addition to supporting the child, the parent learns to apply pedagogical skills during this phase. As a result of the treatment, the parent has a calmer brain, enabling them to learn parenting skills. This is done through cognitive behavioural therapy and video recordings.

Finally, a relapse prevention plan is created with the parent. Possible future triggers are noted, and the plan concretely describes what the parent and significant others could do in case of problems.

24.3.3 Child Treatment

- ***Phase 1: Preparation***

A secure situation is created for the child, both physically and emotionally. Physical safety is achieved by the admission of the family to the clinic, which removes the child from a threatening situation. Emotional safety is promoted by a fixed and predictable daily structure with healthy rhythms for eating, sleeping, and doing activities. The pedagogical climate is also made safe for the child. The family therapists play a crucial role in this. They discuss with the parents how they can support them. The family therapists name the behaviour they see, set boundaries when harmful behaviour occurs, and model healthy parenting behaviour. One of the family therapists has individual meetings and does activities with the child so as to get to know them and build some trust. In addition, the family therapist works with the child and the parent to develop a signalling plan, so everyone knows what they could or should do if tensions build.

In this phase, the trauma therapist identifies the child's need for help, the symptoms, and the traumatic experiences, as has already been done with the parent. This is done in a series of interviews with the child and, if necessary, the parent is involved. Supposed connections between the symptoms and traumatic events are clarified. The child also receives a clinical diagnostic interview to see if there is PTSD: either DITS-LVB (Mevissen et al., 2018) or CAPS-CA DSM-5 (Clinician-Administered PTSD Scale for DSM-5—Child/Adolescent Version; Pynoos et al., 2015).

Should EMDR/IE be indicated, then the trauma therapist provides (age-appropriate) psychoeducation to the child with the parent present. The trauma therapist explains the procedure of EMDR/IE and clarifies what the parent and child might expect as results from the EMDR/IE sessions.

CASE STUDY 24.1 James: Part 5—Preparation for EMDR

James is given individual sessions with a trauma therapist. James has many questions, such as what exactly happens in the therapy sessions and how the light of the EMDR/IE kit works. The therapist builds some trust with him, and explains the therapy and how to respond when negative things happen—in other words, how his symptoms might be related to what he has experienced. The CAPS-CA is used to map out the traumatic events he has experienced and his symptoms. James is good at identifying what he is still suffering from. PTSD is present.

- ***Phase 2: Trauma treatment***

Like the parent, the child undergoes trauma treatment through EMDR/IE. The child also receives several EMDR/IE sessions a day. The duration of the sessions is adapted to the child's attention span. The parent can now offer support to the child from the perspective of a calm brain by being present for the child lovingly and sensitively before and after the EMDR/IE sessions (and even during the sessions, if necessary); at the same time, the parent can ensure a safe and predictable parenting situation.

CASE STUDY 24.1 James: Part 6—EMDR Begins

Based on his symptoms, a step-by-step plan is made with James as to which memories will be treated by EMDR/IE and in what order. All trauma-related memories are treated, starting with the most intrusive memories. James receives EMDR/IE for one week. The EMDR/IE takes place without his mother being present. His mother waits in the waiting room and can be called in, if necessary—for instance, if James wants her to be there as support. Afterwards it turns out that it is not necessary to call his mother in. James is often very tired after the EMDR/IE sessions. During the week he receives EMDR/IE, James displays more difficult behaviour. For example, he does not want to go to sleep and crawls into bed with his mother at night. After the week of EMDR/IE, his behaviour becomes calmer: he is better at listening to his mother and following instructions, he sleeps well again, and he is friendlier and happier.

- ***Phase 3: Integration***

As for the parent, the child's integration phase consists of interventions aimed at generalization and transfer of learning to the home situation (such as behavioural experiments, in vivo exposure, and skill reinforcement). The parent learns parenting skills, which will impact upon the child. This is also a change for the child to get used to. The child learns that their parent is showing different behaviour and that different behaviour is thus also expected from the child (e.g., listening to and following instructions from the parent and being allowed to express feelings to the parent).

The family therapists make a relapse prevention plan with the child and the parent. At this stage, the child transitions to a new school or returns to their original school. Good communication between the clinicians, the parent, the referrer, and the staff of the child's school should promote a good transition. Similar protocols should apply if it turns out that the child still needs individual follow-up support.

CASE STUDY 24.1 **James: Part 7—Follow-Up for James and his Mother**

James's mother has practiced recognizing her son's behaviour and the emotions she sees in him. As a result, there are more moments of contact between them; James feels seen, heard, and understood. There are also more relaxed moments, making it easier for James's mother to practice her 'new' parenting behaviour. She also begins to communicate more clearly. As a result, James is less likely to argue about instructions. Video recordings are used as a tool by the family therapist. By watching the video footage, James's mother gains insight into her own behaviour, and the family therapist shows her alternative and healthier behaviours. For example, there is a recording of a breakfast situation where little is said. The video is stopped at times when she might have spoken. Together with the family therapist, she thinks about what she might say. Finally, personalized relapse prevention plans are made and given to James and to his mother. These include which situations might put them at risk of relapse and what to do to prevent a relapse. After seven weeks in hospital, the family returns home. The outpatient family worker from the referral agency resumes home therapy.

24.4 Empirical Evidence

24.4.1 Behavioural and Mediation Therapy

Within the KINGS treatment, the team looks, thinks, and acts very much from the behavioural therapy frame of reference. The starting point within KINGS is that all members of the treatment team—regardless of their previous training (university or higher vocational education)—are trained in cognitive behavioural therapy (CBT). The therapists use functional analyses to find explanations for why and in what context a particular behaviour (e.g., avoidance) occurs, assuming a non-random relationship between the behaviour and the consequences of that behaviour (Hermans et al., 2018; Spiegler & Guevremont, 2010). To bring about behavioural change in both parent and child, the therapists use various operant techniques for learning and unlearning behaviour (e.g., reinforcement procedures). For a description and underpinning of operant techniques for behaviour change, we refer readers to Cooper and colleagues (2019).

Within the KINGS treatment model, family therapists work with parents directly using these techniques and indirectly through parents to bring about behavioural change in the child. Parents are given specific behavioural instructions based on operant learning principles. This indirect method of intervention is called 'mediation therapy'. For externalizing behavioural problems in children younger than 12 years of age, mediation therapy in a family context (e.g., parent effectiveness training, parent management training, parent training therapy) is considered a first-choice treatment strategy (Chacko et al., 2017; NICE, 2017).

24.4.2 Motivational Interviewing

Motivational interviewing is a widely used method to encourage behavioural change in clients. It aims to increase motivation. Most families receiving KINGS treatment have a long history of family support services. Negative experiences with previous family support services can lead to a lack of confidence and a lack of motivation to change (Tausendfreund et al., 2016). In addition, it takes considerable effort, perseverance, and courage to overcome trauma-related problems. These families will only engage fully with their treatment if they are helped to identify their goals and see how treatment can help them achieve them (Greenwald, 2009, 2013). When applying motivational interviewing in KINGS, practitioners use communication strategies well-suited to families who often need autonomy and recognition. Practitioners' interpersonal skills—demonstrating empathy, warmth, friendliness, reliability, transparency, and an unbiased and respectful attitude—play a central role (Miller & Rollnick, 2013).

The use of motivational interviewing has been associated with increased adherence and willingness to change (Lundahl et al., 2010), including among clients with PTSD (Murphy, 2008). Motivational interviewing can positively contribute to people's well-being—for example, by reducing stress or depressive symptoms (Keeley et al., 2016; Lundahl et al., 2010).

24.4.3 Use of Video in Teaching Parenting Skills

KINGS uses video feedback to improve parenting skills and the quality of parent–child interaction. The approach is based on video home training (as described by Wels, 2001) and a behavioural therapy approach (Cooper et al., 2019). The (everyday) interactions and communication between parent and child(ren) are clarified by systematically analysing and discussing video footage. The emphasis is on increasing the sensitivity and responsiveness of the parent by highlighting the strengths of the parenting behaviour, positive child behaviour, and positive parent–child interactions. Parents are trained in behavioural therapy techniques to systematically influence the antecedents (e.g., giving instructions, providing structure, setting rules) and consequences (e.g., reinforcing, ignoring, punishing) of their child's behaviour.

A meta-analysis by Balldin and colleagues (2018) shows that video feedback is effective in stimulating parental sensitivity and positive (parenting) behaviour, and in inducing a positive behavioural change in children.

Parents receiving the KINGS treatment report that watching video feedback is enlightening, and that positive and successful interactions contribute to self-confidence. Parents become more aware of what they are doing well and what positively affects their children. These experiences are confirmed in a process evaluation of the implementation of video home training in families with children of primary school age (Eliëns et al., 2020).

24.4.4 **Body-Centred Work**

Research shows that there is a correlation between PTSD symptoms and fear of, and less accurate perception of, bodily sensations (Harricharan et al., 2017; Schaan et al., 2019; Tsur et al., 2018; Tsur, 2020). This has led to the hypothesis that clients may benefit more from trauma treatment if they can better tolerate unpleasant bodily sensations and feelings. Within the KINGS treatment model, this led to the development of BET. BET combines techniques from trauma-sensitive mindfulness (Treleaven, 2018) with trauma-sensitive yoga (Emerson, 2015) and compassion training (Gilbert, 2005). The aim of this is to increase both awareness and tolerance of bodily sensations.

An exploratory questionnaire study by Noppers (2020) with 17 parents who participated in BET in phase 1 of KINGS treatment shows a significant reduction in fear of bodily sensations and emotions. International research confirms the potential added value of incorporating body-oriented interventions into regular trauma treatment (Rosenbaum et al., 2015; Van der Kolk et al., 2014).

24.4.5 **EMDR/IE**

Within KINGS, PTSD symptoms in parents and children are treated—according to (inter) national guidelines (NICE, 2018b)—with a combination of the first-choice treatment interventions of EMDR (Shapiro, 2018) and IE (Foa et al., 2007; Van Minnen & Arntz, 2017). There is growing evidence that these first-choice treatment interventions are also effective in treating adults and children with a history of interpersonal and early childhood trauma who suffer from symptoms of complex PTSD (De Jongh et al., 2019; De Jongh et al., 2024a; Jaberghaderi et al., 2019; Oprel et al., 2021). Oprel and colleagues (2021) reported that intensifying IE therapy resulted in a more rapid reduction in symptoms. In line with this are the promising results of intensive trauma treatment for adults and adolescents with a combination of EMDR and IE (Van Woudenberg et al., 2018; van Pelt et al., 2021) and for adolescents who received only intensive IE for complex PTSD (Hendriks et al., 2017). A characteristic of such intensive treatment programmes is that different therapists provide the trauma treatment. This is also the case within KINGS. Therapist rotation is necessary to ensure treatment progress. It also contributes positively to treatment integrity (Van Minnen et al., 2018).

24.4.6 Trauma-Focused CBT

KINGS treatment has a similar structure and uses the same components as trauma-focused cognitive behavioural therapy (TF-CBT: Cohen et al., 2012). Like TF-CBT, KINGS treatment addresses multiple explanatory factors for PTSD, such as dysfunctional cognitions, avoidance, and triggers, and there is a systemic approach with a focus on strengthening skills for the future. The following components of TF-CBT are also covered in KINGS treatment: psychoeducation, parenting skills, relaxation, affect modulation, cognitive coping, and processing. TF-CBT has been studied extensively for its efficacy and has been found to be effective in reducing PTSD symptoms and related problems (e.g., depressive symptoms, anxiety, behavioural problems, parenting distress), including in children with complex PTSD (Cohen et al., 2018; Jensen et al., 2022).

24.4.7 Scientific Rationale for KINGS as a Complete Treatment Programme

A four-year project of a scientific PhD study on the effectiveness of the KINGS treatment model started in 2021 (Zeinstra et al., 2022; Zeinstra, 2026). This research project implies a collaboration between Accare, Erasmus University Rotterdam, and the University of Groningen. The research will add systematic impact evaluation to the positive clinical impressions and indirect evidence of the model's effectiveness. The research project has now been completed. The results are currently being published in peer-reviewed journals and translated into practice.

24.5 Points to Consider

24.5.1 Specific Points Regarding EMDR/IE in this Target Group

- ***Creating conditions***

The stay in the clinic is essential for parents and children of this target group because the clinic provides a safe environment for the family members and allows the family therapists to temporarily take over parenting tasks and provide social and emotional support. From this safe and supportive situation, the parent can be confident that a safety net is in place for them and their child during treatment. Creating these conditions gives both the parent and the child the peace of mind to focus on the trauma treatment.

- ***Case conceptualization***

Because these families have many negative experiences, the KINGS programme carefully considers what will be covered and in what order. This is done using the 'paths for target selection' (see Chapter 4 in this book). Together with the parent, the trauma therapist identifies the intrusive memories. These are treated first. The memories that get in the way of a healthy parenting style are also identified. These memories are also treated so the parent can be available (again) for the child's upbringing.

- ***Psychoeducation***

Turmoil in the brain disrupts one's capacity to absorb and process information. Although we consider this throughout treatment, it is imperative during psychoeducation as this is where a lot of information is given in a relatively short amount of time. For this reason, the parent and child need to hear several times the explanation of how unpleasant past experiences play a role in their current behaviour. Family and trauma therapists must be able to explain these to the parent and child. Family therapists are present 24 hours a day, so they can respond immediately to things they see happening or that the parent or child tells them. For example, if a child reacts angrily to a group of peers, the family therapist can immediately make the connection and give explanations. The family therapist might say 'Because you were bullied a lot at school, you now react very angrily when you see a group of peers. When you see your peers, you think of the bullying again and you react in "fight mode". It prevents you from thinking and reflecting properly. Do you recognize this?'

- ***Predictability***

These parents and children are anxious and distrustful in contact with others. This plays a part in all relationships, including those with the therapist. Because of this distrust, it is pleasant for the parent and child to feel a sense of control, as much as is possible. The trauma therapist can promote this feeling by informing them exactly what will happen and how long something will take, and teaching them how to indicate when something is (temporarily) enough.

To increase predictability for the child, the trauma therapist can agree on exactly how long the EMDR/IE will take. For example, the trauma therapist may use an hourglass, a stopwatch, or a clock on the table. This allows the child to see how long they have to work on the unpleasant memory, which increases their sense of control while reducing anxiety.

24.5.2 Specific Points Regarding the Treatment Setting

- ***Funding***

The clinic's management plays a crucial role in creating the conditions that will facilitate and sustain this form of treatment operational. Essential factors include good working conditions, a shared vision and mission, and providing training and development opportunities for staff. A serious problem is the need for more relevant knowledge among agencies funding psychiatric help. Cutbacks in the care sector also play a role. In the years to come, it will be just as essential to keep insisting on using (new) scientifically proven (or to be proven) treatment methods, besides monitoring results and ensuring that staff are equipped with up-to-date knowledge and skills.

- ***Treatment team support***

Some children persist for a long time in extreme externalizing and dangerous behaviour (e.g., physical aggression, such as hitting others with sticks or squeezing another person's throat), which threatens to exhaust family therapists. It is, therefore, important that everyone involved continues to communicate with each other about how to act in such situations and how to prevent them from arising, as far as is possible. Support from different departments—treatment departments on the same site—can help.

Additionally, the issue of safety/aggression is explicitly addressed at various points in the treatment. Early warning procedures (where necessary) and safety plans (where appropriate) are developed in consultation with the family and referring agency. De-escalation is the watchword. Ongoing training and intervision for trauma and family therapists is essential to understand and manage such situations properly.

- ***Information transfer and attunement***

Children with low trust in adults (because of negative interpersonal experiences) do not find it easy to interact with other people. This is further complicated when there are many different people with whom the child has to 'do something' every day; think of alternating family therapists or teachers. This cannot be avoided entirely in a treatment or school setting. However, one can keep the treatment team as consistent as possible. To promote the child's trust in his environment, there needs to be good coordination and transfer of information to all involved, including the teachers. If everyone 'speaks the same language' to the child, there will be consistency in the approach, and the child will be able to focus on their treatment. Good cooperation and communication with other involved care agencies are also beneficial. This promotes trust among everyone.

24.6 Concluding Remarks

KINGS is a phased inpatient treatment model for children with severe behavioural problems and their parents. Within this treatment model, EMDR/IE is a crucial component for both parent and child. KINGS aims to reduce PTSD symptoms in the child and parent and to improve parent–child interactions, with the ultimate goal of children growing up healthily. Appropriate use of this treatment model requires the entire treatment team to know the potential consequences of trauma and the principles of CBT. It is also vital that the treatment team and the management team of the organization have the courage and the determination to provide a trauma-sensitive treatment environment for these families. Sometimes, this requires stepping off the beaten (treatment) track to jointly achieve the desired reduction in distress for the child and family.

Epilogue

This book informs the reader about the relevance and the state-of-the-art of EMDR for C&A and various subpopulations. Providing an up-to-date overview of a field that is rapidly evolving is a challenging task. Developments in the field are ongoing. Trained therapists can stay updated and be informed of new developments based on research in various ways:

- Through conferences and other meetings organized by national and international organizations, such as EMDR Europe, EMDRIA, EMDRAA, EMDR Africa, EMDR Asia, EMDR Latin America and the Caribbean, and EMDR Middle East and North Africa/Arab countries.
- Through national newsletters and international journals, like the *Journal of EMDR Practice and Research*.

Hopefully, these sources will provide beneficial and resourceful information to C&A therapists.

Future

For the clinical field, this book might help promote international synchronization of EMDR C&A training. For traumatized children, EMDR treatment should become more available worldwide, and the goal of this book is to serve as a resource for enhancing the expertise of therapists. The goal of EMDR therapists is to treat children suffering from problems resulting from (traumatic) stress as efficiently as possible so their developmental opportunities are no longer hindered. Effective treatment of traumatized children will improve their chances of healthy development into adulthood without unnecessary burdens from their past. This, in turn, will contribute to breaking the cycle of intergenerational trauma transmission and increase their chances of becoming psychologically healthy parents in the future.

The focus of this book is on healing the consequences of trauma. Another critical perspective in trauma—prevention of chronic psychopathology after traumatic experiences—is hardly addressed. Children who will continue to grow up in persistently stressful circumstances, such as multi-problem families or war situations, need alternative or additional interventions besides trauma treatment. Enhancing their resilience is vital for these children. A recent meta-analysis of 34 studies involving 54,646 participants revealed that childhood maltreatment accounts for 21% to 41% of common mental health conditions in Australia (Grummit et al., 2024). This indicates a significant burden on many lives. We will never be able to prevent childhood maltreatment, but we can reduce the consequences and lower the number of burdened lives by offering programmes that enhance resilience.

In addition to empirical research testing the effectiveness of treatment methods, other research identifies factors that increase resilience (Masten & Barnes, 2018). By combining research findings from both perspectives, we can develop more effective and efficient treatments, on the one hand, and effective programmes to prevent or reduce the consequences of traumatization, on the other.

Thank You

We embarked on a journey to create this book by collaborating with 31 authors, and it is up to the reader to determine how well we achieved our goal. It was an exciting and fulfilling journey, and we are deeply thankful to everyone who contributed. It has been a demanding project, and we hope that many EMDR colleagues will benefit from the information presented in this book.

First and foremost, we are very grateful to the children and their parents who trusted us and allowed us to treat them. Our insights, as described in this book, are to a large extent the result of our cooperation with the children and parents who shared their experiences.

Secondly, we thank all participating authors for their valuable contributions and collaboration. Their input has enriched the book, featuring 13 balanced chapters full of practical and inspiring information for clinical practice.

We are delighted with Suus van den Akker's fun drawings and the striking photos by Frederique Favreau, who graduated with a project on PTSD from the Amsterdam School of Photography. We thank the children who allowed us to include their drawings.

Finally, we are indebted to the publisher, Oxford University Press, especially Martin Baum, Jade Dixon, and Lavanya Sathiamurthy for their support during the process of creating this book. Additionally, we want to express our sincere gratitude to Helen Cooper for her thoughtful and precise comments on the text, which greatly helped us improve it.

Let's hope this book will help us make the world a slightly better place. Each successful EMDR therapy restores hope and creates chances for a brighter future in traumatized children and adolescents.

Renée Beer and Carlijn de Roos

Bibliography

Abrahamse, M. E., Junger, M., Chavannes, E. L., Coelman, F. J., Boer, F., & Lindauer, R. (2012). Parent-child interaction therapy for preschool children with disruptive behaviour problems in the Netherlands. *Child and Adolescent Psychiatry and Mental Health, 6*, 24. https://doi.org/10.1186/1753-2000-6-24

Abrahamse, M. E., Junger, M., Van Wouwe, M. A. M. M., Boer, F., & Lindauer, R. J. L. (2016). Treating child disruptive behavior in high-risk families: A comparative effectiveness trial from a community-based implementation. *Journal of Child and Family Studies, 25*, 1605–1622. https://doi.org/10.1007/s10826-015-0322-4

Adler-Tapia, R. L., & Settle, C. S. (2008). *EMDR and the art of psychotherapy with children*. Springer Publishing Company.

Adler-Tapia, R., & Settle, C. (2009). Evidence of the efficacy of EMDR with children and adolescents in individual psychotherapy: A review of the research published in peer-reviewed journals. *Journal of EMDR Practice and Research, 3*(4), 232–247. https://doi.org/10.1891/1933-3196.3.4.232

Adler-Tapia, R., & Settle, C. (2012). Specialty topics on using EMDR with children. *Journal of EMDR Practice and Research, 6*(3), 145–153. https://doi.org/10.1891/1933-3196.6.3.145

Adler-Tapia, R., & Settle, C. (2017). *EMDR and the art of psychotherapy with children: Infants to adolescents* (2nd ed.). Springer Publishing Company.

Adler-Tapia, R., & Settle, C. (2023). *EMDR and the art of psychotherapy with children: Guidebook and treatment manual*. Springer Publishing Company.

Adler-Tapia, R., & Settle, C. (2025). Child adaptations to the phases of EMDR therapy. In D. Farrell, S. J. Schubert, & M. D. Kiernan (Eds.), *The Oxford handbook of EMDR therapy*. Oxford Academic. https://doi.org/10.1093/oxfordhb/9780192898357.001.0001

Aduriz, M. E., Knopfler, C., & Bluthgen, C. (2009). Helping child flood victims using group EMDR intervention in Argentina: Treatment outcome and gender differences. *International Journal of Stress Management, 16*(2), 138–153. https://doi.org/10.1037/a0014719

Aelen, F. (2008). Cognitieve systeemtherapie en EMDR. In E. ten Broeke, A. de Jongh, & H.-J. Oppenheim (Eds.), *Praktijkboek EMDR* (pp. 409–429). Harcourt.

Afzal, N., Ye, S., Page, A. C., Trickey, D., Lyttle, M. D., Hiller, R. M., & Halligan, S. L. (2022). A systematic literature review of the relationship between parenting responses and child post-traumatic stress symptoms. *European Journal of Psychotraumatology, 14*(1), 2156053. https://doi.org/10.1080/20008066.2022.2156053

Ahmad, A., Larsson, B., & Sundelin-Wahsten, V. (2007). EMDR treatment for children with PTSD: Results of a randomized controlled trial. *Nordic Journal of Psychiatry, 61*(5), 349–354. https://doi.org/10.1080/08039480701643464

Ahmad, A., & Sundelin-Wahlsten, V. (2008). Applying EMDR on children with PTSD. European Child & Adolescent Psychiatry, 17(3), 127–132.

Aktar, E., Majdandžić, M., De Vente, W., & Bögels, S. M. (2013). The interplay between expressed parental anxiety and infant behavioural inhibition predicts infant avoidance in a social referencing paradigm. *Journal of Child Psychology and Psychiatry, 54*(2), 144–156. https://doi.org/10.1111/j.1469-7610.2012.02601.x

AKWA. (2020). *Care standard for dissociative disorders*. https://www.ggzstandaarden.nl/zorgstandaarden/dissociatieve-stoornissen/introductie

Alexander, J. F., Pugh, C., Parsons, B. V., & Sexton, T. L. (2000). Functional family therapy. In D. S. Elliott (Ed.), *Blueprints for Violence Prevention (Book 3)* (2nd ed., pp. 111–132). Center for the Study and Prevention of Violence, Institute of Behavioral Science, University of Colorado.

Alisic, E., Zalta, A. K., Van Wesel, F., Larsen, S. E., Hafstad, G. S., Hassanpour, K., & Smid, G. E. (2014). Rates of post-traumatic stress disorder in trauma-exposed children and adolescents: Meta-analysis. *The British Journal of Psychiatry, 204*(5), 335–340. https://doi.org/10.1192/bjp.bp.113.131227

American Academy of Child and Adolescent Psychiatry (AACAP). (2011). Practice parameter for the assessment and treatment of children and adolescents with suicidal behavior. *Journal of the American Academy of Child and Adolescent Psychiatry, 50*(12), 1299–1332. https://doi.org/10.1016/j.jaac.2011.09.009

American Psychiatric Association. (2000). *Diagnostic and statistical manual of mental disorders DSM-IV-TR* (4th ed.).

American Psychiatric Association. (2013). *Diagnostic and statistical manual of mental disorders: DSM-5* (5th ed.). https://doi.org/10.1176/appi.books.9780890425596

American Psychiatric Association. (2022). *Diagnostic and statistical manual of mental disorders* (5th ed., text rev.). https://doi.org/10.1176/appi.books.9780890425787

Anderson, M. L., Sortwell, A., Wolf Craig, K. S., & Ziedonis, D. M. (2016). Symptom patterns of posttraumatic stress disorder among deaf trauma survivors. *Journal of the American Deafness and Rehabilitation Association*, *50*(1), 1–19.

Anderson, M. L., Wolf Craig, K. S., & Ziedonis, D. M. (2017). Deaf people's help-seeking following trauma: Experiences with and recommendations for the Massachusetts behavioral health care system. *Psychological Trauma: Theory, Research, Practice, and Policy*, *9*(2), 239–248. https://doi.org/10.1037/tra0000219

Andrade, B. F., Courtney, D., Duda, S., Aitken, M., Craig, S. G., Szatmari, P., Henderson, J., & Bennett, K. (2019). A systematic review and evaluation of clinical practice guidelines for children and youth with disruptive behavior: Rigor of development and recommendations for use. *Clinical Child and Family Psychology Review*, *22*(4), 527–548. https://doi.org/10.1007/s10567-019-00292-2

Andrade, J., Kavanagh, D., & Baddeley, A. (1997). Eye-movements and visual imagery: A working memory approach to the treatment of post-traumatic stress disorder. *British Journal of Clinical Psychology*, *36*(2), 209–223. https://doi.org/10.1111/j.2044-8260.1997.tb01408.x

Àngels Esteller-Cano, A., Buil-Legaz, L., López-Penadés, R., Aguilar-Mediavilla, E., & Adrover-Roig, D. (2022). Retrospective bullying trajectories in adults with self-reported oral language difficulties. *International Journal of Language and Communication Disorders*, *57*(3), 578–592. https://doi.org/10.1111/1460-6984.12708

Antila, H., Arola, R., Hakko, H., Riala, K., Riipinen, P., & Kantojärvi, L. (2017). Bullying involvement in relation to personality disorders: A prospective follow-up of 508 inpatient adolescents. *European Child and Adolescent Psychiatry*, *26*(7), 779–789. https://doi.org/10.1007/s00787-017-0946-6

Armstrong, M. S., & Vaughan, K. (1996). An orienting response model of eye movement desensitization. *Journal of Behavior Therapy and Experimental Psychiatry*, *27*(1), 21–32. https://doi.org/10.1016/0005-7916(95)00056-9

Arntz, A., Rijkeboer, M., Chan, E., Fassbinder, E., Karaosmanoglu, A., Lee, C. W., & Panzeri, M. (2021). Towards a reformulated theory underlying schema therapy: Position paper of an international workgroup. *Cognitive Therapy and Research*, 1–14. https://doi.org/10.1007/s10608-021-10209-5

Artigas, L., & Lehnung, M. (2020). Combining EMDR with play therapy: Principles and practices. *Journal of EMDR Practice and Research*, *14*(1), 45–55.

Atkinson, M., & Hollis, C. (2010). NICE guideline: Attention deficit hyperactivity disorder. *Archives of Disease in Childhood-Education and Practice*, *95*(1), 24–27. https://doi.org/10.1136/adc.2009.175943

Bachem, R., Levin, Y., Zhou, X., Zerach, G., & Solomon, Z. (2018). The role of parental posttraumatic stress, marital adjustment, and dyadic self-disclosure in intergenerational transmission of trauma: A family system approach. *Journal of Marital and Family Therapy*, *44*(3), 543–555. https://doi.org/10.1111/jmft.12266

Baddeley, A. (2012). Working memory: Theories, models, and controversies. *Annual Review of Psychology*, *63*(1), 1–29. https://doi.org/10.1146/annurev-psych-120710-100422

Bae, H., Kim, D., & Park, Y. C. (2008). Eye movement desensitization and reprocessing for adolescent depression. *Psychiatry Investigation*, *5*(1), 60–65. https://doi.org/10.4306/pi.2008.5.1.60

Baio, J., Wiggins, L., Christensen, D. L., Maenner, M. J., Daniels, J., Warren, Z., Kurzius-Spencer, M., Zahorodny, W., Robinson Rosenberg, C., White, T., Durkin, M. S., Imm, P., Nikolaou, L., Yeargin-Allsopp, M., Lee, L-C., Harrington, R., Lopez, M., Fitzgerald, R. T., Hewitt, A., … Dowling, N. F. (2018). Prevalence of autism spectrum disorder among children aged 8 years—Autism and developmental disabilities monitoring network. *Morbidity and Mortality Weekly Report. Surveillance Summaries*, *67*(6), 1–23. https://doi.org/10.15585/mmwr.ss6706a

Bakermans-Kranenburg, M. J., Van Ijzendoorn, M. H., & Juffer, F. (2003). Less is more: Meta-analyses of sensitivity and attachment interventions in early childhood. *Psychological Bulletin*, *129*(2), 195–215. https://doi.org/10.1037/0033-2909.129.2.195

Balldin, S., Fisher, P. A., & Wirtberg, I. (2018). Video feedback intervention with children: A systematic review. *Research on Social Work Practice*, *28*(6), 682–695. https://doi.org/10.1177/1049731516671809

Banoğlu, K., & Korkmazlar, U. (2022). Efficacy of the Eye Movement Desensitization and Reprocessing Group Protocol with children in reducing posttraumatic stress disorder in refugee children. *European Journal of Trauma and Dissociation*, *6*, 100241. https://doi.org/10.1016/j.ejtd.2021.100241

Bardin, A., Comet, J., & Porten, D. (2007). Integrating EMDR and family therapy: Treating the traumatized child. In F. Shapiro, F. W. Kaslow, & L. Maxfield (Eds.). *Handbook of EMDR and family therapy processes* (pp. 325–343). John Wiley & Sons.

Barkley, R. A. (2012). *Executive functions: What they are, how they work, and why they evolved*. Guilford Press.

Barnicot, K., Katsakou, C., Bhatti, N., Savill, M., Fearns, N., & Priebe, S. (2012). Factors predicting the outcome of psychotherapy for borderline personality disorder: A systematic review. *Clinical Psychology Review*, *32*(5), 400–412. https://doi.org/10.1016/j.cpr.2012.04.004

Barol, B. I., & Seubert, A. (2010). Stepping stones: EMDR treatment of individuals with intellectual and developmental disabilities and challenging behavior. *Journal of EMDR Practice and Research*, *4*(4), 156–169. https://doi.org/10.1891/1933-3196.4.4.156

Barron, I. G., Bourgaize, C., Lempertz, D., Swinden, C., & Darker-Smith, S. (2019). Eye movement desensitization reprocessing for children and adolescents with posttraumatic stress disorder: A systematic narrative review. *Journal of EMDR Practice and Research*, *13*(4), 270–283. https://doi.org/10.1891/1933-3196.13.4.270

Barrouillet, P. (2015). Theories of cognitive development: From Piaget to today. *Developmental Review*, *38*, 1–12. https://doi.org/10.1016/j.dr.2015.07.004

Barrowcliff, A. L., Gray, N. S., Freeman, T. C., & MacCulloch, M. J. (2004). Eye-movements reduce the vividness, emotional valence and electrodermal arousal associated with negative autobiographical memories. *Journal of Forensic Psychiatry and Psychology*, *15*(2), 325–345. https://doi.org/10.1080/14789940410001673042

Barrowcliff, A. L., Gray, N. S., MacCulloch, S., Freeman, T. C., & MacCulloch, M. J. (2003). Horizontal rhythmical eye movements consistently diminish the arousal provoked by auditory stimuli. *British Journal of Clinical Psychology*, *42*(3), 289–302. https://doi.org/10.1348/01446650360703393

Barth, R. P., Zeinstra, L. T., Lee, B. R., & Harder, A. T. (2024). Shared family care: Out-of-home care programs for serving parents and children together. *Residential Treatment for Children and Youth*, *41*(1), 24–46. https://doi.org/10.1080/0886571x.2023.2202889

Bastien, R. J. B., Jongsma, H. E., Kabadayi, M., & Billings, J. (2020). The effectiveness of psychological interventions for post-traumatic stress disorder in children, adolescents and young adults: A systematic review and meta-analysis. *Psychological Medicine*, *50*(10), 1598–1612. https://doi.org/10.1017/S0033291720002007

Beaudry, G., Yu, R., Långström, N., & Fazel, S. (2020). Mental disorders among adolescents in juvenile detention and correctional facilities: An updated systematic review and metaregression analysis. *Journal of the American Academy of Child and Adolescent Psychiatry*, *60*(1), 46–60. https://doi.org/10.1016/j.jaac.2020.01.015

Beck, A. T., Davis, D. D., & Freeman, A. (Eds.). (2015). *Cognitive therapy of personality disorders* (3rd ed.). Guilford Press.

Beck, J. S. (2020). *Cognitive behavior therapy: Basics and beyond*. Guilford Press.

Becker, S. P., & Kerig, P. K. (2011). Posttraumatic stress symptoms are associated with the frequency and severity of delinquency among detained boys. *Journal of Clinical Child and Adolescent Psychology*, 40(5), 765–771. https://doi.org/10.1080/15374416.2011.597091

Beebe, B., Jaffe, J., Markese, S., Buck, K., Chen, H., Cohen, P., Bahrick, L., Andrews, H., & Feldstein, S. (2010). The origins of 12-month attachment: A microanalysis of 4-month mother-infant interaction. *Attachment and Human Development*, *12*(1–2), 3–141. https://doi.org/10.1080/14616730903338985

Beebe, B., & Lachmann, F. M. (2014). The predictive power of infant-parent interaction for later attachment: Theory, research, and clinical implications. *Psychoanalytic Inquiry*, *34*(5), 422–439.

Beebe, B., Cohen, P., Sossin, K. M., & Markese, S. (Eds.). (2012). *Mothers, infants and young children of September 11, 2001: A primary prevention project*. Routledge.

Beer, R. (2018). Efficacy of EMDR therapy for children with PTSD: A review of the literature. *Journal of EMDR Practice and Research*, *12*(4), 177–195. https://doi.org/10.1891/1933-3196.12.4.177

Beer, R. (2019). Protocol for EMDR therapy in the treatment of eating disorders. In M. Luber (Ed.), *Eye Movement Desensitization and Reprocessing (EMDR) scripted protocols and summary sheets: Eating disorders, chronic pain, and maladaptive self-care behaviors* (pp. 11–64). Springer.

Beer, R. (2024). EMDR-ED protocol: A transdiagnostic protocol for treating eating disorders in adolescents or adults with EMDR. In A. Seubert & P. Virdi (Eds.), *Trauma informed approaches to eating disorders* (pp. 184–199). Springer.

Beer, R., & De Roos, C. (2017a). De impact van trauma. In R. Beer & C. De Roos (Eds.), *Handboek EMDR bij kinderen en jongeren [Handbook of EMDR for children and young people]* (pp. 32–51). LannooCampus.

Beer, R., & De Roos, C. (2017b). *Handboek EMDR bij kinderen en jongeren*. LannooCampus.

Beer, R., Schubert, S., & De Roos, C. (2024). EMDR with children and adolescents: context, empirical evidence, and challenges. In D. Farrell, S. J. Schubert, & M. D. Kiernan (Eds.), *The Oxford handbook of EMDR therapy*. Oxford University Press. https://doi.org/10.1093/oxfordhb/9780192898357.013.20

Beer, R., Verlinden, E., & Lindauer, R. (2021). Protocol voor classificatie, screening en diagnostiek van kinderen en adolescenten met trauma en stressorgerelateerde stoornissen. https://ntvp.nl/wp-content/uploads/diagnostieprotocol-versie-2020-.pdf

Berg, K. C., & Wonderlich, S. A. (2013). Emerging psychological treatments in the field of eating disorders. *Current Psychiatry Reports*, *15*(11), 407. https://doi.org/10.1007/s11920-013-0407-y

Bernhard, A., Martinelli, A., Ackermann, K., Saure, D., & Freitag, C. M. (2018). Association of trauma, posttraumatic stress disorder and conduct disorder: A systematic review and meta-analysis. *Neuroscience and Biobehavioral Reviews*, *91*, 153–169. https://doi.org/10.1016/j.neubiorev.2016.12.019

Bigelow, A. E., MacLean, K., Proctor, J., Myatt, T., Gillis, R., & Power, M. (2018). Maternal sensitivity throughout infancy: Continuity and relation to attachment security. *Infant Behavior and Development*, *50*, 324–330. https://doi.org/10.1016/j.infbeh.2018.02.002

Bishop, K. (2013). Culturally affirmative adaptations to trauma treatment with deaf children in a residential setting. In N. S. Glickman (Ed.), *Deaf mental health care* (pp. 268–297). Routledge Taylor & Francis Group.

Bisson, J. I., Berliner, L., Cloitre, M., Forbes, D., Jensen, T. K., Lewis, C., Monson, C. M., Olff, M., Pilling, S., Riggs, D. S., Roberts, N. P., & Shapiro, F. (2019). The international society for traumatic stress studies new guidelines for the prevention and treatment of posttraumatic stress disorder: Methodology and development process. *Journal of Traumatic Stress*, *32*(4), 475–483. https://doi.org/10.1002/jts.22421

Blaustein, M. E., & Kinniburgh, K. M. (2015). *Het behandelen van trauma bij kinderen en jongeren. Hoe veerkracht door hechting, zelfregulatie en competenties versterkt kan worden*. SWP.

Blaustein, M. E., & Kinniburgh, K. M. (2018). *Treating traumatic stress in children and adolescents: How to foster resilience through attachment, self-regulation, and competency*. Guilford Press.

Bodden, D. H. M., & Deković, M. (2016). Multiproblem families referred to youth mental health: What's in a name? *Family Process*, *55*(1), 31–47. https://doi.org/10.1111/famp.12144

Boerma, T., Selten, I., & Wijnen, F. N. K. (2023). Aandacht voor taal; Afwijkende taalontwikkeling en psychiatrische symptomen bij kinderen [Attention for language; atypical language development and psychiatric symptoms in children]. *Tijdschrift voor Psychiatrie*, *65*(3), 171–174.

Boeschoten, M. A., Bakker, A., Jongedijk, R. A., Van Minnen, A., Elzinga, B. M., Rademaker, A. R., & Olff, M. (2014). *Clinician-administered PTSD scale for DSM-5 – Nederlandstalige versie [Dutch version]*. Arq Psychotrauma Expert Groep.

Bonta, J., & Andrews, D. A. (2007). Risk-need-responsivity model for offender assessment and rehabilitation. *Rehabilitation*, *6*(1), 1–22.

Borduin, C. M., & Henggeler, S. W. (1990). A multisystemic approach to the treatment of serious delinquent behavior. In R. J. McMahon & R. D. Peters (Eds.), *Behavior disorders of adolescence: Research, intervention, and policy in clinical and school settings* (pp. 63–80). Springer US.

Bosquet Enlow, M., Egeland, B., Carlson, E., Blood, E., & Wright, R. J. (2014). Mother-infant attachment and the intergenerational transmission of posttraumatic stress disorder. *Development and Psychopathology*, *26*(1), 41–65. https://doi.org/10.1017/S0954579413000515

Bowlby, J. (1969). *Attachment and loss: Volume 1. Attachment*. Basic Books.

Bowman, J., Mogensen, L., Marsland, E., & Lannin, N. (2015). The development, content validity and inter-rater reliability of the SMART-Goal Evaluation Method: A standardised method for evaluating clinical goals. *Australian Occupational Therapy Journal*, *62*(6), 420–427. https://doi.org/10.1111/1440-1630.12218

Boyer, B., Geurts, H., Prins, P., Kuin, M., & van der Oord, S. (2013). Two novel CBTs for adolescents with ADHD: The value of planning skills. *European Adolescent and Child Psychiatry*, *24*(9), 1075–1090. https://doi.org/10.1007/s00787-014-0661-5

Boyer, S. M., Caplan, J. E., & Edwards, L. K. (2022). Trauma-related dissociation and the dissociative disorders: Neglected symptoms with severe public health consequences. *Delaware Journal of Public Health*, *8*(2), 78–84. https://doi.org/10.32481/djph.2022.05.010

Brand, B., McNary, S., Myrick, A., Classen, C., Lanius, R., Loewenstein, R., Pain, C., & Putnam, F. (2012). A longitudinal naturalistic study of patients with dissociative disorders treated by community clinicians. *Psychological Trauma Theory Research Practice and Policy*, *5*(4), 301–308. https://doi.org/10.1037/a0027654

Braquehais, M. D., Oquendo, M. A., Baca-García, E., & Sher, L. (2010). Is impulsivity a link between childhood abuse and suicide? *Comprehensive Psychiatry*, *51*(2), 121–129. https://doi.org/10.1016/j.comppsych.2009.05.003

Brenner, J., Pan, Z., Mazefsky, C., Smith, K., & Gabriels, R. (2018). Behavioral symptoms of reported abuse in children and adolescents with autism spectrum disorder in inpatient settings. *Journal of Autism and Developmental Disorders*, *48*(11), 3727–3735. https://doi.org/10.1007/s10803-017-3183-4

Brennstuhl, M. J., Bassan, F., Fayard, A. M., Fisselbrand, M., Guth, A., Hassler, M., Lebourg, K., Pavisse, R., Peter, L., Thiriet, A., Tarquino, P., Rydberg, J. A., & Tarquinio, C. (2019). Immediate treatment following the November 13 attacks: Use of an EMDR emergency protocol. *European Journal of Trauma and Dissociation*, *3*(1), 17–21. https://doi.org/10.1016/j.ejtd.2018.09.004

Brewer, J., De Wit, H., Cortese, A., Denys, D., Hanlon, C. A., Holmes, E. A., Paulus, M. P., Schwarzbach, J., & Tse, P. (2020). Interventions and implications. In P. W. Kalivas & M. P. Paulus (Eds.), *Intrusive thinking: From molecules to free will* (pp. 347–378). MIT Press.

Brewin, C. R. (2014). Episodic memory, perceptual memory, and their interaction: Foundations for a theory of posttraumatic stress disorder. *Psychological Bulletin, 140*, 6997. doi: 10.1037/a0033722

Brewin, C. R. (2015). Re-experiencing traumatic events in PTSD: New avenues in research on intrusive memories and flashbacks. *European Journal of Psychotraumatology, 6*(1), 27180. https://doi.org/10.3402/ejpt.v6.27180

Brewin, C. R., Cloitre, M., Hyland, P., Shevlin, M., Maercker, A., Bryant, R. A., Humayun, A., Jones, L. M., Kagee, A., Rousseau, C., Somasundaram, D., Suzuki, Y., Wessely, S., Van Ommeren, M., & Reed, G. M. (2017). A review of current evidence regarding the ICD-11 proposals for diagnosing PTSD and complex PTSD. *Clinical Psychology Review, 58*, 1–15. https://doi.org/10.1016/j.cpr.2017.09.001

Brewin, C. R., Gregory, J. D., Lipton, M., & Burgess, N. (2010). Intrusive images in psychological disorders: Characteristics, neural mechanisms, and treatment implications. *Psychological Review, 117*(1), 210–232. https://doi.org/10.1037/a0018113

Broekhof, E., Bos, M. G. N., & Rieffe, C. (2021). The roles of shame and guilt in the development of aggression in adolescents with and without hearing loss. *Research on Child and Adolescent Psychopathology, 49*(7), 891–904. https://doi.org/10.1007/s10802-021-00769-1

Brom, D., Pat-Horenczyk, R., & Ford, J. D. (2009). *Treating traumatized children. Risk, resilience and recovery*. Routledge.

Bronner, M. B. (2009). *Traumatic: The psychological impact of paediatric care treatment* [Doctoral Dissertation, Vrije Universiteit Amsterdam]. Gildeprint.

Bronner, M. B., Beer, R., Van Zelm Van Eldik, M., Grootenhuis, M. A., & Last, B. F. (2009). Reducing acute stress in 16 year old using trauma-focused cognitive behaviour therapy and eye movement and desensitization. *Developmental Rehabilitation, 12*(3), 170–174.

Bronner, M. B., Knoester, H., Bos, A. P., Grootenhuis, M. A., & Last, B. F. (2006). *Long term psychological effects in families of survivors of pediatric intensive care* [Abstract poster session]. The European Academy of Paediatrics—EAP (Europaediatrics).

Brown, R. C., Witt, A., Fegert, J. M., Keller, F., Rassenhofer, M., & Plener, P. L. (2017). Psychosocial interventions for children and adolescents after man-made and natural disasters: A meta-analysis and systematic review. *Psychological Medicine, 47*(11), 1893–1905. https://doi.org/10.1017/S0033291717000496

Brundson, V. E., & Happé, F. (2014). Exploring the 'fractionation' of autism at the cognitive level. *Autism, 18*(1), 17–30. https://doi.org/10.1177/1362361313499456

Bryant, R. A., Creamer, M., O'Donnell, M., Silove, D., & McFarlane, A. C. (2012). The capacity of acute stress disorder to predict posttraumatic psychiatric disorders. *Journal of Psychiatric Research, 46*(2), 168–173. https://doi.org/10.1016/j.jpsychires.2011.10.007

Bryant, R. A., Edwards, B., Creamer, M., O'Donnell, M., Forbes, D., Felmingham, K. L., Silove, D., Steel, Z., Nickerson, A., McFarlane, A. C., Van Hooff, M., & Hadzi-Pavlovic, D. (2018). The effect of post-traumatic stress disorder on refugees' parenting and their children's mental health: A cohort study. *The Lancet Public Health, 3*(5), e249–e258. https://doi.org/10.1016/S2468-2667(18)30051-3

Buitelaar, N. J. L., & Ferdinand, R. F. (2013). ADHD undetected in criminal adults. *Journal of Attention Disorders, 20*(3), 270–278. https://doi.org/10.1177/1087054712466916

Bunn, M., Zolman, N., Smith, C. P., Khanna, D., Hanneke, R., Betancourt, T. S., & Weine, S. (2022). Family-based mental health interventions for refugees across the migration continuum: A systematic review. *SSM-Mental Health, 2*, 100153. https://doi.org/10.1016/j.ssmmh.2022.100153

Bürgin, D., Anagnostopoulos, D., Vitiello, B., Sukale, T., Schmid, M., & Fegert, J. M. (2022). Impact of war and forced displacement on children's mental health: Multilevel, needs-oriented, and trauma-informed approaches. *European Child and Adolescent Psychiatry, 31*(6), 845–853. https://doi.org/10.1007/s00787-022-01974-z

Carlson, E. B., Palmieri, P. A., Field, N. P., Dalenberg, C. J., Macia, K. S., & Spain, D. A. (2016). Contributions of risk and protective factors to prediction of psychological symptoms after traumatic experiences. *Comprehensive Psychiatry, 69*, 106–115. https://doi.10.1016/j.comppsych.2016.04.022

Carrière, R. C. (2014). Scaling up what works: Using EMDR to help confront the world's burden of traumatic stress. *Journal of EMDR Practice and Research, 8*(4), 187–195. https://doi.org/10.1891/1933-3196.8.4.187

Centers for Disease Control and Prevention. (2023). https://www.cdc.gov/child-abuse-neglect/about/index.html

Chacko, A., Allan, C. C., Moody, S. S., Crawford, T. P., Nadler, C., & Chimiklis, A. (2017). Behavioral interventions. In S. Goldstein & M. DeVries (Eds.), *Handbook of DSM-5 disorders in children and adolescents* (pp. 617–636). Springer International Publishing.

Chamberlin, D. E. (2019). The network balance model of trauma and resolution—level I: Large-scale neural networks. *Journal of EMDR Practice and Research, 13*(2), 124–142. https://doi.org/10.1891/1933-3196.13.2.124

Chemtob, C. M., Nakashima, J., & Carlson, J. G. (2002). Brief treatment for elementary school children with disaster-related posttraumatic stress disorder: A field study. *Journal of Clinical Psychology, 58*(1), 99–112. https://doi.org/10.1002/jclp.1131

Chmitorz, A., Kunzler, A., Helmreich, I., Tüscher, O., Kalisch, R., Kubiak, T., Wessa, M., & Lieb, K. (2018). Intervention studies to foster resilience: A systematic review and proposal for a resilience framework in future intervention studies. *Clinical Psychology Review, 59*, 78–100. https://doi.org/10.1016/j.cpr.2017.11.002

Civilotti, C., Cussino, M., Callerame, C., Fernandez, I., & Zaccagnino, M. (2019). Changing the adult state of mind with respect to attachment: An exploratory study of the role of EMDR psychotherapy. *Journal of EMDR Practice and Research, 13*(3), 176–186. https://doi.org/10.1891/1933-3196.13.3.176

Clegg, J., Hollis, C., Mawhood, L., & Rutter, M. (2005). Developmental language disorders—A follow-up in later adult life: Cognitive, language and psychosocial outcomes. *Journal of Child Psychology and Psychiatry, 46*(2), 128–149. https://doi.org/10.1111/j.1469-7610.2004.00342.x

Cloitre, M. (2021). Complex PTSD: assessment and treatment. *European Journal of Psychotraumatology, 12*(sup1). https://doi.org/10.1080/20008198.2020.1866423

Cloitre, M., Courtois, C. A., Ford, J. D., Green, B. L., Alexander, P., Briere, J., Herman, J. L., Lanius, R., Stolbach, B. C., Spinazzola, J., Van der Kolk, B. A., & Van der Hart, O. (2012). *The ISTSS expert consensus treatment guidelines for complex PTSD in adults*.

Cloitre, M., & Schmidt, J. A. (2022). STAIR narrative therapy. In U. Schnyuder & M. Cloitre (Eds.), *Evidence based treatments for trauma-related psychological disorders: A practical guide for clinicians* (pp. 307–328). Springer International Publishing.

Cohen, J. A., Bukstein, O., Walter, H., Benson, S. R., Chrisman, A., Farchione, T. R., Hamilton, J., Keable, H., Kinlan, J., Schoettle, U., Siegel, M., Stock, S., Medicus, J., & AACAP Work Group On Quality Issues. (2010). Practice parameter for the assessment and treatment of children and adolescents with posttraumatic stress disorder. *Journal of the American Academy of Child and Adolescent Psychiatry, 49*(4), 414–430. http://www.ncbi.nlm.nih.gov/pubmed/20410735

Cohen, J. A., Deblinger, E., & Mannarino, A. P. (2018). Trauma-focused cognitive behavioural therapy for children and families. *Psychotherapy Research, 28*(1), 47–57. https://doi.org/10.1080/10503307.2016.1208375

Cohen, J. A., Mannarino A. P., & Deblinger, E. (Eds.). (2012). *Trauma focused CBT for children and adolescents: Treatment applications*. Guilford Press.

Cohen, J. A., Mannarino, A. P., & Deblinger, E. (2016). *Treating trauma and traumatic grief in children and adolescents*. Guilford Press.

Cohen, J. A., Mannarino, A. P., & Deblinger, E. (2017). *Treating trauma and traumatic grief in children and adolescents*. Guilford Press.

Conijn, T., De Roos, C., Vreugdenhil, H. J. I., Van Dijk-Lokkart, E. M., Wijburg, F. A., & Haverman, L. (2022). Effectiveness of time-limited eye movement desensitization reprocessing therapy for parents of children with a rare life-limiting illness: A randomized clinical trial. *Orphanet Journal of Rare Diseases, 17*(1), 328. https://doi.org/10.1186/s13023-022-02500-9

Cook, A., Blaustein, M., Spinazzola, J., & Van der Kolk, B. (2003). *Complex trauma in children and adolescents*. White paper from the National Child Traumatic Stress Network. Complex Trauma Task Force.

Cooper, J. O., Heron, T. E., & Heward, W. L. (2019). *Applied behaviour analysis* (3rd ed.). Pearson.

Copeland, W. E., Keeler M. A., Angold A., & Costello E. J. (2007). Traumatic events and posttraumatic stress in childhood. *Archives of General Psychiatry, 64*(5), 577–584. https://doi.org/10.1001/archpsyc.64.5.577

Corrigan, J. P., Fitzpatrick, M., Hanna, D., & Dyer, K. F. (2020). Evaluating the effectiveness of phase-oriented treatment models for PTSD: A meta-analysis. *Traumatology, 26*(4), 447. https://doi.org/10.1037/trm0000261

Couturier, J., Isserlin, L., Norris, M., Spettigue, W., Brouwers, M., Kimber, M., McVey, G., Webb, C., Findlay, S., Bhatnagar, N., Snelgrove, N., Ritsma, A., Preskow, W., Miller, C., Coelho, J., Boachie, A., Steinegger, C., Loewen, R., Loewen, R., … Pilon, D. (2020). Canadian practice guidelines for the treatment of children and adolescents with eating disorders. *Journal of Eating Disorders, 8*(1), 1–80. https://doi.org/10.1186/s40337-020-0277-8

Creswell, C., Waite, P., & Cooper, P. J. (2014). Assessment and management of anxiety disorders in children and adolescents. *Archives of Disease in Childhood, 99*(7), 674–678. https://doi.org/10.1136/archdischild-2013-303768

Croen, L., Grether, J., Yoshida, C. K., Odouli, R., & Hendrick, V. (2005). Antidepressant use during pregnancy and childhood autism spectrum disorders. *Archives of General Psychiatry, 68*(11), 104–112. https://doi.org/10.1001/archgenpsychiatry.2011.73

Cronin, E., Brand, B. L., & Mattanah, J. F. (2014). The impact of the therapeutic alliance on treatment outcome in patients with dissociative disorders. *European Journal of Psychotraumatology, 5*(1), 22676. https://doi.org/10.3402/ejpt.v5.22676

Cuijpers, P., Noma, H., Karyotaki, E., Vinkers, C. H., Cipriani, A., & Furukawa, T. A. (2020). A network meta-analysis of the effects of psychotherapies, pharmacotherapies and their combination in the treatment of adult depression. *World Psychiatry, 19*(1), 92–107. https://doi.org/10.1002/wps.20701

Cuijpers, P., Reijnders, M., & Huibers, M. J. (2019). The role of common factors in psychotherapy outcomes. *Annual Review of Clinical Psychology, 15*, 207–231. https://doi.org/10.1146/annurev-clinpsy-050718-095424

Cyr, C., Euser, E. M., Bakermans-Kranenburg, M. J., & Van Ijzendoorn, M. H. (2010). Attachment security and disorganization in maltreating and high-risk families: A series of meta-analyses. *Development and Psychopathology, 22*(1), 87–108. https://doi.org/10.1017/S0954579409990289

D'Andrea, W., Ford, J., Stolbach, B., Spinazzola, J., & Van der Kolk, B. A. (2012). Understanding interpersonal trauma in children: Why we need a developmentally appropriate trauma diagnosis. *American Journal of Orthopsychiatry, 82*(2), 187–200. https://doi.org/10.1111/j.1939-0025.2012.01154.x

Danese, A., Martsenkovskyi, D., Remberk, B., Khalil, M. Y., Diggins, E., Keiller, E., Masood, S., Awah, I., Barbui, C., Beer, R., Calam, R., Gagliato, M., Jensen, T. K., Kostova, Z., Leckman, J. F., Lewis, S. J., Lorberg, B., Myshakivska, O., Pfeiffer, E., … Weisz, J. R. (2024). Scoping review: Digital mental health interventions for children and adolescents affected by war. *Journal of the American Academy of Child and Adolescent Psychiatry, S0890–8567(24)00243-0*. https://doi.org/10.1016/j.jaac.2024.02.017

Danese, A., McLaughlin, K. A., Samara, M., & Stover, C. S. (2020). Psychopathology in children exposed to trauma: Detection and intervention needed to reduce downstream burden. *BMJ, 371*, m3073. https://doi.org/10.1136/bmj.m3073

Danieli, Y. (Ed.). (1998). *International handbook of multigenerational legacies of trauma*. Plenum Press.

Dashorst, P., Huntjens, R. J., Mooren, T. M., Kleber, R. J., Zu Eulenburg, C., & De Jong, P. J. (2020). Intrusions related to indirectly experienced events in clinical offspring of World War Two survivors. *Journal of Anxiety Disorders, 71*, 102209. https://doi.org/10.1016/j.janxdis.2020.102209

Dashorst, P., Mooren, T. M., Kleber, R. J., De Jong, P. J., & Huntjens, R. J. (2019). Intergenerational consequences of the Holocaust on offspring mental health: A systematic review of associated factors and mechanisms. *European Journal of Psychotraumatology, 10*(1), 1654065. https://doi.org/10.1080/20008198.2019.1654065

Datta, N., Matheson, B. E., Citron, K., Van Wye, E. M., & Lock, J. D. (2023). Evidence based update on psychosocial treatments for eating disorders in children and adolescents. *Journal of Clinical Child and Adolescent Psychology, 52*(2), 159–170. https://doi.org/10.1080/15374416.2022.2109650

Davis, R. S., Meiser-Stedman, R., Afzal, N., Devaney, J., Halligan, S. L., Lofthouse, K., Smith, P., Stallard, P., Ye, S., & Hiller, R. M. (2023). Systematic review and meta-analysis: Group-based interventions for treating posttraumatic stress symptoms in children and adolescents. *Journal of the American Academy of Child and Adolescent Psychiatry, 62*(11), 1217–1232. https://doi.org/10.1016/j.jaac.2023.02.013

De Bellis, M. D., & Van Dillen, T. (2005). Childhood post-traumatic stress disorder: An overview. *Child and Adolescent Psychiatric Clinics of North America, 14*(4), 745–772. https://doi.org/10.1016/j.chc.2005.05.006

De Bildt, A., Servatius-Oosterling, I., & De Jonge, M. (2021). *Autisme bij kinderen. Signalering, diagnostiek en behandeling.* Bohn Stafleu van Loghum.

De Bruin, E., De Nijs, P., Verheij, F., Hartman, C., & Ferdinand, R. (2007). Multiple complex developmental disorder delineated from PDD-NOS. *Journal of Autism and Developmental Disorders, 37*(6), 1181–1191. https://doi.org/10.1007/s10803-006-0261-4

De Bruin, R., Koudstaal, A., & Muller, N. (2013). *Dialectische gedragstherapie voor jongeren met een borderlinestoornis en andere emotieregulatiestoornissen.* Bohn Stafleu van Loghum.

De Graaff, A. M., Cuijpers, P., Twisk, J. W., Kieft, B., Hunaidy, S., Elsawy, M., Gorgis, N., Bouman, T. K., Lommen, M. J. J., Acarturk, C., Bryant, R., Burchert, S., Dawson, K. S., Fuhr, D. C., Hansen, P., Jordans, M., Knaevelsrud, C., McDaid, D., Morina, N., Moergeli, H., … Sijbrandij, M. (2023). Peer-provided psychological intervention for Syrian refugees: Results of a randomised controlled trial on the effectiveness of Problem Management Plus. *BMJ Mental Health, 26*(1), e300637. https://doi.org/10.1136/bmjment-2022-300637

De Haene, L., & Rousseau, C. (2020). *Working with refugee families: Trauma and exile in family relationships.* Cambridge University Press.

De Jongh, A., Bicanic, I., Matthijssen, S., Amann, B. L., Hofmann, A., Farrell, D., Lee, C. W., & Maxfield, L. (2019). The status of EMDR therapy involving the treatment of complex posttraumatic stress disorder. *Journal of EMDR Practice and Research, 13*(4), 284–290. https://doi.org/10.1891/1933-3196.13.4.284

De Jongh, A., Ernst, R., Marques, L., & Hornsveld, H. (2013). The impact of eye movements and tones on disturbing memories involving PTSD and other mental disorders. *Journal of Behavior Therapy and Experimental Psychiatry, 44*(4), 477–483. https://doi.org/10.1016/j.jbtep.2013.07.002

De Jongh, A., & Hafkemeijer, L. C. S. (2024). Trauma-focused treatment of a client with complex PTSD and comorbid pathology using EMDR therapy. *Journal of Clinical Psychology, 80*(4), 824–835. https://doi.org/10.1002/jclp.23521

De Jongh, A., De Roos, C., & El-Leithy, S. (2024a). State of the science: Eye movement desensitization and reprocessing (EMDR) therapy. *Journal of Traumatic Stress, 37*(2), 205–216. https://doi.org/10.1002/jts.23012

De Jongh, A., Hafkemeijer, L., Hofman, S., Slotema, K., & Hornsveld, H. (2024b). The AIP model as a theoretical framework for the treatment of personality disorders with EMDR therapy. *Frontiers in Psychiatry*, *15*, 1331876. https://doi.org/10.3389/fpsyt.2024.1331876

De Jongh, A., Resick, P. A., Zoellner, L. A., Van Minnen, A., Lee, C. W., Monson, C. M., Foa, E. B., Wheeler, K., Ten Broeke, E., Feeny, N., Rauch, S. A. M., Chard, K. M., Mueser, K. T., Sloan, D. M., Van der Gaag, M., Rothbaum, B. O., Neuner, F., De Roos, C., Hehenkamp, L. M. J., Rosner, R., & Bicanic, I. A. E. (2016). Critical analysis of the current treatment guidelines for complex PTSD in adults. *Depression and Anxiety*, *33*(5), 359–369. https://doi.org/10.1002/da.22469

De Jongh, A., Ten Broeke, E., & Meijer, S. (2010). Two Method Questioning Approach: A case conceptualization model in the context of EMDR. *Journal of EMDR Practice and Research*, *4*(1), 12–21. https://doi.org/10.1891/1933-3196.4.1.12

Dekkers, T., Popma, A., Agelink van Rentergem, J., Bexkens, A., & Huizinga, H. M. (2016). Risky decision making in Attention-Deficit/Hyperactivity Disorder: A meta-regression analysis. *Clinical Psychological Review*, *45*, 1–16.

De Palma, M., Rooney, R., Izett, E., Mancini, V., & Kane, R. (2023). The relationship between parental mental health, reflective functioning, co-parenting and social emotional development in 0–3-year-old children. *Frontiers in Psychology*, *14*, 1054723. https://doi.org/10.3389/fpsyg.2023.1054723

De Roos, C. J. A. M. (2021). *Time limited trauma-focused treatment for children and adolescents* [Doctoral dissertation, University of Amsterdam].

De Roos, C., & Beer, R. (2017). EMDR-verhalenmethode: Traumaverwerking bij preverbaal trauma. In R. Beer & C. de Roos (Eds.), *Handboek EMDR bij kinderen en jongeren* (pp. 125–140). LannooCampus.

De Roos, C., & De Jongh, A. (2008). EMDR treatment of children and adolescents with a choking phobia. *Journal of EMDR Practice and Research*, *2*(3), 201–211. https://doi.org/10.1891/1933-3196.2.3.201

De Roos, C., Greenwald, R., Den Hollander-Gijsman, M. Noorthoorn, E., Van Buuren, S., & De Jongh, A. (2011). A randomised comparison of cognitive behavioural treatment (CBT) and eye movement desensitization and reprocessing (EMDR) in disaster exposed children. *European Journal of Psychotraumatology*, *2*, 5694. https://doi.org/10.3402/ejpt.v2i0.5694

De Roos, C., Offermans, J., Bouwmeester, S., Lindauer, R., & Scheper, F. (2025). Preliminary efficacy of eye Movement desensitization and reprocessing for children aged 1.5 to 8 years with PTSD: A multiple baseline experimental design (N=19). *European Journal of Psychotraumatology*, *16*(1), 2447654.

De Roos, C., Van der Oord, S., Zijlstra, B., Lucassen, S., Perrin, S., Emmelkamp, P., & De Jongh, A. (2017). Comparison of eye movement desensitization and reprocessing therapy, cognitive behavioral writing therapy, and wait-list in pediatric posttraumatic stress disorder following single-incident trauma: A multicenter randomized clinical trial. *The Journal of Child Psychology and Psychiatry*, *58*(11), 1219–1228. https://doi.org/10.1111/jcpp.12768

De Voogd, L. D., Kanen, J. W., Neville, D. A., Roelofs, K., Fernández, G., & Hermans, E. J. (2018). Eye-movement intervention enhances extinction via amygdala deactivation. *Journal of Neuroscience*, *38*(40), 8694–8706. https://doi.org/10.1523/JNEUROSCI.0703-18.2018

De Voogd, L. D., & Phelps, E. A. (2020). A cognitively demanding working-memory intervention enhances extinction. *Scientific Reports*, *10*(1), 13002. https://doi.org/10.1038/s41598-020-69587-7

De Wolff, M., Dekker-van der Sande, F., Sterkenburg, P., & Thoomes-Vreugdenhil, A. (2020). *Richtlijn Problematische gehechtheid voor jeugdhulp en jeugdbescherming*. TNO. https://richtlijnenjeugdhulp.nl

De Wolff, M. S., Van Bakel, H. J. A., Juffer, F., Dekker-van der Sande, F., Sterkenburg, P. S., & Thoomes-Vreugdenhil, A. (2015). *Richtlijn problematische gehechtheid voor de jeugdhulp en jeugdbescherming*. TNO.

Deci, E. L., & Ryan, R. M. (Eds.). (2002). *Handbook of self-determination research*. University Rochester Press.

Delage, M. (2008). *La résilience familiale*. Odile Jacob.

Diehle, J., Opmeer, B. C., Boer, F., Mannarino, A. P., & Lindauer, R. J. (2014). Trauma-focused cognitive-behavioral therapy or eye movement desensitization and reprocessing: What works in children with posttraumatic stress symptoms? A randomized controlled trial. *European Child and Adolescent Psychiatry*, *24*(2), 227–236. http://dx.doi.org/10.1007/s00787-014-0572-5

Dimitrova, L., Fernando V., Vissia, E. M., Nijenhuis, E. R. S., Draijer, N., & Reinders, A. T. S. (2020). Sleep, trauma, fantasy and cognition in dissociative identity disorder, post-traumatic stress disorder and healthy controls: A replication and extension study. *European Journal of Psychotraumatology*, *11*(1), 1705599. https://doi.org/10.1080/20008198.2019.1705599

Dimitrova, L. I., Lawrence, A. J., Vissia, E. M., Chalavi, S., Kakouris, A. F., Veltman, D. J., & Reinders, A. (2024). Inter-identity amnesia in dissociative identity disorder resolved: A behavioural and neurobiological study. *Journal of Psychiatric Research*, *174*, 220–229. https://doi.org/10.1016/j.jpsychires.2024.04.026

Dirks, E., Stevens, A., Kok, S., Frijns, J., & Rieffe, C. (2020). Talk with me! Parental linguistic input to toddlers with moderate hearing loss. *Journal of Child Language*, *47*(1), 186–204. https://doi.org/10.1017/S0305000919000667

Dominguez, S. K. (2023). EMDR therapy as a transdiagnostic psychotherapy. In D. Farrell, S. J. Schubert & M. D. Kiernan (Eds.), *The Oxford handbook of EMDR therapy* (online ed.). Oxford Academic. https://doi.org/10.1093/oxfordhb/9780192898357.013.18

Dominguez, S., & Lee, C. W. (2019). Differences in international guidelines regarding EMDR for posttraumatic stress disorder: Why they diverge and suggestions for future research. *Journal of EMDR Practice and Research, 13*(4), 247–260. https://doi.org/10.1891/1933-3196.13.4.247

Doornkate, L. (2008). EMDR bij gezinnen met doven en slechthorenden [EMDR in families with deaf and hearing-impaired people]. *Tijdschrift Kinder en Jeugd Psychotherapie, 35*(2), 45–61. https://www.vkjp.nl/tijdschrift-artikelen/tkjp-2008-2-emdr-bij-gezinnen-met-doven-en-slechthorenden

Dorsey, S., McLaughlin, K. A., Kerns, S. E., Harrison, J. P., Lambert, H. K., Briggs, E. C., & Amaya-Jackson, L. (2017). Evidence base update for psychosocial treatments for children and adolescents exposed to traumatic events. *Journal of Clinical Child and Adolescent Psychology, 46*(3), 303–330. https://doi.org/10.1080/15374416.2016.1220309

Dovis, S., Van der Oord, S., Wiers, R. W., & Prins, P. J. M. (2012). Can motivation normalize working memory and task persistence in children with attention-deficit/hyperactivity disorder? The effects of money and computer-gaming. *Journal of Abnormal Child Psychology, 40*(5), 669–681. https://doi.org/10.1007/s10802-011-9601-8

Draaisma, D. (2015). *Forgetting: Myths, perils, and compensations*. Yale University Press.

Draijer, N., & Nicolai, N. (2020). Transference and countertransference in early childhood traumatisation 'revisited'. *Journal of Psychotherapy, 3*, 1–16.

Dworkin, M. (2005). *EMDR and the relational imperative: The therapeutic relationship in EMDR treatment*. Routledge.

Dyer, K. F., & Corrigan, J. P. (2021). Psychological treatments for complex PTSD: A commentary on the clinical and empirical impasse dividing unimodal and phase-oriented therapy positions. *Psychological Trauma: Theory, Research, Practice, and Policy, 13*(8), 869. https://doi.org/10.1037/tra0001080

Earl, R. K., Peterson, J., Wallace, A. S., Fox, E., Ma, R., Pepper, M., & Haidar, G. (2017). *Trauma and Autism Spectrum Disorder. A reference guide*. Bernier Lab, Center for Human Development and Disability, University of Washington.

Eckers, D. (2010). The method of constant installation of present orientation and safety (CIPOS) in children. In M. Luber (Ed.), *Eye movement desensitization and reprocessing (EMDR) scripted protocols: Special populations* (pp. 51–58). Springer.

Egberts, C. (2015). *Ouders op hun plek. Samenwerken in de driehoek cliënt, ouders en begeleider* [Parents in their place]. Agiel.

Ehlers, A., Hackmann, A., Steil, R., Clohessy, S., Wenninger, K., & Winter, H. (2002). The nature of intrusive memories after trauma: The warning signal hypothesis. *Behaviour Research and Therapy, 40*(9), 995–1002. https://doi.org/10.1016/S0005-7967(01)00077-8

Ehntholt, K. A., Smith, P. A., & Yule, W. (2005). School-based cognitive-behavioural therapy group intervention for refugee children who have experienced war-related trauma. *Clinical Child Psychology and Psychiatry, 10*(2), 235–250. https://doi.org/10.1177/1359104505051214

Ehring, T., Welboren, R., Morina, N., Wicherts, J. M., Freitag, J., & Emmelkamp, P. M. (2014). Meta-analysis of psychological treatments for posttraumatic stress disorder in adult survivors of childhood abuse. *Clinical Psychology Review, 34*(8), 645–657. https://doi.org/10.1016/j.cpr.2014.10.004

Eichengreen, A., Broekhof, E., Tsou, Y-T., & Rieffe, C. (2023). Longitudinal effects of emotion awareness and regulation on mental health symptoms in adolescents with and without hearing loss. *European Child and Adolescent Psychiatry, 32*(4), 705–724. https://doi.org/10.1007/s00787-021-01900-9

Eliëns, M., Konings, M., & Terken, Z. (2020). *Process evaluation video home training in families with children in primary school age children*. Association for Interaction Counselling and Home Treatment (AIT).

Emerson, D. (2015). *Trauma-sensitive yoga in therapy: Bringing the body into treatment*. W. W. Norton.

Engelhard, I. M., Van den Hout, M. A., Janssen, W. C., & Van der Beek, J. (2010). Eye movements reduce vividness and emotionality of 'flashforwards'. *Behaviour Research and Therapy, 48*(5), 442–447. https://doi.org/10.1016/j.brat.2010.01.003

Engelhard, I., Van Uijen, S., & Van den Hout, M. (2010). The impact of taxing working memory on negative and positive memories. *European Journal of Psychotraumatology, 1*(1), 5623. https://doi.org/10.3402/ejpt.v1i0.5623

Eruyar, S., & Vostanis, P. (2020). Feasibility of group ther-a-play with refugee children in Turkey. *Counselling and Psychotherapy Research, 20*(4), 626–637. https://doi.org/10.1002/capr.12354

Eyberg, S. M., Nelson, M. M., & Boggs, S. R. (2008). Evidence-based psychosocial treatments for children and adolescents with disruptive behavior. *Journal of Clinical Child and Adolescent Psychology, 37*(1), 215–237. https://doi.org/10.1080/15374410701820117

Faes, J. (2018). Hoor, ik spreek [Hear, I speak]. *EOS, Psyche & Brein*, 30 October. https://www.eoswetenschap.eu/psyche-brein/hoor-ik-spreek

Fairbank, J. A., & Fairbank, D. W. (2009). Epidemiology of child traumatic stress. *Current Psychiatry Reports*, *11*(4), 289–295. https://doi.org/10.1007/s11920-009-0042-9

Faraone, S. V., Banaschewski, T., Coghill, D., Zheng, Y., Biederman, J., Bellgrove, M. A., Newcorn, J. H., Gignac, M., Al Saud, N. M., Manor, I., Augusto Rohde, L., Yang, L., Cortese, S., Almagor, D., Stein, M. A., Albatti, T. H., Aljoudi, H. F., Alqahtani, M. M. J., Asherson, P., … Wang, Y. (2021). The World Federation of ADHD International Consensus Statement: 208 evidence-based conclusions about the disorder. *Neuroscience and Biobehavorial Reviews*, *128*, 789–818. https://doi.org/10.1016/j.neubiorev.2021.01.022

Farkas, L., Cyr, M., Lebeau, T. M., & Lemay, J. (2010). Effectiveness of MASTR EMDR therapy for traumatized adolescents. *Journal of Child and Adolescent Trauma*, *3*(2), 125–142. https://doi.org/10.1080/19361521003761325

Farrell, Derek, Schubert, Sarah J., & Kiernan, Matthew D. (eds). (2023). *The Oxford handbook of EMDR* (online edn, Oxford Academic). Accessed 2 January 2024. https://doi.org/10.1093/oxfordhb/9780192898357.001.0001

Fazel, M., Reed, R. V., Panter-Brick, C., & Stein, A. (2012). Mental health of displaced and refugee children resettled in high-income countries: risk and protective factors. *Lancet*, *379*(9812), 266–282. https://doi.org/10.1016/S0140-6736(11)60051-2

Felitti, V. J., Anda, R. F., Nordenberg, D., Williamson, D. F., Spitz, A. M., Edwards, V., Koss, M. P., & Marks, J. S. (1998). Relationship of childhood abuse and household dysfunction to many of the leading causes of death in adults: The Adverse Childhood Experiences (ACE) Study. *American Journal of Preventive Medicine*, *14*(4), 245–258. https://doi.org/10.1016/s0749-3797(98)00017-8

Felitti, V. J., Anda, R. F., Nordenberg, D., Williamson, D. F., Spitz, A. M., Edwards, V., & Marks, J. S. (2019). Reprint of: Relationship of childhood abuse and household dysfunction to many of the leading causes of death in adults: the adverse childhood experiences (ACE) study. *American Journal of Preventive Medicine*, *56*(6), 774–786. https://doi.org/10.1016/j.amepre.2019.04.001

Fictorie, V., Jonkman, C., Visser, M., Vandenbosch, M., Steketee, M., & Schuengel, C. (2022). Effectiveness of a high-intensive trauma-focused, family-based therapy for youth exposed to family violence: study protocol for a randomized controlled trial. *Trials*, *23*(1), 46. https://doi.org/10.1186/s13063-021-05981-4

Field, A., & Cottrell, D. (2011). Eye movement desensitization and reprocessing as a therapeutic intervention for traumatized children and adolescents: A systematic review of the evidence for family therapists. *Journal of Family Therapy*, *33*(4), 374–388. https://doi.org/10.3389/fpsyt.2023.1328310

Fleming, J. (2012). The effectiveness of eye movement desensitization and reprocessing in the treatment of traumatized children and youth. *Journal of EMDR Practice and Research*, *6*(1), 16–26. https://doi.org/10.1891/1933-3196.6.1.16

Foa, E. B., Hembree, E. A., & Rothbaum, B. O. (2007). *Prolonged exposure therapy for PTSD: Emotional processing of traumatic experiences: Therapist guide*. Oxford University Press.

Forgash, C., & Knipe, J. (2012). Integrating EMDR and ego state treatment for clients with trauma disorders. *Journal of EMDR Practice and Research*, *6*(3), 120–128. https://doi.org/10.1891/1933-3196.6.3.120

Fraser, G. A. (1991). The dissociative table technique: A strategy for working with ego states in dissociative disorders and ego-state therapy. *Dissociation*, *4*(4), 205–213.

Gerrits, E., Beers, M., Bruinsma, G., & Singer, I. (2017). Handboek Taalontwikkelingsstoornissen *[Handbook of Language Development Disorders]*. Coutinho.

Gersons, B. (2013). Traumaspectrumstoornissen: Van enkelvoudig trauma tot complexe PTSS. In E. Vermetten, R. J. Kleber, & O. Van der Hart (Eds.), *Handboek posttraumatische stressstoornissen* (pp. 65–81). De Tijdstroom.

Gidaya, N. B., Lee, B. K., Burstyn, I., Michael, Y., Newschaffer, C. J., & Mortensen, E. L. (2016). In utero exposure to β-2-adrenergic receptor agonist drugs and risk for autism spectrum disorders. *Pediatrics*, *137*(2), e20151316. https://doi.org/10.1542/peds.2015-1316

Giezen, M. R. (2011). *Speech and sign perception in deaf children with cochlear implants*. LOT.

Gilbert, P. (2005). *Compassion: Conceptualisations, research and use in psychotherapy*. Taylor and Francis.

Gilman, S. R., Iossifov, I., Levy, D., Ronemus, M., Wigler, M., & Vitkup, D., (2011) Rare de novo variants associated with autism implicate a large functional network of genes involved in formation and functioning of synapses. *Neuron*, *70*(5), 898–907. https://doi.org/10.1016/j.neuron.2011.05.021

Gilson, G., & Kaplan S. (2000). *The therapeutic interweave in EMDR: Before and beyond – A manual for EMDR trained clinicians*. http://www.cavershambooksellers.com/search/0970712308

Glickman, N. (2009). *Cognitive-behavioral therapy for deaf and hearing persons with language and learning challenges*. Routledge, Taylor & Francis Group.

Goldsmith, R. E., Barlow, M. R., & Freyd, J. J. (2004). Knowing and not knowing about trauma: Implications for therapy. *Psychotherapy: Theory, Research, Practice,*

Training, 41(4), 448–463. https://doi.org/10.1037/0033-3204.41.4.448

Golier, J., Yehuda, R., Bierer, L., Mitropoulou, V., New, A., Schmeidler, J., Silverman, J., & Siever, L. (2003). The relationship of borderline personality disorder to posttraumatic stress disorder and traumatic events. *The American Journal of Psychiatry, 160*(11), 2018–2024. https://doi.org/10.1176/appi.ajp.160.11.2018

Gomez, A. M. (2013). *EMDR therapy and adjunct approaches with children: Complex trauma, attachment and dissociation*. Springer Publishing Company.

Gomez, A. M. (2024). The journey of the butterfly: G-TEP with children. In R. M. Robinson & S. K. Kaptan (Eds.), *EMDR group therapy: Emerging principles and protocols to treat trauma and beyond* (138–148). Springer Publishing.

Gomez, A. (2025). Generational wounds: The theory and practice of using systemic-attachment informed EMDR therapy with parents and children. In D. P. Farrell, S. J. Schubert, & M. D. Kiernan (Eds.), *The Oxford handbook of EMDR therapy*. Online edn, Oxford Academic, 20 April 2023, https://doi.org/10.1093/oxfordhb/9780192898357.013.36

Gomez-Perales, N. (2015). *Attachment-focused trauma treatment for children and adolescents: Phase-oriented strategies for addressing complex trauma disorders*. Routledge.

González, A., Del Río-Casanova, L., & Justo-Alonso, A. (2017). Integrating neurobiology of emotion regulation and trauma therapy: Reflections on EMDR therapy. *Reviews in the Neurosciences, 28*(4), 431–440. https://doi.org/10.1515/revneuro-2016-0070

Grant, K. E., Compas, B. E., Thurm, A. E., McMahon, S. D., Gipson, P. Y., Campbell, A. J., Krochock, K., & Westerholm, R. I. (2006). Stressors and child and adolescent psychopathology: Evidence of moderating and mediating effects. *Clinical Psychology Review, 26*(3), 257–283. https://doi.org/10.1016/j.cpr.2005.06.01

Green, J. G., McLaughin, K. A., & Berglund, P. A. (2010). Childhood adversities and adult psychiatric disorders in the national comorbidity survey replication I: Associations with first onset of DSM IV disorders. *Archives of General Psychiatry, 67*(2), 113–123. https://doi.org/10.1001/archgenpsychiatry.2009.186

Greenblatt-Kimron, L., Shrira, A., Rubinstein, T., & Palgi, Y. (2021). Event centrality and secondary traumatization among Holocaust survivors' offspring and grandchildren: A three-generation study. *Journal of Anxiety Disorders, 81*, 102401. https://doi.org/10.1016/j.janxdis.2021.102401

Greene, C. A., McCoach, D. B., Ford, J. D., McCarthy, K., Randall, K. G., & Lang, J. M. (2023). Bidirectional effects of parental and adolescent symptom change in trauma-focused cognitive behavioral therapy. *Psychological Trauma: Theory, Research, Practice, and Policy, 15*(S1), S172. https://doi.org/10.1037/tra0001445

Greenwald, R. (1999). *Eye Movement Desensitization and Reprocessing (EMDR) in child and adolescent psychotherapy*. Aronson.

Greenwald, R. (2002). Motivation-adaptive skills-trauma resolution (MASTR) therapy for adolescents with conduct problems: An open trial. *Journal of Aggression, Maltreatment and Trauma, 6*(1), 237–261. https://doi.org/10.1300/J146v06n01_12

Greenwald, R. (2009). *Treating problem behaviours: A trauma-informed approach*. Routledge/Taylor and Francis Group.

Greenwald, R. (2013a). *Behandeling van gedragsproblemen: Een trauma-georiënteerde benadering*. LannooCampus.

Greenwald, R. (2013b). *Treating behavioural problems: A trauma-informed approach*. LannooCampus.

Grummitt, L., Baldwin, J. R., Lafoa'i, J., Keyes, K. M., & Barrett, E. L. (2024). Burden of mental disorders and suicide attributable to childhood maltreatment. *JAMA Psychiatry, 81*(8), 782–788. https://doi.org/10.1001/jamapsychiatry.2024.0804

Gudiño, O. G., Leonard, S., Stiles, A. A., Havens, J. F., & Cloitre, M. (2017). STAIR narrative therapy for adolescents. In M. Landolt, M. Cloitre, & U. Schnyder (Eds.), *Evidence-based treatments for trauma related disorders in children and adolescents*. Springer. https://doi.org/10.1007/978-3-319-46138-0_12

Guidetti, C., Brogna, P., Rosaria Chieffo, D. P., Turrini, I., Arcangeli, V., Rausa, A., Bianchetti, M., Rolleri, E., Santamassimo, C., Di Cesare, G., Ducci, G., Romeo, D. M., & Brogna, C. (2023). Eye Movement Desensitization and Reprocessing (EMDR) as a possible evidence-based rehabilitation treatment option for a patient with ADHD and history of adverse childhood experiences: A case report study. *Journal of Personalised Medicine, 13*(2), 200. https://doi.org/10.3390/jpm13020200

Guild, D. J., Alto, M. E., Handley, E. D., Rogosch, F., Cichetti, D., & Toth, S. L. (2021). Attachment and affect between mothers with depression and their children: Longitudinal outcomes of child parent psychotherapy. *Research on Child and Adolescent Psychopathology, 49*(5), 563–577. https://doi.org/10.1007/s10802-020-00681-0

Gunter, R. W., & Bodner, G. E. (2008). How eye movements affect unpleasant memories: Support for a working memory account. *Behaviour Research and Therapy, 46*(8), 913–931. https://doi.org/10.1016/j.brat.2008.04.006

Gutermann, J., Schreiber, F., Matulis, S., Schwartzkopff, L., Deppe, J., & Steil, R. (2016). Psychological treatments for symptoms of posttraumatic stress disorder in children, adolescents, and young adults: A meta-analysis. *Clinical Child and Family Psychology Review, 19*(2), 77–93. https://doi.org/10.1007/s10567-016-0202-5

Hafkemeijer, L., De Jongh, A., Van der Palen, J., & Starrenburg, A. (2020). Eye movement desensitization and reprocessing (EMDR) in patients with a personality disorder. *European Journal of Psychotraumatology, 11*(1), 1838777. https://doi.org/10.1080/20008198.2020.1838777

Hanetz-Gamliel, K., & Dollberg, D. G. (2022). Links between mothers' ACEs, their psychopathology and parenting, and their children's behaviour problems: A mediation model. *Frontiers in Psychiatry, 13*, 1064915. https://doi.org/10.3389/fpsyt.2022.1064915

Harned, M. S., Rizvi, S. L., & Linehan, M. M. (2010). Impact of co-occurring posttraumatic stress disorder on suicidal women with borderline personality disorder. *American Journal of Psychiatry, 167*(10), 1210–1217. https://doi.org/10.1176/appi.ajp.2010.09081213

Harned, M. S., Wilks, C. R., Schmidt, S. C., & Coyle, T. N. (2018). Improving functional outcomes in women with borderline personality disorder and PTSD by changing PTSD severity and post-traumatic cognitions. *Behaviour Research and Therapy, 103*, 53–61. https://doi.org/10.1016/j.brat.2018.02.002

Harrendorf, S. (2018). Prospects, problems, and pitfalls in comparative analyses of criminal justice data. *Crime and Justice, 47*(1), 159–207. https://doi.org/10.1086/696042

Harricharan, S., Nicholson, A. A., Densmore, M., Théberge, J., McKinnon, M. C., Neufeld, R. W. J., & Lanius, R. A. (2017). Sensory overload and imbalance: Resting-state vestibular connectivity in PTSD and its dissociative subtype. *Neuropsychologia, 106*, 169–178. https://doi.org/10.1016/j.neuropsychologia.2017.09.010

Harvey, S. T., & Taylor, J. E. (2010). A meta-analysis of the effects of psychotherapy with sexually abused children and adolescents. *Clinical Psychology Review, 30*(5), 517–535. https://doi.org/10.1016/j.cpr.2010.03.006

Hase, M., Balmaceda, U. M., Ostacoli, L., Liebermann, P., & Hofmann, A. (2017). The AIP model of EMDR therapy and pathogenic memories. *Frontiers in Psychology, 8*, 1578. https://doi.org/10.3389/fpsyg.2017.01578

Hase, M., & Brisch, K. (2022). The therapeutic relationship in EMDR therapy. *Frontiers in Psychology, 13*, 835470. https://doi.org/10.3389/fpsyg.2022.835470

Haselgruber, A., Sölva, K., & Lueger-Schuster, B. (2020). Validation of ICD-11 PTSD and complex PTSD in foster children using the International Trauma Questionnaire. *Acta Psychiatrica Scandinavica, 141*(1), 60–73. https://doi.org/10.1111/acps.13100

Hauber, K. (2009). An unusual case study (series): The treatment of dissociative identity disorder. *Journal of Psychotherapy, 35*, 109–122.

Hay, P., Chinn, D., Forbes, D., Madden, S., Newton, R., Sugenor, L., Touyz, S., & Ward, W. (2014). Royal Australian and New Zealand College of Psychiatrists clinical practice guidelines for the treatment of eating disorders. *Australian and New Zealand Journal of Psychiatry, 48*(11), 977–1008. https://doi.org/10.1177/0004867414555814

Heffernan, K., & Cloitre, M. (2000). A comparison of posttraumatic stress disorder with and without borderline personality disorder among women with a history of childhood sexual abuse: Etiological and clinical characteristics. *Journal of Nervous and Mental Disease, 188*(9), 589–595. https://doi.org/10.1097/00005053-200009000-00005

Hendriks, L., De Kleine, R. A., Heyvaert, M., Becker, E. S., Hendriks, G.-J., & Van Minnen, A. (2017). Intensive prolonged exposure treatment for adolescent complex posttraumatic stress disorder: A single-trial design. *Journal of Child Psychology and Psychiatry, 58*(11), 1229–1238. https://doi.org/10.1111/jcpp.12756

Henley, J., & Robinson, J. (2011). Mental health issues among refugee children and adolescents. *Clinical Psychologist, 15*(2), 51–62. https://doi.org/10.1111/j.1742-9552.2011.00024.x

Hensel, T. (2009). EMDR with children and adolescents after single-incident trauma: An intervention study. *Journal of EMDR Practice and Research, 3*(1), 2–9. https://doi.org/10.1891/1933-3196.3.1.2

Hensley, B. J. (2020). *An EMDR therapy primer: From practicum to practice.* Springer Publishing Company.

Hermans, D., Isarin, J., Jekeli, I., & Vissers, C. (2021). *Taal in het kwadraat; Kinderen met TOS beter begrijpen* [Understanding children with DLD better]. Pica.

Hermans, D., Raes, F., & Orlemans, H. (2018). *Introduction to behavioural therapy* (7th ed.). Bohn Stafleu van Loghum.

Hilbert, A., Hoek, H. W., & Schmidt, R. (2017). Evidence-based clinical guidelines for eating disorders: International comparison. *Current Opinion in Psychiatry, 30*(6), 423–437. https://doi.org/10.1097/YCO.0000000000000360

Hiles Howard, A. R., Lindaman, S., Copeland, R., & Cross, D. R. (2018). Theraplay impact on parents and children with autism spectrum disorder: Improvements in affect, joint attention, and social cooperation. *International Journal of Play Therapy, 27*(1), 56–68. https://doi.org/10.1037/pla0000056

Hiller, R. M., Meiser-Stedman, R., Elliott, E., Banting, R., & Halligan, S. L. (2021). A longitudinal study of cognitive predictors of (complex) post-traumatic stress in young people in out-of-home care. *Journal of Child Psychology and Psychiatry, 62*(1), 48–57. https://doi.org/10.1111/jcpp.13232

Hiller, R. M., Meiser-Stedman, R., Fearon, P., Lobo, S., McKinnon, A., Fraser, A., & Halligan, S. L. (2016). Research Review: Changes in the prevalence and symptom severity of child post-traumatic stress disorder in the year following trauma—A meta-analytic study. *Journal of Child Psychology and Psychiatry*, *57*(8), 884–898. https://doi.org/10.1111/jcpp.12566

Hiller, R. M., Meiser-Stedman, R., Lobo, S., Creswell, C., Fearon, P., Ehlers, A., Murray, L., & Halligan, S. L. (2018). A longitudinal investigation of the role of parental responses in predicting children's post-traumatic distress. *Journal of Child Psychology and Psychiatry*, *59*(7), 781–789. https://doi.org/10.1111/jcpp.12846

Hoeberichts, K., Roke, Y., Niks, I., & Van Harten, P. N. (2022). Use of a mHealth mobile application to reduce stress in adults with autism: A pre-post pilot study of the Stress Autism Mate (SAM). *Advances in Neurodevelopmental Disorders*, *7*(1), 268–276. https://doi.org/10.1007/s41252-022-00304-3

Hofman, S., Hafkemeijer, L., De Jongh, A., Starrenburg, A., & Slotema, K. (2022). Trauma-focused EMDR for personality disorders among outpatients (TEMPO): Study protocol for a multi-centre, single-blind, randomized controlled trial. *Trials*, *23*(1), 196. https://doi.org/10.1186/s13063-022-06082-6

Holman, R. J. (2018). *Adverse childhood experiences: The impact of toxic stress and complex trauma on the developing child* [Master's thesis, Bethel University]. Spark Repository. https://spark.bethel.edu/etd/299

Hoogstad, A., Mevissen, L., & Didden, R. (2024). EMDR in three adults with severe intellectual disability and posttraumatic stress disorder: A multiple-baseline evaluation. *Journal of EMDR Practice and Research*, *18*(1), 18–30. https://doi.org/10.1891/EMDR-2023-0042

Hoogstad, A., Peters-Scheffer, N., Mevissen, L., & Didden, R. (2025). The impact of traumatic and stressful life events on the relatives of trauma-exposed adults with severe or moderate intellectual disabilities: 'Each time a piece of your strength breaks off'. *Journal of Intellectual & Developmental Disability* http://dx.doi.org/10.3109/13668250.2025.2525661

Hoogstad, A., Bouwmeester, S., Mevissen, L., & Didden, R. (in press). Assessment of posttraumatic stress disorder in adults with severe or moderate intellectual disability using the Diagnostic Interview Trauma and Stressors - Severe Intellectual Disability. *Journal of Intellectual Disability Research*.

Hopewell, S., Chan, A. W., Collins, G. S., Hróbjartsson, A., Moher, D., Schulz, K. F., … & Boutron, I. (2025a). CONSORT 2025 statement: Updated guideline for reporting randomised trials. *The Lancet*, *405*(10489), 1633–1640.

Hoppen, T. H., Meiser-Stedman, R., Kip, A., Birkeland, M. S., & Morina, N. (2024). The efficacy of psychological interventions for adult post-traumatic stress disorder following exposure to single versus multiple traumatic events: A meta-analysis of randomised controlled trials. *The Lancet Psychiatry*, *11*(2), 112–122. https://doi.org/10.1016/S2215-0366(23)00373-5

Howard, S. A. (2021). A causal model of children's vicarious traumatization. *Journal of Child and Adolescent Trauma*, *14*(4), 443–454. https://doi.org/10.1007/s40653-020-00331-z

Hughes, D. A., Golding, K. S., & Hudson, J. (2015). Dyadic developmental psychotherapy (DDP): The development of the theory, practice and research base. *Adoption and Fostering*, *39*(4), 356–365. https://doi.org/10.1177/0308575915610943

Hutsebaut, J., Willemsen, E., Bachrach, N., & Van, R. (2020). Improving access to and effectiveness of mental health care for personality disorders: The Guideline-Informed Treatment for Personality Disorders (GIT-PD) initiative in the Netherlands. *Borderline Personality Disorder and Emotion Dysregulation*, *7*, 16. https://doi.org/10.1186/s40479-020-00133-7

Idring, S., Magnusson, C., Lundberg, M., & Ek, M. (2014). Parental age and the risk of autism spectrum disorders: Findings from a Swedish population-based cohort. *International Journal of Epidemiology*, *43*(1), 107–115. https://doi.org/10.1093/ije/dyt262

Inter-Agency Standing Committee (IASC). (2006). *IASC guidelines on mental health and psychosocial support in emergency settings*. IASC.

Isarin, J. (2013). *Spraaktaal. Een gids voor jongeren met een taalstoornis* [A guide for young people with a language disorder]. Acco.

Isarin, J., Jekeli, I., Hermans, D., & Vissers, C. (2017). *Handreiking sociaal-emotionele problematiek bij kinderen en jongeren met TOS* [Guidelines for social emotional development in children and young people with DLD]. Koninklijke Kentalis.

ISSTD (International Society for the Study of Trauma and Dissociation) (2003). https://www.isst-d.org/publications-resources/resources/child-adolescent-treatment-guidelines/

ISTSS (International Society of Traumatic Stress Studies) (2019). *Post traumatic stress disorder: Prevention and treatment guidelines*. https://istss.org/wp-content/uploads/2024/08/ISTSS_PreventionTreatmentGuidelines_FNL-March-1019.pdfhttps://istss.org/wp-content/uploads/2024/08/ISTSS_PreventionTreatmentGuidelines_FNL-March-19-2019.pdf

Jaberghaderi, N., Greenwald, R., Rubin, A., Zand, S. O., & Dolatabadi, S. (2004). A comparison of CBT and EMDR for sexually abused Iranian girls. *Clinical Psychology and Psychotherapy*, *11*(5), 358–368. https://doi.org/10.1002/cpp.395

Jaberghaderi, N., Rezaei, M., Kolivand, M., & Shokoohi, A. (2019). Effectiveness of cognitive behavioral therapy and eye movement desensitization and reprocessing in child victims of domestic violence. *Iranian Journal of Psychiatry*, *14*(1), 67–75. https://doi.org/10.18502/ijps.v14i1.425

Jarero, I., Artigas, L., & Montero, M. (2008). The EMDR integrative group treatment protocol: Application with child victims of a mass disaster. *Journal of EMDR Practice and Research*, *2*(2), 97–105. https://doi.org/doi:10.1891/1933-3196.2.2.97

Jarero, I., Artigas, L., & Luber, M. (2011). The EMDR protocol for recent critical incidents: Application in a disaster mental health continuum of care context. *Journal of EMDR Practice and Research*, *5*(3), 82–94. https://doi.org/10.1891/1933-3196.5.3.82

Jarero, I., & Artigas, L. (2012). The EMDR integrative group treatment protocol: EMDR group treatment for early intervention following critical incidents. *European Review of Applied Psychology*, *62*(4), 219–222. https://doi.org/10.1016/j.erap.2012.04.004

Jarero, I., & Artigas, L. (2018). AIP model-based acute trauma and ongoing traumatic stress theoretical conceptualization. *Iberoamerican Journal of Psychotraumatology and Dissociation*, *10*(1), 1–10. https://www.revibapst.com/_files/ugd/c70085_bdf830b1ebf14e82afc742a4e11626c1.pdf

Jarero, I., Schnaider, S., & Givaudan, M. (2019). Randomized controlled trial: Provision of EMDR protocol for recent critical incidents and ongoing traumatic stress to first responders. *Journal of EMDR Practice and Research*, *13*(2), 100–110. https://doi.org/10.1891/1933-3196.13.2.100

Jeffries, F. W., & Davis, P. (2013). What is the role of eye movements in Eye Movement Desensitization and Reprocessing (EMDR) for Post-Traumatic Stress Disorder (PTSD)? A review. *Behavioural and Cognitive Psychotherapy*, *41*(3), 290–300. https://doi.org/10.1017/S1352465812000793

Jensen, T. K., Braathu, N., Birkeland, M. S., Ormhaug, S. M., & Skar, A. M. S. (2022). Complex PTSD and treatment outcomes in TF-CBT for youth: A naturalistic study. *European Journal of Psychotraumatology*, *13*(2), 2114630. https://doi.org/10.1080/20008066.2022.2114630

Jiménez, G., Becker, Y., Varela, C., García, P., Nuño, M. A., Pérez, M. C., Osorio, A., Jarero, I., & Givaudan, M. (2020). Multicenter randomized controlled trial on the provision of the EMDR-PRECI to female minor victims of sexual and/or physical violence and related PTSD diagnosis. *American Journal of Applied Psychology*, *9*(2), 42–51. https://doi.org/10.11648/j.ajap.20200902.12

John, S., & Segal, D. L. (2015). Case conceptualization. *The Encyclopedia of Clinical Psychology*, 1–4. https://doi.org/10.1002/9781118625392.wbecp106

Jonkman, C. S., Verlinden, E., Bolle, E. A., Boer, F., & Lindauer, R. J. L. (2013). Traumatic stress symptomatology in children after child maltreatment and single traumatic events: Clinical implications. *Journal of Traumatic Stress*, *26*(2), 225–232. https://doi.org/10.1002/jts.21792

Joshi, P. T., & O'Donnell, D. A. (2003). Consequences of child exposure to war and terrorism. *Clinical Child and Family Psychology Review*, *6*(4), 275–292. https://doi.org/10.1023/b:ccfp.0000006294.88201.68

Juffer, F., Bakermans-Kranenburg M. J., & Van Ijzendoorn, M. H. (2016). Video-feedback Intervention to promote Positive Parenting and Sensitive Discipline (VIPP-SD): Development and meta-analytical evidence of its effectiveness. In H. Steele & M. Steele (Eds.), *Handbook of attachment-based interventions* (pp. 1–26). Guilford Press.

Just, M. A., Cherkassky, V. L., Keller, T. A., & Minshew, N. J. (2004). Cortical activation and synchronization during sentence comprehension in high functioning autism. *Brain*, *127*(Pt 8), 1811–1821. https://doi.org/10.1093/brain/awh199

Kana, R. K., Libero, L. E., & Moore, M. (2011). Disrupted cortical connectivity theory as an explanatory model for autism spectrum disorders. *Physics of Life Reviews*, *8*(4), 410–437. https://doi.org/10.1016/j.plrev.2011.10.001

Kapa, L., & Mettler, H. M. (2021). Language and executive function in preschoolers with developmental language disorder: The role of self-directed speech. *Perspectives of the ASHA Special Interest Groups*, *6*(6), 1315–1326. https://doi.og/10.1044/2021_PERSP-21-00010

Kaptan, S. K., Dursun, B. O., Knowles, M., Husain, N., & Varese, F. (2021). Group eye movement desensitization and reprocessing interventions in adults and children: A systematic review of randomized and nonrandomized trials. *Clinical Psychology and Psychotherapy*, *28*(4), 784–806. https://doi.org/10.1002/cpp.2549

Kaptan, S. K., Varese, F., Yilmaz, B., Andriopoulou, P., & Husain, N. (2022). 'Online delivery gave me privacy and distance from others': Feasibility trial and qualitative evaluation of an online intervention for refugees and asylum seekers; LTP+ EMDR G-TEP. *Counselling and Psychotherapy Research*, *22*(4), 876–888. https://doi.org/10.1002/capr.12580

Karadag, M., Hangül, Z., Ezer, R. N., & Gökçen, C. (2021). Use of EMDR-derived self-help intervention in children in the period of COVID-19: A randomized-controlled study. *Journal of EMDR Practice and Research*, 15, EMDR-D-20-00054. https://doi.org/10.1891/EMDR-D-20-00054

Karatzias, T., Brown, M., Taggart, L., Truesdale, M., Sirisena, C., Walley, R., Mason-Roberts, S., Bradley, A., & Paterson, D. (2019). A mixed-methods, randomized controlled feasibility trial of eye movement desensitization and reprocessing (EMDR) plus standard care (SC) versus SC alone for DSM-5 posttraumatic stress disorder (PTSD) in adults with intellectual disabilities. *Journal of Applied Research in Intellectual Disabilities*, *32*(4), 806–818. https://doi.org/10.1111/jar.12570

Kate, M. A., Jamieson, G., & Middleton, W. (2021). Childhood sexual, emotional, and physical abuse as predictors of dissociation in adulthood. *Journal of Child Sexual Abuse, 30*(8), 953–976. https://doi.org/10.1080/10538712.2021.1955789

Kazdin, A. E. (2007). Mediators and mechanisms of change in psychotherapy research. *Annual Review of Clinical Psychology, 3*, 1–27. https://doi.org/10.1146/annurev.clinpsy.3.022806.091432

Keeley, R. D., Brody, D. S., Engel, M., Burke, B. L., Nordstrom, K., Moralez, E., Dickinson, L. M., & Emsermann, C. (2016). Motivational interviewing improves depression outcome in primary care: A cluster randomised trial. *Journal of Consulting and Clinical Psychology, 84*(11), 993–1007. https://doi.org/10.1037/ccp0000124

Kemp, M., Drummond, P., & McDermott, B. (2009). A wait-list controlled pilot study of eye movement desensitization and reprocessing (EMDR) for children with posttraumatic stress symptoms (PTSD) from motor vehicle accidents. *Clinical Child Psychology and Psychiatry, 15*(1), 5–25. https://doi.org/10.1177/1359104509339086

Ketelaar, L., Wiefferink, C. H., Frijns, J. H. M., Broekhof, E., & Rieffe, C. (2015). Preliminary findings on associations between moral emotions and social behavior in young children with normal hearing and with cochlear implants. *European Child and Adolescent Psychiatry, 24*(11), 1369–1380. https://doi.org/10.1007/s00787-015-0688-2

Kien, Ch., Sommer, I., Faustmann, A., Gibson, L., Schneider, M., Krczal, E., Jank, R., Klerings, I., Szelag, M., Kerschner, B., Brattström, P., & Gartlehner, G. (2019). Prevalence of mental disorders in young refugees and asylum seekers in European countries: A systematic review. *European Child and Adolescent Psychiatry, 28*(10), 1295–1310. https://doi.org/10.1007/s00787-018-1215-z

Kim, J., Chesworth, B., Franchino-Olsen, H., & Macy, R. J. (2022). A scoping review of vicarious trauma interventions for service providers working with people who have experienced traumatic events. *Trauma, Violence, and Abuse, 23*(5), 1437–1460. https://doi.org/10.1177/1524838021991310

King, R. (2010a). Commentary: Complex post-traumatic stress disorder: Implications for individuals with autism spectrum disorders—Part I. *Journal on Developmental Disabilities, 16*(3), 91–100.

King, R. (2010b). Complex post-traumatic stress disorder: Implications for individuals with autism spectrum disorders. *The NADD Bulletin, 13*(5), 5.

Kinniburgh, K. J., Blaustein, M., Spinazzola, J., & Van der Kolk, B. (2005). Attachment, self-regulation and competency: A comprehensive intervention framework for children with complex trauma. *Psychiatric Annals, 35*(5), 424–430. https://doi.org/10.3928/00485713-20050501-08

Kliethermes, M., & Wamser, R. (2012). Adolescents with complex trauma. In J. A. Cohen, A. P. Mannarino & E. Deblinger (Eds.), *Trauma-focused CBT for children and adolescents: Treatment applications* (pp. 175–196). Guilford Press.

Knapen, S., Hutsebaut, J., Van Diemen, R., & Beekman, A. (2020). Epistemic trust as a psycho-marker for outcome in psychosocial interventions. *Journal of Infant, Child, and Adolescent Psychotherapy, 19*(4), 417–426. https://doi.org/10.1080/15289168.2020.1812322

Knipe, J. (2009). 'Shame is my safe place': Adaptive information processing methods of resolving chronic shame-based depression. In R. Shapiro (Ed.), *EMDR solutions II* (Pp. 49–89). Norton Company.

Knipe, J. (2010). The method of constant installation of present orientation and safety (CIPOS). In M. Luber (Ed.), *Eye movement desensitization and reprocessing (EMDR) scripted protocols: Special populations* (pp. 235–241). Springer.

Knipe, J. (2018). *EMDR Toolbox. Theory and Treatment of Complex PTSD and Dissociation* (2nd ed.). Springer Publishing Co Inc.

Knipschild, R., Hein, I., Pieters, S., Lindauer, R., Bicanic, I. A., Staal, W., De Jongh, A., & Klip, H. (2024). Childhood adversity in a youth psychiatric population: Prevalence and associated mental health problems. *European Journal of Psychotraumatology, 15*(1), 2330880. https://doi.org/10.1080/20008066.2024.2330880

Knipschild, R., Klip, H., Van Leeuwaarden, D., Van Onna, M. J., Lindauer, R. J., Staal, W. G., Bicanic, I. A. E., & de Jongh, A. (2023). Treatment of multiple traumatized adolescents by enhancing regulation skills and reducing trauma related symptoms: Rationale, study design, and methods of randomized controlled trial (the Mars-study). *BMC Psychiatry, 23*(1), 644. https://doi.org/10.1186/s12888-023-05073-4

Kofler, M. J., Rapport, M. D., Bolden, J., & Altro, T. A. (2008). Working memory as a core deficit in ADHD: Preliminary findings and implications. *The ADHD Report, 16*(6), 8–14. https://doi.org/10.1521/adhd.2008.16.6.8

Kolthof, K. A., Voorendonk, E. M., Van Minnen, A., & De Jongh, A. (2022). Effects of intensive trauma-focused treatment of individuals with both post-traumatic stress disorder and borderline personality disorder. *European Journal of Psychotraumatology, 13*(2), 2143076. https://doi.org/10.1080/20008066.2022.2143076

Korkmazlar, Ü. (2024). EMDR group protocol for children. In R. M. Robinson & S. K. Kaptan (Eds.), *EMDR group therapy: Emerging principles and protocols to treat trauma and beyond*. Springer Publishing.

Korkmazlar, Ü., Bozkurt, B., & Tunca, D. T. (2020). EMDR group protocol with children: A field study. *Journal of EMDR Practice and Research, 14*(1), 13–30. https://doi.org/10.1891/1933-3196.14.1.13

Korn, D. L., & Leeds, A. M. (2002). Preliminary evidence of efficacy for EMDR resource development and installation in the stabilization phase of treatment of complex posttraumatic stress disorder. *Journal of Clinical Psychology*, 59(12), 1465–1487. https://doi.org/10.1002/jclp.10099

Korrelboom, K., Marissen, M., & Van Assendelft, T. (2011). Competitive memory training (COMET) for low self-esteem in patients with personality disorders: A randomized effectiveness study. *Behavioural and Cognitive Psychotherapy*, *39*(1), 1–19. https://doi.org/10.1017/S1352465810000469

Kosatka, D., & Ona, C. (2014). Eye Movement Desensitization and Reprocessing in a patient with Asperger's disorder: Case report. *Journal of EMDR Practice and Research*, *8*(1). https://doi.org/10.1891/1933-3196.8.1.13

Kotov, R., Krueger, R. F., Watson, D., Achenbach, T. M., Althoff, R. R., Bagby, R. M., Brown, T. A., Carpenter, W. T., Caspi, A., Clark, L. A., Eaton, N. R., Forbes, M. K., Forbush, K. T., Goldberg, D., Hasin, D., Hyman, S. E., Ivanova, M. Y., Lynam, D. R., Markon, K., … Zimmerman, M. (2017). The Hierarchical Taxonomy of Psychopathology (HiTOP): A dimensional alternative to traditional nosologies. *Journal of Abnormal Psychology*, *126*(4), 454–477. https://doi.org/10.1037/abn0000258

Kouwenberg, M. (2013). *Social-emotional factors underlying internalizing problems and peer relations in deaf or hard of hearing youth*. Ponsen & Looijen.

Kowalik, J., Weller, J., Venter, J., & Drachman, D. (2011). Cognitive behavioral therapy for the treatment of pediatric posttraumatic stress disorder: A review and meta-analysis. *Journal of Behavior Therapy and Experimental Psychiatry*, *42*(3), 405–413. https://doi.org/10.1016/j.jbtep.2011.02.002

Kraemer, H. C. (2016). Messages for clinicians: Moderators and mediators of treatment outcome in randomized clinical trials. *American Journal of Psychiatry*, *173*(7), 672–679. https://doi.org/10.1176/appi.ajp.2016.15101333

Kroneman, L. K., & Beer, R. (2013). Stapstenen: Een groepstraining voor adolescenten in de gesloten jeugdzorg met een geschiedenis van complex trauma. *Tijdschrift voor Kinder- en Jeugdpsychotherapie*, *40*(3), 5–19.

Kuyken, W., Padesky, C. A., & Dudley, R. (2008). The science and practice of case conceptualization. *Behavioural and Cognitive Psychotherapy*, *36*(6), 757–768. https://doi.org/10.1017/S1352465808004815

Kvavilashvili, L. (2014). Solving the mystery of intrusive flashbacks in posttraumatic stress disorder: Comment on Brewin (2014). *Psychological Bulletin*, *140*(1), 98–104. https://doi.org/10.1037/a0034677

Lai, M. C., Lombardo, M. V., & Baron-Cohen, S. (2014). Autism. *The Lancet*, *383*(9920), 896–910. https://doi.org/10.1016/S0140-6736(13)61539-1

Laliotis, D., Luber, M., Oren, U., Shapiro, E., Ichii, M., Hase, M., La Rosa, L., Alter-Reid, K., & St. Jammes, J. T. (2021). What is EMDR therapy? Past, present, and future directions. *Journal of EMDR Practice and Research*, *15*(4), 186–201. https://doi.org/10.1891/EMDR-D-21-00029

Landin-Romero, R., Moreno-Alcazar, A., Pagani, M., & Amann, B. L. (2018). How does eye movement desensitization and reprocessing therapy work? A systematic review on suggested mechanisms of action. *Frontiers in Psychology*, *9*, 286360. https://doi.org/10.3389/fpsyg.2018.01395

Landolt, M. A., Ystrom, E., Sennhauser, F. H., Gnehm, H. E., & Vollrath, M. E. (2012). The mutual prospective influence of child and parental post-traumatic stress symptoms in paediatric patients. *Journal of Child Psychology and Psychiatry*, *53*(7), 767–774. https://doi.org/10.1111/j.1469-7610.2011.02520.x

Lazarus, R. S. (1993). From psychological stress to the emotions: A history of changing outlooks. *Annual Review of Psychology*, *44*, 1–21. https://doi.org/10.1146/annurev.ps.44.020193.000245

Lee, C. W., & Cuijpers, P. (2013). A meta-analysis of the contribution of eye movements in processing emotional memories. *Journal of Behavior Therapy and Experimental Psychiatry*, *44*(2), 231–239. https://doi.org/10.1016/j.jbtep.2012.11.001

Lee, C. W., & Drummond, P. D. (2008). Effects of eye movement versus therapist instructions on the processing of distressing memories. *Journal of Anxiety Disorders*, *22*(5), 801–808. https://doi.org/10.1016/j.janxdis.2007.08.007

Lee, C. W., Taylor, G., & Drummond, P. D. (2006) The active ingredient in EMDR: Is it traditional exposure or dual focus of attention? *Clinical Psychology and Psychotherapy*, *13*(2), 97–107. https://doi.org/10.1002/cpp.479

Leeds, A. M. (2009). Resources in EMDR and other trauma focus psychotherapy: A review. *Journal of EMDR Practice and Research*, *3*(3), 152–160. https://doi.org/10.1891/1933-3196.3.3.152

Leeds, A. M. (2016a). *A guide to the standard EMDR therapy protocols for clinicians, supervisors, and consultants* (2nd ed.). Springer Publishing Company.

Leeds, A. M. (2016b). *Mediators, mechanisms and moderators of action for EMDR therapy: A review of multiplex effects in modes of bilateral stimulation* [presentation]. 17th EMDR Europe Association Conference, The Hague, The Netherlands. http://www2.masterapp2.nl/assets/uploads/uploads/45561-Mechanisms-of-Action-Leeds.pdf

Leeds, A. M. (2023). The adaptive information processing model: The theoretical framework for EMDR therapy. In D. Farrell, S. J. Schubert, & M. D. Kiernan (Eds.), *The Oxford handbook of EMDR* (online ed.). Oxford Academic. https://doi.org/10.1093/oxfordhb/9780192898357.013.1

Leef, J. H., Brian, J., VanderLaan, D. P., Wood, H., Scott, K., Lai, M. C., Bradley, S. J., & Zucker, K. J. (2019). Traits of autism spectrum disorder in school-aged children with gender dysphoria: A comparison to clinical controls. *Clinical Practice in Pediatric Psychology*, *7*(4), 383–395. https://doi.org/10.1037/cpp0000303

Leigh, I. W. (2010). *Psychotherapy with deaf clients from diverse groups*. Gallaudet University Press.

Lempertz, D., Wichmann, M., Enderle, E., Stellermann-Strehlow, K., Pawils, S., & Metzner, F. (2020). Pre-post study to assess EMDR-based group therapy for traumatized refugee preschoolers. *Journal of EMDR Practice and Research*, *14*(1), 31–45. https://doi.org/10.1891/1933-3196.14.1.31

Lenferink, L. I. M., Meyerbröker, K., & Boelen, P. A. (2020). PTSD treatment in times of COVID-19: A systematic review of the effects of online EMDR. *Psychiatry Research*, *293*, 113438. https://doi.org/10.1016/j.psychres.2020.113438

Leonard, L. B. (2014). *Children with specific language impairment*. MIT Press.

Leuning, E. M., Van den Berk-smeekens, I., Van Dongen-Boomsma, M., & Staal, W. G. (2023). Eye Movement Desensitization and Reprocessing in adolescents with autism; Efficacy on ASD symptoms and stress. *Frontiers in Psychiatry*, *14*, 981975. https://doi.org/10.3389/fpsyt.2023.981975

Lewis, S. J., Arseneault, L., Caspi, A., Fisher, H. L., Matthews, T., Moffitt, T. E., Odgers, C. L., Stahl, D., Teng, J. Y., & Danese, A. (2019). The epidemiology of trauma and post-traumatic stress disorder in a representative cohort of young people in England and Wales. *The Lancet Psychiatry*, *6*(3), 247–256. https://doi.org/10.1016/S2215-0366(19)30031-8

Liddle, H. A., Dakof, G. A., Parker, K., Diamond, G. S., Barrett, K., & Tejeda, M. (2001). Multidimensional family therapy for adolescent drug abuse: Results of a randomized clinical trial. *The American Journal of Drug and Alcohol Abuse*, *27*(4), 651–688. https://doi.org/10.1081/ada-100107661

Lieberman A. F., Horn P. V., & Ippen C. G. (2005). Toward evidence-based treatment: Child-parent psychotherapy with preschoolers exposed to marital violence. *Journal of the American Academy of Child and Adolescent Psychiatry*, *44*(12), 1241–1248. https://doi.org/10.1097/01.chi.0000181047.59702.58

Lindauer, R. (2014). *Clinician-administered PTSD scale for children and adolescents (CAPS-CA)*. Bohn Stafleu van Loghum.

Linden, D. (2015). *Touch: The science of hand, heart and mind*. Penguin Publishing Group.

Lindsay, G., & Dockrell, J. E. (2012). Longitudinal patterns of behavioral, emotional, and social difficulties and self-concepts in adolescents with a history of specific language impairment. *Language, Speech, and Hearing Services in Schools*, *43*(4), 445–460. https://doi.org/10.1044/0161-1461(2012/11-0069

Lindstrom Johnson, S., Waasdorp, T. E., Gaias, L. M., & Bradshaw, C. P. (2019). Parental responses to bullying: Understanding the role of school policies and practices. *Journal of Educational Psychology*, *111*(3), 475. https://doi.org/10.1037/edu0000295

Linehan, M. M. (1993). *Cognitive behavioral treatment of borderline personality disorder*. Guilford Press.

Liotti, G. (2009). Attachment and dissociation. In P. F. Dell & J. A. O'Neill (Eds.), *Dissociation and the dissociative disorders: DSM-V and beyond* (pp. 53–65). Routledge.

Litschge, C. M., Vaughn, M. G., & McCrea, C. (2010). The empirical status of treatments for children and youth with conduct problems: An overview of meta-analytic studies. *Research on Social Work and Practice*, *20*(1), 21–35. https://doi.org/10.1177/1049731508331247

Littel, M., Remijn, M., Tinga, A. M., Engelhard, I. M., & Van den Hout, M. A. (2017). Stress enhances the memory-degrading effects of eye movements on emotionally neutral memories. *Clinical Psychological Science*, *5*(2), 316–324. https://doi.org/10.1177/2167702616687292

Lobregt-Van Buuren, E., Sizoo, B., Mevissen, L., & De Jongh, A. (2019). Eye movement desensitization and reprocessing (EMDR) therapy as a feasible and potential effective treatment for adults with autism spectrum disorder (ASD) and a history of adverse events. *Journal of Autism and Developmental Disorders*, *49*(4), 151–164. https://doi.org/10.1007/s10803-018-3687-6

Logie, R., Bowers, M., Dent, A., Elliott, J., O'Connor, M., & Russell, A. (2020). *Using stories in EMDR: A guide to the storytelling (narrative) approach in EMDR therapy*. Trauma Aid UK.

Logie, R., & De Jongh, A. (2014). The 'Flashforward Procedure': Confronting the Catastrophe. *Journal of EMDR Practice and Research*, *8*, 25–32. https://doi.org/10.1891/1933-3196.8.1.25

Logie, R., & De Jongh, A. (2016). The 'Flashforward' procedure. In M. Luber (Ed.), *Eye Movement Desensitization and Reprocessing (EMDR) scripted protocols and summary sheets: Treating trauma, anxiety and mood-related conditions* (pp. 81–90). Springer.

Loomes, R., Hull, L., Polmear, W., & Locke, M. (2017). What Is the male-to-female ratio in autism spectrum disorder? A systematic review and meta-analysis. *Journal of the American Academy of Child and Adolescent Psychiatry*, *56*(6), 466–477. https://doi.org/10.1016/j.jaac.2017.03.013

Lovett, J. (1999). *Small wonders: Healing childhood trauma with EMDR*. The Free Press.

Lovett, J. (2015). *Trauma-attachment tangle: Modifying EMDR to help children resolve trauma and develop loving relationships*. Routledge/Taylor & Francis Group.

Luber, M. (Ed.). (2019). *Eye movement desensitization and reprocessing (EMDR) therapy scripted protocols and summary sheets: Treating eating disorders, chronic pain and maladaptive self-care behaviors*. Springer Publishing Company.

Luber, M., & Shapiro, F. (2009). Interview with Francine Shapiro: Historical overview, present issues, and future directions of EMDR. *Journal of EMDR Practice and Research*, *3*(4), 217–231. https//doi.org/10.1891/1933-3196.3.4.217

Luman, M.,Tripp, G., & Scheres, A. (2010). Identifying the neurobiology of altered reinforcement sensitivity in ADHD: A review and research agenda. *Neuroscience and Biobehavioral Reviews, 34,* 744–754.

Lundahl, B. W., Kunz, C., Brownell, C., Tollefson, D., & Burke, B. L. (2010). A meta-analysis of motivational interviewing: Twenty-five years of empirical studies. *Research on Social Work Practice*, *20*(2), 137–160. https://doi.org/10.1177/1049731509347850

Lustig, S. L., Kia-Keating, M., Knight, W., Geltman, P., Ellis, B. H., Kinzie, D., Keane, T., & Saxe, G. (2004). Review of child and adolescent refugee mental health. *Journal of the American Academy of Child and Adolescent Psychiatry*, *43*(1), 31–45. https://doi.org/10.1097/00004583-200401000-00012

Lynn, S. J., Polizzi, C., Merckelbach, H., Chiu, C. D., Maxwell, R., Van Heugten, D., & Lilienfeld, S. O. (2022). Dissociation and dissociative disorders reconsidered: Beyond sociocognitive and trauma models toward a transtheoretical framework. *Annual Review of Clinical Psychology*, *18*, 259–289. https://doi.org/10.1146/annurev-clinpsy-081219-102424

Lyons-Ruth, K., & Jacobvitz, D. (2008). Attachment disorganization: Genetic factors, parenting contexts, and developmental transformation from infancy to adulthood. In J. Cassidy & P. R. Shaver (Eds.), *Handbook of attachment: Theory, research, and clinical applications* (2nd ed., pp. 666–697). Guilford Press.

Madigan, S., Hawkins, E., Goldberg, S., & Benoit, D. (2006). Reduction of disrupted caregiver behavior using modified interaction guidance. *Infant Mental Health Journal*, *27*(5), 509–527. https://doi.org/10.1002/imhj.20102

Maercker, A., Brewin, C. R., Bryant, R. A., Cloitre, M., Van Ommeren, M., Jones, L. M., Humayan, A., Kagee, A., Llosa, A. E., Rousseau, C., Somasundaram, D. J., Souza, R., Suzuki, Y., Weissbecker, I., Wessely, S. C., First, M. B., & Reed, G. M. (2013). Diagnosis and classification of disorders specifically associated with stress: Proposals for ICD-11. *World Psychiatry*, *12*(3), 198–206. https://doi.org/10.1002/wps.20057

Main, M., Hesse, E., & Hesse, S. (2011). Attachment theory and research: Overview with suggested applications to child custody. *Family Court Review*, *49*(3), 426–463. https://doi.org/10.1111/j.1744-1617.2011.01383.x

Malvaso, C. G., Cale, J., Whitten, T., Day, A., Singh, S., Hackett, L., Delfabbro, P. H., & Ross, S. (2022). Associations between adverse childhood experiences and trauma among young people who offend: A systematic literature review. *Trauma, Violence, and Abuse*, *23*(5), 1677–1694. https://doi.org.10.1177/15248380211013132

Mangiulli, I., Jelicic, M., Patihis, L., & Otgaar, H. (2021). Believing in dissociative amnesia relates to claiming it: A survey of people's experiences and beliefs about dissociative amnesia. *Memory*, *29*(10), 1362–1374. https://doi.org/10.1080/09658211.2021.1987475

Manzoni, M., Fernandez, I., Bertella, S., Tizzoni, F., Gazzola, E., Molteni, M., & Nobile, M. (2021). Eye movement desensitization and reprocessing: The state of the art of efficacy in children and adolescents with post-traumatic stress disorder. *Journal of Affective Disorders*, *282*, 340–347. https://doi.org/10.1016/j.jad.2020.12.088

Markus, W., & Hornsveld, H. K. (2017). EMDR interventions in addiction. *Journal of EMDR Practice and Research*, *11*(1), 3–29. https://doi.org/10.1891/1933-3196.11.1.3

Maroufi, M., Zamani, S., Izadikhah, Z., Marofi, M., & O'Connor, P. (2016). Investigating the effect of eye movement desensitization and reprocessing (EMDR) on postoperative pain intensity in adolescents undergoing surgery: A randomized controlled trial. *Journal of Advanced Nursing*, *72*(9), 2207–2217. https://doi.org/10.1111/jan.12985

Marsh, R. J., Dorahy, M. J., Butler, C., Middleton, W., De Jong, P. J., Kemp, S., & Huntjens, R. (2021). Inter-identity amnesia for neutral episodic self-referential and autobiographical memory in Dissociative Identity Disorder: An assessment of recall and recognition. *PloS One*, *16*(2), e0245849. https://doi.org/10.1371/journal.pone.0245849

Martin, A., Naunton, M., Kosari, S., Peterson, G., Thomas, J., & Christenson, J. K. (2021). Treatment guidelines for PTSD: A systematic review. *Journal of Clinical Medicine*, *10*(18), 4175. https://doi.org/10.3390/jcm10184175

Martinussen, R., Hayden, J., Hogg-Johnson, S., & Tannock, R. (2005). A meta-analysis of working memory impairments in children with attention-deficit/hyperactivity disorder. *Journal of the American Academy of Child and Adolescent Psychiatry*, *44*(4), 377–384. https://doi.org/10.1097/01.chi.0000153228.72591.73

Marvin, R., Cooper, G., Hoffman, K., & Powell, B. (2002). The circle of security project: Attachment-based intervention with caregiver–pre-school child dyads. *Attachment and Human Development*, *4*(1), 107–124. https://doi.org/10.1080/14616730252982491

Maslovaric, G., Zaccagnino, M., Mezzaluna, C., Perilli, S., Trivellato, D., Longo, V., & Civilotti, C. (2017). The effectiveness of eye movement desensitization and reprocessing integrative group protocol with adolescent survivors of the Central Italy Earthquake. *Frontiers in Psychology*, *8*, 1826. https://doi.org/10.3389/fpsyg.2017.01826

Mason-Roberts, S., Bradley, A., Karatzias, T., Brown, M., Paterson, D., Walley, R., Truesdale, M., Taggart, L., & Sirisena, C. (2018). Multiple traumatisation and subsequent psychopathology in people with intellectual disabilities and DSM-5 PTSD: A preliminary study. *Journal of Intellectual Disability Research*, *62*(8), 730–736. https://doi.org/10.1111/jir.12505

Masten, A. S., & Barnes, A. J. (2018). Resilience in children: Developmental perspectives. *Children*, *5*(7), 98. https://doi.org/10.3390/children5070098

Matthijssen, S. J., Lee, C. W., De Roos, C., Barron, I. G., Jarero, I., Shapiro, E., Hurley, E. C., Schubert, S. J., Baptist, J., Amann, B. L., Moreno-Alcázar, A., Tesarz, J., & De Jongh, A. (2020). The current status of EMDR therapy, specific target areas, and goals for the future. *Journal of EMDR Practice and Research*, *14*(4), 241–284. https://doi.org/10.1891/EMDR-D-20-00039

Matthijssen, S., Verhoeven, L., Van den Hout, M. A., & Heitland, I. (2017). Auditory and visual memories in PTSD patients targeted with eye movements and counting: The effect of modality-specific loading of working memory. *Frontiers in Psychology*, *8*, 1937. https://doi.org/10.3389/fpsyg.2017.01937

Matthys, W., & Van de Grind, G. (2013). *Richtlijn oppositioneel-opstandige stoornis (ODD) en gedragsstoornis (CD) bij kinderen en jongeren*. De Tijdstroom.

Mavranezouli, I., Megnin-Viggars, O., Trickey, D., Meiser-Stedman, R., Daly, C., Dias, S., Stockton, S., & Pilling, S. (2020). Cost-effectiveness of psychological interventions for children and young people with post-traumatic stress disorder. *Journal of Child Psychology and Psychiatry*, *61*(6), 699–710. https://doi.org/10.1111/jcpp.13142

Maxfield, L. (2019). A clinician's guide to the efficacy of EMDR therapy. *Journal of EMDR Practice and Research*, *13*(4), 239–246. https://doi.org/10.1891/1933-3196.13.4.239

Maxfield, L., Melnyk, W. T., & Hayman, C. A. (2008). A working memory explanation for the effects of eye movements in EMDR. *Journal of EMDR Practice and Research*, *2*(4), 247–261. https://doi.org/10.1891/1933-3196.2.4.247

McDermott, J. (2009). The forgotten victims of posttraumatic stress disorder. *Archives of Pediatrics and Adolescent Medicine*, *163*(6), 587. https://doi.org/10.1001/archpediatrics.2009.108

McDonough, S. (2000). Interaction Guidance: An approach for difficult-to-engage families. In C. H. Zeneah (Ed.), *Handbook of Infant Mental Health* (2nd ed., pp. 485–493). Guilford Press.

McLaughlin, K. A., Green, J. G., Gruber, M. J., Sampson, N. A., Zaslavsky, A. M., & Kessler, R. C. (2012). Childhood adversities and first onset of psychiatric disorders in a national sample of US adolescents. *Archives of General Psychiatry*, *69*(11), 1151–1160. https://doi.org/10.1001/archgenpsychiatry.2011.2277

McLaughlin, K. A., & Lambert, H. K. (2017). Child trauma exposure and psychopathology: Mechanisms of risk and resilience. *Current Opinion in Psychology*, *14*, 29–34. https://doi.org/10.1016/j.copsyc.2016.10.004

Meentken, M. G., Van der Mheen, M., Van Beynum, I. M., Aendekerk, E. W. C., Legerstee, J. S., Van der Ende, J., Del Canho, R., Lindauer, R. J. L., Hillegers, M. H. J., Moll, H. A., Helbing, W. A., & Utens, E. M. W. J. (2020). EMDR for children with medically related subthreshold PTSD: Short-term effects on PTSD, blood-injection-injury phobia, depression and sleep. *European Journal of Psychotraumatology*, *11*(1), 1705598. https://doi.org/10.1080/20008198.2019.1705598

Mehtar, M., & Mukaddes, N. M. (2011). Posttraumatic stress disorder in individuals with diagnosis of autistic spectrum disorder. *Research in Autism Spectrum Disorders*, *5*(1), 539–546. https://doi.org/10.1016/j.rasd.2010.06.020

Meiser-Stedman, R., McKinnon, A., Dixon, C., Boyle, A., Smith, P., & Dalgleish, T. (2019). A core role for cognitive processes in the acute onset and maintenance of post-traumatic stress in children and adolescents. *Journal of Child Psychology and Psychiatry*, *60*(8), 875–884. https://doi.org/10.1111/jcpp.13054

Memarzia, J., Walker, J., & Meiser-Stedman, R. (2021). Psychological peritraumatic risk factors for post-traumatic stress disorder in children and adolescents: A meta-analytic review. *Journal of Affective Disorders*, *282*, 1036–1047. https://doi.org/10.1016/j.jad.2021.01.016

Mevissen, L., Barnhoorn, E., Didden, R., Korzilius, H., & De Jongh, A. (2014). Clinical assessment of PTSD in children with mild to borderline intellectual disabilities: A pilot study. *Developmental Neurorehabilitation*, *17*(1), 16–23. https://doi.org/10.3109/17518423.2013.834998

Mevissen, L., & De Jongh, A. (2010). PTSD and its treatment in people with intellectual disabilities. *Clinical Psychology Review*, *30*(3), 308–316. https://doi.org/10.1016/j.cpr.2009.12.005

Mevissen, L., Didden, R., & De Jongh, A. (2018). *DITS-ID manual: Diagnostic Interview Trauma and Stressors—Intellectual Disability*. Accare Child Study Centre.

Mevissen, L., Didden, R., De Jongh, A., & Korzilius, H. (2020a). Assessing posttraumatic stress disorder in adults with mild intellectual disabilities or borderline intellectual functioning. *Journal of Mental Health Research in Intellectual Disabilities*, *13*(1), 110–125. https://doi.org/10.1080/19315864.2020.1753267

Mevissen, L., Didden, R., Korzilius, H., & De Jongh, A. (2016). Assessment of PTSD in children with mild to borderline intellectual disabilities. *European Journal of Psychotraumatology*, *7*, 29786. https://doi.org/10.3402/ejpt.v7.29786

Mevissen, L., Didden, R., Korzilius, H., & De Jongh, A. (2017). EMDR therapy for PTSD in children and adolescents with mild to borderline intellectual disability: A multiple baseline across subjects study. *Journal of Applied Research in Intellectual Disabilities*, *30*(Suppl. 1), 34–41. https://doi.org/10.1111/jar.12335

Mevissen, L., Evers, M., Serra, M., De Jongh, A., & Didden, R. (2020b). Feasibility and potential effectiveness of an intensive trauma-focused treatment programme for families with PTSD and mild intellectual disability. *European Journal of Psychotraumatology*, *11*(1), 1777809. https://doi.org/10.1080/20008198.2020.1777809

Mevissen, L., Lievegoed, R., & De Jongh, A. (2011). EMDR treatment in people with mild ID and PTSD: 4 cases. *Psychiatric Quarterly*, *82*(1), 43–57. https://doi.org/10.1007/s11126-010-9147-x

Mevissen, L., Lievegoed, R., Seubert, A., & De Jongh, A. (2012). PTSD treatment in people with severe intellectual disabilities: A case series. *Developmental Neurorehabilitation*, *15*(3), 223–232. https://doi.org/10.3109/17518423.2011.654283

Miller, W. R., & Rollnick, S. (2013). *Motivational interviewing: Helping people change* (3rd ed.). Guilford Press.

Molero, R. J., Jarero, I., & Givaudan, M. (2019). Longitudinal multisite randomized controlled trial on the provision of the EMDR-IGTP-OTS to refugee minors in Valencia, Spain. *American Journal of Applied Psychology*, *8*(4), 77–88. https://doi.org/10.11648/j.ajap.20190804.12

Mollica, R., Caspi-Yavin, Y., Bollini, P., Truong, T., Tor, S., & Lavelle, J. (1992). The Harvard Trauma Questionnaire: Validating a cross-cultural instrument for measuring torture, trauma, and posttraumatic stress disorder in Indochinese refugees. *The Journal of Nervous and Mental Disease*, *180*(2), 111–116.

Mooren, T., Van Ee, E., Hein, I., & Bala, J. (2023). Combatting intergenerational effects of psychotrauma with multifamily therapy. *Frontiers in Psychiatry*, *13*, 867305. https://doi.org/10.3389/fpsyt.2022.867305

Morina, N., Koerssen, R., & Pollet, T. V. (2016). Interventions for children and adolescents with posttraumatic stress disorder: A meta-analysis of comparative outcome studies. *Clinical Psychology Review*, *47*, 41–54. https://doi.org/10.1016/j.cpr.2016.05.006

Morris, A., Lee, T., & Delahanty, D. (2013). Interactive relationship between parent and child event appraisals and child PTSD symptoms after an injury. *Psychological Trauma: Theory, Research, Practice, and Policy*, *5*(6), 554–561. https://doi.org/10.1037/a0029894

Morris-Smith, J., & Silvestre, M. (2013). *EMDR for the next generation: Healing children and families*. ACPIL reading.

Morris-Smith, J., & Silvestre, M. (2014). *EMDR for the next generation: Healing children and families* (2nd ed.). Academic Publishing Limited.

Murphy, R. T. (2008). Enhancing combat veterans' motivation to change posttraumatic stress disorder symptoms and other problem behaviours. In H. Arkowitz, H. A. Westra, W. R. Miller, & S. Rollnick (Eds.), *Motivational interviewing in the treatment of psychological problems* (pp. 57–84). Guilford Press.

Murray, K. E., Davidson, G. R., & Schweitzer, R. D. (2010). Review of refugee mental health interventions following resettlement: Best practices and recommendations. *American Journal of Orthopsychiatry*, *80*(4), 576–585. https://doi.org/10.1111/j.1939-0025.2010.01062.x

Muskens, J. B., Velders, F. P., & Staal, W. G. (2017). Medical comorbidities in children and adolescents with autism spectrum disorders and attention deficit hyperactivity disorders: A systematic review. *European Child and Adolescent Psychiatry*, *26*(9), 1093–1103. https://doi.org/10.1007/s00787-017-1020-0

Mutluer, T., Genç, H. A., Morey, A. O., Yapici Eser, H., Ertinmaz, B., Can, M., & Munir, K. (2022). Population-based psychiatric comorbidity in children and adolescents with autism spectrum disorder: A meta-analysis. *Frontiers in Psychiatry*, *13*, 856208. https://doi.org/10.3389/fpsyt.2022.856208

Nauta, M., Braet, C., & Scholing, A. (2011). 16 cognitieve interventies bij kinderen en jongeren [16 cognitive interventions in children and adolescents]. In S. Bögels & P. Van Oppen, *Cognitieve therapie: Theorie en praktijk* (pp. 451–504). Bohn Stafleu van Loghum. https://doi.org/10.1007/978-90-313-8310-8_16

Naveed, S., Saboor, S., & Zeshan, M. (2020). An overview of attachment patterns: Psychology, neurobiology, and clinical implications. *Journal of Psychosocial Nursing and Mental Health Services*, *58*(8), 18–22. https://doi.org/10.3928/02793695-20200717-01

Nestgaard Rød, Å., & Schmidt, C. (2021). Complex PTSD: What is the clinical utility of the diagnosis? *European Journal of Psychotraumatology*, *12*(1), 2002028. https://doi.org/10.1080/20008198.2021.200202

Neuner, F., Catani, C., Ruf, M., Schauer, E., Schauer, M., & Elbert, T. (2008). Narrative exposure therapy for the treatment of traumatized children and adolescents (KidNET): From neurocognitive theory to field intervention. *Child and Adolescent Psychiatric Clinics of North America*, *17*(3), 641–664. https://doi.org/10.1016/j.chc.2008.03.001

NICE. (2017). *Antisocial behaviour and conduct disorders in children and young people: Recognition and management*. NICE Guideline.

NICE. (2018a). *Attention deficit hyperactivity disorder: Diagnosis and management of ADHD in children, young people and adults*. NICE Guideline. www.nice.org.uk/guidance/ng87

NICE. (2018b). *Post-traumatic stress disorder*. NICE Guideline. www.nice.org.uk/guidance/ng116

NICE. (2019). *Depression in children and young people: identification and management (NG134)*. https://www.nice.org.uk/guidance/ng134/resources/depression-in-children-and-young-people-identification-andmanagement-pdf-66141719350981

NICE. (2023). *Personality disorders: Borderline and antisocial. Quality standard* [*QS88*]. https://www.nice.org.uk/guidance/qs88

Nijdam, M. J., Gersons, B. P., Reitsma, J. B., De Jongh, A., & Olff, M. (2012). Brief eclectic psychotherapy v. eye movement desensitisation and reprocessing therapy for post-traumatic stress disorder: randomised controlled trial. *The British Journal of Psychiatry*, *200*(3), 224–231. https://doi.org/10.1192/bjp.bp.111.099234

Nocon, A., Eberle-Sejari, R., Unterhitzenberger, J., & Rosner, R. (2017). The effectiveness of psychosocial interventions in war-traumatized refugee and internally displaced minors: Systematic review and meta-analysis. *European Journal of Psychotraumatology*, *8*(sup2), 1388709. https://doi.org/10.1080/20008198.2017.1388709

Noppers, C. (2020). *Body-oriented exposure training: A method in treating complex trauma in intensive trauma therapy* [Master's thesis, University of Groningen].

Norman, R. E., Byambaa, M., De, R., Butchart, A., Scott, J., & Vos, T. (2014). *The long-term health consequences of child physical abuse, emotional abuse, and neglect: A systematic review and meta-analysis*. Child Rights International Network.

Ogden, P., & Minton, K. (2000). Sensorimotor psychotherapy: One method for processing traumatic memory. *Traumatology*, *6*(3), 149–173. https://doi.org/10.1177/153476560000600302

Ogden, P., Minton, K., & Pain, C. (2006). *Trauma and the body: A sensorimotor approach to psychotherapy*. Norton.

Ohre, B., Uthus, M. P., Von Tetzchner, S., & Falkum, E. (2015). Traumatization in deaf and hard-of-hearing adult psychiatric outpatients. *Journal of Deaf Studies and Deaf Education*, *20*(3), 296–308. https://doi.org/10.1093/deafed/env013

Olivier, E., De Roos, C., & Bexkens, A. (2022). Eye movement desensitization and reprocessing in young children (ages 4–8) with posttraumatic stress disorder: A multiple-baseline evaluation. *Child Psychiatry and Human Development*, *53*(6), 1391–1404.

Omer, H. (2004). *Nonviolent resistance: A new approach to violent and self-destructive children*. Cambridge University Press.

Omer, H. (2021). *Non-violent resistance: A new approach to violent and self-destructive children* (2nd edn.). Cambridge University Press.

Ooms-Evers, M., Van der Graaf-loman, S., Van Duijvenbode, N., Mevissen, L., & Didden, R. (2021). Intensive clinical trauma treatment for children and adolescents with mild intellectual disability or borderline intellectual functioning: A pilot study. *Research in Developmental Disabilities*, *117*, 104030. https://doi.org/10.1016/j.ridd.2021.104030

Oprel, D. A., Hoeboer, C. M., Schoorl, M., Kleine, R. A. D., Cloitre, M., Wigard, I. G., Van Minnen, A., & Van der Does, W. (2021). Effect of prolonged exposure, intensified prolonged exposure and STAIR+ prolonged exposure in patients with PTSD related to childhood abuse: A randomized controlled trial. *European Journal of Psychotraumatology*, *12*(1), 1851511. https://doi.org/10.1080/20008198.2020.1851511

Oras, R., De Ezpeleta, S. C., & Ahmad, A. (2004). Treatment of traumatized refugee children with eye movement desensitization and reprocessing in a psychodynamic context. *Nordic Journal of Psychiatry*, *58*(3), 199–203. https://doi.org/10.1080/08039480410006232

Ornoy, A., Weinstein-Fudim, L., & Ergaz, Z. (2015). Prenatal factors associated with autism spectrum disorder (ASD). *Teproductive Toxicology*, *56*, 155–169. https://doi.org/10.1016/j.reprotox.2015.05.007

O'Shea, K., & Porges, S. (2020). Polyvagal-informed EMDR: A neurobiological approach to healing trauma and attachment wounds. *Frontiers in Psychology*, *11*, 371. https://doi.org/10.3389/fpsyg.2020.00371

Osorio, A., Pérez, M. C., Tirado, S. G., Jarero, I., & Givaudan, M. (2018). Randomized controlled trial on the EMDR integrative group treatment protocol for ongoing traumatic stress with adolescents and young adult patients with cancer. *American Journal of Applied Psychology*, *7*(4), 50–56. https://doi.org/10.11648/j.ajap.20180704.11

Paauw, C. C., De Roos, C., Koornneef, M. G. T., Elzinga, B. M., Boorsma, T. M., Verheij, M. A., & Dingemans, A. E. (2023). Eye movement desensitization and reprocessing for adolescents with major depressive disorder: Study protocol for a multi-site randomized controlled trial. *Trials*, *24*(1), 206. https://doi.org/10.1186/s13063-023-07226-y

Paauw, C., De Roos, C., Tummers, J., De Jongh, A., & Dingemans, A. (2019). Effectiveness of trauma-focused treatment for adolescents with major depressive disorder. *European Journal of Psychotraumatology*, *10*(1), 1682931. https://doi.org/10.1080/20008198.2019.1682931

Pacione, L., Measham, T., & Rousseau, C. (2013). Refugee children: Mental health and effective interventions. *Current Psychiatry Reports*, *15*(2), 341. https://doi.org/10.1007/s11920-012-0341-4

Padesky, C. A. (2020). Collaborative case conceptualization: Client knows best. *Cognitive and Behavioral Practice*, *27*(4), 392–404. https://doi.org/10.1016/j.cbpra.2020.06.003

Pagani, M., Di Lorenzo, G., Verado, A. R., Nicolais, G., Monaco, L., Lauretti, G., Russo, R., Niolu, C., Ammaniti, M., Fernandez, I., & Siracusano, A. (2012). Neurobiological correlates of EMDR monitoring– An EEG study. *PLoS ONE*, *7*(9), e45753. https://doi.org/10.1371/journal.pone.0045753

Pagani, M., Högberg, G., Fernandez, I., & Siracusano, A. (2013). Correlates of EMDR therapy in functional and structural neuroimaging: A critical summary of recent findings. *Journal of EMDR Practice and Research*, *7*(1), 29–38. https://doi.org/10.1891/1933-3196.7.1.29

Panksepp, J. (2009). Brain emotional systems and qualities of mental life: From animal models of affect to implications for psychotherapeutics. In D. Fosha, D. J. Siegel, & M. F. Solomon (Eds.), *The healing power of emotion: Affective neuroscience, development and clinical practice* (pp. 1–26). W. W. Norton & Company.

Panksepp, J. (2010). Emotional causes and consequences of social-affective vocalization. In *Handbook of behavioral neuroscience* (Vol. 19, pp. 201–208). Elsevier.

Parnell, L. (2013). *Attachment-focused EMDR: Healing relational trauma* (pp. 45–73). W. W. Norton & Co.

Pat-Horenczyk, R., Rabinowitz, R. G., Rice, A., & Tucker-Levin, A. (2008). The search for risk and protective factors in childhood PTSD: From variables to processes. In D. Brom, R. Pat-Horenczyk, & J. D. Ford (Eds.), *Treating traumatized children* (pp. 69–89). Routledge.

Peltonen, K., & Kangaslampi, S. (2019). Treating children and adolescents with multiple traumas: A randomized clinical trial of narrative exposure therapy. *European Journal of Psychotraumatology*, *10*(1), 1558708. https://doi.org/10.1080/20008198.2018.1558708

Peltonen, K., Kangaslampi, S., Saranpää, J., Qouta, S., & Punamäki, R. L. (2017). Peritraumatic dissociation predicts posttraumatic stress disorder symptoms via dysfunctional trauma-related memory among war-affected children. *European Journal of Psychotraumatology*, *8*(1), 1375828. https://doi.org/10.1080/20008198.2017.1375828

Penninx Quevedo, R., De Jongh, A., Bouwmeester, S., & Didden, R. (2021). EMDR therapy for PTSD symptoms in patients with mild intellectual disability or borderline intellectual functioning and comorbid psychotic disorder: A case series. *Research in Developmental Disabilities*, *117*, 104044. https://doi.org/10.1016/j.ridd.2021.104044

Perri, R. L., Castelli, P., La Rosa, C., Zucchi, T., & Onofri, A. (2021). COVID-19, isolation, quarantine: On the efficacy of internet-based eye movement desensitization and reprocessing (EMDR) and cognitive-behavioral therapy (CBT) for ongoing trauma. *Brain Sciences*, *11*(5), 579. https://doi.org/10.3390/brainsci11050579

Perilli, S., Giuliani, A., Pagani, M., Mazzoni, G., Maslovaric, G., Maccarone, B., Mahasneh, V. H., & Morales, D. (2019). EMDR group treatment of children refugees: A field study. *Journal of EMDR Practice and Research*, *13*(2), 143–155. https://doi.org/10.1891/1933-3196.13.2.143

Perry, B. D. (2006). The neurosequential model of therapeutics: applying principles of neurodevelopment to clinical work with maltreated and traumatized children. In N. B. Webb (Ed.), *Working with traumatized youth in child welfare* (pp. 27–52). Guilford Press.

Perry, B. D., & Dobson, C. L. (2013). The neurosequential model of therapeutics. In J. D. Ford & C. A. Courtois (Eds.), *Treating complex traumatic stress disorders in children and adolescents: Scientific foundations and therapeutic models* (pp. 249–260). Guilford Press.

Perry, B. D., & Szalavitz, M. (2007). *The boy who was raised as a dog and other stories from a child psychiatrist's notebook: What traumatized children can teach us about loss, love, and healing*. Basic Books.

Perry, B. D., & Winfrey, O. (2023). *What happened to you: Conversations on trauma, resilience, and healing*. Flatiron Books.

Peterson, J. L., Earl, R. K., Fox, E. A., Ma, R., Haidar, G, Petter, M., Berliner, L., Wallace, A. S., & Bernier, R. A. (2019). Trauma and autism spectrum disorder: Review, proposed treatment directions and future directions. *Journal of Child and Adolescent Trauma*, *12*(4), 529–547. https://doi.org/10.1007/s40653-019-00253-5

Pfefferbaum, B., Nitiéma, P., & Newman, E. (2019). A meta-analysis of intervention effects on depression and/or anxiety in youth exposed to political violence or natural disasters. *Child and Youth Care Forum*, *48*, 449–477. https://doi.org/10.1007/s10566-019-09494-9

Phelps, A. J., Lethbridge, R., Brennan, S., Bryant, R. A., Burns, P., Cooper, J. A., Forbes, D., Gardiner, J., Gee, G., Jones, K., Kenardy, J., Kulkarni, J., McDermott, B., McFarlane, A. C., Newman, L., Varker, T., Worth, C., & Silove, D. (2022). Australian guidelines for the prevention and treatment of posttraumatic stress disorder: Updates in the third edition. *Australian and New Zealand Journal of Psychiatry*, *56*(3), 230–247. https://doi.org/10.1177/00048674211041917

Piaget, J. (1970). Piaget's theory. In P. Mussen (Ed.), *Carmichael's manual of child psychology* (3rd ed., vol. I, pp. 703–732). John Wiley & Sons Inc.

Pierce, Z. P., & Black, J. M. (2023). The neurophysiology behind trauma-focused therapy modalities used to treat post-traumatic stress disorder across the life course: A systematic review. *Trauma, Violence, and Abuse, 24*(2), 1106–1123. https://doi.org/10.1177/15248380211048446

Pinkney, C., & Robinson-Edwards, S. (2018). Gangs, music and the mediatisation of crime: Expressions, violations and validations. *Safer Communities, 17*(2), 103–118. https://doi.org/10.1108/SC-01-2017-0004

Ploeg, C., & Wanders-Mulder, E. H. (2019). Child IN Healthy System (KINGS): A trauma-informed treatment for families with multiple and complex problems. In J. Knot-Dickscheit & E. J. Knorth (Eds.), *Families with multiple and complex problems: Theory and practice* (pp. 439–452). Lemniscaat.

Polderman, N., Kellaert-Knol, M. G., & Stams, G. J. J. M. (2011). The basic trust method: An attachment-based specialized form of VIG. In H. Kennedy, M. Landor, & L. Todd (Eds.), *Video interaction guidance: A relationship-based intervention to promote attunement, empathy and wellbeing* (pp. 224–227). Jessica Kingsley Publishers.

Pollard, R. Q., & Barnett, S. (2009). Health-related vocabulary knowledge among deaf adults. *Rehabilitation Psychology, 54*(2), 182–185. https://doi.org/10.1037/a0015771

Porges, S. W. (2022). Polyvagal theory: A science of safety. *Frontiers in Integrative Neuroscience, 16*, 871227. https://doi.org/10.3389/fnint.2022.871227

Porges, S. W., & Dana, D. (2018). *Clinical applications of the polyvagal theory: The emergence of polyvagal-informed therapies* (Norton Series on Interpersonal Neurobiology). W. W. Norton & Company.

Porter, C., Palmier-Claus, J., Branitsky, A., Mansell, W., Warwick, H., & Varese, F. (2020). Childhood adversity and borderline personality disorder: A meta-analysis. *Acta Psychiatrica Scandinavica, 141*(1), 6–20. https://doi.org/10.1111/acps.13118

Potgieter Marks, R., Sabau, A., & Struik, A. (2015). *Guidelines for the assessment and treatment of children and adolescent with dissociative symptoms and dissociative disorders.* Child and Adolescent Committee of the European Society for Trauma and Dissociation (ESTD). http://www.estd.org

Potharst, E. S., Holtkamp, P., Walliser, L., Dommerholt, A. H., van den Heuvel, M. E. N., Spierts, I., & Maric, M. (2025). Improving infant mental health: A pilot study on the effectiveness, acceptability and feasibility of EMDR storytelling in infants with post-traumatic distress after medical procedures. *Evaluation and the Health Professions, 48*(1), 55–70.

Protic, S., Wittmann, L., Taubner, S., & Dimitrijevic, A. (2020). Differences in attachment dimensions and reflective functioning between traumatized juvenile offenders and maltreated non-delinquent adolescents from care services. *Child Abuse and Neglect, 103*, 104420. https://doi.org/10.1016/j.chiabu.2020.104420

Putnam, F. (1997). *Dissociation in children and adolescents: A developmental perspective.* Guilford Press.

Putman, M., Giltaik, H., & Van Gool, A. (2020). Effectiviteit van fasetherapie als behandeling van problematische gehechtheid bij kinderen van 4 tot 12 jaar. *Kinder and Jeugdpsychotherapie, 1*, 64–84.

Pynoos, R. S., Weathers, F. W., Steinberg, A. M., Marx, B. P., Layne, C. M., Kaloupek, D. G., Schnurr, P. P., Keane, T. M., Blake, D. D., Newman, E., Nader, K. O., & Kriegler, J. A. (2015). *Clinician-Administered PTSD Scale for DSM-5—Child/Adolescent Version.* https://www.ptsd.va.gov

Ragsdale, K. A., Watkins, L. E., Sherrill, A. M., Zwiebach, L., & Rothbaum, B. O. (2020). Advances in PTSD treatment delivery: Evidence base and future directions for intensive outpatient programs. *Current Treatment Options in Psychiatry, 7*(2), 291–300. https://doi.org/10.1007/s40501-020-00219-7

Rahko, J. S., Vuontela, V. A., Carlson, S., Nikkinen, J., Hurtig, T. M., Kuusikko-Gauffin, S., Mattila, M. L., Jussila, K. K., Remes, J. J., Jansson-Verkasalo, E. M., Aronen, E. T., Pauls, D. L., Ebeling, H. E., Tervonen, O., Moilanen, I. K., & Kiviniemi, V. J. (2016). Attention and working memory in adolescents with autism spectrum disorder: A functional MRI study. *Child Psychiatry and Human Development, 47*(3), 503–517. https://doi.org/10.1007/s10578-015-0583-6

Rathore, H. E. (2018). Trust and attunement-focused EMDR with a child. *Journal of EMDR Practice and Research, 12*(4), 255–268. https://doi.org/10.1891/1933-3196.12.4.255

Rauvola, R. S., Vega, D. M., & Lavigne, K. N. (2019). Compassion fatigue, secondary traumatic stress, and vicarious traumatization: A qualitative review and research agenda. *Occupational Health Science, 3*, 297–336. https://doi.org/10.1007/s41542-019-00045-1

Raz, R., Roberts, A., Leyall, K., Hart, J., Just, A., Laden, F., & Weiskopf, M. (2015). Autism spectrum disorder and particulate matter air pollution before, during and after pregnancy: A nested case-control analysis within Nurses' Health Study II Cohort. *Environmental Health Perspectives (online), 123*(3), 264–270. https://doi.org/10.1289/ehp.1408133

Reed, R. V., Fazel, M., Jories, L., Panter-Brick, C., & Stein, A. (2012). Mental health of displaced and refugee children resettled in low-income and middle-income countries: Risk and protective factors. *Lancet*, *379*(9812), 250–265. https://doi.org/10.1016/S0140-6736(11)60050-0

Reinders, A. A., Chalavi, S., Schlumpf, Y. R., Vissia, E. M., Nijenhuis, E. R., Jäncke, L., Veltman, D. J., & Ecker, C. (2018). Neurodevelopmental origins of abnormal cortical morphology in dissociative identity disorder. *Acta Psychiatrica Scandinavica*, *137*(2), 157–170. https://doi.org/10.1111/acps.12839

Rentinck, E. M., Van Mourik, R., De Jongh, A., & Matthijssen, S. J. M. A. (2025). Effectiveness of an intensive outpatient treatment programme combining prolonged exposure and EMDR therapy for adolescents and young adults with PTSD in a naturalistic setting. *European Journal of Psychotraumatology*, *16*(1), 2451478.

Resick, P. A., Bovin, M. J., Calloway, A. L., Dick, A. M., Mitchell, K. S., Suvak, M. K., Wells, S. Y., Stirman, S. W., & Wolf, E. J. (2012). A critical evaluation of the complex PTSD literature: Implications for DSM-5. *Journal of Traumatic Stress*, *25*(3), 241–251. https://doi.org/10.1002/jts.21699

Rieffe, C., Kouwenberg, M., Scheper, I., Smit, C., & Wiefferink, K. (2009, April). Inzicht in de eigen emoties bij dove kinderen [Insight into deaf children's own emotions]. *VHZ artikelen*.

Rieffe, C., Netten, A. P., Broekhof, E., & Veiga, G. (2015). The role of environment in children's emotion socialization: The case of deaf or hard-of-hearing (DHH) children. In M. Marschark & H. E. T. Knoors (Eds.), *Educating deaf learners: Creating global evidence base* (pp. 369–388). Oxford University Press.

Rieffe, C., & Wiefferink, C. H. (2017). Happy faces, sad faces: Emotion understanding in toddlers and preschoolers with language impairments. *Research in Developmental Disabilities*, *62*, 40–49. https:/doi.org/10.1016/j.ridd.2016.12.018

Robinson, R. M., & Kaptan, S. K. (Eds.) (2024). *EMDR group therapy: Emerging principles and protocols to treat trauma and beyond*. Springer Publishing Company.

Rodenburg, R., Benjamin, A., Meijer, A., & Jongeneel, R. (2009). Eye movement desensitization and reprocessing in an adolescent with epilepsy and mild intellectual disability. *Epilepsy and Behavior*, *16*(1), 175–180. https://doi.org/10.1016/j.yebeh.2009.07.015

Rommelse, N. J., Geurts, H. M., Franke, B., Buitelaar, J. K., & Hartman, C. A. (2011). A review of cognitive and brain endophenotypes that may be common in autism spectrum disorder and attention-deficit/hyperactivity disorder and facilitate the search for pleiotropic genes. *Neuroscience and Biobehavioral Reviews*, *35*(6), 1363–1396. https://doi.org/10.1016/j.neubiorev.2011.02.015

Rosenbaum, S., Vancampfort, D., Steel, Z., Newby, J., Ward, P. B., & Stubbs, B. (2015). Physical activity in the treatment of post-traumatic stress disorder: A systematic review and meta-analysis. *Psychiatry Research*, *230*(2), 130–136. https://doi.org/10.1016/j.psychres.2015.10.017

Rosoff, A. L. (2019). How we do what we do: The therapist, EMDR, and treatment of complex trauma. *Journal of EMDR Practice and Research*, *13*(1), 61–74. https://doi.org/10.1891/1933-3196.13.1.61

Rossi, E., Cassioli, E., Cecci, L., Arganini, F., Martelli, M., Redaelli, C. A., Anselmetti, S., Bertelli, S., Fernandez, I., Ricca, V., & Castellini, G. (2024). Eye movement desensitisation and reprocessing as add-on treatment to enhanced cognitive behaviour therapy for patients with anorexia nervosa reporting childhood maltreatment: A quasi-experimental multicenter study. *European Eating Disorders Review*, *32*(2), 322–337. https://doi.org/10.1002/erv.3044

Rothschild, B. (2000). *The body remembers. The psychophysiology of trauma and trauma treatment*. Norton.

Rousseau, C., & Drapeau, A. (2003). Are refugee children an at risk group? A longitudinal study of Cambodian adolescents. *Journal of Refugee Studies*, *16*(1), 67–81. https://doi.org/10.1093/jrs/16.1.67

Ruf, M., Schauer, M., Neuner, F., Catani, C., Schauer, E., & Elbert, T. (2010). Narrative exposure therapy for 7- to 16-year-olds: A randomized controlled trial with traumatized refugee children. *Journal of Traumatic Stress*, *23*(4), 437–445. https://doi.org/10.1002/jts.20548

Sachser, C., Berliner, L., Holt, T., Jensen, T. K., Jungbluth, N., Risch, E., Rosner, R., & Goldbeck, L. (2017a). International development and psychometric properties of the Child and Adolescent Trauma Screen (CATS). *Journal of Affective Disorders*, *210*, 189–195. https://doi.org/10.1016/j.jad.2016.12.040

Sachser, C., Keller, F., & Goldbeck, L. (2017b). Complex PTSD as proposed for ICD-11: Validation of a new disorder in children and adolescents and their response to trauma-focused cognitive behavioral therapy. *Journal of Child Psychology and Psychiatry*, *58*(2), 160–168. https://doi.org/10.1111/jcpp.12640

Said, G., & King, D. (2020). Implementing narrative exposure therapy for unaccompanied asylum-seeking minors with post-traumatic stress disorder: A pilot feasibility report. *Clinical Child Psychology and Psychiatry*, *25*(1), 213–226. https://doi.org/10.1177/1359104519864123

Samara, Z., Elzinga, B. M., Slagter, H. A., & Nieuwenhuis, S. (2011). Do horizontal saccadic eye movements increase interhemispheric coherence? Investigation of a hypothesized neural mechanism underlying EMDR. *Frontiers in Psychiatry*, *2*, 4. https://doi.org/10.3389/fpsyt.2011.00004

Samji, H., Wu, J., Ladak, A., Vossen, C., Stewart, E., Dove, N., Long, D., & Snell, G. (2022). Mental health impacts of the COVID-19 pandemic on children and youth: A systematic review. *Child and Adolescent Mental Health, 27*(2), 173–189. https://doi.org/10.1111/camh.12501

Santos, I. (2019). EMDR case formulation tool. *Journal of EMDR Practice and Research, 13*(3), 221–231. https://doi.org/10.1891/1933-3196.13.3.221

Sara, G., & Lappin, J. (2017). Childhood trauma: Psychiatry's greatest public health challenge? *The Lancet Public Health, 2*(7), e300–e301. https://doi.org/10.1016/S2468-2667(17)30104-4

Schaan, V. K., André, S., Julian, A. R., Michael, B., Gregor, D., Hartmut, S., & Claus, V. (2019). Childhood trauma affects stress-related interoceptive accuracy. *Frontiers in Psychiatry, 10.* https://doi.org/10.3389/fpsyt.2019.00750

Schaefer, G. B. (2016). Clinical genetic aspects of autism spectrum disorders. *International Journal of Molecular Sciences, 17*(2), 180. https://doi.org/10.3390/ijms17020180

Scharpf, F., Kaltenbach, E., Nickerson, A., & Hecker, T. (2021). A systematic review of socio-ecological factors contributing to risk and protection of the mental health of refugee children and adolescents. *Clinical Psychology Review, 83*, 101930. https://doi.org/10.1016/j.cpr.2020.101930

Scheck, M. M., Schaeffer, J. A., & Gillette, C. S. (1998). Brief psychological intervention with traumatized young women: The efficacy of eye movement desensitization and reprocessing. *Journal of Traumatic Stress, 11*(1), 25–44. https://doi.org/10.1023/A:1024400931106

Scheeringa, M. S., & Zeanah, C. H. (2001). A relational perspective on PTSD in early childhood. *Journal of Traumatic Stress, 14*(4), 799–815. https://doi.org/10.1023/A:1013002507972

Schild, S., & Dalenberg, C. J. (2012). Trauma exposure and traumatic symptoms in deaf adults. *Psychological Trauma: Theory Research, Practice, and Policy, 4*(1), 117–127. https://doi.org/10.1037/a0021578

Schlattmann, N., Van der Hoeven, M., & Hein, I. (2023). *IGT-K, Integratieve gehechtheidsbevorderende traumabehandeling voor kinderen; gezinstherapie en EMDR*. BSL.

Schlumpf, Y. R., Nijenhuis, E. R., Chalavi, S., Weder, E. V., Zimmermann, E., Luechinger, R., La Marca, R., Simone Reinders, A. A. T., & Jäncke, L. (2013). Dissociative part-dependent biopsychosocial reactions to backward masked angry and neutral faces: An fMRI study of dissociative identity disorder. *NeuroImage: Clinical, 3*, 54–64. https://doi.org/10.1016/j.nicl.2013.07.002

Schore, A. N. (2001). The effects of early relational trauma on right brain development, affect-regulation, and infant mental health. *Infant Mental Health Journal, 22*(1–2), 201–269. https://doi.org/10.1002/1097-0355(200101/04)22:1<201::AID-IMHJ8>3.0.CO;2-9

Schore, A. N. (2019). *Right brain psychotherapy*. W. W. Norton & Company.

Schore, J. R., & Schore, A. N. (2014). Regulation theory and affect regulation psychotherapy: A clinical primer. *Smith College Studies in Social Work, 84*(2–3), 178–195. https://doi.org/10.1080/00377317.2014.923719

Schouten, K. A., De Niet, G. J., Knipscheer, J. W., Kleber, R. J., & Hutschemaekers, G. J. M. (2015). The effectiveness of art therapy in the treatment of traumatized adults: A systematic review on art therapy and trauma. *Trauma, Violence, and Abuse, 16*(2), 220–228. https://doi.org/10.1177/1524838014555032

Sciarrino, N. A., Warnecke, A. J., & Teng, E. J. (2020). A systematic review of intensive empirically supported treatments for posttraumatic stress disorder. *Journal of Traumatic Stress, 33*(4), 443–454. https://doi.org/10.1002/jts.22556

Seubert, N. C. C., & Virdi, P. (Eds.). (2024). *Trauma-informed approaches to eating disorders*. Springer Publishing Company.

Sexton, T. L., & Alexander, J. F. (2002). FBEST: Family-based empirically supported treatment interventions. *The counseling Psychologist, 30*(2), 238–261.

Shapiro, E. (2012). EMDR and early psychological intervention following trauma. *European Review of Applied Psychology, 62*(4), 241–251. https://doi.org/10.1016/j.erap.2012.09.003

Shapiro, E., & Laub, B. (2008). Early EMDR intervention (EEI): A summary, a theoretical model, and the recent traumatic episode protocol (R-TEP). *Journal of EMDR Practice and Research, 2*(2), 79–96. https://doi.org/10.1891/1933-3196.2.2.79

Shapiro, E., & Laub, B. (2014). The new Recent Traumatic Episode Protocol (R-TEP). In M. Luber (Ed.), *Implementing EMDR early mental health interventions for man-made and natural disasters: Models, scripted protocols and summary sheets* (pp. 193–207). Springer.

Shapiro, F. (2001). *Eye movement desensitization and reprocessing: Basic principles, protocols, and procedures* (2nd ed.). Guilford Press.

Shapiro, F. (2014). EMDR therapy humanitarian assistance programs: Treating the psychological, physical, and societal effects of adverse experiences worldwide. *Journal of EMDR Practice and Research, 8*(4), 181. https://doi.org/10.1891/1933-3196.8.4.181

Shapiro, F. (2018). *Eye movement desensitization and reprocessing (EMDR) therapy: Basic principles, protocols, and procedures*. Guilford Press.

Shapiro, F., Kaslow, F. W., & Maxfield, L. (Eds.). (2007). *Handbook of EMDR and family processes*. John Wiley & Sons.

Siegel, D. J. (1999). *The developing mind: Toward a neurobiology of interpersonal experience* (1st ed.). Guilford Press.

Siegel, D. J. (2012). *The developing mind: Toward a neurobiology of interpersonal experience* (2nd ed.). Guilford Press.

Siegel, D. J. (2020). *The developing mind: How relationships and the brain interact to shape who we are*. Guilford Press.

Siegel, A., Brickman, S., Goldberg, Z., & Pat-Horenczyk, R. (2019). Preventing future terrorism: Intervening on youth radicalization. In C. W. Hoven, L. V. Amsel, & S. Tyano (Eds.), *An international perspective on disasters and children's mental health* (pp. 391–418). Springer.

Silberg, J. L. (2013). *The child survivor: Healing developmental trauma and dissociation*. Routledge/Taylor & Francis Group.

Silverstein, M. J., Herress, J., Ostrowski-Delahanty, S., Stavropoulos, V., Kassam-Adams, N., & Daly, B. P. (2022). Associations between parent posttraumatic stress symptoms (PTSD) and later child PTSD: Results from an international data archive. *Journal of Traumatic Stress*, *35*(6), 1620–1630. https://doi.org/10.1002/jts.22864

Silvestre, M., & Tarquinio, C. L. (2022). Systemic family therapy and EMDR therapy: An integrative approach. *European Journal of Trauma and Dissociation*, *6*(4), 100291. https://doi.org/10.1016/j.ejtd.2022.100291

Sim, A., Bowes, L., & Gardner, F. (2018). Modeling the effects of war exposure and daily stressors on maternal mental health, parenting, and child psychosocial adjustment: A cross-sectional study with Syrian refugees in Lebanon. *Global Mental Health*, *5*, e40. https://doi.org/10.1017/gmh.2018.33

Simmons, C., Meiser-Stedman, R., Baily, H., & Beazley, P. (2021). A meta-analysis of dropout from evidence-based psychological treatment for post-traumatic stress disorder (PTSD) in children and young people. *European Journal of Psychotraumatology*, *12*(1), 1947570. https://doi.org/10.1080/20008198.2021.1947570

Sinason, V., & Potgieter Marks, R. (Eds.). (2022). *Treating children with dissociative disorders: Attachment, trauma, theory and practice*. Routledge.

Sleiffer, M. (2013, November 30). Die mimiek, de sierlijkheid van de bewegingen [That facial expression, the gracefulness of the movements]. *Trouw*. https://www.trouw.nl/nieuws/maartje-sleiffer-tolk-gebarentaal-die-mimiek-de-sierlijkheid-van-de-bewegingen~bee09d9a

Sloover, M., Stoltz, S. E. M. J., & Van Ee, E. (2024). Parent–child communication about potentially traumatic events: A systematic review. *Trauma, Violence, and Abuse*, *25*(3), 2115–2127. https://doi.org/10.1177/15248380231207906

Slotema, C. W., Blom, J. D., Niemantsverdriet, M. B. A., & Sommer, I. E. C. (2018). Auditory verbal hallucinations in borderline personality disorder and the efficacy of antipsychotics: A systematic review. *Frontiers in Psychiatry*, *9*, 347. https://doi.org/10.3389/fpsyt.2018.00347

Slotema, C. W., Van den Berg, D. P. G., Driessen, A., Wilhelmus, B., & Franken, I. H. A. (2019). Feasibility of EMDR for posttraumatic stress disorder in patients with personality disorders: A pilot study. *European Journal of Psychotraumatology*, *10*(1), 1614822. https://doi.org/10.1080/20008198.2019.1614822

Slotema, C. W., Wilhelmus, B., Arends, L. R., Franken, I. H. A. (2020). Psychotherapy for posttraumatic stress disorder in patients with borderline personality disorder: A systematic review and meta-analysis of its efficacy and safety. *European Journal of Psychotraumatology*, *11*(1), 1796188. https://doi.org/10.1080/20008198.2020.1796188

Smith, P., Dalgliesh, T., & Meiser-Stedman, R. (2019). Practitioner review: Posttraumatic stress disorder and its treatment in children and adolescents. *Journal of Child Psychology and Psychiatry*, *60*(5), 500–515. https://doi.org/10.1111/jcpp.12983

Smyth-Dent, K. L., Fitzgerald, J., Hagos, Y. (2019). A field study on the EMDR integrative group treatment protocol for ongoing traumatic stress provided to adolescent Eritrean refugees living in Ethiopia. *Psychology and Behavioral Science International Journal*, *12*(4), 1–12. https://doi.org/10.19080/PBSIJ.2019.12.555842

Snider, L., & Hijazi, Z. (2020). UNICEF community-based mental health and psychosocial support (MHPSS) operational guidelines. In S. J. Song & P. Ventevogel (Eds.), *Child, adolescent and family refugee mental health: A global perspective* (pp. 101–119). Springer International Publishing.

Soberman, G. B., Greenwald, R., & Rule, D. L. (2002). A controlled study of eye movement desensitization and reprocessing (EMDR) for boys with conduct problem. *Journal of Aggression, Maltreatment and Trauma*, *6*(1), 217–236. https://doi.org/10.1300/J146v06n01_11

Sonuga-Barke, E., Bitsakou, P., & Thompson, M. (2010). Beyond the dual pathway model: Evidence for the dissociation of timing, inhibitory, and delay-related impairments in attention-deficit/hyperactivity disorder. *Journal of American Academy of Child and Adolescent Psychiatry*, *49*(4), 345–355. https://doi.org/10.1016/j.jaac.2009.12.018

Souverein, F., Dekkers, T., Bulanovaite, E., Doreleijers, T., Hales, H., Kaltiala-Heino, R., Oddo, A., Popma, A., Raschle, N., Schmeck, K., Zanoli, M., & Van Der Pol, T. (2019). Overview of European forensic youth care: Towards an integrative mission for prevention and intervention strategies for juvenile offenders. *Child and Adolescent Psychiatry and Mental Health*, *13*, 1–6. https://doi.org/10.1186/s13034-019-0265-4

Spaans, J., & Van Meekeren, E. (2000). *Borderline hulpboek. Zelf leren omgaan met verschijnselen als impulsiviteit, heftige emoties en conflicten*. Boom.

Spiegler, M. D., & Guevremont, D. C. (2010). *Contemporary behaviour therapy* (5th ed.). Wadsworth.

Spinazzola, J., Van der Kolk, B., & Ford, J. D. (2018). When nowhere is safe: Trauma history antecedents of posttraumatic stress disorder and developmental trauma disorder in childhood. *Journal of Traumatic Stress*, *31*(5), 631–642. https://doi.org/10.1002/jts.22320

Spinazzola, J., Van der Kolk, B., & Ford, J. D. (2021). Developmental trauma disorder: A legacy of attachment trauma in victimized children. *Journal of Traumatic Stress*, *34*(4), 711–720. https://doi.org/10.1002/jts.22697

Staal, W. G. (2016). Autism, vitamin D and early brain development. *Human Genetics and Embryology*, *6*(2), 1–3. https://doi.org/10.4172/2161-0436.1000e114

Staal, W. G., Vorstman, J., & Van der Gaag, R. J. (2016). *Leerboek ontwikkelingsstoornissen in de levensloop*. De Tijdstroom.

Steenen, S. A., Steenen, C. C., van Westrhenen, R., Klausch, T., & de Jongh, A. (2023). *Impact of concomitant psychotropic medication on the efficacy of psychotherapy for post-traumatic stress disorder: A propensity score-matched prospective cohort study.* Available at SSRN 4597991. https://doi.org/10.2139/ssrn.4597991

Stickgold, R. (2007). Of sleep, memories, and trauma. *Nature Neuroscience*, *10*(5), 540–542. https://doi.org/10.1038/nn0507-540

Strand, V. C., Sarmiento, T. L., & Pasquale, L. E. (2005). Assessment and screening tools for trauma in children and adolescents: A review. *Trauma Violence Abuse*, *6*(1), 55–78. https://doi.org/10.1177/1524838004272559

Stratton, P., & Low, D. C. (2020). Culturally sensitive measures of family therapy. In K. S. Wampler (Ed.), *The handbook of systemic family therapy (Volume 4)* (pp. 77–101). Wiley.

Strelchuk, D., Turner, K., Smith, S., Bisson, J., Wiles, N., & Zammit, S. (2023). Provision of online eye movement and desensitisation therapy (EMDR) for people with post-traumatic stress disorder PTSD): A multi-method service evaluation. *European Journal of Psychotraumatology*, *14*(2), 2281182. https://doi.org/10.1080/20008066.2023.2281182

Struik, A. (2019a). *Behandling af kronisk traumatiserede børn. Sleeping Dogs-metoden*. Hans Reitzels Forlag.

Struik, A. (2019b). *Treating chronically traumatized children: The Sleeping Dogs method* (2nd ed.). Routledge.

Struik, A. (2021a). *Slapende Honden? Wakkker maken! Een behandelmethode voor chronisch getraumatiseerde kinderen* (3rd ed.). Pearson Benelux.

Struik, A. (2021b). Structuring treatment for dissociative children with the Sleeping Dogs method. In V. Sinason & R. Potgieter Marks (Eds.), *Treating children with dissociative disorders: Attachment, trauma, theory and practice* (pp. 116–138). Routledge.

Struik, A., Lindauer, R. J., & Ensink, J. B. (2017). I won't do EMDR! The use of the 'Sleeping Dogs' method to overcome children's resistance to EMDR therapy. *Journal of EMDR Practice and Research*, *11*(4), 166–180. https://doi.org/10.1891/1933-3196.11.4.166

Subramanyam, A. A., Mukherjee, A., Dave, M., & Chavda, K. (2019). Clinical practice guidelines for autism spectrum disorders. *Indian Journal of Psychiatry*, *61*(Suppl 2), 254–269. https://doi.org/10.4103/psychiatry

Sullivan, A. L., & Simonson, G. R. (2016). A systematic review of school-based social-emotional interventions for refugee and war-traumatized youth. *Review of Educational Research*, *86*(2), 503–530. https://doi.org/10.3102/0034654315609419

Swimm, L. L. (2018). EMDR Intervention for a 17-month-old child to treat attachment trauma: Clinical case presentation. *Journal of EMDR Practice and Research*, *12*(4), 269–281. https://doi.org/10.1891/1933-3196.12.4.269

Tang, T. C., Yang, P., Yen, C. F., & Liu, T. L. (2015). Eye movement desensitization and reprocessing for treating psychological disturbances in Taiwanese adolescents who experienced Typhoon Morakot. *Kaohsiung Journal of Medical Sciences*, *31*(7), 363–369. https://doi.org/10.1016/j.kjms.2015.04.013

Tarquinio, C., Rotonda, C., Houllé, W. A., Montel, S., Rydberg, J. A., Minary, L., Dellucci, H., Tarquinio, P., Fayard, A., & Alla, F. (2016). Early psychological preventive intervention for workplace violence: A randomized controlled explorative and comparative study between EMDR-recent event and critical incident stress debriefing. *Issues in Mental Health Nursing*, *37*(11), 787–799. https://doi.org/10.1080/01612840.2016.1224282

Tate, R. L., Perdices, M., Rosenkoetter, U., McDonald, S., Togher, L., Shadish, W., Horner, R., Kratochwill, T., Barlow, D. H., Kazdin, A., Sampson, M., Shamseer, L., & Vohra, S. (2016). The Single-Case Reporting In BEhavioural Interventions (SCRIBE) 2016: Explanation and elaboration. *Archives of Scientific Psychology*, *4*(1), 10–31. https://doi.org/10.1037/arc0000027

Tausendfreund, T., Knot-Dickscheit, J., Schulze, G. C., Knorth, E. J., & Grietens, H. (2016). Families in multi-problem situations: Backgrounds, characteristics, and care services. *Child and Youth Services*, *37*(1), 4–22. https://doi.org/10.1080/0145935X.2015.1052133

Teicher, M. H., Andersen, S. L., Polcari, A., Anderson, C. M., Navalta, C. P., & Kim, D. M. (2003). The neurobiological consequences of early stress and childhood maltreatment. *Neuroscience and Biobehavioral Reviews*, *27*(1–2), 33–44. https://doi.org/10.1016/S0149-7634(03)00007-1

Teicher, M. H., & Samson, J. A. (2016). Annual research review: Enduring neurobiological effects of childhood abuse and neglect. *Journal of Child Psychology and Psychiatry*, *57*(3), 241–266. https://doi.org/10.1111/jcpp.12507

Telman, M. D., Overbeek, M. M., De Schipper, J. C., Lamers-Winkelman, F., Finkenauer, C., & Schuengel, C. (2016). Family functioning and children's post-traumatic stress symptoms in a referred sample exposed to interparental violence. *Journal of Family Violence*, *31*(1), 127–136. https://doi.org/10.1007/s10896-015-9769-8

Ter Harmsel, J. F., Noordzij, M. L., Goudriaan, A. E., Dekker, J. J., Swinkels, L. T., Van der Pol, T. M., & Popma, A. (2021). Biocueing and ambulatory biofeedback to enhance emotion regulation: A review of studies investigating non-psychiatric and psychiatric populations. *International Journal of Psychophysiology*, *159*, 94–106. https://doi.org/10.1016/j.ijpsycho.2020.11.009

Ter Harmsel, J. F., Smulders, L. M., Noordzij, M. L., Swinkels, L. T. A., Goudriaan, A. E., Popma, A., & Van der Pol, T. M. (2023). Forensic psychiatric outpatients' and therapists' perspectives on a wearable biocueing app (Sense-IT) as an addition to aggression regulation therapy: Qualitative focus group and interview study. *JMIR Formative Research*, *7*, e40237. https://doi.org/10.2196/40237

Terr, L. C. (1991). Childhood traumas: An outline and overview. *American Journal of Psychiatry*, *148*, 10–20. https://doi.org/10.1176/foc.1.3.322

Theunissen, S. C. P. M, Rieffe, C., Kouwenberg, M., Soede, W., Briaire, J. J., & Frijns, J. H. M. (2011). Depression in hearing-impaired children. *International Journal of Pediatric Otorhinolaryngology*, *75*(10), 1313–1317. https://doi.org/10.1016/j.ijporl.2011.07.023

Timshel, I., Montgomery, E., & Dalgaard, N. T. (2017). A systematic review of risk and protective factors associated with family related violence in refugee families. *Child Abuse and Neglect*, *70*, 315–330. https://doi.org/10.1016/j.chiabu.2017.06.023

Tinker, R. H., & Wilson, S. A. (1999). *Through the eyes of a child: EMDR with children*. Norton.

Tonry, M. (2014). Why crime rates are falling throughout the Western world. *Crime and Justice*, *43*(1), 1–63. https://scholarship.law.umn.edu/faculty_articles/511

Treleaven, D. A. (2018). *Trauma-sensitive mindfulness: Practices for safe and transformative healing*. W. W. Norton.

Trentini, C., Lauriola, M., Giuliani, A., Maslovaric, G., Tambelli, R., Fernandez, I., & Pagani, M. (2018). Dealing with the aftermath of mass disasters: A field study on the application of EMDR Integrative group treatment protocol with child survivors of the 2016 Italy earthquakes. *Frontiers in Psychology*, *9*, 862. https://doi.org/10.3389/fpsyg.2018.00862

Trezise, K., Gray, K., Taffe, J., & Sheppard, D. (2014). Working memory in adolescent males with Down syndrome and males with autism and intellectual disability: Implications for the classroom. *Journal of Intellectual and Developmental Disability*, *39*(1), 24–34. https://doi.org/10.3109/13668250.2013.874550

Trickey, D., Siddaway, A. P., Meiser-Stedman, R., Serpell, L., & Field, A. P. (2012). A meta-analysis of risk factors for post-traumatic stress disorder in children and adolescents. *Clinical Psychology Review*, *32*(2), 122–138. https://doi.org/10.1016/j.cpr.2011.12.001

Tsou, Y-T., Li, B., Eichengreen, A., Frijns, J. H. M., & Rieffe, C. (2021). Emotions in deaf and hard-of-hearing and typically hearing children. *Journal of Deaf Studies and Deaf Education*, *26*(4), 469–482. https://doi.org/10.1093/deafed/enab022

Tsur, N. (2020). 'My own flesh and blood': The implications of child maltreatment for the orientation towards the body among dyads of mothers and daughters. *Child Abuse and Neglect*, *104*, 1–10. https://doi.org/10.1016/j.chiabu.2020.104469

Tsur, N., Defrin, R., Lahav, Y., & Solomon, Z. (2018). The traumatized body: Long-term PTSD and its implications for the orientation towards bodily signals. *Psychiatry Research*, *261*, 281–289. https://doi.org/10.1016/j.psychres.2017.12.083

Turnell, A., & Edwards, S. (1999). *Signs of safety: A solution and safety oriented approach to child protection casework*. Norton & Company.

Turnell, A., & Edwards, S. (2009). *Veilig opgroeien: De oplossingsgerichte aanpak Signs of Safety in jeugdzorg en kinderbescherming*. Bohn Stafleu van Loghum.

Turnell, A., & Essex, S. (2006). *Working with 'denied' child abuse. The resolutions approach*. Open University Press.

Ünver, H., & Karakaya, I. (2019). The assessment of the relationship between ADHD and posttraumatic stress disorder in child and adolescent patients. *Journal of Attention Disorders*, *23*(8), 900–903. https://doi.org/10.1177/1087054716677818

UNHCR (2025). Global trends. Data and statistics. https://www.unhcr.org/global-trends

Valiente-Gómez, A., Moreno-Alcázar, A., Treen, D., Cedrón, C., Colom, F., Pérez, V., & Amann, B. L. (2017). EMDR beyond PTSD: A systematic literature review. *Frontiers in Psychology*, *8*, 1668. https://doi.org/10.3389/fpsyg.2017.01668

Valkenburg, B. (2012). *Without uttering a word* [Doctoral dissertation, Erasmus University].

Van den Bedem, N. P. (2023). *Emotions and the psychosocial development of children with and without developmental language disorder* [Doctoral dissertation, Universiteit Leiden].

Van den Bedem, N. P., Dockrell, J. E., Van Alphen, P. M., De Rooij, M., Samson, A. C., Harjunen E. L. (2018a). Depressive symptoms and emotion regulation strategies in children with and without developmental language disorder: A longitudinal study. *International Journal of Language and Communication Disorders*, *53*(6), 1110–1123. https:/doi.org/10.1111/1460-6984.12423

Van den Bedem, N. P., Dockrell, J. E., Van Alphen, P. M., Kalicharan, S. V., & Rieffe, C. (2018b). Victimization, bullying, and emotional competence: Longitudinal associations in (pre)adolescents with and without developmental language disorder. *Journal of Speech, Language, and Hearing Research*, *61*(8), 2028–2044. https://doi.org/10.1044/2018_JSLHR-L-17-0429

Van den Hout, M., & Engelhard, I. M. (2012). How does EMDR work? *Journal of Experimental Psychopathology*, *3*(5), 724–738. https://doi.org/10.5127/jep.028212

Van den Hout, M. A., Engelhardt, I. M., Rijkeboer, M. M., Koekebakker, J., Hornsveld, H., Leer, A., Toffolo, M. B. J., & Akse, N. (2011). EMDR: Eye movements superior to beeps in taxing working memory and reducing vividness of recollections. *Behaviour Research and Therapy*, *49*(2), 92–98. https://doi.org/10.1016/j.brat.2010.11.003

Van den Hout, M. A., Engelhard, I. M., Smeets, M. A. M., Hornsveld, H., Hoogeveen, E., De Heer, E., Toffolo, M. B. J., & Rijkeboer, M. M. (2010). Counting during recall: Taxing of working memory and reduced vividness and emotionality of negative memories. *Applied Cognitive Psychology*, *24*(3), 303–311. https://doi.org/10.1002/acp.1677

Van der Gaag, R. J. (Ed.). (2009). *Multiple complex developmental disorder*. Benecke.

Van der Hart, O., Nijenhuis, E. R., & Solomon, R. (2010). Dissociation of the personality in complex trauma-related disorders and EMDR: Theoretical considerations. *Journal of EMDR Practice and Research*, *4*(2), 76–92. https://doi.org/10.1891/1933-3196.4.2.76

Van der Hoeven, M. L., Bouwmeester, S., Schlattmann, N. E. F., Lindauer, R. J., & Hein, I. M. (2024). Family therapy and EMDR after child abuse and neglect: Moderating effects of child attachment style and PTSD symptoms on treatment outcome. *European Journal of Psychotraumatology*, *15*(1), 2416288.

Van der Hoeven, M. L., Plukaard, S. C., Schlattmann, N. E. F., Lindauer, R. J. L., & Hein, I. M. (2023). An integrative treatment model of EMDR and family therapy for children after child abuse and neglect: A SCED study. *Children and Youth Services Review*, *152*(1), 107064. https://doi.org/10.1016/j.childyouth.2023.107064

Van der Kolk, B. A. (2005). Developmental trauma disorder: Toward a rational diagnosis for children with complex trauma histories. *Psychiatric Annals*, *35*(5), 401–408. https://doi.org/10.3928/00485713-20050501-06

Van der Kolk, B. A., & Andrea, W. (2010). Towards a developmental trauma disorder diagnosis for childhood interpersonal trauma. In R. Lanius, E. Vermetten, & C. Pain (Eds.), *The impact of early life trauma on health and disease: The hidden epidemic* (pp. 57–69). Cambridge University Press.

Van der Kolk, B. A., Pynoos, R. S., & Cicchetti, D. (2021). The integration of EMDR and attachment-based interventions in the treatment of complex trauma in children. *Journal of Child Psychology and Psychiatry*, *62*(4), 466–480. https://doi.org/10.1111/jcpp.13341

Van der Kolk, B. A., Stone, L., West, J., Rhodes, A., Emerson, D., Suvak, M., & Spinazzola, J. (2014). Yoga as an adjunctive treatment for posttraumatic stress disorder: A randomized controlled trial. *The Journal of Clinical Psychiatry*, *75*(6), 559–565. https://doi.org/10.4088/JCP.13m08561

Van der Molen, M. J., Van Luit, J., Jongmans, M., & Van der Molen, M. W. (2007). Verbal working memory in children with mild intellectual disabilities. *Journal of Intellectual Disability Research*, *51*(Pt 2), 162–169. https://doi.org/10.1111/j.1365-2788.2006.00863.x

Van der Oord, S., & Tripp, G. (2020). How to improve behavioral parent and teacher training for children with ADHD: Integrating empirical research on learning and motivation into treatment. *Clinical Child and Family Psychology Review*, *23*(4), 577–604. https://doi.org/10.1007/s10567-020-00327-z

Van der Ploeg, J. (2013). *Stress bij kinderen*. Bohn Stafleu van Loghum.

Van der Pol, T. M., Van Domburgh, L., Van Widenfelt, B. M., Hurlburt, M. S., Garland, A. F., & Vermeiren, R. R. (2019). Common elements of evidence-based systemic treatments for adolescents with disruptive behaviour problems. *The Lancet Psychiatry*, *6*(10), 862–868. https:/doi.org/10.1016/S2215-0366(19)30085-9

Van der Vleugel, B., Van den Berg, D., De Bont, P., Staring, T., & De Jongh, A. (2016). EMDR for traumatized patients with psychosis. In M. Luber (Ed.), *Eye Movement Desensitization and Reprocessing (EMDR) scripted protocols and summary sheets: Treating trauma, anxiety and mood-related conditions* (pp. 97–148). Springer.

Van Ee, E., De Beijer, D., Florisson, D., & Geuskens, F. (2024). Making sense of change after Intensive Trauma Treatment: A mixed-methods study into adolescents' experience of efficacy. *Child and Adolescent Psychiatry and Mental Health*, *18*(1), 92. https://doi.org/10.1186/s13034-024-00781-5

Van Ee, E., Kleber, R. J., & Jongmans, M. J. (2016). Relational patterns between caregivers with PTSD and their nonexposed children: A review. *Trauma, Violence and Abuse*, *17*(2), 186–203. https://doi.org/10.1177/1524838015584355

Van Ee, E., Kleber, R. J., & Mooren, T. (2012). War trauma lingers on: Associations between maternal PTSD, parent-child interaction and child development. *Journal of Infant Mental Health*, *33*(5), 459–468. https://doi.org/10.1002/imjh.21324

Van Es, C. M., Boelen, P. A., Zwaanswijk, M., Te Brake, H., & Mooren, T. (2021). Family empowerment (FAME): A feasibility trial of preventive multifamily groups for asylum seeker families in the Netherlands. *Journal of Marital and Family Therapy*, *47*(4), 864–881. https://doi.org/10.1111/jmft.12539

Van Es, C. M., Velu, M. E., Sleijpen, M., Van der Aa, N., Boelen, P. A., & Mooren, T. (2023). Trauma-focused treatment for traumatic stress symptoms in unaccompanied refugee minors: A multiple baseline case series. *Frontiers in Psychology*, *14*, 1125740. https://doi.org/10.3389/fpsyg.2023.1125740

Van Essen, J., & Bala, J. (2007). *Als glas in lood: Integratieve behandeling van vluchtelingenkinderen en -gezinnen*. Pharos.

Van Gent, T. (2012). *Mental health problems in deaf and severely hard of hearing children and adolescents*. Universiteit Leiden.

Van Minnen, A., & Arntz, A. (2017). Protocol-based treatment of patients with posttraumatic-stress disorder (PTSD): imagined exposure and exposure in vivo. In G. Keijsers, A. Van Minnen, & M. Verbraak (Eds.), *Protocol-based treatments for adults with psychological complaints 1* (pp. 311–369). Tree.

Van Minnen, A., Wessel, I., & Hagenaars, M. (2005). Intrusies bij de posttraumatische stressstoornis. *Directieve Therapie*, *25*(2), 64–71. https://doi.org/10.1007/BF03060377

Van Minnen, A., Hendriks, L., Kleine, R. D., Hendriks, G.-J., Verhagen, M., & De Jongh, A. (2018). Therapist rotation: a novel approach for implementation of trauma-focused treatment in post-traumatic stress disorder. *European Journal of Psychotraumatology*, *9*(1). https://doi.org/10.1080/20008198.2018.1492836

Van Pelt, Y., De Jongh, A., Ten Broeke, E., Hornsveld, H., Oppenheim, H-J., Weijermans, J., Meijerink-Miedema, M., & Luber, M. (in prepss.). *A practical guide to EMDR therapy: Case conceptualization, and additional treatment strategies*. Springer Publishing. https://www.springerpub.com/a-practical-guide-to-emdr-therapy-9780826156181.html?srsltid=AfmBOoqVXkelqCCfXsbl1oVaLUsB5KXLvKePS6XuKJ8L82SDQEXxZhjB

Van Pelt, Y., Fokkema, P., De Roos, C., & De Jongh, A. (2021). Effectiveness of an intensive treatment programme combining prolonged exposure and EMDR therapy for adolescents suffering from severe post-traumatic stress disorder. *European Journal of Psychotraumatology*, *12*(1), 1917876. https://doi.org/10.1080/20008198.2021.1917876

Van Santvoort, F., Hosman, C. M., Janssens, J. M., Van Doesum, K. T., Reupert, A., & Van Loon, L. M. (2015). The impact of various parental mental disorders on children's diagnoses: A systematic review. *Clinical Child and Family Psychology Review*, *18*(4), 281–299. https://doi.org/10.1007/s10567-015-0191-9

Van Veen, S. C., Van Schie, K., Wijngaards-De Meij, L. D., Littel, M., Engelhard, I. M., & Van den Hout, M. A. (2015). Speed matters: Relationship between speed of eye movements and modification of aversive autobiographical memories. *Frontiers in Psychiatry*, *6*, 45. https://doi.org/10.3389/fpsyt.2015.00045

Van Vliet, N. I., Huntjens, R. J., Van Dijk, M. K., Bachrach, N., Meewisse, M. L., & De Jongh, A. (2021). Phase-based treatment versus immediate trauma-focused treatment for post-traumatic stress disorder due to childhood abuse: Randomised clinical trial. *BJPsych Open*, *7*(6), e211. https://doi.org/10.1192/bjo.2021.1057

Van Woudenberg, C., Voorendonk, E. M., Bongaerts, H., Zoet, H. A., Verhagen, M., Lee, C. W., Van Minnen, A., & De Jongh, A. (2018). Effectiveness of an intensive treatment programme combining prolonged exposure and eye movement desensitization and reprocessing for severe post-traumatic stress disorder. *European Journal of Psychotraumatology*, *9*(1), 1487225. https://doi.org/10.1080/20008198.2018.1487225

Velu, M. E., Martens, I., Shahab, M., De Roos, C., Jongedijk, R. A., Schok, M., & Mooren, T. (2022). Trauma-focused treatments for refugee children: study protocol for a randomized controlled trial of the effectiveness of KIDNET versus EMDR therapy versus a waitlist control group (KIEM). *Trials*, *23*(1), 347. https://doi.org/10.1186/s13063-022-06178-z

Verbist, A. (2010). *The acquisition of personal pronouns in cochlear-implanted children*. Utrecht University.

Verhagen, I., Van der Heijden, R., De Jongh, A., Korzilius, H., Mevissen, L., & Didden, R. (2022). Safety, feasibility, and efficacy of EMDR therapy in adults with PTSD and mild intellectual disability or borderline intellectual functioning and mental health problems: A multiple baseline study. *Journal of Mental Health Research in Intellectual Disabilities*, *16*(3), 1–23. https://doi.org/10.1080/19315864.2022.2148791

Verhulst, F. (2008). *De ontwikkeling van het kind*. Van Gorcum.

Verlinden, E., Opmeer, B. C., Van Meijel, E. P., Beer, R., De Roos, C., Bicanic, I. A., Lamers-Winkelman, F., Olff, M., Boer, F., & Lindauer, R. J. (2015). Enhanced screening for posttraumatic stress disorder and comorbid diagnoses in children and adolescents. *European Journal of Psychotraumatology*, *6*(1), 26661. https://doi.org/10.3402/ejpt.v6.26661

Verlinden, E., Schippers, M., Van Meijel, E. P. M., Beer, R., Opmeer, B. C., Olff, M., Boer, F., & Lindauer, R. J. L. (2013). What makes a life event traumatic for a child? The predictive values of DSM-Criteria A1 and A2. *European Journal of Psychotraumatology*, *4*, 20436. http://dx.doi.org/10.3402/ejpt.v4i0.20436

Vermeire, S. (2023). *Unraveling trauma and weaving resilience with systemic and narrative therapy: Playful collaborations with children, families and networks*. Routledge.

Versluis, A., Mevissen, L., De Jongh, A., Schuengel, C., & Didden, R. (2025). Reliability and validity of the diagnostic interview trauma and stressors - intellectual disability in adults with mild intellectual disabilities or borderline intellectual functioning. *Journal of Mental* Health Research in Intellectual Disabilities, *18*(2), 204–220.

Vervoort-Schel, J., Mercera, G., Wissink, I., Van der Helm, P., Lindauer, R., & Moonen, X. (2021). Prevalence of and relationship between adverse childhood experiences and family context risk factors among children with intellectual disabilities and borderline intellectual functioning. *Research in Developmental Disabilities*, *113*(4), 103935. https://doi.org/10.1016/j.ridd.2021.103935

Vissers, C., Tomas, E., & Law, J. (2020). The emergence of inner speech and its measurement in atypically developing children. *Frontiers in Psychology*, *11*, 279–286. https://doi.org/10.3389/fpsyg.2020.00279

Vissia, E. M., Giesen, M. E., Chalavi, S., Nijenhuis, E. R., Draijer, N., Brand, B. L., & Reinders, A. A. (2016). Is it trauma- or fantasy-based? Comparing dissociative identity disorder, post-traumatic stress disorder, simulators, and controls. *Acta Psychiatrica Scandinavica*, *134*(2), 111–128. https://doi.org/10.1111/acps.12590

Volk, H., Lurmann, F., Penfold, B., Herz-Picciotto, I., & McConnell, R. (2013). Traffic related air pollution, particulate matter, and autism. *JAMA Psychiatry*, *70*(1), 71–77. https://doi.org/10.1001/jamapsychiatry.2013.26

Wadaa, N. N., Zaharim, N. M., & Alqashan, H. F. (2010). The use of EMDR in treatment of traumatized Iraqi children. *Digest of Middle East Studies*, *19*(2), 26–36. https://doi.org/10.1111/j.1949-3606.2010.00012.x

Wadji, D. L., Martin-Soelch, C., & Camos, V. (2022). Can working memory account for EMDR efficacy in PTSD? *BMC Psychology*, *10*(1), 245. https://doi.org/10.1186/s40359-022-00951-0

Walker, J., Dosen, A., Buitelaar, J., & Janzing, J. (2011). Depression in Down syndrome: A review of the literature. *Research in Developmental Disabilities*, *32*(5), 1432–1440. https://doi.org/10.1016/j.ridd.2011.02.010

Walker, H. E., & Wamser-Nanney, R. (2023). Revictimization risk factors following childhood maltreatment: A literature review. *Trauma, Violence, & Abuse*, 24(4), 2319–2332. https://doi.org/10.1177/15248380221093692

Walter, H. J., Bukstein, O. G., Abright, A. R., Keable, H., Ramtekkar, U., Ripperger-Suhler, J., & Rockhill, C. (2020). Clinical practice guideline for the assessment and treatment of children and adolescents with anxiety disorders. *Journal of the American Academy of Child and Adolescent Psychiatry*, *59*(10), 1107–1124. https://doi.org/10.1016/j.jaac.2020.05.005

Wamser-Nanney, R. (2016). Examining the complex trauma definition using children's self-reports. *Journal of Child and Adolescent Trauma*, *9*(4), 295–304. https://doi.org/10.1007/s40653-016-0098-8

Wanders, E. H., Serra, M., & De Jongh, A. (2008). EMDR Versus CBT for children with self-esteem and behavioral problems: A randomized controlled trial. *Journal of EMDR Practice and Research*, *2*(3), 180–189. https://doi.org/10.1891/1933-3196.2.3.180

Wang, S., He, Y., Hu, J., Xia, J., Fang, K., Yu, J., & Wang, Y. (2024). Eye movement intervention facilitates concurrent perception and memory processing. *Cerebral Cortex*, *34*(5), bhae190. https://doi.org/10.1093/cercor/bhae190

Wang, Y., Zhang, Y. B., Liu, L. L., Cui, J. F., Wang, J., Shum, D. H., Van Amelsvoort, T., & Chan, R. C. K. (2017). A meta-analysis of working memory impairments in autism spectrum disorders. *Neuropsychology Review*, *27*(1), 46–61. https://doi.org/10.1007/s11065-016-9336-y

Ward, T., & Brown, M. (2004). The good lives model and conceptual issues in offender rehabilitation. *Psychology, Crime and Law*, *10*(3), 243–257. https://doi.org/10.1080/10683160410001662744

Waters, F. S. (2016). *Healing the fractured child: Diagnosis and treatment of youth with dissociation*. Springer Publishing.

Watkins, J., & Watkins, H. (1997). *Ego-states: Theory and therapy*. W. W. Norton.

Weathers, F. W., Blake, D. D., Schnurr, P. P., Kaloupek, D. G., Marx, B. P., & Keane, T. M. (2013). *Clinician-administered PTSD scale for DSM-5*. National Center for PTSD.

Weaver, J. L., Medyk, N. V., Swank, J. M., Daniels, P. F., & Smith-Adcock, S. (2021). A phenomenological study of Theraplay groups within a middle school. *International Journal of Play Therapy*, *30*(2), 125–135. https://doi.org/10.1037/pla0000139

Wei, Y., Krishnan, G. P., & Bazhenov, M. (2016). Synaptic mechanisms of memory consolidation during sleep slow oscillations. *Journal of Neuroscience, 36*(5), 4231–4247. https://doi.org/10.1523/JNEUROSCI.3648-15.2016

Weine, S., Ware, N., Hakizimana, L., Tugenberg, T., Currie, M., Dahnweih, G., Wagner, M., Polutnik, C., & Wulu, J. (2014). Fostering resilience: Protective agents, resources, and mechanisms for adolescent refugees' psychosocial well-being. *Adolescence Psychiatry, 4*(4), 164–176. https://doi.org/10.2174/22106766040314091 2162410

Weisz, J. R., Kuppens, S., Ng, M. Y., Eckshtain, D., Ugueto, A. M., Vaughn-Coaxum, R., Jensen-Doss, A., Hawley, K. M., Krumholz Marchette, L. S., Chu, B. C., Weersing, V. R., & Fordwood, S. R. (2017). What five decades of research tells us about the effects of youth psychological therapy: A multilevel meta-analysis and implications for science and practice. *American Psychologist, 72*(2), 79–117. https://doi.org/10.1037/a0040360

Weisz, J. R., McCarty, C. A., & Valeri, S. M. (2006). Effects of psychotherapy for depression in children and adolescents: A meta-analysis. *Psychological Bulletin, 132*(1), 132–149. https://doi.org/10.1037/0033-2909.132.1.132

Wels, P. M. A. (2001). *Helping with images: Video in family counselling.* Bohn Stafleu van Loghum.

Went, M. M., Struik, M. A., Möller, E. L., Zijlstra, B. J., Dumoulin, M. A., Van Haaften, M. G., & Rodenburg, R. (2024). Parent-child EMDR therapy for children aged 0–4 years: Protocol, pilot-data, and case study. *European Journal of Trauma and Dissociation, 8*(4), 100475. https://doi.org/10.1016/j.ejtd.2024.100475

Wesselmann, D. (2013). Healing trauma and creating secure attachments with EMDR. In M. Solomon & D. S. Siegel (Eds.), *Healing moments in psychotherapy: Mindful awareness, neural integration, and therapeutic presence* (pp. 115–128). Norton.

Wesselmann, D., Armstrong, S., & Schweitzer, C. (2017a). Interweaves for children with an attachment trauma in foster and adoptive families. In R. Beer & C. De Roos (Eds.), *Handbook EMDR: Children and adolescents* (pp. 399–413). LannooCampus.

Wesselmann, D., Armstrong, S., & Schweitzer, C. (2017b). Using an EMDR integrative model to treat attachment-based difficulties. In K. D. Buckwalter & D. Reed (Eds.), *Attachment theory in action: Building connections between children and parents.* Roman & Littlefield.

Wesselmann, D., Armstrong, S., & Schweitzer, C. (2017c). EMDR for children with attachment trauma in foster- and adoption families. In R. Beer & C. de Roos (Eds.), *Handbook EMDR: Children and adolescents* (pp. 399–413). LannooCampus.

Wesselmann, D., Armstrong, S., Schweitzer, C., Davidson, M., & Potter, A. (2018). An integrative EMDR and family therapy model for treating attachment trauma in children: A case series. *Journal of EMDR Practice and Research, 12*(4), 196–207. https://doi.org/10.1891/1933-3196.12.4.196

Wesselmann, D., Davidson, M., Armstrong, S., Schweitzer, D., Bruckner, D., & Potter, A. E. (2012). EMDR as a treatment for improving attachment status in adults and children. *European Review of Applied Psychology, 62*(4), 223–230. https://doi.org/10.1016/j.erap.2012.08.008

Wesselmann, D., Schweitzer, C., & Armstrong, S. (2014a). *Integrative team treatment for attachment trauma in children: Family therapy and EMDR.* W. W. Norton & Company.

Wesselmann, D., Schweitzer, C., & Armstrong, S. (2014b). *Integrative parenting: Raising children affected by attachment trauma.* W. W. Norton.

Wesselmann, D. (2025a). *EMDR and family therapy: Integrative treatment for attachment trauma in children* (2nd ed.). W.W. Norton.

Wesselmann, D. (2025b). *Attachment trauma in kids: Integrative strategies for parents* (2nd ed.). W.W. Norton.

Wesselmann, D., Schweitzer, C., & Armstrong, S. (2015). Child attachment trauma protocol. In M. Luber (Ed.), *EMDR therapy: Scripted protocols and summary sheets* (pp. 9–44). Springer Publishing.

Wesselmann, D., & Shapiro, F. (2013). Eye movement desensitization and reprocessing. In J. Ford & C. Courtois (Eds.), *Treating complex traumatic stress disorders in children and adolescents* (pp. 213–224). Guilford Press.

What Works Clearinghouse. (2022, August; rev. December). *What Works Clearinghouse procedures and standards handbook, version 5.0* (WWC 2022-008 REV). U.S. Department of Education, Institute of Education Sciences, National Center for Education Evaluation and Regional Assistance.

White, M., & Epston, D. (1990). *Narrative means to therapeutic ends.* W. W. Norton & Company.

Wieland, S. (Ed.). (2015). *Dissociation in traumatized children and adolescents: Theory and clinical interventions* (2nd ed.). Routledge Psychosocial Stress Series.

Wigham, S., Hatton, C., & Taylor, J. (2011). The effects of traumatizing life events on people with intellectual disabilities: A systematic review. *Journal of Metal Health Research in Intellectual Disabilities, 4*(1), 19–39. https://doi.org/10.1080/19315864.2010.534576

Wilcoxon, L. A., Meiser-Stedman, R., & Burgess, A. (2021). Post-traumatic stress disorder in parents following their child's single-event trauma: A meta-analysis of prevalence rates and risk factor correlates. *Clinical Child and Family Psychology Review,* 24(6), 1–19. https://doi.org/10.1007/s10567-021-00367-z

Wizansky, B., & Bar Sadeh, E. (2021). Dyadic EMDR: A clinical model for the treatment of preverbal medical trauma. *Journal of Infant, Child and Adolescent Psychotherapy, 20*(3), 260–227. https://doi.org/10.1080/15289168.2021.1940661

Woolard, A., Boutrus, M., Bullman, I., Wickens, N., Gouveia Belinelo, P., Solomon, T., & Milroy, H. (2024). Treatment for childhood and adolescent dissociation: A systematic review. *Psychological Trauma: Theory, Practice and Policy, 16*(Suppl 3), S483–S491. https://doi.org/10.1037/tra0001615

Woolgar, F., Garfield, H., Dalgleish, T., & Meiser-Stedman, R. (2022). Systematic review and meta-analysis: Prevalence of posttraumatic stress disorder in trauma-exposed preschool-aged children. *Journal of the American Academy of Child and Adolescent Psychiatry, 61*(3), 366–377. https://doi.org/10.1016/j.jaac.2021.05.026

World Health Organization. (2012). *WHO global estimates on prevalence of hearing loss. Mortality and burden of diseases and prevention of blindness and deafness.* https://www.who.int/news-room/fact-sheets/detail/deafness-and-hearing-loss

World Health Organization. (2019*). International Statistical Classification of Diseases and Related Health Problems* (11th ed.). https://icd.who.int

World Health Organization. (2022). *Violence against children.* https://www.who.int/news-room/fact-sheets/detail/violence-against-children

World Health Organization. (2023). *Deafness and hearing loss.* https://www.who.int/news-room/fact-sheets/detail/deafness-and-hearing-loss

World Health Organization. (2024). *Working for a brighter, healthier future: How WHO improves health and promotes well-being for the world's adolescents.* https://www.who.int/publications/i/item/9789240093966

Xie, Y., Zhu, X., Wang, L., Wan, Z., Yang, J., Su, C., Duan, S., Xu, C., & Kan, B. (2024). A network meta-analysis of psychological interventions for children and adolescents after natural and man-made disasters. *BMC Psychiatry, 24*(1), 468. https://doi.org/10.1186/s12888-024-05924-8

Zaidman-Zait, A. (2015). Stress among children who are deaf of hard of hearing and their families. In H. Van Knoors & M. Marschalk (Eds.), *Educating deaf leaners: Creating a global evidence base* (pp. 337–368). Oxford University.

Zanarini, M. C., Frankenburg, F. R., Dubo, E. D., Sickel, A. E., Trikha, A., Levin, A., & Reynolds, V. (1998). Axis I comorbidity of borderline personality disorder. *American Journal of Psychiatry, 155*(12), 1733–1739. https://doi.org/10.1176/ajp.155.12.1733

Zantvoord, J. B., Ensink, J. B., op den Kelder, R., Wessel, A. M., Lok, A., & Lindauer, R. J. (2019). Pretreatment cortisol predicts trauma-focused psychotherapy response in youth with (partial) posttraumatic stress disorder. *Psychoneuroendocrinology, 109*, 104380.

Zeanah, C. H., & Gleason, M. M. (2010). *Proposal to include child and adolescent age-related manifestations and age related subtypes for PTSD in DSM-V*. American Psychiatric Association.

Zeegers, M. A. J., Colonnesi, C., Noom, M. J., Polderman, N., & Stams, G. J. J. M. (2020). Remediating child attachment insecurity: Evaluating the Basic Trust intervention in adoptive families. *Research on Social Work Practice, 30*(7), 736–749. https://doi.org/10.1177/1049731519863106

Zeinstra, L. (2026). *"We're in this Together": Trauma-focused inpatient family treatment: An evaluation of the KINGS program* [Doctoral Thesis]. Erasmus University Rotterdam.

Zeinstra, L., Huyghen, A-M., Harder, A., Post, W., Wanders, F., & Knot-Dickscheit, J. (2024). De klinische en traumageoriënteerde gezinsbehandeling KINGS: Een dossierstudie naar gezinskenmerken [The inpatient and trauma-informed family treatment program KINGS: A case study of family characteristics]. *Jeugd in Ontwikkeling, 4*. https://doi.org/10.54447/JiO.18121

Zeinstra, L., Huyghen, A. M., Knot-Dickscheit, J., Wanders, F., & Harder, A. (2022). KINGS: Trauma-behandeling voor kwetsbare gezinnen: Onderzoek naar effectiviteit [KINGS: Trauma treatment for vulnerable families. Effectiveness study]. *Kind and Adolescent Praktijk, 21*(1), 24–26. https://doi.org/10.1007/s12454-022-0684-x

Zeinstra, L. T., Visscher, L., Huyghen, A. M. N., Harder, A. T., Wanders-Mulder, F., & Knot-Dickscheit, J. (2025). Unraveling trauma-focused inpatient care for families experiencing complex and multiple problems: Practitioner-reported practice and program elements. *Residential Treatment for Children & Youth*, 1–31. https://doi.org/10.1080/0886571X.2025.2540882

Zisser, A., & Eyberg, S. M. (2010). Parent-child interaction therapy and the treatment of disruptive behavior disorders. In J. R. Weisz & A. E. Kazdin (Eds.), *Evidence-based psychotherapies for children and adolescents* (pp. 179–193). Guilford Press.

Zlotnick, C., Franklin, C. L., & Zimmerman, M. (2002). Does 'subthreshold' posttraumatic stress disorder have any clinical relevance? *Comprehensive Psychiatry, 43*(6), 413–419. https://doi.org/10.1053/comp.2002.35900

Zolkoski, S. M., & Bullock, L. M. (2012). Resilience in children and youth: A review. *Children and Youth Services Review, 34*(12), 2295–2303. https://doi.org/10.1016/j.childyouth.2012.08.009

Index

Please note that page references to Boxes include the letter 'b' following the number; References to Figures will be followed by the letter 'f', and Tables by the letter 't'. C&A refers to 'children and adolescents,' whenever it appears in the index.